The middle years of the twentieth century marked a particularly intense time of crisis and change in European society. During this period (1930-1950), a broad intellectual and spiritual movement arose within the European Catholic community, largely in response to the secularism that lay at the core of the crisis. The movement drew inspiration from earlier theologians and philosophers such as Möhler, Newman, Gardeil, Rousselot, and Blondel, as well as from men of letters like Charles Péguy and Paul Claudel.

The group of academic theologians included in the movement extended into Belgium and Germany, in the work of men like Emile Mersch, Dom Odo Casel, Romano Guardini, and Karl Adam. But above all, the theological activity during this period centered in France. Led principally by the Jesuits at Fourvière and the Dominicans at Le Saulchoir, the French revival included many of the greatest names in twentieth-century Catholic thought: Henri de Lubac, Jean Daniélou, Yves Congar, Marie-Dominique Chenu, Louis Bouyer, and, in association, Hans Urs von Balthasar.

It is not true — as subsequent folklore has it — that those theologians represented any sort of self-conscious "school": indeed, the differences among them, for example, between Fourvière and Le Saulchoir, were important. At the same time, most of them were united in the double conviction that theology had to speak to the present situation, and that the condition for doing so faithfully lay in a recovery of the Church's past. In other words, they saw clearly that the first step in what later came to be known as *aggiornamento* had to be *ressourcement* — a rediscovery of the riches of the whole of the Church's two-thousand-year tradition. According to de Lubac, for example, all of his own works as well as the entire *Sources chrétiennes* collection are based on the presupposition that "the renewal of Christian vitality is linked at least partially to a renewed exploration of the periods and of the works where the Christian tradition is expressed with particular intensity."

In sum, for the *ressourcement* theologians theology involved a "return to the sources" of Christian faith, for the purpose of drawing out the meaning and significance of these sources for the critical questions of our time. What these theologians sought was a spiritual and intellectual communion with Christianity in its most vital moments as transmitted to us in its classic texts, a communion that would nourish, invigorate, and rejuvenate twentieth-century Catholicism.

The *ressourcement* movement bore great fruit in the documents of the Second Vatican Council and deeply influenced the work of Pope John Paul II.

The present series is rooted in this renewal of theology. The series thus understands *ressourcement* as revitalization: a return to the sources, for the purpose of developing a theology that will truly meet the challenges of our time. Some of the features of the series, then, are a return to classical (patristic-medieval) sources and a dialogue with contemporary Western culture, particularly in terms of problems associated with the Enlightenment, modernity, and liberalism.

The series publishes out-of-print or as yet untranslated studies by earlier authors associated with the *ressourcement* movement. The series also publishes works by contemporary authors sharing in the aim and spirit of this earlier movement. This will include any works in theology, philosophy, history, literature, and the arts that give renewed expression to Catholic sensibility.

The editor of the Ressourcement series, David L. Schindler, is Gagnon Professor of Fundamental Theology and dean at the John Paul II Institute in Washington, D.C., and editor of the North American edition of *Communio: International Catholic Review,* a federation of journals in thirteen countries founded in Europe in 1972 by Hans Urs von Balthasar, Jean Daniélou, Henri de Lubac, Joseph Ratzinger, and others.

VOLUMES PUBLISHED

Mysterium Paschale
Hans Urs von Balthasar

Joseph Ratzinger in Communio, Volume 1: The Unity of the Church
Pope Benedict XVI

Joseph Ratzinger in Communio, Volume 2: Anthropology and Culture
Pope Benedict XVI

The Heroic Face of Innocence: Three Stories
Georges Bernanos

Maurice Blondel: A Philosophical Life
Oliva Blanchette

The Letter on Apologetics and History and Dogma
Maurice Blondel

Prayer: The Mission of the Church
Jean Daniélou

On Pilgrimage
Dorothy Day

We, the Ordinary People of the Streets
Madeleine Delbrêl

The Discovery of God
Henri de Lubac

Medieval Exegesis, volumes 1-3: The Four Senses of Scripture
Henri de Lubac

ANALOGIA ENTIS

*Metaphysics: Original Structure
and Universal Rhythm*

Erich Przywara

Translated by
John R. Betz and David Bentley Hart

WILLIAM B. EERDMANS PUBLISHING COMPANY
GRAND RAPIDS, MICHIGAN / CAMBRIDGE, U.K.

First published 1962 in German under the title
Analogia Entis I. Metaphysik. Ur-Struktur und All-Rhythmus,
by Johannes Verlag, Einsiedeln.

Published 2014 by
Wm. B. Eerdmans Publishing Co.
2140 Oak Industrial Drive N.E., Grand Rapids, Michigan 49505 /
P.O. Box 163, Cambridge CB3 9PU U.K.

Printed in the United States of America

20 19 18 17 16 15 14   7 6 5 4 3 2 1

Library of Congress Cataloging-in-Publication Data

Przywara, Erich, 1889-1972.
   [Analogia entis. English]
   Analogia entis: metaphysics: original structure and universal rhythm /
   Erich Przywara; translated by John R. Betz and David Bentley Hart.
      pages   cm.
   "First published 1962 in German under the title Analogia Entis I. Metaphysik.
   Ur-Struktur und All-Rhythmus by Johannes Verlag, Einsiedeln."
   Includes bibliographical references and index.
   ISBN 978-0-8028-6859-6 (pbk.: alk. paper)
   1. God (Christianity) — Knowableness.
   2. Analogy (Religion)   I. Title.

BX891.P7813   2013
231 — dc23

                              2013005018

www.eerdmans.com

To our colleagues at
Loyola University Maryland
and the University of Notre Dame

Contents

Translators' Preface   xi

Preface to the 1962 Edition   xviii

From the Preface to the First Edition of
Analogia Entis I (1932)   xx

Translator's Introduction, by John R. Betz   1

     1. Erich Przywara (1889-1972): Life and Writings   12

     2. The Prior Philosophical and Theological History
       of the *analogia entis*   30

     3. The *analogia entis* in Przywara's Early Work (1922-26)   43

     4. The *Analogia Entis* (1932)   61

     5. Philosophical and Theological Criticisms of the
       analogia entis   74

PART I: ORIGINAL STRUCTURE   **117**

    Section One: Metaphysics as Such

    §1. Meta-Noetics and Meta-Ontics   119

    §2. Metaphysical Transcendentalism and
       Transcendental Metaphysics   125

    §3. *A Priori* and *A Posteriori* Metaphysics   132

    §4. Philosophical and Theological Metaphysics   155

Section Two: Analogia Entis

§5. Logos, Logic, Dialectic, Analogy   192

§6. The Grounding of Analogy as *Analogia Entis*
in the Principle of Non-Contradiction   198

§7. The Scope of the Problem of the *Analogia Entis*   238

§8. The *Analogia Entis* as a Principle   307

PART II: UNIVERSAL RHYTHM

1. Philosophies of Essence and Existence   317

2. The Scope of Analogy as a Fundamental Catholic Form   348

3. Philosophy as a Problem   400

4. Metaphysics, Religion, Analogy   409

5. Image, Likeness, Symbol, Mythos, Mysterium, Logos   430

6. Phenomenology, Realogy, Relationology   463

7. Man, World, God, Symbol   480

8. The Religious Gnoseology of St. Augustine   501

9. Between Metaphysics and Christianity   520

10. Beautiful, Sacred, Christian   537

11. *Imago Dei:* On the Theological Message of Max Picard   556

12. Primal Christian Terms: Kerygma, Mysterium,
Kairos, Oikonomia   570

13. Time, Space, Eternity   583

*14. Edith Stein and Simone Weil: Two Fundamental
Philosophical Themes   596

*15. Husserl and Heidegger   613

Index   623

*Chapters 14 and 15 are included as supplemental essays; they were not included
in the original edition.*

Translators' Preface

Erich Przywara's *Analogia Entis: Metaphysics,* which appears here for the first time in English, is the work for which the author is best known, and the work among his writings to which he himself attached the greatest importance. Nevertheless, it remains only a minuscule part of an immense corpus of texts, which includes over forty monographs and as many as 800 articles and reviews. By 1962, many of these pieces were out of print and difficult to obtain.[1] So, in an effort to salvage a core of Przywara's most important writings from neglect and unjust obscurity, his protégé and lifelong friend Hans Urs von Balthasar proposed to undertake a new edition of Przywara's *Schriften.* Projecting as many as eight volumes, he suggested to Przywara that they begin with three. After some discussion, their final arrangement was as follows: the first volume, *Frühe Religiöse Schriften,* would include the early lyrical and scriptural works *Eucharistie und Arbeit* (1917), *Himmelreich: Die Gleichnisse des Herrn* (1922/23), *Kirchenjahr: Die christliche Spannungseinheit* (1923), *Liebe: Der christliche Wesensgrund* (1924), *Wandlung: Ein Christenweg* (1925), and *Majestas Divina: Ignatianische Frömmigkeit* (1925); the second volume, *Religionsphilosophische Schriften,* would include a collection of previously published articles entitled *Weg zu Gott* and other early works such as *Gottgeheimnis der Welt* (1923), *Gott* (1926), and *Religionsphilosophie katholischer Theologie* (1926); and the third volume, bearing the title *Analogia Entis,* would consist of two parts, including the original text of the *Analogia*

---

1. For a bibliography of Przywara's works up to 1962, see Erich Przywara, *Sein Schrifttum 1912-1962,* ed. Leo Zimny, with an introduction by Hans Urs von Balthasar (Einsiedeln: Johannes Verlag, 1963). For a more recent bibliography, including the relevant secondary literature, mainly in German, see www.helmut-zenz.de/hzprzywa.html.

Entis (1932) and a selection of later essays apposite to its themes. The projected other volumes were never published.

The arrangement of the final volume into two parts is due to Przywara's original conception of the *Analogia Entis* as a two-volume work. According to his original preface, the first volume, which appeared in 1932, was intended to introduce the "formal problem" of metaphysics as such, and so bore the subtitle "Principle." The projected second volume was intended to fill out the basic material features of metaphysics, now specified as an analogical metaphysics, in terms of "consciousness, being, and world." For various reasons, however, this second volume was never completed. In the 1962 edition, therefore, Przywara and von Balthasar attempted to capture something of Przywara's original aim for this second volume by the addition of essays either on analogy or exhibiting the principle of analogy, written between 1939 and 1959. Comprising the original 1932 text of the *Analogia Entis* (now designated as Part I) and the later essays (Part II), the third volume of Przywara's *Schriften*, which is translated here in its entirety, thus presents the complete *Analogia Entis* as Przywara more or less intended it. In order to prevent any misunderstandings of what he had meant by the term "Principle" on the title page of the 1932 edition, Przywara also re-christened Part I "Original Structure" *("Ur-Struktur")* and gave Part II of the new edition the complementary title "Universal Rhythm" *("All-Rhythmus")*. The only other changes he made were the additions of a new preface and a new final paragraph at the conclusion of the original text.

As for the essays that make up Part II, von Balthasar thought they constituted "a splendid exercise in analogical thought" and, as such, a fitting supplement to the original 1932 text.[2] But how to arrange such disparate materials was by no means clear. At first, he proposed a loosely topical arrangement: from the more philosophical essays to the more theological, with a coda made up of "Beautiful, Sacred, Christian," "Time, Space, Eternity," and perhaps "Imago Dei."[3] He was also of the opinion that one essay in particular, "The Religious Gnoseology of St. Augustine," provided the key to all the rest and should accordingly appear in the collection either first or last.[4]

---

2. See Manfred Lochbrunner, *Hans Urs von Balthasar und seine Theologen-Kollegen* (Würzburg: Echter Verlag, 2009), p. 85.

3. Lochbrunner, *Hans Urs von Balthasar*, p. 85.

4. This accords with the importance von Balthasar attached to Przywara's Augustine anthology *Augustinus: Die Gestalt als Gefüge* (Leipzig: Hegner, 1934), particularly Przywara's monograph-length introduction, which von Balthasar later published separately as *Augustinisch: Ur-Haltung des Geistes* (Einsiedeln: Johannes Verlag, 1970).

Przywara, however, preferred that the essays be arranged chronologically, on account of what he saw as a significant unfolding of his understanding of analogy from the earlier essays ("Philosophies of Essence and Existence," "The Scope of Analogy as a Fundamental Catholic Form," and "Philosophy as a Problem") to those written later; so in the end the chronological arrangement was adopted.[5]

The only difference between the texts translated here and those that appeared in the third volume of the 1962 edition is the inclusion of two additional essays, which were originally published in French translations. They have been translated here from original typescripts preserved in the Archive of the German province of the Society of Jesus. The first, "Edith Stein und Simone Weil: Zwei philosophische Grund-Motive," appears here for a number of reasons — the enduring importance of the two figures it discusses, its intrinsic value, the splash of personal color it adds to an otherwise rather abstract volume — but principally because von Balthasar and Przywara at one point considered including it in the new edition.[6] The second essay, from 1960, concerns Husserl and Heidegger; its inclusion follows not so much from the quality of the piece as compared to Przywara's other works, but from the light it sheds on Przywara's understanding of their projects, seeing in them and the intertwining antitheses of their thought the analogical conclusion not only of German philosophy but of philosophy itself.

Since this is the first volume of Przywara's *Schriften* to be translated in its entirety, one might legitimately wonder why we have begun with the third volume, and not, say, more logically, with the first. Our reason is twofold: first, the already noted centrality of the *Analogia Entis* within Przywara's corpus, which looks back to his earlier works and, together with the subsequent essays, forward to his latest works, making it an optimal midpoint from which any further study or translation of Przywara could expand; second, Przywara's own intention that this work should come first, "and in a *single volume* together *with the essays*. Next to my *Mensch,* the corresponding col-

5. Przywara also suggested that von Balthasar include in between the two parts of the third volume, as a fitting intermezzo, von Balthasar's early review of the *Analogia Entis,* which he considered excellent. See Lochbrunner, *Hans Urs von Balthasar,* pp. 87f.; von Balthasar, "Die Metaphysik Erich Przywaras," *Schweizerische Rundschau* 33 (1933): 489-99. Von Balthasar, however, declined the offer, apparently deciding it would be better to leave his own contribution for the introduction to the Przywara bibliography, which he published around the same time.

6. Lochbrunner, *Hans Urs von Balthasar,* p. 84.

lected essays are among the most important things that I have written in recent years."[7]

There is, however, also a disadvantage to beginning with this volume: the *Analogia Entis* is, without question, Przywara's most demanding work, not only on account of its content, which presumes the reader's familiarity with more than two millennia of philosophical and theological reflection, but also on account of Przywara's lapidary — at times positively hieroglyphic — style, which over the years has proved daunting even to the most patient and educated readers of German theology. As von Balthasar noted in his review of the original work, "An exposition of this thought-world, which is compressed into 150 pages, would ordinarily require as many as 1000 pages of philosophical epic."[8] All of which makes the *Analogia Entis* arguably one of the most challenging works of philosophical theology ever written and, absent some prior acquaintance with Przywara's thought and earlier writings, almost inaccessible. Of necessity, therefore, given both the inherent difficulty of the work and the complicated history of its reception, the present translation includes a sizeable introduction, whose length is commensurate with its fourfold aim: first, given Przywara's relative obscurity today, to introduce his life and writings; second, given the text's very complicated philosophical and theological background, to sketch out the history of analogy as a philosophical and theological concept; third, given the inherent difficulties of this text, to introduce the *analogia entis* as a concept in Przywara's early work, as well as to summarize the basic argument of the *Analogia Entis* itself; and, fourth, given that the *analogia entis* is so controversial and freighted by philosophical and theological prejudices, to present and respond to the two most significant criticisms of the concept, stemming respectively from Karl Barth and from Martin Heidegger.

If the *Analogia Entis* presents great challenges even to the well-educated reader, it goes without saying that it presents great challenges to the translator as well, in large part because so many difficulties attend any attempt to read it in German. The first challenge (as for any reader of a difficult text) is hermeneutical; but here the hermeneutical difficulties are greater than usual because almost every sentence in the text requires considerable efforts at reflective disentanglement. For instance, at any given juncture in the text, if one

---

7. Lochbrunner, *Hans Urs von Balthasar*, p. 83. Letter to von Balthasar, February 14, 1962. The reference is to Przywara's *Mensch: Typologisch Anthropologie*, vol. 1 (Nürnberg: Glock und Lutz, 1959).

8. Von Balthasar, "Die Metaphysik Erich Przywaras," p. 489.

hopes to understand Przywara's point — in order even to *begin* to translate it — the same sentence may have to be read many times. And often the hermeneutical labor can feel like a true *Sisyphusarbeit*. Compounding the challenges posed by the content is a style of writing that is almost a parody of critical concision, a kind of philosophical shorthand or *Dicht-ung* in the etymological sense of the word: what would normally require pages of elaboration, Przywara often condenses into a single paragraph, or even into a single, undulously convoluted sentence — replete with multiple dashes, semicolons, subordinate clauses, delayed resolutions, and wantonly proliferating pronouns — that can run on for nearly a page at a time. Moreover, this same outlandish concision is frequently embodied in one or another of a host of bewildering semantic congelations and composite neologisms, such as *"in-über"* (which literally means "in-over," but is generally translated here as "in-and-beyond"), *"Spannungs-Einheit"* ("unity-in-tension"), *"Spannungs-Schwebe"* ("suspended tension"), and so forth — none of which translates well into English (hence the large number of our "translators' notes," which in most circumstances would be annoyingly obtrusive and superfluous).

At times, frankly, it was tempting to write a paraphrase of the text rather than a translation, wondering whether by doing so we might make Przywara more immediately understandable than a literal rendering would. In the case of Przywara, however, whose style of exposition was deliberate, compelling one to think if one is to understand him, the risks of paraphrase are greater than those of being too literal. Such an approach would have produced not a translation so much as a single possible interpretation of the text, and the original meaning of many passages might well have been not merely obscured but altogether lost. For this reason, we have tried to follow the model of translation suggested by Przywara's close friend and now canonized saint, Edith Stein, who was herself a translator (at Przywara's suggestion) and who was also one of the first persons to read and comment upon the *Analogia Entis:* "The translator has to be like a windowpane that lets in the light without itself being seen."[9] So, in the interminable twilight struggle between fidelity and felicity, the former has emerged victorious from every engagement in these pages; we have tried, however, to assure that the terms of armistice would be as generous as possible to the latter.[10]

9. Quoted in Teresia Renata de Spiritu Sancto, *Edith Stein: Lebensbild einer Philosophin und Karmelitin,* 7th ed. (Nürnberg: Glock und Lutz, 1957); also cited in Edith Stein, *Briefe an Hedwig Conrad-Martius* (Munich: Kösel Verlag, 1960), p. 7. It is a fitting motto for a saint, whose life was itself such a translation.

10. As it happens, the inherent limitations of translation with regard to an original,

In closing, we would like to thank those who in one way or another have given us aid and encouragement in the task of completing this translation. Among them our thanks goes to Dr. Hans-Anton Drewes, former director of the Karl Barth Archive in Basel, whose seminar on Barth, Przywara, and von Balthasar in Tübingen in the summer semester of 1997 originally inspired this project; thanks also to Professor Eberhard Jüngel for the pleasure of occasional conversations about Przywara, Barth, and Heidegger, which confirmed Przywara's importance to modern theology and the preposterousness of the negligible interest in him today. Among those who have facilitated the translation, our thanks goes to Bill Eerdmans and David L. Schindler, who initially agreed to this project and who waited patiently, beyond all reasonable expectations, for its completion. Thanks also to the Alexander von Humboldt Foundation for a grant to research Przywara's *Nachlass* at the Munich School of Philosophy, and in particular to Professors Harald Schöndorf, S.J., and Gerd Haeffner, S.J. Thanks also to Dr. Clemens Brodkorb, director of the Archive of the German province of the Society of Jesus, and to Fr. Andreas Batlogg, S.J., director of the Karl Rahner Archive. A special thanks also goes to Professor Manfred Lochbrunner for his hospitality and for his inestimably helpful scholarship, and to Dr. Martin Walko, director of the Dombibliothek Freising, for a consistently quiet place to study.

We would also like to thank friends and colleagues who have offered helpful advice along the way, or whose conversation has in one way or another helped to shape this project: Patricia Bellm, Paul Richard Blum, Peter Casarella, Christophe Chalamet, Lawrence Cunningham, Marian David, Reinhard Hütter, Keith Johnson, Grant Kaplan, Sean Kelsey, Graham

and the dynamic of its ceaseless movement between accuracy and readability, afford an analogous sense of what Przywara means by the "suspension" and rhythmic interplay of creaturely being *as* analogy. Indeed, for Przywara, the rhythm of analogy that defines creaturely being *eo ipso* defines the nature of language itself as a kind of dynamic translation. As he put it in reference to a Benedictine reviewer who had attempted to summarize his style, "He has grasped that my so-called '*analogia entis*' as the original structure of being is, with a similar necessity, the original structure of all thought, and therefore of all language. If being in itself is analogical, in the sense of the Fourth Lateran Council . . . , this necessarily applies to thought and language as well. But this means that both thought and language are an 'ever-transcending' movement [*ein 'je über hinaus*']. There is no such thing as possessive saturation in a concept or a formula. Rather, one can only make every thought and word transparent 'beyond itself,' which is to say that I think and speak in a 'transcendental dynamic' way: always beyond every concept and every word in ever renewed movement" (Erich Przywara, *Zwiegespräch an seinem 65. Geburtstag am 12. Oktober, 1954* [Nürnberg: Glock und Lutz, 1954], pp. 9f.).

McAleer, Gerald McKenny, Balázs Mezei, Francesca Aran Murphy, Kenneth Oakes, Cyril O'Regan, Aaron Pidel, S.J., Troy Stephano (who compiled the index), and Adrian Walker. We would also like to thank Jenny Hoffman, associate managing editor at Eerdmans, for her great patience in seeing this project — through multiple drafts, revisions, and, hence, a lengthier than usual redaction process — to completion. Our thanks also goes to Laura Betz, who has, with great patience, awaited the completion of this project, and who has read and helpfully commented upon much of this text; to Solwyn Hart, who endured the whole process with amazing equanimity and offered some indispensably trenchant observations on certain phrases in our English text; and to a number of doctoral students at Notre Dame who read an initial draft of the translation in the context of a seminar on Przywara, and who caught a number of typographical errors that had eluded us: Brian Dunkle, S.J., Stephen Gaetano, Patrick Gardner, Michael Hahn, Han-Luen Kantzer Komline, and Anthony Pagliarini. And thanks, finally, to Keith Johnson for his helpful correspondence, for his admirable scholarship, and — in a reprise, but in reverse, of Przywara's visit to Barth's seminar in 1929 — for graciously discussing Barth's view of the *analogia entis* in our doctoral seminar at Notre Dame in the spring semester of 2011.

JOHN R. BETZ *and* DAVID BENTLEY HART
July 31, 2012
Feast of St. Ignatius Loyola

Preface to the 1962 Edition

In the years since the publication of *Analogia Entis* I[1] in 1932, the author has not succeeded in completing a planned second volume to the *Analogia Entis* that would have developed its present structure into a sufficiently complete philosophy and theology. This was due to labor on other works and, during the war, frequent lecturing at the behest of Cardinal Faulhaber, who had commissioned the author to assist with the pastoral care of retired academics in Munich. In the absence of this second volume, the *analogia entis* increasingly made its way into all manner of spoken and written discourse, until the treatises appearing since 1956, especially those that appeared in the *Archivio di filosofia* in Rome, finally provided a deeper and more precise exposition of the *analogia entis* in the areas of philosophy and theology. As a unified corpus, these essays fulfill what was intended for the second volume; and for this reason they have here been appended to *Analogia Entis* I as "Part II."

Taken together with two early essays in *Scholastik* and three previous *Festschrift* contributions, these essays are at the same time the author's response to the discussion about the *analogia entis*. In spite of flat-out misunderstandings, which not infrequently occurred (on all sides), the concept has come to have a certain currency today: both in contemporary philosophical

---

1. What is here titled "Analogia Entis I" originally appeared in 1932 as the first volume of a planned two-volume work. According to the 1932 preface, the first volume (the first part of the present translation) was intended to introduce the "formal problem" of metaphysics as such and thus bore the subtitle "Principle." The projected second volume, which was never completed, was intended to fill out the basic material features of metaphysics, now specified as an analogical metaphysics, in terms of "consciousness, being, and world." — Trans.

circles as well as in certain circles of Protestant and Catholic theology. The misunderstanding, for which the author himself is not free of blame, has to do with his having chosen the word "Principle" for the title of the first volume — in order then, however, from the outset, to understand this "principle" as a dynamic primordial movement. In the new edition, therefore, the first volume from 1932 bears the title "Original Structure," while the subsequent collection of investigations concerning the *analogia* [*sic*] in various domains bears the title "Universal Rhythm." The final sentence of "*Analogia Entis* I," which was especially open to this misunderstanding, has also been supplemented in the present edition with a new concluding sentence.

In the context of the collected *Schriften*, the present volume, *Analogia Entis*, thus contains as its first principal part the unaltered text of "*Analogia Entis* I" from 1932 (with its sections "*Metaphysics as Such*" and "*Analogia Entis*"), and as its second principal part the essays on this theme spanning the period from 1939 to the present. Aside from the present *Schriften*, the *analogia entis*, as the "original structure" of philosophy and theology, is further elaborated in the following books: *Deus semper major* (1938-41; new edition Vienna, 1963), *Alter und Neuer Bund* (Vienna, 1956), and *Mensch* (Nuremberg, 1959).

At this point the author wishes to express his thanks to Hans Urs von Balthasar, the director of the Johannes Verlag, for generously undertaking a new edition of his out-of-print works.

Spring 1962

From the Preface to the First Edition
of Analogia Entis I (1932)

The decisive impetus of this work was a study of Thomas Aquinas's *Quaestiones disputatae* and *De ente et essentia* during the years 1912-13. At issue was the question of the distinction between essence and existence — *Sosein und Dasein*. As an alternative to the antithesis between the customary solutions of the schools, I sought a formula that would do justice to the way that the question of essence and existence appears in Thomas himself. In this regard I was decisively influenced by an intensive study, which I undertook between 1914 and 1918, of *Augustine* and *Dionysius the Areopagite*, as well as of German mysticism. This led me in the direction of a dynamic solution, and towards an emphatic *theologia negativa*. At the same time, and to a great extent over the years to come, this influence needed to be clarified by an engagement with modern forms of dynamic and aporetic thought: from *Goethe's* "polarity" and the philosophy of *Romanticism* (Baader and, above all, Görres), to *Nietzsche's* "dynamic heroism," to *Simmel's* "aporetics," to *Troeltsch's* "ethical dynamism." Then, in 1920-21, I reached an especially important conclusion to these studies in my engagement with *Newman's* "dynamic antithetics."[1] My engagement with Kant, Hegel, and Kierkegaard took place in subsequent years, mainly around the time when my writings on them appeared.

Equally, however, my work was influenced by relationships with contemporaries. I name them in chronological order. From Nietzsche the path led directly to the collected essays of *Max Scheler*. For me, his sociology (in his "material value-ethics") was intimately connected to the philosophy of

---

1. J. H. Newman, *Christentum. Ein Aufbau*, trans. Otto Karrer, ed. E. Przywara (Freiburg: Herder, 1922). [This was a large collection of German translations of Newman's writings, edited and provided with an interpretive introduction by Przywara. — Trans.]

Romanticism (Baader, Görres, Möhler). But it was his *On the Eternal in Man* that first led to an actual engagement.[2] My work is indebted to Scheler on two counts: for providing me with a vibrant connection to the phenomenological method and for compelling me (through Scheler's "immediacy of the religious") towards the explicit problematic of the *analogia entis*. It was therefore a happy coincidence that, in the same year in which my book on Scheler appeared, I came to see the necessity of a confrontation[3] with *Karl Barth* — though this did not lead to a personal, fruitful encounter until we met in Münster in 1929. It was in engagement with him that the theological aspect of the *analogia entis* developed into its proper form. Its philosophical elaboration[4] was chiefly the result of vibrant connections with phenomenology, which proved significant in that I became involved to a considerable extent with *Edith Stein's* efforts to put Husserl in conversation with Thomas. It was Edith Stein who paved the way for fruitful connections with *Husserl,* which exercised an initial influence upon the formation of my method. But it was influenced no less by my engagement with *Martin Heidegger,* which clarified the concept of creatureliness, especially over the course of my lectures in Davos (1929) and Freiburg (1930). Finally, my work ended up in a surprising parallel to *Johann Plenge;* in his tabulation of the method and system of sociology, he forged ahead towards an ontology of relation, and thus, necessarily, towards the problematic of analogy. Our works were to no small extent intertwined.

All of these influences did not come to fruition, however, until the years between 1929 and 1931, when the work itself compelled me to steep our contemporary problematic directly in the original tradition.[5] It was, above all, a more intensive study of Plato, Aristotle, and Thomas Aquinas that finally led to a breakthrough.

From the beginning my writings have been associated with the idea of the *analogia entis,* even though my first formulation of it arose out of my en-

---

2. See my *Religionsbegründung. Max Scheler — J. H. Newman* (Freiburg: Herder, 1923).

3. Przywara uses the old German term *Waffengang* here, which means an armed encounter or passage at arms in the course of a battle (for instance, an impromptu *duellum* between two knights). — Trans.

4. *Ausgestaltung.* Przywara seems to be picking up on the word "form" *(Gestalt)* in the previous sentence, implicitly suggesting something about the theological priority of the *analogia entis,* which is then elaborated in philosophical terms. — Trans.

5. *Ur-Tradition.* — Trans.

gagement with Max Scheler (late in 1922). In its objective form, and above all in my religious writings, it was associated with the Augustinian formula "*God in us and God beyond us.*" The first thing this indicated was my fundamental intention, which first emerged in the introduction to *Unsere Kirche* (1915): to understand the "ultimate" relation between God and creature. This led to my further concern with the relation between a *theologia positiva* and a *theologia negativa* (above all in the works from 1926, *Gott* and *Religionsphilosophie katholischer Theologie*). Thus, my inquiry was finally aimed at the question of the fundamental comportment of religious life (in *Himmelreich der Seele* I-V, 1922-23). The *Deus incomprehensibilis* "in us" — as a way of underscoring the all-pervading, living, personal proximity of the God who works all things — was seen to correspond to a final, unreserved, and unconditional self-surrender to his guidance. The *Deus incomprehensibilis* "beyond us" — as a way of underscoring the difference and separation between the God of sublime majesty above all things and "the human being who dwells on the earth" — was seen to correspond to the reverent comportment of sober service, soberly attentive to our earthliness and to the struggle of our earthly labor. But this was to pose the problem of the oscillating[6] "in-and-beyond."[7] It first went by the name "*dynamic polarity*" (in *Gottgeheimnis der Welt*, 1924), understood as a "*unity-in-tension*"[8] (in *Kirchenjahr*, 1923) *within constant "change"* (in *Wandlung*, 1925). This amounted to saying that the mystery of God is vibrantly experienced only in the back-and-forth of the experience of the inexhaustibility of the various aspects in which he has declared himself within the creaturely — aspects that mutually determine one another in a "*polar*" way; and that the difference between God (as the Is) and the creaturely (as that which "becomes") is clarified to the extent that one experiences the mutability of the creature. The words "dynamic" and "tension" are employed because, and insofar as, God is infinite and the creature is mutable. The words "polarity" and "unity," on the other hand, are employed because God's infinity is not an undulation of opposites, but the

---

6. *Schwingend.* Rendered here as "oscillation," this word, which recurs throughout Przywara's writings in connection with the *analogia entis*, generally indicates a vibrant — and ultimately musical — swinging and swaying back and forth. — Trans.

7. *In-über.* No term is more central to Przywara's special idiom than this. We have chosen, here and below, to render the phrase as "in-and-beyond" rather than, say, "in-over" or "in-and-above," because — as will become obvious — for Przywara, the "*über*" indicates the full scope of divine transcendence, the "ever greater" difference between Creator and creature. — Trans.

8. *Spannungseinheit.* — Trans.

immutability of his infinite unity; and because, on this account, the creature's "constant change" is grounded and flows within the (relative) immutability of a single uniform relation to and connectedness with God. The implication here is twofold: the positive aspect of being-given-over without reserve, and the negative aspect of having "no ground beneath one's feet." As a matter of course, therefore, what I intended with this acquired a twofold name: *"love"* (in *Liebe*, 1924) *and "night"* (in *Wandlung*, 1925, *Das Geheimnis Kierkegaards*, 1929, and *Karmel*, 1932). Naturally, therefore, it could equally be stated in the language of Paul's epistles (*Christus lebt in mir*, 1929), of Ignatius Loyola (*Majestas Divina*, 1925), and of Carmel (in *Wandlung*, 1925, *Das Geheimnis Kierkegaards*, 1929, and *Karmel*, 1932).

Then, corresponding to this, there was the question of method. The intellectual comportment indicated by the *analogia entis* (as a principle of method) appeared, on the one hand, as a *method of immanent historical understanding that aimed at an objective synthesis:* in my philosophical-historical works on Augustine, Thomas, Kant, Hegel, Kierkegaard, and the contemporary philosophical scene (*Newman, Christentum*, 1922; *Religionsbegründung*, 1923; *Gottgeheimnis der Welt*, 1924; *Gott*, 1926; *Religionsphilosophie katholischer Theologie*, 1926; *Ringen der Gegenwart* I and II, 1929; *Das Geheimnis Kierkegaards*, 1929; *Kant Heute: Eine Sichtung*, 1930; *Augustinus-Synthesis*, 1932). But, on the other hand, the lines of the *formal unity of philosophy and theology*, which were latent in the (unpublished) corpus of my lectures, became ever more pronounced. On the one hand, my writings present a theory that (in contrast to the *individuum de ratione materiae* of scholastic Thomism) seeks to comprehend the individually diversified fullness of things: a *differentiated universalism* of the "unity-in-tension between individual and community"; on the other hand, however, they present a theory that intends (over against a humanistic rationalism that goes all the way up to neo-scholasticism) a radical humbling of every (ontic) end-in-itself of self and community and of every rounded (noetic) calculation under the sovereignty of God: a *theocentrism* — *relativizing* all things human — of "God in Christ in the church."

Munich, February 1932

Translator's Introduction

John R. Betz

The totality of Przywara's work defies classification; it is not something that one can be finished with, and so most have chosen to ignore it. But whoever has gone through his school, wherever one later ends up, will carry the impression of this encounter in one's thought and life; and every return to the old master will leave one oddly shaken, perhaps because one comes to realize how much younger this old master has remained than all who have come after him.

HANS URS VON BALTHASAR[1]

For various reasons this translation of Erich Przywara's *Analogia Entis* (1932) and a collection of later essays is long overdue. Not only is the *Analogia Entis* a philosophical-theological tour de force, which boldly posits a Catholic analogical ontology in response to the history of philosophy from the pre-Socratics to Martin Heidegger; it is also one of the most controversial works in the history of modern theology, having inadvertently renewed a long-standing ecumenical debate over the relevance of metaphysics and natural theology to the Christian faith. As Przywara's protégé and lifelong friend Hans Urs von Balthasar put it, "No one who would wish to grasp the theological and philosophical currents of our time can avoid an engagement with Przywara's significant work."[2] What is more, as late as 1966 he speaks of Przywara's thought, as embodied in the *Analogia Entis*, as "*the* pharmakon

---

1. Erich Przywara, *Sein Schrifttum 1912-1962*, ed. Leo Zimny, with an introduction by Hans Urs von Balthasar (Einsiedeln: Johannes Verlag, 1963), p. 18.
2. See Manfred Lochbrunner, *Hans Urs von Balthasar und seine Theologen-Kollegen* (Würzburg: Echter Verlag, 2009), p. 97.

for the philosophy and theology of our time."[3] And yet, notwithstanding the work's historical significance, its arguably unparalleled intellectual heft, and the importance von Balthasar himself attached to it,[4] it is a work to which few have devoted serious attention. As a result, the term *analogia entis*, which originated in the Thomistic tradition and which Przywara reintroduced in the 1920s as a fundamental principle of Catholic theology, is typically employed in contemporary theology with little if any understanding of what it meant to Przywara himself. In the words of the eminent Protestant theologian Eberhard Jüngel, "The *analogia entis* has doubtless been invoked more often than it has even remotely been understood."[5] All of which makes an introduction to this troubled concept, and in particular Przywara's own understanding of it, something of a necessity.

Of course, in the English-speaking world the neglect of Przywara's work has largely been due to a lack of translations.[6] But even for readers of German one must immediately acknowledge several factors that have hindered scholarship and continue to present serious challenges to understanding Przywara today. Firstly, Przywara is difficult to categorize, being equally a

3. See "Erich Przywara," in *Tendenzen zur Theologie im 20. Jahrhundert. Eine Geschichte in Porträts* (Stuttgart: Olten, 1966), p. 357.

4. See Werner Löser, "Weg und Werk Hans Urs von Balthasars," *Philosophisch-Theologische Hochschule Sankt Georgen. Frankfurt am Main-Virtueller Leseraum:* "Von Balthasar never wavered in his conviction that the doctrine of the *'analogia entis'* was of decisive significance for every right-thinking philosophy and theology. It determines, whether implicitly or explicitly, all the expressions of his thought." See also Aidan Nichols, *The Word Has Been Abroad: A Guide Through Balthasar's Aesthetics* (Edinburgh: T. & T. Clark, 1998); and G. De Schrijver, *Le merveilleux accord de l'homme et Dieu: Études de l'analogie de l'être chez H. U. von Balthasar* (Louvain: Leuven University Press, 1983). See also von Balthasar's revealing correspondence with the director of the Kösel Verlag in 1939: "I can now confide to you that for a long time I have stood in front of your 'store' like a child in front of a Christmas display, with a finger in his mouth and ever widening eyes. And the object of these acquisitive looks? You won't be surprised: Przywara: *Analogia entis, Homo, Gott*. If I am being too immodest, then . . . 'just' send me the *Analogia*. For I can barely live without it" (Lochbrunner, p. 53). Why von Balthasar needed a copy since he already knew the work and reviewed it in 1933 is unclear; he merely indicates that for a time he was "forced to do without it."

5. Eberhard Jüngel, *Gott als Geheimnis der Welt*, 6th ed. (Tübingen: Mohr-Siebeck, 1992), p. 357. While the connection between them is somewhat tenuous, the title of this work bears an allusion to Przywara's *Gottgeheimnis der Welt* (1923).

6. While translations of the *Analogia Entis* have appeared in French (1990) and Italian (1995), thus far the only other works of Przywara to have been translated into English are his *Majestas Divina*, trans. Thomas Corbishley (Cork: Mercier Press, 1951) and *Religionsphilosophie katholischer Theologie*, which appeared under the title *Polarity: A German Catholic's Interpretation of Religion*, trans. A. C. Bouquet (London: Oxford University Press, 1935).

philosopher and a theologian, and so he tends to be neglected by philosophers unversed in theology and by theologians unversed in philosophy. Secondly, one must contend with the highly demanding nature of his thought, which presupposes a familiarity with the history of philosophy and theology and purports to lay bare in and through this history the formal structure of metaphysics "as such," beyond every particular metaphysics that has been or could be conceived. Thirdly, one must contend with his exceedingly concise and idiosyncratic prose style, which has proved daunting even to the most patient of readers and presents great, almost insurmountable challenges even to the most intrepid of translators.[7] As von Balthasar put it in his review of the *Analogia Entis*, pinpointing the difficulty, "an exposition of this thought-world, which is compressed into 150 pages, would ordinarily require as many as 1000 pages of philosophical epic."[8] Thus, even so competent a philosopher as Josef Pieper, who recounts being profoundly affected by Przywara's lectures in Whylen between 1924 and 1926, could find their later condensation in the *Analogia Entis* "virtually unreadable."[9] Finally, one must reckon with the unpopularity of metaphysics in our day, stemming variously from Kant's critical philosophy, Protestant critiques of natural theology (most notably on the part of Karl Barth), postmodern critiques of metaphysics by Nietzsche, Heidegger, and Derrida, and, last but not least, the mind-numbing horrors of the twentieth century, in view of which metaphysical investigations have come to seem, at best, woefully inadequate. Indeed, for these and other reasons, not a few philosophers and theologians have been happy to announce the "end of metaphysics," as though this could not happen soon enough.[10]

7. It is not without reason, therefore, that an initial French translation was abandoned. See Gustav Wilhelmy (pseudonym for Sigrid Müller), "Erich Przywara. Ein Überblick," in *Erich Przywara. 1889-1969. Eine Festgabe* (Düsseldorf: Patmos Verlag, 1969), p. 17. For Przywara's own understanding of his difficult style, see his interview with Stefan Varnhagen: *Erich Przywara. Zwiegespräch an seinem 65. Geburtstag am 12. Oktober, 1954* (Nürnberg: Glock und Lutz, 1954).

8. Hans Urs von Balthasar, "Die Metaphysik Erich Przywaras," *Schweizerische Rundschau* 33 (1933): 489.

9. "It is a shame that Przywara did not manage to publish the comprehensive, albeit perhaps too 'unguarded' conception [of analogy] that he presented in these philosophical-theological lectures; the unfinished and virtually unreadable *Analogia Entis*, which he himself declared to be the quintessence of these lectures, gives absolutely no picture of the concrete plenitude that he spread out before us at that time." See Josef Pieper, *Autobiographische Schriften*, ed. Berthold Wald (Hamburg: Felix Meiner Verlag), p. 82.

10. See, for example, such recent titles as Mark A. Wrathall, ed., *Religion after Meta-*

But if it is not surprising that Przywara's metaphysics has been neglected and frequently misunderstood, it *is* surprising that Przywara himself
continues to be a *quantité négligeable* even to most Catholic theologians.[11]
This is all the more baffling when one considers that Przywara was one of
the most brilliant and prolific theologians of the twentieth century, author-
ing over forty monographs and as many as 800 articles and reviews; that he
was the representative Catholic theologian at the Davos seminar in 1928 and
1929 (where Heidegger and Cassirer famously clashed); that he was an inspiration to Karl Rahner[12] and an unparalleled influence on the young von
Balthasar;[13] that Karl Barth regarded him as his most serious opponent, indeed, as "the giant Goliath incarnate"[14] whom he necessarily had to engage
(much as Luther had to face Cajetan); that he was a leading editor of the important Jesuit journal *Stimmen der Zeit* until the journal was shut down by
the Gestapo in 1941; that he was the first to introduce Newman to the world
of German theology, editing and introducing the first German edition of
Newman's works; that he was one of the first Catholic theologians to engage
modern phenomenology (most notably, Husserl, Heidegger, and Scheler);
that he was a friend and mentor to Edith Stein, steering her toward metaphysical questions and her first studies and translations of Thomas Aquinas;
that he was one of the first Catholic theologians to take Luther seriously on
the basis of a thorough study of the Reformer's works, and remained up to

physics (Cambridge: Cambridge University Press, 2003); John Panteleimon Manoussakis,
God after Metaphysics (Bloomington: Indiana University Press, 2007); and Kevin Hector,
Theology without Metaphysics (Cambridge: Cambridge University Press, 2011).

11. See, for example, Fergus Kerr, *Twentieth-Century Catholic Theologians* (Oxford:
Wiley-Blackwell, 2007), in which Przywara is barely mentioned.

12. As Rahner put it in 1965, "One must not forget Father Erich Przywara. For the
Catholics of Germany in the twenties, thirties, and forties he was considered one of the
greatest minds. He had a great influence on all of us when we were young." See Paul Imhof,
ed., *Karl Rahner in Dialogue: Conversations and Interviews, 1965-1985* (New York: Crossroad,
1986), p. 14.

13. Von Balthasar refers to him as an "unforgettable guide and master" and "the greatest spirit" he was ever permitted to meet. See *My Work: In Retrospect* (San Francisco: Ignatius
Press, 1993), pp. 50, 89: ". . . Erich Przywara, an unforgettable guide and master. Never since
have I encountered such a combination of depth and fullness of analytic clarity and all-
embracing synoptic vision. The publication of three volumes of his works in my house is intended as an external sign of thanks; but none of my own books should hide what it owes to
him."

14. See Barth, Letter to Pastor Horn, February 12, 1929 (Karl Barth Archive). See also
Barth's letters to Eduard Thurneysen in *Karl Barth–Eduard Thurneysen Briefwechsel*, vol. 2,
1921-1930 (Zürich: TVZ, 1974), pp. 638, 651-54, 708-9.

the Second Vatican Council in the vanguard of ecumenical dialogue;[15] and, finally, when one considers that he was a genuinely *Catholic* thinker, so much so that many regarded him as the *"doctor universalis."*[16] Thus, commenting on his astounding range and charity of intellect, in a *laudatio* from 1967 Karl Rahner speaks of Przywara's "lifelong dialogue with the past and the present, with the entirety of western intellectual history from Heraclitus to Nietzsche," and of "his openness to all in order to give to all."[17]

Of course, Przywara was also a thinker of his generation and for his generation, as is especially evident from his two-volume *Ringen der Gegenwart,* which is, among other things, an engaging commentary on the philosophical and theological issues of the early twentieth century. But as both Rahner and von Balthasar stress, Przywara's thought transcends his time, possessing an almost timeless quality, indeed an abiding novelty. To be sure, Rahner admits that in the noisy marketplace of ideas, Przywara's voice is hardly heard anymore. But, he asks, "Does this mean that the Catholic generation of today has learned what it had to learn from him and, now that it is able to forget the old teacher, can continue to march nonchalantly along the path of the future of the Church without him?"[18] "Without being a prophet," he continues, "I feel compelled to say that we, the generation after him, as well as future generations still have critical things to learn from him."[19] And in this regard he predicts, "The whole Przywara, especially the late Przywara, is yet to come. He stands at a place in the road that many in the Church have yet to get past."[20]

Given their close student-teacher relationship, which grew into a lifelong friendship,[21] von Balthasar's lamenting of Przywara's fate is even more

---

15. See, for example, Erich Przywara and Hermann Sauer, *Gespräch zwischen den Kirchen. Das Grundsätzliche* (Nürnberg: Glock und Lutz Verlag, 1956).

16. See, for example, the publisher's *Werbetext* for *Humanitas: Der Mensch Gestern und Morgen* (1952).

17. Karl Rahner, *Gnade als Freiheit. Kleine theologische Beiträge* (Freiburg: Herder, 1968), p. 268. See also Karl H. Neufeld, S.J., "Vertiefte und gelebte Katholizität. Erich Przywara — 100 Jahre," *Theologie und Philosophie* 65 (1990): 161-71. See also Walter Warnach, "Erich Przywara zum 75. Geburtstag am 12. Oktober 1964," *Frankfurter Allgemeine Zeitung,* 12 October 1964, where Przywara is described as "perhaps the most Catholic theologian of the twentieth century."

18. Rahner, *Gnade als Freiheit,* p. 271.

19. Rahner, *Gnade als Freiheit,* p. 271.

20. Rahner, *Gnade als Freiheit,* p. 272.

21. Von Balthasar's long relationship with Przywara, whom he variously addresses in their correspondence as "Dear Friend," "Dear Master [*Meister*]," etc., began during his

JOHN R. BETZ

poignant: "Erich Przywara's immense theological undertaking — whose profundity and breadth is without comparison in our time — could have provided critical therapy for Christian thought in our day."[22] And in what, for von Balthasar, did this critical therapy consist? His answer may surprise us if we have mistakenly come to associate Przywara's thought with an overweening metaphysics or natural theology:

> [Przywara] had long anticipated the opening of the Church to the world that came with the [Second Vatican] Council, but he also possessed the corrective that has not been applied in the way that the Council's [teachings] have been inflected and broadly put into practice: namely, the elemental, downright Old Testament sense for the divinity of God, who is a consuming fire, a death-bringing sword, and a transporting love. Indeed, he alone possessed the language in which the word *God* could be heard without that touch of faint-heartedness that has led to the luke-

philosophical studies in Pullach between 1931 and 1933, the conclusion of which was his philosophical dissertation, "Erich Przywaras Philosophie der Analogie." See von Balthasar, *Our Task* (San Francisco: Ignatius Press, 1994), pp. 37, 103, where he notes being "chaperoned at a distance by Przywara," whose "influence on my first attempts at philosophy is obvious," and whom he credits, along with his other teachers de Lubac and Adrienne von Speyr, for having "showed me, in contrast to a narrow scholastic theology, the world-spanning dimensions of what is Catholic." After his theological studies in Lyon, von Balthasar returned to Munich, where from 1937 to 1939 he lived and worked in the same house with Przywara on the editorial staff of *Stimmen der Zeit*. While their contact lessened after von Balthasar's return to Switzerland and failed plans for Przywara to join him there, he never ceased to feel and express his indebtedness to him, as in his letter from October 6, 1964: "Caro Maestro . . . First of all thanks — and an obvious thanks, because I cannot imagine what I would have become without you — though whenever I read you anew I feel myself outclassed, as in the beginning. Thanks be to God that he made and sent you, even if your life has become such a chain of sorrows" [from Przywara's *Nachlass*]. For a definitive treatment of their relationship, see Lochbrunner, *Hans Urs von Balthasar und seine Theologen-Kollegen*, pp. 17-146.

22. Von Balthasar, "Erich Przywara," pp. 354-55. In a letter to Przywara from November 27, 1962, von Balthasar indicates that today's situation is the opposite of what the Church faced, and Przywara was responding to, in the various systems and absolutisms of the nineteenth and early twentieth century. For "what do we have today? A complete metaphysical impotence and lack of vision, such a formal functionalism that the original motivation for the *Analogia Entis* is no longer even felt and its necessity is no longer even perceived . . ." (Przywara's *Nachlass*). In other words, as von Balthasar here suggests, no metaphysics, as is the tendency today, is just as bad as an absolute metaphysics. Hence, to draw von Balthasar's implicit conclusion, the Church has a perennial need for some kind of metaphysical vision — not, to be sure, an absolute metaphysics, but a vigorous *creaturely* metaphysics of the kind provided by Przywara's *analogia entis*.

6

warm chatter of the average theology of today. He lives like the mythical salamander in the fire: there, at the point where finite, creaturely being arises out of the infinite, where that indissoluble mystery holds sway that he baptized with the name *analogia entis*.[23]

That is to say, far from "domesticating" God by bringing him down to the level of creaturely concepts by means of analogy (which is the most common and most mistaken notion of what Przywara means by the *analogia entis*), Przywara was in von Balthasar's estimation a prophet of the Divine Majesty, who was commissioned to shake the foundations of a self-assured, secular culture and humble it before the mystery of the ever-greater God revealed in Christ. Commenting further on Przywara's pathos and extraordinary vocation, he writes:

> [Przywara] like no other broke to pieces all the putative absolute formulas outside and in the Church as though they were nothing but toys, razed every "high tower set against God," literally decimated all concepts, in order to take "every thought captive to Christ" and to point through the flaming contradictions of the Crucified and Resurrected One to the unfathomable depths of God. There is really no one far and wide, either domestic or abroad, who has received a charism of similar dimensions to provide an effective indication of the absoluteness of God; it is therefore indispensable to go through his school, in order to learn with the help of his inexhaustible insights and formulas, born out of the greatest religious passion, how to speak appropriately about God.[24]

Certainly, anticipating the Second Vatican Council, Przywara also possessed for that time an unparalleled degree of theological openness to

---

23. Von Balthasar, "Erich Przywara," pp. 354-55.

24. Von Balthasar, "Erich Przywara," p. 357. Similarly, von Balthasar writes, "Like everyone who encounters the living God and is called to proclaim Him, Przywara was more than simply a 'thinker.' If with one half of his being he was such a sharp and implacable thinker, like no other in his time, this was simply the way that he fulfilled the Pauline duty 'to use weapons of . . . divine power to destroy strongholds, to unmask sophistries, to raze every high tower that would exalt itself against the knowledge of God, and to take every thought captive to obedience to Christ' (2 Cor. 10:4-5). One can only understand the passion with which he cleared the floor, broke every possibility of a system and forced it into the yoke of relativity if one understands it as he himself understood it, as obedient service to the mystery that, were it not for this clearing away, could not be descried" (Erich Przywara, *Sein Schrifttum*, p. 6).

the world — to philosophy, literature, and culture — as is obvious from the remarkable diversity of his corpus and such wide-ranging individual works as his *Humanitas;* and von Balthasar clearly learned much from his teacher in this regard, saying that Przywara helped him to appreciate the "world-spanning dimensions of what is Catholic."[25] Equally, though, and just as importantly, von Balthasar saw in Przywara an antidote to every facile identification of God and humanity (leading to the degradation of true, God-centered worship and even true love of Christ as *God*). Thus von Balthasar writes in 1948, still hopeful that Przywara would find an audience among those involved in future reforms of the Church: "Few have a clearer vocation to advise, to clarify, to illuminate and, even if they cannot join in the planning themselves, train those who would do so for their mission, than Erich Przywara."[26] But mindful of Przywara's prophetic fate, he laments that "our age has chosen the easier path of not engaging him" — indeed, of "ignoring him."[27] As he puts it at the beginning of another, almost elegiac late tribute:

> The prophets who were rapt by angels and transported to the throne of glory in order that they might experience there how much they would have to "suffer for His name" — such as these could not help but remain solitaries. . . . Their words burn; they do not baptize in water, but in spirit and fire; zeal for God's house consumes them; they are most certainly ablaze. And when, having been misunderstood, inhospitably turned away, and undervalued by their own and those closest to them, when despised, derided, betrayed, and tired to death they finally give their soul back to God, it could be that Consuming Fire will send his chariot of fire to bring them home.[28]

Like Rahner, however, von Balthasar also believed that Przywara's thought would one day have a significant impact. As he put it in a letter from 1969 just a few years before Przywara's death, "My thoughts are always with you, and no less my thanks for all the indispensable things I have received [from you]. I also believe that your hour will once again come and have a very great impact, and this could happen very soon, once the God-is-dead

---

25. Von Balthasar, *Our Task,* p. 103.

26. Von Balthasar, foreword to Przywara's *Vier Predigten über das Abendland* (Einsiedeln: Johannes Verlag, 1948), p. 8.

27. Von Balthasar, "Erich Przywara," p. 354; Erich Przywara, *Sein Schrifttum,* p. 18.

28. Erich Przywara, *Sein Schrifttum,* p. 5.

wave has been smashed to bits on the rock. Then no other way will remain but yours."[29]

But if von Balthasar is right, if Przywara has been misunderstood, and if he continues to be neglected and ignored, the Church has not entirely forgotten him. For as John Paul II remarked in a papal address in Germany in 1980, Przywara remains one of the great theologians of the German Catholic tradition, along with Albert the Great, Nicholas of Cusa, Johann Adam Möhler, Matthias Scheeben, and Romano Guardini — theologians "who have enriched and continue to enrich not merely the Church in Germany, but the theology and life of the entire Church."[30] As far as John Paul II's own theology is concerned, one sees something of Przywara's legacy in the encyclical *Fides et Ratio,* in which the late pope calls for a philosophy of "*genuinely metaphysical* range," affirms an "intimate relationship" between faith and metaphysical reasoning, sees metaphysics as playing "an essential role of mediation in theological research," and, in keeping with this vision, exhorts fundamental theologians to recover and express "to the full the metaphysical dimension of truth."[31] What is more, in the same encyclical John Paul II not only underscores the importance of analogy to theology, but cites the very passage from the Fourth Lateran Council that Przywara consistently identified as the dogmatic basis and summary of his doctrine.[32] All of which represents, one could argue, a papal vindication of Przywara's basic insights. Indeed, one could argue that after decades of neglect, during which even Catholic theologians have abjured metaphysics, John Paul II has called Catholic theologians to recover and pursue precisely the kind of metaphysics that Przywara proposed in his *Analogia Entis.*

Not surprisingly, given his roots in the German theological tradition, Benedict XVI is no less familiar with Przywara, having studied both his early

29. Letter to Przywara from October 10, 1969; quoted in Lochbrunner, *Hans Urs von Balthasar und seine Theologen-Kollegen,* p. 121.

30. Papal address to theologians in Altötting, Germany (November 18, 1980): "Sie stehen in einer großen Tradition, wenn ich nur an den hl. Albert den Großen, Nikolaus von Kues, Möhler und Scheeben, Guardini und Przywara denke. Ich nenne diese hervorragenden Theologen stellvertretend für viele andere, die in der Vergangenheit wie in der Gegenwart nicht nur die Kirche des deutschen Sprachraums, sondern die Theologie und das Leben der ganzen Kirche bereichert haben und noch ständig bereichern."

31. *Fides et Ratio,* §§83, 97, 105.

32. *Fides et Ratio,* §84; see Denzinger-Schönmetzer, 806: *inter creatorem et creaturam non potest tanta similitudo notari, quin inter eos non sit maior dissimilitudo notanda* (between the Creator and the creature no similarity can be noted, however great, without compelling one to observe the greater dissimilarity between them).

and his late work.[33] In a review of Przywara's late work, which he describes as "masterful" and as possessing a "salutary sobriety," he not only displays a profound grasp of Przywara's doctrine of the *analogia entis*, but also masterfully illustrates how Przywara's understanding of the *analogia fidei* (as the analogy between the two covenants centered in Christ) is ultimately connected to his understanding of the *analogia entis*, namely, as the latter's representation *par excellence*.[34] For the "ever greater God" of the *analogia entis*, Benedict (then Joseph Ratzinger) points out, is nowhere so manifest as in the crossing oppositions of the *admirabile commercium* of the Cross; indeed, it is in the glory of the Cross that we see precisely a coincidence of a *"theologia analogiae fidei"* and a *"theologia analogiae entis."*[35] In Benedict's estimation, therefore, Przywara's late work, especially his epilogue to *Alter und Neuer Bund*, demands serious attention, constituting a "significant theological prolegomenon" whose "objective weight" is in every respect comparable to his *Analogia Entis*.

While it is difficult to say to what extent Benedict himself may have been influenced by Przywara, it is significant that in his Regensburg address from 2006 he speaks of the principle of analogy as fundamental to the faith of the Church: ". . . the faith of the Church has always insisted that between God and us, between his eternal Creator Spirit and our created reason there exists a real analogy, in which — as the Fourth Lateran Council in 1215 stated — unlikeness remains infinitely greater than likeness, yet not to the point of abolishing analogy and its language."[36] The significance of this statement in the present context is that here again, as in *Fides et Ratio*, the implicit reference is to Przywara, who was the first to advance the notion of analogy as a "fundamental form" of Catholic theology, and who likewise did so by connecting it to the teaching of the Fourth Lateran Council. Thus, one could argue, Przywara stands obscurely in the background of the thought of John Paul II and Benedict XVI, making the recovery of his thought, especially for Catholic theology today, that much more relevant.

33. For Przywara's influence on Benedict, see Aidan Nichols, O.P., *The Thought of Pope Benedict XVI: An Introduction to the Theology of Joseph Ratzinger* (New York: Continuum, 2005), pp. 28, 49f.; see also Tracey Rowland, *Ratzinger's Faith: The Theology of Pope Benedict XVI* (New York: Oxford University Press, 2008), p. 24, where she names Przywara as an influence, along with Augustine, Newman, and Guardini.

34. Joseph Ratzinger, "Erich Przywaras Alterswerk," in *Wort und Wahrheit* 13 (1958): 220-21.

35. Ratzinger, "Erich Przywaras Alterswerk," pp. 220-21.

36. Cf. Joseph Ratzinger, *The Spirit of the Liturgy* (San Francisco: Ignatius Press, 2000), pp. 44-50.

To this end, given how little is known about Przywara in the English-speaking world, the following introduction begins with a brief account of his life and work, particularly as it informs his understanding of the *analogia entis*. Subsequent sections will then discuss the philosophical and theological background of the *analogia entis,* the *analogia entis* in Przywara's early work, and the basic argument of the original 1932 text (Part I of the present translation). On this basis, it is hoped, the reader will find it easier to follow the path of Przywara's thought, and to appreciate how the original, highly abstract *magnum opus* of 1932 is complemented and filled out by the later essays written between 1939 and 1959, which were selected by Przywara in consultation with von Balthasar and comprise the content of Part II.[37]

Finally, whether or not one is inclined to agree with Przywara that the *analogia entis* is simply a way of articulating the metaphysics implied by the Christian doctrine of creation, one cannot overlook the fact that this concept has been vigorously contested, most notably by Karl Barth. As Barth famously declared in the preface to his *Church Dogmatics:* "I regard the *analogia entis* as *the* invention of Antichrist, and I believe that because of it it is impossible ever to become a Roman Catholic, all other reasons for not doing so being to my mind shortsighted and trivial."[38] Whether or not this statement was justified; whether or not it illustrates Barth's penchant for rhetorical fireworks (as with his similarly vehement response to Emil Brunner); whether or not it was a turn of old-fashioned Protestant rhetoric intended to disabuse his Protestant confreres of charges of his crypto-Catholicism;[39] or, whether, seen in the best possible light, it was a kind of joke, as Przywara magnanimously seems to have taken it,[40] the effect of Barth's pronouncement on the history of Przywara's reception and the subsequent history of twentieth-century theology and ecumenical dialogue

37. The only exception to their selection for the 1962 edition is the inclusion in the present translation of two supplemental essays that originally appeared in French and have been newly translated on the basis of the German typescripts in the archive of the German Province of the Society of Jesus in Munich: the essay on Edith Stein and Simone Weil, which Przywara and von Balthasar had at one point considered including in the volume, and the essay on Husserl and Heidegger.

38. *Church Dogmatics* I/1, 2nd ed., trans. G. W. Bromiley (Edinburgh: T. & T. Clark, 1975), p. xiii.

39. See Bruce McCormack, "Karl Barth's Version of the *Analogia Entis:* A Dialectical No and Yes to Roman Catholicism," in *The Analogy of Being: Invention of the Antichrist or the Wisdom of God* (Grand Rapids: Eerdmans, 2010), p. 107.

40. See Przywara, *In und Gegen. Stellungnahmen zur Zeit* (Nürnberg: Glock und Lutz, 1955), p. 278.

cannot be denied. Nor, if one is to assess the currency of Przywara's metaphysics today, can one fail to appreciate the state of philosophy after Heidegger and the confident assertions on the part of countless postmodern philosophers and theologians that metaphysics is a problematic inheritance that must either be dispensed with — in the name of postmodern ontology or biblical theology — or, at the very least, like an inveterate temptation, overcome. Of necessity, therefore, the final section will address some of the most common criticisms of the *analogia entis*, stemming, on the one hand, from Barth, and, on the other, from Heidegger.

1. Erich Przywara (1889-1972): Life and Writings[41]

Of Polish and German descent (his mother was German), Erich Przywara was born in 1889 in the upper Silesian city of Kattowitz, today Katowice, in southern Poland. As he described the region years later, it was a land of intersecting empires (Germany, Russia, and Austria) and a culture full of contradictions: between Pole and German, East and West, Romanticism and modern technological rationalism.[42] Not surprisingly, therefore, he speaks of his roots in terms of a "unity of opposites." In subsequent years, in the context of his early musical training, he also came to appreciate this theme in the polyphony of Palestrina and Orlando di Lasso, as well as in Bach and Liszt (not the popular Liszt, but the "profound Liszt" of his choral work "Christus"). All of which proved significant to his later thought; for it was his appreciation of "music as form" that not only shaped his religious poetry, but also his understanding of "polarity," "unity-in-tension" [*"Spannungseinheit"*], and ultimately "analogy."[43]

---

41. The following draws primarily upon Gustav Wilhelmy, "Erich Przywara. Ein Überblick," in *Erich Przywara. 1889-1969. Eine Festgabe* (Düsseldorf: Patmos Verlag, 1969). See also Berhard Gertz, "Erich Przywara (1889-1972)," in *Christliche Philosophie im katholischen Denkendes 19. und 20. Jahrhunderts*, ed. Emerich Coreth (Graz: Styria, 1988), vol. 2, pp. 572-89; Thomas O'Meara, O.P., *Erich Przywara, S.J. His Theology and His World* (Notre Dame: University of Notre Dame Press, 2002); and Friedrich Wulf, "Christliches Denken. Eine Einführung in das theologische-religiöse Werk von Erich Przywara, S.J. (1889-1972)," in *Gottes Nähe*, ed. Paul Imhof (Würzburg: Echter, 1990), pp. 353-65.

42. Przywara, *In und Gegen*, pp. 12-13.

43. Przywara, *In und Gegen*, pp. 12-13.

1.1. Przywara's Education and Early Works

In 1908, Przywara entered the Jesuit novitiate in Exaten in the Netherlands (given the anti-Jesuit laws that were still in effect in Germany).[44] From this period his novice master, Johann Baptist Müller, stands out as an important early influence, having helped him to appreciate Ignatius' profound love of the liturgy as the "secret basis" of the *Spiritual Exercises,* and for having modeled the dictum of his namesake, *illum oportet crescere, me autem minui* (John 3:30). In short, Müller modeled for him the life of a Jesuit as one of selfless service as a "friend of the bridegroom."[45] From 1910 to 1913 he continued his formation with philosophical studies in Valkenburg, also in the Netherlands. It was at this time that he began an intensive study of Thomas Aquinas, beginning with the *Quaestiones disputatae* and Thomas's early work *De ente et essentia.* Other important influences include Gerhard Gietmann and the biblical scholar Franz von Hummelauer. The most influential teacher from this period, however, seems to have been Joseph Fröbes. For it was in Fröbes's classes, if not earlier, that Przywara would have been introduced to the concept of the *analogia entis.*[46] In no sense therefore is the term *analogia entis* original to Przywara. On the contrary, it was a common topic among Jesuit scholastics ever since Suarez's *Disputationes Metaphysicae,* and can be traced back even earlier to the Dominicans, specifically to Cajetan and John of St. Thomas.[47]

From 1913 to 1917 Przywara spent his so-called "college" years at Stella

44. At the time, given the continued ban on the Society of Jesus in Germany (dating back to the *Kulturkampf* between 1871 and 1878), this was one of the two Jesuit novitiates of the German province.

45. Wilhelmy, "Erich Przywara. Ein Überblick," p. 9.

46. In Fröbes's codex on ontology, for example, we find a heading that included the following explanation: "Conceptus entis ut sic est analogus, et quidem quoad Deum et creaturam, quoad substantiam et accidens analogia attributionis intrinsicae." And in the same textbook we also find the following: "non possunt Deus et creatura connumerari quasi duo entia, quia modus essendi tam infinite distat in utroque casu." See Julio Terán-Dutari, "Die Geschichte des Terminus 'Analogia Entis' und das Werk Erich Przywaras," in *Philosophisches Jahrbuch der Görres-Gesellschaft* 77 (1970): 164-65.

47. Terán-Dutari, "Die Geschichte des Terminus 'Analogia Entis,'" pp. 164-65. See, for example, Disputations 28, §3 and 32, §2. See also John P. Doyle, "Suarez on the Analogy of Being," *The Modern Schoolman* 46 (March 1969): 219-49; (May 1969): 323-41. As we shall see, however, Przywara was more than a mediating figure; for, in reintroducing the *analogia entis,* he endowed it with a far more comprehensive significance, transforming it "from a scholastic technicality into the fundamental structure of Catholic theology." See Rahner, *Gnade als Freiheit,* p. 270.

Matutina in Feldkirch, Austria, where he served as the prefect of music, and together with Josef Kreitmaier, produced a collection of hymns that originally appeared under the title *Unsere Kirche* (1915) and in subsequent editions as *Gloria*. During this time he also dedicated himself to intensive study of Augustine, Pseudo-Dionysius, German mysticism, as well as to what he refers to as the "dynamic" and "aporetic" thought of Goethe, Baader, Görres, Nietzsche, Simmel, and Troeltsch.[48] From early on, therefore, and as the scope of his own corpus shows, Przywara was never a pure neo-scholastic — as much as he regarded Thomas Aquinas as "the teacher" — but was decidedly engaged with modern thought. In fact, anticipating the Second Vatican Council, he was one of the first Catholics of his generation to break out of the confines of a narrow scholasticism, engage modern culture, and show how its intrinsic philosophical and cultural problems ultimately demand a religious answer. As he put it in the epigraph to his first work, *Eucharistie und Arbeit* (1917), which was subsequently translated into four languages, "The question of our time is fundamentally a religious one, and politics and society are nothing but the wrappings of its hidden existence."[49] But as this first work also shows, while Przywara was always engaged with modern culture, his thought was centered upon Christ in the Eucharist. Indeed, the express content of his first work is none other than a series of meditations on the empowering Eucharistic presence of "Christ in you," which should transform everything we say and do.

In the same year, 1917, Przywara returned to Valkenburg, where he continued with his theological studies and in 1920 was ordained a priest. While he continued to study the church Fathers, especially Augustine, during the final years of his doctorate he began to take an interest in John Henry Newman and Max Scheler. Przywara was impressed by Newman and defended him against popular suspicions of modernism. In fact, he was so impressed by "the great cardinal," viewing him as a modern-day church Father, indeed as Augustine *redivivus,* that he took up the task of editing and introducing the first German edition of his works, which appeared in 1922.[50] In

---

48. See the preface to the first edition of the *Analogia Entis.*

49. *Schriften,* vol. 1, p. 1. The quote is from Martin Deutinger.

50. See J. H. Kardinal Newman, *Christentum. Ein Aufbau,* 8 vols., trans. Otto Karrer (Freiburg: Herder, 1922), the fourth volume of which is Przywara's perspicacious summary of Newman entitled *Einführung in Newmans Wesen und Werk.* An English edition of Przywara's selection of Newman's texts was published under the title *A Newman Synthesis* (London: Sheed & Ward, 1930) and has since been reprinted under the new title *The Heart of Newman* (San Francisco: Ignatius Press, 1997). Unfortunately, however, in both English edi-

Przywara's view, what connected Newman to Scheler (next to Husserl, the other great early phenomenologist) was that both had raised anew, and in Scheler's case at an explicitly philosophical level, the question of religion's foundation; and it was precisely this topic that Przywara explored in his first major work, *Religionsbegründung,* which is essentially a critical reception of Scheler in light of Newman.[51]

The next phase of Przywara's productivity coincided with his transition in 1922 to the editorial staff of the Jesuit journal *Stimmen der Zeit* in Munich, which for nearly two decades, until the journal was shut down by the Gestapo in 1941, was his principal outlet as a theological critic of contemporary thought and culture. In addition to regular articles and reviews, Przywara also continued to produce monographs at an extraordinary, almost superhuman rate. For example, between 1922 and 1932 he produced 230 articles and reviews, gave 237 lectures all over Germany and central Europe, and in between managed to produce seventeen books. That is, on average, roughly every other week he produced an article, on alternate weeks he gave lectures, and roughly every seven months he produced a book. In the *annus mirabilis* of 1923, for instance, he produced no less than four books, seventeen articles (not counting reviews), and gave twenty-six lectures. In addition to his *Religionsbegründung,* the three other books from this year were a five-volume devotional work on Christ's parables, entitled *Himmelreich der Seele; Gottgeheimnis der Welt,* in which he began to spell out his philosophy

---

tions Przywara's commentary was omitted, leaving the reader without a sense of how Przywara actually read Newman and his reasoning behind this particular arrangement.

51. Przywara, *Religionsbegründung. Max Scheler — J. H. Newman* (Freiburg: Herder, 1923). What Przywara especially valued in Scheler (and the early Husserl, for that matter) was his reversal of Kant's "Copernican revolution," his reorientation of philosophy toward an objective realism, and the prospect this presented, after centuries of opposition, of a rapprochement between modern philosophy and scholasticism, most specifically, Thomas Aquinas. In other words, with the so-called "Kant crisis" and the rise of phenomenology, it was once again philosophically respectable to claim that we can actually have knowledge of an objective order of being. As Scheler himself noted around this time, the phenomenological movement "has a profounder affinity with the basic principles of traditional Christian philosophy than any other modern philosophical school since Cartesius." See Scheler's preface to Otto Gründler, *Elemente zu einer Religionsphilosophie auf phänomenologischer Grundlage* (München: Kösel & Pustet, 1922); quoted in *Religionsbegründung,* p. 2. In the end, however, Przywara criticizes Scheler's essentialist phenomenology, above all his principle of an "immediate" knowledge of God, for failing to appreciate the scholastic *analogia entis,* the tension between essence and existence, and the mediate, earthbound quality of any knowledge of God that this implies. See in this regard also Przywara, *Christliche Existenz* (Leipzig: Jakob Hegner, 1934), pp. 13-14.

of polarity; and, finally, a book of meditations on the liturgical calendar also inspired by the theme of polarity, entitled *Kirchenjahr: Die christliche Spannungseinheit.* Then in rapid succession came such works as *Liebe: Der christliche Wesensgrund* (1924); *Wandlung: Ein Christenweg* (1925); *Majestas Divina: Ignatianische Frömmigkeit* (1925); *Gott* (1925); and, as a capstone to his phenomenal early period, his *Religionsphilosophie katholischer Theologie* (1926).

At this point Przywara was beginning to be recognized as an important Catholic thinker both in Germany and abroad, speaking in such distinguished venues as the first and second international Davos conferences in 1928 and 1929. As one commentator observed, "Next to Guardini and Peter Lippert, Przywara is the most important intellectual [*geistige*] phenomenon in the realm of contemporary German Catholicism."[52] What most seems to have impressed his contemporaries, however, was Przywara's "genuinely Catholic range of intellect," i.e., his ability to feel his way into all kinds of systems and redeem from them at least a kernel of truth. Accordingly, the *Courrier de Genève* referred to Przywara's great "intellectual charity," adding that "when he criticizes, it is not to tear down, but to build up, so that in between the years 1920 and 1930 one could call him Germany's greatest constructive critic in the area of philosophy."[53]

In this regard the single most important testament to Przywara as a critic is his *Ringen der Gegenwart* (1929), a two-volume collection of articles written between 1922 and 1927. To give some sense of the variety of this collection, Przywara here discusses such themes as metaphysics, Romanticism, contemporary philosophy and theology, ecumenism, and the liturgical movement, as well as a host of figures, past and contemporary, such as Karl Adam, Hermann Bahr, Karl Barth, Emil Brunner, Martin Buber, Hermann Cohen, Karl Eschweiler, Nicolai Hartmann, Friedrich Heiler, Hegel, Wilhelm Herrmann, Husserl, Kant, Paul Natorp, Nietzsche, Matthias Scheeben, Schelling, Georg Simmel, Nathan Söderblom, Ernst Troeltsch, Josef Wittig, Georg Wobbermin, and Peter Wust — not to mention such standard figures in Przywara's corpus as Augustine, Aquinas, and Newman. In short, *Ringen der Gegenwart* is a treasury of theological commentary and an important resource for our knowledge of this period. But it also contains seminal philo-

52. From *Berliner Börsenkurier,* February 24, 1926; quoted in Wilhelmy, "Erich Przywara. Ein Überblick," p. 60. As another commentator put it in 1929, "I know of no other Catholic thinker who has so vigorously thought through the movements of our time." See *Jong Dietschland,* Nr. 28 (1929); quoted in Wilhelmy, p. 55.

53. *Courrier de Genève,* September 18, 1930; quoted in Wilhelmy, p. 58.

sophical and metaphysical reflections that would be developed in later works; and in this regard — as a further testament to his familiarity with the philosophical currents of the time — it is significant that Przywara was often in conversation with Husserl and Edith Stein. In fact, in his acknowledgments, he expressly thanks Husserl and Stein not only for stimulating conversations, but also for their help in determining the work's final arrangement.

1.2. Przywara's Encounter with Karl Barth

It was also around this time that, in a modern clash of titans, Przywara met Karl Barth.[54] In some sense their clash was inevitable. In a series of articles, which had appeared in *Stimmen der Zeit* between 1923 and 1925, Przywara had presented from a decidedly Catholic perspective his assessment of the dialectical theology of what he called the "Barth-Gogarten-Thurneysen" school. On the one hand, he views this school as a "genuine rebirth" of the spirit of the Reformation, in comparison with which the liberal Protestantism of Otto and Harnack represented a "falling away."[55] On the other hand,

---

54. Przywara first came to the attention of Barth in 1923 through his friend Eduard Thurneysen, who had read an article by Przywara in *Stimmen der Zeit*. See "Gott in uns oder Gott über uns? Immanenz und Transzendenz im heutigen Geistesleben," *Stimmen der Zeit* 105 (1923): 343-62. Reprinted in an abbreviated version in *Ringen der Gegenwart*, vol. 2 (Augsburg: Benno Filser-Verlag, 1929), pp. 543-78. In his letter to Barth from September 30, 1923, Thurneysen writes, "Obtain a copy of issue 11 of *Stimmen der Zeit*, August 1923, Herder Freiburg. There you will find a remarkably perceptive and extensive essay about us from the side of the Catholic partner. It is interesting because it makes the Catholic standpoint very clear. There are also essential and detailed remarks on Augustine. It is an expert who speaks there. We come off well, even though our most proper concern is not seen." See *Briefwechsel Barth-Thurneysen*, vol. 2 (Zürich: Theologischer Verlag, 1974), p. 190. For the best of recent scholarship on Barth and Przywara, see Keith Johnson, *Karl Barth and the* Analogia Entis (London: T. & T. Clark, 2010); Christophe Chalamet, "Est Deus in Nobis?" in Martin Leiner and Michael Trowitzsch, eds., *Karl Barths Theologie als europaeisches Ereignis* (Göttingen: Vandenhoeck & Ruprecht, 2008), pp. 271-90; and Benjamin Dahlke, *Karl Barth, Catholic Renewal, and Vatican II* (London: T. & T. Clark, 2012), pp. 15-18. See also Bernhard Gertz, *Glaubenswelt als Analogie: Die theologische Analogielehre Erich Przywaras und ihr Ort in der Auseinandersetzung um die analogia fidei* (Düsseldorf: Patmos Verlag, 1969); and Eberhard Mechels, *Analogie bei Erich Przywara und Karl Barth. Das Verhältnis von Offenbarungstheologie und Metaphysik* (Neukirchen-Vluyn: Neukirchener Verlag, 1974).

55. *Ringen der Gegenwart*, vol. 2, pp. 553-54. With regard to Przywara's appreciation for dialectical theology as representing a more genuine opportunity for ecumenical dialogue than liberal Protestantism, see also "Gott in uns oder Gott über uns," p. 343: "The period of

he let it be known that, in his view, Barth, Gogarten, and Thurneysen were at odds with Catholicism inasmuch as they were committed to Luther's doctrine of God's *Alleinwirksamkeit* and a corresponding denial of any analogical understanding of secondary causes within God's *Allwirksamkeit*.[56] Thus, here already we see that, for Przywara, the differences between the confessions are not incidentally but, at the end of the day, *fundamentally* about the *analogia entis*. As Przywara put it, the problem with dialectical theology is that

> [w]hatever belongs to the divine is diametrically opposed to whatever is human. . . . The only relation between God and creature is . . . that of the absolute "No." We thus see here the actual antithesis to the Catholic concept of God in that the "analogy" between God and creature is replaced with a pure "negation." Whereas the *analogia entis* proper to the Catholic concept of God entails the mysterious tension of "similar-dissimilar" . . . , in the Protestant conception of God the "similar" is completely abolished. God is the absolutely and completely "Other," as Rudolf Otto conceives it, or the "No" to the creature, the "No" of a "Yes" that alone is real [*alleinwirklich*] and effective [*alleinwirksam*].[57]

In other words, in Przywara's view, inasmuch as it places all the emphasis upon divine transcendence, dialectical theology ends up denying the reality of God's analogical immanence to creation. Accordingly, it fails to register the "both-and," which Catholicism affirms, of divine immanence and divine transcendence.[58] Moreover, in Przywara's view, inasmuch as (in the name of revelation) dialectical theology overrides human nature and reason, making them strictly passive with regard to the divine, and inasmuch as it denies any

the history and psychology of religion is on its death bed. . . . The 'awakening' of the question of God in the genuinely philosophical, i.e., ultimately metaphysical sense, in sharp and explicit contrast to the old psychologizing and historicizing, is undeniable."

56. *Ringen der Gegenwart*, vol. 2, p. 553.

57. *Ringen der Gegenwart*, vol. 2, p. 553.

58. For Przywara, this polarity is best captured in the theology of Augustine. "This is the great thought of Augustine. . . . Deus interior et exterior, 'God in all and above all,' God more inward to us than we are to ourselves, and yet surpassing and surmounting us as the one who is infinite and incomprehensible." From this it follows, for Przywara, that God is to be loved in his intimacy and revered in his majesty — the love corresponding to "God in us," and the fear corresponding to "God above us." See *Ringen der Gegenwart*, vol. 2, p. 543. Among other references to Augustine, see *Confessions*, III, 6 (11): "you were more inward than my inmost, and higher than my highest."

natural knowledge of God, rendering null and void the revelation of creation, dialectical theology unwittingly falls victim to a form of "theopanism" (inasmuch as salvation is the work of God *alone,* who works the salvation of human nature essentially without human nature and human cooperation). Here again, therefore, Przywara sees a fundamental incompatibility with Catholic theology, inasmuch as the latter affirms an *analogia entis,* i.e., an ultimately inscrutable but real analogical relation between the saving God who works "all in all" and the real secondary causes of creation, which are vitiated by the Fall but whose integrity (and ability to correspond to grace) is never fully destroyed.[59] For Przywara, however, in Barth's early, dialectical theology, there is no relation — not even the vaguest of analogies — left to redeem; there is only contradiction: for human nature, which is fallen *tout court,* stands entirely under divine judgment. Thus, Przywara avers, for this type of theology, which rules out any notion of divine immanence, "Religion is essentially eschatology, and therefore essentially the opposite of Church."[60]

Whatever one makes of this criticism, which would require significant qualifications in light of Barth's mature theology,[61] it shows that in Przy-

---

59. In this regard Przywara can thus claim that the *analogia entis* is essentially a concise articulation of Thomas's doctrine of secondary causes *(causae secundae);* for "though the creature is entirely from God and similar to God, God nevertheless transcends the creature and is unconditionally separate from the creature; hence the creature is endowed with its own being [*Eigen-Sein*] and efficacy [*Eigen-Wirksamkeit*]" (*Ringen der Gegenwart,* vol. 1, p. 57). Importantly, in this same context, Przywara emphasizes that the *analogia entis* does not entail a competitive relation between two discrete, autonomous agents of varying magnitudes, as though divine agency could somehow be constrained by human agency; rather, it entails a relation between the sovereign omnificence [*Allwirksamkeit*] of God and the properly limited agency of the creature. Certainly, these secondary causes are terribly vitiated by the Fall, but the Fall does not destroy the *analogia entis.* On the contrary, for Przywara, an adequate doctrine of sin (and redemption) is predicated precisely upon the misuse (and rectification) of the real causative power that the creature, according to the *analogia entis,* is understood to possess. For sin, according to Catholic theology, can only be explained as a privation of a created good, a misuse of created freedom; it can wear down and terribly disfigure but not entirely efface the image that God created.

60. Przywara, *Ringen der Gegenwart,* vol. 1, p. 49.

61. Since von Balthasar's book on Barth, *The Theology of Karl Barth* (San Francisco: Ignatius, 1992), originally published in 1951, much has been made of Barth's so-called turn to analogy; and, in view of Barth's mature theology, this "turn" becomes more credible with Barth's use of the term *analogia fidei (relationis)* and his doctrine of humanity as a "covenant partner" in the third volume of the *Church Dogmatics.* All of which would seem to invalidate Przywara's charge of "theopanism." See Kenneth Oakes, "The Question of Nature and Grace in Karl Barth: Humanity as Creature and as Covenant-Partner," *Modern Theology*

wara's view the differences between Catholic and Lutheran-Reformed theology are not so much ecclesiological or soteriological as *metaphysical*, stemming from fundamentally different conceptions of the relation between God and world — a difference that subsequently plays out in varying degrees of Protestant suspicion with regard to any real creaturely cooperation with grace (as regards justification) or any real creaturely mediation of grace (as regards the church and sacraments). For whereas Catholic theology maintains the similarity-in-difference between God and creature (a similarity that the sinfulness of human beings cannot altogether destroy), dialectical theology, precisely to the extent that it denies any *potentia oboedientialis*, ironically collapses the very difference between God and creature that it seeks at all costs to maintain.[62] Simply put, to the extent that the creature is reduced to nothing — having lost even the capacity to respond to grace — God becomes everything. And it is precisely against this concept of God, whose metaphysical presupposition is what Przywara calls "theopanism" and which leads to a devaluing of creation as creation, i.e., as a genuine *other* of the divine life that nevertheless *participates* in it analogically, that Przywara consistently reasserts the Thomistic doctrine of the relative dignity of secondary causes.

Whether or not Przywara correctly understood Barth's pathos, his crit-

---

23 (2007): 595-616. It is notable, however, that Przywara never retracted his rejection of Barth's "theopanism," just as Barth, in turn, never retracted his rejection of the *analogia entis*. Indeed, while opinions vary as to whether and to what extent Barth and Przywara may have misunderstood one another, it seems clear in light of Keith Johnson's recent study that Barth rejected the *analogia entis* on the basis of his commitment to Reformed theology and his corresponding denial of any analogy between nature and grace, reason and faith. Nor, for Johnson, is Barth's rejection of the *analogia entis* qualified by his later adoption of an *analogia fidei*, inasmuch as it is by faith alone that there *is* any relation between God and (a fallen) creation. If Johnson is right, then it would seem that, as far as their basic methodologies are concerned, Barth and Przywara understood one another well enough. For Barth, there is no analogy outside of faith; for Przywara, the absence of any analogy between nature and grace entails theopanism (in which case the creature is absorbed into God) or pantheism (in which case God is absorbed into the creature).

62. See *Ringen der Gegenwart*, p. 497: "The Barth-Thurneysen theology of the 'negation' [*das Nicht*] of the creaturely is at bottom simply the instantiation of Luther's primal vehemence, in which, in his radical experience of the night of sin, he, so to speak, forced God into his arms. 'Night' here is not pervaded by the trembling of the reverent creature before the infinity of God. . . . 'Night' here is ultimately the despair of the unrestrained drive toward the most ardent proximity and certainty. . . . Luther's God is ultimately the deification of his tempestuous longing. Luther's 'night' is that of a storm; the 'night' of John of the Cross is complete silence."

icisms evidently gave Barth pause, causing the Reformed theologian to reflect more deeply upon his own theology and upon the merits of Catholic theology in general. Indeed, one could argue that Przywara instigated a "Catholic turn" in Barth's theological development, so much so that in his Münster lectures between 1926 and 1928 Barth himself positively employed the concept of the *analogia entis* that he later rejected.[63] Thus one could say that between 1923 and 1930 Barth's theological development took a turn toward and then away from Catholicism. In any event, it seems there was still room for discussion and Barth was still open to the Catholic "partner," when toward the end of 1928, in a generous and novel ecumenical gesture, he invited Przywara to Münster the following February to deliver a lecture on the Catholic understanding of the Church and to speak at his seminar on Thomas Aquinas.[64] Przywara accepted the invitation and later recalled their first encounter: "Karl Barth had set it up to be a kind of symbol. . . . For the discussion itself two chairs were placed behind the podium, and in his introductory remarks Barth did not fail to point out that, once again, for the first time in centuries, a Protestant and Catholic theologian sat together 'at one table' for a strictly objective 'conversation' about dogmatics, in which what was at issue was not cheap compromises but final clarity about the opposing positions."[65]

To judge from Barth's subsequent letter to Thurneysen from February 9, Barth was deeply impressed by Przywara's lecture, which "from an artistic standpoint" he considered to be "a masterpiece," and by what Przywara had to say during Barth's seminar and at Barth's home on the evenings of February 5 and 6. As he relates their encounter:

> [Przywara] "overwhelmed me" with how . . . at least in the Catholic Church, [our] dear God overwhelms human beings with grace . . . in such a way that the formula 'God in-and-beyond the human being' be-

63. See in this regard Amy Marga's helpful work, *Karl Barth's Dialogue with Catholicism in Göttingen and Münster* (Tübingen: Mohr-Siebeck, 2010), pp. 36-37. For more on this topic and a lucid assessment of the stages in Barth's dialogue with Catholic theology, see Keith Johnson, "A Reappraisal of Karl Barth's Theological Development and His Dialogue with Catholicism," *International Journal of Systematic Theology* 14 (2012): 3-25.

64. Przywara's lecture, entitled "Das katholische Kirchenprinzip," was held in response to Barth's previously published article "Der Begriff der Kirche." Przywara's lecture was subsequently published in *Zwischen den Zeiten* 7 (1929): 277-302.

65. Erich Przywara and Hermann Sauer, *Gespräch zwischen den Kirchen* (Nürnberg: Glock und Lutz), p. 7.

comes a shorthand for man's existence and the resolution in the peace of the *analogia entis* of all the cramped Protestant and modern, transcendent and immanent stupidities. . . . You have to imagine a little man with a big head . . . who somehow always knows how to give an intelligent and well-suited answer to everything, and I mean everything, that one says to him . . . always with Trent and Vatican [I] close at hand, who knows Augustine inside and out, Thomas, Duns Scotus, Molina, etc., always the Church, the Church, the Church, but rightly understood the Church as it circles with the greatest vibrancy and diversity around the fixed pole of dogma, which is becoming ever more manifest, and whose visible center he appeared to constitute. (I once asked him "whether he himself would by rights have to be pope?" No, definitely not, but the *gladium ecclesiae* . . . though he himself be nothing but a grain of seed that must die.) Moreover, [he is] "thoroughly" [versed] in history, philosophy, psychology, but also notoriously at home in the Bible, his favorite apostle being none other than Paul. But at the end of the day [he is] also able to question himself . . . , concluding his final discussion in the seminar with the beautiful *credo:* we human beings are all rascals! (in response to our question about how sin relates to the [formula] 'God in-beyond man from God'); [he is] actually ready to make concessions — not, of course, as far as doctrine is concerned, but with regard to his formulations. . . . Precisely because for him we Protestants exist simply as the wise fathers of Trent have portrayed and rejected us, there is the possibility not simply of treating us kindly, but of rejoicing in finding, in what Trent does not discuss, our share in the *veritas catholica* as well. Obviously, we are not ripe for the *analogia entis* (in response to my question he confirmed that instead of *analogia entis* one could possibly . . . say Mary!), and so we are sadly abandoned to the contortions of doctrine between transcendentalism and immanentism. . . . At the same time [he is] open to all good things, even . . . a drink of beer, and his friendliness delighted our children, who were anxious to see the Jesuit in person. Indeed, Eduard, what am I to make of that? And what are we really to make of Catholicism, which, *despite* all our celebrating of the Reformation, is *so* alert and with it? Was it an angel of the Antichrist or a chosen instrument of the Lord? *The* grand inquisitor or really a disciple of the "apostle to the Gentiles"?[66]

66. Karl Barth to Eduard Thurneysen, *Briefwechsel Barth–Thurneysen,* vol. 2 (Zürich: Theologischer Verlag, 1974), pp. 652-54.

The justification for so lengthy a quote, aside from the personal color it adds to an otherwise abstract and vexing debate, lies in what it reveals about Barth's deliberations prior to his final rejection of the *analogia entis* as the "invention of Antichrist": it shows that he wavered, and that his rejection of the *analogia entis* was not ill-considered; it also suggests that the vehemence of his final rejection of the *analogia entis* corresponded to the degree to which he himself had been drawn by Przywara into the orbit of the Catholic Church, to the point of arousing suspicions among his own Protestant colleagues about his loyalties.[67] As he also put it to his friend Pastor Horn, expressing to him his mixed feelings of admiration and suspicion:

> [Przywara] also knows everything, everything which we think we know, except that . . . he does not make use of it. The Catholic Church is becoming for me more and more *the* amazing phenomenon. In comparison, our Protestant opponents look very much like dwarfs, don't you think? . . . This Jesuit was really something I had never seen before. He also told me that I too am for him *the* opponent *par excellence*. He is a little man with a large head, but that doesn't mean he is not the giant Goliath incarnate.[68]

Still, Barth and Przywara remained on friendly terms, as one can gather from the fact that in 1931 Barth once again invited Przywara to his seminar, this time in Bonn, where Przywara gave a talk on the topic of natural theology. Whatever Przywara may have said in his talk, the writing was by now on the wall. For it seems that from this point on — whether or not there is really any isomorphism here — Barth was unable to dissociate the *analogia entis* from natural theology; and if Barth was to reject the one (as with his later, and equally famous repudiation of Emil Brunner), he would perforce have to reject the other. And so it happened: in the summer of 1931 Barth rendered his verdict — regrettably, before having read or digested the *Analogia Entis* itself, which Przywara considered to be the mature theological formulation of his doctrine and his own initial response to Barth's concerns.

---

67. See McCormack, "Karl Barth's Version of the *Analogia Entis:* A Dialectical No and Yes to Roman Catholicism," p. 107.

68. Letter to Pastor Horn, February 13, 1929 (Karl Barth Archive), here in Christophe Chalamet's translation.

JOHN R. BETZ

1.3. The Analogia Entis *and Other Works*

At the same time as Przywara was engaged with Barth, attempting to clarify Catholic teaching over against Reformed theology, he was also engaged with the philosophical issues of the time, producing two notable monographs, one on Kierkegaard, *Das Geheimnis Kierkegaards* (1929), which the Protestant theologian Hermann Diem called "the most intelligent book yet written on Kierkegaard,"[69] the other on Kant, entitled *Kant Heute: Eine Sichtung* (1930). What these two works have in common is Przywara's attempt to get to the bottom of the philosophical and theological movements of the time, be it phenomenology (as a conscious response to and overcoming of Kant) or existentialism and dialectical theology (which derive their inspiration from Kierkegaard). Then in 1932 came the *Analogia Entis,* which is itself, in part, a response to Hegel. In no sense, therefore, is the *Analogia Entis* a dated, pre-critical scholastic metaphysics. On the contrary, it was developed precisely in conversation with the entire history of philosophy, up to and including the various strands of phenomenology represented by Scheler, Husserl, and Heidegger.[70]

While the *Analogia Entis* is certainly the most important work from this period — to the point that Przywara himself is more or less identified with it — it is often forgotten that during this same period he also produced several works of religious poetry, *Karmel* (1932), *Homo* (1933), and *Hymnus* (1936); that he translated and produced an anthology on Augustine, *Augustinus: Die Gestalt als Gefüge* (1934), which includes a substantial introduction that was highly valued by von Balthasar; that he produced several works that addressed the larger existential and cultural crisis of the time, including *Christliche Existenz* (1934) and *Heroisch* (1936); that throughout this period he continued conducting the *Spiritual Exercises* for small circles of enthusiastic participants; that he concurrently produced a massive and influential three-volume commentary on Ignatius' *Spiritual Exercises,* entitled *Deus Semper Maior* (1938); and that he had been thinking a great deal about the problem of Nietzsche, whom he contrasts with Ignatius Loyola in *Crucis Mysterium* (1939).

With the appearance of *Crucis Mysterium* and the outbreak of the Second World War, Przywara's authorship fell silent. He produced no mono-

69. See *Zwischen den Zeiten* 10 (1932); quoted in Wilhelmy, "Erich Przywara. Ein Überblick," p. 55.
70. See "Drei Richtungen der Phänomenologie," *Stimmen der Zeit* 115 (1928): 252-64.

graphs, but only occasional articles and reviews. Moreover, by 1941 his editorial office had been shut down by the Gestapo, which says something about how he and his fellow Jesuits were perceived by the Nazi party.[71] To give an indication of his attitude toward the Nazis, as early as 1930 he was criticizing with foreboding the combined implications of Nietzsche and Bakunin; by 1933 he publicly called Nazism "a distortion of the Christian *imperium* of the past";[72] and in the same year in Berlin he publicly criticized Friedrich Hielscher for confusing Christianity with a pantheism of "blood and soil."[73] Furthermore, in 1934 — the same year in which Barth and the Confessing Church published the Barmen declaration — Przywara published an article that similarly could be taken as a call to civil disobedience, reminding German Christians that they belonged first and foremost not to any state, but to Christ. Indeed, repudiating the notion of a *Volkskirche*, Przywara reminded them that they did not even belong to any particular people: "What Paul has to say in his epistles is therefore fundamental to Christianity: that the Christian, just as he has died to himself, such that Christ becomes his very self (Gal. 2:20), is equally without a people [*'entvolkt'*] and without a state [*'entstaatlicht'*]."[74] And as for Przywara's attitude toward Jews, if this be in question, one need only point out his friendships with Husserl and Edith Stein, his personal contacts with Martin Buber and Leo Baeck, and his respectful intellectual engagement with any number of contemporary Jewish thinkers, from Hermann Cohen to Franz Rosenzweig.[75]

---

71. Nazi records from this time indicate that Przywara was under surveillance as "the most dangerous exponent of militant Catholicism." See Wilhelmy, "Erich Przywara," p. 18.

72. See O'Meara, *Erich Przywara,* p. 8. In opposition to Hielscher's 1931 work *Das Reich,* Przywara's lecture centered upon the fundamentally correlated concepts of kingdom and Cross. See *Logos* (Düsseldorf: Patmos Verlag, 1964), pp. 105-18, as well as Przywara's late reflection on the event, pp. 169-70.

73. See Wilhelmy, "Erich Przywara. Ein Überblick," p. 19.

74. See "Nation, Staat, und Kirche," *Stimmen der Zeit* 125 (1934): 377.

75. See Wilhelmy, "Erich Przywara. Ein Überblick," pp. 19-20. There has nevertheless been one recent attempt to discredit Przywara on the basis of his supposed national socialist and anti-Semitic sympathies. See Paul Silas Peterson, "Erich Przywara on *Sieg-Katholizismus,* Bolshevism, the Jews, Volk, Reich and the *analogia entis* in the 1920s and 1930s," *Journal for the History of Modern Theology* 19 (2012): 104-40. It should be noted here that this is a follow-up to a previous article in which Peterson makes the same charges against von Balthasar. While the author's sensitivity to anti-Semitism, especially in Christian theology, is laudable, it is unfortunate (since it is far easier to put a label on someone than to remove one) that in his reading of an article by Przywara from 1926, entitled "Judentum und Christentum," which serves as the basis for his incrimination, Peterson takes Przywara's statements about Judaism out of the context in which they occur, where one will find an intellectually rigorous and candid presen-

The war years, however, also took their toll. Whether due to the anxiety of being under surveillance, or to bombing raids, or to wandering nearly penniless from residence to residence for six years (his meager allowance was apparently five marks a month), Przywara's health steadily declined.[76] To all appearances, he was no longer the "man without nerves" his fellow Jesuits once took him to be. As Thomas O'Meara has put it, "The priest who had appeared to possess energy without limits became anxious, incapable of work, and erratic, a condition only heightened by the opinions of others that it was partly psycho-somatic, exaggerated, or easily remedied."[77] Whatever the nature of Przywara's illness, which appears to have been a kind of nervous disorder, his strength returned somewhat in 1941, when he was commissioned by Cardinal Faulhaber with the pastoral care of elderly academics in Munich. Though the exact nature of this commission is unclear, in addition to leading small academic circles in private homes on such topics as Hölderlin, Nietzsche, and Rilke, he also held regular evening lectures in the old Bürgersaal and in the basements of local churches. Apparently, these lectures provoked the suspicion of Himmler in Berlin, who came to Munich to investigate them, but their content was subsequently judged to be "too elevated" to constitute a serious threat.

By the war's end the matter of Przywara's health had reached a point of crisis, involving considerable efforts on von Balthasar's part to help him.[78]

---

tation of the differences between modern Judaism and Christianity. To be sure, there is an element of supersessionism in Przywara's account of Judaism (only recently has this become a term of opprobrium); and, like Buber and Cohen themselves (in their critical statements about Christianity), he presents the relationship between modern Judaism and Christianity as a clash of worldviews. But this hardly warrants the conclusion that he was anti-Semitic — any more than the candidly critical statements of Buber and Cohen about Christianity entail that they had a personal animus toward Christians. In fact, in the same article that Peterson cites to discredit him, Przywara not only shows admiration for the Jewish philosophers he criticizes — Leo Baeck, for one, is described as "masterful" and "brilliant" — but even uses the word "grotesque" to describe the anti-Semitism of the time, concluding his article in a hopeful spirit with Paul's theology of Israel from Romans 11:12, 26, 29.

76. Wilhelmy, "Erich Przywara. Ein Überblick," p. 22.

77. See O'Meara, *Erich Przywara*, p. 9.

78. Since 1942 von Balthasar had tried to arrange for Przywara to be transferred to Switzerland, where they could once again live and work together, and where he could more readily care for him, but the war years had made this impossible. By 1947, though, von Balthasar had a plan: in September he would pick Przywara up in Bad Wiessee, near Munich, and take him back to Switzerland. In a letter dated May 11, 1947, he writes to Przywara, "I am looking forward beyond words to seeing you again and picking you up; it will be a new life for you as well as for me." Unfortunately, the plan failed: Przywara soon had to be taken to

Nevertheless, in the postwar years he managed to produce the following important works, which incorporated some of the insights of his wartime sermons and lectures, including *Gebete in die Zeit* (1946); *Was ist Gott? Summula* (1947); *Vier Predigten über das Abendland* (1948), in which, as von Balthasar observes in the work's preface, Przywara sees through the apocalyptic flames of a destroyed Germany to the final depth of things; *Nuptiae Agni* (1948), a quasi-expressionistic translation of the Roman liturgy, which was originally composed in 1934 and is prefaced by an extraordinary meditation on the nature and meaning of the liturgy; *Hölderlin* (1952), who came to represent a prophet of this "apocalyptic time" and is read *contra* Heidegger in light of such late works as "Patmos"; *Humanitas* (1952), a massive 900-page compilation of breathtaking scope, which, despite its size, saw several editions, was widely discussed, and once again put Przywara back in the theological spotlight; and, finally, two works that signal Przywara's increasing preoccupation with scriptural exegesis and his increasingly Christological anchoring of the *analogia entis*: *Christentum gemäß Johannes* (1954), which was the first work of a planned series of scriptural commentaries, and *Alter und Neuer Bund* (1956), which is a poignant memorial of his wartime theology, deriving from lectures given in 1944. In the words of Joseph Ratzinger, the latter work opens "new horizons of theological thought," presenting the *analogia entis* now in light of Scripture and a "masterful exposition" of the Catholic understanding of the *analogia fidei*.[79]

1.4. Late Works and Reception

The final phase of Przywara's life and work as a philosopher, theologian, scholar, and critic roughly coincides with his return to the theological spotlight and a corresponding series of radio talks delivered between 1949 and 1955

---

the Claraspital in Basel (where on October 1 Karl Barth also visited him); and despite von Balthasar's (and Adrienne von Speyr's) good intentions, Przywara decided upon returning to Munich, where he was cared for by Sigrid Müller, a very capable nurse, until his death. See Lochbrunner, *Hans Urs von Balthasar und seine Theologen-Kollegen*, pp. 54-70.

79. See Joseph Ratzinger, "Erich Przywaras Alterswerk," *Wort und Wahrheit* 13 (1958): 220-21. Inasmuch as this work is critical to any final assessment of Przywara's theology, which stands fixed at the intersection, the crossing, between philosophy and theology, between an *analogia entis* and an *analogia fidei*, it is also critical to any final assessment of the debate between Przywara and Karl Barth — and, by implication, between Catholic and Reformed theology.

for the *Südwestdeutsche Rundfunk*. A handful of these talks were eventually gathered into a volume entitled *In und Gegen. Stellungnahmen zur Zeit* (1955), along with other short essays from this period. This volume not only sheds valuable light on Przywara's theology to date (one will find here, for example, a brief summary of his doctrine of the *analogia entis*), but also reveals much about the man himself — from his views on such varied topics as "Mary," "the Trinity," "Pius X," "pastoral care," "the metaphysics of sexuality," "church, culture, and state," etc., to his vignettes of Simone Weil, Paul Claudel, Rudolf Bultmann, and Martin Heidegger, to his friendships with Edith Stein, Gertrud le Fort, Reinhold Schneider, Hermann Bahr, Hans Urs von Balthasar, and others. The volume also reveals much about Przywara's method as a critic, as one who is at once "in" his time — and who charitably attempts to understand his contemporaries before criticizing them — but who also stands in important respects as a Catholic theologian in contradiction to his time, in short, "against it." And to this extent his cultural criticism in some sense mirrors his understanding of the *analogia entis*, which likewise rests upon a distinction between "in" and "beyond," or "in" and "over against."

But Przywara's health soon took another turn for the worse, and in 1950, for the purposes of convalescence, he permanently retired from community religious life in Munich — eventually settling in the country in a tiny village called Hagen, which lies on the outskirts of Murnau in view of the Zugspitze. It was here, in spite of poor health and extremely modest, almost ascetical living conditions, that he edited some of his last manuscripts and produced his last works, among them: *Ignatianisch* (1956), which was written for the four hundredth anniversary of Ignatius' death; *Idee Europa* (1956), which was based on a series of radio talks; *Gespräch zwischen den Kirchen* (1957), an ecumenical dialogue with the Protestant theologian Hermann Sauer; a beautiful series of meditations entitled *Demut, Geduld, Liebe. Die drei christlichen Tugenden* (1960); *Christ und Obrigkeit* (1962), which in the form of a dialogue with Paul Schütz gives an account of his political theology; a work on ecclesiology, *Kirche in Gegensätzen* (1962); *Hymnen des Karmel* (1962), comprising his own translations of Teresa of Avila, John of the Cross, and Thérèse of Lisieux; *Logos* (1963), which further illustrates the increasingly Christological center of his understanding of analogy; and a final work, a collection of ecclesiological writings that appeared under the title *Katholische Krise* (1967). The most important of Przywara's late works, however, is undoubtedly his monumental anthropology, *Mensch*, the first volume of which appeared in 1959. Upon its publication, Vatican radio announced it as "a formal anthropology of all anthropologies, a history of the spiritual life of man in all its forms, a comprehensive vision of which Przywara alone is capable."[80] Given that Przywara was taken up with finishing the other works from this period, however, the second, planned volume was never completed. The work, whose scope is matched by its profundity, thus stands as a monumental, nearly 450-page fragment.

Though ailing and increasingly isolated, in his last years Przywara was honored in various ways: with a *Festschrift* edited by Siegfried Behn, entitled *Der beständige Aufbruch* (1959), which included a brief greeting from Karl Barth and articles by such well-known theologians as Heinrich Fries, Karl Rahner, and Johannes Baptist Lotz; a three-volume collection of his *Schriften* (1962), edited by von Balthasar;[81] a bibliography of his extant works, published in 1963 under the title *Erich Przywara. Sein Schrifttum, 1912-1962*, edited by Leo Zimny, along with a substantial tribute and introduction by von Balthasar; an article by Walter Warnach commemorating Przywara's seventy-fifth birthday in the 12 October 1964 issue of the *Frankfurter Allgemeine Zeitung;* a second tribute to Przywara by von Balthasar, which appeared in 1966 in a volume edited by Hans Jürgen Schultz;[82] a *laudatio* given by Karl Rahner in 1967 on the occasion of Przywara's reception of the Upper-Silesian culture prize; a *Festgabe* edited by Sigrid Müller (under the pseudonym Gustav Wilhelmy), which appeared in 1968 and contains both a biography and a bibliography of all the secondary literature on Przywara to date; and, finally, for the occasion of his eightieth birthday, the first major treatment and defense of his work by Bernhard Gertz, *Glaubenswelt als Analogie. Die theologische Analogielehre Erich Przywaras und ihr Ort in der Auseinandersetzung um die analogia fidei*, which appeared in 1969.

Przywara died on September 28, 1972 and was interred in the Jesuit cemetery in Pullach. Two months later, on December 10, a Mass was celebrated in his honor in the Jesuit *Michaelskirche* in Munich, during which the following quote from his works was adduced:

The essential requirement of Catholic philosophy is that it not go condemning and cursing through the world, but rather "searching for what

80. See Wilhelmy, "Erich Przywara. Ein Überblick," pp. 28-29.
81. Though by no means exhaustive, von Balthasar considered the writings in this collection to be the most valuable and indispensable. For the details of the production of the edition, which involved extensive correspondence between von Balthasar and Przywara over the course of 1962, see Lochbrunner, *Hans Urs von Balthasar und seine Theologen-Kollegen*, pp. 75-105.
82. "Erich Przywara," in *Tendenzen zur Theologie im 20. Jahrhundert. Eine Geschichte in Porträts* (Stuttgart: Olten, 1966), pp. 354-59.

was lost"; that with regard to all individual philosophies it should have as its defining comportment a tireless searching for their kernel of truth, a searching for the *sperma tou logou*. For it can only fulfill its sacred trust . . . by orienting itself to this One immutable truth, which is the One in the many. Logically, therefore, it exercises its office of distinguishing truth from error most decisively when it seeks to find in the error that part of truth that has become one-sided and distorted. For, in keeping with the profound wisdom of the scholastics, everything positive is true and good, [whereas] error and evil are a "privatio." . . . Accordingly, the destiny of genuine Catholic philosophy is that its greatness be bound to the vision of the whole Logos-Christ; that it condemns itself with premature judgment and self-isolation and shuts itself off from Christ, whose [full] luminosity is first [visible] in the whole body. . . . Man must have this one concern: increasingly to expand beyond the narrow confines of his self, which he so readily confuses with God, into the immeasurable breadth of the eternally new and eternally different shining of the infinite God. . . .[83]

In twentieth-century theology it would be difficult to find a theologian who so profoundly embodied this Ignatian spirit of "finding God in all things" — not in order to validate all things as they are, but rather in order to redeem all things for the sake of the full visibility and radiance of the *totus Christus*.

2. The Prior Philosophical and Theological History of the *analogia entis*

Before introducing Przywara's doctrine of the *analogia entis*, it is important to recall that the term itself is not original to him. As we have seen, it can be traced back to Cajetan and Suarez, and can be found thereafter as a *terminus technicus* among the religious orders.[84] It is therefore — as Barth rightly recognized — very much part of the Catholic tradition. But the basic idea of the *analogia entis* is much older. Indeed, in its rudimentary forms it is as old as philosophy itself, being rooted in specific metaphysical problems posed

---

83. The homily, which is retained in the archives of the German Province of the Society of Jesus, was given by Fr. Anibal Edwards, S.J.

84. See Julio Terán-Dutari, "Die Geschichte des Terminus 'Analogia entis' und das Werk Erich Przywaras," *Philosophisches Jahrbuch der Görres-Gesellschaft* 77 (1970): 163-79.

by Greek antiquity. It is not surprising, therefore, that in §7 of the present work Przywara treats the historical scope of the *analogia entis* — from Plato and Aristotle to Augustine and Aquinas.

Like Edith Stein, who along with von Balthasar was one of the first readers of the *Analogia Entis,* we might reasonably wonder why this section appears relatively late in the work; and, in fact, Stein suggested to Przywara that this section should come earlier.[85] Nevertheless, Przywara kept the placement of this section, maintaining that the historical forms of the *analogia entis* are historical expressions of an objective problematic that is given with the fact of creation and are therefore formally posterior to it. For present purposes, however (and given that his "historical" section is hardly serviceable as a general introduction), it seems prudent to follow Edith Stein's advice and begin with a historical introduction to the concept of analogy: from its origins in Greek mathematics to its philosophical use in Plato and Aristotle to its theological use in Thomas Aquinas.

2.1. The Origins of Analogy as a Term and a Concept

While the term *analogy* was first employed in ancient Greek mathematics, in which context it meant, quite simply, a proportion of four terms (a:b::c:d), the philosophical use of the term, including any notion of an analogy of being, evolved only gradually along with the development of the Greek metaphysical tradition. In fact, one could argue that the Greeks never had a doctrine of the analogy of being, inasmuch as the Greeks had no doctrine of creation in the Christian sense of the term (i.e., no doctrine of creation out of nothing), and therefore made no clear distinction between essence and existence upon which the *analogia entis,* for Przywara, properly depends. Instead, as Étienne Gilson argued, what we typically find in the Greeks are philosophies of essence of one kind or another, which inevitably reduce being to a univocal concept (however graded by priority and posteriority, according to an improper "analogy of inequality"), and so compromise the kind of distinction between God and creation that the *analogia entis* absolutely maintains.[86]

---

85. See *Finite and Eternal Being,* trans. Kurt F. Reichardt, in *The Collected Works of Edith Stein* (Washington: ICS Publications, 2002), vol. 9, p. xxix.

86. See Étienne Gilson, *Being and Some Philosophers* (Toronto: Pontifical Institute of Medieval Studies, 1952); see also James Anderson, *The Bond of Being: An Essay on Analogy and Existence* (St. Louis and London: Herder, 1949).

Nevertheless, even if the *analogia entis* is a properly theological term and cannot be found as a term either in Plato or in Aristotle, or even in the later neo-Platonic tradition from which it is sometimes derived,[87] one could argue that the Greeks had begun to think analogically inasmuch as they had begun to consider the question of unity in view of the patent diversity of being, i.e., the problem of the One and the Many.[88] And to this extent, according to Eberhard Jüngel, analogy can already be found in Heraclitus and Parmenides as an implicit *Denkform* governing the metaphysical relation between the One (or in Heraclitus's case the Logos), which "is" and abides, and the Many, which by comparison "are not."[89] However one might evaluate Jüngel's reading of Heraclitus and Parmenides, this much is certain: that the philosophical concept of analogy developed in response to the differences traditionally ascribed to them.[90] Whereas for Parmenides being alone is real, and change is an illusion (εἰ γὰρ ἔγεντ᾽, οὐκ ἔστ᾽), for Heraclitus there is no being, no permanence, but only becoming (πάντα χωρεῖ καὶ οὐδὲν μένει).[91] Accordingly, as historically received, the philosophies of Parmenides and Heraclitus came to represent dialectical extremes, "all is being" and "all is

87. See Pierre Aubenque, "Les Origines de la Doctrine de l'Analogie de l'Être," *Les études philosophiques* 103 (1978): 3-12; "Néoplatonism et l'analogie de l'être," in *Néoplatonisme: Mélanges offerts à J. Trouillard* (Fontenay-aux-Roses: Les Cahiers de Fontenay, 1981), pp. 63-76.

88. Importantly, the problem of the One and the Many *qua* problem should not immediately be confused with the modern pantheistic solution of the problem, which understands the ancient phrase Ἕν καὶ Πᾶν in terms of an ultimate identity.

89. Cf. Eberhard Jüngel, "Zum Ursprung der Analogie bei Parmenides und Heraklit," in *Entsprechungen: Gott — Wahrheit — Mensch*, 3rd ed. (Tübingen: Mohr-Siebeck, 2002). According to Jüngel, analogy is implied in Parmenides' understanding of the relation between thought and being: "Parmenides setzt in B 3 Denken und Sein in einen Selbigkeitsbezug. Es geht ihm dabei um mehr als um die Auskunft 'A = A'. Es geht ihm auch nicht um die Ineinssetzung von einander Widersprechendem. Parmenides lehrt vielmehr einen Selbigkeitsbezug von einander Entsprechendem. Das Denken entspricht dem Sein. Denn das Sein spricht sich dem Denken zu" (p. 67). For a classical treatment of analogy in antiquity as a background to its use in Thomas Aquinas, see Hampus Lyttkens, *The Analogy between God and the World: An Investigation of Its Background and Interpretation of Its Use by Thomas of Aquino*, trans. A. Poignant (Uppsala: Almqvist & Wiksell, 1952), pp. 15-110.

90. See *Analogia Entis*, pp. 239-40 herein. Hereafter cited as *AE*, either by page or by section number.

91. "For if it came into being it is not"; "everything gives way and nothing abides." See Plato, *Cratylus* 402a: "Heraclitus somewhere says that all things are in process and nothing stays still, and likening existing things to the stream of a river he says that you would not step twice into the same river." Quoted in *The Presocratic Philosophers*, 2nd ed., ed. G. S. Kirk, J. E. Raven, and M. Schofield (Cambridge: Cambridge University Press, 1983).

becoming," with no *analogia entis* in sight: on the one hand, a monistic philosophy of absolute identity (to the point that change is an illusion); on the
other hand, a philosophy of absolute flux and difference (to the point that
permanence is an illusion and all that is real is the revolution of opposites).

2.2. Analogy in Plato and Aristotle

Such was the metaphysical conundrum inherited by Plato and Aristotle,
which their own philosophies respectively attempted to resolve.[92] With
Heraclitus, both of them affirmed that our experience of finite being is not
an illusion and that finite things do, in fact, change; in short, they affirmed
the commonsense view that real things really come into being and pass away.
On the other hand, in keeping with Parmenides' fundamental intuition, they
recognized that the world of change is not real in any ultimate sense, but
points beyond itself to some kind of being or substance or ideal realm of
Forms that exists truly, immutably, and eternally. And to this extent, inasmuch as they sought a "mean" (and implicitly a kind of analogy as a mean)
between absolute identity and absolute difference, they navigated precisely
between the extremes represented by Heraclitus and Parmenides.[93] Thus, at
the conclusion of Book V of the *Republic,* Plato speaks of the world of
change as something "intermediate," as something between being and non-
being, and likewise as something between the Forms and the formless.[94] All
of which is developed in Books VI and VII of the *Republic* into a more or less
analogical understanding of finite things as so many images of the archetypal forms in which they participate. For to the extent that they "are," they
"are" by participation (μέθεξις) in the Forms, apart from which they are
nothing; and to this extent Plato could be said to have laid the foundation
for an "analogy of being."

To speak of the participatory relation between image and archetype as

92. See, for example, Plato, *Theaetetus* 180e; Aristotle, *Metaphysics* I, 5, 986b-87b; IV, 5,
1010a, *et passim.*

93. See *Nicomachean Ethics* V, 3, 1131b, where Aristotle calls analogy a "mean": τὸ γὰρ
ἀνάλογον μέσον.

94. For a recent Catholic metaphysics that develops this theme of the "in-between" as
definitive of creaturely being, and in many ways bears comparison with the metaphysics of
Przywara, see the work of William Desmond, e.g., *Being and the Between* (Albany: State University of New York Press, 1995), and, most recently, *God and the Between* (Malden, MA:
Blackwell, 2008).

an analogy, however, is, strictly speaking, to overstep the bounds of Plato's usage. For when Plato uses the word *analogy* he tends to mean a proportionality in keeping with the mathematical origin of the term, as when the term is employed in the cosmological context of the *Timaeus* (31a-d) where it is called the "most beautiful" of arrangements. So too, when the word is used in the *Republic,* it refers to the proportions of Plato's "line," which is arranged according to an analogy (ἀνὰ λόγον), i.e., a proportionality, between the order of knowledge and the order of being, since the proportion between opinion and knowledge is analogous to the relation between image and archetype.[95] But even if an analogy is, strictly speaking, a proportion involving four terms, for Przywara, one can clearly make out the fundamental "in-over" or "in-and-beyond" structure of the *analogia entis,* namely, in the instantiation "in" nature of Forms that are "superior" to it. Moreover, in the Platonic doctrine of Eros (*Symposium* 203 b-d), one can already glimpse something of the theological dimension of the *analogia entis,* inasmuch as the world of becoming is not resident in itself, but, like Eros, a "homeless hunter," constituted by a transcendent orientation to the being of the divine and fixed *in change* over against it. Thus, vis-à-vis Parmenides and Heraclitus, Plato precisely does not reduce reality to being or becoming; instead he presents the reality of the one as a moving image of the other.[96] Therein, one could argue, lies his essentially analogical solution to the pre-Socratic dialectic: being and becoming are not ultimately opposed — notwithstanding the so-called χωρισμός or "divide" posited between the forms and the sensible particulars that participate in them (*Parmenides* 130-33) — nor is the one reduced to the other; rather, they are genuinely related, one could say analogically related, according to a fundamental similarity-in-difference.

At the end of the day, however, according to Przywara, Plato's unbaptized philosophy falls short of a genuine *analogia entis* inasmuch as his philosophy lacks a genuine transcendence. For, as Przywara sees it, Plato's transcendence is not a genuine "beyond" of immanence, but rather the "goad" of an "interior expansion."[97] In other words, given the fundamental essentialism of Plato's philosophy (which, in the absence of a doctrine of *creatio ex nihilo,* knows no real distinction between essence and existence), the difference between immanence and transcendence, image and archetype,

---

95. *Republic* 511e. In other words, for Plato, "Being bears the same relation to becoming as truth does to belief." See Lyttkens, *The Analogy between God and the World,* p. 24.
96. See in this regard especially the *Timaeus* 31a-d.
97. *AE* §7, 4.

is ultimately one of degree. Furthermore, the Platonic "analogy" lacks any interval based upon the difference between the finite and the infinite (since the Forms are divine, whereas for the Greeks the infinite is precisely what characterizes the non-divine).[98] Thus, given that difference here is merely one of intensity or degree, an analogy merely according to priority and posteriority *(per prius et posterius),* the Platonic or neo-Platonic "analogy" is sometimes called an improper "analogy of inequality" or a "pseudo-analogy of gradation."[99] Indeed, one could argue that it is not an analogy at all, inasmuch as predication here is ultimately univocal. As Penido put it regarding this type of analogy, "The accomplished artist knows how to make a cord vibrate in such a way as to draw from it a piercing note, which little by little fades away and finally disappears. *The intensity varies, but it is always the same note.*"[100]

Turning now to Aristotle, when he uses the term *analogy,* like Plato he invariably means a proportion of four terms, as in the following passage from the *Poetics,* where he defines analogy as a species of metaphor: "That [kind of metaphor] from analogy is possible whenever there are four terms so related that the second is to the first, as the fourth to the third. . . . Thus a cup is in relation to Dionysus what a shield is to Ares. The cup accordingly will be described as the 'shield of Dionysus' and the shield as the 'cup of Ares.'"[101] Analogy thus functions to compare things that are otherwise fundamentally different. But, for Aristotle, its use is not limited to figures of speech; for it is precisely in this way that he uses the term in other works, most notably, on natural history, where analogy is defined as a more distant

---

98. We thus see here two ways in which the Platonic analogy was radically transformed (and necessarily so) by Christianity: first, by the doctrine of *creatio ex nihilo* (which entails the radical non-necessity of created being and therewith a fundamental distinction between essence and existence); second, as first occurs in Gregory of Nyssa, by the radical attribution of infinity to God. As much as the attribution of infinity to God *adds* to divine transcendence, however, by itself (that is, apart from a doctrine of *creatio ex nihilo*), it is not sufficient to maintain a proper doctrine of divine transcendence — and therewith a properly Christian doctrine of the *analogia entis* — since this could be taken as merely extending an analogy of degrees to infinity.

99. See James F. Anderson, *The Bond of Being* (St. Louis and London: Herder, 1949), p. 84.

100. M. T.-L. Penido, *Le rôle de l'analogie en théologie dogmatique* (Paris: Vrin, 1931), p. 55; quoted in James F. Anderson, *The Bond of Being* (St. Louis and London: Herder, 1949), p. 60.

101. *Poetics* 1457b16f., trans. I. Bywater, in *The Complete Works of Aristotle,* vol. 2, ed. Jonathan Barnes (Princeton: Princeton University Press, 1984). See also, for a brief but helpful treatment of the topic of analogy in Aristotle, Eberhard Jüngel, *Gott als Geheimnis der Welt* (Tübingen: Mohr-Siebeck, 1992), pp. 364ff.

and imprecise relation than classification according to number, genus, and species.[102] The word *analogy* also appears in the *Metaphysics*, where after naming some of the more direct ways that things can be related (viz., unity in number, species, and genus), Aristotle names analogy as a fourth kind of unity, according to which things are only proportionally and thus only indirectly related (ὥς ἄλλο πρὸς ἄλλο).[103]

When it comes to metaphysics, however, and the question, specifically, of analogy's application to ontological questions, matters are more complicated, since in Aristotle's usage the word *analogy* is limited to proportional analogies of the kind just described, and since Aristotle does not explicitly use the term in his discussion of being. Instead he speaks of being in connection with so-called "πρὸς ἕν equivocals," which are so called inasmuch as diverse things sharing a common denomination are related "to one" *(pros hen)* primary instance from which their different meanings derive.[104] Whether or not "πρὸς ἕν equivocals" are rightly regarded as a kind of analogy — and here it depends upon whether one follows medieval commentators, who tend to employ the word *analogy* in this connection, or whether one insists with some more recent commentators upon a strict adherence to Aristotle's terms — some kind of "analogy of being" is clearly suggested at the beginning of Book IV of the *Metaphysics*, where Aristotle famously says that "being can be said in many ways" (τὸ δὲ ὂν λέγεται μὲν πολλαχῶς) and then proceeds to elaborate precisely in this connection what has come to be known as a *pros hen* (πρὸς ἕν) analogy.[105] The now-famous example he adduces is that of health: "Everything which is healthy is related to health, one thing in the sense that it produces it, another in the sense that it is a symp-

---

102. See, for example, *History of Animals* 486b19-21; *Generation of Animals* 715b19-21; *Parts of Animals* 645b25. Cf. *Nicomachean Ethics* 1131a30: "For proportion [analogy] is equality of ratios, and involves at least four terms."

103. *Metaphysics* V, 6, 1016b.

104. For a classical study, see Joseph Owens, *The Doctrine of Being in the Aristotelian 'Metaphysics': A Study in the Greek Background of Medieval Thought* (Toronto: Pontifical Institute of Medieval Studies, 1951), pp. 123ff. The most famous examples of "pros hen" equivocals are the various senses of "health" or "medical" (see below). According to Owens, analogy constitutes a separate class of equivocal reference vis-à-vis both *pros hen* equivocals and those types of equivocation that are purely the result of chance and thus equivocal in the truest sense: as is the case, for example, with the homonym "bank," which as a matter of chance can mean things as diverse (and totally unconnected) as a financial institution, the side of a river, and a kind of aeronautical maneuver.

105. *Metaphysics* IV, 1, 1003a32: "τὸ δὲ ὂν λέγεται μὲν πολλαχῶς ἀλλὰ πρὸς ἓν καὶ μίαν τινὰ φύσιν καὶ οὐχ ὁμωνύμως." Cf. *Metaphysics* V, 1, 1028a10.

tom of health, another because it is capable of it."[106] In other words, according to this kind of analogy, the health of a person or animal is the "primary analogate" from which the other senses of healthy (as when speaking of food, medicine, or urine) derive. The case is similar, Aristotle then suggests, with regard to the various senses of being: "Some things are said to be because they are substances, others because they are affections of substance, others because they are a process towards substance, or destructions or privations or qualities of substance, or productive or generative of substance, or of things which are relative to substance, or negations of some of these things or of substance itself. It is for this reason that we say even of non-being that it *is* non-being."[107]

For Aristotle, then (if one admits a broader definition of analogy), there is clearly an analogical community among the various senses of being, just as there is an analogical community among the senses of the word *healthy.* And, importantly, it is an *ordered* community, inasmuch as the various senses of being all refer to being *qua* substance as the "primary analogate." Indeed, this is why the science of metaphysics, which is concerned with the question of being qua being, is concerned chiefly with being qua substance as that manner of being upon which all other things, insofar as they have being, depend. But we can take matters further. For just as one may speak of an analogical ordering among the diverse modes of being, substance being primary, one may also speak of an analogical ordering among the various substances themselves. Accordingly, being is said primarily of divine substance, which is eternal and unmoved (Aristotle's prime mover), in another sense of eternally moving substances (e.g., Aristotle's spheres), and in a still more removed sense of substances, like plants and animals, that are moving but finite and perishable. Thus, to employ more recent terminology, the lines of Aristotle's argument lead us from a horizontal and "predicamental" analogy (concerning the relative being of accidents with regard to substance) to a vertical and "transcendental" analogy of being.

2.3. Analogy in Thomas Aquinas

It was not until the Middle Ages, however, that the significance and larger implications of Aristotle's few remarks on analogy were seriously consid-

106. *Metaphysics* IV, 1, 1003a32.
107. *Metaphysics* IV, 2, 1003b6-11.

ered. And in this respect Thomas Aquinas stands out as Aristotle's most important medieval commentator — both for having clarified received notions of analogy and for assessing its theological uses.[108] In his commentary on the foregoing passage from the *Metaphysics* (1016b-1017a), for example, Thomas helps to clarify the two basic kinds of analogy that have come down to us from Aristotle. He says that analogy can be understood here in two ways: either as two things being related to a third (in reference to the example of health, which is predicated differently but not equivocally of man, urine, and medicine, where man is the primary analogate); or in the sense that two things are proportionally similar to two other things (as in the relation of the tranquility of the sea to the serenity of the air).[109] The first kind of analogy is what we have identified as a *pros hen* (πρὸς ἕν) analogy, since two things are ordered "to one" primary thing (in this case man), whereas urine and medicine are "healthy" only in an analogical sense, as, respectively, a sign and cause of health. Since Cajetan, this kind of analogy has also come to be known as an analogy of attribution *(analogia attributionis)*, which can be distinguished further according to whether or not the attribution is intrinsic or extrinsic.[110] The second kind of analogy, which Cajetan considered

---

108. For a masterful synopsis of Aquinas on the analogy of being, see John F. Wippel, *The Metaphysical Thought of Thomas Aquinas: From Finite Being to Uncreated Being* (Washington, DC: Catholic University of America Press, 2000), pp. 65-93. See also Lyttkens, *The Analogy between God and the World*; C. Fabro, *Participation et causalité de l'être d'après saint Thomas d'Aquin* (Louvain-Paris: Publications Universitaires, 1963); George Klubertanz, *St. Thomas Aquinas on Analogy* (Chicago: Loyola University Press, 1960); and Bernard Montagnes, *The Doctrine of the Analogy of Being according to Thomas Aquinas*, trans. E. M. Macierowski (Milwaukee: Marquette University Press, 2004). See also, more recently, the articles by Reinhard Hütter and Bruce Marshall in *The Analogy of Being: Invention of the Antichrist or the Wisdom of God*, pp. 209-45, 280-313.

109. Aquinas, *In Duodecim Libros Metaphysicorum Aristotelis Expositio* V, lec. 8; *Commentary on Aristotle's Metaphysics*, trans. John P. Rowan (Notre Dame: Dumb Ox Books, 1961), p. 317. Cf. Thomas's discussion of this first example in *Summa Th.* I, q. 16, a. 6; the second example derives from Aristotle's *Topics* 108a.

110. For example, "health" is attributed extrinsically to "urine" and "medicine," since these things are not in themselves, strictly speaking, "healthy." If, however, one is talking about such concepts as *ens* or *bonum,* and if it is God who causes these perfections in creatures, and if, as for Aquinas and the medievals in general, effects in some way resemble their causes, according to the principle *omne agens agit sibi simile,* then it is clear that, while these concepts refer primarily to God, they also refer to something, however deficient, intrinsic to creatures themselves. See, for example, *De Veritate* q. 21, a. 4: ". . . omne agens invenitur sibi simile agere; unde si prima bonitas sit effectiva omnium bonorum, oportet quod similitudinem suam imprimat in rebus effectis; et sic unumquodque dicetur bonum sicut

to be the only proper analogy, is known as an analogy of proportionality *(analogia proportionalitatis)*, since it is based upon a comparison of two different proportions and recalls the origins of analogy in Greek arithmetic. While it cannot be decided here which of these analogies is more proper,[111] the second analogy *(analogia proportionalitatis)* clearly comports with metaphor and thus could be said to imply a greater dissimilarity between the things compared. And this, in fact, is how Przywara understands this type of analogy. What both forms of analogy have in common, however, is that both are ways of expressing a relationship between (or among) otherwise different things.

Now, when it comes to the theological use of analogy, whether conceived in terms of an analogy of attribution or an analogy of proportionality, there are two traditional applications: one regarding the order of knowing *(ordo cognoscendi)*, the other regarding the order of being *(ordo essendi)*. The most famous instance of the first kind, traditionally called an analogy of names *(analogia nominum)*, is Aquinas's use of analogy in question 13 of the *Summa Theologiae*, where analogy is said to govern the naming of God, i.e., the attribution to God of creaturely perfections such as wisdom or goodness. While the role of analogy in Aquinas is a matter of much dispute (among other things about whether or not Thomas favored an analogy of attribution or an analogy of proportionality), here in question 13 his discussion is rather straightforward: analogy functions to strike an important balance between univocity and equivocity, i.e., pure identity and pure ambiguity of meaning. Accordingly, in keeping with Aristotle's understanding of analogy as a mean,[112] analogy functions to preserve religious language from two opposing errors: on the one hand, the error of presumption (of assuming that our words mean the same thing when applied to God and creatures); on the

---

forma inhaerente per similitudinem summi boni sibi inditam, et ulterius per bonitatem primam, sicut per exemplar et effectivum omnis bonitatis creatae." See Lyttkens, *The Analogy between God and the World*, pp. 207-8, 246ff.

111. Whereas Cajetan favored an analogy of proportionality, Suarez favored an analogy of intrinsic attribution; and it is along these lines, as far as this particular issue is concerned, that the orders have traditionally divided, with the Dominicans largely following Cajetan and the Jesuits, Suarez. What Przywara sought to show, though, is that *both* are right, and that a properly Catholic understanding of the *analogia entis* demands that one recognize the merits of each school's interpretation — the one, as it were, balancing out the other. Indeed, Przywara sought to show the same with regard to the debate between the Thomists and the Scotists (and Molinists) concerning the "real distinction." See *Ringen der Gegenwart*, pp. 926-29. See *AE* §6.

112. See *Nicomachean Ethics* V, 3, 1131b: "τὸ γὰρ ἀνάλογον μέσον."

other hand, the error of agnosticism (of assuming, whether on the basis of skepticism or false humility, that our words, when applied to God, have only an ambiguous reference). As Thomas puts it, "no name is predicated univocally of God and of creatures," but "neither, on the other hand, are names applied to God and creatures in a purely equivocal sense."[113] The reason for the former, Thomas explains, is that no effect, not even a creaturely perfection, fully resembles its cause; it is merely a similitude of what exists truly and perfectly only in God. The reason for the latter, Thomas explains, is that God is not unknown, since creation itself is already a form of revelation, as Paul declares in Romans 1:20. Thus, for Thomas, when we say that God is "good" or "wise," we are to understand that, when applied to God, what these words mean is neither the same as nor totally different from their creaturely reference — at least not so totally different that one no longer has any conception of what one is saying.

The second theological use of analogy, which is the subject of greater controversy, especially on the ecumenical front, is that with which the present work is explicitly concerned: the use of analogy to describe the existing relation between the being of God and the being of creation. In other words, here it is not merely a question of an analogy of names or an analogical judgment that God "is" or is "wise," etc., a kind of analogical discourse that could conceivably be confined to a particular religion and justified on the basis of its own scriptures; rather, leaving aside for now the question of whether or not it can be recognized independently of Scripture or special revelation, here it is a question of a real ontological analogy, traditionally referred to by the term *analogia entis,* which obtains simply due to the fact of creation. As already mentioned, the first thing to be noted about this term is that it is a development of the Thomist school (Thomas himself does not use the phrase) — a fact that has led several venerable scholars to disown the notion, claiming that it is without foundation in the teaching of the Angelic Doctor. Instead, it is argued, in the most extreme variant of such scholarship, that the role of analogy in Aquinas is simply that of a regulative grammar, a "comment on our use of certain words," which is to say that analogy functions simply in the manner described above.[114]

---

113. *Summa Th.* I, q. 13, a. 5, corp.

114. See Herbert McCabe's commentary in *Summa Theologiae,* vol. 3: *Knowing and Naming God* (London: Eyre & Spottiswoode, 1964), p. 106: "Analogy is not a way of getting to know about God, nor is it a theory of the structure of the universe, it is a comment on our use of certain words." See also David Burrell, *Analogy and Philosophical Language* (New Haven: Yale University Press, 1973), pp. 119ff.; *Aquinas, God and Action* (Notre Dame: University

Pace recent scholarship, however, one need look no further for a real analogy of being in Thomas than question 4 of the *Summa Theologiae,* where Thomas discusses the question of whether creatures can be considered like God.[115] In response to the stated objections, Thomas argues that indeed they can, citing, in a fascinating conjunction of the protological and the eschatological, both the familiar verse from Genesis 1:26, "Let us make man to our image and likeness," and the verse from 1 John 3:2, "When He shall appear we shall be like to Him."[116] Clearly, in view of these verses, some

---

of Notre Dame Press, 1979); and Ralph McInerny, *The Logic of Analogy* (The Hague: Martinus Nijhoff, 1961); *Studies in Analogy* (The Hague: Martinus Nijhoff, 1968); *Aquinas and Analogy* (Washington: Catholic University of America Press, 1996), pp. 152ff. In other words, so the argument goes, analogy in Thomas has a merely linguistic function and is not directly tied to ontological or metaphysical questions — even though "being" for Thomas is an analogical term, along with other terms such as "good" and "wise." Thus McInerny distinguishes (and sees a disconnection) between an "analogy of being" and an "analogy of 'being'" — the first being a matter of real relations, the *ordo rerum,* the second being a matter merely of naming, the *ordo nominis* (*Aquinas and Analogy,* pp. 161-62). But, surely, for Thomas, the very possibility of an analogy of names, if it is to have any content and not to be a nominalist charade, is predicated upon a real analogy of being, apart from which our words would be just words, without any objective reference in the order of being, and theology would be consigned to agnosticism. As even Eberhard Jüngel has pointed out in his masterful treatment of the topic (*Gott als Geheimnis der Welt,* pp. 357-58), an analogy of names cannot be separated from an analogy of being. For the "being" of God and the "being" of the world are related not merely by a convention of speech, a mere analogy of names, but by the *reality* of causal dependence of the one upon the other and the *reality* of a created participation of the one in the other that this implies. In short, as Alister McGrath puts it, "For Aquinas, the capacity of analogies to model God rests upon a *created correspondence* between the creation and creator." See *A Scientific Theology,* vol. 3 (London: T. & T. Clark, 2003), p. 110. See also Rudi te Velde, *Participation and Substantiality in Thomas Aquinas* (Leiden: Brill, 1995). Notably, in recent years, for all his appreciation of McInerny, even Burrell seems to have moved closer to a traditional Thomist position. See "From Analogy of 'Being' to the Analogy of Being," in *Faith and Freedom: An Interfaith Perspective* (Oxford: Blackwell, 2004), p. 119: ". . . when said of the cause of being [analogous terms] cannot be predicated as attributes, strictly speaking, but as part of what it is to be the One whose essence is simply to be. The role of *participation,* then, is to remind us that there could be no such set of terms were the universe not itself derived from a source from which all that is, and notably what is perfect about what-is, flows. So the ontological ground of the set of terms lies in the fact that all-that-is participates in the One from whom everything derives, and their proper use demands that we bring this grounding fact to awareness."

115. *Summa Th.* I, q. 4, a. 3.

116. What makes Thomas's conjunction of these verses fascinating is that, given the *différance* between a protological and an eschatological "likeness," the "likeness" of Genesis 1:26 could be understood as a proleptic likeness, that is, as a promise, which is to be effected

sort of real, ontological likeness, which in the corpus of question 4 Thomas calls an analogy, is commended by Scripture. At the same time, for Thomas, even apart from Scripture, an analogy of being is commended by reason, inasmuch as creation is an effect of the Creator, and inasmuch as all effects bear, however remotely, some likeness to their cause. Of course, since God is not confined to any genus, this likeness is all the more remote; nevertheless, the effect (creation) may still be said to participate in the likeness of the cause (God) "according to some sort of analogy; as existence is common to all. In this way all created things, so far as they are beings, are like God as the first and universal principle of all being."[117]

The analogy of being is thus implied in Thomas inasmuch as it is implied by his metaphysics of creation, which, as an effect of God, is neither wholly alien to God (since "the effect must in some way resemble the form of the agent"), nor wholly like God (since the effect falls short of its cause "not merely in intensity and remission, as that which is less white falls short of that which is more white; but because they are not in agreement, specifically or generically").[118] In sum, being at once similar *and* dissimilar to God creation *is* a kind of analogy. But, *nota bene,* for Thomas the analogy must not be misconstrued in a way that would overstate the similarity between God and creatures according to a so-called "analogy of inequality," as was described above, in which case one thing simply shares in a given perfection to a greater degree than another. For, as he says, God is precisely *not* confined

---

historically through Christ and his Spirit, in whom "we are transformed from glory to glory" (2 Cor. 3:18), and which awaits the eschatological realization of 1 John 3:2, when the Church, the Bride, will be presented without blemish to Christ, the Bridegroom (Eph. 5:27). Unfortunately, Thomas does not discuss the relation between the protological and the eschatological here, even though the whole question of the analogy of being would seem to turn on it. For the question is not *whether* there is an analogy of being — Scripture clearly commends it. The question is whether the analogy is to be affirmed already as a matter of protology (in spite of the subsequent reality of sin) as a terminus a quo (which not even the reality of sin can destroy), or whether the analogy is to be affirmed only eschatologically, as a terminus ad quem, which is produced only through faith in Christ and the work of the Spirit. This would seem to be the crux of the matter as far as the debate between the churches is concerned. Przywara, essentially following Thomas, affirms the *analogia entis,* though filled out and perfected by grace, already at the level of nature; Barth affirms an analogy (in the form of an *analogia fidei*) *only* as a matter of grace. But perhaps the whole debate is best resolved simply by positing the traditional Orthodox distinction between "image" and "likeness" — which does not confuse but makes explicit the difference between nature and grace that Przywara himself (and Catholic theology in general) affirms.

117. *Summa Th.* I, q. 4, a. 3.
118. *Summa Th.* I, q. 4, a. 3.

to any genus, which is to say that He cannot be classified as an instance of something in which both He and the creature commonly share. On the contrary, He transcends every genus *(Deus non est in genere)*. Thus, for Thomas, while "it may be admitted that creatures are in some sense like God, it must nowise be admitted that God is like creatures; because, as Dionysius says (Div. Nom. ix): 'A mutual likeness may be found between things of the same order, but not between a cause and that which is caused.' For we say that a statue is like a man, but not conversely; so also a creature can be spoken of as in some sense like God; but not that God is like a creature."[119] Accordingly, for Thomas, whatever similarity one may attribute to God and creatures (keeping in mind the order of relation just described), the dissimilarity between them is always *greater*. And, as we shall see, this is precisely what Przywara means by the analogy of being.

3. The *analogia entis* in Przywara's Early Work (1922-26)

Given the foregoing, and given Przywara's self-understanding as a student and faithful expositor of tradition, the first thing to be noted is that he never regarded the *analogia entis* as *his* doctrine, but as a fundamental doctrine of the Catholic Church, something implicitly held by *all* the doctors of the Church, and which he merely sought to articulate and explicate: on the one hand, that creation is not divine and must never be confused with the divine (as happens with the various monisms and pantheisms); on the other hand, that creation, however corrupted by sin, is not *in its created essence* a reality alien to God (as is the case with the dualistic Gnostic religions). In short, being neither (univocally) identical to God nor totally (equivocally) different from him, the being of creation is mysteriously *analogous* to the being of God.[120] For, on the one hand, creation expresses something about the Cre-

---

119. *Summa Th.* I, q. 4, a. 3.

120. Of course, the dimensions of the analogy of being are considerably altered in light of sin, on the one hand, and redemption, on the other (as will be crucial to note again in response to Karl Barth's concerns). For, on the one hand, to the degree that creation is in bondage to sin, to that same degree it is *unlike* God and *alienated* from God (even if sin, being a privation, is never able utterly to destroy creation and obliterate the analogy of being). On the other hand, when creation is finally glorified in the saints, who are "like" Christ (1 John 3:2), creation will reveal a far *greater* likeness than a sinful humanity looking in the dark mirror of the present world can imagine (though even so great a likeness does not negate the *analogia entis* and the interval between the Creator and the creature).

ator who is declared in his works (Ps. 19:1; Wisd. 13:5; Rom. 1:19-20), and to this extent, in a general way that is to be distinguished from God's redemptive indwelling of creation in Christ, God can be said to be manifest "in" his creation. On the other hand, however much God is declared in his works and reflected in his image (Gen. 1:26-27), even in the saints who are his redeemed and glorified image, creation is in no way to be confused with him who remains in the words of *Dei Filius* "in reality and in his nature distinct from the world . . . and ineffably exalted above all things that exist or can be conceived."[121] In the words of Isaiah, "Heaven is my throne and the earth is my footstool; what is the house which you would build for me?" (Isa. 66:1). Or in the words of the psalmist, "Who is like the Lord our God, who is enthroned on high?" (Ps. 113:5). Thus Scripture itself suggests that creation is at once like God (*being* a revelation of God) *and* unlike God — not, though, in such a way that balances the likeness against the unlikeness, but in such a way that every similarity is necessarily qualified by *and gives way to* an ultimate and *greater* dissimilarity.

Far, then, from being original to Przywara, the doctrine of the *analogia entis* is a fundamentally *biblical* doctrine (as biblical, say, as the doctrine of the Trinity, which, like the *analogia entis,* is clearly implied by Scripture, but nowhere explicitly stated or defined). As we have also seen, it is a doctrine commended by tradition and understandably associated with Thomas Aquinas.[122] Nevertheless, it would be a mistake to think that Przywara was merely an expositor of Scripture and tradition, or that he was merely a student of Aquinas. For, as Rahner rightly pointed out, with Przywara not only is the *analogia entis* reformulated with an unparalleled degree of rigor and precision (precisely in the context of twentieth-century phenomenology), it is also endowed with a far more comprehensive meaning and a hitherto unparalleled degree of importance.[123] This is true, firstly, with regard to the Catholic Church's engagement with modern philosophy, Protestant theology, other religions, and modern secular culture.[124] In other words, far from

121. *Dogmatic Constitution on the Catholic Faith,* c. 1 (April 24, 1870).

122. According to Przywara (see *AE* §7, 6), the *analogia entis* is so perfectly expressed in Thomas as to be indelibly stamped with his name.

123. To reiterate Rahner's observation, Przywara transformed the *analogia entis* "from a scholastic technicality into the fundamental structure of Catholic theology." See Rahner, "Laudatio auf Erich Przywara," p. 270.

124. We have already seen how the *analogia entis* is posed against pantheism (and, it goes without saying, scientific naturalism). Equally, we have seen how it is posed against "theopanism," as Przywara termed the fundamental metaphysical tendency of Protestant

being a scholastic technicality, the *analogia entis* was to Przywara the standard of a properly Catholic understanding of reality, and, as such, crucial to the apologetics of the Catholic Church in the modern world. It is true, secondly, with regard to the Church itself, in which it continues to have a regulative function *within* the *analogia fidei* (since God remains ever greater than we can conceive even in light of revealed doctrine); the same also applies, therefore, to visionary theologies and claims of special revelation (as was at issue in the Church's response to Joachim of Fiore). For here, too, one must always observe the principle of God's ever-greater dissimilarity within every similarity, however great.[125] Thus, for Przywara, the *analogia entis* is fundamental to reason *and* to faith, as well as being a kind of bridge between them. Such is its comprehensive importance.

Since Przywara's formulation of the *analogia entis* goes through a series of stages or (better) refinements, however, in the following it will be important to spell out more precisely what he himself understood by the term over the course of his career: from the early 1920s when he first used it in the context of his engagement with Scheler's phenomenology, to the *Analogia*

theology, i.e., Lutheran and Reformed theology, which (in Przywara's view) led to the similarly conflationary religious philosophy of Hegel. As regards secular culture, if the *analogia entis* is a metaphysical truth, and if it can be grasped at some level by reason, then, from the Catholic Church's perspective, no culture can presume to be ignorant of its metaphysical dependence upon God as the source of all being, to whom, in a second-order reflection, all instances of truth, goodness, and beauty ultimately refer; nor can it idolatrously confuse itself with God in a reenactment of the fall *(eritis sicut Deus)*, as happened with the fascism of National Socialism and the atheism of the Soviet Republic. The same could be said of modern western democracies when, inadvertently or not, they make public opinion, "the people," into God (inasmuch as the people's consensus, however debased, is *de facto* the *summum bonum*), thereby forming the anti-Republic to Plato's Republic, forgetting the analogical interval between truth and opinion, divine and human knowledge. For these reasons the *analogia entis* thus remains a first line of argument in the Church's engagement with modern culture. See von Balthasar, "A Résumé of My Thought," in *Hans Urs von Balthasar: His Life and Work*, ed. David L. Schindler (San Francisco: Ignatius, 1991), p. 3: "The One, the Good, the True, and the Beautiful, these are what we call transcendental attributes of Being, because they surpass all the limits of essences and are coextensive with Being. If there is an insurmountable distance between God and his creature, but if there is also an analogy between them which cannot be resolved in any form of identity, there must also exist an analogy between the transcendentals — between those of the creature and those in God."

125. This, incidentally, is why Przywara could never accept Gottlieb Söhngen's proposal (vis-à-vis Karl Barth) of an *"analogia entis* within an *analogia fidei."* In fact, on Przywara's view it is precisely the reverse, in that the *analogia entis* is both epistemologically prior and ontologically ultimate.

Entis of 1932, to his clarification of the term in an essay from 1940, which is included in Part II of the present translation, entitled "The Scope of Analogy as a Fundamental Catholic Form." In doing so we will see, among other things, how the *analogia entis* initially describes a basic metaphysical insight, how it is subsequently employed as a *via media* between the metaphysical extremes of pantheism and "theopanism," and how it is finally reaffirmed, in light of Augustine, Thomas, Pseudo-Dionysius, and the IV Lateran Council, as a "fundamental form" of Catholic theology.

3.1. The analogia entis *as a Metaphysical Principle*

When Przywara first uses the term *analogia entis* in the early 1920s it is simply a way of saying that the world of becoming, the world of finite, mutable things, is not grounded in itself, but derives from and is dependent upon an absolute and infinite existence.[126] In Przywara's words, it means "that in their ultimate essence mutable and finite things are grounded in something immutable and infinite that is essentially distinct from them"; moreover, in such a way that "every perfection of the creature is a similitude of the infinite perfection of the Creator, and such that the Creator declares Himself in creatures on the basis of [His being] this essential ground of being."[127] For Przywara, therefore, to affirm the *analogia entis* is essentially to affirm two things: on the one hand, that the finite is grounded in the infinite and derives its being from absolute being (herein lies the moment of similarity, proximity, and likeness); on the other hand, that finite being cannot be equated with its divine ground but remains both essentially distinct from it and infinitely transcended by it (therein lies the moment of dissimilarity, distance, and insurmountable difference). Thus, for Przywara, in view of this similarity and difference, likeness and unlikeness, one may speak of an essentially *analogical* relation between the finite and the infinite.

Still, though, the nature of the relation between God (conceived philosophically as creation's infinite ground) and creation (as the universe of finite, contingent things) stands in need of further specification. For what exactly do we mean by finite being? Drawing out the implications of Aquinas's so-called "real distinction" between essence and existence,

126. See "Gotteserfahrung und Gottesbeweis," in *Schriften*, vol. 2, p. 7.
127. "Gotteserfahrung und Gottesbeweis," in *Schriften*, vol. 2, p. 7.

Przywara speaks of finite being as a *tension* [*Spannung*] between essence and existence.[128] For "what" one is, one's essence, is not the same as the sheer "fact" of one's existence. Rather, to be a creature is to be a wholly gratuitous "unity-in-tension" [*Spannungs-Einheit*] of essence and existence. It is, furthermore, this *non-identity* of essence and existence that accounts for the inherent mutability and movement of the creature as a being that is strictly "in becoming" *(in fieri)*. In Przywara's peculiar idiom, which specifies the nature of the tension between essence and existence, the essence of the creature is always "in-and-beyond" existence as that which, on the one hand, in-forms the existing creature, making it *what* it is, but at the same time mysteriously transcends existence in the given moment as something, as it were, yet to be attained; so that in some sense, compared to the being of God, who alone IS (Exod. 3:14), the being of the creature, being marked precisely by this *différance* [*sic*] between essence and existence, is never fully there.[129] In the paradoxical Augustinian phrase, the creature both "is and is not" *(est non est)*, as it awaits that eschatological realization when its being will finally be disclosed — and realized — in the parousia of Christ, the God-man (1 John 3:2).[130] Far, then, from being easily identified, objectified, and mastered, creaturely being is itself a mystery that exceeds our grasp. And, for Przywara, it is only once one begins to appreciate the mystery and gratuity of creaturely being that one can begin to intimate the far greater mystery, which declares itself within this mystery — as the secret of its being — of God himself.

For Przywara, therefore, creaturely being, as a dynamic unity of essence and existence, is fundamentally distended and ecstatic (since it is precisely not self-possessed but finds its being beyond itself), and to this extent (notwithstanding the incurvature of sin and the harmatiological possibility of "missing the mark") it points metaphysically as "being-in-becoming" to the Being of God on which it depends. Still, though, the question arises as to what, more specifically, constitutes the analogy between them. Without getting into the details of what type of analogy is most proper here, whether the

---

128. See, for example, *Ringen der Gegenwart, Gesammelte Aufsätze 1922-1927* (Augsburg: Benno Filser-Verlag, 1929), vol. 2, pp. 906-62. See also Przywara, "Thomas von Aquin als Problematiker," *Stimmen der Zeit* 109 (June 1925): 188-99. For Thomas on the real distinction, see John F. Wippel, *The Metaphysical Thought of Thomas Aquinas*, pp. 146ff.; *Metaphysical Themes in Thomas Aquinas* (Washington, DC: Catholic University of America Press, 1984), p. 136.

129. See Przywara, "Die Problematik der Neuscholastik," in *Kant-Studien* 33 (1928): 81.

130. See Augustine, *In Ps.* 121, 12; *Confessions*, XII, 6.

so-called "analogy of attribution" or the so-called "analogy of proper proportionality," each of which Przywara discusses in §6 of the *Analogia Entis,*
following Przywara the simplest answer to this question is to say that there is
an analogy between the unity of essence and existence in creatures and the
unity of essence and existence in God. The all-important difference, however, is that whereas creatures are a wholly *gratuitous* and *contingent* unity of
essence and existence, and whereas in creatures this unity is one of *tension*
between essence and existence, which remain forever *distinct,* and whereas
creatures therefore exist only in a state of constant *becoming,* in God the
unity of essence and existence is from all eternity an essential and absolute
identity, inasmuch as God's essence is to be. In the words of Thomas, *sua
igitur essentia est suum esse.*[131] Therein, to put it simply, in this kind of relational difference between the being of God and the being of creatures, lies
the analogy of being.

Once again, however, one must immediately emphasize that for
Przywara (as for Aquinas) the stress of the analogy falls not on the similarity
but rather on the *difference* between God and creatures. This must be said in
light of common misunderstandings of the *analogia entis* as a form of metaphysical bridge-building, which (it is thought) subsumes God and creatures
under a common concept (namely, being) and thereby presumes, in a form
of metaphysical Prometheanism, to span the gulf between them. As
Przywara emphatically puts it in a 1925 essay, "Thomas von Aquin als Problematiker," which renders all such charges otiose:

> For [Thomas] too, therefore, his final word is the famous and much mis-
> understood '*analogia entis.*' That is to say, there is nothing absolutely
> common between God and creature. On the contrary: in the very thing
> in which they correspond, namely, in being, they are separated from one
> another as by an abyss. God's being is essentially pure being [*reines
> Sein*]; the being of the creature is essentially spanned between essence
> and existence [*Sosein-Dasein-gespanntes Sein*]. Consequently (as follows
> from the correlation of being and knowledge), the summit of all
> creaturely knowledge of God is: to comprehend God's incomprehensi-
> bility. It is in penetrating through all peripheral conceptions to the in-
> comprehensible mystery of its being that the creature opens its true eye
> to the true God.[132]

131. *Summa Th.* I, q. 3, a. 3, corp.; *Ringen der Gegenwart,* vol. 2, p. 945.
132. *Ringen der Gegenwart,* vol. 2, p. 928.

Far, then, from being comprehensible, the fundamentally *analogical* being of the creature, being already at an immanent level a mysterious correlation of opposites — from the most basic metaphysical correlation of essence-existence to the highest natural correlation of man-woman — is *itself* a mystery; and only *as such, in its mysteriousness,* is it an analogue of the (ever) *greater* and incomprehensible mystery of God. Thus, in his late works Przywara can summarize the correlated alterities of the *analogia entis* in terms of *homo abyssus* and *Deus abyssus,* recalling thereby the words of the psalmist, *abyssus abyssum invocat* (Ps. 42:7).[133]

In no sense, therefore, can Przywara's *analogia entis* be said to objectify being, since it precisely deconstructs every metaphysics of presence that would fix or determine being either as existence or as essence (i.e., it militates equally against every pure essentialism and every pure existentialism); much less can it be said to objectify or determine the being of God or put God within the creature's grasp (as though one had to do here with just another version of "onto-theology"), since God appears here, at the level of natural theology, through the *mystery* of the tensions of creaturely being as "through a glass darkly."[134] On the contrary, while admitting a certain similitude by virtue of the fact of creation, the point of the *analogia entis* is precisely to *loosen* our grasp upon being (whether this grasping be in the form of reductive naturalism, logical positivism, or absolute idealism) and to humble every proud system of thought, in order to make way for silent adoration of the *Deus tamquam ignotus,* the God who is revealed *in* creation as infinitely *beyond* it — and hence infinitely beyond our grasp. As Przywara puts it at the conclusion of the same essay, denying that Thomas himself was a systematician (viewing him instead as, more truly, an "aporetic thinker") or that Thomas can be turned into a system (as happens in the schools): "Only God can have something like a completely closed picture of the world.

133. See "The Religious Gnoseology of Augustine" in Part II of the present volume, but above all Przywara's *Mensch,* p. 101; and *Humanitas,* p. 741, *et passim.*

134. This is why any possible objection to the *analogia entis* on the grounds that it is an instance of natural theology that works its way up to God upon the secure (ontic or noetic) foundation of nature or reason is entirely misplaced. And here, one could argue, Przywara overcomes some of the more simplistic versions of Thomism, for which nature and reason can be thought to provide this secure foundation. For the entire (profoundly Augustinian) point of the *analogia entis* (understood immanently) is that the creature has no resting place in itself: that its ground (whether conceived ontically or noetically) is not one of identity, but one of relation — a relation that is ultimately inscrutable — making every allegedly secure and fixed philosophical foundation impossible.

The task of the creature is ever more humbly and resignedly to get over the delusions of all seemingly self-contained systems and to recognize the creature's true vocation: worshipful silence before the mysteries: *Adoro te devote, latens Deitas.*"[135]

3.2. *The* analogia entis *Between Pantheism and Theopanism*

Przywara's novelty, however, consisted not so much in his explication of the late-scholastic doctrine of the *analogia entis* — though it may certainly be considered a creative development within Thomism — as in the way that he used this doctrine to engage modern thought.[136] And in this regard he notes profound differences between modernity and the carefully balanced theologies of the Middle Ages. To put it simply, whereas the great scholastics, such as Bonaventure, Thomas, and Scotus, notwithstanding their differences, appreciated the fundamental tensions between intellect and will, divine and human freedom, the omni-causality of God and the secondary causality of creatures, in modernity, according to Przywara, in the wake of the Reformation, these tensions give way to two destructive dialectics: on the one hand, a dialectic between rationalism and voluntarism; on the other hand, and more fundamentally, a dialectic between what he calls pantheism and theopanism.[137]

To understand how the *analogia entis* relates to these dialectics (as a corrective to them), it is important to note that the *analogia entis*, as Przywara understands it, functions on two different registers: the first, at an immanent level, concerns the creaturely tension between essence and existence; the second concerns the transcendent relation of creaturely being, thus constituted, to the Creator. Whereas the *analogia entis*, considered according to the first register, preserves the tension between philosophies of essence and philosophies of existence, in modernity this tension mutates into an either-or: between an abstract, universal, and ultimately sterile rationalism disconnected from history and tradition (characteristic of the Enlightenment) and a radical, individualistic voluntarism (stemming from Luther's existentialist-nominalist theology) that can make out no universal

---

135. *Ringen der Gegenwart,* vol. 2, p. 929; Przywara's emphasis.

136. *Ringen der Gegenwart,* vol. 2, pp. 958ff.

137. While Przywara mints it anew, the term "theopanism" seems to have originated with Rudolf Otto. See *Schriften,* vol. 2, p. 352.

rational norms and terminates in the historicism, relativism, and will to power of Nietzsche. In the case of the second register, instead of the tension between the omni-causality [*Allwirksamkeit*] of God and the secondary causality of the world, which the *analogia entis* is intended to preserve, modernity fluctuates between a theopanism of "God alone" (whereby God is or does essentially everything and the creature is or does essentially nothing) and a pantheism of the "world alone" (whereby the world is essentially everything and God is essentially nothing).[138] In the first case, the world either lacks density, being a mere manifestation or emanation of the divine or the ideal (as one sees in various idealisms, neo-Platonisms, and Eastern philosophies), or it lacks integrity, being stripped as a consequence of the fall and a despotic conception of divine sovereignty of any cooperation with grace.[139] In the second case, which is the dialectical flipside of the first and is represented by modern Western secularism, it is God who is unreal, being nothing but a conceptual projection or epiphenomenon of the real. For whereas idealism cedes all reality to the infinite and absolute, depriving the contingent world of any real being or agency (as is the case with Bud-

---

138. This, incidentally, is why Przywara strikingly refers to Heidegger's philosophy of *Sein als Nichts* precisely as a form of pantheism. Cf. *Logos*, p. 112: "All that remains is an either-or between a piety toward God that is hostile to the world and a piety toward the world that is hostile toward God. Such is the either-or between the Reformation taken to its logical conclusion (as in the early Barth) and secularism taken to its logical conclusion (as with Lenin and Stalin)."

139. In other words, with theopanism the world is not a genuine other of the divine but in reality nothing but an emanation *of* the divine (a *genitivus subjectivus*!) or a moment in the self-development or self-interpretation of the divine — as is the case, *mutatis mutandis*, with Neo-Platonism, Hegelianism, and, in Przywara's view, the dialectical theology of the 1920s, inasmuch as the posited dialectic between God and world (faith and reason, grace and nature) ultimately and *ironically* collapses into the Lutheran-Reformed doctrine of God's exclusive agency or sole-causality *(Alleinwirksamkeit)*. In short, as Przywara sees it, it is a radical theology of difference that ends in a fateful theology of identity. Over against the Lutheran-Reformed doctrine of *Alleinwirksamkeit*, Przywara thus posits the *analogia entis*, which grants to creation the integrity of secondary causes without thereby compromising the Catholic doctrine of God's *Allwirksamkeit*, i.e., the doctrine that God nevertheless — in and through the reality of created freedom — works all in all. To be sure, theopanism is often cloaked in a language of hyper-transcendence, as part of a pious and well-intentioned attempt precisely not to confuse God with the world, but rather to give God the glory. At the end of the day, however, as Przywara sees it, Barth's dialectic (lacking an analogy of being) ironically collapses into an unwitting form of identity — the very thing he wishes to avoid — in that faith is a work of God alone and the believing creature is simply a site of divine *self*-interpretation. For Przywara's reading of Barth, see *Humanitas*, p. 174.

dhism and *mutatis mutandis* Lutheran-Reformed theology to the extent that the latter denies any cooperation with grace), Western secular materialism cedes all reality to this world and denies that God is anything more than a product of self-alienation (Feuerbach-Marx), mythopoesis (Nietzsche), or wish fulfillment (Freud).

When Przywara employs the term *analogia entis* in his early work it is therefore always in the name of a Catholic doctrine of creation (and a Thomistic doctrine of secondary causes) as a way of steering between the Scylla of pantheism (and secularism) and the Charybdis of theopanism — each of which, for all their obvious differences, amounts to a denial of the *analogia entis*. For, to put it simply, in neither of these cases can one speak of a real *relation* between God and world: neither in the case of pantheism, nor, Przywara contends, in the case of a strict Lutheran-Reformed theopanism, since the integrity of creation is here so denigrated on account of the fall as to become an illusion (as when Luther calls the free will a fiction, or when Barth denies that nature has any capacity even to respond to grace). Instead, the relational tension of the *analogia entis* between the infinite and the finite, Being and becoming, is collapsed into one or another form of identity: in the case of theopanism, God in effect is or does everything and creation in effect is or does nothing (rendering human being and freedom an illusion); in the case of pantheism and modern secularism, the world is all there really is and God is as nothing (whether God is explicitly affirmed to be an illusion, as with the fathers of modern atheism, who were still religious *ex negativo*, channeling their religious zeal and residual messianic hopes into a secular-redemptive psychology [Freud], politics [Marx], science [Comte], and art [Nietzsche]; or whether God is treated in practice, if not in theory, in the spirit of the mindless nihilism of Nietzsche's blinking "last men," as if he did not exist).[140] In-

140. As Przywara strikingly puts it, "As for this identity [*Identität-Eins*] of God and world, which replaced polarity's unity-in-tension [*Polaritäts-Spannung-Eins*] of God and world, what does it fundamentally matter whether one call it God or world, whether one call it Spinoza's world-denying theopanism or Schopenhauer-Nietzsche's God-denying pantheism? Either way, its inevitable consequence was the frightful reeling of modernity between a sensual, pleasure-seeking intoxication with the world and a fanatical, eschatological hatred of the world: is not this the deadly fever that is shaking Europe even now?" *Ringen der Gegenwart*, pp. 960-61. The fact that Przywara here identifies Spinoza (the typical pantheist) with theopanism is not a category mistake but an indication of greater precision on his part — Hegel, too, on this reading, is a "theopanist" — and is therefore not at odds with his similar reading of Lutheran-Reformed theology. On the contrary, it shows that, for Przywara, Spinoza-Hegel is precisely a genealogical development of this kind of theology. See Przywara, "Die religiöse Krisis in der Gegenwart und der Katholizismus," in Przywara,

deed, so truly is pantheism the metaphysical inverse and parody of theopanism that just as a resigned Buddhism wishes the contingent world away (as a source of suffering) or a resigned Luther wishes the free will away (as something dreadful), modern secular atheism wishes God away (as an imagined source of oppression or at least as an obstacle to the fulfillment of carnal desires and secular political agendas).

In Przywara's view, therefore, what is needed over against the extremes of Lutheran-Reformed theology and modern secular atheism (each of which, he contends, is the dialectical flipside of the other) is a properly Catholic metaphysics of the *analogia entis*. For it is precisely in the *analogia entis* that the relational tension between God and creation, grace and nature, is preserved — namely, in the form of God "in-and-beyond" creation and grace "in-and-beyond" nature (since nature itself is already an unmerited gift), thereby doing justice to divine immanence in a real world of secondary causes, and thus to human freedom (*contra* theopanism), as well as to God's sovereign transcendence of the world (*contra* pantheism). In sum, as Przywara incisively puts it: "Instead of the congenital illness of the modern 'God *alone* [is] everything,' the native wholeness of the Thomistic 'God [is] all *in all*': instead of 'God above us *or* in us' (either a world that is absorbed into God *or* a God that is dissolved into the world) the great, vital and liberating 'God above us *and* in us.'"[141]

3.3. *The* analogia entis *and Natural Theology*

Przywara thus brings us to a metaphysical crossroads, for "either one identifies the mutable and finite with what is immutable and infinite," as inevitably happens with both pantheism and theopanism, or one recognizes the actual state of affairs that the *philosophia perennis* describes by the "*analogia entis*."[142] But if he sees the *analogia entis* as the answer to the fitful dialectics of modernity, this makes the question all the more pressing whether it is

---

Katholische Krise, ed. Bernhard Gertz (Düsseldorf: Patmos Verlag, 1967), p. 51: "The inner dialectic of the religiosity of the Reformation turns out to be precisely the *Urgrund* of the dialectic of modernity: between the negation and apotheosis of culture. This dialectic is inherent in the almost indiscernible coincidence of God and creature that follows from the doctrine of God's *Alleinwirksamkeit*. If God and creature are so nearly blurred into one, it is ultimately a matter of indifference whether I call this one thing God or the universe."

141. *Ringen der Gegenwart*, p. 961.

142. See "Gotteserfahrung und Gottesbeweis," in *Schriften*, vol. 2, p. 7.

properly a matter of faith or reason. Certainly, for Przywara, it is not a question of whether faith confirms or clarifies the *analogia entis* (for him it does both); rather, the question is to what extent the *analogia entis* can in principle be recognized by reason and, as such, belongs to our natural knowledge of God. Przywara's answer to this question in his early work is clear: the *analogia entis* is *"the origin, ground of truth, content and extent of our natural knowledge of God."*[143] For we can know as a matter of the natural light of reason that all the perfection of the creature is but an image — an analogy — of the infinite perfection of the Creator, who declares himself in creatures as this essential ground of being.[144] Elaborating on this natural knowledge, he writes:

> The more specific ways in which God can be known can be very different: at one moment, one might ascend from the perfections of finite things to the infinite source of all perfection; at another moment one might catch a glimpse of the majesty of the immutable shining through the flitting back and forth of mutable things; at another moment one's experience of other persons may give one a lively sense of the personality of God as the fulfillment of everything we intimate in personal greatness; or, at yet another moment, we might happen to perceive in the restless activity of creation the "active repose and reposing activity" of the Creator.[145]

In other words, in such experiences we intimate something of the transcendent declared within the immanent, and therewith the basic "in-over" [*in-über*] or "in-and-beyond" structure of the analogy of being. For while God is

---

143. "Gotteserfahrung und Gottesbeweis," p. 10. In the words of the first Vatican Council, "The same Holy mother Church holds and teaches that God, the source and end of all things, can be known with certainty from the consideration of created things, by the natural power of human reason." *Dogmatic Constitution on the Catholic Faith,* chapter 2. Thus, expressly affirming the *duplex ordo* of Vatican I, Przywara says that the knowledge of God's existence is, strictly speaking, a matter of reason, since it is "positively reasonable," as contrasted with faith in mysteries, which can merely be shown to be "not contrary to reason" (*Schriften,* vol. 2, p. 8).

144. "Gotteserfahrung und Gottesbeweis," p. 7. Regarding the ground of creaturely essences, Przywara explains with added emphasis, "The **analogia** entis points to God as the *ipsa forma* of the *forma rerum,* i.e., to God as *causa exemplaris;* as for the ground of creaturely existence, on the other hand, the *analogia* **entis** points to God as the *principium* (i.e., *causa efficiens*) and *finis* (i.e., *causa finalis*). Thus all three causal relations between God and world . . . are comprised within the one *analogia entis.*"

145. "Gotteserfahrung und Gottesbeweis," p. 10.

"in all things" as the effective ground of things, apart from whom they would not be, He is always also "beyond all things" — "sensible [*faßlich*] in His creatures, who are His image, yet incomprehensible in His inmost being [*Wesen*]."[146] Again, more or less summarizing his early doctrine of the *analogia entis,* he writes: "as the *effective* ground of the *being* of the creature, God is ineffably 'interior' to the creature; as the effective *ground* of the being of the creature, he is infinitely 'beyond' the creature: 'similar' and yet 'dissimilar,' 'in' and yet 'beyond.'"[147]

Whether or not Barth was right to reject the *analogia entis,* he was therefore right to perceive a connection between the *analogia entis* and natural theology; for all of this can in principle be thought (according to a *cognito directa*) or subsequently theorized (according to a *cognitio reflexa*) apart from any special revelation.[148] But if one is accurately to represent and appreciate Przywara's doctrine, several clarifications are crucial. The first, which cannot be stressed enough, is that according to the *analogia entis,* however much one may glimpse God in the likeness of creatures, the likeness of creation is *only* a likeness, and therefore the ultimate stress of the *analogia entis* is that of an "in-and-*beyond.*" Secondly, one must appreciate that, for Przywara, the purchase of the *analogia entis,* as glimpsed from the vantage of the sinful, fallen creature without the light of faith, is severely limited. Indeed, for Przywara, natural theology, apart from faith, is always on the verge of idolatrously collapsing the distance between Creator and creature that the *analogia entis* holds open.[149] Thirdly, one must appreciate that, for Przywara, the *analogia entis* precisely *cannot* be reduced to natural theology for the simple reason that it stands as a corrective not only to all misguided natural theologies (and

---

146. "Gotteserfahrung und Gottesbeweis," p. 7.

147. "Gotteserfahrung und Gottesbeweis," p. 21.

148. "Gotteserfahrung und Gottesbeweis," p. 11.

149. See, for example, Przywara's fascinating footnote on Romans 1:21-22 (*AE* §6, 5), where, following Aquinas, he makes a fundamental distinction between formal and material knowledge of the divine. In light of this passage it is clear that for Przywara one can have a formal knowledge of the divine as something shared in by Catholics and pagans, in the minimal sense of recognizing *(Erkennen)* a divine ground of the world, which is distinct from the world (cf. *Summa Th.* I, q. 13, a. 10 ad 5; q. 13, a. 9 ad 2), and yet fail to give due recognition *(Anerkennen)* to God as God. Thus, for Przywara, vis-à-vis the one triune God of Christianity, even Aristotle's "God" is ultimately an *idol*, being merely the immanent unity of the cosmos: the unity of the ontic cosmic cycle (κυκλοφορία) with the noetic cycle of thought in and to itself (νόησις νοήσεως). The natural knowledge of God afforded by the *analogia entis* is therefore by no means a guarantee that one will properly worship the God to whom it points.

all alternative metaphysical philosophies), but even to all positive and ostensibly biblical theologies that, in the name of revelation, would forget or unwittingly slight the difference between God and creatures. In other words, the *analogia entis* is equally a *theological* principle and, as such, pertains even to theologies formulated in light of revelation, as was the case with the Fourth Lateran Council's response to the Trinitarian theology of Joachim of Fiore.

To be sure, Przywara also employs the *analogia entis* in order to affirm that creation possesses a certain ontological integrity and density, a certain similitude of being, in order to affirm, furthermore, that the creature is in principle able, notwithstanding its fallen condition, to recognize in this similitude, as through a glass darkly, the Creator who is declared in his works (as Vatican I teaches). And to this extent, it bears an analogy to the kind of natural theology that Barth rejected. Again, however, anticipating our response to Barth (and Heidegger) in the final section, the ultimate point of the *analogia entis* is precisely to humble all natural (and even all supernatural) knowledge of God, to deconstruct every closed system (whether philosophical or theological), in short, to break to pieces every conceptual idol, and to insist that all our knowledge of God, no matter how exalted by grace, is "patchwork" (cf. 1 Cor. 13:12) — a knowledge in "images and likenesses" that break and fail and thereby point to a God who is *beyond* comparison, indeed, "beyond all analogy."[150] Not surprisingly, therefore, von Balthasar contends that Barth (though he may have had other misgivings about the *analogia entis*) fundamentally misunderstood Przywara's pathos:

> The term [*analogia entis*] passed over into the common vocabulary without an understanding and concomitant appropriation of its true pathos. How could a pathos be systematized? In this etiolated, academic, and no longer identifiable form Karl Barth could brand the *analogia entis* the invention of Antichrist, when in fact it was at the time what most resembled his own pathos: both took a stand against Kantianism and Hegelianism, against Schleiermacherian or modernist methods of immanence, against every form by which the human being, whether pious or not, would usurp the living God. Przywara's radicalism shows this interconfessional conflict to rest upon a misunderstanding, provided that one grants the validity of his analysis of original Protestantism (as theopanistic dialectic).[151]

150. "Gotteserfahrung und Gottesbeweis," p. 10; *Schriften*, vol. 2, p. 404.
151. Przywara, *Sein Schrifttum*, p. 6.

Again, this is not to say that the *analogia entis* does not comport in its abstract philosophical formulation with natural theology. But, as von Balthasar here points out, there is nothing in the *analogia entis* — "nothing whatever" of that "ogre that Barth has made of it — that should be cause for concern."[152] For, properly understood, the *analogia entis* cannot in any sense be said to comport with the modern philosophies and theologies of immanence from Kant to Schleiermacher, which inevitably threaten to confuse the divine with reason or feeling, and which Barth understandably rejected. On the contrary, the explicit intention of Przywara's *analogia entis,* as the metaphysical basis of any *genuine* natural theology, is precisely to explode the confines of immanence, by analogically relating it to a God who — as becomes even clearer in light of revelation — is exceedingly *beyond* it. In any event, the ultimate point of the *analogia entis,* as deployed by Przywara, is precisely *not* by philosophical means to close the gap between God and creatures, grace and nature, reason and revelation (as Barth seems to have feared), but rather to widen it. And in this respect, *pace* Barth, the *analogia entis* actually serves revelation, inasmuch as the novelty of God's revelation to creatures (which Barth understandably emphasized) first requires an appreciation of the *distance* (which can be recognized by reason) between them.[153]

Accordingly, if one attends to the proper stress of the *analogia entis* and if one appreciates the pathos with which Przywara employed it during the 1920s and 1930s, one will find that Barth and Przywara were actually *united* in their efforts to combat the "crisis" and potentially disastrous consequences of modern rationalism and humanism.[154] One will find, more-

152. Von Balthasar, *The Theology of Karl Barth,* trans. E. Oakes (San Francisco: Ignatius, 1992), p. 50.
153. See footnote 24, above.
154. Consider, for example, Przywara's incisive lecture on December 1, 1925, at the University of Munich, "Die religiöse Krisis in der Gegenwart und der Katholizismus," reprinted in *Katholische Krise,* pp. 42-53. As Przywara puts it, in sharp criticism of humanism: "The quintessence of humanity, its inner unity, is God. God is nothing but the essential ground of humanity. It is therefore clear that God arises in creation; he has no other meaning but to be the inner ground of the being of creation and the inner [essence] of humanity. To put it sharply, God is the world, is humanity. Through a slow process, this conception of European rationalism is then incorporated into the philosophy of religion proper: from the so-called universal religious theism up to Schleiermacher" (p. 42). Przywara then goes on to criticize what Heidegger would later call "onto-theology" in various forms, in Leibniz, in modern science, in Kant, et al., for which God is nothing but the "inner ground" of the purposefulness of the world or of the lawfulness of the world or of the harmony of virtue and happiness. "In the end God is simply and solely there to connect the oppositions of world

over, that their differences lay not so much in what they hoped to achieve as in their methods and in their perceived solutions to the *same* problem: what Barth sought to do by means of a dogmatic theology recentered *upon* revelation, the Jesuit Przywara sought to achieve from *within* philosophy and its language — by means of an implacable demonstration of the thoroughgoing relativity of all creaturely thought and being — in order, like John the Baptist, to prepare the way *for* revelation: to demolish all idolatrous systems of thought, which would domesticate God in human concepts, and thereby dispose creaturely thought *qua* creaturely thought to revelation *qua* revelation. In short, as von Balthasar observes, just as Barth was animated by the zeal of Calvin's *soli Deo gloria*, Przywara, the Jesuit, was animated by zealous service to the "ever-greater" God of his order's founder — as can be seen from his 1925 poetic work on Ignatian spirituality, *Majestas Divina*, not to mention his monumental three-volume commentary on the *Spiritual Exercises*, whose title, *Deus Semper Maior*, is in itself a clear indication of the spiritual pathos animating his metaphysics.[155]

3.4. The analogia entis *as Dynamic Polarity*

All of this is further explicated in another article from Przywara's early period entitled "God in us and God above us," where he says that the God of the *analogia entis* is none other than the God of Augustine — a God who is *interior intimo meo,* but at the same time *superior summo meo,* "more inward than my inmost" and "higher than my highest."[156] "*Deus interior* and *Deus*

---

and humanity. And so it is now self-evident that this entire development concludes with Schleiermacher's philosophy of religion, where God is nothing but the unity of the universe. . . . God is world. The real calamity of this philosophy of religion, however . . . is that it has made its way into religion itself" (pp. 42-43).

155. See von Balthasar, "Analogie und Dialektik," *Divus Thomas* 22 (1944): 211-12. As Aidan Nichols aptly puts it, summing up the shared pathos of Przywara and von Balthasar, both hoped to "combine the mind of St Thomas with the heart of St Augustine, all in the spirit of St Ignatius Loyola, that burning obedience — at once interior and missionary — to the Word of God" (*The Word Has Been Abroad*, p. 8). For one of the best recent works on Przywara, which admirably captures the Ignatian dimensions of his metaphysics, see Christian Lagger, *Dienst. Kenosis in Schöpfung und Kreuz bei Erich Przywara S.J.* (Innsbruck-Wien: Tyrolia Verlag, 2007). For an earlier treatment of the Ignatian aspect of Przywara's metaphysics, see James Zeitz, *Spirituality and the Analogia Entis According to Erich Przywara, S.J.* (Washington, DC: University Press of America, 1982).

156. *Confessions* III, 6 (11).

exterior," he writes, 'God in all and above all,' God more inward than we are to ourselves, and yet surmounting and transcending [all things] as infinite and incomprehensible."[157] And so he concludes (in what amounts to a metaphysical justification for Newman's "opposite virtues"): "because God reveals himself as at once a God of blessed, mystical intimacy and a God of the coolest distance, the fundamental disposition of the believing soul should be one of 'fearing love and loving fear' — a fear that springs from love inasmuch as love fears to lose the beloved; and a love that through fear maintains a holy sobriety and a tender reverence."[158] Thus, for Przywara, not only does the *analogia entis* sum up the Catholic concept of God (i.e., as a God who is at once immanent and transcendent), it is also the measure of authentic religious life.

Accordingly, in his 1923 work *Gottgeheimnis der Welt*, he argues that what is needed vis-à-vis all one-sided philosophies and theologies is a genuinely Catholic philosophy of "dynamic polarity" that would do justice to the respective poles of divine immanence and divine transcendence. And, in fact, throughout the 1920s the term *polarity* is more or less equivalent to what Przywara means by the *analogia entis,* inasmuch as the *analogia entis* comprises both the immanent polar tension in creatures between essence and existence and, vertically intersecting this polarity, the polar tension between divine immanence and transcendence. For Przywara, however, it is again crucial to observe: the *analogia entis* is not to be confused with an equilibrium or static midpoint between the poles of divine immanence and divine transcendence, as though the *analogia entis* could be summed up by a simple "both-and." On the contrary, for Przywara, the back-and-forth rhythm of the *analogia entis* is an explicitly *dynamic* one, tending always in

---

157. *Ringen der Gegenwart. Gesammelte Aufsätze 1922-1927* (Augsburg: Benno Filser Verlag, 1929), vol. 2, p. 543. Importantly, by divine "immanence," Przywara hardly means to equate God with things or to endorse anything remotely resembling pantheism. On the contrary, even in God's immanence to creation, being *more interior* to it, he is beyond it. Thus, at no point does the *analogia entis* give the creature a hold on God.

158. *Ringen der Gegenwart,* vol. 2, p. 543. Cf. *Schriften,* vol. 2, p. 22: "God in creatures, and therefore love; God above and beyond creatures, and therefore fear: 'loving fear and fearing love.'" See Augustine, *In Ps.* 118 (22, 6). Cf. John Henry Newman, *Parochial and Plain Sermons,* vol. 1 (London: Longmans, Green and Co., 1907), p. 322: "The fear of God is the beginning of wisdom; till you see him to be a consuming fire, and approach him with reverence and godly fear, as being sinners, you are not even in sight of the strait gate. I do not wish you to be able to point to any particular time when you renounced the world (as it is called), and were converted; this is a deceit. Fear and love must go together; always fear, always love, to your dying day."

the direction of a greater transcendence. As he puts it, recalling the theme of divine infinity in Gregory of Nyssa and Augustine, "Even if we were to have the most sublime experience of mystical union, would we then have any right to come to a stopping point and dream of having finally attained a state of 'immediacy' or a state of 'maximal knowledge' or a state of 'ultimate proximity'?" He answers with a single paradoxical phrase from Augustine: *Invenitur quaerendus!* ["He is found in order to be sought!"] In other words, with respect to God, "Even the greatest finding is but the beginning of a new searching."[159] Przywara beautifully makes the same point a few years later in a lecture from 1926:

> Thus all our wandering in Him and to Him is itself a tension between an ineffable proximity and an ineffable distance. Every living thing . . . everything that happens, is full of His presence. 'He is not far from us; for in Him we live and move and have our being.' But we grow in our sense of His fullness only in the measure that we do not equate Him with any created thing or circumstance, that is, in the measure that we stand at an ultimate distance from every particular shining of His face. He is the one who lights up before us when we stand at a distance, and who lights up before us to urge us on. He is the infinite light that becomes ever more distant the closer we come to Him. Every finding is the beginning of a new searching. His blessed intimacy [*Inne-Sein*] is the experience of His infinite transcendence [*Über-Sein*]. No morning of mystical marriage is a definitive embrace of His fullness; no mystical night of despair a detachment from His presence. . . . He compels us into all the riches and changes of world and life in order that we might experience Him anew and more richly as beyond this world and life. And, ultimately, this indissoluble tension of proximity and distance to Him is but the innermost revelation of His own primal mystery, by which He is *in* us and *beyond* us, closer to us than we are to ourselves, such that we love him as proximity *itself*, and, yet again, farther away from us than any other distance, such that we revere Him with trembling as distance *itself*. God in us *and* God beyond us.[160]

159. *Schriften*, vol. 2, p. 231. Cf. Augustine, *In Jo. Tract.* LXIII, i: "Ut inveniendus quaeratur, occultus est; ut inventus quaeratur, immensus est. Unde alibi dicitur, 'Quaerite faciem ejus semper'" (Ps. 105:4). ("He is hidden in order that you might seek him; and in order that you might not cease in your search once you have found him, he is infinite. Thus is it said . . . 'Seek his face evermore.'")

160. *Schriften*, vol. 2, p. 281; cf. p. 404.

Here again we see the basic point of the *analogia entis,* which Przywara reiterates throughout his early work: there is no genuine natural *or* supernatural experience of God that does not give way to reverent distance and silent adoration.[161] Nor does his point fundamentally change. It is only refined and deepened. What this particular passage makes clear, though, and must be kept in mind if one is properly to understand the *analogia entis,* is that it is not simply a code word for a particular metaphysics but a profound expression of genuine religious experience. Indeed, just as the *lex credendi* follows the *lex orandi,* one could say that Przywara's metaphysics is simply a philosophical expression for what the saints have always known in their prayer life and the Church has always expressed in its liturgical life. For, as he puts it in 1927, "What is meant by *analogia entis* is precisely this: that in the very same act in which the human being comes to intimate God in the likeness of the creature, he also comes to intimate Him as the one who is beyond all likeness."[162]

4. The *Analogia Entis* (1932)

Building upon the foregoing, Przywara's mature doctrine of the *analogia entis* is set forth in two principal works: first in his *Religionsphilosophie katholischer Theologie* (1926) and then, more thoroughly, in his *Analogia Entis* (1932).[163] The difference between these and earlier works is that here Przywara takes a further, bolder step, attempting to show how the dynamic of the *analogia entis,* as a truly fundamental principle, is manifest in the structures of consciousness and the principles of thought itself. At the same time Przywara attends in these works more clearly to questions of intentionality; and to this extent he could be said to adopt more of a phenomenological approach.[164]

161. See "Mysticism and Distance," in *Schriften,* vol. 2, pp. 66-90, 72-73: "Even the Church is inwardly conscious of Him only insofar as she reveres Him as above her. . . . Both individual and ecclesial mysticism are essentially bound to the law of distance. Both the individual soul and the community live Christ [*leben Christus*] to the extent that they have a lively consciousness of the ultimate distance between Him and them."

162. *Schriften,* vol. 2, p. 404.

163. *Religionsphilosophie katholischer Theologie* (München and Berlin: Oldenbourg, 1927), which is included in *Schriften,* vol. 2.

164. In this regard it is important to recall that Przywara was a close friend of Edith Stein and, through her, personally acquainted with Husserl. He was also one of the first Catholic theologians to assess the importance of phenomenology from a Thomist perspective. See his early work *Religionsbegründung,* which is his engagement with Scheler, as well as his "Drei Richtungen der Phänomenologie," *Stimmen der Zeit* 115 (1928): 252-64.

Thus, in *Religionsphilosophie katholischer Theologie* he begins with a rigorous examination of the possible orientations of consciousness as such, from which the possible types of religious consciousness — and corresponding philosophies of religion — emerge.[165] Likewise, in the *Analogia Entis* he develops the concept of "metaphysics as such," which turns out to be an analogical metaphysics, upon the basis of the tensions between a transcendental philosophy of consciousness (which attends to essences) and a philosophy of being (which attends to the question of being and our historical-existential being-in-the-world), thereby implicitly touching upon the conflict that had recently emerged from within the school of phenomenology (and from Przywara's perspective inevitably so) between Husserl and his one-time assistant, Heidegger.[166] What both of these works have in common is that they expose with incredible rigor and perspicacity the tensions that animate *all* philosophical reflection — tensions that ultimately trace back to the "real distinction" in creaturely being between essence and existence. Indeed, drawing out the full implications of Thomism's "real distinction," Przywara shows that the *analogia entis* is secretly at the heart of all thought — being always already "in" philosophy and informing its very dynamic as the ultimately theological solution to its inherent tensions and contradictions.

4.1. The analogia entis *as the Original Structure of Metaphysics*

Needless to say, it is impossible here to go through all the steps required to see how the *analogia entis* emerges from and ultimately resolves (theologically) the problems intrinsic to philosophy. For the sake of the reader, however, who might reasonably wish for some guidance through the thicket of Przywara's argument in *Analogia Entis* (§§1-4), one might summarize these steps as fol-

165. For example, if consciousness is fundamentally oriented to itself as the unity of its own experience, this will tend to be expressed in a religious philosophy of *immanence;* if consciousness is fundamentally oriented toward an external unity beyond it, this will tend to be expressed in a religious philosophy of *transcendence;* if, finally, consciousness can discover no unity, internal or external, nor any rest, but conceives of unity as an infinite task, never to be finished, this will tend to be expressed in a *transcendental* philosophy of religion. The first type, more or less represented by Schleiermacher, tends in the direction of an aesthetic religion of a pure "condition" *(reinen "Zustandes");* the second type tends in the direction of an intellectual religion of "objects" *(der "Gegenstände");* the third type, whose purest instantiation Przywara sees in Cohen's neo-Kantianism, tends in the direction of an ethical, voluntaristic religion of the "imperative" *("des Sollens").*

166. See "Drei Richtungen der Phänomenologie."

lows. First, in §1, Przywara begins with the essentially epistemological problem of the relation between being and consciousness — a problem that is reflected methodologically in one of two basic options: either a "meta-ontics," which begins with the question of being, or a "meta-noetics," which begins with consciousness or, more specifically, the act of consciousness. He then shows that neither of these methodological starting points is pure, absolute in itself, but that each points to the other and is, in fact, implied by the other. Thus any rigorous philosophy will have to take into account this dynamic tension and ultimate correlation between a meta-ontics and a meta-noetics.

Przywara's next step is to argue that this dynamic tension inherent in epistemology is ultimately rooted in a dynamic ontological tension between essence and existence, which is ontologically prior to any methodological considerations. In other words, for Przywara, the epistemological instability that manifests itself in the ineluctable back-and-forth between a meta-ontics and a meta-noetics is ultimately a reflection, at the level of method, of the inherent instability of creaturely being as such. For just as epistemology is without any firm footing, so too is the creature's fundamental being, since unlike God, whose essence is to exist, the essence of the creature is precisely *not* identical to its existence. Rather, essence and existence are related in the creature in such a way that the essence of the creature is never fully given, i.e., never identical or reducible to its existence, but is always on the horizon of its existence as something to be attained. This is more or less what Przywara means by his gnomic and idiosyncratic formula "essence in-and-beyond existence," understood as the basic formula of a creaturely metaphysics.[167] To be sure, the essence of the creature informs the *fact* of the creature's existence, making it *what* it is; therein lies the "in" of "essence *in*-and-beyond existence." Radically speaking, however, the creature is never fully there, since its essence is at the same time always that *to which* it is underway.[168] Indeed, to draw out the

---

167. See *AE* §§1-4, *et passim.*

168. Thus Przywara speaks of "a tension (that can never be mastered in thought) between a being that is 'such' [*so*] and 'there' [*da*], yet whose 'such' in fact always remains 'to be attained,' so that in its purity it is never really 'there.'" See Przywara, "Die Problematik der Neuscholastik," *Kant-Studien* 33 (1928): 81. In this respect the *analogia entis* bears comparison to the existentialism of Heidegger. The difference here is that this dynamic of *Dasein*, to use Heidegger's expression, is analogous to Being — to *Sein* — itself. It is an image of the God, whose essence is to exist. And for this reason the ecstatic projection of *Dasein* — or of Przywara's "essence in-and-beyond existence" — does not ultimately run up against death or Nothing (as for Heidegger), but against the One of whom it is an image, and in whose active repose its restless mutability finds its supernatural rest.

metaphysical implications of Scripture, we cannot even be said to be *what* we are, for "*what* we will be has not yet been revealed" (1 John 3:2).

But, as Przywara goes on to argue in §2, what is meant by meta-noetics and meta-ontics stands in need of further clarification. For just as νοῦς (from which "noetic" is derived) ultimately designates in Aristotle the crowning of a hierarchy that includes scientific, ethical, and artistic modes of consciousness — modes that are aimed, respectively, at the true, the good, and the beautiful — so too ὄν (from which "ontic" is derived), far from indicating a pure, factual presence, turns out to be similarly bound up with the transcendentals.[169] Thus, according to Przywara, the tension between a meta-ontics and a meta-noetics is inevitably inflected in the form of a tension between a "transcendental metaphysics" of the kind that predominated in antiquity (with its predominantly meta-ontic starting point) and a "metaphysical transcendentalism" of the kind that predominates in modernity since Descartes (with its predominantly meta-noetic starting point). What we discover from this inevitable correlation, however, is *no foundation,* but only a further confirmation of the creaturely tensions that no philosophy has yet resolved or even can resolve.

As Przywara proceeds to argue in §3, these tensions manifest themselves still further in the tension between an *a priori* metaphysics (with its emphasis upon the purity of a transcendental subject and its alleged capacity for timeless, superhistorical truth) and an *a posteriori* metaphysics, which takes history, the senses, tradition, and embodiment seriously as that through which any superhistorical truth is mediated. According to Przywara, this is illustrated *mutatis mutandis* by the difference — and the tension — between Kant and Thomas Aquinas.[170] If the one direction tends (in its extreme rationalistic form) to make truth ahistorical, the other tends (in extreme forms of historicism) to dissolve truth into history. Rightly understood, however,

---

169. See *AE* §2, 1. For instance, the nature of creaturely being is so constituted in terms of *potentia* and *actus* (δύναμις and ἐνέργεια) as to be directed to a truth, an essence, beyond it (as is even the case, *mutatis mutandis,* with the *"je seine Möglichkeit"* of Heidegger's *Dasein*). Thus here again we see an instantiation of the formula "essence in-and-*beyond* existence." So too, if one emphasizes the practical aspect of this dynamic, as pertains to the life of virtue, the same formula once again appears, though now under the form of an "ontic good." And, finally, the beautiful appears as the realization or ideal unity of essence and existence in the work of art.

170. See *AE* §3, 3. We might find Thomas Aquinas an odd choice for comparison with Kant on this point, but Przywara is contrasting him with Kant here inasmuch as for Thomas, following Aristotle, knowledge is *per sensibilia.*

truth, which is "beyond history," is known only "in history," and thus, according to Przywara, we arrive at the formula "truth in-and-beyond history."[171] But truth, he goes on to say, belongs to the region of essence; and history, to the region of existence. Thus, in the formula, "truth in-and-beyond history," and in the historical aporetic it involves, we again encounter the more basic formula, "essence in-and-beyond existence." That is to say, we once again discover that the creature is ultimately and irreducibly a *non-identity* of the ideative and the real, the essential and the existential, and that truth and history must therefore be understood in correlative terms.

At this point, having laid bare the tensions intrinsic to philosophy — from the tension between a meta-ontics and a meta-noetics (§1), to the tension between a transcendental metaphysics and a metaphysical transcendentalism (§2), to the tension between an *a priori* and an *a posteriori* metaphysics (§3) — and having thereby demonstrated the inevitable *relativity* of all creaturely thought and being, Przywara shows that *the concept of God is already implied in any formal consideration of metaphysics as such.* Thus we come to the question of the relation between philosophy and theology (§4). The concept of God (of theology) is implied, most obviously, in the metaphysical question of the relation between that which is "grounded, directed, and determined" and its "ground-end-definition" [*"Grund-Ziel-Sinn"*].[172] In short, it is implied in any consideration of the relation between the absolute and the relative; as Aquinas puts it, *"res divinae . . . prout sunt principia omnium entium."*[173] The all-important question here, however, is whether God is reducible to the absolute of a *philosophical* metaphysics (whether in the form of an *a priori* or an *a posteriori* metaphysics).[174] For if this is the case, then philosophy would already be theology, or what (to adopt Heidegger's idiom) we might call "onto-theology." It would mean that the absolute posited by the creature and determined by its concepts would be the absolute of God himself.

171. *AE* §3, 3, p. 152.
172. *AE* §4, 1, pp. 155ff.
173. Things divine . . . insofar as they are the principles of all beings. *AE* §4, 2, p. 163. See *In Boeth. De Trin.* q. 5, a. 4, corp.
174. Whereas an *a priori* metaphysics proceeds deductively from the ideative to the real (in which case the world appears to pure eidetic vision as a more or less direct expression of divine ideas), an *a posteriori* metaphysics proceeds inductively from the empirical, from the breadth of the many, to a concept of their unity, to a concept of the universe, understood as the perfection of the whole. Whereas the former tends in its extreme form to theopanism, the latter tends in its extreme form to pantheism.

But a *theological* metaphysics, Przywara crucially points out, is concerned not with God as conceived philosophically, but with God as he has *freely revealed himself,* transcending all philosophical conceptions and preconceptions. Thus, according to Przywara, we are presented with a fundamental choice: "either the absolutizations of the immanent poles of the creaturely (as we saw in the cases of absolute *a priori* and absolute *a posteriori* metaphysics) or the absolute beyond-and-in them."[175] The problem with the absolutizations, however, is that they fail to do justice to the creaturely quality of finite being as a dynamic unity (in the form of "in-and-beyond") of essence and existence. In the first case, that of an absolute *a priori* metaphysics, "the creaturely solidifies (into an eternity of essence: in the systematic rigidity of a pure apriorism); in the second case, that of an absolute *a posteriori* metaphysics, it dissolves (into the *apeiron* of existence: in the 'in infinitum' of purely *a posteriori* experience)."[176] In neither case, however, do we truly have a creature. Thus, through the *failures* of the respective absolutes of a philosophical metaphysics, and through a concern to achieve a metaphysics that is adequate to the *mystery* of creaturely being, we come to the prospect of a *theological* metaphysics — a metaphysics that does justice to the creature *qua* creature, as well as to divine freedom and transcendence. In short, to spell out the matter according to Przywara's peculiar idiom, we come to see that the tension intrinsic to creaturely being ("essence in-and-beyond existence"), which can be made out at the level of philosophy, points to and is "vertically intersected" by the still more basic *theological* formula "God *beyond*-in creation."

Now we are finally in a position to see how, for Przywara, creaturely being is inherently *analogical* (being a dynamic, never fixed relation of difference between essence and existence); and how philosophy itself points toward theology and to a theological conception of the *analogia entis.* To this end, however, given Przywara's rather broad and, at the same time, somewhat idiosyncratic use of the term *analogy,* it is important first to observe the particular way in which he appropriates Aristotle's definition of analogy as a "mean" or something "intermediate" (τὸ γὰρ ἀνάλογον μέσον).[177] When Aristotle gives this definition in the *Nicomachean Ethics,* it is in the context of a discussion of justice. Here, though, it is applied to the nature of creaturely being and, specifi-

175. *AE* §4, 1, p. 159.
176. *AE* §4, 1, p. 159.
177. See *Nicomachean Ethics* 1131b. See *AE* §7, 3, p. 247. Equally, though, Przywara draws here upon Plato.

cally, to the characteristic tensions (between extremes) that we have already described. Thus, in view of the fundamentally dynamic tension between essence and existence (according to the formula "essence in-and-beyond existence"), Przywara speaks of creaturely being as a kind of "middle." More specifically, given the way that creaturely being, i.e., its actuality (ἐνέργεια) at any given moment, is suspended between its potentiality (δύναμις) and its end (τέλος) — an end that is curiously "in" but at the same time "beyond" the creature (ἐν-τελέχεια) — he speaks of creaturely being as a kind of "*suspended middle*" [*"schwebende Mitte"*].[178] Indeed, for Przywara, the creature only "is" in this *rhythmic* "back-and-forth": back to the virtual infinity of potentiality, which is limited in every act, and forth to the end "in-and-beyond" every actuality. Therein lies the first aspect — which Przywara calls the "immanent analogy" — of the *analogia entis.*

But given that, according to the terms of this "immanent analogy," creaturely being has no firm footing in itself, given that its essence is precisely not identical to its essence, given that it is therefore not self-possessed (cf. 1 Cor. 6:19-20) but ecstatically constituted — given, moreover, that it essentially "is and is not" (in Augustine's phrase, *est non est*), "being" only in constant movement — the very being of the creature also points beyond itself to that which "Is."[179] And thus, given the traditional identification of God with being (Exod. 3:14), we are driven to the question of a further analogy, a "theological analogy," between God and creation (in the form of "God *beyond*-in creation"). At this point we come to see that the first analogy, which points beyond itself toward a transcendent participation (as a *"teil-nehmendes Über-hinaus-bezogen-sein"*), presupposes and is vertically intersected by the grace of a second, profounder analogy, understood in *donative* terms as a *"'self-imparting-relation-from-above'* of the divine Is (Truth, etc.)."[180] In other words, whereas the first analogy is inferential and emphasizes a participatory "sharing," even a "taking" *(teil-nehmend),* of creaturely being in the divine (in accordance with a strictly Platonic understanding of analogy), the second analogy emphasizes that being "is" only *as* the "imparting" of a gift; moreover, that the creature only "is" insofar as it is between nothing and the Creator *ex nihilo.* Thus, for Przywara, the full form of the *analogia entis* must be understood in terms of the *intersection* of these

178. See *AE,* pp. 159-63, 209. In other words, creaturely being is suspended inasmuch as it "is" only within this back-and-forth between its potentiality and end.
179. See Augustine *In Ps.* 121, 12; *Confessions* XII, 6; see *AE* §4, 4, p. 190; §6, 5.
180. *AE* §6, 5, p. 214.

two analogies — the latter of which fills out the former with its properly theological height and depth — and thus, by implication, in terms of an intersection of philosophy and theology.

4.2. *The* analogia entis *as the Intersection of Philosophy and Theology*

The nature of the relationship between philosophy and theology, however, still stands in need of further clarification. On the one hand, as we have already seen, some form of *theologia naturalis* is immanent to the concept of metaphysics as such — both in terms of the question of the creature's origin *(principium)* and end *(finis),* and in terms of the suggestion of a divine identity of essence and existence, a divine "Is," to which the real distinction of essence and existence in creaturely being (as "essence in-and-beyond existence") obscurely points.[181] Thus Przywara affirms the teaching of Vatican I that God, at least as a "positive limit-concept," can be known by the natural light of reason.[182] And to this extent, one may say, theology is always already "in" philosophy.[183] On the other hand, as we have also seen, *contra* Hegel, theology is not reducible to philosophy. For theology's proper concern is with the supernatural mystery of "things divine as they are in themselves" *(res divinae prout sunt in se).*[184] Accordingly, again *contra* Hegel, the supernatural mysteries of faith never become comprehensible. On the contrary, for Przywara, following Augustine, theology is precisely a *reductio in mysterium,* "an entry into the mystery of God in order more deeply 'to grasp his incomprehensibility as such.'"[185] In the words of Augustine, whom Przywara frequently cites, "He is hidden in order that you might seek him; and in order that you might not cease in your search once you have found him, he is infinite. Thus is it said . . . 'Seek his face evermore'" (Ps. 105:4).[186] Quite the opposite, therefore, of reducing to a Hegelian Concept [*Begriff*], theology is, properly speaking, a reduction to the *Deus tamquam ignotus* of Aquinas and the "superluminous darkness"

---

181. *AE* §6, 5, pp. 212-13.

182. *AE* §4, 3, p. 168; Denz. 1799.

183. *AE* §4, 4, pp. 172-73.

184. *AE* §4, 2, p. 16; Aquinas, *In Boeth. de Trin.* q. 5, a. 4, corp.

185. *AE* §4, 5, p. 18; *De Trin.* XV, ii, 2.

186. *In Jo. Tract.* LXIII, i: "Ut inveniendus quaeratur, occultus est; ut inventus quaeratur, immensus est. Unde alibi dicitur, 'Quaerite faciem ejus semper'" (Ps. 105:4).

(ὑπέρφωτος γνόφος) of the Areopagite.[187] And so, while theology is always already positively "in" philosophy, it is always also "beyond" its grasp; hence Przywara's succinct formula "theology in-and-beyond philosophy."[188]

But if theology is beyond philosophy, it is also that at which philosophy aims. Indeed, for Przywara, theology is not only formally *in* philosophy, but also its proper *telos*. In other words, in yet another instantiation of the analogical "in-and-beyond" [*"in-über"*] structure, theology is the *en-telechy* (ἐντελέχια) of philosophy.[189] For to the extent that philosophy is as incomplete and unstable as the being of the creature it seeks to understand, it ineluctably points beyond itself and its own inherent tensions to a theological region of mystery — precisely in the way that the *pro-fane* points to the sacredness of the temple *(fanum)*. But to this extent, for all their differences, like the profane and the sacred, philosophy and theology also truly belong together (ἄλλο πρὸς ἄλλο). And for Przywara, essentially following Thomas, they belong together and are ultimately configured in the same way as the relation of reason to faith: *fides (theologia) non destruit, sed supponit et perficit rationem (philosophiam)*.[190] Accordingly, one may speak of an analogical ordering of philosophy to theology — as of natural desire to its fulfillment. Of course, this does not mean that philosophy is able of itself to make out the mysteries with which theology is properly concerned — no more than Adam, for all his natural desire, could envision Eve before she was given to him. For as of yet, from a purely philosophical perspective, nothing whatsoever can be made out about who God is or what God has revealed, or even that there is such thing as revelation. All that can be made out metaphysically with any degree of certainty apart from revelation is that creaturely being is not its own ground, that it is not being itself, that it "is" only in the form of becoming, and that theology, i.e., the science of a God of revelation, is a reasonable possibility or, to put it in Przywara's still more minimalist terms, a "non-impossibility."[191]

---

187. *AE* §4, 5, p. 18; Aquinas, *In Boeth. de Trin.* q. 1, a. 2, corp. et ad 1; Pseudo-Areopagite, *Mystical Theology* I, 1.

188. *AE* §4, 6, p. 190.

189. As Przywara puts it (*AE* §4, 4, p. 174), "it is through the theological, as its 'inner telos' (ἐντελέχεια), that the 'ascending movement' (δύναμις) of metaphysics reaches its 'final actualization' (ἐνέργεια)."

190. *AE* §4, 5, p. 178.

191. *AE* §4, 4, p. 177.

4.3. Between Logic and Dialectic: The analogia entis and the Principle of Non-Contradiction

Thus far we have seen how analogy emerges from philosophy as the principle of metaphysics as such; we have also seen how philosophy points to theology, and how a theological analogy fills out the "in-and-beyond" of the so-called "immanent" analogy with its properly theological height and depth. Now, in §§5-6, Przywara returns to the subject of analogy and points to a basis for analogy in the foundations of logic (§§5-6), specifically, in the principle of non-contradiction.

As Aristotle formulates this foundational principle, "just as the same attribute cannot simultaneously be affirmed and denied of the same subject, neither can one simultaneously take something to be and not to be" (τὸ γὰρ αὐτὸ ἅμα ὑπάρχειν τε καὶ μὴ ὑπάξειν ἀδύνατον τῷ αὐτῷ καὶ κατὰ τὸ αὐτό . . . ἀδύνατον γὰρ ὁτινοῦν ταὐτὸν ὑπολαμβάνειν εἶναι καὶ μὴ εἶναι).[192] The reason why this principle is fundamental to Przywara's argument for the *analogia entis* — indeed, why he goes so far as to call it the "foundation" for the *analogia entis* — is twofold. Firstly, in this principle (as the most basic principle of thought) we see precisely the kind of correlation of ontic and noetic forms that Przywara claimed was the case in §1 with regard to a meta-ontics and a meta-noetics. Thus we have a basis in logic for the entire argument developed thus far. Secondly, vis-à-vis the various philosophies of identity (pure logic) and contradiction (pure dialectic), which either in Promethean fashion seek a more basic logic of identity (A = A) or in false humility deny even the minimalist position that the principle of non-contradiction affords, it turns out that the principle of non-contradiction is preserved in analogy alone, since both analogy (as the fundamental form of being) and the principle of non-contradiction (as the fundamental form of thought) fall precisely *between* the extremes of contradiction and identity.[193] In other words, for Przywara, an *analogical* metaphysics is the only metaphysics that reflects and properly corresponds to the most fundamental principle of thought; indeed, the former is the metaphysical articulation (and presupposition) of the latter.

But if the principle of non-contradiction provides a foundation for

---

192. For the same attribute cannot, in the same way, both belong and not belong to a thing . . . for it is not possible to believe something both to be and not to be. *AE* §6, 1, pp. 198-99; *Metaphysics* IV, 3, 1005b, 19-24. Cf. *Metaphysics* X, 5, 1061b-1062a.

193. *AE* §6, 1, pp. 198-99.

analogy in logic, as the most "basic possibility for the activity of thought as such," it is important to note that it is not a stable foundation, or even a particularly positive one. Rather, for Przywara, it merely provides a minimal "basis for movement" as a "negative reductive formality": for "even if one denies everything, one cannot deny this."[194] In other words, like the principle of non-contradiction, the *analogia entis* (its metaphysical correlate) does not amount to a positive determination; rather, it merely allows one to say that creaturely being is "not not being," and to distinguish it thereby from being as such, which can be predicated of God alone.

4.4. *The* analogia entis *and the Thomistic Doctrine of Obediential Potency*

But if the *analogia entis* is grounded in the principle of non-contradiction — if, that is, it may be substantiated philosophically — it is, once again, only from a theological perspective that it fully appears. For, as we have seen, the full form of the *analogia entis* consists precisely in an intersection of two analogies — the immanent (in the form of "essence in-and-beyond existence") and the theological (in the form of "God in-and-beyond creation"). And here again the Thomistic maxim *fides (gratia) non destruit, sed supponit et perficit rationem (naturam)* holds true, inasmuch as the former analogy, which is presupposed, points to and is fulfilled in the latter. The problem with the first analogy, taken by itself, is that the creature ends up cramped in itself — in its own possibility (Heidegger's *"je seine Möglichkeit"*). Seen in light of the theological analogy, however, the potentiality of creaturely being appears more radically, between nothing and the Creator out of nothing, as a *potentia oboedientialis*. That is to say, the potentiality of the creature now appears as a potentiality for a supernatural end *(finis ad quem homo a Deo praeparatur).*[195]

But it is not, *contra* Pelagius (and implicitly in response to Barth's concerns), a potentiality in the creature's power.[196] Nor is it an end to which the natural desire of the creature could lay any claim. On the contrary, it is expressly a "free gift from above."[197] At the same time, neither is the creature

---

194. *AE* §6, 1, p. 199.
195. *AE* §6, 7, p. 227; *De Ver.* q. 27, a. 1, corp. Cf. *AE* §6, 8.
196. *AE* §6, 7, p. 228; *De Ver.* q. 8, a. 3, corp.; *Summa Contra Gentiles,* III, cc. 52, 53.
197. *AE* §6, 7, p. 229.

negated in its creatureliness or reduced to inactivity with regard to its own end (as would be the case with a full-blown theopanism). Rather, the wonder of creaturely being (as seen from the perspective of the theological analogy) is that the maximum of God's proximity to the creature (God "in" creation) is at the same time "the greatest liberation of the creature for active, free self-movement" *(quanto aliqua natura Deo vicinior, tanto minus ab eo inclinatur et nata est seipsam inclinare).*[198] Indeed, the more that human beings are "in" God by virtue of the gift of God (cf. John 4:10), i.e., by virtue of the gift of the Holy Spirit, who is received "from above" (Luke 24:49), the more human beings come into their *own* as the active *image* of God they were always intended to be — to the point of sharing not only in God's own causal agency as the "origin of all good" *(quod sint causa bonitatis aliorum),*[199] but also in God's own providential office *(non solum quod sint provisae, sed etiam quod provideant).*[200] Thus, from a consideration of potentiality — having come to see more clearly how profoundly God is "in" creation, communicating to creatures his own perfections — we come back to the question of the theological analogy between God (as the cause of creaturely perfections) and creation (now understood as a realm of analogous, secondary causes). In other words, we now see more clearly how creation, in human beings, is an image of God (Gen. 1:26-27), and therefore rightly understood to constitute an analogy to God.

4.5. *The* analogia entis *as an Explication of Lateran IV*

Again, though, as we have often repeated, for Przywara the stress of the theological analogy falls not on the side of similarity, proximity, and divine immanence, but on the side of dissimilarity, distance, and divine transcendence. And in this respect he can claim that the *analogia entis* is simply an explication of the Fourth Lateran Council's edict against Joachim of Fiore: *"Inter creatorem et creaturam non potest tanta similitudo notari, quin inter eos non maior sit dissimilitudo notanda"* ["One cannot note any similarity between creator and creature, however great, without being compelled to ob-

198. The nearer any nature is to God, the less inclined it is to be moved by another and the more capable it is of moving itself. *AE* §6, 7, p. 230; *De Ver.* q. 22, a. 4, corp.

199. That they might be the cause of goodness in others. *AE* §6, 7, p. 230; *De Ver.* q. 5, a. 8, corp.

200. That they be not only provided for, but provident. *AE* §6, 7, p. 230; *De Ver.* q. 6, a. 5, corp.

serve an ever greater dissimilarity between them"].²⁰¹ In order to emphasize this, at the conclusion of §6 Przywara elaborates the theological analogy in terms of the two traditional models of analogy that were discussed above: an *analogia attributionis,* otherwise known as a *pros hen* (πρὸς ἕν) analogy, and an *analogia proportionalitatis,* understood not, as in the case of an *analogia attributionis,* as an ordering to one *(ad aliquid unum),* but as *"a relation of mutual alterity,"* as one proportion to another (ὡς ἄλλο πρὸς ἄλλο).²⁰² Whereas the former emphasizes a degree of similarity between God and creation (inasmuch as the creature can point to God as the ground and cause of its perfections), the latter emphasizes an ultimate dissimilarity. For in the latter case one can speak only of a suspended analogy between two radically different proportions, i.e., two radically different ways of being: on the one hand, in the creature a relation of essence and existence, which has the form of a "unity-in-tension" [*Spannungseinheit*]; on the other hand, in the case of God, an essential identity [*Wesenseinheit*] of essence and existence.²⁰³ Consequently, the most one can say is that there is some kind of relation, some kind of analogy between being and becoming, which are related *not directly,* but as one proportion to *another.*

Properly understood, therefore, the *analogia entis* (in the form of the theological analogy) comprises two moments: a *tanta similitudo* expressed in the *analogia attributionis* and a *maior dissimilitudo* expressed in the *analogia proportionalitatis.* Accordingly, "analogy lies between univocity *(univocatio)* and complete equivocity *(aequivocatio)."*²⁰⁴ But, again, two

---

201. See *Schriften,* vol. 2, p. 402; *AE* §6, 8. See Denzinger, *Enchiridion Symbolorum,* 43rd ed., ed. Peter Hünermann (San Francisco: Ignatius Press, 2012), p. 269 (806). N.B.: Some manuscripts seem to include the "tanta" in *tanta similitudo,* while others do not. In any case, Przywara generally reads it as *tanta similitudo;* he also tends to read the Ignatian "ever greater" *(semper maior)* into the Lateran *maior dissimilitudo.*

202. *AE* §6, 8; Aristotle, *Metaphysics* V, 6, 1016b. Of course, everything turns on how one understands these different analogies. Traditionally, for the Thomist school following Cajetan, the analogy of proportionality stands as a corrective to the analogy of attribution, which is sometimes thought insufficiently to safeguard divine transcendence. This, for example, is how Przywara understands this analogy. For others, like David Burrell, it is the analogy of attribution that best underscores the singularity of the first cause and in this way safeguards the difference between God and creatures, which the analogy of proportionality, understood as a proportional sharing in a common term, threatens to undercut. See Burrell, *Faith and Freedom,* p. 119. See, however, Eberhard Jüngel (*Gott als Geheimnis der Welt,* pp. 375-76), for whom the analogy of proportionality is, at the end of the day, implied in the analogy of attribution.

203. *Schriften,* vol. 2, p. 403; cf. p. 39; cf. *Summa Th.* I, q. 80, a. 1.

204. *Summa Th.* I, q. 13, a. 5, corp.

JOHN R. BETZ

things are crucial to observe here, upon which a proper understanding of Przywara's doctrine depends. Firstly, for Przywara, following Thomas (*De Ver.* q. 2, a. 11), the stress falls on the second analogy, the *analogia proportionalitatis*. For one must always observe the "alterity *(diversas proportiones)* within whatever *one* term is predicated *of* both God and creature (*ad aliquid unum:* e.g., being, good, etc.)."[205] Secondly, in giving due priority to the *analogia proportionalitatis*, it is not as though the similarity implied by the *analogia attributionis* is "simply 'balanced out' by the dissimilarity of the mode *(modus)* whereby this same *one* is in both God and creature (like and unlike, *simile 'et' dissimile*)."[206] For then, "it would not be the divine Is (Truth, etc.) that is ultimately decisive, but instead this suspended equilibrium between God and creature."[207] "No," Przywara says, "the positive commonality of the *ad aliquid unum* is led beyond itself into the genuinely Areopagitic 'dazzling darkness' of the *diversas proportiones* — into, that is, an 'ever greater dissimilarity': *creaturae . . . quamvis aliquam Dei similitudinem gerant in seipsis, tamen maxima dissimilitudo subest.*"[208] Indeed, the simple point of the *analogia entis* (as far as its ultimate stress is concerned) is that any analogy between God and creatures is ultimately *only* an analogy — one that at a certain point fails, breaks off, pointing beyond every similitude, "however great," to an "ever greater" God, who is "beyond all analogy."[209]

5. Philosophical and Theological Criticisms of the *analogia entis*

Given the comprehensive nature of Przywara's *analogia entis*, and the way in which he attempts to relate within analogy both reason and faith, nature and grace, philosophy and theology, it is not surprising that this particular solution would elicit criticism from a number of philosophers who, wanting to preserve the *purity* of philosophy, deem it to be too theological, and a number of theologians who, wanting to preserve the *purity* of theology, deem it to be too philosophical. Such, for instance, is what we find in Martin

205. *AE* §6, 8.
206. *AE* §6, 8; *De Ver.* q. 2, a. 11, ad 1.
207. *AE* §6, 8.
208. *AE* §6, 8; *De Ver.* q. 1, a. 10, ad 1 in contr. [although creatures bear within themselves a certain likeness to God, there is nevertheless present the greatest unlikeness]. For this reason, Przywara says at the conclusion of the *Analogia Entis* that the "resonance" of the first analogy gives way to the "silence" of the second.
209. *Schriften*, vol. 2, p. 404.

Heidegger, who rejects any notion of a Christian philosophy (i.e., any admixture of theology in philosophy), and Karl Barth, who rejects in turn any kind of natural theology (i.e., any admixture of philosophy in dogmatics). What both have in common, however, in addition to the methodological purity they respectively seek, is a conception of metaphysics — and of the *analogia entis* — as something that needs to be banished, whether for the sake of a postmodern ontology (like Heidegger's) or a dogmatic theology of revelation (like Barth's). And in this respect, notwithstanding Heidegger's Catholic background as a one-time Jesuit novice, both stand in the anti-scholastic and anti-metaphysical tradition of Luther.[210]

For its part, of course, from the Stoic Logos metaphysics of Justin Martyr, to the Platonism of the Cappadocians, Augustine, and Dionysius, to the Aristotelianism of Thomas Aquinas, the Catholic Church has never been reluctant to incorporate philosophy into its theology; nor, in keeping with the principle of the *spolia Aegyptiorum,* has it seen metaphysics as something necessarily problematic as long as it is corrected in light of revelation. On the contrary, as is figured for Gregory of Nyssa in Moses' two mothers, and is expressed for Thomas in the principle that faith (grace) does not destroy but presupposes and perfects reason (nature), the Catholic Church has long regarded philosophical metaphysics as helpful, even if it is inadequate. And in this respect, from an intra-Catholic standpoint, the *analogia entis* — which for Przywara summarizes the Catholic metaphysical tradition — stands in need of no particular justification. It is, one could argue, simply a concise articulation of the Catholic metaphysics of creation.

But Barth and Heidegger, it goes without saying, are not incidental voices in the history of modern theology and philosophy; and under their influence many prominent theologians, such as Dietrich Bonhoeffer, and even many prominent Catholic philosophers, such as Jean-Luc Marion, *have* come to see metaphysics as a problematic inheritance — one that does not lead to, but in one way or another obscures the (real) God of revelation.[211]

210. See *Luther's Works,* ed. Jaroslav Pelikan, Hilton Oswald, and Helmut Lehmann, 55 vols., vol. 25 (Philadelphia: Fortress, 1999), p. 153: "But alas, how deeply and painfully we are ensnared in categories and questions of what a thing is; in how many foolish metaphysical questions we involve ourselves." Cf. Luther, *WA, Tr,* III, 563-66, no. 3722: "The reason why Thomas is so loquacious is that he was seduced by metaphysics. Now it has been more than twenty years since God has miraculously led us out of that. . . ." For a recent discussion of the influence of Luther on Barth and Heidegger, see Timothy Stanley, *Protestant Metaphysics after Karl Barth and Martin Heidegger* (Eugene, OR: Cascade Books, 2010).
211. See, for instance, Bonhoeffer, *Act and Being,* in *Works,* vol. 2 (Minneapolis: For-

Indeed, in the spirit of Heidegger's deconstructive zeal (for the sake of a new revelation of Being) and of Barth's Reformed iconoclasm (for the sake of divine glory), many have come to regard metaphysics as a subtle and therefore more insidious form of idolatry, requiring that Christian theology be delivered from its seductions as from a kind of Egypt.[212] If, therefore, Przywara's work, and the present work in particular, is to have any currency today — and if any larger effort to recover the Catholic metaphysical tradition is not to be viewed as, at best, a quixotic retreat to an outdated scholasticism — one cannot avoid addressing Barth's and Heidegger's concerns, from which all of the others follow.

5.1. Heidegger and "Onto-Theology"

While no adequate defense of Przywara's *analogia entis* can be developed here,[213] and while Przywara's work really speaks for itself, a provisional response to these charges would have to raise the question of what one means by "metaphysics," and whether Przywara's understanding of the *analogia entis* in any way resembles what in postmodern discourse is commonly understood by this term. To this end, let us first consider what Heidegger means by metaphysics. For Heidegger, risking simplification, "metaphysics is onto-theology," by which he means the double positing of a universal ground of beings and, simultaneously, the positing of this ground of beings as the supreme being.[214] In other words, so Heidegger alleges, the question of being is not even asked before it is answered in terms of beings, i.e., in

---

tress, 1996), pp. 73-75. See also Jean-Luc Marion, *The Idol and Distance,* trans. Thomas Carlson (New York: Fordham University Press, 2001); *God without Being,* trans. Thomas Carlson (Chicago: University of Chicago Press, 1991).

212. As Kevin Hector puts it, "if idolatry is 'the subjection of God to human conditions for the experience of the divine' (as Jean-Luc Marion asserts), it would appear that metaphysical theism is unquestionably idolatrous . . ." (*Theology without Metaphysics,* p. 13).

213. For a more robust defense of Przywara's *analogia entis* against Barthian and postmodern charges, see John R. Betz, "Beyond the Sublime: The Aesthetics of the Analogy of Being," in two parts, *Modern Theology* 21 (July 2005): 367-411, and *Modern Theology* 22 (January 2006): 1-50; "The Beauty of the Metaphysical Imagination," in *Metaphysics and Belief,* ed. Conor Cunningham and Peter Candler (London: SCM Press, 2007), pp. 41-65; "After Barth: A New Introduction to Erich Przywara's *Analogia Entis,*" in *The Analogy of Being: Invention of the Antichrist or the Wisdom of God,* pp. 35-87.

214. "The Ontological Constitution of Metaphysics," in *Identity and Difference,* trans. Joan Stambaugh (Chicago: University of Chicago Press, 2002), p. 54.

ontic terms: beings are simply an effect of the supreme being understood as first cause. And since the ground of beings is directly equated with the supreme being, the difference between being [*Sein*] and beings [*Seiendes*] is forgotten, being concealed from view, and therefore goes unthought. Hence under the regime of metaphysics we never become real philosophers because we never leave the circle of onto-theology to allow ourselves to be startled by the question of being.

A further criticism is that, inasmuch as metaphysics (supposedly) turns being into an object (for only "objects" exist) that is represented to a subject, and inasmuch as it turns truth into "certainty" regarding the correspondence between a subject and an object, metaphysics as a regime of *representation* not only obscures the question of being (since being defies objectification) but also does violence to beings, which are made to fit predetermined categories.[215] In other words, under the regime of metaphysics, neither Being nor beings are free to be — to be *other* than they appear to a rational, positing subject, who *eo ipso* becomes the usurped ground and measure of all things (hence for Heidegger the complicity of metaphysics and humanism). Consequently, the indictment goes on: as enshrined in Leibniz's principle of sufficient reason, according to which nothing is without a cause, Western metaphysics has effectively stripped the world of wonder and given rise to the disenchanted, instrumental "world picture" of the modern age.[216] In effect, therefore, metaphysics is a system of obfuscation, which makes modern technology and scientific materialism possible, but, inasmuch as it forestalls the *question* of being, allows neither being nor beings — or, more precisely the *gift* of being in beings — to appear. Finally, metaphysics cannot even be said to promote good theology, since the God of metaphysics, as *causa sui,* is not the God of faith but a rationally posited "god" of the philosophers, before whom "man can neither fall to his knees in awe nor . . . play music and dance."[217] Thus, for Heidegger, if we are to think what remains unthought, resist the dangers of unquestioned technology, prepare ourselves for a new revelation of being, and even prepare the way for

215. Heidegger, *Off the Beaten Path,* trans. Julian Young and Kenneth Haynes (Cambridge: Cambridge University Press, 2002), p. 66.

216. Heidegger, *The Principle of Reason,* trans. Reginald Lilly (Bloomington: Indiana University Press, 1996).

217. "The Ontological Constitution of Metaphysics," in *Identity and Difference,* trans. Joan Stambaugh (Chicago: University of Chicago Press, 2002), p. 72. For a consistent attempt to follow Heidegger along these lines, see Laurence Paul Hemming, *Heidegger's Atheism: The Refusal of a Theological Voice* (Notre Dame: University of Notre Dame Press, 2002).

a new theological beginning, the task of philosophy requires a regressive "destruction" of the metaphysical tradition to the unthought difference between being and beings.

Now the pressing question as far as the present work is concerned is whether the *analogia entis* fits this description of metaphysics. For his part, at least, Heidegger gives every indication that it does. Indeed, for Heidegger analogy functions precisely to secure the hegemony of metaphysics and the binding of beings within a causal network: "Beings 'correspond,' follow in what and how they are, obey the ruling cause as something caused. . . . *Analogy belongs to metaphysics,* in the double sense: 1. That beings themselves 'correspond' to the highest being. 2. That one thinks and explains with regard to correspondences, similarities, universals. Where, on the other hand, one thinks in terms of Being itself, 'analogy' no longer has any basis."[218] The implication is clear: the *analogia entis* is part and parcel of the problematic tradition of Western metaphysics, being complicit not only in a "nihilistic" displacement of meaning (away from this world), which is the standard criticism of metaphysics since Nietzsche, and not only in the obscuring of the difference between being and beings, which is the fundamental criticism of Heidegger, but also in the categorical violence to beings that its regime of representation entails, since beings are not allowed to appear in their *givenness,* but only insofar as they correspond to ideal essences. Thus we come to the widespread notion of the violence of metaphysics.

Of course, it may well be that this description of metaphysics is itself a form of Procrustean violence, insofar as every metaphysics, however apophatic (Przywara's included), is made to conform to it, and insofar as it conceals by indirection that Heidegger's philosophy is itself a kind of metaphysics — a metaphysics of Being as nothing, which prioritizes potentiality over actuality — and not, as it pretends to be, an alternative to it.[219] For that matter, far from being a pure philosophical ontology, Heidegger's own philosophy — from his early readings of Luther, to his influential dialogue with Bultmann, to his doctrine of the fallenness of *das man,* to his Eckhartian apophaticism, to his deference to poetry as revelation and poets as prophets, to his eschatological expectation of being's arrival and apocalypse, to the Christological trope of being's *kenosis* in beings — is itself obviously pervaded by theological themes.

218. Martin Heidegger, *Schelling's Treatise on the Essence of Human Freedom,* trans. Joan Stambaugh (Athens: Ohio University Press, 1985), p. 192.

219. See Przywara, "Katholische Metaphysik," *Stimmen der Zeit* 125 (1933): 228, where he contrasts Heidegger's "magical metaphysics" of Being as Nothing with the "mystical metaphysics" of Catholicism.

Thus in *In und Gegen* Przywara gives a brief synopsis of Heidegger's thought under the title "Theological Motifs in Martin Heidegger's Work," where, among other things, he points out that, whether he would deny it or not, Heidegger himself implicitly subscribes to the rhythm of the *analogia entis* (as a rhythm between positive and negative theologies), as is manifest in his understanding of the play between being's unconcealment in beings and its, as it were, "greater" concealment from beings. Indeed, according to Przywara, while the work of the early Heidegger is only implicitly theological, being to all appearances a "radically atheist" philosophy (which in the name of an ostensibly pure phenomenology brackets and dispenses with the question of God), in the late Heidegger the formerly banished God reappears in the features of Being, so that one could even regard Heidegger himself as a "convert," and his work as a kind of *philosophia praeambula*.[220]

In any event, at a time when we are wont to think of Heidegger's philosophy as a kind of authoritative tribunal, as once Kant's was regarded, to which all philosophy and even all Christian theology must submit, this is important to keep in mind: that Przywara, who was no less of a thinker, was also a keen reader and critic of Heidegger — from his 1928 essay, "Three Directions of Phenomenology," to the *Analogia Entis,* which is as much a response to Heidegger as it is to Hegel, to the late essay on Husserl and Heidegger from 1960, which is included in the present volume. And what one finds, keeping in mind the development of Heidegger's philosophy (and Przywara's tracked reading of it), is that just as Heidegger positions Catholic metaphysics within his own history of onto-theology as the forgetfulness of being, Przywara variously positions Heidegger's philosophy within his own history of cramped, unredeemed philosophy: as Plato (and Buddhism) inverted, as a "heroism of despair," as a "tragic existentialism under the secret standard of an existential philosophy of essence," as a "secular theology," as a "secular doctrine of salvation," as (for lack of a better word) "onto-mythology," as a Lutheran form of Scotism wavering between revolutionary titanism and passive mysticism, and, finally, as a "theosophical cosmosophy" and "negative eschatology" "under the symbol of Trakl's decadent, death-obsessed Western civilization."[221]

Of course, by themselves such catchphrases do not fully capture what Heidegger is up to; nor do they amount to anything approximating an argu-

220. See *In und Gegen,* pp. 58-59.
221. *Humanitas,* p. 34; *In und Gegen,* pp. 55-60; see also in Part II of the present volume "Philosophies of Essence and Existence," "The Scope of Analogy as a Fundamental Catholic Form," "Image, Likeness, Symbol, Mythos, Mysterium, Logos," and "Husserl and Heidegger."

ment — no more than brandishing the phrase "onto-theology" does. Nevertheless, one can gather from Przywara's scattered comments and observations that, in his view, Heidegger's early philosophy is internally confused: for, on the one hand, in a gesture toward transcendence, it radically relativizes all subjective knowledge and value, giving priority to the objective [*sachlich*] "self-giving of Being"; on the other hand, as a philosophy of heroic atheism, it defiantly abandons "every region of ideal objectivity for the finite region of care and death."[222] In other words, Heidegger longs for a kind of transcendence, even as he denies it; for Being is nothing, and so there is nothing but being-in-the-world as care. This is why in the *Analogia Entis* Przywara denies that Heidegger's philosophy is a genuine philosophy of difference, claiming that it remains formally a philosophy of identity — one whose "productive Nothing," which usurps the divine "I Am," leaves the creature tragically curved "in-the-world" upon itself, with nothing to "project" but its "ownmost possibility."[223] All of which could be said to explain the increasingly eschatological shift in Heidegger's philosophy toward a "saving" doctrine of "Being as advent." In any event, when one is dealing with a thinker as powerful and versatile as Przywara, the tables can easily be turned, even to the point of alleging that Heidegger's metaphysics of immanence and corresponding emphasis upon the *anthropos praktikos* (against Plato's *anthropos theoretikos*) is precisely what legitimates the very technology he abhors; and perhaps nowhere is such table-turning so evident as in Przywara's explicitly *Johannine* reading of a shared interest: Hölderlin.

But while Heidegger's own thought can certainly be challenged and perhaps even out-positioned in the ways that Przywara suggests, this by itself does not speak to Heidegger's specific concerns about analogy and onto-theology. For present purposes, therefore, let us summarize the main points of his criticism: as the linchpin of "onto-theology," the analogy of being short-circuits phenomenality, because through its economy of representation it obscures the difference between being and beings, allowing neither truly, freely, to appear. Furthermore, because it conceives of God as the self-caused ruling cause to which beings, as effects, necessarily correspond, it supposedly leaves us with a philosophical God before whom "man can neither fall to his knees in awe nor . . . play music and dance."[224] Hence the analogy of being, along with the history of metaphysics, must be dismantled —

222. *Humanitas*, p. 28.
223. *AE* §6, 3, p. 202.
224. "The Ontological Constitution of Metaphysics," p. 72.

not only for the sake of a genuine phenomenology of being, but (as Heidegger suggests) even for the sake of an authentic and pious theology. And so, by way of Heidegger (and an admixture of the mystical theology of Pseudo-Dionysius) we come to the anti-metaphysical and even post-ontological phenomenology of Jean-Luc Marion. In the words of Thomas Carlson, "Just as Marion's theology would pass beyond metaphysics by freeing God's self-revelation in distance from every limiting concept that would seek to render that God present under idolatrous conditions of thought, so his phenomenology would pass beyond metaphysics by freeing the phenomenon's self-showing from any *a priori* conditions, whether those of the thinking subject or those of a metaphysical God."[225] Thus, just as Marion would have us transcend metaphysics and do theology "without being," by implication he would also have us do without the *analogia entis.*[226]

Fortunately, we have already covered enough ground in the preceding sections to show that what is presented here as "onto-theology" has little to do with Przywara's *analogia entis,* and that any attempt to identify the one with the other would be to misunderstand not only the theological *overcoming and redemption* of philosophical metaphysics that occurs in Przywara's understanding of the *analogia entis,* but the entire pathos of Przywara's thought (as von Balthasar, for one, consistently described it). Indeed, since it is expressly formulated against Hegel as a reduction not to a concept but to a mystery — a *reductio in mysterium* — the *analogia entis* can *itself* be read, and should be read, as a critique of "onto-theology." As Przywara puts it in his late essay, "Religion, Metaphysics, Analogy," the *analogia entis,* as what is ultimate to metaphysics and religion, ultimately "explodes the limits of metaphysics as such."[227]

In any event, as an explicitly *negative* theology in the tradition of the Areopagite, like Marion's, Przywara's *analogia entis* can in no way be said to

---

225. *The Idol and Distance,* p. xix.

226. It is notable, however, and an indication that Marion is not necessarily inhospitable to Przywara's metaphysics, that at the climax of an important essay he invokes Przywara's favorite formula for analogy from Lateran IV: *inter creatorem et creaturam non potest tanta similitudo notari, quin inter eos major sit dissimilitudo notanda* (Denz. 806). See "In the Name: How to Avoid Speaking of 'Negative Theology,'" in *God, the Gift, and Postmodernism,* ed. John Caputo and Michael Scanlon (Bloomington: Indiana University Press, 1999), p. 39.

227. *AE,* p. 427. To be sure, there is a crossing of philosophy and theology within the *analogia entis,* but it is a crossing in which philosophy suffers a kind of death; and in this regard Przywara goes so far as to suggest that "only Catholic metaphysics, as illuminated by the Cross of Christ, is 'metaphysics' as such" ("Katholische Metaphysik," p. 230). *Vide supra,* p. 57 n. 154.

JOHN R. BETZ

subject beings, much less God, to a stable economy of representation. This is already clear from the first pages of the *Analogia Entis,* whose entire point is to show by way of a thoroughgoing *deconstruction* of every allegedly pure and secure starting point (whether in thought or in being) that creaturely being is a rhythmic mystery that can *in no way* be fixed or conceptually mastered.[228] And, as far as any supposed conceptual mastery of God himself is concerned, as Przywara tirelessly repeats with Augustine, "If you comprehend [him], it is not God" (*si comprehendis non est Deus*). Indeed, lacking none of the deconstructive or iconoclastic zeal one finds in Heidegger, Barth, or Marion, the point of Przywara's *analogia entis* and his own animating pathos is precisely to clear away all conceptual idols, to demolish every foundation that the creature by virtue of its being or its thought would presume to have in itself, to *loosen* our grasp on being, and to point through the *mystery* of creaturely being to the profounder, even more inscrutable mystery of God, leaving no foundation but for the creature to cling to God over the depths of its own nothingness.[229]

In no sense, therefore, can the *analogia entis* be classified and explained away as "onto-theology." Nor can it be classified as metaphysics if by this one means "the attempt to secure human knowledge by identifying the fundamental reality of objects — their being as such — with our ideas about them."[230] For, according to the *analogia entis,* the essences of things are known at best, from a creaturely standpoint, only in part — their full reality being eschatologically deferred — and never in any purity apart from constant becoming. Nor can it be said to obscure the difference between being and beings inasmuch as the *analogia entis* is predicated precisely upon this difference — not, to be sure, upon an alternative Heideggerian difference between beings and being as *Nichts,* nor even upon a difference between beings and God as the first and highest being, but upon the difference between beings and God as being itself *(ipsum esse).* Nor, finally, can the *analogia entis* be said to obscure the phenomenality, the sheer givenness of beings in their appearing, requiring a

---

228. In fact, for Przywara, not only is creaturely being out of the reach of our grasping, it also never fully appears, inasmuch as its essence, while manifest in its existence, is also hidden in God, so that the only plausible criticism here is that Przywara, as a true metaphysician, like C. S. Lewis, endows beings with too much depth.

229. As Przywara puts it, "It is the mystery of Augustine's favorite phrase from the Psalms: *adhaerere Deo.* 'To be suspended in God' means that the one who is suspended has only an 'abyss of emptiness' beneath him. But then it means that for just this reason he is completely surrendered to Him 'in' whom he is suspended" (*AE* §7, 5, p. 269).

230. Hector, *Theology without Metaphysics,* p. 9.

surpassing of metaphysics by phenomenology, unless one forgets what is meant by the real distinction between essence and existence and the wonder of existence that flashes from it. For what, after all, does the real distinction mean if not the gratuity of being?

Granted, Heidegger suggests that we will not experience this gratuity unless we bracket the notion of Being as Creator in order to wonder at givenness as such — a givenness that has no "why," just as "the rose is without why."[231] And this should give us pause before we advance directly and thoughtlessly from the real distinction to a posited divine identity that automatically explains it. For Przywara's *analogia entis*, like Heidegger's own philosophy of "ontological difference," can easily be cheapened, turned into a system or slogan, and thereby stripped of its pathos. Rightly understood, however, both Heidegger's philosophy of ontological difference and Przywara's *analogia entis* see the gift of beings out of nothing, and both are open to wonder; and in this both are genuinely philosophical, inasmuch as all genuine philosophy arises out of wonder (though Heidegger would have us forget that this was also the experience of Plato and Aristotle).[232] The final question, therefore, which is posed by Przywara and Heidegger, is which is more wonderful: a Christian metaphysics of a mysterious analogy between beings out of nothing and Being as triune difference or a neo-pagan philosophy of the difference, ruled ultimately by the offerings of fate [*Schicksal*], between beings and Being (as nothing).

5.2. *Karl Barth and "The Invention of Antichrist"*

The final topic to consider, which has been the subject of much recent scholarship, is Karl Barth's controversial rejection of the *analogia entis* as "the invention of Antichrist" and the chief reason why he felt he could never "become a Roman Catholic, all other reasons for not doing so being to my mind shortsighted and trivial."[233] Fortunately, we have already covered some

231. Heidegger, *The Principle of Reason,* p. 35f.

232. See *Theaetetus,* 155d; *Metaphysics,* 982b. As von Balthasar wrote of Przywara, "He lives like the mythical salamander in the fire: there, at the point where finite, creaturely being arises out of the infinite, where that indissoluble mystery holds sway that he baptized with the name *analogia entis*" ("Erich Przywara," p. 355).

233. *Church Dogmatics* I/1, 2nd ed., trans. G. W. Bromiley (London: T. & T. Clark, 1975), p. xiii. See Thomas Joseph White, ed., *The Analogy of Being: Invention of the Antichrist or the Wisdom of God* (Grand Rapids: Eerdmans, 2010).

ground on this topic too, having discussed Barth's relationship with Przywara and the connection between the *analogia entis* and natural theology. But, while Barth's reasons for rejecting the *analogia entis* were clear to him, they are not so easily discerned today, especially when one is presented with a clear account of what Przywara himself understood by the term. All of which leads to the difficult question of whether Barth's judgment was based upon a misunderstanding (as von Balthasar argued in defense of his teacher), causing Barth, after the clarifications of von Balthasar and Gottlieb Söhngen, to change his mind and withdraw his earlier criticism of the *analogia entis* (as Peter Oh has argued), or whether it was deliberate, well-grounded, and firmly held, being based upon Barth's own intractable Reformed convictions and a clear understanding of Przywara's doctrine (as Keith Johnson has argued).[234]

Admittedly, there is no easy answer to this question; and one can be fairly certain that at the end of the day it will be decided along confessional lines. Until it is answered, however, or at least until one attempts to answer it, there can be no free and untrammeled investigation of Przywara's thought. Reformed Christians will find no good reason to read his work (considering the *analogia entis* to be part of the dubious inheritance of Greek metaphysics, which is alien to the gospel), and even Catholic Christians might legitimately wonder what stake the Catholic Church should have in a metaphysical doctrine that presented so great an obstacle to ecumenical dialogue in the twentieth century. It is thus necessary to address some of Barth's concerns about the *analogia entis,* bearing in mind that he issued his anathema, regrettably, without having read the *Analogia Entis,* which was written *after* Przywara's "fruitful encounter" with him in 1929.[235] For not only did

---

234. See von Balthasar, "Analogie und Dialektik. Zur Klärung der theologischen Prinzipienlehre Karl Barths," *Divus Thomas* 22 (1944): 171-216; "Analogie und Natur. Zur Klärung der theologischen Prinzipienlehre Karl Barths," *Divus Thomas* 23 (1945): 3-56; *The Theology of Karl Barth,* trans. E. Oakes (San Francisco: Ignatius Press, 1992); Bernhard Gertz, *Glaubenswelt als Analogie. Die theologische Analogielehre Erich Przywaras und ihr Ort in der Auseinandersetzung um die analogia fidei* (Düsseldorf: Patmos Verlag, 1969); Keith Johnson, *Karl Barth and the* Analogia Entis (London: T. & T. Clark, 2010); Eberhard Mechels, *Analogie bei Erich Przywara und Karl Barth. Das Verhältnis von Offenbarungstheologie und Metaphysik* (Neukirchen-Vluyn: Neukirchener Verlag, 1974); Peter Oh, *Karl Barth's Trinitarian Theology: A Study in Karl Barth's Analogical Use of the Trinitarian Relation* (London: T. & T. Clark, 2006).

235. See the preface to the first edition. It is even possible that Barth, who was by then considerably preoccupied with his *Church Dogmatics,* never read the *Analogia Entis,* having turned down Przywara's request that he review it, claiming, understandably, that he did not have the time to do it justice (letter to Przywara from May 6, 1932). See Johnson, *Karl Barth and the* Analogia Entis, p. 150.

Przywara write the *Analogia Entis* with Barth in mind, in the work's preface he even credits their encounter for having helped him to clarify the *theological* aspect of his doctrine. All of which further complicates the task of sorting out Barth's criticisms (to which version of the *analogia entis* do they apply?) and Przywara's actual views (did they develop in such a way that would have qualified Barth's initial verdict?).

In the foregoing we have already indicated something of the nature of Barth's concerns, chiefly, that the *analogia entis* represented to him the kind of natural theology that he subsequently rejected in his response to Brunner. We have also shown that Barth hesitated in rendering his verdict, not least of all given that he himself made use of the concept of the *analogia entis* in his early lectures, and also because he was profoundly impressed by his initial encounter with Przywara in early February, 1929. What remains to be shown for present purposes is what Barth was thinking about the *analogia entis,* and more generally about the relationship between philosophy and theology, between 1929 and 1932, that is, in the crucial years leading up to the *Church Dogmatics.* And in this regard two lectures from 1929 are decisive: "Fate and Idea in Theology," which was delivered only weeks after his first encounter with Przywara and is obviously (if implicitly) in conversation with him; and "The Holy Spirit and the Christian Life," which was delivered in October of the same year and is more negative in tone, clearly adumbrating his final position.

5.2.1. Barth's "Fate and Idea in Theology" (1929)

Without going into the details of these lectures,[236] in "Fate and Idea in Theology" Barth assesses the differences between realism and idealism as philosophical points of departure, and the extent of their usefulness to theology. He begins with realism: "'God is' — what does that mean if not that God takes part in being? Then of course the next proposition leads to the idea that God is himself being, the origin and perfection of everything that is. In their classical form, as set forth by Thomas Aquinas, these propositions combine with a third which can logically be regarded as the consequence, namely, everything that is as such participates in God."[237] That Barth is also

236. For further discussion of these lectures, see Johnson, *Karl Barth and the* Analogia Entis, pp. 93-121.
237. "Fate and Idea in Theology," in *The Way of Theology in Karl Barth: Essays and Comments,* ed. H. Martin Rumscheidt, with an introduction by Stephen W. Sykes (Eugene, OR: Pickwick, 1986), p. 33.

thinking of Przywara here, as a representative of Thomistic theological realism, is clear from what he then goes on to say:

> Everything that is exists as mere creature in greatest dissimilarity to the Creator, yet by having being it exists in greatest similarity to the Creator. That is what is meant by *analogia entis*. The realist confidently supposes that in what is given he is able to encounter something similar to God. . . . For he teaches that God must be inferred from the given (necessarily from the given and not from anywhere else). . . . It is thus the case that we stand in relation to God by virtue of the fact that we ourselves *are* and that things outside of us *are*. . . . *Analogia entis* means the dissimilarity and similarity to God which I myself have as knower and the thing outside of me has as the known.[238]

On the basis of a cursory reading of these passages one could think that Barth has given an accurate account of the *analogia entis*. But here already one can pick up a certain amount of distortion in his reproduction of Przywara's doctrine. *Firstly,* he does not give the *analogia entis* the proper stress that for Przywara, as we have seen, is crucial: for the *analogia entis* precisely does not mean a neatly balanced ontology of the "greatest similarity" and "the greatest dissimilarity," as Barth puts it, but an ultimately negative theology of "ever greater" dissimilarity. In fact, when presented the way Barth presents it, the dynamic rhythm of the *analogia entis* ossifies into a balanced equation that Przywara himself would certainly have rejected. For then, as Przywara puts it, "it would not be the divine Is (Truth, etc.) that is ultimately decisive, but instead this suspended equilibrium between God and creature."[239] Accordingly, to use an analogy, understanding Przywara's *analogia entis* is not simply a matter of seeing the notes of a musical score, the major and the minor keys, i.e., the similar and the dissimilar, but of hearing with a musical ear the proper *stress* of its rhythm. *Secondly,* and even more fundamentally, while these passages from Barth's lecture alone cannot be considered conclusive, it is fairly clear in light of other statements that Barth understands by the *analogia entis* an attempt to refer God and creatures to a *tertium quid,* in this case "being," in which both God and creatures respectively share. As he put it in a late statement, suggesting that

---

238. "Fate and Idea in Theology," p. 33.

239. *AE* §6, 8, p. 233; *De Ver.* q. 1, a. 10, ad 1: "although creatures bear within themselves a certain likeness to God, there is nevertheless present the greatest unlikeness."

he was always operating under this assumption: "My criticism of the *analogia entis* consisted in that the *analogia entis* — as Thomas understood it — calls for a common ground between God and human beings; and this ground was found in the concept of being. God is, the human being also is. To this extent there is an analogy between God and world, etc. And it was against this concept that I had to fight."[240] If this really were the teaching of Thomas (and Przywara), then Barth's vigorous rebuttal would not only be understandable, but called for. In reality, however, while such an interpretation may apply to certain degraded forms of neo-scholasticism, it in no way applies to Przywara or to Thomas himself, neither of whom can be said to make God a species of being *(Deus non est in genere!)* or to subordinate theology to ontology.

Let us return, though, with these important clarifications in mind, to the remaining substance of Barth's criticisms: for Barth the *analogia entis* means that by virtue of their mere being creatures are automatically (and, as it were, fated to be) in relation to God. As a result, the God who appears as the creature's "fate," as necessarily bound to the creature as its origin and end, is himself fated to be a "given," the end of a chain of creaturely reasoning, in short, an "inference." But this, Barth contends, is something altogether different from the "self-giving" God of the Bible, who is encountered and known only in the event of his "coming," i.e., his self-revelation.[241] That is to say, for Barth, the God of Christianity, if he is God at all, far from being a "given," an "object" that is simply "there" in constant reserve, only gives himself to the creature freely as a *subject* in the sovereign event of his self-revelation. Moreover, in Barth's view, if theology begins methodologically with philosophy and with this kind of ontology, then the novelty of the Word of God cannot break through. Thus Barth concludes (along with Bonhoeffer) that the *analogia entis,* as an ontological superstructure, threatens not only the sovereignty of God, but the very concept of revelation, which comes not on our terms, but on God's terms, as something altogether new and unexpected, indeed as light to darkness.[242] All of which leads Barth to distinguish his own Protestant theology — as centered upon the dynamic, active, momentary, interruptive "event-character" of God's self-revelation

---

240. Karl Barth, *Gespräche, 1959-1962* (Zürich: TVZ, 1995), p. 294.

241. As he puts it, "Doesn't realism come dangerously near to conceiving of God as given by fate at the very point where God has nothing in common with fate, namely, at the point of his coming? Aren't we threatened here with the idea of a God whose being is merely there instead of a God who comes?" ("Fate and Idea in Theology," p. 42).

242. See Bonhoeffer, *Act and Being,* p. 75.

— from the supposedly static Catholic metaphysics of the *analogia entis* that he finds in Thomas and Przywara.[243]

Needless to say, what all of these criticisms have in common is Barth's profound suspicion of philosophy and of what he takes to be (in Thomas and Przywara) a philosophical as opposed to a dogmatic point of departure — signaling his eventual rejection of every attempt to provide "for theology a foundation, support, or justification in philosophical existentialism."[244] In other words, what informs Barth's criticism of the *analogia entis* from the start is his well-known stance on natural theology. Indeed, this would seem to be the real nerve of his criticism, since, as he correctly perceived, the *analogia entis* provides the requisite ontological *foundation* and *presupposition* for any natural theology, making it (in his view) all the more dangerous.

At this point we are still a few years away from his vehement assertion in the *Church Dogmatics,* but here already in this 1929 lecture, with natural theology as supported by the *analogia entis* in view, he poses the dramatic question: "Wouldn't it perhaps be better for this God to be called simply nature? And might it not be better for the theology of this particular God to be called demonology rather than theology?"[245] And even more shockingly, he concludes, in language reminiscent of Luther: "A theology ignorant that even its best concept of God, informed by the pinnacle of human thought, is in itself no witness to God can only be, strictly speaking, a witness to the devil."[246] Barth concedes that such a drastic way of formulating the matter makes it "difficult to determine whether with these questions we have not departed hopelessly from a Thomas or a Schleiermacher, to say nothing of the realists in contemporary theology," presumably like Przywara. (And this important qualification seems to be a sign that at this point he is still wavering in his judgment.) "But," he goes on to say, "we did need to speak of the boundary that visibly emerges here, of the danger against which theology must ever be on the alert. The *Deus sive natura* is not the God who reveals himself in his Word."[247] In other words, as Barth would remind us with

---

243. Needless to say, Thomas himself understands God as the "pure act" of being, as Barth certainly recognizes, but Barth says that "it is being propounded here in a completely different way than was true in his case" ("Fate and Idea in Theology," p. 40).

244. *Church Dogmatics* I/1, p. xiii. For a nuanced account of Barth's attitude toward philosophy, see Kenneth Oakes, *Karl Barth on Theology and Philosophy* (Oxford: Oxford University Press, 2012).

245. "Fate and Idea in Theology," p. 42.

246. "Fate and Idea in Theology," p. 59.

247. "Fate and Idea in Theology," p. 42.

Pascal, the God of Abraham, Isaac, and Jacob is *not* the God of the philosophers — the one is a necessary postulate and object of reason, the other is a
sovereign subject and free — and (of all people) theologians should be the
first not to confuse them.

Leaving aside Barth's hyperbolic identification of natural theology
with demonology (which adumbrates his acerbic remark in the *Church Dogmatics*), his point here is a legitimate one, which no Catholic need or should
wish to dispute — it was, after all, a Catholic (Pascal) who first made it.[248]
For if we confuse theology with philosophy it may be that the object of our
theology is no longer the living God of revelation, but merely a "deified concept" of our own reasoning or imagining.[249] And precisely here we touch
upon the Reformed concern about idolatry, now regarding human conceptions of God, that animates Barth's theology as a dogmatic theology based
strictly upon revelation. The all-important question here, however — if one
is to avoid conceding everything to Feuerbach — is how one reads the "not"
in Pascal's memorial. For, on the Catholic view, this "not" does not have to
be read dialectically, as though theology (faith) necessarily implied the negation of philosophy (reason), but can also be read analogically, such that the
God of revelation, while different from the God of reason (and thus *not* the
God of reason), is not entirely unrelated to the God of reason. In other
words, on the Catholic view (and Przywara's view), one does not have to embrace fideism in order to avoid rationalism. But here again, as Luther
redivivus, Barth takes things one step further (further even than his second
Romans commentary), essentially claiming that the natural light of reason
knows nothing of God but *entia rationis,* i.e., idols of its own fabrication.[250]

---

248. For that matter, one need only recall the Catholic Church's consistent condemnation of rationalism, its response to the Modernist crisis, and its express condemnation of
the philosophies of Günther and Hermes. To this extent, therefore, Barth and the Catholic
Church are agreed: faith is not reason, and theology is not philosophy.

249. "Fate and Idea in Theology," p. 58.

250. For example, as Charles Lewis of Wake Forest University has pointed out, in his
1922 Romans commentary (London: Oxford University Press, 1933) Barth was still happy to
speak of the "memory" of our lost relationship with God, which even the pagans possess
(p. 230). By 1929, however, in a move reminiscent of Kierkegaard's critique of immanence in
the *Philosophical Fragments*, Barth denies any such remembrance of God as one finds at the
bottom of Augustine's natural theology. See *The Holy Spirit and the Christian Life*, trans.
R. Birch Hoyle (Louisville: Westminster/John Knox, 1993), p. 5: "The discontinuity between
God the Lord and man must certainly mean, in light of the relation between Creator and
creature, that between the one who is commanding and the one who is commanded there is
an irreversibility which excludes the presentation of God as already present as an object of

Accordingly, because for Barth there is no such thing as natural theology, since this would put God on our level and at *our* disposal (which is impossible), all knowledge of God is *eo ipso* supernatural knowledge of God, and therefore already (noetic) participation in the life of the Trinity.[251]

Another fundamental concern about the *analogia entis* that emerges from Barth's remarks in "Fate and Idea in Theology" is that the *analogia entis* gives human beings a foothold from which confidently to assert their similarity to God (for this, at least as popularly conceived, is what analogy does: it bridges the gap between dissimilar things), invariably obscuring and giving one a perilous philosophical excuse to disregard humanity's actual *separation* and *alienation* from God due to sin. In other words, inasmuch as it treats man "as such" and not "man in Adam," the *analogia entis* as an abstract theory fails to register our concrete situation and thereby tempts one to think that one is related to God when one is not.[252] And this leads Barth to affirm (in a radical dogmatic move to banish this temptation once and for all) that creatures are related to God not by virtue of their being, not by any *analogia entis,* but solely by virtue of faith in the one and only mediator, Jesus Christ, through whom God, who must be sovereign in this relationship, *relates himself to us* (which is precisely what Barth intends by opposing his *analogia fidei* to the *analogia entis*). Accordingly, for Barth the continuity between God and creatures comes not from below (as something established by natural theology, which is just another version of "works righteousness"), but only from above (as something established by revelation). For apart from Christ we are but sinners and separated from God; and it would be the

---

our memory, as a *'pulchritudo antiqua.'* On the contrary, it characterizes the knowledge of God as the revelation of something really and radically new, without any possibility of a primordial prior knowledge of it" (Chalamet's revised translation). In other words, for Barth God is "given" neither as the highest object outside us in an inventory of reality, as for the theological realist, nor is he given to the theological idealist inside us at the bottom of our cognition or memory; and in this regard, alerting his audience to what he takes to be the inherent dangers of Augustine's theology, he goes so far as to speak of Augustine's "terrible" *(schrecklichen) Confessions (The Holy Spirit and the Christian Life,* p. 22).

251. "Fate and Idea in Theology," p. 27: "Theology can know about God only to the extent that God makes himself accessible to us." Indeed, for Barth, God is not given in reality, according to an *analogia entis,* since this would turn revelation into a constant, a "given," but only in the ever "momentary" event of his self-revelation (p. 40).

252. See Bonhoeffer, *Act and Being,* p. 32: "Concepts of being, insofar as they are acquired from revelation, are always determined by the concepts of sin and grace, 'Adam' and Christ. There are in theology no ontological categories that are primarily based in creation and divorced from those latter concepts."

height of presumption to attempt to establish our relatedness to God on any other basis. Barth's rejection of the *analogia entis* is thus a principled one, matching (at the ontological level) his rejection of natural theology (at the epistemological level).

5.2.2. *Barth's* The Holy Spirit and the Christian Life *(1929)*

Some months later in *The Holy Spirit and the Christian Life*, Barth reiterates these concerns. But whereas in "Fate and Idea in Theology" he still showed a certain amount of admiration for Przywara, who is unnamed but everywhere present as the representative theologian who does philosophy,[253] now for the first time he openly states his disagreement with him:

> If creaturehood is to be understood strictly as a reality desired and posited by God in distinction from His own reality, as the miracle of a reality which has place and existence next to His own reality by virtue of His love, then the continuity between God and the creature too, the true *analogia entis* in virtue of which He, the uncreated Spirit, can be revealed to the created spirit, cannot belong to the creature as such but only to the Creator *in His relating* to the creature. It cannot be understood as an original endowment of the creature, but rather only as a second miracle of the love of *God;* as an incomprehensible, unmerited, divine *giving*. The human as creature is not in a place from which he can establish and survey his relation to God (for example, in a scheme of a unity of similarity and dissimilarity) and, on that basis, understand himself as "open upwards" and therefore he is not able to attribute his knowing to a revealedness of God proper to him as such.[254]

This passage is revealing on multiple levels. For one thing, as Christophe Chalamet has pointed out, we already see here in what Barth calls the "true *analogia entis*" the rudiments of his *analogia fidei*.[255] For, in Barth's view, it is not that we *are always already related* to God by virtue of our creation, i.e., by virtue of the *analogia entis,* but that God, by virtue of his eternal election

---

253. For instance, Barth suggests that Przywara is like an Aaron among the philosophers battling their serpent-staves with the staff of a genuine *philosophia sacra* (*The Holy Spirit and the Christian Life*, p. 28). "The great temptation and danger," however, consists in this, that the theologian will actually become what he seems to be — a philosopher" (p. 29).

254. *The Holy Spirit and the Christian Life*, p. 5 (Chalamet's translation).

255. See "Est Deus in Nobis?" p. 285.

of humanity in Christ, *sovereignly relates himself* to us. For another thing, it gives us a clear indication of how Barth was reading Przywara's 1926 work *Religionsphilosophie katholischer Theologie,* from which the phrase "open upwards" [*nach oben offen*] is taken, and whose title by itself undoubtedly suggested to him a problematic confusion of philosophy and theology. Simply put, it shows that Barth thinks of the *analogia entis* as virtually synonymous with a created capacity for grace, with a *potentia oboedientialis,* with, in other words, precisely the kind of creaturely "point of contact" *(Anknüpfungspunkt)* that he later rejected in his response to Emil Brunner.[256] But as he goes on to say: "the created spirit is in no wise 'open upward' in itself: it is not within the compass of any cleverness or ability of mine, but it is purely and simply the office of the Holy Spirit to be continually opening our ears to enable us to receive the Creator's word."[257] Accordingly, for Barth, just as there is no *ontological* relation to God apart from Christ, who mediates what in no way can be compared, there is at an *epistemological* level no creaturely knowledge of God (not even the most meager natural theology) apart from the sovereign, ever-momentary working in us of the Holy Spirit.

Whether or not one subscribes to Barth's corresponding dogmatic positions, which in Przywara's view have serious metaphysical problems of their own (principally that they exacerbate the tendency of Lutheran and Reformed theology to denigrate the creature as creature and to embrace what Przywara called "theopanism," which is but the inverse of pantheism and secularism), the force of Barth's criticisms cannot be denied; and in contrast to Heidegger they are all the more serious inasmuch as they stem from a genuine Christian pathos. As with Heidegger, however, the question here is whether what Barth was criticizing truly resembles what Przywara was proposing. And so we come back to our guiding question: Did Barth misunder-

---

256. As he put it a few months before, "No inherent grace or capacity for grace can be claimed by virtue of which the knower and the known would exist in relation to God through the *analogia entis*" ("Fate and Idea in Theology," p. 39).

257. *The Holy Spirit and the Christian Life,* p. 8. Clearly, in keeping with the title of his lecture, Barth's understanding of the *analogia fidei* is based upon a certain understanding of the Spirit as the *Creator* Spirit and a radical reading of John 3:8, "The Spirit blows where it wills." For it is not simply that the Holy Spirit is the power of salvation, relating us (who are fallen but still made in God's image) to Christ, but that we are ontologically related to God *only* on the basis of the event of the Spirit's ever momentary coming. For Barth, therefore, axiomatically, there can be neither a Catholic *analogia entis,* which preserves a fixed ontological relatedness to God, nor a Catholic doctrine of grace *(gratia infusa et inhaerens),* nor a Catholic understanding of the sacraments *(ex opere operato),* since all of these doctrines (ostensibly) put God at our disposal and turn the free event of grace into a ready possession.

stand Przywara (as von Balthasar argued), or in light of later clarifications did he change his mind about the *analogia entis* (as Peter Oh has argued), or was his judgment from the beginning well informed and conclusive, being based upon a clear-headed and unwavering commitment to Reformed theology (as Keith Johnson has argued)?

5.2.3. Retraction or Confirmation?
Barth's Final Position on the analogia entis

As already indicated, this question is not easily decided, not least of all because Barth issued his verdict before Przywara had the opportunity to clarify his views, first in the *Analogia Entis* itself, and also because Barth's own position appears to change with his own adoption of the language of analogy in the form of an *analogia fidei*.[258] The matter is further complicated in that by 1940 Barth seemed to be appeased by Gottlieb Söhngen's argument for an *analogia entis* within an *analogia fidei*. As he puts it in the second volume of his *Church Dogmatics*: "If this is the Roman Catholic doctrine of the *analogia entis*, then naturally I must withdraw my earlier statement that I regard the *analogia entis* as 'the invention of the anti-Christ.'"[259] Thus, noting Barth's more conciliatory tone and (along with von Balthasar) Barth's own move toward an *analogia fidei*, Peter Oh has argued, "It is certain that Balthasar's affirmation of the complementary concept of analogy, '*analogia entis* within *analogia fidei*,' has sufficiently convinced Karl Barth himself."[260] But two things need to be noted here: firstly, the view Oh ascribes to von Balthasar is really that of Söhngen, which neither Barth nor von Balthasar considered to be the normative Catholic position; secondly, as both Barth and von Balthasar recognized, it would be premature to equate Przywara's doctrine with Söhngen's formulation of it — not least of all because Przywara's doctrine comports with (even if it cannot be reduced to) the natural theology insisted upon by Vatican I.[261]

---

258. It should be noted here that Barth's use of the term *analogia fidei* is, in contrast to its traditional meaning, a neologism. In Romans 12:6 it simply means that the charism of prophecy should be tested "according" to the rule of faith, and in the Catholic tradition it also means the analogy of the two covenants. In Barth it has a decidedly different meaning, referring to the conformity of God and creatures in the act of faith. See *Church Dogmatics* I/1, p. 243.

259. See *Church Dogmatics* II/1, p. 82.

260. See Peter Oh, *Karl Barth's Trinitarian Theology*, p. 16.

261. See also von Balthasar's letter to Barth from April 25, 1940: "As with your earlier

JOHN R. BETZ

In this regard Keith Johnson's scholarship brings a new level of clarity to the discussion. For as he convincingly shows, even if Barth's tone softens over time (in view of the clarifications of Söhngen and von Balthasar), and even if he gradually came to realize that analogy is somehow indispensable to theology, he never really changed his mind about Przywara's *analogia entis*. As Barth put it in response to a question at Princeton in 1962:

> . . . it is true that in the first volume of the *Church Dogmatics* I said something very nasty about the *analogia entis*. I said it was the invention of the anti-Christ. Later on I began to see that the notion of analogy cannot totally be suppressed in theology. I didn't at first speak of an *analogia entis*. I spoke of *analogia relationis* and then in a more biblical way of the analogy of faith. And then some of my critics said: "Well, after all, an *analogia relationis* is also some kind of *analogia entis*." And I couldn't deny it completely. I said: "Well, after all, if *analogia entis* is interpreted as *analogia relationis* or analogy of faith, well, then I will no longer say nasty things about the *analogia entis*. But I understand it in *this* way." So I have not changed my mind.[262]

For Johnson this important quote resets the terms of the ecumenical discussion about the *analogia entis* and frees it from "many misconceptions that have shaped this debate for decades."[263] For now we can see that Barth did not change his mind; indeed, for Johnson, Barth's mature doctrine of a continuity between God and human beings based upon an *analogia fidei (relationis)* "stands as the strongest possible rejection of [an *analogia entis*], because nothing like that analogy is conceivable on Barth's terms."[264] And, true enough, notwithstanding a certain resemblance in vocabulary, Barth's

---

works I have also read the new volume of your dogmatics with great interest. But, as a Catholic theologian, I was not in every respect satisfied with your engagement with the *analogia entis*, since it seems to me that the ultimate Catholic positions were not everywhere confronted. . . . It is not as if I would possibly want to identify myself with Söhngen, whom you rightly characterize as not representing the normative Catholic position." Quoted in Lochbrunner, *Hans Urs von Balthasar und seine Theologen-Kollegen*, p. 267. From the rest of von Balthasar's letter, which defends Przywara at length, it is clear that he considers Przywara's position to be the more or less normative Catholic position.

  262. Barth, *Gespräche, 1959-1962* (Zürich: TVZ, 1995), p. 499, here in Johnson's translation, p. 12.

  263. Johnson, *Karl Barth and the* Analogia Entis, p. 12.

  264. Johnson, *Karl Barth and the* Analogia Entis, p. 11.

analogia fidei — and the entire methodology of his *Church Dogmatics* — is conceived precisely in terms of his opposition to the *analogia entis*. Thus, for Barth to admit that he was mistaken about the *analogia entis* would be to call into question the validity of his entire theological program.

For Reformed theologians who are committed to Barth's theology — as a Protestant theology with a legitimate protest to make — it is therefore crucial that Barth not be wrong about Przywara. Accordingly, Johnson is at pains to show not only (*contra* Oh) that Barth did not change his mind about Przywara, but also (*contra* von Balthasar) that Barth did not misunderstand him. As he puts it, "the debate about Barth's interpretation of the *analogia entis* should begin from the basis that Barth's criticism of the *analogia entis* was not based upon a mistake."[265] But this part of Johnson's argument, it must be said, is much harder to make, because it assumes that von Balthasar, who knew both Barth and Przywara, and was as knowledgeable of their actual positions as very few have been or could claim to be, was himself mistaken — not so much about whether or to what degree Barth himself made a move toward analogy, which is debatable, but about perceiving that his mentor had been unfairly criticized, implying at some level that Przywara *had* been misunderstood. As von Balthasar famously put it in his book on Barth, attempting to set the record straight and pave the way for more fruitful ecumenical dialogue, "nothing whatever can be found of that ogre Barth has made of the analogy of being."[266] Thus, everything comes down to the question of whether Johnson or von Balthasar is right; or whether, as a final possibility (and springboard for ecumenical discussion in which the real similarities and real differences are clearly seen), both could be right. To this end, let us first examine whether Barth's criticisms match up with Przywara's actual views.

5.2.4. Boiling Down Barth's Criticisms

We have already noted that in both of the lectures from 1929 Barth took the *analogia entis* to mean a scheme of unity between similarity and dissimilarity, which gives the creature the confidence to establish and survey its relationship with God. Clearly, however, Barth has not presented Przywara's *analogia entis* so much as a caricature of it.[267] For as we have seen, the *analogia entis*, as an ul-

---

265. Johnson, *Karl Barth and the* Analogia Entis, p. 12.
266. Von Balthasar, *The Theology of Karl Barth*, p. 50.
267. It should be noted that while Barth occasionally shows a more nuanced reading

timately *negative* theology, is in no sense a simple balancing of the similar and the dissimilar; much less does Przywara ever present the *analogia entis* as something that could give the creature a secure basis for "surveying" (!) its relationship with God. Rather, it is explicitly a doctrine of God's *ever greater* dissimilarity, which, in the spirit of Ignatius, is meant to *humble* the creature for service to an *ever greater* God. Furthermore, if God is "given" in creation, as Barth puts it, then he is given for Przywara only analogously (with all of and more than the distance of metaphor that this implies) and certainly not in the way that an object is given to us. For, to put it very simply, if a "smiling" meadow fails to capture what we mean by a human smile, *a fortiori* creation itself, as an analogy, fails to capture or reveal the mystery of God himself, which would always require a *personal* revelation (as occurs in the incarnation).[268] Thus, to conceive of the *analogia entis* as some kind of a metaphysical straightjacket into which God is forced, or by means of which God is somehow compelled to unveil himself or become a "given," would indeed be a misunderstanding of Przywara's doctrine.

In this regard, in order to see just how Barth reads Przywara, and whether one may fairly claim that he misunderstood or at least misrepresented him, it is illuminating to compare his remarks from *The Holy Spirit and the Christian Life,* which were cited and discussed above, with the following corresponding passage from Przywara's *Religionsphilosophie katholischer Theologie:*

---

of the "greater dissimilarity" of the *analogia entis* (as in *Church Dogmatics* I/1, p. 239), his tendency is plainly to read it as an all-too-pliable doctrine that allows one to shift easily from dissimilarity back to similarity. Thus he imputes to the *analogia entis* an "innocuous indirectness of low potency that can easily be changed into directness" (p. 173), essentially *reversing* the actual and intended direction of the doctrine, which allows him, rather inconceivably, to align the *analogia entis* without any hesitation with other "menaces" such as "mysticism and identity philosophy" (p. 242).

268. Johnson is therefore right to say that, for Przywara, creation (in the human being) does not provide a *direct* (but only an *indirect*) revelation of God (though even here the word "indirect" does not sufficiently capture the ultimate distance and failure of representation that obtains for Przywara between God and creation). His account of Przywara becomes misleading, though, when he goes on to say that for Przywara the mere existence of the human being is a "'window' through which God's being is revealed" (*Karl Barth and the* Analogia Entis, p. 75), since this suggests the very immediacy to God's being that Przywara's *analogia entis* emphatically disallows; or when he says that "Przywara's doctrine is predicated upon the notion that God's revelation can be read directly off of creaturely realities. Barth had rejected this same error 15 years earlier . . ." (p. 121). But Przywara could never have made such statements, being inconceivable according to his own terms; thus, if this was the "error" that Barth was rejecting, then the error was actually Barth's own.

[T]he Catholic grounding of religion . . . conceives of the relation between God and creature as "open upward." This entails two things. On the one hand, this means that God is neither the absolute positing of any particular aspect of creation — neither the spiritual [*des Geisthaften*] nor the cosmic [*des Allhaften*], neither will nor thought, neither the personal nor the ideal — nor is He the ideal "unity" of the antitheses of these "sides" of creation. He is absolutely transcendent, as Thomas Aquinas puts it, *tamquam ignotus*, beyond all conceivable contents. Seen from this perspective, the creature is that which is never "completed"; it is the inconclusive "openness" of its tensions. On the other hand, this totality of the creaturely — in its antitheses . . . — is a "revelation" of God "from above," i.e., it is not an analogy [*Gleichnis*] into which God could in any way be "compelled" [*"vernotwendigt"*], as though by means of this analogy He could be calculated in His living essence and activity . . . but an analogy that points beyond itself to a God who is beyond all analogy [*übergleichnishaft*], who happened to choose this particular "analogy" according to an inscrutable decree and could choose thousands of others. God is thus, on the one hand, the mysterious "meaning" to which the totality of creation points. . . . At the same time, however, He is neither the "inner" meaning of creaturely reality . . . nor is "this" creaturely reality in any way a "necessary" revelation of His nature and activity or a limitation of new ways of His Self-revelation.[269]

Again, to judge from Barth's criticisms, which we know to be based in part upon this passage, one would think that the *analogia entis* is a form of metaphysical bridge-building that "domesticates" God, puts him into a metaphysical straightjacket, threatens divine sovereignty, and shackles divine freedom. Such, at least, are the more common objections to the *analogia entis,* which without question trace back to Barth. As this passage shows, however, such criticisms are groundless since for Przywara God is "absolutely transcendent," indeed, "beyond all analogy." Thus, in the interest of ecumenical dialogue, it may be hoped that such criticisms can finally be set aside as a misunderstanding.

But three more serious and interrelated criticisms remain, which one might summarize as follows. The *first,* which Keith Johnson rightly regards as basic, is that for Przywara creation is a self-revelation of God, whereas, for Barth, Christ *alone* is the source of revelation and "[n]othing else, be it hu-

269. *Schriften,* vol. 2, pp. 400ff.

man reason, consciousness, nature, or history, can serve as a source of revelation."[270] Thus, on Barth's dialectical view, the *analogia entis,* inasmuch as it posits a general self-revelation, automatically forestalls the novelty of God's self-revelation in Christ and God's ability through his self-revelation in Christ to *contradict* a fallen creation. Furthermore, it gives fallen human beings a perilous excuse to feel comfortable about themselves as images and likenesses of God, neutralizing the need for a decision in response to the event of revelation, which, since everything is already a revelation of God, cannot even break through.[271]

A *second* criticism is that the phrase "open upward" (ostensibly) means that human beings are always already open to God and related to God apart from the justifying grace of Christ, when in fact they are closed in upon themselves *(incurvatio in se ipsum)* and shut out from a relation with God due to sin. Consequently, on Barth's view Przywara's *analogia entis* is an abstract metaphysical doctrine dangerously out of touch with the reality of sin and our actual separation from God because of it. On the face of it, this criticism seems fair, for in his more philosophical works, the *Analogia Entis* included, Przywara tends to treat the topic of creation rather abstractly, not in terms of humanity's fallen condition, but in terms of its fundamental structure, as when he says in his 1926 philosophy of religion:

> The Catholic *analogia entis* bears within it the possibilities for a genuine *Menschwerdungskosmos,* which includes body and soul, community and individual, since in their totality (taking into consideration, of course, the upward relation from dead matter to pure spirit) they are "open" to God. From the standpoint of the Catholic *analogia entis,* the creature in its totality looks within analogy beyond all analogy to the God who transcends all analogy; and in this respect the creature is a receptive preparedness for Him: in its ultimate essence it already cries out, as it were, "Behold the handmaid of the Lord: may it be done unto me according to Thy Word!"[272]

---

270. Johnson, *Karl Barth and the* Analogia Entis, pp. 75, 104-5.

271. See *Church Dogmatics* I/1, p. 41. As Barth puts it, "[the] continuity between God and me in my creatureliness is not (as Przywara asserts) my 'tranquil, assured' quality" (*The Holy Spirit and the Christian Life,* p. 8). The reference here is to Przywara's *Religionsphilosophie katholischer Theologie* (*Schriften,* vol. 2, pp. 483-84).

272. *Schriften,* vol. 2, pp. 441-42. Importantly, this passage occurs in the context of Przywara's discussion of two basic ways of construing the God-world relation that he says are alien to a Catholic perspective and, specifically, to a Catholic understanding of the incar-

Here again we see that the problem with the *analogia entis* cannot be that it somehow "domesticates" God or compromises divine transcendence. To judge from Barth's reaction to this passage in the *Church Dogmatics*,[273] however, this is not his main concern. His main concern is rather that, according to the *analogia entis,* the creature is structurally, in spite of sin, already open to God — not, certainly, to the point of demanding an incarnation, but to the point of being in its essence, like Mary, a *potentia oboedientialis,* i.e., a preparation for it. In other words, Barth objects to the *analogia entis* because of the Mariology — and the essentially open relation between man and God, nature and grace — that he saw in it, since for him nature is precisely (due to sin) not ready for grace, but must at every moment be disposed by grace to grace (corresponding to his view that human beings have no inherent capacity even to cooperate with grace).[274]

Accordingly, concomitant with Barth's rejection of Przywara's *Menschwerdungskosmos,* i.e., a cosmos whose essence becomes transparent in the Mother of God as a readiness for God and a preparation for divine indwelling, we can identify a *third* criticism, namely, of the standard analogy in Catholic theology between nature and grace, according to which nature (the order of creation) is a preparation for grace (the order of redemption).[275] In

---

nation. The first way reduces God to some aspect of the world — even the highest, absolute unity of the world. In this case, Przywara says, the incarnation is made impossible precisely because God and world are already "melted together" and God possesses no freedom vis-à-vis the world. The second way of construing the God-world relation safeguards God's transcendence, but is characterized by an essentially docetic-Gnostic view of the incarnation as touching only upon the "invisible interior" of the soul, in which case the incarnation is rendered essentially invisible. Whereas in the first case God is so much "in" the world as ultimately to be a part (or the whole) of the world, in the second case, God, though free with respect to world, does not enter into it profoundly enough. Against both forms of religion, Przywara argues that a proper understanding of the incarnation is preserved only in the Catholic understanding of the *analogia entis.*

273. *Church Dogmatics* I/2, §15, pp. 144-45.

274. See Johnson, *Karl Barth and the* Analogia Entis, p. 56. As Johnson rightly points out, "This critique is crucial for understanding Barth's relationship to the *analogia entis,* because this continuity between divine and human action is precisely what Barth is rejecting when he rejects Przywara's version of the *analogia entis*" (p. 113). Of course, it would be preposterous to suppose that Catholic theology did not have its own carefully worked-out doctrines of prevenient grace, or that Mary's preparation to be the immaculate Mother of God was not itself the work of grace. The difference here rather comes down to Barth's denial of any natural creaturely cooperation with grace on the grounds that the human remains, in keeping with the Reformed tradition, "*totally* sinful" (p. 115; my emphasis).

275. Johnson, *Karl Barth and the* Analogia Entis, p. 108.

other words, what unites all of Barth's criticisms is his rejection of the Thomistic maxim, which is central to Przywara's argument in the *Analogia Entis,* that grace (faith) does not destroy but presupposes and perfects nature (reason) — as a corollary of which, Barth thinks, one begins methodologically in Catholic theology with nature, with history (perhaps the history of religions), with man in general (anthropology), with merely human thinking (philosophy), and not with God's definitive self-revelation in Christ. And in this respect it seems, notwithstanding the radical differences between them, Barth could see little difference between Roman Catholicism and his other declared enemy, liberal Protestantism, both of which — and with equal force — had to be rejected.

Consequently, with these fundamental criticisms in view, Keith Johnson is right to conclude that Barth objects to the *analogia entis* on the basis of Reformed theological principles, which Barth not only confirms but also extends: allowing no knowledge of God except by faith (in novel epistemological extension of *sola fide*) and no relation to God except through Christ (in novel ontological extension of *solo Christo*).[276] For here it is not, as for Catholic theology, that faith in Christ presupposes, illuminates and perfects (admittedly fallible) reason, but that reason gets one, theologically speaking, nowhere; nor is it the case, as for Catholic theology, that the greater gift of grace presupposes and perfects the prior gift of creation (which, however corrupted by sin, is still a gift), but that creation of itself does not even have any capacity to fulfill; nor is it the case, as for Catholic theology, that nature intimates something about God even to the pagan, who is therefore "without excuse" (Rom. 1:18), but that nature of itself has nothing to say, no secrets to reveal, and (apart from faith in Christ) is not even considered a revelation. Thus, for Barth, the *analogia entis* was indeed more than a metaphysical technicality; inasmuch as it represented and conveyed age-old Catholic principles, it was in his mind grounds for being Protestant. Nor, as Johnson rightly concludes, did Barth's position significantly change with his adoption of the language of an *analogia fidei,* which for Barth means that there is no ontological relation to God, not even an indirect, analogical one, outside of faith. For here too the final word as far as the relation between nature (reason) and grace (faith) is concerned is *not* analogy but dialectic — a

---

276. And here, one could argue, it is not so much Barth's commitment to Reformed principles as his radical *extension* of them, beyond even the teachings of Calvin on natural theology, that bedevils ecumenical dialogue. See in this regard the currently unpublished paper by Han-Luen Kantzer Komline entitled "Przywara's *Analogia Entis* and Calvin's *Institutes* I.1-5: A Case of Dissimilarity amid Greater Similarity."

dialectic that is overcome, analogized, only in Christ.[277] The final question to consider, therefore, given the sharp lines that Barth draws between the confessions, is whether and to what extent he may have *overdrawn* them, and whether he may have misunderstood or misrepresented Przywara and Catholic theology in the process, as von Balthasar and Przywara believed was the case. To this end, we conclude first with a brief discussion of von Balthasar's view of the debate, and, finally, with a selection of Przywara's own implicit and explicit responses to Barth's criticisms.

5.3. Von Balthasar's Dialogue with Barth about the analogia entis

Von Balthasar's defense of Przywara and Catholic theology in his book on Karl Barth is well known; it is less well known that this book was long in process, grew out of his frustration with Barth's reading of Przywara, and originally bore the title "*Analogia Entis:* A Dialogue with Karl Barth."[278] Nor is it well known that in 1940 von Balthasar wrote a lengthy and rather forward letter to Barth, in which he says that in his reading of the *Church Dogmatics,* which he otherwise admires, he was "continually held up" by what he believed to be "a genuine misunderstanding of analogy and its proper sense."[279] Indeed, he says, "I had the feeling that you were often battling against a phantom or, to be honest, against a misuse of Catholic theology."[280]

277. In this regard, therefore, Bruce McCormack is absolutely right to say in his significant work that Barth's "*analogia fidei* is itself an *inherently dialectical concept*." See his *Karl Barth's Critically Realistic Dialectical Theology* (Oxford: Clarendon, 1995), p. 16.

278. See von Balthasar, *Our Task,* p. 101: "Barth's dialogue with Erich Przywara had broken down ('*Analogia entis* as Antichrist'). I wanted to get things moving again and clear away some of the chief obstacles in ecumenical dialogue by using ideas from de Lubac's *Surnaturel* [Supernatural] and *Sur les chemins de Dieu* [On the Pathways to God]." See Lochbrunner, *Hans Urs von Balthasar und seine Theologen-Kollegen*, p. 284; for a full-length study of their encounter in English, see Stephen Wigley, *Karl Barth and Hans Urs von Balthasar: A Critical Engagement* (Edinburgh: T. & T. Clark, 2007).

279. Letter from May 4, 1940; quoted in Lochbrunner, *Hans Urs von Balthasar und seine Theologen-Kollegen*, p. 277.

280. Lochbrunner, *Hans Urs von Balthasar und seine Theologen-Kollegen*, p. 277. By "misuse" of Catholic theology von Balthasar means an "inexcusable" separation (beyond the necessary distinctions) and extrinsicism between the orders of nature and grace that had become current in neo-scholasticism (and which, he argues, can be attributed neither to Augustine nor to Thomas nor to Przywara). Accordingly, in von Balthasar's view, Barth's mistake was to have applied legitimate criticisms of neo-scholasticism (and of popular notions of Molinism) to Przywara and to Catholic theology in general.

And so, in an effort to correct what he perceived to be serial misunderstanding on Barth's part, he makes several important clarifications.

Firstly, he denies that the *analogia entis* somehow subordinates God (and creatures) to a *tertium quid,* i.e., being, in which both God and creatures differently participate. Secondly, he distinguishes Jesuit theology from popularized Molinism, saying that the *analogia entis* is in no way an affront to divine freedom and sovereignty. Thirdly, he denies that the *analogia entis* in any way establishes the "independence" of the creature against God only to exalt its own inherent godlikeness, which would be utterly contrary to the content and spirit of Przywara's doctrine. Fourthly, he denies that the "upward openness" of nature through the human spirit, as posited by the *analogia entis,* in any way guarantees the "givenness" of God in a personal encounter; rather, it is simply a way of saying that the human spirit, while powerless to transcend its own nature, is nevertheless in principle capable of being addressed by God. Fifthly, he denies that the *analogia entis* entails a methodologically independent starting point in nature (or reason), as though Przywara's philosophical theology were not undertaken from the perspective of faith in what is ultimately *one* order of salvation (from sin) in Christ.[281] Accordingly, he rejects the notion that the *analogia entis* and the *analogia fidei* are necessarily opposed, "as though the *analogia entis* were valid only with regard to "nature" and the *analogia fidei* only with regard to the "supernatural." And in this regard he makes an important clarification, specifying what he takes to be the authentic Catholic understanding of the *analogia entis:*

> It is clear, of course, that in the Catholic view the *analogia entis* has a natural (one could say: philosophical) and a supernatural (theological) form. The first is plainly implied in the second insofar as the "formal outline" of the God-creature relation is not negated [*aufgehoben*], even as it

281. For this reason, von Balthasar goes on to argue, since the notion of a separate sphere of nature is an abstraction from the one concrete order of salvation, for Przywara (no less than for Augustine or Thomas) there can be no natural knowledge of God that is not ultimately connected to this one concrete order of salvation. For that matter, he points out, Catholic theology has never posited a realm of pure nature that is not destined for supernatural elevation. Barth has therefore confused Przywara and Thomas with the worst of neoscholasticism. For, like Thomas, Przywara too thinks from faith, but like Thomas he nevertheless finds it theologically necessary to distinguish nature from grace as that to which grace applies, since otherwise all and nothing is grace; and this is "not sinful hubris, but authentic service to the *intelligentia fidei*" (Lochbrunner, *Hans Urs von Balthasar und seine Theologen-Kollegen,* p. 275).

is made completely new in terms of content. But the first is implied in the second only as an abstraction, and in this sense it is negated [*aufgehoben*], insofar as the entire revelation of God as *principium et finis* is sublated and submerged in the revelation of the living and personal God of Christ and the Church. *In concreto,* therefore, the *analogia* is *in no sense a philosophical but rather a purely theological principle,* within which one may nevertheless (retrospectively) sketch out a sphere of nature. . . . Such knowledge is not idle speculation, forbidden, as it were, by the existential character of revelation, but rather an indispensable moment within the full understanding of what the concrete relation to God is.[282]

That is to say, for von Balthasar, a correct understanding of the *analogia entis* navigates a middle path (not unlike the *analogia entis* itself!) between two possible extremes: between Barth's dialectical opposition of the *analogia entis* and the *analogia fidei* (which radically rules out any continuity or compatibility) and Gottlieb Söhngen's proposal of an *analogia entis* only within an *analogia fidei* (which essentially collapses the former into the latter). For, as he observes, Catholic theology *can* distinguish between an *analogia entis* proper to philosophy, which sketches out the bare formality of the relation between God and creature, and a concrete *analogia entis* within the one order of salvation that is proper to theology.[283]

Finally, von Balthasar dismisses the notion that the *analogia entis,* as a philosophical principle, represents a conceptual attempt to "lay hold" of God (in a refined philosophical rendition, as it were, of the grasping after deity of the original sin). For the *analogia entis,* he explains, "is precisely not any formula (as Przywara has repeatedly and rightly emphasized) but rather that which *makes every formula that would grasp and usurp [the divine] impossible*."[284] For that matter, when one affirms the *analogia entis* from the perspective of faith in Christ, the thinker cannot even be tempted to compare God and the creature on the same plane ["*Eins und Eins gegenüberzustellen*"] or "to smuggle in one or another form of univocity in place of the incomparable superiority of God and the complete dependence of the creature."[285]

---

282. Lochbrunner, *Hans Urs von Balthasar und seine Theologen-Kollegen,* p. 275.

283. Lochbrunner, *Hans Urs von Balthasar und seine Theologen-Kollegen,* p. 276. For "the movement of grace," von Balthasar writes, "is inscribed in this fundamental relation of nature, which is also posited by God," and "this and this alone is what is meant by the maxim: *Gratia non destruit, sed perficit et elevat naturam.*"

284. Lochbrunner, *Hans Urs von Balthasar und seine Theologen-Kollegen,* p. 276.

285. Lochbrunner, *Hans Urs von Balthasar und seine Theologen-Kollegen,* p. 276.

Nevertheless, von Balthasar goes on to say that while the *analogia entis* is understood, as for Przywara, from a position of faith, "this incomparability remains evident on the (sublated but formally filled out) basis of the relation between God and creature: for here too, and precisely here, it continues to be *God* and the *creature* who encounter one another in a completely new way."[286] In other words, for von Balthasar, the fact that there is ultimately only *one* order of salvation (through grace) does not mean that there is no discernible order of creation (nature), or that the formal relation between God and creature cannot in principle be discerned by reason. Rather, grace presupposes a nature to which it applies and which it fulfills. And to explain his point he draws an analogy between the animal and rational nature of the human being, which are conceptually distinct, even if they do not designate two separate realities. "Granted," he tells Barth,

> that the first is for the sake of the second, it is nevertheless also the case, as you yourself say somewhere else, that *the second is through the first.* If the first is excluded from the second, then Christ would not be *all* in all; so I cannot understand why on p. 575 you refuse to allow that creaturely freedom is taken up into the freedom of grace. Not as something "competing" with God — for creaturely freedom, which in itself is certainly not evil, does not necessarily entail willful opposition to God [*Gegen-Gott-sein-Wollen*] — but rather as a creaturely possibility something that is redeemable from defiance and, as such, *"elevabilis"* [i.e., capable of being elevated]. To be sure, the nature of the creature is always in proximate danger of hubris. But, conceptually, the definition of the created spirit (as a being capable of a *reflexio completa*) is certainly not the same as that of the admittedly very similar definition of sin (as the *conversio creaturae ad se ipsam* or *ad creaturas*). Rather, if it should occur in the right way — which would certainly not happen without the grace of God — then it is precisely the creature's *reflexio completa* that reveals its createdness, and hence its being-from-God and its being-to-God, its total relativity.[287]

In no sense, therefore, for von Balthasar, can the *analogia entis* be said to compromise divine sovereignty; on the contrary, it leads precisely to a recognition of it. Equally, though, as far as the question of creaturely freedom is

---

286. Lochbrunner, *Hans Urs von Balthasar und seine Theologen-Kollegen*, p. 276.

287. Lochbrunner, *Hans Urs von Balthasar und seine Theologen-Kollegen*, pp. 276-77. The reference here is to a passage from *Church Dogmatics* II/1, §31, p. 512.

concerned, von Balthasar clearly defends Przywara's understanding of the integrity of nature as a realm of secondary causes that can be redeemed from the possibility of defiance and transformed by grace.

Accordingly, with the *analogia entis* properly in view, von Balthasar expresses the wish that in his most recent volume of the *Church Dogmatics* Barth had engaged in more serious debate with Przywara, "whose doctrine of analogy is the only truly perspicuous one" and who "is the only one on the Catholic side who could see your [Barth's] concerns," instead of having taken as his chief interlocutors more minor Catholic theologians such as Fehr, Bartmann, and Diekamp.[288] Had he done so, von Balthasar suggests, Barth's chief fears about the *analogia entis* would have been allayed: "For precisely here [in Przywara] it becomes clear that God and creature in no way fall under a higher category, since the creature itself stands *within* analogy (ontically and noetically) and so cannot leap beyond its own creaturely sphere."[289]

5.4. Przywara's Actual Positions and Clarifications

Przywara's own response to Barth can be gleaned, initially, from his doctrine of the *analogia entis* itself, since it was formulated in part and from early on against Barth's dialectical theology; and in Przywara's view it certainly retains its validity as a response to Barth to the extent that Barth never advanced to a genuine doctrine of analogy.[290] His most extensive response to Barth (among other critics), however, is found in an article from 1940 entitled "The Scope of Analogy as a Fundamental Catholic Form,"[291] in which he reiterates that the *analogia entis* is a *theological* principle based in the

288. Lochbrunner, *Hans Urs von Balthasar und seine Theologen-Kollegen*, p. 270.

289. Lochbrunner, *Hans Urs von Balthasar und seine Theologen-Kollegen*, p. 270.

290. Accordingly, following the lines of Przywara's own argument, the best defense of the *analogia entis* would be to point out the theopanistic or pantheistic consequences of denying it — showing *ex negativo* that it is a truly fundamental and indispensable doctrine, which is necessary precisely to establish the *difference* between God and creation, without which grace would not be grace and revelation would not be revelation, and whereon (as Przywara himself insisted) even a proper understanding of the incarnation as a real incarnation depends. See footnote 272, above.

291. Importantly, one will also find here a highly nuanced account of what the Catholic tradition understands by *potentia oboedientialis* and a rejection of the notion that this means a "neutral 'becoming'" or participation in the divine that is unaffected by original sin. Indeed, Przywara speaks of "the impotence — puffed up by sin — of the man who seeks to be God." *AE*, p. 386.

teachings of the Fourth Lateran Council and in no way is reducible to natural theology; on the contrary, it is a principle that the Church has consistently maintained (implicitly or explicitly) in view of every (naturalizing or supernaturalizing) attempt to conflate God with the world — even as it also stands as a check against every radical sundering of God and the world.

How, though, more specifically, does Przywara respond to Barth's criticisms — say, that the *analogia entis* posits an understanding of creation as revelation or that it follows the Thomistic principle that grace does not destroy but presupposes and perfects nature? To the first of these criticisms Przywara simply gives no response; he stands with Bonaventure and the majority, if not entirety of the Catholic tradition: "Whoever is not enlightened by such great splendor in created things is blind; whoever remains unheedful of such great outcries is deaf; whoever does not praise God in all these effects is dumb; whoever does not turn to the First Principle after so many signs is a fool."[292] That is to say, for the Catholic tradition, *contra* Barth, creation *is* a revelation, which *should* elicit praise of the Creator, even if it is only a general revelation, and even if one's perception of God in this revelation (as Augustine emphasized no less than the Reformers) is greatly obscured by sin. Consequently, the Catholic tradition has never denied a modicum of natural theology. Nor, by the same token, has it ever posited a contradiction between God's unique and complete self-revelation in Christ (as *the* revelation of the Logos) and a general revelation in creation (as a work and manifestation of the same Logos), as though traces of the Logos could not be found in creation even amid the wreckage of the world of original sin. For, according to Scripture, "all things came into being through him" (John 1:3), and, according to a metaphysical reading of John 1:11, "He came unto *his own*, and *his own* received him not."

As a matter of fidelity to Scripture itself, therefore, it is impossible for Catholic theology to posit, notwithstanding the reality of original sin, a *metaphysical* contradiction between the one revelation and the other; it is rather that sin contradicts what is fundamentally, metaphysically, and originally an *analogy*, which Christ came to redeem. All of which relates to the second criticism, which Przywara equally cannot deny, since for Catholic theology grace *does* presuppose nature and *is* predicated upon a prior but incomplete revelation through creation — just as the New Testament presupposes the Old Testament, which it fulfills.[293] Thus, as far as these two criti-

---

292. *The Journey of the Mind to God,* trans. Philotheus Boehner (Indianapolis: Hackett, 1993), p. 10.

293. See, for example, Przywara's article, "Der Grundsatz, 'Gratia non destruit sed

cisms are concerned, Barth genuinely does force a choice between himself and the Catholic tradition, which leaves as the strongest remaining criticisms: 1) that the *analogia entis* nevertheless presents a misleading picture of our relation to God as "open upward," failing sufficiently to register the effects of sin; 2) that Catholic theology, as exemplified in the *analogia entis,* has things methodologically backwards in that it begins with reason and philosophy and not with faith and revelation; and 3) that the *analogia entis* relates God and creation already as a matter of philosophical metaphysics and thereby threatens the uniqueness of Christ as the mediator.

Regarding the first of the remaining criticisms, Barth appears to have a point; for in Przywara's early works he tends not so much to emphasize the sinfulness of human beings as to note in creation and its antitheses a mysterious analogue and proto-revelation of Christ, who unites all things in himself. As he poetically put it in his first work *Eucharistie und Arbeit:*

> *Christ is the eternal archetype of the inner and outer world.* All the beauty of the cosmos — the majesty of the high mountain range, the lovely simplicity of the verdant fields, the brilliant concert of birds in the springtime forests and the cracking and thundering of storms at night, the still solitude of the mountain retreat and the powerful rushing together of the industrial city — is a manifold image of his unity.[294]

From Barth's perspective, certainly, such passages would seem to blur the difference between God and creation (which is precisely how he also read Przywara's later formulations of the *analogia entis*), calling for his dialectical rebuttal. But if the problem of sin does not feature prominently in Przywara's earliest works, by the time of his 1926 philosophy of religion, upon which Barth's criticisms were largely based, Przywara clearly makes a point of it: "Between supernatural elevation and supernatural redemption stands, according to Catholic teaching, the *mysterium iniquitatis* of original sin . . . which is wiped away only by the God-man as the Redeemer."[295] So, too, in the *Analogia Entis* he treats the tragic conclusions reached by the philosophies of Plato and Aristotle in terms of this same theologoumenon of original sin and redemption.[296] And in later works he continues to take sin into

---

supponit et perficit naturam.' Eine ideengeschichtliche Interpretation," *Scholastik* 17 (1942): 178-86.

294. *Schriften,* vol. 1, p. 7; Przywara's emphasis.
295. *Schriften,* vol. 2, p. 506.
296. See *AE* §7, 4-6.

account, as when he says in "Philosophies of Essence and Existence": "What we mean by Christianity is, firstly, *redemption from original sin,* the sin in which man wanted to be 'like God, knowing the difference between good and evil'"; or when he speaks of original sin as that "final tragedy" whereby the human being resists "love in the Cross" and redemptive participation in the authentic human nature of God in Christ. In sum, for Przywara, original sin is precisely what *contradicts* (without destroying) the original analogy of the *imago Dei* and is overcome solely by participation in the justifying mediation of Christ.[297]

In no sense, therefore, does the *analogia entis,* concretely understood, fail to account for the reality of sin or the need for redemption — though, given Barth's concerns, one could reasonably wish that Przywara had distinguished more clearly between a natural "relation" between God and creatures, i.e., a natural *analogia entis,* which obtains in spite of the Fall simply by virtue of the Creator-creature relation, and a saving "relationship" with God (and redemption of the original analogy) through Christ.[298] For when Przywara says that the creature is "in its essence" structurally "open upward" to God, this in no way means that the creature is necessarily open to God in an existential sense.[299] Nor by any stretch of the imagination does the

---

297. See *AE,* pp. 337-38. See also the highly relevant essay in the present volume *"Imago Dei"*: "On the one hand, it is not the case that this *consortium anti-Dei* would extinguish the *imago Dei* (for even in the *consortium anti-Dei* the human being remains human 'in nature' and so, as such, the *imago Dei*). On the other hand, it *is* the case "the human being becomes a contradiction between the *imago Dei,* which originates with God, and the *consortium anti-Dei,* which is subject to Satan — as distinct from the original state of an analogy between the *imago Dei* and the *consortium Dei*" (*AE,* p. 566).

298. Doubtless some of the confusion here has to do with Przywara's early formulation of the *analogia entis* as "God in us and God above us," which could give the mistaken impression that for Przywara human beings are already in a "right relationship" with God by virtue of their mere existence (cf. Acts 17:28). Clearly, however, this is not the case. For to say that God is "in us" according to a natural *analogia entis* is merely to say (1) that God, though absolutely transcendent of the creature, is also the ultimate ground and interior of the creature by virtue of God's omnipresence to and interior sustaining of creation and (2) that God is analogously expressed in his creation and, in particular, in human beings as his image. But, since creation is also fallen, none of this is to be confused with a supernaturally redeemed and elevated *analogia entis,* whereby through faith in Christ God truly and more profoundly indwells his creation, being now interior to the will of the creature that has received him, liberating it from sin and refashioning it into a *genuine* likeness.

299. This must be said in response to Johnson's conclusion that, for Przywara, by virtue of the *analogia entis,* "[h]uman existence itself, because it occurs within the tension of this relationship, pushes the creature towards God as the One in whom it lives and has its be-

analogia entis, as a created structure, automatically entail salvation — no more than nature automatically entails grace. For that matter, at a purely structural, metaphysical level, while immanent to existence as an entelechy, the essence of the creature is also, paradoxically, something to be attained (according to the metaphysical formula "essence in-and-beyond existence"), this being, in turn, the metaphysical foundation for the equally paradoxical moral imperative to "become what you are," i.e., to *be* the image of God. And even then, in addition to the metaphysical possibility of failure, it is clear that for Przywara the attainment of the creature's essence is obstructed by original sin, requiring the grace of redemption through Christ, in whom alone, by virtue of membership in his body, the Church, one becomes who one is.

The second of Barth's remaining criticisms, concerning Przywara's methodology and, by extension, Vatican I's doctrine of a *duplex ordo* between nature and grace, is harder to dispel given the nature of Przywara's vocation as a philosophical theologian, who works immanently through the problems of philosophy, as well as popular, Neo-scholastic conceptions of the *duplex ordo* as entailing two fundamentally separate spheres — as it were, one secular, the other sacred. But as von Balthasar (also the student of de Lubac) points out, for Przywara nature and grace cannot be construed as two orders that are essentially extrinsic to one another, leaving the surd of an imaginary realm called "pure nature," whose investigation would constitute the proper philosophical point of departure for theology. For one thing this ignores the problem of original sin we have just addressed, which rules out the possibility of nature or history providing a sure foundation, i.e., an unambiguous deposit of truths, upon which theology had only to build; for another thing, while grace presupposes nature (in keeping with one aspect of the Thomistic maxim), nature is also, as for de Lubac, always already ordered *to* the grace that redeems and perfects it (in keeping with the other aspect of the Thomistic maxim).

Thus, for Przywara, while nature and grace are analogically distinct, as two different gifts, there is ultimately only *one* economy of salvation *within* which nature is ordered *to* grace.[300] As he puts it in "Philosophy as a Prob-

---

ing" (*Karl Barth and the* Analogia Entis, p. 81). This might apply to an abstract *analogia entis,* but not to the one and only concrete *analogia entis* that obtains within the one order of original sin and redemption.

300. See in this regard Przywara's early essay, "Einheit von Natur und Übernatur?" *Stimmen der Zeit* 105 (1923): 428-40; reprinted in *Schriften,* vol. 2, pp. 27-45.

lem": "there is only one concretely existing order between God and creature in this concretely existing world: the order between original sin in Adam and redemption in Christ, the crucified."[301] Nor, for Przywara, can this single ordering of nature to grace be said to compromise the *novelty* of revelation and grace in Christ, as Barth feared. For, as he clearly states already in his philosophy of religion from 1926, "the incarnation of God is nothing that could in any way be calculated"; equally, however, for reasons we have seen and because there is ultimately only one order of salvation within which creation and redemption take place and unfold, it cannot be something contradictory.[302] Accordingly, summing up his analogical approach as the only way to avoid either conflating or radically sundering the orders of nature and grace, the natural and the supernatural, he writes: "In *God* nature and the supernatural are inseparably united according to their objective essence in that the 'gift of participation' [*Teilgeben*] in the supernatural is simply the unanticipated and unmerited fulfillment of that analogous 'gift of participation' that is the essence of nature: the 'participation in the divine nature' [should be understood] as the blessed crowning of 'in him we live and move and have our being.'"[303]

But what of the final criticism, namely, that the *analogia entis* posits a general revelation in creation and a general relatedness of creatures to God that supposedly detracts from the uniqueness of Christ as the mediator? Once again, part of the problem here is that in Przywara's early work, and in passages we have already adduced, he does not distinguish clearly enough between God's "self-revelation" in creation and his self-revelation in Christ, when it may have been better (and less politically troubling) to avoid the personal prefix in the case of the former. But even here it should be clear on other grounds that Przywara uses the term *self-revelation* analogically, since nature and grace are *analogically* related, which makes nature, *at best*, an in-

---

301. *AE*, pp. 402-3. Indeed, he goes on to say, "The concretely existing face of philosophy (every philosophy, that is, found within the concretely existing world and its history) is not visible except from the perspective of this order (within which, as an objectively universal order, every concretely existing human being stands, whether he knows it or not)." Cf. *Deus Semper Maior*, vol. 3, pp. 374, 384, quoted by von Balthasar in *The Theology of Karl Barth*, p. 360: "The mystery of salvation, that is, its ultimate fulfillment in the course of salvation history from creation to exaltation, from original sin to redemption, [is] in fact first in the counsels of God, since God 'has chosen us from before the foundation of the world, adopting us as his children'"; "For ultimately the priority of the mystery of Christ over the mystery of the Antichrist is the real inner meaning of all things."

302. *Schriften*, vol. 2, p. 442.

303. *Schriften*, vol. 2, p. 34; *Ringen der Gegenwart*, p. 429.

direct revelation, whose testimony is corrupted and made ambiguous by sin.[304] If, though, Barth could reasonably have had such worries prior to 1932, from the *Analogia Entis* onward such criticisms are more than adequately addressed. As Przywara notes in his discussion of analogy in Thomas, all forms of creaturely mediation "fall short of the *personal* revelation of God as middle in 'the mediator.' Christ appears as *the* reality of the way in which God-the-middle takes up the All: as the "infinity that assumes *(infinita virtus assumentis),* he is the unifying head of everything from the invisible to the visible, not only of all persons of every age, but also of pure spirits."[305] Similarly, in his *Summula,* which is based on a series of lectures originally given in 1941, he writes:

> Anything that could be considered a path to God and an image of God is but a shadowy intimation whose corresponding visible form is revealed only in the one who is God's only "interpretation." Indeed, he alone is God's "pro-ceeding" *(ex-egesis),* God's visibility: Jesus Christ. According to his own eternal decree (Eph. 1ff.), God is revealed nowhere else but in Christ. . . . Consequently, everything that might be a way to God or an image of God is only a glimmer or a first intimation of what alone is revealed in Christ. All the traits in which God shines before the creature are themselves drawn out and interpreted only in Christ. [They are traits] of the only true and only real God only insofar as they are aspects of the God who steps forth and interprets himself in Christ: the God who is only God as Father, Son and Holy Spirit. There is no other God beside him, and thus all general traits of God are either the prior or subsequent radiance of Father, Son and Holy Spirit.[306]

304. This must be said in response to Johnson's problematic claim that, for Przywara, "the whole of creation is an 'incarnation-cosmos' and is *just as much* a self-revelation of God as the incarnate Jesus was, because the direction of the revelation is the same: 'above to below'" (*Karl Barth and the* Analogia Entis, p. 75; my emphasis). If this were really what Przywara believed, then on grounds of orthodoxy it would have to be rejected; but, clearly, it was not.

305. *AE* §7, 6, p. 301.

306. Przywara, *Summula* (Nürnberg: Glock und Lutz, 1946); quoted by von Balthasar in *The Theology of Karl Barth,* p. 328 (translation slightly revised). For Przywara, accordingly, it is in Christ alone, surpassing every shadowy and indirect intimation of divine presence, that God is fully present *in* — immanent to — the finite; and in him alone, therefore, as "Immanuel," that we also *see* the absolute *transcendence* of God. For comprising in himself the full span of the "in-and-beyond" of analogy, Christ alone *is* the measure of being, in relation to whom every other manifestation of God is but an analogy and approximation:

And, finally, as he unambiguously puts it in "Between Metaphysics and Christianity": "It is precisely in the unresolved and irresolvable *Mysterium Crucis* in the Crucified Christ that we see *the* 'Logos' and 'icon' and 'mirror' and 'reflection' and 'image' and 'appearance and exegesis' of the God 'whom no one has ever seen or can see' (1 Tim. 6:16)."[307] This is why von Balthasar can speak without hesitation of Przywara's "Christocentric starting point" as determinative even of his metaphysics, and advise that these and similar passages "should by no means be overlooked if we are to contrast Przywara with Barth" or "use Przywara as our way of responding to Barth's *Dogmatics*."[308] For in the end (if not already well before) it is clear that for Przywara the real bond, the real *analogia entis,* between God and world is no abstract analogy (based upon a merely metaphysical Logos and a merely philosophical doctrine of participation), but precisely the *incarnate* Logos, the Logos-made-Flesh; and not only the incarnate Logos, but the Logos who was "slain from the foundation of the world" (Rev. 13:8). As he puts it in his remarkable commentary on the gospel of John: "This is *the* message of 'John the theologian': how God and cosmos are correlated [*zueinander*] in the 'Logos-Lamb who was slain.'"[309]

One can hardly be surprised, then, in view of both his late *and his early work,* that Przywara considered Barth's representation of his doctrine to be a "grotesque distortion" of his views.[310] As he put it in a late clarification from 1955: "If [the *analogia entis*] is the invention of Antichrist . . . (and if his use of this phrase is anything other than a joke to be received in the spirit of camaraderie as I have long taken it to be), then my dear old friend Karl Barth should relearn from the old Greek monks the meaning of the phrase 'discernment of spirits.'"[311] And in the same context he gives an important clarification of his doctrine that is worth quoting in full, adding that the doctrine is ultimately so "simple" — the idea that God is "ever greater" — that it too, in fulfillment of the gospel (Matt. 11:25), is "hidden from the wise and the intelligent, but revealed to babes":

---

from the natural revelation of creation, with its basic "in-and-beyond" structure, to his greater self-revelation in the saints, his mystical body, who are truly indwelled by him and shaped by the Holy Spirit into his likeness.

307. *AE,* p. 535.

308. *The Theology of Karl Barth,* pp. 328, 39.

309. See *Christentum gemäß Johannes,* p. 25; see also and especially Przywara's late work from 1963, *Logos.*

310. *In und Gegen,* p. 278.

311. *In und Gegen,* p. 278.

Analogia entis is an abbreviated way of stating what the Fourth Lateran Council . . . defined in 1215: that even in the most exalted regions of the supernatural (as was here at issue with the Trinitarian mysticism [of Joachim of Fiore]), "one cannot note any similarity between creator and creature, however great, without being compelled to observe an ever greater dissimilarity between them." Thus *analogia entis* in no way signifies a "natural theology"; on the contrary, it obtains precisely in the domain of the supernatural and the genuinely Christian. Nor does it signify a "theological-philosophical doctrine, according to which the created world is directed to God"; still less does it signify a comprehensible ontological nexus between Creator, creation, and creature. On the contrary, *analogia entis* signifies that what is decisive in "every similarity, however great," is the "ever greater dissimilarity." It signifies, so to speak, God's "dynamic transcendence," i.e., that God is ever above and beyond [*je-über-hinaus*] "everything external to him and everything that can be conceived," as was stressed in the "negative theology" of the Greek fathers and transmitted like a "sacred relic" from Augustine to Thomas to the [first] Vatican Council. My dear friends — from Karl Barth to Söhngen to Haecker to Balthasar — have apparently never grasped that "analogia," according to Aristotle, is a "proportion between two X" (see my *Analogia Entis!*).[312]

312. *In und Gegen,* pp. 277-78. In what way Przywara may have felt misunderstood even by von Balthasar is less certain, and may have to do with tensions in their relationship at this time, owing to issues related to Przywara's illness, his care, and the management of his affairs. See Lochbrunner, *Hans Urs von Balthasar und seine Theologen-Kollegen,* p. 74. To judge from their correspondence, however, this much seems clear: upon a first reading of *The Glory of the Lord,* Przywara concluded that Balthasar's aesthetics moved too much in the opposite direction of his *analogia entis,* that is, not toward an ever greater dissimilarity *in infinitum,* and thus into mystery, but toward the greater similarity, no longer qualified by analogy, of the manifestation of the "beautiful in itself." See his letter to von Balthasar from January 13, 1962 (Lochbrunner, p. 77). For his part, on the other hand, von Balthasar expresses a concern that the rhythm of the *analogia entis* is ultimately so dynamic as to compromise the givenness of the *form* of revelation. See *Theodramatik* II/1 (Einsiedeln: Johannes Verlag, 1976), p. 325. In short, from Przywara's perspective, von Balthasar seemed too kataphatic; from von Balthasar's perspective, Przywara seemed too apophatic. Von Balthasar's response to Przywara, though, would seem to resolve any misunderstanding between them and express well what both of them believed: that the *maior dissimilitudo* of God is revealed in the form of Christ without being exhausted, since God's self-revelation in Christ cannot be understood apart from the mystery of the Trinity, which precisely in its revelation "is more profoundly veiled as *anexeraúneton* [unsearchable] and *anexichníaston* [inscrutable] [Rom. 11:33]." Indeed, for von Balthasar it is precisely this presence of the *excessive* — of the abso-

Clearly, Przywara felt misunderstood — and not without good reason. For, leaving aside his mature works, we have seen that many of Barth's criticisms, and certainly the more popular versions of them, do not apply even to Przywara's *early* formulations of the *analogia entis*, and that, right from the start, one can pick up a certain amount of distortion in Barth's reproduction of Przywara's doctrine. To use an analogy: it is like a musical score that is played using only half of the instruments that the composer had intended for it, or a piece of music that is played out of tune, or with some instruments played too loudly, others too softly; in which case, what one hears both is and is not the actual score. All of which would seem to demand that one hear the actual score as it was intended — and the *full* score, including the essays included in Part II of the present volume — before passing judgment on it.[313]

5.5. Rapprochement?

So what, in the end, is one to make of Barth's criticisms? On the one hand, *pace* Keith Johnson, whose important and admirable work has greatly clarified Barth's reasons for rejecting the *analogia entis*, one cannot proceed as though the debate about the *analogia entis* has not been plagued by misunderstanding. On the other hand, even after all the historical misunderstandings are cleared up and the distortion is removed, Johnson has convincingly shown that Barth felt compelled to reject the *analogia entis* on the basis of his own theological commitments and those underlying aspects of Przywara's

---

lutely transcendent fully *in* the immanent, of *Deus excessus* fully *in* the form of Christ — that makes Christ the "concrete *analogia entis*" and makes God's self-revelation in Christ a revelation of his glory [*kabôd*]. See Lochbrunner, *Hans Urs von Balthasar und seine Theologen-Kollegen*, p. 81. See von Balthasar, *Theo-Drama*, vol. 3 (San Francisco: Ignatius Press, 1993), pp. 221-22.

313. Admittedly, in Barth's defense, the *analogia entis* is a doctrine that can all too easily be read without the crucial footnotes and clarifications; and so perhaps the most charitable reading of his harsh response to Przywara is to say that (beyond establishing his own theological position) he was responding to the very real danger that the *analogia entis* (like Brunner's natural theology) could provide a metaphysical basis for seeing a "self-revelation" of God in contemporary cultural movements like National Socialism. But, of course, such a use of the *analogia entis* would never have been anything but a grotesque misuse and misunderstanding of the doctrine; for that matter, it ignores the fact that Przywara employed the *analogia entis* throughout the 1920s and 1930s precisely as a bludgeon against every conflation of God and humanity, as he found in both the immanentism of liberal Protestantism *and* the "blood and soil" ideology of National Socialism.

doctrine that remained incompatible with them — such as the Catholic doctrines that creation *is* a revelation and that this *can* be recognized by reason; that grace (faith) does not destroy but presupposes and perfects nature (reason); and that the effects of original sin, however great, have not totally destroyed the capacity of human beings to respond to grace on the basis of their created natures as secondary causes. Indeed, it seems that in this regard Barth understood Przywara (and Catholic theology) perfectly well; and to this extent his criticisms of the *analogia entis,* far from being incidental to ecumenical discussion, inevitably force a choice, not just between his views and Przywara's, but between his views and those of the Catholic Church.

To conclude on a positive note, however, it cannot be denied that Barth's criticisms caused Przywara to think more deeply about his own position, just as Przywara's early criticisms of Barth caused Barth to think more deeply about the problems with his early dialectical theology. And in this regard the encounter with Barth must be considered a mutually "fruitful one," as Przywara himself indicates in the preface to the *Analogia Entis* — causing him to be clearer about the "theocentric" nature of the *analogia entis,* and possibly playing a factor in his ever more explicit centering of the *analogia entis* in Christ as *the* measure of the relation between God and creation (Eph. 4:7-10), in whom all things hold together (Col. 1:17). One could even see the debate between Barth and Przywara as Otto Hermann Pesch, in his classic work, viewed the relation between Luther and Thomas Aquinas, which it in some ways mirrors, namely, in terms of the complementary difference between a predominately "existential" and a predominately "sapiential" theology.[314] To be sure, this is a simplification, but at least superficially Barth (like Luther) is more concerned about the *novelty* of revelation in the *event* of faith, in which the individual is sovereignly grasped and saved by a sovereign God; whereas Przywara (like Thomas) is at least superficially more concerned about the total mystery of the being of the cosmos as arising from God and returning to God in and through Christ. Clearly, such emphases need not — and ultimately cannot — be opposed; and so, in conclusion, one might dare to hope that the differences between the confessions are not so great and insurmountable as the debate between Barth and Przywara could lead one to suppose.

314. See Otto Hermann Pesch, *Die Theologie der Rechtfertigung bei Martin Luther und Thomas von Aquin* (Mainz: Matthias Grünewald Verlag, 1967), pp. 935-48.

PART I

Original Structure

Prior to any material metaphysics stands the question of its formal principle: so much so, in fact, that its very character as a critical science depends upon whether and to what degree this question — before every other that might be asked — has been examined.

But then, logically, it is a double question. It is addressed firstly and most basically to metaphysics "as such": What kind of fundamental structure is manifest within its formal concept? For it is in this fundamental structure, understood as the formal principle of metaphysics "as such," that the further question concerning the formal principle of "this" particular metaphysics finds its critical measure. The formal principle of "this" metaphysics will be critically justified not only insofar as it can "prove itself" against the formal principle of metaphysics "as such," but insofar as it in fact "corresponds" to it — indeed, ideally speaking, is actually "demanded" by it.

It is in this sense that we begin with the problem of metaphysics as such.

§1 Meta-Noetics and Meta-Ontics

1. *Metaphysics* was originally, as is well known, merely the bibliographical designation assigned to the collection of Aristotle's ontological writings that followed (μετὰ) his *"Physics."* It is a quite irreversible fact, however, that the word *metaphysics* developed into a technical designation for a specific field of inquiry, and so, given this fact, it is still best to derive our formal problem from this term.

Today it is common to think of the "physical" as the antonym of the "psychical," and ultimately (in virtue of an idealism of "pure validity" and modern psychology's principle of actuality)[1] in terms of the opposition between "being and consciousness," or even between "reality and ideality." For Aristotle, however, the relation between the two is that of the more universal to the particular. *Physis* is that mode of being whereby an entity relies on itself for its existence and operations (ἔχοντα ἐν ἑαυτοῖς ἀρχὴν κινήσεως καὶ στάσεως).[2] *Psyche*, on the other hand, as the "defining-shape"[3] (εἶδος-μορφὴ)

---

1. *Aktualitäts-Psychologie*. Przywara seems to have in mind here the theory of actuality proposed by the modern psychologist Wilhelm Wundt (1832-1920), for whom the soul has no substance but is more or less the product and sum of its acts. — Trans.

2. Having in itself the principle of movement and of rest. *Phys.* II, 1, 192b, 13.

3. *Sinn-Gestalt*. The phrases rendered below as "ground and end and definition" and "place of definitions" are in the German *"Grund und Ziel und Sinn"* and *"Sinn-Ort."* In choosing to use *"Sinn"* rather than *"Idee"* as the equivalent for εἶδος, at least in regard to Aristotle's thought, Przywara is exploiting a range of connotations contained in the German word to which no available English word quite corresponds. One might plausibly prefer to translate the word here as "scheme" or "paradigm," but it seems best to use the word "definition" (or, alternatively, "determination") because it possesses several of the connotations *Sinn* seems to have in this context (the *finis* in "definition," for instance, offers at least an echo of the "directedness" of *Sinn*). More importantly, the crucial phrase *"Grund und Ziel*

of the body — and especially in the νοῦς, the apex of *psyche* — is the most exalted form of this power of self-grounding: it is such a "ground and end and definition in itself" (ἐν-τελ-έχεια) that it is ultimately the very "place of definitions as such" (τόπος εἰδῶν),[4] the "*eidos* of *eidē*."[5] "Meta-physics," accordingly, means a "going behind" into the "back-grounds" of the being proper to *physis,* whose highest instance is *psyche.* What is at issue, then, is the formal question of this "ground and end and definition in itself," which poses itself here from the question of being as being.

2. But already with the posing of this question we discover the first formal problem of such a metaphysics. The question poses itself in the questioner with regard to the question's object: my "act of consciousness" interrogates being regarding its "ground and end and definition." And it is a matter of indifference here whether I say, "My question is the self-expression of Being, which questions" (as does Heidegger) or "My question is the question of consciousness concerning being" (as does German idealism). It is also a matter of indifference (though to a lesser degree) whether I say (along with the whole of modern philosophy, from Descartes and Kant on through Heidegger), "My question is more originally the question concerning being in the consciousness that questions" or (along with the Scholastics) "My question proceeds through consciousness and beyond it to being." In all these ways of framing the matter, some more formal principle has been predetermined, which this last version of the question certainly hints at, but still fails to articulate. For prior to either approach to the issue lies a neutral duality between the act of cognition, which questions, and the object of cognition, at which its question is directed. Of course, between these poles are located both the objective sense of the question in itself and the objective orientation of the answer in itself (which leads to the ideative construct of an "objective answer"). But these are both already concerned with the question's procedure, not its presuppositions. Moreover, they themselves already participate in one very particular explanation of these presuppositions: namely, the theory that objective idealism provides regarding the nature of this question-posing act of knowledge. The only thing that remains strictly neutral is the duality to which we adverted above: the act of knowledge and the act of being, understood as the object of the act of knowledge. This duality establishes our first formal problem, which should,

---

und Sinn" is later complemented by the phrase "*begründet, gerichtet, und bestimmt*" — grounded, directed, and determined. — Trans.

4. Place of the ideas. *De Anima* III, 4, 429a, 27f.

5. *De Anima* III, 8, 432a, 2.

accordingly, be phrased thus: Is a metaphysics (understood as the question concerning the "ground and being and definition in itself"[6] of being) primarily one that takes its point of departure from a reflection upon the act of knowledge (and so from a *meta-noetics* of knowledge *qua* knowledge)? Or is it primarily one whose intention proceeds immediately towards the object of knowledge (and is thus a *meta-ontics* of being *qua* being)? This question has precedence, because it is also raised even in those instances when it is the being of the act of knowledge itself that is under interrogation: that is, even in *this* question, one must distinguish between the act of knowledge, which questions, and the *being* of the act of knowledge, which is questioned. On the other hand, it becomes obvious from this that our question concerns which of these definitions of metaphysics is *primary,* but not which definition is *exclusive.* We pose our either-or not between a meta-noetics and a meta-ontics, but between a meta-noetics that provides the point of departure for a meta-ontics and a meta-ontics that finds its reflection, at the last, in a meta-noetics. When the issue is formulated thus, the historical opposition that otherwise holds between a pure meta-noetics (as in the case of a closed idealism of consciousness) and a pure meta-ontics (as in the case of certain directions within phenomenology) has already resolved itself. This neutral duality — which cannot simply be interpreted away — between the act of knowledge and the object of knowledge (in the sense given above) leaves open no possibility of a retreat on the part of either into the enclosure of its own "purity." The meta-noetic transcends itself, in a forward intentionality, towards the meta-ontic. The meta-ontic moves backward in self-critique, reflexively, towards the meta-noetic. The question, therefore, is simply which of these two forms of metaphysics objectively has priority — or whether, as may be the case, both point beyond themselves to their mutual interpenetration.

3. The *first form* of metaphysics has in its favor that it appears to leave no presupposition unexamined. According to its logic, an account of the *act* of knowledge (under the scrutiny of a critical examination from the very beginning) manifestly precedes any account of the *objects* of knowledge. Arguing against it, however, is firstly a certain *"in infinitum"* in its account of knowledge. For if it requires an account of the act of knowledge, then it clearly also requires a further account of this initial account itself, and so on. And it avails one nothing to turn for support to a so-called "concomitant reflection,"[7] for obviously such a reflection either constitutes a purely practical

---

6. *"In sich selbst Grund und Sein und Sinn."* — Trans.
7. *Mitvollziehende Reflexion.* — Trans.

accompaniment, in which case its attendance is one of observation, not examination; or it is truly critically reflective, in which case it is itself subject to the imperative of examination. The second consideration is still more serious. No account can be given at all that is not cast in the form of certain ontological categories. This is most conspicuous in the very term "act of knowledge": for "act" implies "potency," and "act" and "potency" are ontology's most general categories. Indeed, this, moreover, is what proves strangely inevitable in general for all talk — even if it be concerned only with method — of a so-called "pure consciousness." Not only does any comprehension of pure consciousness (whether it be comprehended as one's own or as other than oneself) occur by way of objects (at the very least, in the inevitability with which the "I" rings out, and then in the intricate intertwinings of the I in "things" and "fellow I's"), but even the inner form of this comprehension has itself the character of an object. Even Kant's pure categories of judgment bear the form of ontological categories: quality, quantity, modality, etc. Even Hegel's retreat to the inner and most formal species of judgment runs up against an expression proper to ontology: identity and opposition. Even the most formal comportment of consciousness as such — relation (that between act and object) — has an ontological shape. And even what is most proper to "pure consciousness" (in the sense given this phrase by objective idealism) succumbs to this reality: in the permanence of "validity" there rings out the "there" — the "*Da*" — of a *Dasein* (existence); in the ideality of "validity," the "thus" — the "*So*" — of *Sosein* (essence).

So it would seem that everything militates in favor of the *second form* of metaphysics (i.e., the construction of a method of meta-ontics, which only subsequently re-flects itself in a critical meta-noetics). The same arguments adduced against a meta-noetic point of departure provide positive arguments for beginning from the meta-ontic. Against this, however, there stands the consideration that such a method still makes practical use of a very particular epistemology. And while it may be the privilege of the lived life to rest content merely with its factical situation, it is the duty of metaphysics, as a scientific endeavor, to persevere in critical examination. The epistemology that this method in practice employs is one that presumes a complete adequation between knowledge and being: so complete, in fact, that knowledge is nothing other than being brought to expression — indeed, being manifesting itself to itself (because only then can a tension between the "what" and the "how" be ruled out). Hence, if I hold that an epistemology is to be erected upon the basis of the reasons just given, then obviously an explanation of these reasons would objectively have to precede any implementation (insofar as what is at issue here is a science, not merely lived life). But this means that primacy as regards method belongs to meta-noetics. And naturally this is even more the case if I then add qualifications (as in, for example, scholasticism, with its distinction between the *modus quo* and the *id quod* of knowledge).

It becomes obvious then, from how intrinsically these considerations follow from one another, that even in the case of an extreme, predominantly meta-ontic method, the meta-noetic point of departure is unavoidable. According to its own formal structure, therefore, metaphysics must begin from the problem of the act. Thus, on the one hand, it will be concerned with an immanent meta-noetics (that is, not with a problematic of the act that stands under the regime of meta-ontic categories introduced adventitiously, but one that proceeds in accordance with laws immanent to itself). On the other hand, it must be a meta-noetics that is conscious that it is pervaded from the start by the meta-ontic. In this respect, it will not only take aim from consciousness "towards" being (as do various forms of epistemological realism), but will develop its meta-ontic categories within and out of consciousness' own immanent reflection. The subsequent problem of a meta-ontics is then the explicit consideration of the meta-ontic categories themselves. It is, to be sure, in keeping with the radicality of the problem of being, a new and independent starting point. But, on the one hand, it rests upon the meta-noetic to the extent that its development of meta-ontic categories immanent to its act comes to clear *expression* in the meta-ontic. On the other hand, we have arrived anew at the meta-noetic, since now the circumference of its problem becomes visible, within the meta-ontic, from the vantage of the ontic. Clearly, if consciousness and being are thus connected to one another in the problems both of act and of being, then the final problem of metaphysics must be just this mutual belonging — this "to one another"[8] — itself (which is to say, the structure of the "world," which subsists in this "to one another"). Here we see the culmination of this formal structure — that of "inaugurating a new beginning by simultaneously pointing back towards and recapturing what has gone before." For, on the one hand, this "to one another" is an altogether new problem. On the other hand, it is the most incisive way of stating our conclusion with regard to our first two problems: the confluence of the meta-noetic and the meta-ontic. It is here that the problem of the meta-noetic and the meta-ontic is for the first time posed

8. *Zu einander.* — Trans.

fully, and so it is here, also, that all that has gone before resumes its most proper shape. The most formal and comprehensive structure of metaphysics, therefore, lies in this: by virtue of the ultimate correlation — *Zueinander* — of consciousness and being, its three problems unfold out of one another so intrinsically, from the first to the third, that, taken in reverse, from third to first, they show themselves to have been contained within one another from the beginning.

What we have here, however, is the most formal foundation of a "*creaturely* metaphysics." It is creaturely according to its most formal object: because it concerns the suspended tension[9] between consciousness and being (and not the *absoluteness* of the self-identity of either consciousness or being). It is creaturely, moreover and more decisively, according to its most formal method: because it proceeds according to the *in fieri* — becoming[10] — of a back-and-forth relation (and not by way of a discrimination between self-sufficient unities). This "creaturely metaphysics" is the metaphysics that arises immanently from the most formal problem of metaphysics as such.

It is clearly "creaturely," though, in that it is grounded upon the suspended tension of the correlation (in its object) and upon the becoming proper to the back-and-forth relation (in its method). In this regard, the suspended tension of the correlation (between consciousness and being) expresses the same thing as becoming proper to the back-and-forth relation. For the latter, as method, develops directly out of the former, taken as object: as, that is, the method intrinsically adequate to the object, or as — so to speak — "the object become method." But this becoming, which is proper to the back-and-forth relation, is none other than the venerable "Become what you are": the *thus* towards which becoming proceeds already is at the same time the *there* of that which becomes: which is to say, "the thus beyond the there" and yet "the thus in the there": hence, "the thus in-and-beyond the there." If we take into account that the meta-ontic is, in any case, the objectively prior and comprehensive category (while still granting methodological priority to the meta-noetic), then the formally constitutive basic formula of creaturely metaphysics, as it follows from the basic problem of metaphysics as such, can be stated thus: essence in-and-beyond existence.[11]

---

9. *Spannungs-Schwebe.* — Trans.
10. *Werdehaft.* — Trans.
11. *Sosein in-über Dasein.* — Trans.

§2 Metaphysical Transcendentalism and Transcendental Metaphysics

1. The terms *meta-noetic* and *meta-ontic* stand in need of further clarification. This becomes especially evident if we turn back to Aristotle. The νοῦς (whence comes the term "noetic") is the crowning instance within a hierarchy that comprises τέχνη (meaning a kind of making, γένος ποιήσεως, concerned with the beautiful, καλόν), ἐπιστήμη (meaning "pure science"), and φρόνησις (meaning a practical habit, ἕξις πρακτική, concerned with things good and bad, ἀγαθὰ καὶ κακά).[1] By the same token, διάνοια, thought, is expressly divided into three parts (practical, "poetical," and theoretical): πρακτική (the "good"), ποιητική (the "beautiful"), and θεωρητική (the "true").[2] The noetic is thus the unity (to employ a provisional term) of the scientific, ethical, and artistic comportments of consciousness. Correspondingly — when we turn to the meta-ontic — it is likewise evident that ὄν in no way signifies a purely factual presence. Ὄν, for Plato and Aristotle alike, is simply synonymous with the "proper being" of "the true, the good, and the beautiful." This is pointedly expressed by Aristotle, inasmuch as the categories of ὄν are simultaneously those of the true, the good, and the beautiful.[3] In turn, however, this is grounded in the intrinsically "energetic" character of ὄν, which presents itself as the relation "potency-act" (δύναμις-ἐνέργεια). As for the "ownmost possibility" (as Heidegger would render it) of the possible, δυνατόν, this points to a certain "essence beyond (existence)" and thus to something ontically "purely true."[4] But when instead

1. *Eth. Nic.* VI, 3-13, 1139b ff.

2. *Met.* VI, 1, 1025b, 25; *Eth. Nic.* VI, 2, 1139a, 27ff.

3. Cf. *Met.* II, 1, 993a, 30ff.; *Eth. Nic.* I, 4, 1096a, 23ff.; *Met.* XIII, 3, 1078a, 36ff.; *Poet.* 7, 1450b, 36ff., etc.

4. Cf. *Met.* V, 12, 1019b, 27f.; *je seine Möglichkeit.* — Trans.

the accent is put upon ἐνέργεια, it indicates the realm of virtue (ἀρετή) and so of the good (ἀγαθόν).[5] Which is to say that we gain a glimpse into an "ontic good": in the sense of the energetic becoming — the *in fieri* — of an "(essence) in-and-beyond (existence)." The Aristotelian distinction then between act, ἐνέργεια, and work, ἔργον[6] — in its correlation with the distinction between the done, πρακτόν, and the made, ποιητόν (which is equivalent to the beautiful, καλόν)[7] — grants one a definitive perspective upon the essential liminality of a being, ὄν, that *ideally* has "become" (ἔργον): by which one means an ideal unity of essence and existence, whether in the case of a "real ideality" ("ontically beautiful" in the sense of "pure shape"), or of a "reality rounded out" ("ontically beautiful" in the sense of "pure rhythm").

This yields the second formal problem of metaphysics. Truth, goodness, and beauty go by the name of the "transcendentals": in the thought of antiquity, they are principally meta-ontic; in Kantian transcendentalism, they are principally meta-noetic — as the inner formality of the acts of "pure reason" (the true), "practical reason" (the good), and synthesizing "judgment" (the beautiful). So our new problem is that of this transcendentalism in metaphysics.

2. Initially it can be phrased thus: Is this unity of transcendentalism and metaphysics of such a kind that the transcendentals are to be construed as determinations of the noetic? Or is it rather of such a kind that they hold true as determinations of the ontic? In the former case, it would be a matter of the metaphysics of a meta-noetic transcendentalism (in concrete terms, an immanent metaphysics of Kantian transcendentalism); in the latter case, conversely, a matter of a meta-ontic transcendentalism (in concrete terms, an unfolding of the prevailing meta-ontic tendencies in Plato and Aristotle). From this, however, it becomes clear that this first question was already implicitly decided in §1 above.

A second question may also have been decided: that, namely, concerning the inclusion within our method of the transcendentals as such. For, first of all, they are already objectively comprised, primordially, within the structure of *any* philosophy. The seemingly purest positivism of the "factual" and the seemingly purest formalism of "method" flow, both alike, into an ethics and an aesthetics. But this is also subjectively the case with the concept of

---

5. *Eth. Nic.* I, 1, 1094a, 3ff.; II, 1, 1103a, 26ff.
6. *Eth. Nic.* I, 1, 1094a, 4ff.
7. *Eth. Nic.* VI, 4, 1140a, 1ff.

knowledge as such (as later we shall see more precisely). In the positivism of "pure experience" the accent lies of course upon verification, which belongs to the "true" — but it is, at the same time, an accent modulated by resonances of a certain ethical "probity" and aesthetic "purity of style." So too, critical formalism, however much the purely "true" is vouchsafed it by the practice of critique, contains within itself (on account of the *"in infinitum"* of critique's articulation) both the infinity of the "pure striving" of the ethical and (on account of its "spontaneity") the "creating" and "shaping" of the artistic (whence, of course, it speaks of "matter" and "form"). And so, consequently, our question really concerns only this: whether one may simply rest content with this *de facto* play of the transcendentals within one's method, or whether one must rather consciously and critically include the transcendentals in one's method at the outset. To phrase the question thus, however, is already to have given the answer.

3. All that is at issue, then, is how to undertake this inclusion consciously and critically. On the one hand — in keeping with all the customary considerations — as far as method is concerned, it seems necessary to proceed from the outset from this sort of conscious and critical analysis, and so proceed within a kind of convergence of logical ("true"), ethical ("good"), and aesthetic ("beautiful") perspectives, which "transcend" towards being. What would obviously be at issue in this case would be an inner metaphysics of the transcendentals, and so a *metaphysical transcendentalism.*

Arguing against this, however, is that, of the three transcendentals, it is the "true" with which the metaphysical enterprise is distinctively associated. Certainly ethics and aesthetics can then constitute elements of such a metaphysics, but still only in subordination to the concern peculiar to metaphysics: that is, the intelligible "true." Indeed, inasmuch as they are elements of metaphysics (which also means, in the critically conscious form described above, elements of a convergence of perspectives), ethics and aesthetics are for this very reason no longer distinct as ethics and aesthetics. This is a consequence of the Aristotelian division of the three γένη: θεωρητικόν, πρακτικόν, ποιητικόν — the theoretical, practical, and productive. And this is expressed even more incisively by Thomas Aquinas, in that the inner relation between soul and thing, *anima* and *res,* which is properly common to the "true" and the "good," tends in two entirely opposite directions. With respect to the "true," it is said that it has its term in the soul: *terminatur ad animam;*[8] which culminates in the proposition that "true and false are in the

---

8. *De Ver.* q. 1, a. 2, corp.

mind": *verum et falsam . . . sunt in mente.*[9] With respect to the "good," however, it is said that it has its term in the thing: *terminatur ad res;*[10] which culminates in the antithesis, "good and evil are in things": *bonum et malum . . . sunt in rebus.*[11] And this dialectic between, on the one hand, a truth related to and immanent within the soul and, on the other, a good related to and immanent within things is resolved only in the factical objectivity of the *circulus,* which plays upon the path between consciousness *(anima)* and being *(res).*[12] From a reflexive and subjective standpoint, there are only two ways by which one might comprehend this circle.

First, one could do so by translating into method what Thomas says about the beautiful: namely, that on the one hand it goes together with the "true" by reason of its formal cause, *de ratione causae formalis,*[13] while on the other it is included within the good *(quicumque appetit bonum, appetit hoc ipso pulchrum).*[14] It would then be a matter of aesthetics as a synthesis of metaphysics (in the strict sense of the logically true) and ethics, which is what Kant clearly had in mind for his *Critique of Judgment* (as a synthesis between the *Critique of Pure Reason,* with its concern for the true, and the *Critique of Practical Reason,* with its concern for the good). In fact, even Romantic "contemplation" and Bergsonian and Schelerian "intuition" aim at the same thing. It is that *"one"* peculiar to the beautiful, whether found in the nuptial passivity of the "contemplation" of the work of art, or in the artist's creative parturition, wherein "soul" and "thing" are so thoroughly at one that whatever belongs to the thing is also "soul" (in its orientation towards the true), just as what belongs to the soul is also "thing" (in its orientation towards the good). This is, however, the inner formal problematic of aesthetics, which is posed between an aesthetics of the person (be it a psychological aesthetics or an aesthetics of shape) and an aesthetics of matter (be it a purely material aesthetics, like Semper's, or an aesthetics of the pure forms [of things]). Thus it becomes clear that the method we are attempting to use merely grasps what is peculiar to the beautiful itself. The circle between *anima* and *res* is ambiguous. It signifies, in one sense, the site of the beautiful — but not yet on this account the superordinated site of the

9. *Summa Th.* I, q. 82, a. 3, corp.

10. *De Ver.* q. 1, a. 2, corp.

11. *Summa Th.* I, q. 82, a. 3, corp.

12. *De Ver.* q. 1, a. 2, corp.

13. *Summa Th.* I, q. 6, a. 4.

14. Whosoever seeks the good seeks also, for that very reason, the beautiful. *De Ver.* q. 22, a. 1, ad. 12.

relation of the true, the good, and (distinguishing itself over against both) the beautiful.

Consequently, there remains only one way by which one might seek to grasp the circle in this, its superordinated sense. Thomas Aquinas points to it both in deriving the ontic transcendentals (the true, the good, and the beautiful, considered as the "properties of things") from the priority of *esse*,[15] and in finding the noetic transcendentals (truth, goodness, and beauty, but taken as orientations of consciousness: *intellectus, voluntas,* and — in addition — the Augustinian *memoria*) within the unity of the subject of consciousness.[16] The proper way forward would thus seem to demand that one grasp the correlation between this meta-transcendental *esse* and this meta-transcendental *homo* or, as the case may be, *anima*. But precisely such a path, as a path of "comprehension,"[17] is bound to what is distinctly proper to the transcendentals. For otherwise *esse* or, as the case may be, *homo-anima,* and *a fortiori* their correlation would be merely a one-sided metaphysicizing of one of the three transcendentals (in actual practice, the true).

Fundamentally, however, the problem does not come fully into view until we take into consideration the scholastic formula of the *notiones transcendentales,* which enumerates four transcendentals: *esse, unum, verum, bonum. Verum* and *bonum,* along with *pulchrum* (which, as with Thomas, is always implied), constitute the expression of the transcendentals in the narrower sense. *Esse* is, in the narrower sense, classified under metaphysics (following both Aristotle and Thomas Aquinas). *Unum,* however (as the problem of unity and multiplicity), concerns that concept of mathematics which stands at the center of philosophical method for Plato, Aristotle, Augustine *(incommutabilis veritas numerorum),* and Thomas Aquinas (to say nothing of the moderns), as the governing concept for both (objective) system and (subjective) rigor. This is surely also the case with Kant: the intention informing his (noetic) transcendentalism is that of a critical metaphysics (as Heidegger and Herrigel very rightly recognize) under the sovereign ideal of mathematical precision.

At this point the problem is cast in sharper relief, as offering three possibilities: a transcendentalism, which intrinsically becomes a metaphysics and a mathematics (this was the initial possibility of a "metaphysical transcendentalism" identified earlier); a metaphysics, which advances from a

---

15. *De Ver.* q. 1, a. 1, corp.; *De Ver.* q. 21, a. 1, corp.
16. *De Ver.* q. 10, a. 9, ad. 3 in contr.
17. *Erfassung.* — Trans.

meta-transcendental grasp of being (after the fashion, say, of Bergsonian intuition, understood as an immediate "oneness with life," or of the Heideggerean self-declaration of Being) to truth, goodness, and beauty, as the "three rays of being," and thus lays hold of this triplet's inner unity with itself (the *unum*); and finally a mathematics, conceived on the Pythagorean model — as, say, a meta-mathematics of ordinary science and technology — which discovers the essence of being and its threefold radiance (the three transcendentals) in the problem of unity and multiplicity. But inasmuch as history shows us that the (specifically mathematical) problem of unity and multiplicity is inevitably the final formal problem of every possible system (whether that of Plato, Aristotle, Augustine, Thomas Aquinas, Kant, or Hegel), what are in themselves three possibilities can be reduced yet again to two: a "metaphysical transcendentalism" and, over against it, a *transcendental metaphysics,* in the sense of the second possibility just sketched out.

The difficulty that is posed by these two possibilities is clearly the result of the points of departure proper to their respective methods: in the case of metaphysical transcendentalism, a comprehension of the threefold radiance of truth, goodness, and beauty, which aims at a comprehension of being *(esse)* in its unity *(unum);* in the case of transcendental metaphysics, a pre-transcendental, pure comprehension of being, which moves, according to its intention, towards a comprehension of being's threefold radiance *(verum-bonum-pulchrum)* and its unity *(unum).*

Examined dispassionately, both points of departure look like versions of a utopian "unconditioned purity of style." The former is contradicted by the fact that any "comprehension" is always a matter of somehow "knowing" something. It may be that the good and the beautiful are distinguished (noetically) from the true by the posture of a "knowing through and in striving (or, creating)." But this remains a "knowing." From this it becomes manifest how the relation of the transcendentals to one another is that of an implication of one by the other, but as subject to the varying formal primacy of one over the other (as must be clarified further below). Thus metaphysics will be distinctively associated with the true in such a way that the good and the beautiful will be comprised within it. The same holds true for ethics and aesthetics. In place of a "pure" threefold radiance, we thus have a threefold radiance that is characterized by three relations of prevalence. This also takes care of the difficulty posed by the second point of departure. A "pre-transcendental, pure comprehension of being" might well be the intended result of its theoretical system. But it is a fantasy. For all comprehension, be it ever so "elementary," falls under the rule of the true. Neutrality in this matter can therefore mean no more than this: that the act of comprehension, which is in fact subordinate to the true from the start, and so to the true's intrinsic relation to the good and the beautiful, will advance in its reflections at first only gradually towards a full recognition of this, its own formal configuration. In this way we reach an accord between the approaches proper to a metaphysical transcendentalism and a transcendental metaphysics.

The meta-noetic (as the first problem of metaphysics) will thus have to commence from a general problematic of consciousness, from which the threefold radiance of the transcendentals will then be gradually abstracted, in order thereby to guide this general problematic to its proper depth. Likewise, the meta-ontic (as the second problem) will allow a general problematic of being to evolve from within into a consideration of being in its transcendental aspect,[18] and thus into its more precise form. And, finally, in an explicit meta-physics (as we may well denominate the third problematic of the "correlation"[19] of consciousness and being), it is this very correlation (of the "world") that must proceed along the same path: from its most general shape, to an explicit recognition of its fully transcendental dimension (i.e., the correlation of the noetically and the ontically transcendental), to its ultimate formal structure.

We have seen how the problematic of the transcendental rolls out the intrinsic breadth of tension contained in "essence in-and-beyond existence." We have seen, furthermore, how the particular problematic of the *unum* (in the form of the mathematical) brings implications of "system" and "rigor" to the fundamental problem, as it is played out between a narrower transcendentalism and metaphysics, but therefore "system" and "rigor" as they intrinsically correspond to this intrinsic breadth of tension proper to "essence in-and-beyond existence" — which is to say, a "creaturely" system and a "creaturely" rigor. It is not simply that in the problematic of transcendentalism and metaphysics, the formal mode of becoming (proper to the back-and-forth relation) returns and, in this way, more forcefully confirms the structure of a "creaturely metaphysics." Rather, in addition to this, having previously identified "essence in-and-beyond existence" as the formally constitutive basic formula for this metaphysics, we now see the greater scope of its domain.

18. *In das Seins-Transzendentale.* — Trans.
19. *Zueinander.* — Trans.

§3 *A Priori* and *A Posteriori* Metaphysics

1. Earlier (in §1) we saw how the inner problematic of the word *metaphysics* yielded the phrase "ground and end and definition in itself" as metaphysics' most formal object. Regarded thus, metaphysics is the "going behind" into the "back-grounds" of being. But implicit in this, and pervading our entire problematic up to this point, is a very particular way of phrasing the question concerning the relation between these "back-grounds" and their "fore-grounds," between the "ground and end and definition" and that which is established by this ground, directed by this end, and determined by this definition.

Considered objectively, it is certainly the case that the "ground and end and definition," understood as "back-grounds," come "first," in that it is by these that everything else is established, directed, and determined. For this reason Aristotelian metaphysics is oriented towards being *qua* being, ὄν ἦ ὄν, as distinct from the various concrete regions of being. For this reason the ὄν ἦ ὄν proper to metaphysics is presented in categories: the most formal determinations of being common not only to all the concrete regions of being, but even to the transcendentals, the triad "true-good-beautiful." For this reason the concrete regions of being (the anorganic, the organic world, the animal world, man, spirit) become the subject of metaphysics only with regard to the respective "prime being," the πρῶτον ὄν, of each: i.e., each region's respective primordial or first form, in comparison with which the concrete plenitude of forms appears as so many variations. For this reason even the true-good-beautiful comes into consideration for metaphysics only insofar as what is at issue is not the concrete compass of logic, ethics, and aesthetics, but rather that true-in-itself, good-in-itself, and beautiful-in-itself by which this compass of logic, ethics, and aesthetics is inwardly established, directed, and determined.

Considered subjectively, therefore, all of this constitutes merely the formal object of a metaphysics: the categories of ὄν ᾗ ὄν, the πρῶτον ὄν (be it the Platonic εἶδος or the Aristotelian μορφή, ideal or real primordial form, *universalia ante rem* or *universalia in rebus,* Kantian ideas or Schellingian potencies), and finally the αὐτὸ καθ' αὐτό, of the true-good-beautiful. It is a doctrine of categories with the breadth of a doctrine of universals, in the threefold figure of logic, ethics, and aesthetics. Metaphysics is *a priori* in this double sense, because — and to the extent that — it is objectively directed towards the objective *prius* of being.

But it is obviously another thing altogether when what is at issue is the subjective, formal method appropriate to such an objective, formal *a priori* metaphysics. On the one hand, it would seem that its formal object demands the choice of a method that would facilitate the greatest possible immediacy to this formal object. Hence it would be a method for directly understanding not only the three kinds of content proper to this formal object (categories and universals within logic, ethics, and aesthetics), but also, and precisely, their character as the objective *prius* of being's concrete compass. It would be (in terms of subjective method) an *a priori metaphysics,* not only in the sense of the *"priori"* — an immediate grasp of the first principle — but also and precisely in the sense of the *"a"* — seeing *from* the vantage of the first principle: seeing, that is, what is established, directed, and determined as such *from* the vantage of the ground and end and definition. On the other hand, one cannot deny that the metaphysician does not, in actuality, simply have being's concrete compass naturally and immediately spread out before him; rather, he himself, even in his seemingly purest cerebrations, is a part of it. As regards both object and act, he stands naturally and immediately not in the back-grounds, but in the fore-grounds; not within the ground and end and definition, but within the established, directed, and determined. Indeed, it is from precisely this position that the question of metaphysics is derived. *Because* it is the ground and end and definition, understood as "back-grounds," that are the "questionable," it is they that are the questioned. *Because* concrete beings[1] are, as the foreground, the "self-evident," the question commences from them. They become transparent to the questioner: he begins from their simple presence at hand, in which they appear as grounded, directed, and determined, and then penetrates through this to their ground and end and definition. From this perspective, then, our subjective method appears to be a "(setting) out from" what actually comes "after" (what is

---

1. *Das konkret Seiende.* — Trans.

prior): that is (as far as subjective method is concerned), an *a posteriori metaphysics*.

Thus far we have achieved only the most formal configuration of our problem. At the concrete level, however, our problem has a dual aspect. It seems to be most accessible from the side of the object: a deductive metaphysics (= an *a priori* of the object) or an inductive metaphysics (= an *a posteriori* of the object). But the question as posed from the side of the act falls just as much within our purview: Is a so-called "pure subject" of metaphysical thought possible (in the sense, that is, of a purely *a priori* metaphysics of the act)? Or is it possible only by way of a critical convergence and crystallization of concrete subjects (in the sense, that is, of an *a posteriori* metaphysics of the act: whether it be of a more empirical subjective nature, aided by a psychological classification of individual thinkers as particular human types; or whether it be of a more typological subjective nature, aided by a typology of the various particular orientations of thought)? The full extent of the problem thus consists in the correlation and coinherence of these its two sides.

2. The *problematic of the object* presents itself first. It is the most immediate concrete figure for what we encountered above in its most formal configuration. In and of itself, it would seem to present a twofold problem. The first problem would fall between ontology and metaphysics (in the idiom of phenomenology), i.e., between the question concerning "essence" *(Sosein)* and the question concerning facticity or "presence" *(Dasein)*. The other would then concern the formulation of the question from within the concretely existing world: a deductive metaphysics that would explain foreground existence *from* background existence — or an inductive metaphysics that would explain foreground existence by going *towards* background existence. Understood more precisely, however, the two problems interpenetrate. For one thing, the first problem is subject to the form of the second. For the "region of essential unities"[2] is understood as that through which all factical existence is first explicable. Consequently, one may draw a distinction between ontology and metaphysics only insofar as one fails to take "metaphysics" as something formal and instead directly equates it with a particular metaphysics. Aristotle is right in this regard to give formal precedence to the concept of causality, either formal or efficient. Both express the same thing: whether one proceeds from the cause to the effect (an *a priori* of the object: that is, a deductive metaphysics) or from the effect to the cause

2. *Region der Wesenseinheiten.* — Trans.

(an *a posteriori* of the object: an inductive metaphysics). But, on the other hand, even here the contrary holds sway. Metaphysics is ultimately a question of the "what." To be sure, a metaphysics that moves backwards from effect to cause must, before considering the "what it is," objectively inquire after the "that it is" of the cause, just as a metaphysics that ventures forward from cause to effect must, before considering the "what it is," objectively inquire after the "that it is" of the effect. Nevertheless, in both cases the question concerning the "that" is still raised on the basis of the question concerning the "what." In the case of an *a priori* metaphysics of the object, the question proceeds from the presupposed "that" of cause and effect alike towards the besought "what" of the relationship of cause to effect. In the case of an *a posteriori* metaphysics of the object, the question moves from the presupposed "that" of the effect to its besought "what" and, in this way, to the "that" and "what" of the cause. Thus, in either case, the question concerning the "what" determines the metaphysical intention. This means that Plato is right to characterize every question of science, ἐπιστήμη, as a question concerning the εἶδος. The general form — whether of an *"a priori"* or of an *"a posteriori"* metaphysics of the object — is concretely expressed in either the metaphysics of an ideative "what" (the Platonic "form," the austere εἶδος abiding beyond all things: which is to say, an *eidetic metaphysics*) or a metaphysics of a real "what" (the Aristotelian "form," the immanent μορφή of things: which is to say, a *morphological metaphysics*).

Eidetic metaphysics aims at the "what" from cause to effect and thus, ultimately, at that which constitutes the peculiar primacy of the cause: the ideative pre-containment of its effect within it (in the supreme instance, the *ordo idearum* within God). Deductive metaphysics is therefore the inner working out of such an eidetic metaphysics: in the sense that a contemplation of this ideative pre-containment precedes any observation of the effect following from the cause. Morphological metaphysics, on the other hand, approaches the "what" by going from effect to cause, and thus finds its limits and its measure in seeing through the inner shape of the effect — that is, in exhausting the full reality of the effect. Morphological metaphysics thus works itself out in inductive metaphysics: as the telos that gives it its direction. The actual problematic of the object thus oscillates between these two unities, neither of which, however, is an identity unto itself:[3] *deductive meta-*

---

3. *Selbigkeiten,* a difficult word to translate felicitously or unambiguously. Neither deductive nor inductive metaphysics is sufficient unto itself, however complete a unity it constitutes; only the transcendentals themselves can be accorded the status of the αὐτὸ καθ᾽

physics from eidetic metaphysics and *inductive metaphysics from morphological metaphysics.*

On the one hand, it seems self-evident (as already became clear at the
most formal level, in the comparison between *a priori* and *a posteriori* metaphysics) that, at the very least, the rudiments of a soberly critical metaphysics would have to lie "in the things": that is, it would have to be subject to the
primacy of an inductive morphological metaphysics. Of course, such a
metaphysics already, in itself, admits of a certain tension between the *a priori*
and the *a posteriori*: between a morphological method that inwardly guides
the observational method from the beginning, so that the perception of the
"shape" precedes, at least objectively, the perception of "sensations" (a predominantly morphological metaphysics); and an observational method
that, by virtue of its "experimental precision," aims at the perception of
"shape" as the convergence or even the sum of "sensations" (a predominantly inductive metaphysics). Still, though, "shape" remains "the shape of
the real," and thus the *a priori* of a predominantly morphological metaphysics is actually always only an inner *a priori* of the *a posteriori,* which is to say,
an *a posteriori a-priori.* To be sure, an inductive morphological metaphysics
moves logically towards the sphere in which the "that" — no less than the
"what" — of "this" world has its ground, end, and definition. What is more,
given that even a metaphysics as calibrated for "experimental precision" as
that of the natural sciences has called for a "formula of the world" during the
final decades of the past century, an extreme inductive metaphysics directly
designates an eidetic metaphysics as its goal: a deduction of the real world
from its "idea." Notably, however, this formula of the world points to an immanent numerical relation — to, that is, the mathematical symbol of the Aristotelian κυκλοφορία, the cycle of the world recurring into itself. That is to
say, for an inductive morphological metaphysics, an eidetic deductive metaphysics is a limit concept: in the sense of the limit idea that provides a standard for its method (in the manner of the "natural scientific" Kant) or, at
most, in the sense of a positive limit (in the manner of Thomas Aquinas in
his Aristotelian aspect, for whom the principles appear formally in the
sensibile and have their limit therein — and for whom God appears materially only as *principium et finis,* i.e., strictly within the bounds of the question
concerning the world, and not therefore in his *quid est*).

αὐτό, while we must remain within the reciprocal tension between the eidetic and the morphological, pursuing now one course and now the other, depending on which for the moment is prior (neither can ever be exclusive). — Trans.

Yet precisely this type of metaphysics — in which an eidetic deductive metaphysics remains inwardly the limit concept of an inductive morphological metaphysics — opens for us a prospect upon the other side of the relation. For even the most extreme instance of empirical experimental metaphysics cannot avoid a theoretical point of departure for its experiments (as Hugo Dingler has convincingly demonstrated). Every "it is assumed that" already implies an antecedent theory, which affects the order of the experiment and thus constitutes at least a negative *a priori*. A Kantianism of "pure method" (furthermore) signifies, by this very phrase, simply that the steps of its research are guided from the outset by this limit concept of "pure method." Determination by this limit concept thus objectively precedes every initial step, and is intrinsically *a priori* to it. Thus Aristotle — also and precisely in his emphasis upon real, scientific "proof," ἀπόδειξις — begins from an analysis (or what we would today call a formal ontological analysis) of his basic concepts. The "thing rendered evident by induction," the "δῆλον ἐκ τῆς ἐπαγωγῆς, which he thus allows to follow this analysis, appears almost to be, at this point, a mere exemplification, not a development from the purely empirical. Ultimately, Thomas Aquinas's Aristotelianism is, in the *reductio in sensibile* of the *principia*,[4] penetrated to its core by his theory of the *a priori* circle in which these same *principia* are enclosed[5] — and within which, logically, all science is "seminally" contained.[6] But a science is mere "uncontrolled opinion" (δόξα) so long as its presuppositions go unclarified and the course of all the steps that follow from these presuppositions goes unexamined; and so, clearly, from this point on, metaphysics' very character as a rigorous science (ἐπιστήμη), and nothing less, depends upon whether an eidetic deductive metaphysics provides, at the very least, its scaffolding. But then it holds true not only that an *a priori* eidetics is the presupposition of an *a posteriori* empiricism, but that this very *a posteriori* is preceded by its own *a priori* — as truly, that is to say, as the event of experience is preceded by its concept. What is at issue, therefore, is nothing less than the *a priori* of an ***a priori a-posteriori.***

Thus the problematic of an *a priori* and *a posteriori* metaphysics of the object is situated precisely between an *a posteriori a priori* metaphysics (of the morphological "in" the empirical) and an *a priori a posteriori* metaphysics (of the eidetic "of" the empirical). Its solution, however, is to be found where Plato, Aristotle, and Thomas Aquinas all found it: in a final correla-

---

4. *De Ver.* q. 12, a. 3, ad 2-3.
5. *De Ver.* q. 10, a. 8, ad 10.
6. *Summa Th.* I, q. 58, a. 3, corp.; *De Ver.* q. 10, a. 13; q. 12, a. 3, corp.; etc.

tion and coinherence (as is most incisively expressed in the analyses of *Metaphysics* V, where Aristotle explicates the pure inner possibility of the concepts while yet, at the same time, remaining entirely within the realm of the empirical). In the orientation particularly stressed in an eidetic deductive metaphysics, the emphasis lies firstly upon the distinctive formality of metaphysics, and secondly upon its relation as premise to the real sciences. In the first case, because the formal object of this metaphysics, the "ground, end, and definition," intrinsically demands that one must now genuinely be concerned specifically with this formal object (as distinct from the real sciences). In the second case, because the real sciences of themselves presuppose a clarification of their formal basic concepts and methods. They themselves are occupied with the path from hypotheses to conclusions, from ὑποθέσεις to τελευτή (in the real researches they undertake within the ambit of the empirical world); objectively, though, they rest upon an examination of their ὑποθέσεις, which is to say, upon a path leading back from these ὑποθέσεις to their principle, their ἀρχή — which is to say that they rest upon an eidetics (εἴδεσιν αὐτοῖς δι' αὐτῶν εἰς αὐτά).[7] The orientation particularly stressed in an inductive morphological metaphysics, on the other hand, comprehends firstly the concreteness of the formality of metaphysics and, secondly, its limitation with regard to — and determination by — the real sciences. In the first case, because even an eidetics must always be one that is concerned with the real *eidē* of real being: one that is occupied not with essences and the relations among essences "in themselves," but rather with the things of "this world" — with, that is, the *essentiae* **rerum** — because these alone are actually "given" to us. From this perspective, every investigation of "possibilities in themselves" (the scholastic *possibilia,* the Kantian pure forms, the phenomenological *eidē*) is, at first, merely a demarcation of the furthermost bounds of "this" world. It oversteps those bounds only to the extent that it is able to advance into the real "ground and end and definition" of this world, in order to survey "possibilities" from that vantage; though even then, strictly speaking, it views these possibilities not "in themselves," but rather within the stringent circumscriptions dictated by an ultimate limit to our knowledge of this "ground and end and definition" (i.e., by its *theologia negativa*). From this follows the second case: such a metaphysics, precisely because and insofar as it means to function as the premise of the real sciences, lies in advance of them, so as to realize itself in them. Its first step is also a step proper to the real sciences. For it concerns the same terri-

---

7. Reasoning from ideas, through ideas, to terminate in ideas. Plato, *Rep.* VI, 511b-c.

tory: "this" world. But then neither are any of its subsequent steps simply independent. To be sure, the quiddity — the "what" — of "humanity" precedes the various ramifications of the anthropological real sciences, and is therefore developed in its self-sameness, as opposed to being transformed, according to the terms of these sciences, into "plant" or "animal" or "pure spirit." Nevertheless, it remains the case that humanity really unfolds. In this sense a minimal metaphysics precedes the ramification and unfolding of the real sciences, so that in them it may expand into a maximal metaphysics — without being (by virtue of the formal distinction in method between the eidetic and the empirical) a formal metaphysics "at the mercy of" the real sciences.

The solution to all of this is that eidetic deductive metaphysics imposes sobriety upon itself by a transition from a purely ideal to a real metaphysics, and from an absolute metaphysics to one that unfolds itself (in the ramification and unfolding of the real sciences); while, conversely, inductive morphological metaphysics purges itself of its alloy of the real sciences so as to become a (realogical) eidetics, and frees itself from its bondage to the vicissitudes of observation so as to become a (realogical) system of principles. This solution touches the point where μορφή and εἶδος meet. Μορφή, understood as the intrinsically real "shapeliness of things,"[8] signifies an "actualized essence" or, as we prefer to say, "essence in existence"; εἶδος, on the other hand, signifies the intrinsically ideal "idea of things," the "essence as what guides actualization" or, as we prefer to say, "essence beyond existence." The problem of the reciprocal relation between morphological and eidetic metaphysics thus brings us back to the "in-and-beyond," which is the oscillating unity of the two. But then — with ultimate logical consistency — induction, understood as the realogical *in fieri* of μορφή ("thither towards form"), and deduction, understood as the ideative *in fieri* of εἶδος ("hither from the idea"), are the shifting accents of this "in-and-beyond": induction as the rhythm of the in towards the beyond (in → beyond); deduction as the rhythm of the beyond towards the in (in ← beyond). This can be further differentiated by taking into account the sequence of themes proper to metaphysics. To be sure, a meta-noetics cannot proceed but from concrete human consciousness, and so in the direction of an inductive morphological metaphysics. Nevertheless, it is equally the case that it aims from the first to provide neither an empiricism nor a morphology of anthropological consciousness, but rather the essence of knowledge

8. *Gestaltigkeit der Dinge.* — Trans.

as such. From the very outset, therefore, the inductive morphological point of departure is subordinate to an eidetic deductive intention. This intention also necessarily dictates the further differentiation of perspectives[9] proper to a meta-noetics. We see this, for example, in the positive intention of Husserl's immanent phenomenology. But the negative moment here is removed: in place of the bracketing-out of concrete existence, we have instead a gradual transition from the inductive morphological to the eidetic deductive; for this reason, the "sphere of immanence" is not contracted and enclosed within the absoluteness of "pure consciousness," but rather opens out again from within itself to concrete being. In an (explicit) meta-ontics, the inductive morphological point of departure will need further fortification, because a contemplation of being is manifestly dependent, in greater measure, upon being's concrete presence. On the other hand, however, even the contemplation of being in an (explicit) meta-ontics does not proceed towards an inductive morphology of being's concrete presence; on the contrary, the contemplation of concrete being is the pathway to the contemplation of being in itself. Thus, here too the eidetic deductive intention is present from the start. Still, though, the inductive morphological is here not merely a point of departure but, at the very least, a continuous point of departure; and so any further perspectives one might differentiate will necessarily bear in themselves the mark of this "continuation."[10] This shifting of accent toward the inductive morphological will culminate, then, in an (explicit) metaphysics of the "world," which would seem to entail a morphology of the concrete world. For the world is "concrete" not only in that it "exists" (and thus essence and existence "concresce": literally, "grow together"), but in that it exhibits, even in its most universal structure, a certain correlation of particular beings — which is to say, their "having-grown-together *(con-crescere)*" into a "world." Even so, however, the intention of this metaphysics remains fixed upon the eidetic deductive from the outset. For, as we saw earlier (§1), the concern here is with the form of the "correlation" as such — with the "world as such." To be sure, the variously differentiated perspectives will be dictated predominantly from the vantage of "this" world, but they are thus determined only so that, through them, the form of the "world as such" might be disclosed. We thus observe a shifting of accent between a relative preponderance of the eidetic deductive (in the meta-noetic) and a relative preponderance of the inductive morpholog-

9. *Einteilungs-Gesichtspunkte.* — Trans.
10. *Fortdauern.* — Trans.

ical (in the metaphysics of the world), but in constant observance of the law that an inductive morphological point of departure must be directed from the outset by its intention towards the eidetic deductive.

We thus have in many respects — in the problem of an *a priori* and an *a posteriori* metaphysics of the object — an underscoring and intensification of the character of "creaturely metaphysics": its formally constitutive basic formula, "essence in-and-beyond existence," does not merely determine the nature of these individual possibilities (μορφή-εἶδος, induction-deduction); rather, the formal range of oscillation of the "in-and-beyond" is itself the law of the variably oscillating unity between them. But this formula is not simply an underscoring and intensification. Rather it indicates here — from the side of the object — the particular formal configuration of creaturely metaphysics: precisely in this oscillating correlation and coinherence of μορφή (understood as "essence in existence") and εἶδος (understood as "essence beyond existence"); of induction (understood as "in → beyond") and deduction (understood as "in ← beyond").

3. All of this is thrown into sharper relief, however, by the *problematic* of an *a priori* and an *a posteriori* metaphysics *of the act*. In all of the preceding, it has been tacitly assumed that the thinker of a metaphysics, "as" thinker, is not "this" concrete human being as distinct from "that" one, but the thinker "as such" — simply thought "*itself*" *in actu*. The range of variation that opened up within the "suspense"[11] characterizing the solution we reached above was presented as something purely objective: that is, as something conditioned not by the person of the thinker, but by the scope of objective possibilities. Of course, insofar as individual possibilities bear the names of particular persons (Plato, Kant, etc.), it did in fact consist in affixing personal names to objective possibilities, or, conversely, in objectifying personal standpoints. But it was in fact an *a priori* of thought "*itself*," as opposed to concrete historical thought. It was in fact an *a priori* metaphysics of the act put into practice. If this is so, then it becomes obvious how the problem of *a priori* and *a posteriori* metaphysics is first seen in its entirety — indeed, first seen at all in clear focus — when one raises the question concerning the relation between thought "*itself*" (an *a priori* metaphysics of the act) and concrete historical thought (an *a posteriori* metaphysics of the act).

In the problematic of the object, the question was posed not between metaphysics and an a-metaphysical empiricism, but between two possibilities proper to actual metaphysics. By the same token, the scope of the prob-

---

11. *Schwebe*. — Trans.

lematic of the act cannot be characterized as an either-or between a kind of thought that is capable of "Truth" and an empiricist relativism. To be sure, an *a posteriori* metaphysics of the act aims most definitely at truth-in-itself, but it operates under the condition that it positively include within itself a concrete historical differentiation of distinct standpoints — whereas in the case of an *a priori* metaphysics of the act this differentiation has no application, since the only kind of thought with which this metaphysics is ever concerned is thought "itself." The occurrence of this thought, however, is essentially one and the same, independent of person and history alike: *a priori,* that is, to the realm of experience proper to them. The problem at issue here is manifest in, say, Aristotle's method: on the one hand, in his syllogistics, and in its foundations in an axiomatics rooted in the principle of non-contradiction, he aims at a pure *a priori* of the act; and yet, on the other hand, he in fact not only develops his problematic from an aporetics of the solutions actually proposed throughout the course of history,[12] but arrives even at his principle of non-contradiction by way of struggle with Heraclitus ("everything changes") and Parmenides ("everything remains the same").[13] One sees this in almost sharper relief in Thomas Aquinas: on the one hand, he erects a self-enclosed *a priori* structure of pure *principia,* against which thought not only proves its correctness,[14] but within which,[15] indeed by means of which (as *semina*), thought occurs;[16] yet, on the other hand, at the same time, the method he actually employs portrays itself as a concord struck among the various historical *auctoritates,* and this not only in a kind of extension of the theological method of "tradition," but with the explicit founding of the superhistorical *principia* upon the intrahistorical *providentia divina et dispositio (necessitas principiorum dictorum consequitur providentiam divinam et dispositionem).*[17] The task at hand, then, is to reflect critically upon just this actual "togetherness" — *Nebeneinander* — and "coinherence" — *Ineinander.*[18] Specifically, the following three standpoints are under consideration: superhistorical thought versus intrahistorical

12. *Met.* I, 3-10, 983b-993a.
13. *Met.* IV, 8, 1012b, 22-31.
14. *De Ver.* q. 1, a. 12, corp.; q. 10, a. 1, corp.; *Summa Th.* I, q. 85, a. 6, corp.
15. *De Ver.* q. 10, a. 13, corp.; q. 12, a. 3, corp.; q. 9, a. 5, corp., etc.
16. *Summa Th.* I, q. 58, a. 3, corp.; *De Ver.* q. 9, a. 5, corp., etc.
17. The necessity of the principles we have enunciated depends upon divine providence and disposition. *De Ver.* q. 5, a. 2, ad 7.
18. Concerning these translations of *Nebeneinander* and *Ineinander,* see footnote 21 below. — Trans.

thought; objectively aporetic thought versus historically aporetic thought; and progressive thought versus regressive thought.[19] In these three forms, an *a priori* metaphysics of the act shifts ever nearer to an *a posteriori* metaphysics of the act, though without the ultimate difference between them being annulled. The difference is merely transposed.[20]

In its strict form, an *a priori metaphysics of the act* will have the *character of a superhistorical system.* Viewed from the vantage of such a metaphysics, every argument between one thinker and another is concerned always and simply with the overcoming of falsehood's multiplicity by the *one* truth. Consequently, thought is the one region within the thinker that is an exception to the creatureliness that otherwise characterizes him — an exception, that is, to his individual limitation (in his "togetherness") and his historical mutability (in his "succession," his *Nacheinander*).[21] It is therefore a region *a priori* to the entire shape of the thinker as a creature. Hence the tractates of Eckhart discovered by Martin Grabmann draw the correct conclusion when they speak of such thought as true divinity. It is the divinity of pure thought, such as will later dominate all of German idealism: Kant's "transcendental

---

19. It should be noted that, here and below, "objectively" is the (admittedly unsatisfactory) translation for *"sach" (sach-aporetisch).* Therefore it may not be entirely obvious to the English-language reader that Przywara does not mean "objects" in the sense of concrete empirical particulars, but *Sachen* in an almost Husserlian sense: timeless "essences," so to speak, enduring possibilities of metaphysics that — however specific their instantiations may be in time — can be considered in abstraction from the contingencies of history. One should also note that the slightly perplexing terms "regressive" and "progressive" must be understood as complements of the "back-and-forth" dynamism of both creaturely being and creaturely thought: "regressive thought" retreats inductively to the "in" (the μορφή) of concrete, empirical, historical fact, while "progressive thought" ventures out deductively from the "beyond" (the εἶδος) of abstract, ideative, timeless essence. — Trans.

20. *Es übersetzt sich nur.* — Trans.

21. Here Przywara's idiom has expanded to take in, as a complement of the earlier *Zueinander* and *Ineinander* (rendered above as "correlation" and "coinherence"), the terms *Nebeneinander* and *Nacheinander* (rendered here as "togetherness" and "succession"). In the simplest sense, Przywara is speaking of the principal features of finite existence, particularity (in relation) and change, and so these words might plausibly have been rendered as "individuation" and "mutability," or more literally as "side by side" and "one after another." As terms for existence in space and time, they might be rendered as "contiguity" and "sequentiality." When discussing the constraints of method, they might be taken to refer to the inseparability, within the creaturely, of "synchrony" and "diachrony" (in the structuralist sense); and, since Przywara turns below towards analogical speech and, finally, the imagery of music, it could be tempting to write (in the first case) "hypotaxis" and "syntaxis" and (in the second) "counterpoint" and "development." — Trans.

subject," Hegel's "absolute Spirit" — as, in either case, divinity immanent within empirical humanity. It is the position directly contrary to that of articles 5 and 6 of *Quaestio* 1 of Thomas Aquinas's *De Veritate,* which know nothing of any *veritas aeterna creata;* they know only of the positive reduction of all creaturely knowledge of truth — through and beyond the creatureliness of created thought — to the one divine subject of thought beyond the creature; thus the *one* eternal truth of God reveals itself noetically in creaturely truth in the same way that divine being reveals itself ontically in creaturely being — that is, within the variety produced by this "togetherness" and "succession" (since the true and being are convertible: *cum verum et ens convertantur*).

The milder form of an *a priori* metaphysics of the act, in advocating an *objective aporetics,* clearly takes this incisive critique into account. Such an objective aporetics intends three things. Firstly, a reduction to ultimate *impasses (a-poroi).* But then, further, an unmasking of all so-called "solutions," which present, in each case, only "one" side of a given problem. And finally, logically, a reduction of the historical course of philosophical thought to an immanent objective dialectic of its problems. From this, however, it is clear how an objective aporetics nevertheless fails to do justice to Thomas's critique, which is grounded in his emphasis upon the difference between God and creature even — and precisely — within thought. An objective *a priori* metaphysics, however, precisely does away with this distinction; it merely does so more subtly than was the case in superhistorical metaphysics. On the one hand, it evacuates thought of Eternal Truth of all divinity, converting this Truth into the absoluteness of an Eternal Dialectic. On the other hand, though, it divinizes creaturely searching, turning it into an Absolute Dialectic. So the objectively *a priori* is, in point of fact, simply another version of thought *as* divinity, immanent within empirical humanity. It is both superindividual and superhistorical, and hence (because this "togetherness-and-succession" is an essential characteristic of the creature) a supercreaturely "pure dialectic."

An *a priori* metaphysics of the act thus makes one last attempt to include the differentiation of (individual) "togetherness" and (historical) "succession" within its apriorism.[22] A "pure dialectic" is "pure" (in the sense of *a priori* absoluteness), above all, in that its inner form is that of a circle's

---

22. To be clear, German idealism, as it passes from transcendental to absolute, seeks to gather particularity and change into an *a priori* metaphysics *of the act,* rather than into — as was classically the case — an *a priori* metaphysics of the object. — Trans.

recurrence back into itself. But the circle is the very symbol of self-sufficient completeness: from Aristotle's "perfect circle," κύκλος τέλειος,[23] to the "summing up," the εἰς κορυφὴν . . . συνάγεσθαι, by which Dionysius of Alexandria describes the movement of the intra-divine tri-personal life of God.[24] The form of *progression* would seem to have made this dispensable. For it is the nature of creaturely being that it be mutable "forwards" — not that it simply, purely *be* its "thus," its essence, but rather that it *become* its essence. Thus creaturely thought is fully creaturely only in being mutable "forwards" — in being, that is, progressive. In that it is truth in *becoming,* it would appear to have given due respect to the creaturely. At the same time, in that it is *truth* in becoming, the a priori is thought to be preserved. For by "progression" is meant the forward, unidirectional increase of truth, liberated from the up-and-down vicissitudes of human history. Of course, progression is possible only by way of the agents of this human history — and to this extent the "togetherness and succession" of the creaturely enters into this progression. But as soon as it is introduced the agents of human history must rise above and "trans-pose" themselves out of this "togetherness and succession," which is their most proper condition; that is to say, they must transpose themselves out of the ups-and-downs of development and decline into the logical linearity of constant progress (to borrow the idiom, principally, of the Enlightenment). Yet it becomes clear how even here — indeed, precisely here (because subtlety is in fact intensification) — the same old notion of the divinity of pure thought prevails. The logical linearity of constant progress stands *a priori* to the reality of this creaturely up-and-down. On the one hand, progress entails, as noted above, a de-divinization: namely, of the immutability of Eternal Truth into an eternal progress (of the "evolving God-Spirit"). For this very reason, though, it is at the same time a divinization: of the im-purity of the ups-and-downs of the creaturely into a "pure progress." On the one hand, becoming is incompatible with Eternal Absolute

23. *Phys.* VII, 3, 246a, 14f.

24. Fragm. ex Ep. 2. [The reference is to the mid-third-century trinitarian debates between, broadly speaking, "subordinationism" and "modalism." Dionysius of Alexandria, writing against Sabellianism, employed certain phrases that aroused the suspicion in some — not least among them another Dionysius, the (somewhat modalist monarchian) bishop of Rome — of subordinationist tritheism. In response to Roman criticisms, Dionysius defended his use of the term "three hypostases" to describe the trinity, accepted the further term "homoousios," and encapsulated his doctrine in the formula "We expand the monad into the triad without division, and we sum up the triad in the monad without subtraction." — Trans.]

Truth. But, on the other hand, specifically *creaturely* becoming is no pure progression. It is, at the very least, just as likely to be a regression — that is, an explication of something given, which is present at hand, but which to this extent bears reference to primordial conditions: the tree, which ever and again renews itself from its roots. But, moreover, this is not an immanent, pure dialectic of the two processes, progress and regress; it is rather, in an entirely special sense, the unsystematizable im-purity within their coinherence: the remainder that cannot be resolved. It is not simply a matter of ups-and-downs, but a matter of ups-and-downs to which no rhythmic formula can be applied.

From this perspective, an *a posteriori metaphysics of the act* certainly stands in an easier position. Having the form of pure *intrahistoricality*, it elevates to the status of method precisely that which always appeared to constitute an objection to it: the separation between superhistorical truth and the "ups-and-downs" of the intrahistorical. Superhistorical truth is then the idea upon which the intrahistoricality of thought, in all its multiplicity, converges. Accordingly, truth is known to the degree that the eye that surveys the universality of the intrahistorical turns its gaze upward to contemplate superhistorical truth. But here another nasty dilemma arises. *Either* one takes this genuine historicality seriously, which means, firstly, that the "eye of universality" is itself a pure limit idea (since the "universal observer" is himself an "item" contained within the intrahistorical); and, secondly, that — even if this "eye of universality" could be made a reality — the divide between the course of history and superhistorical validity remains. *Or* one attempts by every means available to fashion out of the multiplicity of historical standpoints a, so to speak, intrahistorical καθόλου, a "common denominator," the result of which is a mixture of history and philosophy. The consequence of such a mixture, though, must then be either a de-objectification of objective truth, reducing it to the level of factical eventuality (making it, that is, an asseveration regarding not what is true, but rather what is held to be true over the course of time), or a de-historicization of historical eventuality (into merely the self-manifestation of the logical).[25]

A *historical aporetics* is located in precisely this point of difficulty. It is distinguished from objective aporetics (as the second form of an *a priori* metaphysics of the act) by a reversal of perspectives. Whereas objective

---

25. By this last opposition, it seems clear enough, Przywara means something like a choice between the Heideggerean hermeneutical approach and the Hegelian dialectical. — Trans.

aporetics looks from the superhistorical to the intrahistorical, historical aporetics tends from the intrahistorical towards the superhistorical. Whereas an objective aporetics understands any system of historical thought to be a partial step in the developing objective system of a problem-in-itself, for a historical aporetics it is fundamental that one first recognize the peculiar inner completeness of whatever specific system is in question, in order then to discern more deeply within the totality of the historical system — and positively transparent throughout — the "one" prevalent form in the objective system of the problem-in-itself. The form best suited to its method of comparing historical systems will thus prove to be that of "transposition," which Maréchal so brilliantly knew to employ when framing his "debate" between Thomas and Kant. This means that everything depends upon finding the thought of one thinker anew in the historically contingent perspective and idiom of another, transcribed from, say, the F major key of the historical contingency of the one into the A-flat minor key of the historical contingency of the other. From there the method advances to a comparative critique of whatever remains of either of these historical contingencies, in order thus to arrive asymptotically at an objective aporetics. But precisely here it becomes apparent how the intractable surd bedeviling the first form of our *a posteriori* metaphysics of the act has at this point merely mutated. That is to say, if one takes the strict historicality of a historical aporetics seriously, there will always be historical remainders. A historical aporetics cannot simply be translated without remainder into an objective aporetics. The two are, of course, extremely close to one another with respect to what is entailed in any aporetics — that is, in their concern for the limited, the mutable, and the ultimately impassable. But in a genuinely historical aporetics one is engaged in a real factical aporetics. The relative systematicity of a typological construct (e.g., "Kantianism as such") provides the limit concept for a style of reflection oriented towards the determination of facts, which knows itself to be "genuine" to the degree that it stays close to the purely factical "existence" of unconnected facts. Conversely, a genuine objective aporetics is an ideative aporetics. The relatively unsystematic nature of the self-ramification of the problem-in-itself (e.g., "noetic transcendentalism," understood as the "objective aporetic aspect of historically aporetic Kantianism") provides the limit concept for a style of systematic reflection that seeks to exhaust all possibilities objectively and to ground them as far as possible in an ultimate principle. Precisely this encounter between historical and objective aporetics, therefore, lays bare the still more acute difference between them: in the former, intrahistorical eventuality, in the latter superhistorical truth.

The final form of an *a posteriori* metaphysics of the act tries to take this difference seriously — but still in such a fashion as to attempt somehow to capture it within the intrahistorical. We mean by this a *regression,* as it is articulated in the tradition (as the opposing concept to "progressive Enlightenment"). Nothing intrahistorical is simply a steady progression. Quite the contrary: history displays originary moments, in which something new really does "originate." A historical method that one-sidedly consigns itself to the "closed causality" of the natural sciences will disregard these irruptions (what Franz Overbeck called "original history") and can, to this extent, do no more than classify them as "prehistorical." For the neutral observer, however, these two things — origin (primordial history) and course (history) — are most certainly to be distinguished. What "originates" thus attains a certain superhistoricality. Its "course" is to some extent the self-declaration of this superhistorical form in its intrahistorical development. The superhistorical form is the enduring criterion of its intrahistorical formations. The *ineffabile* of its original appearing (in the moment of original history) is the fountain of youth to which everything aged returns. This is not only the case with the historical formation of Christianity; it is approximated in other historical formations as well. For one speaks of the "tradition" of a people, a nation, a race, a federation, etc. It is clear how this applies to our present case. Plato and Aristotle are both historically contingent participants in history. But in them a *single* philosophy "originates" and begins to take shape — one that has persisted throughout the course of history, unfolding and diversifying itself in and through them. Superhistorical truth thus has an intrahistorical course. Every step of the way is living tradition, not only measuring itself against its "original form," but vitally declaring this original form in ever new ways. In becoming a *telos* within history, the superhistoricality of truth is thus transposed from the level of the ideative to that of the real-factical: as the final cause that provides the caused course of history with its origin, it is objectively "prior" (an a-prioristic *a priori*); as the inwardly guiding final cause that presides over the guided course of history, it is always ever "before and beyond" (an a-posterioristic *a priori*). This approach certainly does incomparably more justice to what is distinctive to the creaturely than did the corresponding model of "progression" (in the *a priori* metaphysics of the act). For the creature — understood as the one enjoined to "become what you are!" — is not a "becoming *in infinitum,*" but a "becoming what is (once) given." Progression, on the other hand (corresponding to the "ultimate emphasis" peculiar to an *a priori* metaphysics of the act), is rather a "making creaturely of the divine" — that is, a making creaturely of divine infinity in the form of an "infinity that becomes." By contrast, "regressive" tradition means an intensified limitation (corresponding, in similar fashion, to the "ultimate emphasis" in the *a posteriori* metaphysics of the act): the limited "thus" — the "*So*" — of a particular truth (of, say, the Peripatetic system), which unfolds itself not only gradually, but also always only within the limits of its originary form. It is precisely a sober historical account of these "traditions," however, that shows very clearly that here no inner synthesis between history and truth actually comes to pass. The history of all "traditions" is characterized by an unending conflict between a strictly historical and an objectively logical interpretation of a given "author." A strictly historical interpretation of Thomas, for example, has the advantage of historical fidelity to what Thomas really said. But with it comes the tendency not only to relativize the author, but also thereby to reduce him to the object of a kind of research concerned purely with facts. Which is to say that it kills him as the "author" of a living "tradition." Of course, an objective logical interpretation avoids doing this to such an extent that it permits the living Thomas to "say ever more" (in the consequences unfolding from his thought). But this, at the same time, brings about a dehistoricization. "What Thomas really said" turns into "what Thomas logically must be saying" (with the interpreter's own doctrine being interpolated in each case as the syllogism's middle term). Now at the mercy of his interpreters — not only of their "schools" but, also and precisely, of each of them as individuals — a historical author is turned into a *universale a parte rei*, one moreover that has become uncontrollable. Thus what appeared to be a solution really only takes us back to our original problem: intrahistorical event, superhistorical truth. The division between them now proves to go deeper than the relation between superhistorical telos and intrahistorical course. Nor is this division rendered any more innocuous by being situated within the factually real as such. For this leads either to a historicism of truth (even — and indeed precisely — in the case of regressive tradition) or to a logicism of history. Instead the division is set, and remains fixed, between the ideative and the real.

But if this is the case our problem will be one of striking a kind of balance between an *a priori* and an *a posteriori* metaphysics of the act — a balance that will do justice not only to this division between the ideative and the real, but also to the peculiar form of the order that obtains between them. It is neither that truth is derived from history, nor that history is derived from truth. It is rather that in the connection between them (while preserving the distinction) truth indicates the formal direction, since metaphysics is concerned not with knowledge of what historically has been said to be true, but with knowledge of what *is* true. At the same time, however, history must be the positively conscious medium in which such knowledge comes about. For the retrospective view of historically conditioned thought, this means that it must grow out of the tradition, positively and consciously. For the contemporaneous view (looking at the present), it means that this outgrowth of the tradition must be one that is fecundated by being made to live as universally as possible in community with the intellectual motifs of the present. For the prospective view, finally (looking into the future), it means the anticipation of a creative thinking that will not obstruct the flow of historically enduring thought (of a living *philosophia perennis*) with the unyielding rock of the latest "infallible systems" — any attempt so to do would naturally be in vain — but that will ultimately do no more than place itself at the service of the current; for such creative thinking is (ideally) a silent "concurrence" with the current, and in this way goes "beyond itself."

Logically, then, the method that is being developed here will conform itself to this threefold perspective. The form taken by the retrospective view (looking at what grows positively out of the tradition) will be one of stepping into the current as near to its sources as one can, because only in this way is it possible to take hold of the current's welling force (or better, to be taken by it and feel its flow).[26] Thus, for the contemporary thinker it will not suffice to work from an internal debate with Descartes, Spinoza, Kant, Hegel. For, in the first place, modern philosophy presupposes the problems of Scholasticism (as the recent researches of Koyré, Heimsoeth, *et al.* increasingly prove). In the second place, as Hegel demonstrated in the most unadorned fashion in his lectures on the history of philosophy, modern philosophy bears in itself the form, specifically, of Protestant theology, and constitutes the *intelligere* of its *credere*. Seen in light of the former consideration, modern philosophy points to the whole unabbreviated spectrum of the problematic that flowed into Scholasticism (while not being exhausted by it): Plato, Aristotle, Augustine, Thomas Aquinas. Seen in the light of the latter consideration, modern philosophy must trace its Protestant theological form back still further, to its origin — i.e., it must come to understand its Protestant form from the perspective of the entire undiminished spectrum of Catholic theology. What contemporary Protestant theology — which wants to be a theology proper, and not the study of religion — is attempting anew today (in Karl Barth's theology, for example) is precisely what also constitutes the special concern of contemporary metaphysics: a positive de-

26. *Von ihm erfasst und durchfaßt zu werden.* — Trans.

bate with Catholic theology. Thus one can speak in a special sense of a positive outgrowth of the *original tradition*. The concomitant view (of the present) realizes itself then in the life of the sources *now*, at *this* point in the course of their flow. It is already for the historian a utopian hope that one could withdraw oneself artificially from the present, in order to live originally and immediately in the period of one's researches. But for the metaphysician, who may not investigate the tradition historically, but who still seeks to live *out of* the tradition *towards* superhistorical truth, it is even more so the case. So there remains but one possibility: to live the life of the sources now, today, in the current that flows from them. This could be described as a method of *critical reflection*. Critical, insofar as one remains conscious of the difference between the way one formulates the question today and the ways in which it was posed by the authors of the tradition. Reflection, insofar as such discriminating critique nevertheless has the positive purpose of making contemporary life sensible to the force of the current of the one tradition. The third perspective, finally, would then consist in the attempt to achieve the greatest possible unity with the *one* current flowing through and shaping all time's stages. In the ideal case, this will come to pass if the metaphysics at issue becomes almost, as it were, a metaphysics *of* this *one* current, i.e., of the fundamental law that makes the current of the tradition, throughout its many variations, *one* current, from the past to the present and into the future. In its humblest form, such a metaphysics would be a very special and limited research that would conduct itself in constant consciousness of this fundamental law. In its most ambitious form, such a metaphysics would be nothing less than what, at bottom, Hegel desired: a *comprehension of the fundamental law* itself. But Hegel's own peculiar philosophical intention is impossible to realize. For it would imply a standpoint not only outside the tradition's current, but one situated already at the end, at the very mouth of the stream. But this standpoint is God's alone. For the creature, only something similar (though precisely for this reason essentially dissimilar) is possible: firstly, moving "with" the current, which is to say, maximally, giving oneself up to it; secondly, moving "in" the current, which is to say moving in the conscious awareness that even the most vigorous attempt to move "with" the current never grasps the whole of it (because both its past as well as its coming possibilities always loom out of the reach of any attempt, concomitantly, to grasp it), but is instead ever more deeply grasped by it. Seen thus, all "comprehension" must know itself, consciously and from the first, as a "being comprehended." In the course of this work itself, we shall see how the theme of the *Analogia entis* takes such a method as its own proper mode of operation — how, that is, it formalizes itself in such a method: in every "comprehending of something" (and therein union with it) there is the greater "above-and-beyond" of "being comprehended by it" (and therein the increasing distance that transcends all unity).

In this threefold way, history can become a positively conscious medium. But then, as such, it must explicitly carry within itself the intentionality towards objective truth that the concept of medium implies. This means that the growing-out of the original tradition (this being the first step along the path of the emphatically historical) is a genuine step of metaphysics only insofar as it is guided by this intentionality and hence is guided toward its fulfillment. Thus, in terms of method, it must proceed from an (antecedent) pure, objective problematic[27] towards a (consequent) pure, objective solution. This relation is something ultimate. On the one hand, critical reflection upon the original tradition (as the predominant *a posteriori* of the act) cannot be prosecuted without an inner knowledge of the objective problems that lie at its foundation, nor without an orientation towards their evolving solution. On the other hand, a treatment of these objective questions (which, for its part, represents the predominant *a priori* of the act) will never actually be "pure," but will rather be already intrinsically determined by the thinker's historical position within the entirety of the tradition in which he lives, even if he does not know it. Certainly, truth, as what is "beyond history," makes itself known always only "in history," but it reveals itself "in history" as "beyond history." So our formula must read: truth in-and-beyond history.

If we compare this formula to the formally constitutive basic formula of creaturely metaphysics, it is evident that it spells out the formal configuration of its problem of the act. For truth is the region of the pure "thus" — *So;* history, the region of the "there" — *Da.* Hence one hears, speaking through this formula of "truth in-and-beyond history," the more original formula of "essence in-and-beyond existence." This is what is ultimately irreducible in the creature: that in the creature there is no identity of the ideative and the real, and that there is therefore a span, one to the other, between truth and history.[28] Yet precisely because it is the problem of the act that is decisive for the prosecution of a metaphysics, we gain for our "creaturely metaphysics" not only the formal configuration of its "problem of the act," but — precisely herein — nothing less than its definitive anchor.

27. *Sach-Problematik.* — Trans.
28. *Sich zueinanderspannen.* — Trans.

4. There is, however, an intrinsic correlation within *a priori* and *a posteriori* metaphysics between the problematic of the object and the problematic of the act. Not only is this correlation between the *problematic of the act* and *the problematic of the object* the concrete Gestalt of the general formal problematic of *a priori* and *a posteriori* metaphysics (as we saw in §3, 1 above); compared to the latter, which it passes through and goes beyond, it is also the more complete and more incisive form of the problem posed between transcendental (§2) meta-noetic and meta-ontic (§1) metaphysics.

Logically, therefore, what is at issue is not simply a matter of the fact — the "that it is" — of this correlation. For, clearly, the meaning of this "that it is" has three forms. The first is the correlation between an eidetic deductive metaphysics (understood as an *a priori* metaphysics of the object) and a superhistorical, objectively aporetic, progressive metaphysics (understood as an *a priori* metaphysics of the act). This would give us the pure form of a general *a priori* metaphysics, the classical form of which one could see, in part, in Husserl. The second would be the correlation between inductive morphological metaphysics (understood as an *a priori* metaphysics of the object) and an intrahistorical, historically aporetic, regressive metaphysics (understood as an *a posteriori* metaphysics of the act). This would be the pure form of a general *a posteriori* metaphysics — though it has scarcely any historical precedent, because (as we shall presently see) every style of thought will somehow be in search of an *a priori*. Finally, the correlation proper to creaturely metaphysics would consist (as the logical conclusion drawn from the foregoing) in the correlation between the form of the object and the form of the act proper to the "creaturely"; specifically, in a correlation between a realogical eidetics (which is shorthand for "essence in-and-beyond existence" as it concerns the problematic of the object) and an objective thinking from and in critical reflection upon the fundamental law of the original tradition (which is shorthand for "essence in-and-beyond existence" as it concerns the problematic of the act).

But the fact — the "that it is" — of this correlation is insufficient. First of all, this can be seen historically from something we have already been obliged to note: that there has never been a pure form of universal *a posteriori* metaphysics. And this truth is mirrored in another: that even a seemingly pure universal *a priori* metaphysics invariably introduces an *a posteriori* factor. The classical example of this is precisely Plato, who juxtaposes a pure eidetics (on the side of the object) with an aristocratic individualism (on the side of the act): not "thought in itself," which would be independent of the differences among individual persons, but precisely that kind of thought proper to the elect individual, the ἄριστος, as opposed to the πολλοί.[29] By contrast, Aristotle comes to see his καθόλου precisely in the colors of "how everyone thinks," inasmuch as the objective side of his philosophy appears as predominantly *a posteriori*. In other words, all of these actual historical philosophies tend towards an internal equilibrium, in their systems, between the *a priori* and the *a posteriori*. But this equilibrium is a more stringent version of their "purity." As we saw above, these pure correlations immediately betray themselves as one-sided, and thus point beyond themselves. If an equilibrium between the *a priori* and the *a posteriori* is integrated into the form of the correlation itself, however, it would appear to overcome all one-sidedness, like a circle closing in upon itself. Here, on the one hand, a real recognition of the formal configuration of creaturely metaphysics has been achieved (in that there is a span here, one to the other, between the *a priori* and the *a posteriori*). On the other hand, however, it is not translated into action, but remains stalled in the form of a deceptive hybrid — one that, instead of surrendering its "purity," "disguises" it.

The correlation proper to creaturely metaphysics, between the creaturely form of the object and of the act, is now more strikingly apparent, as logically following from the (disguised) concession. For in this correlation there is first of all the fact, the "that," of the coordination between two suspended equilibria (in the object as well as in the act); it does not, consequently, form a closed circle, in the sense of two halves completing one another so as to create a whole. Secondly, neither of these equilibria in itself constitutes a closed circle; on the contrary, they constitute (as their formula "in-and-beyond" indicates) the becoming of a back-and-forth movement that is never completed. Nor, finally, is the "that" of this coordination a neutral one; rather, the creaturely form of the act ("truth in-and-beyond history") more penetratingly intrudes itself into the creaturely form of the object: since eidetic deductive metaphysics and inductive morphological metaphysics, as well as their suspended correlation — insofar as they are "truth" — are subject ever anew to the "in-and-beyond" of "truth in-and-beyond history."

The implication here is twofold. For one, we see how creaturely metaphysics is established at its root: as coming from and proceeding toward the problem of the act. For another, we are hereby presented with the complete formal configuration of a creaturely metaphysics: in both the fact — the "that" — and the manner — the "how" — of the correlation between its formal object and its formal act.

29. E.g., *Phaedo* 90a-b.

§4 Philosophical and Theological Metaphysics

1. We discovered at the outset — by way of the etymological problematic of the word — that "metaphysics" concerns the *meta* of *physis:* that wherein *physis* is at once "ground and end and definition in itself." Setting out from this determination, we have thus far discussed only the first part of this phrase: "ground and end and definition." We have dealt with it, firstly, with respect to what "ground and end and definition" is related to: consciousness or being. This was the problematic of the meta-noetic and the meta-ontic (§1) and of the transcendental as such (§2). But, then, we have also dealt with it with respect to the correlation between this ground-end-definition and the grounded, directed, and determined. This was the problematic of the *a priori* and the *a posteriori* (§3). What remains to be considered, therefore, is the second part of the phrase, the "in itself." As a question of metaphysics, this obviously does not constitute a positive assertion *that* the being of *physis* contains within itself the *meta* of the ground-end-definition in such a manner that it would be itself a ground-end-definition. Rather, it is a question of the "how" of a neutral, factical "that": for how is one to understand this "being in," given that, on the one hand, all being in fact carries within itself a ground-end-definition; and given that, on the other hand, metaphysics moves by virtue of its essence towards the *meta* — to the degree that it is manifest in the *physis* — of this ground, end, and definition? This implies, firstly, that metaphysics inquires not only about the "in between" set between the ground-end-definition and the grounded, directed, and determined, but about the ground-end-definition itself. Secondly, if metaphysics inquires about the ground-end-definition, then it certainly does so, on the one hand, from within the back and forth motion of this "in between" (the complete configuration of which we discovered at the conclusion of §3); yet it does so in such a

way that the question concerning the ground-end-definition is addressed to this "in between" itself, and thus goes through and beyond it.

We would therefore do best to set out from this "in between" as it was presented to us in our last investigation (§3). What takes place in an *a priori* metaphysics, whether of the object or of the act, is manifestly, in the highest degree, a deduction of the grounded, directed, and determined from its ground, end, and definition. This ground, end, and definition, as regards the object, is the eidetic dimension of real things. But insofar as real things are deduced "absolutely" from it, this ground, end, and definition appears, as regards the act, as absolute truth. By virtue of this absolute truth, the consistent *a priori* metaphysician determines the groundedness, directedness, and determinate being of real things by way of the eidetic as their ground, end, and definition. Accordingly, what ultimately figures in this kind of metaphysics is a certain relation between God and creature: namely, a oneness with a God of the "Ideas" and of "Truth," to the point of reproducing[1] the groundedness, directedness, and determinateness of all reality from this God. In a pure *a posteriori* metaphysics, whether of the object or of the act, we see the reverse movement: from below to above. For its aim, as regards the object, is to open a prospect upon the ground, end, and definition within the universality of the grounded, directed, and determined; at the same time, as regards the act, it understands truth to be the final integration of all the various perspectives regarding the truth. Here, obviously, the ultimate relation between God and creature lies in the play between a "summation" and a "sum" or, more precisely, between an all *in potentia* and an all *in actu*. In his co-realization of[2] the "all in becoming," the consistent *a posteriori* metaphysician mounts upward to the limit idea of the "all in existence." If, in pure *a priori* metaphysics, the ultimate lay in a relation between God and creature, the form of which was that of a devolution (from above to below), here it lies in a relation of an evolution (from below to above). This implies two things. On the one hand, that the question of the relation between the *a priori* and the *a posteriori* inexorably breaks through to the question of the relation between the absolute and the relative (completing the way in which the same question broke through into our previous questions). But then one sees how the most extreme solutions go astray precisely in that they identify them-

---

1. *Mitvollzug*. One might almost read this as "co-agency" or "co-enactment"; a more customary use of the word, however, would be to indicate the way in which, say, a student repeats a demonstration lesson. — Trans.

2. *Mitvollzug mit.* — Trans.

selves with the latter question (completing the way in which, as we saw earlier, extreme solutions were rendered impossible by their own desire to be absolute). Hence, the conclusion to be drawn from this is also twofold. First, the pure formal problem of metaphysics as such leads to the *question of the relation between God and creature*. Second, we are confronted here by an either-or: either we equate this question with the previous questions or we distinguish it from them. Since equating it with those previous questions would lead back to the objectively impossible solutions we encountered in them, however, the only possibility that remains is that of distinguishing it from them. But such a distinction implies that the question of the relation between God and creature lies beyond the reach of our earlier questions. Thus, even the concept of God, which is formally immanent to the question thus distinguished, is situated beyond the reach of those concepts of God that were revealed in the forms of their equation: beyond, that is, either the "God who descends" to the creature (in an *a priori* metaphysics of the object or of the act: divine ideativity and creaturely reality) or the "God who comes to be" from the creature (in an *a posteriori* metaphysics of the object or of the act: creaturely multiplicity and divine all-unity). It follows, therefore — given that these concepts of God stem from positing the intra-creaturely problem of the *a priori* and the *a posteriori* as absolute — that the concept of God proper to this "distinction" should have the formal fundamental form³ of "God beyond the creature."

But then, when the relation between God and creature is thus clarified, everything positive that remains of the extreme forms of purely *a priori* and purely *a posteriori* metaphysics will still be included within this relation. For the question concerning God and the creature is, as we have seen, the final consequence of the question concerning the ground, end, and definition, in that this latter is addressed to the "in between" set between the *a priori* and the *a posteriori*, whether of the object or of the act. But the relation between the ground, end, and definition and the grounded, directed, and determined — which is itself at play within the question of the *a priori* and the *a posteriori* — is a direct likeness of the question concerning the "ultimate" ground, end, and definition. And insofar as the relation between the ideal-real (in a purely *a priori* metaphysics) and multiplicity-universality (in a purely *a posteriori* metaphysics) is concerned with the intra-creaturely problem of essence and existence (as we saw in §3), it nevertheless forces itself through this problem and beyond it, to the question of an "absolute" ideal and an

3. *Die formale Grundform.* — Trans.

"absolute" universal — as is shown in those cases where one side or the other is taken as absolute. But when we say "ideal" and "universal" it becomes clear that these questions strive to grasp the absolute in its particular instantiation — its *In-sein* — within the creaturely. Hence they are questions concerning the innermost rhythmic beat between God (as the absolute) and the created (as what is grounded, directed, and determined by this absolute), in that they are concerned with the innermost beat of becoming (between essence and existence) in the creature. In that they grasp the "in" of the creature, they touch upon the "in" of God *to* the creature. That is, on the basis of "God beyond the creature" (as we saw above), these questions point to the special sense of "God in the creature." This is the *positivum* that itself, in the extreme forms of metaphysics, was made into a false absolute: in that it was transformed from a relation of "in" to one of "as": "God as creature" or, as the case may be, "the creature as God." Corresponding to the differences between *a priori* and *a posteriori* metaphysics, "God in the creature" (as the final form common to both) is differentiated into two versions. In the first, the "in" within the formula "God in the creature" (understood as the *positivum* of *a priori* metaphysics) tends to mean that the creature is simply a (passive) "manifestation of God." *A priori* metaphysical thought goes from the ground, end, and definition to the grounded, directed, and determined. In this respect, it therefore involves in its ultimate depth a reproduction of God's own standpoint (of his knowledge *per modum quo artifex cognoscit artificiata* — that is, of his knowledge from the vantage of the ideative and the creative, as Thomas says: *scientia speculativa artificis*),[4] and so, as such, is truly a "manifestation of God." Then, in the second version of "God in the creature," we see the distinct *positivum* of *a posteriori* metaphysics. Here the "in" means a kind of (active) "potency" of the creature "towards God," insofar as the creature is able to measure out the expanse of being (from below to above), even to its ultimate foundations. To the degree, though, that the expanse of existing being is measured out in this way, what is ultimately being sketched is an outline of the other side of divine knowledge: the *scientia visionis* which sees through the whole universe. On the basis of the creature's "potency towards God," the "in" in "God in the creature" thus appears to mean "in the power of God," inasmuch as this "potency" (which is in becoming) is an image of the power of God's *scientia visionis* (which *is*). In the end, therefore, this too is one formal side of "God in the creature."

---

4. In the way in which the artisan knows the things he has made/the speculative knowledge of the artisan. *De Ver.* q. 2, a. 8, corp.

In this double way (both by overcoming the absolutizations and by including the *positiva*), the formula "essence in-and-beyond existence" (understood as the formal configuration of the problem of the *a priori* and the *a posteriori*) is clarified — transcending and yet returning to itself — in the formula "God beyond-and-in the creature" (understood as the formal configuration of the problem of the absolute and the relative). The attaining of this ultimate foundation of the formal configuration of metaphysics as such thus depends upon our preserving a double aspect within the formal configuration of the problem of the *a priori* and the *a posteriori*. Firstly, it requires the "in-and-beyond" that characterizes the relation between essence and existence. The extremes of a purely *a priori* and a purely *a posteriori* metaphysics succumb either to an "absolute unity" (Parmenides' immobile ideative being of essence) or to an "absolute movement" (Heraclitus's utterly mobile being of existence). In the first case, the creaturely solidifies (into an eternity of essence: in the systematic rigidity of a pure apriorism); in the second case, it flows away (into the *apeiron* of existence: in the *"in infinitum"* of purely *a posteriori* experience). In the "in-and-beyond," by contrast, unity and movement are bound together in a suspended middle that oscillates back and forth: it is a *unity* of movement, to the degree that (as we saw in §3) we are concerned with the *a priori* (of both object and act) — but, by the same token, it is equally a unity of *movement,* because our concern with the *a priori* is realized in and through the *a posteriori* (likewise of both object and act). Secondly, it requires that, right within this de-absolutization, the tendency towards the absolute more profoundly spring up. In the forms of absolutization, this tendency became the death of the creature. But neither can this tendency simply sink down and away into a "suspended back-and-forth," as though this were ultimate. For, as regards the object, it aims at the primal origin *(principium)* and ultimate defining end *(finis)* of the motion of becoming (in its back-and-forth); while, as regards the act, it aims at an unconditioned truth *(veritas prima)* from which (as the omnificent origin) the movement towards truth issues, and towards which (as the defining end that guides all things) this movement is ideally directed. To posit a "self-enclosed creatureliness," therefore, is arbitrarily to freeze a "transition" into a fixed "state." "Essence in-and-beyond existence" is an "ultimate quality" — one that, in itself, is "a transcending relation because it is transcended." In arriving at creatureliness as a quality, one also arrives at createdness as a relation. All that remains is an either-or: either the absolutizations of the immanent poles of the creaturely (as we saw in the cases of absolute *a priori* and absolute *a posteriori* metaphysics) or the absolute beyond-and-in them.

In this way it becomes clear how "God beyond-and-in the creature" necessarily appears as what is ultimate within the formal problem of metaphysics — as, that is, its formal ground. Thus we have a *theologia naturalis* inherent in the concept of metaphysics as such, and prior to the particular *theologia naturalis* advanced by any particular metaphysics. Here too, therefore, we have the *formal ground of the formal configuration of "creaturely metaphysics"*: its "essence in-and-beyond existence" is vertically transected by "God beyond-and-in the creature." But if thorough consideration of the formula "essence in-and-beyond existence" yielded the formula "God beyond-and-in the creature," then obviously the latter formula is visible in the features of the former. That is to say that here even the *absoluta,* which we encountered in the problem of the relation between the *a priori* and the *a posteriori,* become transparent: in that their name declares the name of God. They are absolutes because and insofar as they posit an "as" in the place of an "in-and-beyond": "essence as existence." In this, each is a (usurpatious) divine "Is." But in that the *absolutum* of the *a priori* posits the ideative as absolute, it accentuates "*essence* as existence"; whereas, conversely, the *absolutum* of the *a posteriori,* which speaks of a "real unity of the all," is to be heard as "essence as *existence.*" The unity of these two names thus yields, immanently, the name for the *absolutum* of creaturely metaphysics. Its *complete formal configuration* can be depicted as follows:

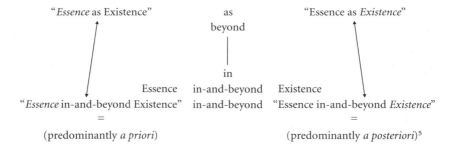

5. The reader might reasonably find this somewhat hermetic device more a cause for perplexity than an aid to understanding. Some exposition may be of use. The reality of creaturely being is that of the dynamism — the incommensurability and yet inseparability — of essence and existence: essence is always that which we are, have been, and are yet to be; "what we are" is ours only in becoming, and so lies in and beyond us. In this we are at once analogous to God (in whom essence and existence perfectly coincide) and infinitely different from God; and so he is thus at once in and beyond creaturely reality. Because essence and existence are distinct and yet inseparable in us, metaphysics may concern itself principally

2. For our definitive formal configuration of metaphysics, however, it is decisive that its transcending relation was rendered fundamentally as "God *beyond* the creature." This does not simply mean that the divine absolute as it appears "from" the creaturely can be only "beyond (everything creaturely)." On the contrary, this "beyond" is "beyond" in the fullest sense only when the appearing of the divine absolute is not bound in any way intrinsically to this "from (the creaturely)," but instead presides independently over the manner of its own appearing — such that now, conversely, this "from" appears from "beyond." Indeed, one might ask whether the "beyond" does not show itself as "beyond" until it is seen not "from (the creaturely)," but from Itself. This then raises the more pointed question: Is metaphysics (as we have conceived of it thus far) fully possible "from the creaturely" or does it intrinsically entail the necessity of a self-revelation of the divine absolute "from Itself"? It is the *question concerning philosophical and theological metaphysics:* both general and concrete.

Plato contrasts philosophy, understood as *philo-(sophia)*, with *sophia* proper; *sophia* is what is proper to God alone (θεῷ μόνῳ πρέπειν). The human being is capable only of a "loving towards . . ." this wisdom, which is God. If φιλία designates that personal fellowship that has its original form in the family (the fellowship of man and woman, siblings, father-children-servants),[6] then philosophy would be a participation in the wisdom that God is by virtue of personal participation in God. In this sense, even Aristotle, who no longer draws this distinction between philosophy and σοφία, characterizes σοφία as οὐκ ἀνθρωπίνη . . . κτῆσις.[7] Accordingly, at the level of subjective method, the act of philosophy is directly likened to a mystery rite.[8] In Plato *(inter alia),* it is likened to the funerary mysteries of the Βάκχοι[9] and to the

---

either with the former (*a priori* metaphysics) or with the latter (*a posteriori* metaphysics), but it can never do so in such a way as to escape dependency upon the side of the equation it neglects. The difference here between the *a priori* and the *a posteriori* is simply that, in their common orientation towards the absolute (essence as existence), the one places its stress upon *essence* and the other upon *existence.* Moreover, in the ambition they share of making their special objects each comprehensive of the other, they point beyond themselves to God's simple and essential act of being. And indeed, one might add, the very impossibility of assigning either species of metaphysics priority (or of, as above, elevating either the meta-ontic or the meta-noetic above the other) testifies to the simplicity of the prior act of being and knowing in which all finite reality participates. — Trans.

6. Aristotle, *Eth. Nic.* VIII, 10, 1160a, 32f.

7. Not a human . . . possession. *Met.* I, 2, 982b, 28f.

8. *Mysterien-Akt.* — Trans.

9. *Phaedo,* 69cd.

priesthood of Apollo's swans;[10] in Aristotle, to a proximity to the mystical (φιλόμυθος ὁ φιλόσοφος)[11] and to a priestly celebration performed in contemplative leisure (σχολάζειν τὸ τῶν ἱερέων ἔθνος).[12]

It is in this sense that Thomas Aquinas will describe theology as *maxime sapientia*.[13] That is to say that, at least in an objective and factical way, he will equate it with that *sophia* by participation in which *philo-sophia* occurs (as we just saw). On the one hand, therefore, theology appears precisely as the immanent apex of knowledge *(ordinans et iudicans ex altissima causa)*.[14] On the other hand, philosophy projects itself into theology. As a "statement about God" (λέγειν θεόν), theology is, on the one hand, the true "metaphysics" *(in qua considerantur res divinae non tamquam subiectum scientiae, sed tamquam principium subiecti)*:[15] the relation between God and creature figuring as the *principium* — i.e., the innermost "ground, end, and definition" of the objects of philosophy. But then, on the other hand, as a "statement by God" (θεὸς λέγων), theology constitutes a completely different genus over against the *philosophicae disciplinae*,[16] since it deals fundamentally (corresponding to the form of the act of a "statement by God") with the divine for its own sake *(ipsas res divinas considerat propter seipsas ut subiectum scientiae)*.[17]

If we take the generic difference between philosophy and theology as fundamental (which alone allows for a clear discrimination of the two), then what obviously distinguishes them from one another — however much interplay there may be between them *(vide infra)* — is that in philosophy it is the "philo" that is decisive and in theology the "theo." The distinctive meaning of "philo" is that the creature is the formal subject of the *act* (insofar, at least, as the "with" in "participation"[18] signifies the participant and not the participated). The distinctive mark of "theo," by contrast, is that it places the

10. *Phaedo*, 85b.
11. The lover of wisdom is a lover of myth. *Met.* I, 2, 982b, 18.
12. The caste of priests (was allowed to be) at leisure. *Met.* I, 981b, 24f. [Aristotle is explaining why the mathematical arts were established first in Egypt. — Trans.]
13. *Summa Th.* I, q. I, a. 6, corp.
14. Ordering and judging in light of the highest cause. *Summa Th.* I, q. I, a. 6, corp.
15. Wherein things divine are considered not as the subject of its science, but as the principle of its subject. *In Boeth. De Trin.* q. 5, a. 4, corp.
16. *Summa Th.* I, q. 1, a. 1, ad 2.
17. It considers things divine themselves, for their own sake, as the subject of its science. *In Boeth. De Trin.* q. 5, a. 4, corp.
18. Przywara is thinking in Greek; he means the μετά in such words as μέθεξις, μετοχή, μετάληψις, and μετουσία. — Trans.

stress on God as the formal subject of the act (insofar, at least, as even a "speculative theology" essentially rests upon foundations grounded solely in the authority of God's self-expression). Logically, then, from these distinctions in the act, follow distinctions in the realm of *content*. Philosophy tarries, fundamentally, within the ambit of creatureliness, and so the divine belongs to philosophy as an object only insofar as the divine falls under the question of creatureliness — as, that is, its "ground, end, and definition" *(res divinae . . . prout sunt principia omnium entium)*;[19] thus the divine is not treated "in itself," but ultimately only as the "above-and-beyond," and hence "negatively" *(quod Deus est super illud quod de ipso intellectui nostro repraesentatur, . . . et ideo non videmus de Deo quid est, sed quid non est)*.[20] Theology's domain, on the other hand, is the divine itself *(res divinae . . . prout sunt in se res quaedam)*,[21] while the creaturely comes into question only as (and "insofar" as it is) the site and way and mode of the self-declaration of the divine *(est principaliter de Deo sicut de subiecto; de creaturis autem multa assumit ut effectus Eius vel quomodolibet habentia habitudinem ad ipsum)*.[22] — This is certainly not to say that philosophy would thus have God as its negative limit concept, and theology the creature. On the contrary: this would constitute the most extreme cleft between the philosophical "methodological atheism" of a "creatureliness suspended in itself" (which has already shown itself to be self-refuting, in §3, 1) and a theological *theologia archetypa* (which considers God as what he is in and to himself, and not what he is to us).[23] Nor is it the case that, just as philosophy has the "divine in itself" as its limit, so too theology would have the "creaturely in itself" as its limit. For limit is a concept proper to the realm of the creature, not to that of God. But it is, of course, nevertheless the case that, whereas philosophy confines itself to the realm of creatureliness, theology confines itself to that of God, so that everything else is limited to an "insofar as" by these material formal objects: in philosophy, "God" by the "creature"; in theology, "the

19. Things divine . . . insofar as they are the principles of all beings. *In Boeth. De Trin.* q. 5, a. 4, corp.

20. For God is beyond what our intellect can of itself represent, . . . and therefore what we can see of God is not what he is, but what he is not. *De Ver.* q. 8, a. 1, ad 8.

21. Things divine . . . insofar as they are what they are in themselves. *In Boeth. De Trin.* q. 5, a. 4, corp.

22. Principally it takes God as its subject; it does, however, take up many things proper to creatures, as effects of God or as having an orientation towards him. *In Boeth. De Trin.* q. 5, a. 4, ad 8.

23. Cf. *Summa Th.* I, q. 1, a. 6, ad 1.

creature" by "God." This "insofar as" is the most formal commonality between them.

If we compare this problematic with the one yielded by our earlier problematic of *a priori* and *a posteriori* metaphysics, then it is obvious at first glance that the two are peculiarly aimed at one another. For the antitheses "from above to below" and "from below to above," as presented by the problem of *a priori* and *a posteriori* metaphysics, seem also to ground the relation between theology and philosophy. The question of theological and philosophical metaphysics will thus depend upon the clarification of this — at least apparent — equivalence. If they are equivalent to the point of coincidence, then the question of theological and philosophical metaphysics falls away (because it would already have been dealt with as the question of *a priori* and *a posteriori* metaphysics). If there is no equivalence whatsoever, then the question cannot be posed at all (because then it would not arise from within the question concerning metaphysics as such).

It should now be clear that our question can be posed only from the perspective of a "creaturely" metaphysics, and not from that of the absolute of purely *a priori* or purely *a posteriori* metaphysics. Theology, as clearly distinct from philosophy, is possible only on the basis of "God beyond the creature," understood as the fundamental relation between God and creature. "God as creature" — this being the formal ground of the fundamental relation between God and creature within the *absoluta* of purely *a priori* and purely *a posteriori* metaphysics — excludes any independent theology, because here philosophy as such is already theology. In a purely *a priori* metaphysics, one sees a theology of the "God of the ideas" within the absoluteness of eidetic vision and mathematical deduction; in a purely *a posteriori* metaphysics, on the other hand, a theology of a "God of the all" is latent within the absoluteness of the purely empirical and of a self-rounding perfection that is in itself and to itself (as we sketched out above). So much has the absolute of God become the absolute of the creature that the creature's self-expression is an expression of the divine: "God speaking his word," θεὸς λέγων λόγον. Thus it can come as no surprise when we observe that, even in historical terms, those modern philosophies that seek to be absolute are in fact theologies emptied of theological content — derived from a theology, to be sure, that had already of itself annulled the differences between God and creature: the Reformation's theology of God alone working all things.[24]

---

24. It is worth calling attention to this point, as it entirely inverts the accusation often made against Przywara by some forms of Barthian theology. For Przywara, it is precisely the

Hence follows the correlate that theologies of this type degenerate into philosophies, as we have adequately demonstrated in earlier works.

However, as we also argued in those works, this holds true not only for
this particular historical case, but in general. Borrowing from our earlier terminology, we can say that the differences between God and creature are annulled by way either of theo-pan-ism or of pan-the-ism. "Theo-pan-ism"
means that, proceeding fundamentally "from above to below," God becomes
the all. This is the form of "devolution" that ultimately is immanently implicit
in a purely *a priori* metaphysics (as we saw above, §4, 1). "Pan-the-ism" then
means that, proceeding fundamentally "from below to above," the all becomes
God. Hence, this is the form of "evolution" that ultimately is immanently implicit in a purely *a posteriori* metaphysics. Thus theopanism is the formal
ground of purely *a priori* metaphysics, and pantheism the formal ground of
purely *a posteriori* metaphysics. In the former case, the confusion of theology
and philosophy occurs in such a way that at the beginning stands theology,
and at the end a philosophy that is theology and a theology that is philosophy.
The particular historical instance of this is the theology of the Reformation.
And we can take as an example of this the way in which Hegel's philosophy
originates from and grows out of theology, and conversely (as in the case, say,
of Biedermann) the way in which it leads to the transformation of theology
into philosophical dialectic. But we can also see this in the contemporary unity
of theological and philosophical dialectic, specifically, in that one sees behind
"dialectical theology" a universal spiritual[25] "aporetics," while, conversely, in
Heidegger's pure philosophy, one sees the theological impulse of Kierkegaard
at work. In the latter case (that of a formal pantheism of purely *a posteriori*
metaphysics), the same confusion of theology and philosophy takes place, but
in such a way that a philosophy, which is conceived as absolute, stands at the

---

failure of Protestant thought to allow a real analogical interval between God's *actus essendi
subsistens* and the actuality of the creature that causes the distinction between God and creation to collapse, by making creation nothing but the manifestation of sovereign divine
arbitrium. A purely dialectical style of theology, without the analogical "middle" that "liberates" the creature for free "service" *(vide infra)*, does not in fact safeguard the transcendence
of God; it reduces divine action towards creatures to a kind of efficiency univocal with
creaturely action, erases the distinction between the primary causality of God's freedom and
the secondary causality of creaturely freedom, and ultimately binds God to the world by
supplanting genuine creaturely contingency with an absolute fatalism. Dialectical theology,
that is, is effectively indistinguishable from metaphysical monism; and a theology reducible
to "God alone working all" is effectively indistinguishable from a Promethean unwillingness
to be a creature. — Trans.
    25. *Geistige.* — Trans.

beginning — one whose original impulse is either expressly mystical (as in the Platonism of the Renaissance) or one that is emphatically apostate, that is, "religious, but with all the symbols inverted" (as with all the forms of positivism, but especially those commencing in our day). At the end of either, one consequently finds a theology immanent to philosophy: i.e., a "mythos" — be it that of a "cosmic mysticism" (as in Spinoza and Giordano Bruno), or of a "chthonic Dionysian world" (as in Nietzsche), or of "number, measure, and weight" (as in the various positivisms), etc. One can see here how Jewish messianism is at work in one way or another.[26] This is implicit in its formal ground: in the deification of the "law" and thus the dependence of God on the working of human beings (reaching its extreme in the Talmudic mysticism of "the becoming of God in and through man").

If we now consider how all the remaining forms are gathered within this fateful relation between theopanism and pantheism,[27] the only form left (considered purely from the question of the formal ground) is Catholic theology, because and insofar as it knows neither extreme. For the same reason that we can pose our question concerning theology and philosophy only from the vantage of a "creaturely metaphysics," we can pose it also only from the perspective of Catholic theology. For Catholic theology (alone) carries within itself, as its formal ground, the formula "God beyond-and-in the creature," which alone overcomes the relation between theopanism and pantheism, as we have shown in earlier works.[28] As we saw above (from §1 on-

---

26. If this seems a curious conclusion to reach — and if the identification below of such messianism with a species of pantheism seems bizarre — it is necessary to keep in mind that Przywara is writing in the light of the school of German Jewish idealist messianism that produced the quasi-Kantian Hermann Cohen, the quasi-Schellingian Franz Rosenzweig, and their intellectual progeny (particularly Martin Buber). The distinction Przywara is at pains to make, here and hereafter, is one between a (largely Barthian) theology that reduces the creature to a mere manifestation of God's absolute will and a form of modern idealism that sees God as achieving his identity in and through the creature; in either case, quite contrary to what either school supposes or intends, the real difference — the analogical interval — between the divine and creaturely is effectively negated. — Trans.

27. I refer here only briefly to "God" (1925), reprinted in *Religionsphilosophische Schriften* (Einsiedeln: Johannes-Verlag, 1962); *Religionsphilosophie katholischer Theologie* (1925) [in English: *Polarity*, trans. A. C. Bouquet (London: Oxford University Press, 1935)]; *Ringen der Gegenwart*, vol. 2 (Augsburg: Brenno Filser, 1929); and *Geheimnis Kierkegaards* (München: Oldenbourg, 1930). But even Albert Schweitzer aims in the same direction (*Das Christentum und die Weltreligionen*, 1924).

28. Earlier I used the term "God in-and-beyond the creature." But (from the perspective governing us here) "God beyond-and-in the creature" is actually more precise. The internal relation between these two forms is the object of the present work.

ward), this same "God beyond-and-in the creature" showed itself to be the formal ground of "creaturely" metaphysics (this metaphysics being the only solution to result intrinsically from the problematic of metaphysics as such). According to its intrinsic logic, therefore, the question of philosophical and theological metaphysics has become concrete in the *question of creaturely metaphysics and Catholic theology.*

3. Still, though, we have before us only the question in its concrete form, not its answer. We have reached the conclusion that we can pose the question of the relation between philosophical and theological metaphysics only when the philosophical does not exclude a theology (which is the case with "creaturely" metaphysics as we have explicated it up to this point) and when the theological is not the immanent theology of a philosophy (which is the case only in Catholic theology, because and insofar as it alone is distinguished from both of the forms of immanent theology — theopanism and pantheism). But we have not yet dealt with the actual *relationship between philosophy and theology within a single metaphysics.*

We will best be able to lay out this relationship if we compare the conceptual determinations that resulted from our consideration of metaphysics (§4, 1) and philosophy and theology (§4, 2).

On the one hand, it would seem that metaphysics is so much a part of philosophy that, while it does not exclude theology (which would be contrary to what we have shown above), it nevertheless does not require theology for its own inner formal configuration. For, first of all, metaphysics in the most general sense (as we have explicated it from the parts of the word) is the "going behind" into the "backgrounds" of *physis:* the backgrounds, that is, of being, insofar as it — as what is grounded, directed, and determined — points to a ground, end, and definition at work within it. The movement of the intellect here is plainly one that proceeds "from" and "within" that which is grounded, directed, and determined. Since the formality ground-end-definition is fulfilled perfectly only in God (not only because the creature, in this respect, points beyond itself to him, but also because he alone, therefore, is the ground-in-itself, end-in-itself, and definition-in-itself), this ground, end, and definition is in truth something like a "positive limit concept" of the metaphysical movement of thought. That is to say that the "insofar as" peculiar to philosophy is active within this movement: God is an object *insofar as* the creature is an object. Nor then, secondly, can the span[29] between the *a pri-*

---

29. *Spanne.* Here, however, as is the case throughout the text, Przywara uses this word in a way that suggests also *Spannung,* "tension," which is how both the French and Italian

ori and the *a posteriori* here constitute an objection. For both of these appear as aliases for theology and philosophy only insofar as what is at issue is, say, a *pure a priori* that would presume to fathom being from its ultimate origin (and thus presume for itself the position of God, who alone knows the creature from its origin — which is to say, from himself: the divine "knowledge of things in the Divine Essence," *cognoscere res in Essentia Divina*). As we have already seen, once their *positiva* are liberated from claims to absoluteness, the *a priori* and *a posteriori* reflect only the immanent span of the creaturely itself: between *eidos* (as "essence beyond existence") and *morphe* (as "essence in existence"). Seen thus, metaphysics would be something distinct from theology and would occupy a distinctly philosophical position. Theology, even where such a thing exists, would not be a possibility belonging essentially to the inner range of possibilities proper to metaphysics. Historically, this conception was envisaged by Catholic philosophy with the development of Scotism — a tradition that acquired its first manual in the *Disputationes metaphysicae* of Suarez, though it did not actually achieve a more conscious breakthrough until the debates with the "Pure Philosophy" that had been regarded as an ideal (however unrealized) since Descartes. It is sharply formulated in the words of the Vatican Council, which underscore not only a *duplex ordo cognitionis non solum principio, sed obiecto distinctus,*[30] but also and expressly the proper principles, proper method, and due liberty of each sphere (*propria principia, propria methodus,* and *iusta libertas*).[31] The same doctrinal definition that tells us that God belongs as "the principle and end of all things" *(rerum omnium principium et finis)* to the essential realm of "the natural light of human reason" *(naturale humanae rationis lumen)*[32] also tells us in the same terms we have seen with respect to the concept of philosophy what the material range of this domain is: God (as object) insofar as the creature (is object). Here we have *metaphysics as a philosophy that includes God as its positive limit concept* (which, for all its positivity, is still so decidedly a limit concept that, according to the acts of the Council, *creatio ex nihilo* does not belong to the realm of the philosophical concept of God).[33]

---

editions of the work render it. We, however, have elected a more literal — if far less felicitous — translation to avoid importing anything into the metaphor not intended by Przywara. — Trans.

    30. A twofold order of knowledge, distinct not solely according to principle, but according to object. Denz. 1795.

    31. Denz. 1799.

    32. Denz. 1786.

    33. *Coll. Lac.* VII, 79.

On the other hand, however, historical fact obliges us to consider the reality that certain theologies have[34] an inner disposition towards certain philosophies. This is the fact with which we were confronted above (§4, 2). The (theopanistic) theology of the Reformation tends to lead towards variants of purely *a priori* metaphysics. Jewish messianic (pantheistic) theology turns out to be the formal ground of the versions of purely *a posteriori* metaphysics. A "creaturely" metaphysics, however, stands eye to eye with Catholic theology.[35] Of course, from the perspective of an objective problematics, it is possible (as we have already done) to criticize certain kinds of metaphysics as being methodologically impossible (and to refute, logically, at their root, the theologies that belong to these metaphysics, by way of a kind of negative, philosophical apologetics). Nor can one say, insofar as this objective problematics is subject to verification and thoroughly objectively verifiable, that it itself is simply a concealed theology — namely, Catholic theology. Still, after taking all of this into account, it remains the case that, as a matter of objective fact, the "creaturely" metaphysics that resulted from such an objective problematics has its match in Catholic theology; and also the case that, as a matter of historical fact (in terms of subjective method), such metaphysics arises for all intents and purposes (however unconsciously) only on Catholic soil.

But, secondly, it is still not so clear that metaphysics, in confining itself to the essence of the creature (in the sense of this "insofar as"), is distinctly demarcated from theology. This was already suggested to us as we were developing the concept of philosophy and theology, since the *sophia* in philosophy itself bore a resemblance to theology. This becomes entirely clear from the perspective of Catholic theology. It has two formal principles that encompass everything within it. The one holds true for the noetic: "faith does not destroy, but presupposes and perfects reason," *fides non destruit, sed supponit et perficit rationem.* The other refers specifically to the ontic: "grace does not destroy, but presupposes and perfects nature," *gratia non destruit, sed supponit et perficit*

---

34. Literally, "are": *sind.* — Trans.

35. *Steht Aug in Aug zur katholischen Theologie.* Przywara seems to mean here that a "creaturely" metaphysics finds its match in Catholic theology, inasmuch as Catholic theology is not conflatable with philosophy and does not reduce (or tend to reduce) to one or the other kind of philosophical metaphysics (purely *a priori* or purely *a posteriori*). Instead, here the difference (and distance) between philosophy and theology is preserved, and therewith also the possibility of a genuine "eye-to-eye" encounter and relationship between them. The phrase "eye-to-eye" thus implies a matching (a relationship) predicated upon difference. — Trans.

naturam. Both have a foundation in Thomas's work.[36] *Fides* and *gratia* signify what belongs strictly to the domain of theology. *Ratio* and *natura* signify the "creaturely" domain proper to philosophy: the noetic *(ratio)* and the ontic *(natura)*. It is proper to the essential domain of *ratio* that it come to a sure recognition of God as the *principium et finis* of *natura* (as was said above). This *ratio* and this *natura*, furthermore, are not negated by the theological *(fides* and *gratia)*, but rather preserved each in its own essence *(non destruit, sed supponit)*. It remains the case, however, that this is only the negative side of a positive: of, namely, the theological *(fides* and *gratia)* as the "ultimate transfiguration[37] into its perfect form" *(per-ficit)* of the philosophical *(ratio* and *natura)*. If philosophical metaphysics is concerned noetically with *ratio* and ontically with *natura*, then it is concerned with them as "perfected"[38] — and so alone "real" — only insofar as they are explicitly regarded as such. A metaphysics that "disregards" this would not be false (because disregard is not "denial"); with respect to its proper object (the "creature"), however, it would be provisional. It is "definitive" only insofar as it takes into consideration the factual, objective "finality" of the creature: *fides* and *gratia* as shorthand for the creature understood as "supernaturally exalted and redeemed" consciousness *(fides)* and being *(gratia)*. But to say that metaphysics is "provisional" as philosophy is to say that it first attains "finality" through theology — to be sure, "through" and not "as" theology (since it remains the case that the formal object of a philosophical metaphysics is the "insofar as" of the creature).

If this is so, then the relation between the *a priori* and the *a posteriori* is not an alias of — but a transparency to — an internal relation between theology and philosophy within a *single* metaphysics. *A priori* metaphysics, in its own proper sense, moves from the supertemporal idea of things to the intratemporal form of its appearance: from *eidos* (= the essence, which is "valid in itself"), as ground-end-definition, to the *pragma* (= the instantiated thing), understood as the grounded, directed, and determined.[39] This movement becomes intrinsically transparent to the theological, as it is un-

---

36. *De Ver.* q. 14, a. 10, ad 9; *Summa Th.* I, q. 1, a. 8, ad 2; q. 2, a. 2, ad 1.

37. *Überformung.* One could perhaps risk the rebarbative neologism "super-formation" to convey the special connotations of Przywara's word, which here and below seems to mean in some sense "being formed from above" or "being formed into something higher." — Trans.

38. *Ausgeformt.* — Trans.

39. For the sake of simplicity, we give this example from the perspective of the problem of the object, though the mode of the problem of the act is included along with it (according to the above, §3, 1).

derstood from within the *one* metaphysics: in practice, this is what earlier "speculative theology" had done. It is not without reason that, for Thomas Aquinas, in accord with the ancient tradition, theology in the truest sense means *Sacra Scriptura* — i.e., the positivity of God's revealed Word. But since, according to its strict concept, it cannot suffice for theology to have the revealed word of God merely as its material object (theology as "speaking the word of God," λέγων λόγον θεοῦ), it must be a *Sacra Scriptura* that also has God as the subject of its act (theology as "God speaking the word of God," θεὸς λέγων λόγον θεοῦ). Since, finally, according to its concept, theology is a movement of God into humanity, and thus a visible entrance into this visibility (otherwise it would remain a *theologia archetypa*: of God in himself), it must intrinsically — as having a divine subject to its act — be an act that is *visibly* divine. This is, according to its concept, the infallible magisterium of the church. Theology, therefore, strictly speaking, is prosecuted as the offering of the positive word of revelation through the infallible magisterium of the church. It is an ecclesial theology of revelation that, over the course of time, unfolds the fullness of the given word of revelation. Within this theology, then, reflection upon the content of revelation (which takes place in the "theological schools") is the material principle, as it were, while its formal principle is represented by the positive verdict of the infallible magisterium. It is at this point that a relatively independent "speculative theology" forks off from actual (positively ecclesial) theology. The "reflection" of the "theological schools" takes the form, as Thomas explains, of conclusions drawn from those *articuli fidei* that serve as their *principia*.[40] Insofar as this manner of thinking is one that merely un-"folds," and that does so formally as an organ of the infallible magisterium (or at least with its consent), it is real theology. Insofar as its goal is a complete and pervasive philosophical vision, however, one must characterize it as the kind of "speculative theology" for which theology proper constitutes merely the point of departure. It becomes a thinking from the *principium qui et loquor* (John 8:25),[41] from the *a priori* of the God who expresses himself as the "speaking ground (end, definition)" of things. It becomes that to which *a priori* metaphysics is transparent, through and beyond itself.

40. *Summa Th.* I, q. 1, a. 2 and 8.

41. Przywara is exploiting the notorious Latin mistranslation of Christ's Τὴν ἀρχὴν ὅ τι καὶ λαλῶ ὑμῖν *(Principium, qui et loquor vobis);* rather than "I am first of all what I tell you I am," or "I am what I say I am from the beginning," or "why do I speak to you at all?," or any of the other renderings now normally proposed, he takes it to mean "I am the principle who also speaks to you." — Trans.

It is clear, though, how a "provisional" (purely philosophical) metaphysics and a "definitive" (theological) metaphysics relate to one another. Theological metaphysics has the formal primacy. But since it itself intrinsically refers back to the authentic ecclesial theology of revelation (inasmuch as this is where its *principia* reside), it itself is relative with respect to this authentic theology. We are entrusted with a *corpus,* as is especially characteristic of patristic and scholastic theology. The method of Greek and Roman patristic thought is *credere-intelligere-videre,* which is to say, theology as the explicit point of departure for philosophy. Classical scholasticism, in the form of the Summa, attends to the unity between a theological thinking undertaken from philosophical perspectives (of the way of God to the world and of the world to God) and a philosophical thinking undertaken in a theological light and with regard to theological objects. And even modern Catholic philosophy (which, as we have seen, essentially aims at "pure philosophy") cannot escape this. In its epistemology, for example, taking theology into consideration, it will extensively treat the topic of "knowledge from authority." From a theological perspective, it will investigate entire complexes of questions in ontology, cosmology, or psychology (the concept of the person, real accidents, etc.). In particular, its theodicy and ethics will be distinguished in no small measure by their emphasis upon the so-called *argumenta ex ratione* of the theological treatises *De Deo uno* and *De Deo creante* as well as those of moral theology. Thus it will recognize theology principally as a *norma negativa.* The [First] Vatican Council is simply being consistent, therefore, when it declares that the church (as the formal organ of theology) has a right to intervene in the realm of the sciences: *ius et officium habet falsi nominis scientiam proscribendi;*[42] a right, moreover, not merely in the sense of an "external discipline," but one that entails a decision regarding truth and falsehood: *non solum prohibentur tanquam legitimas scientiae conclusiones defendere, sed pro erroribus potius, qui fallacem veritatis speciem prae se ferant, habere tenentur omnino.*[43] If metaphysics consists in the unity of (philosophical) "provisional" metaphysics and (theological) "definitive" metaphysics, then it is *metaphysics under an ultimate formal primacy of theology,* even though, here too, it can in no way be considered formal theology.

42. [The church has] the right and duty of proscribing whatever is falsely called knowledge [1 Tim. 6:20]. Denz. 1798.

43. Not only are [faithful Christians] prohibited from defending [such opinions] as the legitimate conclusions of science, but they are altogether bound to regard these opinions as errors that present a false semblance of the truth. Denz. 1798.

4. The solution lies — as our explication to this point has adequately sketched out — in the inner connection of the two sides. This is evident, fundamentally, in the way that the relation between *a priori* and *a posteriori* metaphysics is completely transparent (through and beyond itself) to the relation between theological and philosophical metaphysics. For the former relation we earlier coined the term "realogical eidetics" (or, for the problem of the act, the term "truth in history"). In more general terms, we could call it an *a priori* that unfolds itself in an *a posteriori* fashion. If we apply this transparently to our present case, we can call it a (speculative) theological metaphysics that gradually opens up by way of philosophical metaphysics (in the sense given it with regard to the "first side" of our question — §4, 3). In looking at the relation between the *a priori* and the *a posteriori* we found that, on the one hand, the *a priori* is always already there, prior to the very first step of the *a posteriori;* on the other hand, though, the *a priori* can be envisioned only through and in the *a posteriori*. It is here that this relation, which is in fact a "making explicit of the implicit," arrives at its pinnacle, having ascended from the problem of the meta-noetic and the meta-ontic, to the problem of the transcendentals, and from there to the problem of the *a priori* and the *a posteriori*. Insofar as the theological resides — as, at the very least, an undeniable possibility — within the God-creature relation ("God beyond the creature"), which constitutes the ultimate formal ground of the philosophical (within a "creaturely" metaphysics); and insofar as, for this reason, the theological in fact has the ultimate formal primacy (as we saw above), as either an "idea," in its possibility, or as a "reality," if it in fact is real ("if," that is, God speaks); to this extent the theological has a formal primacy that is at work in the very first step of the philosophical and that, therefore, objectively precedes it. To this extent the *theological* constitutes a "telos," which, though *ultimum in executione,* is nevertheless *primum in intentione:* rising up before us as ultimate, and yet, from the beginning, not only looked towards, but exercising an active influence: ascending in its influence from the minimum of a "negative disposition" (in the sense of the *norma negativa* of neo-scholasticism) to the maximum of a positive imparting of content (in theological metaphysics, understood as "definitive" metaphysics). But insofar as the goal of all this is not a theology, but a metaphysics (that is, an undertaking that, with respect to its formal method, still has its home within the philosophical, however much it may reach into the realm of the theological); and insofar, furthermore, as theology is not somehow objectively grounded in philosophy, but is nonetheless something recognizable (with respect to subjective method) — as regards both its possibility and its actual existence — from considerations proper to

the realm of the philosophical (a principled recognition that faith and revelation are at least not impossible; and a recognition, in historical terms, of revelation's actual presence in history); to this extent the formal primacy of the theological, to which we have already adverted, is formally realized within the framework of the philosophical. In no way is it the case that the metaphysics in question constitutes a *"tertium quid"* — a "third" — that bridges the separation between philosophy and theology. On the contrary, any formally philosophical undertaking carries within itself a formal primacy of the theological because, and insofar as, the theological as such super-forms[44] the entire creaturely realm. The formal primacy of the theological is therefore an immanent consequence of the distinctive essence of metaphysics (as we have also argued). Thus the theological is a "telos" (in the sense described above) as, and insofar as it is, the "inner telos" of the metaphysical. Aristotle's word for such an inner telos, *en-telecheia,* refers back to a "putting-into-action" (ἐν-έργεια) and "power-as-possibility" (δύναμις). Having already observed how the formal primacy of the theological developed from the notion of a "definitive" metaphysics (§4, 3), we can now observe that the formula *"the theological as the entelechy of metaphysics"* accords with Aristotle's usage. Through the theological, as its "inner telos" (ἐντελέχεια), the "ascending movement" (δύναμις) of metaphysics arrives at its "definitive actualization" (ἐνέργεια).[45]

Still, though, there is an ambiguity at play in this formula; for it makes it seem as though the theological were an "entelechy" in the same sense that there is force in matter, or the life-principle in life, or the soul in the body, all of which — even if the terms of each of these couplets cannot be derived from one another — are nevertheless connected to one another on the same plane. In fact, however, one must observe the same intensification within this correlation that Augustine described in his famous formula: as the body is to the soul, so is the soul to God. The common element of the "as . . . so" is

---

44. A literal translation, again, of *"überformt,"* which is even more impenetrable here. Clearly, Przywara is not using the word with the sense of "transforms," and it is possible that he means simply that the theological "extends over" the entire realm of the creaturely; but it is also possible that it should be read as possessing a somewhat more active sense: it may constitute a complement (following from the analogical dynamism of the "beyond-in") of "informs." — Trans.

45. This cannot, however, be translated into the scholastic formula *potentia-actus,* since not only does this formula make a duality out of the Aristotelian triad, but also because (in this formula) *potentia* is already conceived merely as "possibility" without the additional sense of "power held in tension."

then understood to mean not that the terms are "bound together on the same plane," but rather that in both relations a higher term, by remaining the higher term (soul, God), has a formal primacy with respect to the lower, such that the lower term (body, soul) arrives at its actuality not "in itself," but "beyond itself." If the distance between the higher and the lower grows greater (as it does here: from body-soul, as the distance between creature and creature, to soul-God, as the distance between creature and God), so too must grow, incomparably, the magnitude of the descent (of the soul to the body, of God to the soul) and thus of the ascent (of the body to the soul, of the soul to God). This is by all means transferable from the question of ontic content to that of noetic method. We thus have here a series of intensifications: from the problem of the *a priori* and the *a posteriori* (§3), to the God-creature relation implicit in it (§4, 1), to the concluding relation between theology and philosophy, all within the *one* metaphysics.

What they all have in common is that in each case it is always a matter of the *one* metaphysics. What they also have in common is that, as is already the case with the relation of the *a priori* to the *a posteriori,* a derivation of one from the other is infeasible. As we have seen, neither are "principles" (or "truth") derived from "experience" (or "history"), as is the aim of a purely *a posteriori* metaphysics, nor is experience derived from "principles" (or "truth"), as is the aim of a purely *a priori* metaphysics. And, finally, here too it is already the case that this impossibility of derivation is graded. A purely *a posteriori* metaphysics is impossible because principles or truth (as the higher term) can in no way be inferred from experience or history (understood as an "application of principles" or a "manifestation of truth"). A purely *a priori* metaphysics, by contrast, is impossible simply because "an application of principles" (or "manifestation of truth"), even if it follows from its principles (or truth), is not an ideative necessity. This is the sense of the neo-scholastic distinction between *possibilitas interna* and *externa:* the reality of human beings is certainly a realization of the idea of the human being; but from this idea one can derive neither any instance — the "that it is" — of its realization, nor any more proximate determination of the particular nature of this instance (by which "our" human world would be distinguished from other possible human worlds).

Nevertheless, the problem between the *a priori* and the *a posteriori* is an intra-creaturely one: between the idea of being and the actuality of being. There is thus a common plane: creaturely being, which, as such, divides into idea (essence) and actuality (existence). This ceases to be the case for the other two problems, which are at play between God and creature. For, between God and creature, there can be no univocity whatsoever, in that, as the "Is" and the "becomes," they are distinguished from one another in the innermost constitution of being. And even here there is an intensification, going from the general problem of the relation between God and creature to the specific problem of the relation between theology and philosophy. For whereas, in the first instance, the constitution of the creature is unthinkable apart from its relation to God (as creator), the specific relation of God to the creature, which falls within theology's ken, is characterized by its complete "gratuity." For nowhere in the essence of the creature is there any kind of claim upon this relation, however intrinsically the creature may be objectively "open" to it (in its *potentia oboedientialis,* as Thomas phrases it).[46] Accordingly, what we have already identified as the ultimate commonality in the relations of the *a priori* and the *a posteriori,* of God and creature, of theology and philosophy — namely, the impossibility (which itself admits of various grades) of any derivation of one term from the other — will most clearly express the differences among these intensifications. In the problem of the *a priori* and the *a posteriori,* this graded impossibility of derivation manifests itself in a method in which real experience, from the first and constantly, tends beyond itself towards the *eidos.* The God-human relation is manifest at the level of method in a kind of thinking that — in its "knowledge of God in his image in the creature" — must, from the first and constantly, say along with Augustine: "This only can I say, that which he is not."[47] That is to say (to use the pointed language of the Greek fathers): the knowledge of God goes, from the first and constantly, beyond itself towards an unknowing. Indeed, it comes to pass precisely in such, and as such, an unknowing: as Thomas says, we come *ad cognoscendum de eo quid est . . . , in quantum de eo cognoscimus quid non est.*[48] This reaches its apex in the problem of theology and philosophy. For, in the case of the general God-creature relation, the relationship between "knowing" and "unknowing" is still contained within the concept of God: "If it concerns God in any way, it

---

46. In view of Przywara's clear point here, it is worth emphasizing that the most common Reformed criticism of the *analogia entis* — namely, that it puts God within the creature's grasp, or involves some sort of natural claim upon grace or seamless transition from philosophy to theology — is based upon a misunderstanding. That being said, it is also the case, given Przywara's remarks in the preface of this work, that his debate with Karl Barth helped him to clarify his own position. — Trans.

47. *In Ps.* LXXXV, 12.

48. To the knowledge of what he is . . . to the degree that we know what he is not. *De Ver.* q. 10, a. 12, ad 7.

can have only the nature of a 'knowing in unknowing,'" as is pointedly expressed in Augustine's maxim, *"si comprehendis, non est Deus."*[49] But the content of theology — to the extent that it is genuine theology — lies wholly in the freedom of God. To be sure, a "knowing in unknowing" already explodes the kind of knowledge whose aim is to comprehend in concepts. But a necessary connection still holds sway between "knowing" and "unknowing," insofar as the *cognoscimus . . . quid non est* stands within the internal connection of the *in quantum* to the *cognoscendum . . . quid est.* In the problem of theology and philosophy, however, this connection is only that of an "antecedent possibility" or, better, a "non-impossibility" (that God would reveal himself and thereby ground theology), and a "factual" relationship ("if God has, in fact, revealed himself"). The (first) connection, which has the character of an internal connection, says nothing about actuality. The (second) connection, which does speak of actuality, contains no trace of necessity. Thus "above-and-beyond" here really means what 1 Corinthians says about the relationship between revelation and thought: "scandal" and "folly" in the sign of the "cross." "Pure thought"[50] is "routed,"[51] forced to flee undecidably either to "necessity without actuality" or to "actuality without necessity." And precisely thus is it philosophy: participation in the truth, which is God. For the *one* metaphysics, *theology* is the ἐντελέχεια (in the sense of our earlier explanation) — that is, its ultimate life-giving form — in that it appears (from the perspective of our earlier considerations) to be the στέρησις of philosophical thought — that is, its bursting open to the point of a hollowing-out: "life in death." In that, as Thomas says,[52] the relationship of the theological to the philosophical is one of *excedere* (the "bursting open" in the "above and beyond" to the point of a "hollowed-out abandonment"), it is one of *per-ficere* (of a "thorough crafting-to-the-end" to the point of "perfection").

5. The corresponding *practical method,* too, therefore, is best encapsulated in the two maxims that we have already formulated in view of these fundamental considerations. For the meta-noetic side of the metaphysical

49. If you understand it, it is not God. *Serm.* CVII, iii, 5.

50. *Reinliches Denken.* — Trans.

51. *Zu Paaren getrieben.* By this felicitous phrase, which is difficult to translate, Przywara seems to mean that pure thought, which would seek to be exact, is at once routed and dispersed (like a defeated army) into two equally valid alternatives. The etymology of the word "Paar" also suggests that pure thought is hereby "herded" back into its proper confines. — Trans.

52. *De Ver.* q. 14, a. 10, ad 9.

problem, the maxim holds true: *fides (theologia)*[53] *non destruit, sed supponit et perficit rationem (philosophiam)*. The maxim corresponding to the meta-ontic side of the problem is: *gratia non destruit, sed supponit et perficit naturam*. In their interplication (as *Thomas* is quite happy to formulate the matter)[54] these two maxims constitute "the" methodological principle for the metaphysical world-picture that is expressed in the unity of these two sides of the metaphysical problem. In its unity with the *perficit*, the *non destruit* establishes, in each case, the *point of departure* for these three themes. On the one hand, it is a thoroughly positive philosophical point of departure (by virtue of the *non destruit*); on the other hand, it is positive by virtue of the theological — and not simply because the theological does not render such a point of departure impossible *(non destruit)*, but because the theological explicitly makes it possible as such (since the *non destruit* is the "fore-shadowing" of the *per-ficit*). It is, therefore, a genuine philosophical positivity, but one that is from the outset "open" to the theological — not, however, in a purely negative sense (out of a kind of "failure"), but rather in a precisely positive sense (because it receives *from* the theological the ground of what distinguishes it over against the theological).

The *supponit*, in its unity with the *perficit*, points the way for this point of departure's *unfolding* towards its goal. *Supponit* means, firstly: a genuine advance and passage through the whole undiminished breadth of the philosophical (since, as regards both question and content, the "pre-supposed" is distinguished from the "super-imposed"). Secondly, *supponit* has even this sense: that the theological is genuinely established by a philosophy that is distinguished by its autonomy (because that which is "super-imposed" is actually "posed upon" that which is "pre-supposed"). Finally, however (and thirdly), *supponit* means: an internal transition of the philosophical into the theological as its completion (because the "presupposed" is intrinsically "underway towards" the "superimposed"). It is thus not the case that philosophy simply "fails," in a purely negative manner, when it reaches certain limits. Rather, it is positively "liberated" to go "beyond itself" into the theological, in that the *intelligere* that moves "within" the (explicitly) theological is the inner completion of the *intelligere* that moves "towards" the (explicitly) theological. It is the method of the Augustinian relation between "I under-

---

53. This parenthesis indicates that, in this entire presentation, what is at issue is not the more precise concept of theology, as opposed to faith, etc., but rather what they have in common that distinguishes them from philosophy.

54. *Summa Th.* I, q. 1, a. 8, ad 2; q. 2, a. 2, ad 1.

stand so that I may believe," *intelligo ut credam,* and "I believe so that I may understand," *credo ut intelligam.*[55] There is a real *intelligo ut credam* — one that proceeds, that is, from the innermost essence of the act and of the content of the philosophical. And yet, from the start, it proceeds (by virtue of the *perficit*) intrinsically "beyond itself" into the *credo ut intelligam,* because this latter is its *per-ficere* — i.e., its intrinsically superordinated form.

For this reason too, finally, there is no *tertium quid* — no "third"; rather the theological is itself the sea into which the philosophical *flows.* One could say that philosophical thought in itself comes first, pure *credere* second, and *credo ut intelligam* third. But insofar as the "pure *credere*" is understood not as an act of the self-revealing God, but as an act of the human being who receives the revelation, it cannot be prosecuted with such "purity." Augustine rightly derives the *credo ut intelligam* from this: that the *credere* itself already contains the *intelligere,* because, as a human act, it is "to think with assent," *cum assensione cogitare: cogitat omnis qui credit, et credendo cogitat et cogitando credit.*[56] To be sure — as we ourselves prosecute it — "genuine" (positive, ecclesial) theology is to be distinguished from what the theological means within the enterprise of metaphysics. But (as we saw at the proper juncture above — §4, 3) this is merely a distinction *a potiori.*[57] And not only that: in the practice of theological research, positive ecclesial theology and theological metaphysics interpenetrate. The definition of the immaculate conception arises, historically, out of the Scotist school; and in its historical development it is intimately bound to that school's peculiar metaphysics, with its emphasis upon the freedom of God's positing will, and so forth. In its definition, however, the doctrine is completely independent of that metaphysics (because it is a formal act of the infallible teaching authority). In this sense too, therefore, there is no "third" to be achieved: with pure philosophy first, positive ecclesial theology second, and theological metaphysics third. For the distinction between the latter two permits no order of succession,[58] since they already fork off from one another in the very first act of convergence. This, after all, is simply the result of what is inseparably given along with any real theology: the, as it

55. *Serm.* XLIII, vii, 9.

56. Everyone who believes thinks, and thinks in believing and believes in thinking. *De Praedest. Sanct.* II, 5.

57. That is to say, this is not a difference in kind, but a distinction in degree with regard to the "stronger" or more eminent case: "positive" or revealed theology, as opposed to "the theological" within metaphysics as such. — Trans.

58. *Nacheinander.* — Trans.

were, noetic *unio hypostatica* within it: that a human act, while being thoroughly human, has a personal form that is divine. From the one side there arises theological metaphysics (as the emphatic self-representation of the theological in creaturely, human forms); from the other side, there arises a positive ecclesial theology (as the proper authority[59] of the theological in the authority of the personal God). Our theological metaphysics thus carries in itself the positively ecclesial as the determining ground of its life. Indeed, the *tantum-quantum* of its progressive thought is essentially the *tantum-quantum* of positive ecclesiality. At the same time, however, it is formally and from the start a "private human labor" and not the "language of the church": taking the authority of God in the church as a determinative form for itself but not for others. It is positively ecclesial in the sense that it is "determined by the positively ecclesial," but not in the sense that it is "exercising the authority of the positively ecclesial." Thus one may speak of theological metaphysics as resting upon theology "proper," without itself being "proper" theology. For such "proper" theology aims at a form of binding ecclesial judgment (even if only in that lowliest of forms, the "theological qualification").

The other possibility of a "third" would then consist in the supposition of a "third" that could be attained beyond the theological (which, as we have just seen, cannot be divided). This is the possibility that has, as a matter of historical fact, actually been tried. Augustine refers to it as the ascent through the *transitorium* of the Word made flesh, the *Verbum caro factum,* to the incommutable truth, *veritas incommutabilis,* of the *Deus Verbum:*[60] from *credere* to *intelligere* to *videre.*[61] Thomas conceives[62] the idea of an *intellectus* that reverts again into its own immanence (after the *intellectus* has been led by the will in pure *credere* and strives, in the believing *intellectus,* to come to itself), but in such a way that this occurs only transcendently, by way of the *prima veritas* as *apparens* — that is, in the *videre* of the *visio.*[63] Hegel speaks of "absolute knowledge," which "is the revealed religion." But precisely his example makes it clear that this is no intratemporal possibility. Though Hegel's conception in fact rests upon Augustine and Thomas, he disregards the wise admonition that Augustine never tires of intoning: *antequam validi simus ad capiendum Verbum, non*

59. *Selbst-Autorität.* — Trans.
60. *In Ps.* CIX, v, 12.
61. *De Trin.* IX, i, 1.
62. *De Ver.* q. 14, a. 2, ad 14; Ibid. a. 9, ad 1 et 2.
63. *De Ver.* q. 18, a. 3, ad 1.

recedamus a fide lactis nostrae.[64] That is to say: the "third" is a possibility that is fulfilled solely in the measure that "God is all in all," and is thus ever more greatly beyond every grasping and comprehending by way of concepts. Not in the measure that the mystery becomes a concept, but in the measure that the concept is overcome in the mystery.[65]

On the path leading from the philosophical into the theological, we touch upon mystery at two points. It happens once at the point where the end of the philosophical becomes the (explicit) beginning of the theological. Here we encounter mystery in the sense of the (neo-scholastic) *mysterium naturale.* It is the mystery of God as *principium et finis* of the creature. It is what is meant by the Augustinian maxim: "so that he who is to be found should be sought, he is hidden," *ut inveniendus quaeratur occultus est.* It is mystery inasmuch as it corresponds to the search under way "towards" God *(inveniendus quaeratur)*: more negatively, it is mystery as something guarded *(occultus est).* Mystery appears a second time where the theological itself runs up against its limits: where the profoundest of theologians is forced to conclude, along with Thomas, that: *quamvis . . . per revelationem elevemur ad aliquid cognoscendum quod alias nobis esset ignotum; non tamen ad hoc quod alio modo cognoscamus nisi per sensibilia.*[66] Even the most exalted theology does not overcome the limits of the senses, which concede to all that is purely intellectual only a knowledge *per remotionem et negationem,* and so no knowledge of the thing in itself, the *quid est.* What is more: *impossibile est quod aliquis intellectus creatus divinam essentiam comprehendat.*[67] It is an entry into the mystery of God in order more deeply "to grasp his incomprehensibility as such," as Augustine says.[68] It is thus the (neo-scholastic) *mysterium supernaturale,* i.e., the mystery of "things divine as they are in themselves," *res divinae prout sunt in se.*[69] This is what is meant by the rest of Augustine's maxim: "so that he who has been found might be sought, he is unending," *ut inventus quaeratur, immensus est.*[70]

---

64. Before we are strong enough to receive the Word, let us not be weaned from the milk of [the church's] faith. *In Ps.* CXXX, xi.

65. *In das Geheimnis ubermächtigt wird.* — Trans.

66. Though . . . we may be raised by revelation to the knowledge of something that would otherwise be unknown to us; nevertheless that to which we are raised we can know in no way other than through sensible things. *In Boeth. de Trin.* q. 6, a. 3, corp.

67. It is impossible that any created intellect should comprehend the divine essence. *De Ver.* q. 8, a. 2, corp.

68. *De Trin.* XV, ii, 2.

69. *In Boeth. de Trin.* q. 5, a. 4, corp.

70. *In Jo. Tract.* LXIII, i.

It is mystery, as it corresponds to the search as it takes place "in" God *(inventus quaeratur):* mystery that is positively open into mystery *(immensus est).* The night of God as unknown, *Deus tamquam ignotus,* which for Thomas stands at the "summit of our (earthly) knowledge,"[71] is thus, on the one hand (at the limits of the philosophical), "a darkening night"[72] and, to this extent, induces that "blindness" that alone leads into the theological (the *non videre* of the *credere*). But, on the other hand (at the limits of the theological), it is an "encompassing night" and therein that "super-luminous darkness" (ὑπέρφωτος γνόφος) of the Areopagite,[73] which announces the essence of the theo-logical: where, in the "Word (of God)," the "(Word) of God" is revealed: the depth of his invisibility in the depth of his visibility.

In practical terms, this is to say two things. It is to say, firstly, that a so-called "third" is realized within the theological itself: in its ever greater self-reduction (in all three themes of metaphysics) into the "depths of God," but thereby into the inner-personal life of God — into, that is, the *Trinitarian.* Theological metaphysics is here properly enjoined to undertake a renewal of Augustine — though in the medium of the "holy sobriety" of Thomas Aquinas, who in this respect develops the kind of critique that Augustine himself sets forth in the final books of *De Trinitate.*

It is to say, secondly, that the relation between *"concept" and "mystery"* is found at every point along the way. What is at issue is best described by the full meaning of the phrase that we have long since employed for this, *reductio in mysterium.* "Mysterium," on the one hand, means the opposite of *profanum. My-sterium* signifies that which is "closed off" (μύω), insofar as it is demarcated over against that which lies "before" the "temple precincts" and yet is essentially "for" the "temple precincts" — that is, it points the way towards the temple *(pro-fano).* Thus the *mysterium,* understood as "mystery,"[74] is the inner meaning of the "clearly paved street" that leads into it, but that — as a street — necessarily breaks off before the doors of mystery. The "street" breaks off before the door of separation (μύω) and, in this way, enters through it. In this sense, the concept leads, as concept, into the mystery: it is a *re-ductio in fieri,* an incursion of the bright corona of the conceptual into the dark center; and, in that it is a *re-ductio,* it is a being led along paths according to a plan. It is in this form that concept and mystery are con-

71. *In Boeth. de Trin.* q. 1, a. 2, corp. et ad 1.
72. *Aufdunkelnde Nacht.* A neologism that is impossible to translate, suggesting the rising darkness of night. — Trans.
73. *Myst. Th.* I, 1.
74. *Geheimnis.* — Trans.

nected along the path that leads from the philosophical into the theological. But *"mysterium"* (understood as *in facto esse*) also means having been inducted into what is "closed," and a being closed in together with it. Thus, the "concept" arises here anew out of "mystery": as a "being comprehended" by "mystery":[75] just as the night unveils its countenance only so far as the light has faded. We have here, consequently, a twofold sense of "concept." In that the "mystery" "grasps"[76] us, we feel (passively) its "grasp." The theological concept is therefore the primary and strictest concept: not as the goal towards which philosophy laboriously strives, but rather as "truth defined thus and not otherwise." It is a *re-**ductio*** altogether free of doubt, a state of being blindly led by the hand: absolute authority. But mystery grasps us in order to com-pre-hend us.[77] It leads us in order to lead us back into itself (hence the *re* in *re-ductio*). This is the full significance of 1 Corinthians 8:2-3: not simply a sinking of philosophical "knowing" (γνῶναι) before a theological and conceptual determination provided by definite revelation (ἔγνωσται), but more profoundly a sinking into the infinity of union (εἰ δέ τις ἀγαπᾷ τὸν θεόν, οὗτος ἔγνωσται ὑπ᾽ αὐτοῦ). In other words, even the concept of "defined truth" leads to mystery. But, whereas the philosophical concept breaks off into mystery, in the theological concept mystery is the fullness of the concept. It is not the case that a (super-theological) critique could assume a position superior to the "symbolism" of the dogmas, in order to relativize them by reducing them to a "pure meaning," and thus take them simply as "ways of speaking" of God's character as mystery. On the contrary, the positive maximum of the theological obedience of faith is the maximum of an immersion into the mystery of the depths of God. Otherwise the theological would have ceased to be *theo*-logical.

By now it should be clear that we are contending here with *Hegel.* But our argument is not yet sufficiently rigorous; for, having just explicated the manifold relation between concept and mystery, we still have to emphasize the ambiguity of its inner dynamic. For two reasons, this dynamic is not something that can be reduced to a concept, and it is therefore a dynamic in the most formal sense. On the one hand, it is a negative irreducibility: the

---

75. *"Begriff" entsteht hier mithin neu vom "Geheimnis" her: als "einbegriffen sein" durch das "Geheimnis."* The wordplay in this sentence and those following is more obvious in the German, where words with Latin roots do not appear; the "grasp" in "concept" — *Begriff* — is immediately audible, and allows more elegantly for the (very un-Hegelian) image of the "con-cept" being itself "com-prehended" by mystery. — Trans.

76. *Greift.* — Trans.

77. *Um uns ein-zu-be-greifen.* — Trans.

final failure and, hence, brokenness of creaturely concepts over against God. In this regard it is a dynamic in the ancient Greek sense: a relapse of the πέρας of delimiting concepts into the ἄπειρον of a limitless flooding. But, then, it is also a positive irreducibility: the living fullness of the divine infinity, which, far from having any "concept of God" above itself (in the sense of "God's self-concept"), is — "as" this infinity — God's true self-concept. Here it is not the case that a definite πέρας is plunged into a chaotic ἄπειρον. On the contrary, a positive ἄπειρον, understood as eternal life, constitutes the proper πέρας of the form. Both modes of the dynamic are connected, however, in that the negative of the first (creaturely) dynamic appears to be purely negative only from the perspective of an artificial disregard. For, when it is seen over against this same infinity of God — which in itself is a positive dynamic of eternal life — what appeared to be a "disintegration" turns out to be a "likeness."[78] The scattering is the scattering of the clouds in the light that pervades them. Precisely thus is the dynamic of the creature, which appears to be negative in its flowing away (in its mutability and multiplicity), a declaration of the positive dynamic of God (in his unity and immutability). This is the great insight of Thomas Aquinas: just as, ontically, the meaning of the mutable multiplicity of being is its mirroring of the infinity of God,[79] just so, noetically, the *Una . . . veritas prima increata* reveals itself in the *variare* of truth[80] and its multiplicity *(multae veritates)*;[81] and so, finally, God expresses himself in the *pluralitas* of our *diversae conceptiones* of God as the one who is altogether one and simple, the *omnino unus et simplex.*[82] This culminates in the threefold sense of the *"antithetics"* that is peculiar to the Augustinian dynamic (and that leads directly to Hegel). It is, first of all, a creaturely *antithetics:* such that creaturely thought, to the extent that it seeks to grasp something in the most precise concept possible, can do so only in concepts that cross themselves out and that, consequently, conspire to disrupt whatever uniform sense each might otherwise possess (for example, *diligere timendo, operando requiescere*).[83] Because, and in that, this *antithetics* is revealed in such measure as creaturely thought touches upon the region of God, however, it is more profoundly an antithetics between a comprehension of God (as "within ev-

78. *Zerfall, Gleichnis.* — Trans.
79. *Comp. Th.* c 102.
80. *De Ver.* q. 1, a. 4, ad 3.
81. *De Ver.* q. 27, a. 1, ad 7.
82. *Summa Th.* I, q. 13, a. 12, corp.
83. To love by fearing, to rest by acting. . . .

ery thing," *interior omni re*) and his transcendence of all comprehension (as "beyond every thing," *exterior omni re*).[84] But at the same time, because our *mens* is, in its ultimate depth, "the" image and likeness of the *Mens Divina*, it is here — in the way that, in our mental life, the mind in its reflection *(intellectus sui)* "opposes" itself to its own un-reflective self-presence *(memoria sui)* so as to take itself in conscious embrace *(voluntas sive dilectio sui)* — that a view opens (from a perspective illumined by faith) into the intra-divine vitality of the Father *(Memoria Sui)*, the Son *(Intellectus Sui)*, and the Holy Spirit *(Voluntas Sui)*.

Such is the basic record. What characterizes Hegel is that he directly grasps the super-conceptual rhythm of the intra-trinitarian life as the thought form governing the creature's intellectual life.[85] Hence, for him, on the one hand, the flowing antithetics of the intra-creaturely is forced to suffer a hardening absoluteness: in a supplanting of the category of "opposition"[86] — which is the only category that is objectively warranted — by that of "contradiction."[87] On the other hand, the eternity of the Logos of truth itself is compelled to assume within itself the διά of the creature's intrinsic oppositionality: in a supplanting of the "manifestation" or "self-communication" of *eternal* truth by a "dialectic," which is regarded as divine. This "dialectical contradiction" is diametrically opposed to what, for us, most fully expresses *the inner unity of philosophy and theology* at which we are aiming here: namely, an inner unity between the (material) centrality of the Trinitarian and the (formal) dynamic unity of concept and mystery. Here the three spheres of dynamic antithetics not only remain separate, as we have seen; they also remain separate in such a way that, logically, our path commences strictly with the first sphere (the intra-creaturely) — not in order to derive the other spheres from the intra-creaturely (which would lead to a new theological rationalism), but in order that the intra-creaturely might surmount itself by passing over into them — or, better yet, by letting itself be borne over into them. Logically, therefore, it is here that we are most fully engaged in critical reflection upon the Augustinian-Thomistic tradition.[88]

6. Since the debate with Hegelianism forms the historical background to

---

84. *De Gen. ad Litt.* VIII, 26.
85. *Geistesleben.* — Trans.
86. *Gegensatz.* — Trans.
87. *Widerspruch.* — Trans.
88. By "Augustinian-Thomistic" I mean not a school, but Augustine and Thomas Aquinas.

the [First] Vatican Council's chapter *De fide et ratione*,[89] this chapter provides us with the most precise formulation of the method we are here attempting to sketch out. First of all, at *a fundamental level,* there is the formal primacy of the theological (*Ecclesia . . . ius et officium divinitus habet falsi nominis scientiam prohibendi,* such that *omnes Christiani fideles huiusmodi opiniones . . . pro erroribus . . . habere tenentur omnino*),[90] which primacy, however, does not result in any restraint being placed upon knowledge, but rather in a liberation of knowledge; for what this chapter teaches is precisely that knowledge possesses an autonomy both objective *(propriis principiis)*[91] and subjective *(propria methodo).*[92] It is not that limits are set to "truth." On the contrary: because the theological either stands or falls on its character as the theological, its claim to formal primacy is advanced exclusively in the name of the *one* truth, which is grounded in God *(cum idem Deus, qui mysteria revelat et fidem infundit, animo humano rationis lumen indiderit, Deus autem negare se ipsum non possit nec verum vero unquam contradicere).*[93] Thus, to submit to the church purely on "grounds of compromise" would go not only against the autonomy and freedom that this same church asserts *(iustam . . . libertatem),*[94] but directly against God, understood as the God of the *one* unconditional truth. Rather, such submission — even and precisely in those cases that demand a sacrifice of one's own understanding — can take place only on the basis of an obligation to this *one* unconditional truth. Since this truth resides in God, however, in the God who speaks immediately in the theo-*logical* as the *theo*-logical, it bears within itself that fundamental law of God: "My thoughts are not your thoughts, nor my ways your ways." Far, then, from entailing a break with truth, it is, to the contrary, precisely in this way that the authentic breakthrough to the truth occurs: as a breaking out of the narrow confines of "truth in the I" to the "Truth, which is God." This is the practical realization of what is involved in Augustine's exhortation *"transcende te ipsum":* that, at bottom, the transcendence of "truth" over the "thinking soul" is none other than the transcen-

89. Sess. 3, ch. 4.

90. [The church has] the right and duty of proscribing whatever is falsely called knowledge [1 Tim. 6:20]/all faithful Christians are altogether bound to regard these opinions as errors. Denz. 1798.

91. Denz. 1799.

92. Denz. 1799.

93. For the same God who reveals mysteries and infuses faith has also imparted the light of reason to the human soul; moreover God cannot negate himself nor ever contradict one truth with another. Denz. 1797.

94. Denz. 1799.

dence of God over the I, and thus the depth of a genuine objectivism regarding truth turns out to be the *se abnegare* of the gospel: *noli remanere in te, transcende et te: in illo te pone qui fecit te.*[95] The profound significance of this, therefore, comes from Trinitarian doctrine: submission to the church is a being-formed-in-Christ, who as the Eternal Son of the Father is the Logos, the *Intellectus Sui* within the intra-divine life. Thus, what might look like "disciplinary cowardice" is actually a noetic mysticism of participation in the intra-divine procession of Eternal Truth.

At this fundamental level, then, it is not that some compromise is struck between the semi-theological and the semi-philosophical; rather, a genuine and unanxious theology and a genuine and unanxious philosophy are one in the *one* God of the *one* truth, and for this reason — secondly — the *working out* of their union, as it takes shape, will be equally free of anxiety. As sharply as theology and philosophy are separated, they just as completely interpenetrate. They are separated in terms of an actual *duplex ordo cognitionis*,[96] at the root both of the formal act *(distinctum . . . principio . . . , quia in altero naturali ratione, in altero fide divina cognoscimus)*[97] and of the formal object *(objecto . . . , quia praeter ea, ad quae naturalis ratio pertingere potest, credenda nobis proponuntur mysteria in Deo abscondita).*[98] But they interpenetrate in such a way that each reaches toward the root of the other; and the mutuality of this intervention,[99] far from violating the independence of theology and philosophy one from the other, in fact establishes it. Philosophy becomes the groundwork for the "foundations" of theology, even to the point of providing the "methodological tools" for its "construction" *(cum recta ratio fidei fundamenta demonstret eiusque lumine illustrata rerum divinarum scientiam excolat).*[100] For its part, theology comes to be, formally, the inner liberation of the act of philosophy *([cum] fides . . . rationem ab erroribus liberet)*[101] and, materially, the widening of its horizons *(. . . eamque*

95. Do not remain within yourself, but transcend yourself; place yourself in him who made you. *Serm.* CLIII, vii, 19.

96. Denz. 1795.

97. It is distinct . . . according to its principle . . . , because we know in the one case by natural reason and in the other by divine faith. Denz. 1795.

98. [And distinct] according to its object . . . , because, in addition to those things to which natural reason can attain, to us are propounded mysteries in which we must believe but which are hidden in God. Denz. 1795.

99. *Dieses Eingreifens.* — Trans.

100. Since right reason explains the foundations of faith and, illumined by its light, refines our knowledge of divine things. Denz. 1799.

101. [While] faith . . . liberates reason from errors. Denz. 1799.

multiplici cognitione instruat).[102] But inasmuch as, in the relation of the philosophical to the theological, what is at issue are the ***fidei fundamenta,*** the "groundwork" is one in which that which lays the ground "surrenders itself," through and beyond itself (in the offering up of the *intrinseca rerum veritas naturali rationis lumine perspecta* to the *auctoritas ipsius Dei revelantis).*[103] And inasmuch as, in the relation of the theological to the philosophical, the concern is specifically with the *ratio* and the negative of an *ab erroribus liberet,* it proves to be "liberation" in the fullest sense of the word: that is, not a derivation of philosophy from theology, but rather a free *(iustam liberet)* edifice standing upon its own ground *(propriis principiis)* and having its own manner of construction *(propria methodo).*

Here too, therefore, everything *flows* into mystery — presenting a clear front against both the rationalism of the philosophical concept, as represented by the Catholic Hegelianism of Georg Hermes, Anton Günther, and Jakob Frohschammer,[104] and the kind of theological rationalism that would seek to derive everything from the theological.[105] In the first of these confrontations (against the "concept from below") what is stressed is that even the profoundest theology, bound to the most rigorous kind of philosophy, ultimately becomes a *reductio in mysterium (divina enim mysteria suapte natura intellectum creaturarum sic excedunt, ut etiam revelatione tradita et fide suscepta ipsius tamen fidei velamine contecta et quadam quasi caligine obvoluta maneant).*[106] The second confrontation, though (against the "concept from above"), insists that this way into mystery be a genuinely positive one, and not the false mysticism of some obscure feeling of being seized by something, which frustrates the capacities of genuine research *(ratio . . . fide illustrata, cum sedulo, pie et sobrie quaerit, aliquam Deo dante mysteriorum intelligentiam eamque fructuosissimam assequitur tum ex eorum, quae naturaliter cognoscit analogia tum e mysteriorum ipsorum nexu inter se et cum fine et hominis ultimo).*[107] The ***reductio in mysterium*** (which is also and pre-

102. . . . and provides it with manifold understanding. Denz. 1799.

103. The intrinsic truth of things perceived in the light of natural reason/ the authority of the revealing God himself. Denz. 1789.

104. Denz. 1618f., 1642f., 1655f., 1666f.

105. Denz. 1622f., 1649f., 1659f.

106. For the divine mysteries, by their own nature, so far exceed the intellect of creatures that, even when handed down by revelation and received by faith, they nevertheless remain covered by the veil of faith itself and wrapped as it were in a certain mist. Denz. 1796.

107. Reason . . . illumined by faith, diligently, piously, and soberly seeks, and — with God's help — achieves an understanding of these mysteries, and a most fruitful understand-

cisely the church's final word) is thus a way into the mystery *"in" the concept and "beyond" the concept* — in response to Hegel's attempt to grasp the mystery "as" concept (in "absolute knowledge"), for whom it is primarily the concept which appears "as" mystery (namely, as the "self-concept" of a Trinitarian-dialectical God).

The problem of philosophical-theological metaphysics is thus inscribed as ultimate within the structure of a "creaturely metaphysics," just as we saw at the outset of our most recent considerations (§4, 1). On the one hand, it seems that, within this structure, everything was comprised within the logical consistency of the concept (essence-existence), whereas now the concept is overcome in the mystery. On the other hand, however, having just made clear how the mystery "in" the concept goes "beyond" the concept — that is, how, between concept and mystery, there holds sway as a formal relation the same "in-and-beyond" that characterized the earlier structure — it follows from our argument thus far that the relationship between philosophical and theological metaphysics is integrated into this same structure. Not, of course, as a new content: for the essence of God, from which theology comes and towards which philosophy goes, was already the apex. Nevertheless, at this apex the relation between philosophical and theological metaphysics gives expression both to the particular inner span between concept *(theologia positiva)* and mystery *(theologia negativa)* and, herein, to the double emphasis of its "in-and-beyond" with regard to the creaturely realm: the "from the in to the beyond" as the special intention of the philosophical; the "from the beyond to the in" as the special intention of the theological:

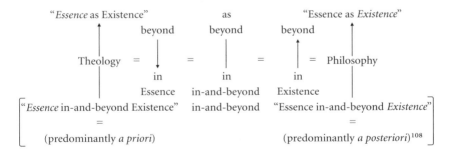

_____

ing at that, first by analogy to those things that it can naturally know, and then by the connections of these mysteries one with another and with the last end of man. Denz. 1796.

108. See n. 5 above. This diagram elaborates upon the earlier by showing how philosophy and theology figure in the configuration of a creaturely metaphysics. — Trans.

But then one must recall how we arrived at this configuration: how the relation between *a priori* and *a posteriori* metaphysics became transparent — through and beyond itself — to the relation between a metaphysics of God's manifestation and a metaphysics of potentiality towards God (§4, 1); and how, yet again — through and beyond this relation — it became transparent to the relation between philosophical and theological metaphysics (§4, 2; §4, 4). Hence one should designate this threefold in-and-beyond (whose three stages stand "in-and-beyond" one another) as, so to speak, the "exponent" of the configuration laid out above, in terms of which this configuration should be read three times, in each case with a stress towards the beyond. This then is the principle of metaphysics as such:

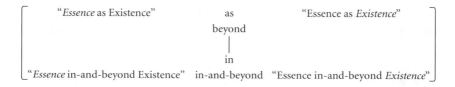

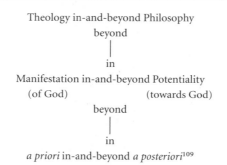

In summary: The "in-and-beyond" has shown itself to be the fundamental formal relation within this our principle of metaphysics as such. It is, firstly, a relation — that is, the suspension of a "between" (§1, 3) — as distinct from some demarcated position from which one could directly draw conclusions. It is, secondly, and precisely for this reason, a relation pointing above and beyond itself (§4, 1) — as distinct from a relation oscillating in and to itself. It

---

109. The import of this final diagram is fairly straightforward: the material in brackets at the top is simply a condensed form of the basic configuration of the earlier diagrams, and it is placed as it is to indicate that the dynamism that it represents is found at each of the three levels of our investigations to this point (which are represented at the bottom). — Trans.

is herein, thirdly, a relation whose inner form increasingly surpasses itself (§4, 4) — as distinct from a relation whose formula remains always and un-equivocally the same. Hence, fourthly, it is a relation of dynamic antithetics (§4, 5) — as distinct from one that is exhausted in a concept. And so it is, fifthly and finally, a relation that leads us through and beyond its positive ar-ticulation to a negative declaration (§4, 5) — as opposed to a relation that can be positively and completely articulated. Thus, by way of these five char-acteristics — the suspended relation, the pointing ever-beyond-itself, the in-creasing transcendence, the dynamic antithetics, the positive-negative — we have already demonstrated that the principle of metaphysics as such, under-stood as a "creaturely metaphysics," must be called analogy. Consequently, the formal principle of metaphysics as such is the formal principle of "this" particular metaphysics (which has been the object of our investigation).

Two considerations, however, require us to explicate the formal princi-ple of analogy in its own right. Firstly, in order explicitly to demonstrate this equation between analogy and the principle of metaphysics as such. Secondly, so that in this way the groundwork we have thus completed can be achieved at a still more radical level: from the concept of logos (§5) and from the prin-ciple of non-contradiction (§6). At the same time, however, the investigation itself will necessarily be the application of the method of metaphysics as such (laid out in Section One), just as our exposition of this method was itself al-ready the practice of this method. In particular, the principle that one must undertake "objective research in critical reflection upon the original tradi-tion" will have to be put abundantly into practice, because analogy is a histor-ically received notion, which concerns a specific objective problem — and thus one must set out *from* this problem (§§5 and 6) in order to aim, through critical reflection upon the original tradition (§7), *at* the problem (§8).

§5 Logos, Logic, Dialectic, Analogy

In the spirit of the conclusions we reached regarding meta-noetic and meta-ontic metaphysics, the most general observation we can make is that the connection between "*ana-logia*" and "*ens*" reveals an intentional[1] "ordering" (ἀνὰ λόγον λέγειν) — an ordering that not only (intentionally) announces an objective "order of being" (ἀνὰ λόγον τοῦ ὄντος λέγειν), but that, in itself (structurally as "principle"), is that wherein this "order of being" declares itself (the ontic law of the ἀνὰ λόγον τοῦ ὄντος εἶναι as the noetic law of the ἀνὰ λόγον λέγειν, and only thus as a fundamental law).

But, in this most general sense of an "ordering order," *ana(-logia)* agrees not only with its stem, *logos,* but also with the *dia(-logon)* (in "dialectic"). For all of their differences, what ἀναλογίζεσθαι, διαλογίζεσθαι, and λογίζεσθαι have in common is that they indicate a kind of "measured consideration,"[2] which is to say, an order that is realized in this very act of consideration, judgment, etc.; in short, our "ordering order." This ordering order is distinguished by prefixlessness (λογίζεσθαι) or by a difference of prefix (between δια- and ἀνα-λογίζεσθαι).

1. The range of meanings corresponding to *logos* resonates with the range of the problematic of the logic of language, as classically formulated in Plato's *Cratylus:* there is a prior "meaning," which ex-presses itself subsequently in the "word" (as the pro-duct of this meaning);[3] or the "word" is

---

1. *Akthaftes.* In keeping with Przywara's discussion of the problem of the act in §3, 3 above, "*akthaft*" here does not mean "active" in the standard sense of the term, but instead signals the "act" of intentionality. — Trans.

2. *Überlegens nach Maßstäben.* — Trans.

3. *ein vor-gegebener "Sinn," der sich in das (nach-gegebene und vom Sinn aus-gegebene) "Wort" aus-spricht.* — Trans.

simply posited in a factical sort of way, and its "meaning" is co-posited along with it. The two designations "reason" and "reflection"[4] (understood as "reason *in actu*") are informed by this ambiguity: between *"Vernunft"* or "reason" in the sense of *"in sich vernehmen,"* that is, in the sense of a "taking-in" or "receiving" (reason thus as the site of the manifestation of "meaning": in the act of its "being-given"), and *"Vernunft"* or "reason," which takes *"vernehmen"* in the active sense of a juridical procedure, as in "taking someone to court for interrogation" (reason thus as the site of the "efficacious word": in the act of "positing"). "Concept" and "object"[5] — as our final pair of significant terms — thus form a kind of tension-filled limit-circle. As "object," *logos* is a kind of "concept" in which the object "comprehends itself." The being (of the "object") is its own being-manifest (as "concept"). *Logos* as "meaning" (which is prior to and productive of the "word") is then (in this limited sense of *logos* as "object") the region of an "onto-(logy)" — that is, the region of "being as meaning," which can be "taken" "in" by reason (conceived as passive).[6] We have here, historically speaking, one side of Hegel's thought, in which all logic appears as the logic of being ("whatever is is rational") — including its renascence in noematic phenomenology, but especially in Heidegger. Opposed to this stands *logos* as "concept." Here *logos* is an active "ap-prehending"[7] of the "object" in order to com-prehend[8] it (on every side). Thus the concept is measured according to its "clear usefulness."[9] Thus it is the means of turning "things not understood" into things "commonly in use." That is to say that it corresponds (in one form) to the mode of a "positing" logic of language: the "words" by which "objects" become "useful" arise according to the measure of this "usefulness": i.e., according to the laws of common practice. *Logos,* understood as the "word" which is practically "posited" and which co-posits its "meaning," is then (in our present, limited sense of *logos* as "concept") the region of an "(onto)-logy": i.e., the region of a spontaneous translation of being (as "matter") into the categories (as real forms of predication) of "pure sense" "through" a reason (actively conceived) that subjects "objects" to a "juridical interrogation." Here we have, historically speaking, the other side of Hegel's thought,

---

4. *Vernunft* and *Überlegung.* — Trans.

5. *Sache.* — Trans.

6. Literally, "which is 'perceptible' 'in' reason (conceived as passive)": *das "in" der (passiv gefaßten) Vernunft "vernehmlich" ist.* — Trans.

7. *Er-greifen.* — Trans.

8. *Be-greifen.* — Trans.

9. *Handlichkeit.* — Trans.

in which all objective being must be reduced to the predicative form of judgment (under the forms of identity and difference); and in which, consequently, every structure of the object must be reduced to the structure of the (active) concept, such that every structure of the object ultimately reveals itself to be the concept's form of self-manifestation (in its dialectical movement). This is the Hegel who has his resurrection — in a clarified form — in the "transcendental subjectivity" of the late Husserl: in the reduction of everything noematic to the noetic of the *cogito*.

2. Seen from this perspective, which takes into consideration the breadth of *Logos* in itself, λογίζεσθαι, *understood as "pure logic,"* would be a form in which *logos* is "immediately" given. Indeed, for this reason it carries no distinguishing prefix. It thus expresses that towards which (as we have seen) all the "pure forms" of metaphysics strove (§1-4): the intrinsic linearity of "logy" as is expressed in the constructions "anthropo-logy," "cosmo-logy," etc. But if *Logos* comprises within itself, as we saw, a manifold problematic, then such an unbroken logic proves to be impossible from the outset. Rather (as we have also seen above), such a logic constitutes a desire "to be like God." For it is modeled upon the ideal of divine knowledge, which comprehends everything from the One (from, namely, itself), and thus comprehends the fullness of reality from its idea.

3. Pure λογίζεσθαι is thus opposed by its antithesis, the διαλογίζεσθαι found *in dialectic.* The purely grammatical meaning of διά is that of an "in between," in the two senses of "through" — *durch* — and "apart" — *zer.* The presupposition here, of course, is that the act of δια-λογίζεσθαι takes place within the interval between possibilities that are antithetical, at least in the sense that they are distinguished by opposition to one another. Thus, here, the situation that had presented an impediment and an objection to a simple λογίζεσθαι is precisely the site where the δια-λογίζεσθαι comes to pass: the antithesis of differing possibilities — which either are represented in the guise of persons, in the case of "dialogue," or, beyond the level of the person, constitute the tension of an objective "dialectic." If this situation were to stand under the ensign of the διά in the sense of "apart" (as in, for example, δι-αιρέω, understood as "taking apart"), then δια-λογίζεσθαι would constitute the supreme antithesis of λογίζεσθαι. For, far from providing a way of solution, it rather certifies the antitheses in their insolubility, because it expresses only the incompatibility between different possibilities. It is the confirmation of a (perduring) "in between" as an "in between" — and "solution" here means only the recognition of this in between. Here, therefore, we see the specifically *Platonic dialectic,* which reduces all "knowing" (εἰδέναι) to

a "knowing that I do not know" (εἰδέναι με οὐκ εἰδέναι), and every "effortless passage" (εὐ-πορεῖν) to an "impasse" (ἀ-πορεῖν). The watchword for this Platonic dialectic is therefore the Platonic "a-poria" (which logically has its resurrection in Kierkegaard). It is an aporia not as (in the Aristotelian sense) the object of some future solution, but rather as, in itself, an ideal path of knowledge. Augustine, the Christian Plato, put it in the most incisive terms: *si intelligentia tibi placet in natura hominis . . . , intellige quid non intelligas, ne totum non intelligas.*[10] But this same situation can also bear the sign of διά in the sense of "through." In this case, to stand in the interval in between possibilities betokens that a solution is completely guaranteed upon the path of thinking by way of separation and discrimination. This is the specifically *Aristotelian dialectic* (which has its most pronounced resurrection in Hegel). Here all knowledge of antitheses aims to order the antitheses in such a way that this ordering itself turns out to be the most compelling of logical proofs. Seen thus, either διαλεκτική is a preliminary "attempt" (πειραστική) — which must pass over into the "clear knowledge" (γνωριστική) of φιλοσοφία (understood as proof, ἀπόδειξις)[11] — and is thus a lingering in the "contingent facticity of concrete plurality" (the accidental, the συμβεβηκότα), whereas φιλοσοφία (understood as ἀπόδειξις) concerns being only insofar as it is being, ὄν αὐτὸ καθ᾽ ὅσον ὄν.[12] Or διαλεκτική is the γένος whose specific probative forms are induction and syllogism, ἐπαγωγή and συλλογισμός[13] — that is, it is logical proof (ἀπόδειξις) in *potentia*. If one expands on this, as does Hegel, to such a degree of refinement that a "contradiction" of antitheses (as is characteristic of the supreme instance of διά in the sense of "apart") reveals the "identity" of the one Logos, then it turns out that διαλογίζεσθαι, in its inner movement, is really so sharply contrasted with λογίζεσθαι (in Platonic aporetic dialectic) only in order that it might relapse (in Aristotelian syllogistic dialectic) into yet more unconditional unity with it. It is the distance of a tension, the two terms drawn apart only that they might spring back together all the more passionately.

4. But, taken in this sense, the entire meaning of διαλογίζεσθαι points beyond itself. It is dialectic in the profound Augustinian sense of a self-revelation of the mind's movement between a critical distancing from and a

10. Since understanding is what so pleases you in human nature . . . understand what it is that you do not understand, lest you fail to understand anything. *De Nat. et Orig. An.,* IV, xi, 15.

11. *Met.* IV, 2, 1004b, 25f.

12. *Met.* XI, 3, 1061b, 8f.

13. *Top.* I, 1, 105a, 11.

sheer mystical fusion with truth: *in hoc se ipsa ratio demonstrat, atque aperit quae sit, quid velit, quid valeat.*[14] But this requires that one pass through the passion of this movement to an investigation of its quiet fundamental law, the lineaments of which are distorted[15] by this passion raging between contradiction and identity, between extremest night and extremest day. This fundamental law is called ἀναλογίζεσθαι. "Logic" (in the ideative sense discussed above) is a self-deluding escape into the region of the divine. "Dialectic," in and for itself, is a "creaturely realism," but one caught in a delirium, reeling irredeemably between a defiant self-recusing (into its own night of antitheses) and a passionate desire for fusion (understood not as a desire for self-submission, but as a desire for self-mastery). *"Analogy"* is the inner balancing of this confusion: defiant self-recusing yields to humble self-discrimination, and passionate desire for fusion to loving self-surrender. As such, it represents the *Aufhebung* of the antithesis between logic and dialectic: neither "logical dialectic" (which, with Hegel, makes dialectic into a logic of the divine), nor "dialectical logic" (which, with Heidegger, knows all truth only as the being underway of the inherently autonomous creature), but rather "creaturely logic," as the immanent (and most formal) method of "creaturely metaphysics."

A decisive feature of this most general concept of "analogy" is that ἀνά, grammatically speaking, means "according to an orderly sequence" and, at the same time, goes together with ἄνω, and so signifies an "upward movement."[16] On the one hand, this sequence therefore has its principle in the "above": as a movement "towards" the origin — "upstream," as in ἀνὰ ποταμόν. On the other hand, however, the "above" principle works itself out in this sequence, inasmuch as every sequence ensues "according" to it. We thus have here: a sequence "of" the origin — just as it is possible to move "upstream" only because the current of the source itself is active within its flowing forth (as a river), and so can be "followed back." If all thought, as λογίζεσθαι, is directed towards λόγος, then it is here — in the relation between λογίζεσθαι and λόγος — that we will find the concept of analogy most fundamentally established. The λογίζεσθαι of pure logic serves here to emphasize the relation of the ἐν: thought, as the being-in of Logos, is the "Logos in effect."[17] The διαλογίζεσθαι of dialectic bears within it the relation

14. In this reason shows itself, and reveals what it is, what it wills, and of what it is capable. *De Ord.* XIII, 38.

15. *Verzerrt.* — Trans.

16. *Nach der Reihe* and *oben hinauf.* — Trans.

17. *Logos im Vollzug.* — Trans.

of the διά: thought, as the contradiction (διά in the sense of "apart") of (pure) Logos, is the breakthrough (διά in the sense of "through") precisely of this Logos. In its ἀνά, then (as we have just seen), the ἀναλογίζεσθαι of analogy says that thought, as a distanced obedience to the Logos (ἀνά in the sense of "according to" an "above"), is the pervasive working of the Logos in all things (ἀνά in the sense of an "above that orders"). The most formal fundamental relation of the λογίζεσθαι of "pure logic" is "identity from beginning to end"; while that of the διαλογίζεσθαι of dialectic, on the other hand, is "identity in contradiction"; but that of the ἀναλογίζεσθαι of analogy is a "self-ordering within a being-ordered."

§6 The Grounding of Analogy as *Analogia Entis* in the Principle of Non-Contradiction

What we have just seen is something fundamentally decided on the grounds of what has always been the basic question of thought as such: the "principle of non-contradiction" *(principium contradictionis)*.

1. Aristotle formulates the principle in such a way that its noetic[1] and ontic forms interpenetrate. At one point, he states it thus: because something cannot in the same respect simultaneously both "be" and not be, neither, by the same token, can it be "validated" as in the same respect both true and not true (οὐκ ἐνδέχεται τὸ αὐτὸ καθ' ἕνα καὶ τὸν αὐτὸν χρόνον εἶναι καὶ μὴ εἶναι . . . ὥστ' . . . τὴν ἀντίφασιν ἀδύνατον ἀληθεύειν κατὰ τοῦ αὐτοῦ).[2]

But then, at another point, he also says: because it is not possible in the same respect both to affirm and to deny something of something, neither can something in the same respect simultaneously both be and not be (τὸ γὰρ αὐτὸ ἅμα ὑπάρχειν τε καὶ μὴ ὑπάρχειν ἀδύνατον τῷ αὐτῷ καὶ κατὰ τὸ αὐτό . . . ἀδύνατον γὰρ ὁτινοῦν ταὐτὸν ὑπολαμβάνειν εἶναι).[3]

---

1. "Noetic," naturally, means Truth-Goodness-Beauty, in the fullest sense (§2). Indeed, Aristotle extends the principle of non-contradiction so far that the pair "true-false" comes to comprise the pair "good-bad" as well (*Met.* XI, 6, 1062b, 15f.), which is to say that it also comes to comprise the pair "beautiful-ugly" (in passages we touched upon earlier, §2). Thus I use the term "to be valid" for "noetic," since this is the term that best captures the additional sense of "good-beautiful" — even though our practical exposition of the matter can scarcely do otherwise than give preference to the presence within "valid" of the (never exclusive) sense of "true."

2. The same thing cannot simultaneously be and not be . . . and hence . . . it is impossible to make contradictory true assertions regarding the same thing. *Met.* XI, 5, 1061b, 36-1062a, 20.

3. For the same attribute cannot, in the same way, both belong and not belong to a

This interpenetration presents us with the most basic and most formal ground of the interpenetration between the meta-noetic and the meta-ontic (as we saw in §1). Here we have a formal position that precedes even the most elementary position regarding material content. It is, furthermore, the most negative of formal positions[4]: in that the principle of non-contradiction is distinguished over against the principle of identity, which is conceived positively: "what is (valid), is (valid)." It is, finally, a formal position that is negative in a reductive sense: "even if one denies everything, one cannot deny 'this.'" In this regard it was Augustine who gave the principle its sharpest formulation: "the doubt that doubts everything still cannot doubt that it doubts" (*si dubitat, unde dubitet, meminit: si dubitat, dubitare se intelligit: si dubitat, certus esse vult . . . Quisquis igitur aliunde dubitat, de his omnibus dubitare non debet: quae si non essent, de ulla re dubitare non posset*).[5]

Given that the principle of non-contradiction — in this mode of a "negative reductive formality" — constitutes the most fundamental possibility for the activity of thought as such, it is clear that it is also present in each of the three basic modes we encountered above: pure logic, dialectic, and analogy. In the first two modes, however, the principle must suffer a transposition; only in the third is it preserved in the form in which it is given as what is most fundamental to the activity of thought as such: as, that is, a negative reductive formality. Thus we obtain decisive proof that, of the three, analogy is the only real possibility.

2. It is proper to the standpoint of *pure logic* (λογίζεσθαι) that it takes the principle of non-contradiction simply as a form of expression of the *principle of identity* ("what is [valid], is [valid]"). In this, it is guided by a genuine intention to gain an "initial foothold."[6] But the very intensity of the striving for this basis tempts one to treat it as absolute. The ontic version of the principle of identity, "what is, is," thus implies an immediacy to the "I am who am," understood as *the* name of God. In Augustinian terms: the *est,* which belongs to God

---

thing . . . for it is not possible to believe something both to be and not to be. *Met.* IV, 3, 1005b, 19-24.

4. *Eine möglichst negative Formal-Position.* — Trans.

5. If one doubts, one remembers why one doubts: if one doubts, one understands that one doubts: if one doubts, one wishes to be certain. . . . Whosoever, therefore, has doubts about anything still ought not be in doubt regarding all of these things (life, memory, understanding, will, thought, knowledge, judgment): for if these things were not, one should be unable to doubt anything at all. *De Trin.* X, x, 14.

6. *Das "erste Bodenfassen."* — Trans.

alone, is here asserted of the creaturely *est non est.*[7] Logically, this gives rise to the *apriorism of being*[8] of German rationalism and ontologism, which derive the structure of being and the world of being from "pure being" as it is grasped intuitively (in the ontic principle of identity). But then the noetic version of the principle of identity, "what is valid, is valid," equally implies an immediacy to immutable and eternal truth (goodness, beauty). In Augustinian terms: the "lamp *(lucerna)* that receives" the light is taken for the immediate self-manifestation of the light.[9] This is the theory of truth that intrinsically corresponds to the apriorism of being: "pure being" is known in *"pure truth."* But even Descartes and Kant fit this pattern, despite their antagonism to any apriorism of being. For the Cartesian immediacy of pure truth within the *cogito* is what establishes the infallibility of Descartes's mathematical method. With Kant, it is the effective absoluteness[10] that resides in the system of categories. In a mitigated form, one could also include here those trends in neo-scholastic thought that, in their unconscious dependence upon German rationalism, attempt to derive *"principles"* immediately from the principle of non-contradiction. In this respect they stand in sharp opposition to Thomas. For even if he calls for a *reductio in principia,*[11] and designates these principles as the *primum a quo* and the *ultimum in quod,*[12] and calls the principle of non-contradiction the highest principle among them,[13] for him they nevertheless constitute the lowest level of participation in eternal truth;[14] as the *necessitas naturalis* of the *intellectus*[15] and as the instruments of the agent intellect, *instrumenta intellectus agentis,*[16] these principles effectively operate entirely within the realm of the senses, such that — though they are valid *in se nota*[17] and *cognita in ratione entis*[18] — even a *resolutio* in *sensibile*[19] obtains. Whereas here everything remains at the level of the performed act,[20] in the so-called

7. *In Ps.* CXXI, 12.
8. *Seins-Apriorismus.* — Trans.
9. *In Ps.* LVIII, s.1, 18.
10. *Akthafte Unbedingtheit.* — Trans.
11. *De Ver.* q. 1, a. 1, corp.; *De Ver.* q. 14, a. 1, corp.
12. *De Ver.* q. 14, a. 1, corp.; *Summa Th.* I/I, q. 79, a. 8 and 12, corp.
13. *Summa Th.* II, q. 1, a. 7, corp.; *In Boeth. de Trin.* q. 6, a. 4, corp.
14. *De Ver.* q. 8, a. 15, corp.; *De Ver.* q. 11, a. 1, ad 18; *De Ver.* q. 11, a. 3, corp.
15. *Summa Th.* I, q. 82, a. 1 and 2, corp.
16. *De Ver.* q. 9, a. 1, ad 2; *De Ver.* q. 10, a. 13, corp.; *De Ver.* q. 11, a. 3, corp.
17. *De Ver.* q. 1, a. 12, corp.
18. *De Ver.* q. 5, a. 2, ad 7.
19. *De Ver.* q. 12, a. 3, ad 2 and 3.
20. *Alles im Aktvollzug bleibt.* — Trans.

neo-scholastic "theory" it is isolated and objectified. The principle of non-contradiction is turned into a thing. But, logically, this makes it indistinguishable from the principle of identity, however well many of the adherents of this "theory" may know to distinguish between the two. In the language of St. Thomas, one is obliged to say that this neo-scholastic method concerning principles — as the last vestiges of "innate ideas" — involves the inadmissible transfer to human beings of the mode of knowledge proper to pure spirit (since God alone knows things in and from their "ideas," while pure created spirits participate in that knowledge).[21] From this perspective, *Husserl* is absolutely right (in his "Formal and Transcendental Logic") to distinguish between a "consequential logic or a logic free from contradiction" and a "logic of truth" — whereby the former concerns simply the "form" of judgments, and only the latter their "theme." But then, even here, both kinds of logic end up gliding back to Descartes — back, that is, to the noetic principle of identity. While the principle of non-contradiction is merely a negative reductive formality, in a "consequential logic" it becomes deductive (in the mode of the neo-scholastic doctrine of principles). But, on the other hand, in that this leads to the development of a strictly "formal" logic, it prepares the way for the unconditionality[22] of the (eidetic) "logic of truth." This then, logically, becomes the Cartesian immediacy of truth in the *cogito* (= Husserl's "transcendental subjectivity") — so much so that God does not stand above the *cogito*, but instead signifies the ultimate inner telos of the *cogito's* teleological structure. By contrast, the principle of non-contradiction, precisely as thought's minimum "ground," is immanent to this thought precisely insofar as it journeys towards (material) truth — signifying by its negative form, in the sharpest possible way, the innermost creatureliness of this "journey towards" truth. The principle of non-contradiction thus stands or falls with this unity. Detached from the "journey towards truth," it becomes a thing and is thus transformed into the principle of identity. Detached from the principle of non-contradiction, the "journey towards truth" comes "to be the site of truth,"[23] and so the (noetic) principle of identity appears once again.

3. From the standpoint of *dialectic* (διαλογίζεσθαι) — in view of the shipwreck of the absoluteness of pure logic — one is so eager to avoid any proximity to the principle of identity that one aims, even further, at a dissolution of that stability which has its foundation in the principle of non-

---

21. *De Ver.* q. 8, a. 15, corp.; q. 11, a. 1, ad 18; a. 3, corp.
22. *Uneingeschränktheit.* — Trans.
23. *Ort der Wahrheit sein.* — Trans.

contradiction. The aim here is "pure contradiction." But the antithesis of dialectic to pure logic has the effect that this dissolution remains intrinsically guided by the ideal of pure logic, so that it is suddenly converted into pure logic and unmasks itself as a more refined version of the same. This is most clearly the case with *Hegel.* "Contradiction" is the form in which self-identical "ontic truth" or self-identical "noetic being" is immanent to the mutable world from above, so much so that the world is the rhythm of its dialectical unfolding. This is to say that the noetic-ontic principle of identity remains determinative in the background (however much Hegel, against Fichte and Schelling, seeks to decommission it), but works itself out in the absoluteness of contradiction. The relation of creature and God (ontically and noetically) is one of an identity that, by contradicting itself, becomes its own opposite. Whereas the neutral principle of non-contradiction expresses the maximum of the (ontic-noetic) "ground" of the creature, in this Hegelian "contradiction-identity" the ground of God is usurped: not simply in the naïve form of pure logic, whereby the absolute appears immediately "within" the creaturely; nor even simply in the intensified form of a usurpatious grasping of that moment when the creature originates "out of" God; but directly in the titanic form of a laying hold of the inner rhythm of the divine life, since the origination of the creature out of God is the (trinitarian) "origination of God" (the Son). The dialectic that has its basis in Kierkegaard's *Philosophical Fragments* and is developed in Heidegger's existential phenomenology thus attempts actually to eliminate the principle of identity. Both the absolute of being and the absolute of truth give way to the pure becoming of a creature incurvated upon itself (as shaped by "care" "in the world"). Just as being comes to mean becoming, truth comes to mean a "needless freedom."[24] That is to say, the purely logical is truly eliminated. But this ontic-noetic becoming excludes only the static and material mode of the principle of identity. At a dynamic-formal level, the principle of identity remains, here too, the final form. (Ontic-noetic) becoming is underway to itself in an infinity of intensity: as nothing but "ever its own possibility." And the expression for this circular self-containment of becoming is its being "in the world." The Hegelian "contradiction" has been radicalized in the Heideggerean "Nothing." But this Nothing, as Nothing, is the fundamental principle determining and producing all things. This "productive Nothing" utters the ontic-noetic "I am who I am" of the principle of identity. Conse-

---

24. *Notgewendete Freiheit.* An idiomatic phrase from Heidegger. Literally, an unencumbered freedom in which the only necessity is its absence, as when any pressing need or crisis has been "averted." — Trans.

quently, both dialectics (Hegel's and Heidegger's) are related to one another as the theopanistic dialectic and the pantheistic dialectic of the *one* principle of identity.

4. From just this relation between contradiction and identity, however, we can now derive the authentic version of the principle of non-contradiction as it is realized from the standpoint of *analogy* (ἀναλογίζεσθαι).[25] The fundamental argument that Aristotle gives for the principle of non-contradiction clearly shows that this principle arises as the minimum of a dynamic synthesis, and is therefore situated within the movement of this synthesis. That is to say, it is not something "from" which one can make deductions; rather, it itself is simply the basis for a back-and-forth debate, whose dynamic is ever again renewed. It is the ever renewed *debate* that takes place *between Heraclitus and Parmenides*.

On the one hand, real creaturely consciousness and being are characterized by a constantly surging flux of oppositions, which suggests being lost upon a chaotic sea, since the human hand is impotent to capture "origin and end" like a ring in its grasp: "τοὺς ἀνθρώπους διὰ τοῦτο ἀπόλλυσθαι," says Alcmaeon, "ὅτι οὐ δύνανται τὴν ἀρχὴν τῶι τέλει προσάψαι."[26] Of course, this is what science, taken in the literal sense of ἐπιστήμη ("to stand upon"), seeks to do, in that one of its branches goes from hypotheses to a conclusion, ἐξ ὑποθέσεων . . . εἰς τελευτήν — from a multiplicity of streams to their *one* confluence — while the other aims at a principle from hypotheses, ἐπ᾿ ἀρχὴν . . . ἐξ ὑποθέσεων — from multiplicity back to the *one* origin. But even in this Platonic conception,[27] there is no easing of the tension. Thus the ἀντικείμενα, pure oppositions, appear to be the final word. The soul is a daemonically surging infinity: ψυχῆς πείρατα . . . οὐκ ἂν ἐξεύροιο, says Heraclitus;[28] ψυχῆς ἐστι λόγος ἑαυτὸν αὔξων;[29] ἦθος ἀνθρώπωι δαίμων.[30] The world is both a heap of cast-off rubbish (σάρμα εἰκῆ

25. I am going here a step beyond my argument in *Kant heute* (pp. 71-72) concerning the relation between the principle of non-contradiction and analogy. There I said that, in its negative form, the principle is *in potentia* "towards" analogy, which is itself positive. I would go further now and say that, in its authentic form, analogy declares itself to be "fundamental." The principle of non-contradiction is thus the *in potentia* "of" analogy (towards its greater actuality).

26. Men perish because they are unable to join the beginning to the end. Diels (5th ed.), 24, 2.

27. *Rep.* VII, 510b.

28. The soul's bounds . . . one could never discover. Diels, 22, 45.

29. The logos of the soul gives increase to itself. Diels, 115.

30. Man's character [or ethos] is his daemon. Diels, 119.

κεχυμένον)³¹ and an ever living fire (πῦρ ἀείζωον).³² God is thus the absolute locus of opposites — day-night, winter-summer, war-peace, plenty-
want — and even the fire of transformation (ἡμέρη εὐφρόνη, χειμὼν θέρος,
πόλεμος εἰρήνη, κόρος λιμός, . . . ἀλλοιοῦται . . . ὅκωσπερ πῦρ).³³

On the other hand, however, the very same Heraclitus cannot help but
envision a λόγος for both the noetic³⁴ and the ontic³⁵ — to the point of recognizing a real rhythmic measure of opposites within the living fire
(ἁπτόμενον μέτρα καὶ ἀποσβεννύμενον μέτρα),³⁶ and an "utterly beautiful
harmony" of "differences" (a καλλίστη ἁρμονία of διαφέροντα).³⁷ An enduring order thus raises its imperturbable head. In riposte to Alcmaeon's metaphor of the sea upon which we are lost (since origin and end never meet), one
can thus cite Diogenes of Apollonia's apophthegm that all being comes from
the same, is the same, and returns to the same (πάντα τὰ ὄντα ἀπὸ τοῦ αὐτοῦ
ἑτεροιοῦσθαι και τὸ αὐτὸ εἶναι . . . πάντα ἐκ τοῦ αὐτοῦ ἑτεροιούμενα ἄλλοτε
ἀλλοῖα γίνεται καὶ εἰς τὸ αὐτὸ ἀναχωρεῖ).³⁸ Thus is laid the foundation of
Parmenides' vision. The opposition between thought as act (νοεῖν) and the
content of thought (νόημα) becomes one and the same (ταὐτὸν δ᾽ ἐστὶ νοεῖν
τε καὶ οὕνεκέν ἐστι νόημα),³⁹ in such measure as being, as the being of the
perduring order, is the expression of ordering thought (οὐ γὰρ ἄνευ τοῦ
ἐόντος, ἐν ὧι πεφατισμένον ἐστίν, εὑρήσεις τὸ νοεῖν).⁴⁰ The oppositions
proper to "mortals" — becoming and perishing, being and non-being,
change of place and of form — are merely vain echoes, not truth (τῶι πάντ᾽
ὀνομ[α] ἔσται, . . . γίγνεσθαί τε καὶ ὄλλυσθαι, εἶναι τε καὶ οὐχί, τόπον
ἀλλάσσειν διά τε χρόα φανὸν ἀμείβειν).⁴¹ For being, as the thought-being⁴²

31. Diels, 124.
32. Diels, 30.
33. Day-night, winter-summer, war-peace, plenty-want . . . he changes . . . like fire.
Diels, 67.
34. Diels, 2, 16.
35. Diels, 1.
36. In measure kindled and extinguished. Diels, 30.
37. Diels, 8.
38. All beings are differentiated from the same and are the same . . . and all become
something else at different times and return to the same. Diels, 64, 2.
39. Thinking is the same as what is thought. Diels, 28, 8, 34.
40. For you cannot find thinking apart from the being in which it is expressed. Diels,
8, 35-36.
41. All these are only a name . . . becoming and perishing, being and non-being,
change of place, and alternations of shining colors. Diels, 8, 38-121b, 8, 41.
42. *Denk-sein.* — Trans.

of "order *as* being" (τὸ γὰρ αὐτὸ νοεῖν ἐστίν τε καὶ εἶναι)[43] is the being of eternal truth, which as such is one and undivided, being in itself uniformly the same (ἀγένητον ἐὸν καὶ ἀνώλεθρον . . . , οὐθὲ διαιρετόν . . . , ἐπεὶ πᾶν ἐστιν ὁμοῖον . . . , ταὐτόν τ᾽ ἐν ταὐτῶι τε μένον καθ᾽ ἑαυτό).[44] Since the Nothing gapes open wherever there is a span of oppositions, the Nothing also disappears with the oppositions. All that remains is being as eternal truth and eternal truth as being (ἔστιν τε καὶ . . . οὐκ ἔστι μὴ εἶναι . . .· οὔτε γὰρ ἂν γνοίης τό γε μὴ ἐὸν [οὐ γὰρ ἄνυστον] οὔτε φράσαις).[45] While the symbol for Heraclitus's thought is that of eternally tangled tongues of flickering fire (πῦρ ἀείζωον), the symbol that best captures Parmenides' vision is that of the sphere (εὐκύκλου σφαίρης),[46] understood as the being of perfection[47] in the stillness of consecration (τετελεσμένον),[48] in the inner equality of proportion of the center to all sides (μεσσόθεν ἰσοπαλὲς πάντηι),[49] in its center circumbounding itself (ἐν πείρασι κύρει),[50] in itself Itself.

The point of this exposition thus becomes clear: to show how the principle of non-contradiction is decisively grounded in the minimum of the constantly renewed and counterbalanced debate between thought's two deepest antitheses. Aristotle characterizes the view of Heraclitus as "all is movement" (πάντα κινεῖσθαι); and that of Parmenides as "all is rest" (πάντα ἠρεμεῖν): neither standpoint can, in itself, be realized (φανερὸν δ᾽ ὅτι οὐ δ᾽ οἱ πάντα ἠρεμεῖν λέγοντες ἀληθῆ λέγουσιν οὐ δ᾽ οἱ πάντα κινεῖσθαι).[51] The standpoint of Parmenides entails the denial that the creature changes either noetically — between true and false — or ontically — between being and non-being. But since the creature does in fact undergo this twofold change between its oppositions, the standpoint of Parmenides leads one to take truth and falsity, being and non-being as the same (ταὐτόν), and thus,

43. For what is thought is the same as what is [or, the same thing is available both to thinking and to being; or, what can be thought is the same as what can be; or, it is the same thing to think and to be]. Diels, 3.

44. Being is ungenerated and imperishable . . . , nor is it divisible . . . , since it is all alike . . . , for remaining the same and in the same place, it rests in itself. Diels, 8, 3-29.

45. It is . . . and cannot not be. . . . For you could not know what is not [for this is not possible] nor speak of it. Diels, 2, 3, 7-8.

46. A well-rounded sphere. Diels, 8, 43.

47. *Vollendungs-Sein.* — Trans.

48. Completed. Diels, 8, 42.

49. Equally balanced from the center out in every direction. Diels, 8, 44.

50. It reaches its limits. Diels, 8, 49.

51. Clearly neither those who say all things are at rest nor those who say all things are in motion are correct. *Met.* IV, 8, 1012b, 22-24.

noetically and ontically, to eliminate the principle of non-contradiction (εἰ μὲν γὰρ ἠρεμεῖ πάντα, ἀεὶ ταὐτὰ ἀληθῆ καὶ ψευδῆ εἶναι, φαίνεται δὲ τοῦτο μεταβάλλον· ὁ γὰρ λέγων ποτὲ αὐτὸς οὐκ ἦν καὶ πάλιν οὐκ ἔσται).[52] The standpoint of Heraclitus, of course, emphasizes change. But because every-thing changes, there is neither any truth (since the true can turn into the false), nor any being (since being can turn into nothing). Consequently, there is no longer any ultimate difference between true and false, being and non-being, and the principle of non-contradiction, noetically and ontically, is done away with once again (εἰ δὲ πάντα κινεῖται, οὐδὲν ἔσται ἀληθές, πάντα ἄρα ψευδῆ).[53] If, then, the principle of non-contradiction is the fun-damental, dynamic middle between the Heraclitean "all is movement" and the Parmenidean "all is rest," this indicates a dynamic "measured equilib-rium"[54] within it. But this happens to be the most general sense of analogy. (Pure) logic is the immediacy of a single law of the world — in this case ei-ther an immanent Heraclitean logic of movement or an immanent Parmenidean logic of rest. Dialectic is the either-or of abrupt change, as it is found in an identity-of-contradiction — in this case the abrupt back-and-forth between Heraclitus and Parmenides. Analogy alone is a measured equilibrium, and this, as we have seen, is precisely the sense of the principle of non-contradiction, understood as the most basic midpoint of equilib-rium between Heraclitus and Parmenides. In keeping with this understand-ing Aristotle will equate *analogy* with the *middle:* τὸ γὰρ ἀνάλογον μέσον.[55] It is thus in the principle of non-contradiction — understood as middle — that analogy establishes itself as the foundation of all thought.

5. This middle is not something fixed, however — and here Aristotle completes the laying of his foundation — but, rather, the basis of a move-ment,[56] albeit now a movement that is directed, and as such "rest in motion."

Through their dissolution of the principle of non-contradiction, Heraclitus and Parmenides effectively bring about an "identity of opposites"

---

52. For if all things are at rest, the same statements will always be both true and false, which clearly is not so; for even the one making a statement once was not and one day will again not be. *Met.* IV, 8, 1012b, 24-26.

53. If all things are in motion, nothing will be true, and so everything will be false. *Met.* IV, 8, 1012b, 26-27.

54. *Ausgleich im Maß.* — Trans.

55. *Nic. Eth.* V, 4, 1131b, 11.

56. *Fußpunkt von Bewegung,* which looks like an almost exact translation of ἀρχὴ κινήσεως (i.e., efficient cause), but which might also be rendered as the "footing" or "foot-hold" (almost like a starting block) for movement. — Trans.

(ταὐτὸν τἀναντία),[57] which in Heraclitus takes the form of an explosive contradiction (ταὐτὸν . . . *τἀναντία*), and in Parmenides the form of a motionless One (*ταὐτὸν . . . τἀναντία*). But this "identity of opposites" is characteristic only of what upholds the creaturely at its lowest level (as what most sharply distinguishes it from God): the constant "possibility towards everything" as a "dynamic towards everything" (δύναμις understood here in the sense of the transition from possible to impossible, and from dynamic to static).[58] As accords with its concept, this "dynamic possibility towards everything" implies an "identity of opposites" (ὅσα . . . κατὰ τὸ δύνασθαι λέγεται, ταὐτόν ἐστι δυνατὸν τἀναντία),[59] because this lowest "possibility as such" (ὕλη, *potentia pura, materia prima*) is logically oriented towards the entire possible compass of the creature as such, which is to say towards the entire web of contraries within this compass (ἡ αὐτὴ γὰρ δύναμις τοῦ ὑγιαίνειν καὶ κάμνειν, καὶ ἠρεμεῖν καὶ κινεῖσθαι, etc.),[60] including even the span of contradiction between being (valid) and not-being (valid) (δύναμις ἅμα τῆς ἀντιφάσεως ἐστιν . . . · τὸ ἄρα δυνατὸν εἶναι ἐνδέχεται . . . καὶ μὴ εἶναι);[61] thus here the principle of non-contradiction, either noetically or ontically, fails to apply. It is another thing, however, when what is at issue is a possibility that has been actualized, "en-acted" (ἐν-έργ-εια). Actuality, understood as an "actualized possibility" (τοὔνομα ἐνέργεια λέγεται κατὰ τὸ ἔργον),[62] means the realized, discriminating choice of one possibility over others. The "en-acted possibility," as "enacted," entails the exclusion of its contrary possibility: if, from the contraries health and illness, the former is in a particular case chosen for actualization, then the latter is in that particular case excluded. This means that there is no "identity of opposites" in the sphere of enacted possibility (τὰς ἐνεργείας . . . ἅμα ἀδύνατον ὑπάρχειν . . .).[63] Consequently, the principle of non-contradiction is, noetically and ontically, valid *a fortiori:* with the en-act-ment[64] — and hence actuality — of a possibility, it both "is (valid)" and "is

57. *Met.* IX, 9, 1051a, 6.

58. *Met.* V, 12, 1019a, 35f.; 1019b, 22f.

59. Whatever we say to be capable of something is capable likewise of the opposite. *Met.* IX, 9, 1051a, 5.

60. For the same potentiality for health is that for illness, for rest is that for motion. . . . *Met.* IX, 8f.

61. A potentiality is simultaneously a potentiality for its own opposite . . . ; the same thing has the possibility of being . . . and of not being. *Met.* IX, 8, 1050b, 8-9; 11-12.

62. We speak of actuality in regard to the act. *Met.* IX, 1050a, 22-23.

63. These actualities . . . cannot be simultaneously present. *Met.* IX, 9, 1051a, 12.

64. *Ins-Werk-Setzung.* — Trans.

not not (valid)." For herein lies what is decisive for en-act-ment — and hence actuality (ἐνέργεια) — as opposed to pure possibility (δύναμις).

In their inner relation to one another, however, actuality (ἐνέργεια, *actus*) and possibility (δύναμις, *potentia*) bear witness to an oscillating rhythm, back and forth, which Aristotle directly designates as analogy (λέγεται δὲ ἐνεργείᾳ . . . τὸ ἀνάλογον).[65] In the most formal sense, it consists in this: that the relation between actuality — understood as "the" enacted possibility — and possibility is like that between the activity of "building" and that which is "build-able" (ὡς τὸ οἰκοδομοῦν πρός τὸ οἰκοδομικόν).[66] But, concretely, there is a correlation between the two. On the one hand, the sphere of pure possibility implies a "limitless expanse" (ἄπειρον): not only in the togetherness of contrary possibilities, but — by virtue of the "identity of opposites" (ταὐτόν . . . τἀναντία) — in the immensity of an authentic "dynamic" of an "all in everything" (ἐν ἅπαντι πᾶν).[67] The sphere of actuality, understood as en-act-ment, is by contrast a "case-by-case limitation" (πέρας). It is like an unstable dam set against the tempestuous ocean of possibilities, while the sea itself, admitted by the dam "in rations," surges within its bounds and causes them to tremble. Seen thus, possibility and actuality are related as the infinite to the finite. What is more: every instance of actuality is always something that is merely provisional with respect to the "infinite possibilities" that ever and again exceed it. And what is yet more: each en-act-ment is merely an instrument in the hand of these "infinite possibilities," which press on towards their fullest possible actualization. Insofar as (today) we understand possibility as something "dynamic," however, it is seen as a "charged possibility": δυνατόν in contrast to στατικόν, as the point of departure of a movement pressing towards actualization (ἔχον κινήσεως ἀρχὴν ἢ μεταβολῆς).[68] But it is equally "pure possibility," which is in need of actualization, so that the very concept of possibility already "presupposes" that someone is there who actualizes it, and who thus is already actuality in himself. In this sense, not only is it the case that "en-act-ment into actuality" is the defining goal of possibility (τέλος δ' ἡ ἐνέργεια καὶ τούτου χάριν ἡ δύναμις λαμβάνεται).[69] For, in addition to this,

65. [Things are] said to be actual . . . by analogy. *Met.* IX, 6, 1048b, 6-7. [That is, actuality is not a univocal but an analogical term when one is speaking of how the potential is made actual. — Trans.]

66. *Met.* IX, 1048a, 37-b, 1.

67. *Met.* XI, 6, 1063b, 29.

68. It possesses a beginning of movement and of change. *Met.*, V, 12, 1019a, 34-35.

69. And actuality is the end and that for which potentiality is acquired. *Met.* IX, 8, 1050a, 9-10.

the august fundamental law of Aristotelianism also holds true: that in the region of being and of the transcendentals actuality is prior to possibility (πάσης δὲ τῆς τοιαύτης [δυνάμεως] πρότερα ἐστὶν ἡ ἐνέργεια).[70]

Here, then, is the "analogy" that constitutes the relation between possibility and actuality:[71] it is, in practical terms, the dynamic quality of suspendedness proper to (creaturely) actuality. On the one hand, actuality (as the "actualization of 'one' possibility out of 'infinitely many'") is oriented backwards: as limited actuality it is a quaking ground, the establishing of limits upon the deceptive surface of the infinitely surging sea. Here actuality is on the way towards possibility. But, on the other hand, there is here, decidedly, a pressing of possibility towards actuality. Every instance of actuality is oriented forwards, beyond itself, towards a new "end," an end that is the actualization of an orientation that is predetermined and that thus has this end "in itself." Possibility (δύναμις) is on the way towards actuality (ἐνέργεια) as its end (τέλος δ' ἡ ἐνέργεια)[72] in that actuality, by "having an end in itself" (ἐν-τελ-έχεια), is directed beyond itself (ἐνέργεια understood as ἡ πρὸς τὴν ἐντελεχείαν συντιθεμένη).[73] (Creaturely) actuality is thus indeed "energetic" (ἐνέργεια): passively by virtue of its backward relation (ἐπ' ἀρχήν)[74] to possibility, actively by virtue of the forward relation (τέλος) implicit in its "having an end in itself" (ἐντελέχεια). If (creaturely) actuality, then, constitutes the actual formal plane of the principle of non-contradiction, then the latter is situated most formally within the energetic transitoriness of this plane: between the abyss of the principle's negation (in the ταὐτὸν τἀναντία of possibility) and its superelevation into the most definite possible "is" (wherein the principle of identity is fulfilled). The principle of non-contradiction is comprehensible only as the energy of this movement between the limit concepts of "pure contradiction" (in δύναμις) and "pure identity" (in an ἐντελέχεια brought to completion). It is (according to the logic of our analyses) the foundation of *analogy* understood as an *immanent dynamic middle directed to an end*. For the rhythm of analogy is grounded in the "middle" (understood as the back-and-forth of ἐνέργεια between δύναμις and ἐντελέχεια). The "end-directedness," on the other hand, shows the "measure from above" (which lies in the ἄνω of ἀνά).[75]

70. To all such [potentiality] actuality is prior. *Met.* IX, 8, 1049b, 10.

71. *Met.* IX, 6, 1048b, 6-7.

72. *Met.* IX, 8, 1050a, 9.

73. Actuality [understood as that which] is connected with entelechy. *Met.* IX, 3, 1047a, 30-31.

74. *Met.* IX, 1050a, 7.

75. Thus even the most basic judgment of logic subsists solely upon finite being's irre-

But it is precisely this "end-directedness" that ultimately leads this foundation beyond itself. According to Aristotle,[76] neither the (more cosmological) "all is movement" (μεταβολή) of Heraclitus, nor the more (anthropological) subjective "all is change" of Protagoras can overturn the principle of non-contradiction, because they always refer to the quantitative-formal (ποσόν), never to the qualitative-material (ποιόν). Both "all is movement" and "all is change" entail movement and change between alternating forms (both present and future). This is already true of the real immanent forms of the world: the ontic forms[77] (οὐσία).[78] It is all the more true of the ideal ontic forms, understood as their defining forms[79] (εἶδος).[80] The boundlessness of "all is movement" and "all is change" is the inner character of purely formal movement as such (τὸ . . . ποσὸν τῆς ἀορίστου).[81] The bounded, by contrast, is characterized by the qualitative-material aspect of the (energetic) unity of ontic and defining form (ἡ δ' οὐσία κατὰ τὸ ποιόν, τοῦτο δὲ τῆς ὡρισμένης φύσεως).[82] Thus, here, for the first time, a certain transcendence is mixed into what till now has been immanence. It is not simply that — as it has been to this point — the principle of non-contradiction signifies (both noetically and ontically) a rhythmic middle. It is rather that there is a stress upon "end-directedness," which becomes more clearly an "end towards which. . . ." The changing movement of the creature is (both noetically and ontically) not only like the surging back and forth of the sea's same ultimate elements (the ποιόν understood as οὐσία-μορφή), but also, and precisely, like the turbulent infinity of the sea governed by the everlasting stars (the ποιόν understood as εἶδος). The principle of non-contradiction thus has a stress towards the principle of identity, but in such a way as to be "directed" towards it, not equated with it. It is not identity that holds sway between

---

ducible dynamism, that of the synthesis *in fieri* of possibility and actuality. The principle of non-contradiction, properly speaking, holds true neither in the realm of pure potency (of the chaotic, of indefinite *materia prima,* of unrealized *possibilia*) nor in the realm of pure act (of supereminent *actus purus,* the one simple act of all that is), but only in the realm of contingent reality. Thus finite being has no ground in itself — not even the surety of its most incontrovertible logical principle — but *is* only *per analogiam.* — Trans.

76. *Met.* IV, 5, 1010a, 7-25; XI, 6, 1063a, 22-28.

77. *Seins-Formen.* — Trans.

78. *Met.* XI, 6, 1063a, 27ff.

79. *Sinn-Formen.* — Trans.

80. *Met.* IV, 5, 1010a, 25.

81. Quantity is indeterminate. *Met.* XI, 6, 1063a, 28.

82. But substance is dependent upon quality, and this is of a determinate nature. *Met.* XI, 6, 1063a, 27-28.

them, but analogy itself: an analogy from the moving earth of the creature to a "heavenly identity." On the one hand, this identity has the appearance of "rest as the depth of all movement": in that "all is movement" and "all is change" "presuppose" the abiding constancy of (alternating) ontic forms and defining forms (ἔκ τινος γὰρ εἴς τι ἡ μεταβολή).[83] But, on the other hand, it also has the appearance of "rest as the measure above all movement": in that "all is movement" and "all is change" have their "guiding and directing measure" in the totality of ontic forms and defining forms, and in the entire range of possibilities of change ("permutations") that obtain among — and relative to — these forms. The analogy that holds sway here thus appears to coincide with the problematic of number, as is precisely the case from a historical perspective as well (cf. especially Philolaus): number taken here as the expression of purely formal variation (that is, of the "all is movement" within a limitless ποσόν), but, at the same time and equally, as the most poignant expression of immutable Eternal Laws (that is, of immutability within a bounded ποιόν): between the mathematics of a radical positivism and the *incommutabilis veritas numerorum* of Augustine.[84] *Analogy* appears here as an *immanent transcending between movement and number*.[85]

But one must go beyond this to something still more ultimate. Against these very positions (and at the same places in his text), Aristotle reconceives both a transcendence towards that which is unmoved in its "is-ness,"[86] as well as an ultimate immanence of this transcendence (from above). Even were the (noetic-ontic) "all is movement" (within "all is change") really to obtain, as a movement it would still point beyond itself to a mover that, as a mover, would have to be independent of that movement, and hence would have to be an "unmoved mover" (κινοῦν ἀκίνητον).[87] As "unmoved," it is distinguished from any Heraclitean (noetic and ontic) construal of creatureliness. As "causing movement," it bespeaks an inner liveliness, which distinguishes it from any Parmenidean (thing-like) fixity.[88] For this reason, it is not the immanent pole

83. For change is from one thing to another. *Met.* IV, 8, 1012b, 28-29.

84. *De Libero Arbitrio* II, xi, 30.

85. That is, the back-and-forth dynamic of analogy is manifest here in the way that creaturely movement points to the problematic of number and vice versa. For as much as the question of creaturely movement points to the problematic of number, even this seemingly higher problematic (as it would appear, say, from a Pythagorean or Platonic perspective) is stamped by the same dynamic movement. Thus, here too, "analogy" obtains. — Trans.

86. *Ist-haft Unbewegten.* — Trans.

87. *Met.* IV, 8, 1012b, 31.

88. *(Es-haften) Starrheit.* — Trans.

at the limit of the Heraclitean "all is flux" (in which case, logically, it would fall within the sphere of creatureliness), but is rather, positively, a "mover," whose intrinsic "eternity"[89] (ἀεὶ κινεῖ τὰ κινούμενα)[90] is that of a living immovability,[91] which — as first cause and ground[92] — stands over against the "eternity" of the perpetually being-moved of perpetual movement. As this "eternity" (ἀεὶ), it alone is the site of authoritative[93] truth (goodness, beauty) (ἐκ τῶν ἀεὶ κατὰ ταὐτὰ ἐχόντων καὶ μηδεμίαν μεταβολὴν ποιουμένων τἀληθὲς θηρεύειν).[94]

Thus the sphere of creatureliness, as the sphere of the principle of non-contradiction — in contrast to this (divine)[95] sphere of the principle of

89. *Immer.* — Trans.

90. It forever moves those things that are moved. *Met.* IV, 8, 1012b, 31.

91. *Lebenshaften Unbewegtheit.* — Trans.

92. *Ur-Sach-Grund.* — Trans.

93. *Maßgebend.* — Trans.

94. We must, if we pursue the truth, set out from those things that remain ever the same and undergo no change whatsoever. *Met.* XI, 6, 1063a, 13-14.

95. Here, "divine" means — in reference to Aristotle — the divine in its formal aspect. It is something else entirely to ask what reality Aristotle accords to this formal aspect. We shall have to see how Romans 1:21ff. holds true here: "they, knowing God (in the formality of the divine) . . . exchanged the glory of the changeless God for an image made in the likeness of changeable man." For what is really divine is, for Aristotle, the unity of the cosmic cycle of change (κυκλοφορία) with the noetic "circle circling into itself" (νόησις νοήσεως). This distinction between the formal and material doctrines of God is expressed best by Thomas Aquinas (*Summa Th.* I, q. 13, a. 10, ad 5), where he allows that there is a harmony between the *Catholic* and the *pagan* in regard to "what is meant by 'God'" (in the *eadem significatio*) — God, that is, in the sense of a ground of the creaturely "is (valid)," which as such is independent of and distinct from this "is," and thus "beyond it" (by virtue of this distinction), as the "pure Is (Truth, etc.)" (all persons know God "according to some concept of causality or excellence or remotion," *secundum aliquam rationem causalitatis vel excellentiae vel remotionis* — Ibid.; for the name "God" signifies something "existing above all things, which is the principle of all things and remote from all things," *supra omnia existens, quod est principium omnium, et remotum ab omnibus* — *Summa Th.* I, q. 13, a. 8, ad 2). This harmony is not incompatible with the sharpest divergence in material doctrine: between the heathen's world of idols and the Catholic's *one* tri-personal God; "thus the Gentile is able to take this name 'God', when he declares 'this idol is God', in the same fashion as does the Catholic when he declares 'this idol is not God'," *secundum hoc in eadem significatione accipere potest gentilis hoc nomen 'Deus', cum dicit: Idolum est Deus, in qua accipit ipsum catholicus, dicens: Idolum non est Deus (Summa Th.* I, q. 13, a. 10, ad 5). The ground of the possibility of this divergence is the distinction Romans draws between "knowledge" ("erkennen") and "acknowledgment" ("anerkennen"), a distinction whose own ground, however, is the freedom of man, who — knowing precisely what is meant by "God" — can make something creaturely into his God. Athe-

identity — "has" (ontically) being and (noetically) truth (goodness, beauty) in such measure as it is related, beyond itself, to this latter, superordinated sphere. That is to say: *analogy* is established *as a participatory being-related-above-and-beyond.*

As a genuine consequence of such an "above-and-beyond," however, one must ultimately grant at least an objective priority to the "from-above." If the sphere of eternal movement (noetically and ontically) *is* by virtue of a movement produced by the eternal mover, then (ontically) the former "is" properly speaking "in the latter," and not "in itself" (δεῖ ἄρα τὸ κινούμενον εἶναι ἐν ἐκείνῳ ἐξ οὗ κινήσεται καὶ οὐκ εἶναι ἐν αὐτῷ, καὶ εἰς τοδὶ κινεῖσθαι καὶ γίγνεσθαι ἐν τούτῳ).[96] By the same token, it (noetically) has truth (goodness, beauty) "in" the mover, and not "in itself" (τὸ δὲ κατὰ τὴν ἀντίφασιν μὴ ἀληθεύεσθαι κατ' αὐτοῦ).[97] Here we have the notion that finds its classical formulation in Augustine: the principle of non-contradiction designates, both ontically and noetically, a "ground" that "trembles above the nothing," and thus shows that those standing upon it are of themselves "nothing," rather than that they of themselves (ontically and noetically) "are": *si . . . accedendo illuminamini et recedendo tenebramini: non erat in vobis lumen vestrum, sed in Deo vestro* (the noetic side). . . . *Si accedendo vivitis, recedendo morimini, non erat in vobis vita vestra* (the ontic side). *Ipsa est enim vita vestra, quae est lux vestra* (from a noetic-ontic identity to a unity of the noetic and ontic).[98] This Aristotelian notion is further clarified, however, by Thomas Aquinas's profounder notion that the "is (valid)" "is (valid) in the Is (Truth, etc.)" *(dicuntur omnia esse in Deo, in quantum conti-*

---

ism is an imprecise concept. Ultimately, there is only the either-or between God and idol, and thus between *Catholic* and *pagan.*

96. Thus that which is moved must necessarily be in that from which it will move, and then not in it, and move into the other and come to be therein. *Met.* XI, 6, 1063a, 19-20.

97. Contrary statements are not simultaneously true. *I Met.* XI, 6, 1063a, 21.

98. If . . . you are illumined by drawing near to him and darkened by withdrawing, your light was not in yourselves but in your God. . . . If you live by drawing near to him and die by withdrawing, your life was not in yourselves. For that which is your life is the same as that which is your light. *In Joh. Tract.* XIX, xii. [The pregnant concluding words in parentheses here signal the distinction (and the direction of the distinction) between the identity of the noetic and ontic in God (whose light is his life), just as his essence is his existence, and the contingent conjunction (or unity-in-tension) of the noetic and the ontic (essence and existence) in creatures. From §1 we have now arrived at the point where the original tension between the noetic and the ontic (essence and existence) points beyond itself to the noetic-ontic (essence-existence) identity from whom the creaturely unity of the noetic and the ontic (essence and existence) ultimately derives. — Trans.]

nentur ab ipso)[99] because, fundamentally, the "is (valid)" signifies the "being of the Is (Truth, etc.) in all things" *(Deus est in rebus sicut continens res).*[100] This "is (valid)," which expresses what is positive within the principle of non-contradiction, reveals itself as essentially "from" the Is (Truth, etc.) *(cum . . . Deus sit ipsum esse per suam essentiam oportet quod esse creatum sit proprius effectus eius);*[101] and for this reason it is in its ultimate essence the self-impartation and, hence, self-presence of "the" Is (Truth, etc.), just as the luminosity of the air is the luminosity of the sun *(sicut lumen causatur in aere a sole, quamdiu aer illuminatus manet).*[102] God as the Is (Truth, etc.) is the innermost depth and the deepest interior of every "is (valid)": *esse . . . est illud quod est magis intimum cuilibet, et quod profundius omnibus inest . . . Unde oportet quod Deus sit in omnibus rebus et intime.*[103] Thus analogy, as a participatory being-related-above-and-beyond, has as its profounder premise an *analogy as the self-imparting-relation-from-above*[104] of the divine identity of the Is (Truth, etc.).

But then both senses of analogy are interlinked in a new way. In that the former ("from below to above") has the latter ("from above to below") as its objective foundation, it is in the latter that the "above-and-beyond" reveals its proper depth: as the "transcending" of a being-in — *Inne-Sein* — of the Is (Truth, etc.) within the "is (valid)" toward the very being-beyond — *Über-Sein* — of this Is (Truth, etc.): the "trace" and "effect" of God, as "God in things," points beyond itself to "God in himself": the *(Deus) in omnibus rebus ut causans omnium esse*[105] points above and beyond to the *Deus . . . supra omnia per excellentiam suae naturae.* By contrast, in the second analogy ("from above to below") there is such a being-beyond of the Is (Truth, etc.) that it becomes an all-effecting *(causans omnium esse)* and all-containing *(continens res)* being-in: *Deus est supra omnia per excellentiam suae naturae,*

99. All things are said to be in God in that they are contained by him. *Summa Th.* I, q. 8, a. 1, ad 2.

100. God is in all things as containing them. *Summa Th.* I, q. 8, a. 1, ad 2.

101. Since . . . God is being itself according to his own essence, created being is necessarily his proper effect. *Summa Th.* I, q. 8, a. 1, corp.

102. As light is caused in the air by the sun, so long as the air remains illumined. *Summa Th.* I, q. 8, a. 1, corp.

103. Being . . . is that which is more inward to each thing and which inheres more deeply in all things. . . . Hence it must be that God is in all things, inwardly. *Summa Th.* I, q. 8, a. 1, corp.

104. *Analogie als teilgebendes Sich-von-oben-hinein-beziehen.* — Trans.

105. [God] in all things as the cause of the being of all things. *Summa Th.* I, q. 8, a. 1, ad 1.

et tamen est in omnibus rebus ut causans omnium esse.[106] This is the fully explicated meaning of Augustine's "God most inward and God most transcendent": *interior omni re, quia in ipso sunt omnia, et exterior omni re, quia ipse est super omnia.*[107] It is established along these lines by Gregory the Great's more incisive formulation, which interchangeably interweaves the antithetical couplets inner-outer and above-below: *implendo circumdat et circumdando implet et implendo transcendit et transcendendo implet et sustinendo transcendit et transcendendo sustinet;*[108] *unde superius praesidens, inde inferius sustinens: et unde exterius ambiens, inde interius replens.*[109] This means, on the one hand (according to the analogy "from below to above"): the Is (Truth, etc.) in → beyond the is (valid); and then (according to the analogy "from above to below"): the Is (Truth, etc.) beyond → in the is (valid). On the one hand, as a matter of intention,[110] the first rests upon the second: the "above-and-beyond" (towards God) presupposes the "from-above-into" (of God). Therefore, "analogy" does not mean that the Is (Truth, etc.) is "similar" to the "is (valid)," but rather, conversely, that the "is (valid)" (as the participating image) is "similar" to the Is (Truth, etc.) (as the imparting archetype): *Deus nullo modo similis creaturae dicendus est, sed creaturae similes possunt dici Deo aliquo modo.*[111] But, on the other hand, the second truly bears an intention toward the first. The Is (Truth, etc.), which is God, is essentially ("as" the Is) self-sufficient. If there is an "is (valid)," which derives its existence from the Is (Truth, etc.), the Is (Truth, etc.) is not therefore "related" to it, as if the Is stood in need of the is. Rather this "is (valid)" cannot be (valid) if it is not intrinsically related to the Is (Truth, etc.). So understood, a self-im-partation of God (in the analogy "from above to below") proceeds properly towards a participation of the creature (ontically and noetically) in him (proceeds, that is, towards the analogy "from below to above"): *ut sic Deus dicatur relative ad creaturam, quia creatura refertur ad*

---

106. God . . . above all things by the excellence of his nature. *Summa Th.* I, q. 8, a. 1, ad 1.

107. Within everything because all things are in him, and outside everything because beyond all things. *De Gen. ad Litt.* VIII, xxvi.

108. He encompasses [all things] in filling [them], and fills in encompassing, and transcends in filling, and fills in transcending, and transcends in sustaining, and sustains in transcending. *Moralia* XVI, xv.

109. On the one hand he is above presiding and on the other below sustaining; and on the one hand he is without and surrounding and on the other within and replenishing. *Moralia* II, viii.

110. *Sinngemäß.* — Trans.

111. God must in no wise be said to be similar to the creature, but creatures can be said in a certain way to be similar to God. *De Ver.* q. 2, a. 11, ad 1.

ipsum;[112] *cum ea ratione referatur Deus ad creaturam, qua creatura referatur ad ipsum.*[113] Analogy is, at this highest point, analogy *as a dynamic back-and-forth between the above-and-beyond (of a transcending immanence) and the from-above-into (of an indwelling transcendence).*[114]

6. This formulation of analogy, however, points back to our earlier definition of analogy as a back-and-forth within the immanence of creatureliness itself (§6, 5): as an "immanent dynamic middle" — as we phrased it — of actuality (ἐνέργεια) between dynamic possibility (δύναμις) and an inner end-directedness (ἐντελέχεια). What these two have formally in common is, first of all, the equation drawn between analogy and middle (μέσον), from which arises the concept of a "dynamic" or "moving" or "suspended" middle. Then, secondly, it is the concept of an end-directedness within this "moving suspended" middle. But it is precisely here that we discover the decisive differences between them. For the analogy intrinsic to the immanence of creatureliness (or, more simply, the "intra-creaturely analogy") is distinguished by this characteristic: that, according to an inner necessity, it points beyond itself (as we have seen) to the transcending analogy with which we have just dealt (or, more simply, the "analogy between God and creature"). The latter, however, stands or falls with this: that God, as the Is (Truth, etc.), is so little related by "necessity" to the creature, understood as the "is (valid)," that, to the contrary (as we said above), God is not even "related" to the creature; rather their relatedness consists in the creature being related to him. There is thus a contrast not only between the "above and beyond" (which was the result of the intra-creaturely analogy) and the "from-above-into" (as the most characteristic feature of the analogy between God and creature), but also between the "freely independent" of the latter and the "necessarily dependent" of the former. The difference lies not simply in the direction of movement: "from below to above" as opposed to "from above to below" (or, equally, inasmuch as God, understood in Augustinian terms as the "Above," is the all-forming and all-directing "within" of creatureliness: "from exterior to interior" as opposed to "from interior to exterior"). Rather, to put it more pointedly, it is a difference in the manner of movement: "necessarily dependently receptive" (and thus movement as a "needful becom-

112. We speak of "God" relative to the creature, since the creature is related to him. *Summa Th.* I, q. 13, a. 7, ad 4.
113. Since God is related to the creature only in that the creature is related to him. *Summa Th.* I, q. 13, a. 7, ad 5.
114. *Zwischen Überhinaus (transzendierender Immanenz) und Von-Oben-hinein (immanierender Transzendenz).* — Trans.

ing" between the "*in infinitum* of possibilities" in the "nothing" and, in each case, a "limited" actuality: *esse contingens,* accidental being, that which "just comes about") as opposed to "freely independently giving" (and thus movement as "independent creation" on the part of the infinity of the Is, which, far from being a "possibility becoming actual," is on the contrary, as the Is that imparts to all things their ground and end and definition, the actuality that cannot be conceived as possibly not-being and that is thus the "impossible non-possible" — that is, "necessary actuality," *esse necessarium*).

This, at the same time, designates what is ultimate: the positive reciprocal relationship between the two analogies. Just as the differences between them were found in the back-and-forth (of the end-directed, moving middle) that they formally have in common, so too it is here that we discover their positive reciprocal relationship. To be sure, the result of the unity of the back-and-forth proper to the intra-creaturely analogy (back to δύναμις, forth to ἐντελέχεια) is the one above-and-beyond, wherein is comprised that particular "back"[115] proper to the analogy between God and creature (the "back" to God of the creaturely, which ontically and noetically originates from God). It is a unity, however, not an identity, and thus expresses its components *in* this unity. The "back" of the intra-creaturely analogy (from ἐνέργεια to δύναμις) distinctly indicates the negative contingency of the "is (valid)." This intra-creaturely "back" is thus, in a special way, the site of the manifestation of the "forward"[116] of the relation between God and creature (the "indwelling transcendence" of which we earlier spoke): the "is (valid)" as the sign of the *Deus interior omni re.* Conversely, the "forward" of the intra-creaturely analogy (from ἐνέργεια to ἐντελέχεια) distinctly expresses the negative mutability *(semper fieri)* of the "is (valid)." Within this constant "self-transcending"[117] of the surpassing of every attained stage of being (truth, etc.) by another, however, we immediately hear the distinctive rhythm of the "back" of the relation between God and creature (the "transcending immanence" of which we earlier spoke). The liveliness within the "self-transcending" of perpetual becoming is that of Augustine's "restless . . . till it rest in Thee," *inquietum . . . , donec requiescat in Te.* On the one hand, the *cor inquietum* bears in itself the drive towards a perfection of is-ness: *Est . . . simplex quaero, Est verum quaero, Est germanum quaero.*[118] On the other

---

115. *Das besondere Zurück.* — Trans.
116. *Hin.* — Trans.
117. *Über sich hinaus.* — Trans.
118. I seek the simple Is, the true Is, the authentic Is. Augustine, *In Ps.* XXXVIII, vii.

hand, just as everything creaturely (ontic and noetic), "as" creaturely, is a negative mutability, what the *cor inquietum* experiences is a coming to be only to pass away: *nondum habetur, dum non venit: non tenetur, dum venerit . . . Est et non est.*[119] Thus it points beyond itself to the *Deus exterior omni re.*

The first relation — between the "back" of the intra-creaturely analogy and the "forward" of the analogy between God and creature — is a certain span[120] of extremes. The one extreme would be a self-enclosing of the creaturely "is (valid)" within the negativity of its "back" towards "pure possibility" (δύναμις), which, inasmuch as it is prior to being, places the accent on non-being. That is to say, inasmuch as the creaturely (ontic and noetic), in its tendency to self-enclosure, seeks to be grounded-in-itself, it can be thus grounded only insofar as the nothing becomes the ground of its being (as is, quite logically, the teaching of Heidegger). The other extreme is what we have repeatedly called theo-pan-ism. The "pure being-given" of the "is (valid)" (in the "forward" of the relation between God and creature) becomes the immediate "self-donation" of the Is (Truth, etc.) of God; the "being of God *in* all things" passes over into the "being of God *as* the being of things." There is a similar spanning of extremes in the second relation, between the "forward" of the intra-creaturely analogy and the "back" of the analogy between God and creature. Here the one extreme is a self-enclosure of the creaturely "is (valid)" in its (negative) "mutability *in infinitum*" (from the ἐνέργεια of δύναμις to ἐντελέχεια). Here too, therefore, such self-enclosure ultimately leads to a nothing, albeit a nothing understood in the sense of the "away from and towards" of the "into the infinite" — not as the nothing of "pure possibility," but as the nothing of a "pure transition" in the sense of a "passing-over."[121] The opposite extreme, then, is what we have repeatedly called pan-the-ism. God becomes the immanent defining end of creaturely (ontic and noetic) movement. Here, creaturely movement is intrinsically a "God-in-becoming"; and so it is proper to this perspective that the "all (pan)" — once it is achieved — "is" God (pan-theos). It was characteristic of the "back" of the analogy between God and creature that the creaturely "is (valid)" goes "forth" "towards" the divine Is (Truth, etc.) as its "end." To this extent, God is in a genuine sense the measure of all things, *mensura omnium rerum.*[122] But, to the extent that God becomes the imma-

---

119. It is not yet possessed so long as it has not arrived, it cannot be held onto once it has arrived. . . . It is and is not. Augustine, *In Ps.* XXXVIII, vii.

120. *Spanne.* — Trans.

121. *Das Nichts des "reinen Übergangs als Vorübergangs."* — Trans.

122. *De Ver.* q. 23, a. 7, corp.

nent end, this slides over into pantheism: *Deus non est mensura proportionata mensuratis.*[123]

In the foregoing, however, we have worked out something common to both spans. Each is, first of all, a span, which is to say neither an identity nor a contradiction, but rather a coordinated relation, and thus an analogy. Consequently, the *relation between the intra-creaturely analogy and the analogy between God and creature is itself an analogy.* Obviously, then, this analogy is in every respect the decisive analogy. Secondly, it is an analogy that is itself, once again (in a higher sense), characterized by the suspended middle between theopanism and pantheism. In the self-enclosure of the creaturely "is (valid)" (in both of the above relations) there is a tendency towards being self-enclosed "like God." Such is the pan-theistic tendency: to be "rounded unto oneself." At the opposite extreme, however, that of the express divinity of the creature (passively in the first relation, actively in the second), its intention is concealed: to comprise God within the sphere of the creature, so that he might be its Being and its All. Such is theo-pan-ism.

7. What is decisive for our last analogy (as the culminating problem of the principle of non-contradiction) lies in the relation between the lowest pole of the intra-creaturely analogy, that of "pure possibility" (δύναμις), and the highest pole of the analogy between God and creature, the Is of God in himself, because here the unity of the two analogies has its most extreme and comprehensive span. It is the expanse taken in by the vision of Thomas Aquinas: between *pura potentialitas* and *actus purus.* The point of this span is that *the potentiality of the creaturely with regard to God* in no way be taken as a usurping of God. For such usurpation was the final sense of the pairs of extremes that we looked at above. The result in these cases was that both poles of the span were dissolved. God was not God — i.e., the authentic Is (Truth, etc.) that the principle of non-contradiction shows him to be — because he was a function of potentiality. By the same token, even this potentiality was not really a potentiality standing "in need of God," but rather a disguised actuality that "masters" God. Our final analogy thus adheres primarily to the truth of the ἄνω in "ana": to the above as authentically above.

The first thing thus established is a *"negative potentiality."* It is rooted — firstly — in that which constitutes the apex of the Aristotelian problematic of δύναμις and ἐνέργεια: the fundamental, ultimate priority of ἐνέργεια

---

123. God is not a measure proportionate to the things measured. *Summa Th.* I, q. 13, a. 5, ad 3.

(πρότερα ἐστὶν ἡ ἐνέργεια).[124] While it is true that (in the sphere of the creaturely) actuality (ἐνέργεια), as an actualized possibility, derives from possibility in the sense of potentiality, it does so nevertheless always by virtue of something already actual (ἀεὶ γὰρ ἐκ τοῦ δυνάμει ὄντος γίγνεται τὸ ἐνεργείᾳ ὂν ὑπὸ ἐνεργείᾳ ὄντος).[125] So too, therefore, with regard to what is ultimate, there stands at the beginning not an "eternal potentiality" (ἔστι δ' οὐθὲν δυνάμει ἀΐδιον),[126] but rather something "eternally actual" (ἀεὶ ἐνεργεῖ[127]).[128]

It logically follows — secondly — that this potentiality itself, as potentiality, is not ultimately its own; rather, even as regards "what is possible," the last word belongs to the "eternal actual," the divine Is (Truth, etc.). As Thomas Aquinas inexorably concludes, the potentiality of the creaturely, properly understood, is not something "possible in and of itself, which, on this basis, could demand actualization by God" *(posse creari ab Ipso);*[129] on the contrary, the potentiality of the creaturely is at bottom decidedly a "possibility originating from the freedom of God" *(creare posse aliquid).*[130]

If this is the case, then — thirdly — this potentiality itself shifts into the sphere of creative eternal actuality. Potentiality is an equivocal term. On the one hand (materially),[131] it implies a "what" that is possible, and thus signifies the sphere of the neo-scholastic *possibilia* (of an *interna possibilitas*). But it signifies equally the "how" of possibility as such, and is thus a term for the most pronounced aspect of creatureliness, which we denominated above as "pure possibility": the neo-scholastic notion that there is "no incompatibility with existence," *non repugnare ad existendum* (as the intra-creaturely correlate of the *externa possibilitas,* understood as "the capacity to be created by God"). The shifting of material potentiality[132] into the divine

124. Act is prior. *Met.* IX, 8, 1049b, 10.
125. For the actual is always produced from the potential by something actual. *Met.* IX, 8, 1049b, 24.
126. Nothing eternal exists in potential. *Met.* IX, 8, 1050b, 7-8.
127. By this Aristotle naturally means to indicate his revolving cosmic cycle. But, as we have already seen above, this changes nothing with respect to the formal doctrine of God, upon which such an inversion (the material doctrine of God) must rest.
128. *Met.* IX, 8, 1050b, 22.
129. Capable of being created by him. *De Ver.* q. 2, a. 10, ad 2 in contr.
130. Capable of creating something. *De Ver.* q. 2, a. 10, ad 2 in contr.
131. *Inhaltlich.* — Trans.
132. Again, the word "material" here is a rendering of the word *"inhaltlich";* that is to say, it does not refer to potentiality simply in the sense of "matter" — ὕλη, *materia prima* — but in the sense of "contents": the fullness of all that might ever be. — Trans.

sphere is hereby indicated in that, according to Thomas Aquinas, there is not some ideative world of ideas or values or essences (in the sense of a paradigm of actualizable "whats")[133] that "stands over against" God; rather the diverse plenitude of all "possible whats" leads us back to the manifold and limitlessly "representable" essence of God: *una prima forma, ad quam omnia reducuntur, est ipsa essentia divina secundum se considerata.*[134] In place of the ideas (values, etc.) *(loco harum idearum quas Plato ponebat)*,[135] there is a "measuring out" *(ratio)*, whereby God himself, in the irreducible independence of his essence, grounds the "ambit of essences" of possible creatures *(rationes omnium creaturarum)*[136] in his essence. Accordingly, this *essentia divina* is not only in a general sense the defining-ground *(ratio)*[137] of material possibilities *(communis omnium ratio, in quantum est res ipsa una, quam omnia imitantur)*[138] but also, in the most formal sense, the ground of their inner qualitative multiplicity *(propria huius ratio vel illius, secundum quod res eam diversimode imitantur)*.[139] There is no uncreated "world of essences" *(ipsa quidditas creari dicitur)*,[140] but rather the "creative essence" of God *(creatrix essentia)*.[141] But then formal potentiality likewise ends up in this sphere. For only then can there be a complete creative independence of God and (correlatively) a complete being "from-Him" of the creature — when precisely the formal form[142] of the creature's creatureliness also comes from God. But this is what we mean by formal potentiality. In this, everything creaturely, in its entirety, is immediately from God: not by way of a sorting-out of the particular *(singulare)* from ideative universal forms *(universalia)*, nor by way of an "activation" of some "lowest potentiality" *(materia prima)*

---

133. *Inbegriff verwirklichbarer Washeiten.* — Trans.

134. The one prime form, to which all things are reduced, is itself the divine essence considered according to itself. *De Ver.* q. 3, a. 2, ad 6.

135. In place of the ideas posited by Plato. . . .

136. The types [ratios] of all creatures. *Summa Th.* I, q. 84, a. 5, corp.

137. The ambiguity of *ratio* (understood as "measuring out," "ambit of essences," "defining-ground") is itself a pronounced expression of the point being made here. This includes additionally the sense of *ratio* as "understanding" and the sense of *ratio* as "concept." Cf. *De Ver.* q. 8, a. 7, ad 3.

138. The type [ratio] common to all things insofar as it is itself the one thing that all things imitate. *De Ver.* q. 2, a. 4, ad 2.

139. A type [ratio] proper to this thing or that, in that things imitate it in a diversity of modes. *De Ver.* q. 2, a. 4, ad 2.

140. The essence is itself said to be created. *De Pot.* q. 3, a. 5, ad 2.

141. *De Pot.* q. 3, a. 5, ad 2.

142. *Formale Form.* — Trans.

already at hand; rather, God is the *one* ideative origin *(una idea respondet singulari, speciei et generi, individuatis in ipso singulari),*[143] and as such the *one* origin of material *(forma)* and formal *(materia)* potentiality[144] *(ponimus Deum esse causam singularis et quantum ad formam et quantum ad materiam),*[145] and, as such, consequently, the origin of the positive multiplicity of the "what" of the *formae rerum*[146] and of the creature's most basic "potentiality toward everything" (the *materia prima).*[147] He is therefore, finally, an unexhausted and inexhaustible origin that is "beyond" each and every thing that originates from him, because otherwise he would be the inner correlate of his creations, the "act" that is "there" "for the purpose of" their enactment. But since the material and formal potentiality of everything that ever could originate from him is "in him," as we have seen, he is "necessary" only with respect to himself: *finis . . . naturalis divinae voluntatis est eius bonitas.*[148] Consequently, the "potentiality" that is ordered intrinsically and exclusively towards the "act," which is God, is God himself: the "possible" God who, as the possible "God," can be none other than the God who is "necessarily actual." No potentiality of the creature, therefore, is able by its enactment to exhaust this act that is interiorly related to itself: *fini huic non commensurantur creaturae.*[149] The ultimate aspect of the creaturely "is (valid)" is thus not only its potentiality, but its "provisionality" in every instant, and, what is more, its provisionality *"in infinitum."* Always, in every moment, an ever new and different "is (valid)" is possible: *potest* (namely, *Eius bonitas) manifestari per alias creaturas et alio modo ordinatas.*[150]

But then — fourthly — creaturely potentiality does not, of itself, place limits on God, but rather receives its limits from God. Thus these limits are not ultimately something irrevocably fixed in the essence of this potentiality, but

---

143. One idea corresponds to the particular, the species, and the genus, and whatever is individuated within the particular itself. *De Ver.* q. 3, a. 8, ad 2.

144. This is not a mistake. Simply said, matter and form are each potential to the other. — Trans.

145. We assert that God is the cause of the particular as regards both its form and its matter. *De Ver.* q. 3, a. 8, corp.

146. *Comp. Th.* c. 102.

147. *Summa Th.* I, q. 44, a. 2. The differences among *potentia (actus), materia (forma),* etc. are here left without further explanation; what is at issue here is always simply the minimum expressed in the principle of non-contradiction.

148. The natural end of the divine will is God's own goodness. *De Pot.,* q. 1, a. 5, corp.

149. To this end creatures are not proportionate. *De Pot.,* q. 1, a. 5, corp.

150. [His goodness] can be manifested in such various creatures as he ordains and in a variable mode. *De Pot.,* q. 1, a. 5, corp.

rather a provisional halting point imposed by the illimitability of God's free decree. Every potentiality expressed within the concept of the creaturely (ontic or noetic) *(potentia . . . naturalis, quae potest tota impleri, quia haec non se extendit nisi ad perfectiones naturales)*[151] — every such "natural" potentiality — is ultimately ground-less, to the point of an unlimited disposability before God, in the *potentia oboedientiae, secundum quod potest recipere a Deo.*[152] Here we have a breaching of the natural limits of the creaturely: it is a potentiality to the incomprehensibilities of supernature, which are revealed only through theology *(sicut dicitur aliquid esse in potentia ad illa quae supra naturam Deus in eo potest facere).*[153] Here we have an abiding provisionality with regard to limitless possibilities, as God incalculably wills them: *potentia oboedientiae, secundum quam in creatura fieri potest quidquid in ea fieri voluerit Creator.*[154] Consequently, here we have the limitless possibility of an ever new above-and-beyond: *talis capacitas non potest impleri, quia quidquid Deus de creatura faciat, adhuc remanet in potentia recipiendi a Deo.*[155] The measure lies decidedly beyond the creature, in the incomprehensibility of the measure of divine giving: *modus . . . , qui crescente bonitate crescit, sequitur magis mensuram perfectionis receptae quam capacitatis ad recipiendum.*[156]

The effective implication of these first four aspects of negative potentiality, however, is that a boundary is established, not only against an (active) pantheism of the creature, but equally against a (passive) theopanism that interprets "possibility" in such a way as to distort it into the "magic of impotence." This is immediately evident in view of certain subtle details that Thomas likes to inscribe within these four potentialities, and which aim at something we might call *"positive potentiality."* Precisely because the material and formal potentiality of the creature lies so very much "in God," it is not simply a "powerless nothing." Because it proceeds both materially and

151. Natural potentiality, which has the power of being fulfilled entirely because it extends to nothing but natural perfections. *De Ver.* q. 29, a. 3, ad 3.

152. A potential of obedience, inasmuch as it is capable of receiving from God. *De Ver.* q. 29, a. 3, ad 3.

153. Thus something is said to be in potency to those things above its nature that God can cause in it. *De Ver.* q. 8, a. 4, ad 13.

154. The potential of obedience according to which the Creator can cause whatsoever he wishes to come about in the creature. *De Ver.* q. 8, a. 12, ad 4.

155. Such a capacity cannot be filled, because whatever God does with a creature, still the creature remains in potency to receive from God. *De Ver.* q. 29, a. 3, ad 3.

156. The mode [of reception] . . . , which increases in the increase of the good, is determined by the measure of what is received rather than by the capacity to receive. *De Ver.* q. 29, a. 3, ad 3.

formally from the pure Is (Truth, etc.), it is already, as such, filled with the breath of this positivity of the pure Is (Truth, etc.). Thus — firstly — the creaturely "is (valid)" does not, by virtue of its abiding inner potentiality, have of itself an "orientation towards nothing," but rather towards an ever new "is (valid, etc.)": *tendere in nihilum non est proprie motus naturae, qui semper est in bonum, sed est ipsius defectus.*[157] For so little does the activity of the divine Is (Truth, etc.) — because it is the positivity of an Is — intend for the creature to sink back into nothingness[158] that, on the contrary, the (enduring) positivity of the creature mysteriously merges with God's own (eternal) positivity. Because the creature reveals God, as Thomas formulates it, one can say equally that God wills the creature for its sake and that he wills it for himself: *idem est dictu, quod Deus propter se ipsum fecit, et quod creaturas fecerit propter earum esse.*[159]

But then — secondly — this very positivity of the creaturely "is (valid)" enters into the form of its potentiality. There is, in a true sense, something that is "impossible" for God: namely, the abrogation of the permanence of the principle of non-contradiction and all that it entails *(non potest facere quod affirmatio et negatio sint simul vera, nec aliquid eorum in quibus hoc impossibile includitur)*;[160] hence God is confronted by something that is truly "possible in itself," and the *"omni-"* in his "omnipotence" concerns "all" that is "possible in itself" *(ad omnia . . . se extendit quae contradictionem non implicant . . . , potest omnia quae sunt possibilia secundum se).*[161] It is not as if God were "confronted" by limits, but that his own positivity "obliges" him, as it were, to "positivity as such."

Thus it becomes understandable — thirdly — how the potentiality of the creaturely can comprise within itself a gradation: from the realm of "pure potentiality" (in the proper realm of matter: *illae solae res in sua natura possibilitatem habent ad non esse, in quibus est materia contrarietati subjecta)*[162]

157. To tend towards nothingness is not the proper motion of nature — which tends rather always towards the good — but is a defect thereof. *De Pot.* q. 5, a. 1, ad 16.

158. *De Pot.* q. 5, a. 4, corp.; ad 10.

159. It is the same to say that God made creatures for himself and that he will have made them for the sake of their own being. *De Pot.* q. 5, a. 4, corp.

160. He is not able to make an affirmation and a negation simultaneously true, nor to create anything in which this impossibility would be included. *De Pot.* q. 1, a. 3, corp.

161. It extends to all things that do not imply a contradiction . . . , he is capable of all such things as are possible in themselves. *De Pot.* q. 1, a. 7, corp.

162. Only those things wherein matter is subject to contrariety have in their nature the possibility of not being. *De Pot.* q. 5, a. 3, corp.

to that of a true "necessity of being" (in the realm of spirit: *aliis . . . rebus secundum suam naturam competit necessitas essendi, possibilitate non essendi ab earum natura sublata).*¹⁶³ Potentiality thus oscillates between a potentiality towards the "possibility of non-being" *(possibilitas ad non esse)* and a potentiality towards the "impossibility of non-being" *(non possibilitas ad non esse).* For if God creates the spiritual, he can create it only as spiritual, i.e., as in its nature imperishable. Potentiality is so positive that God can endow something with the "impossibility of not being." But even then the full "negative potentiality," as we sketched it out above, remains: the absence of any necessity that any creature whatsoever should exist *(simpliciter non esse, non est in se impossibile quasi contradictionem implicans):*¹⁶⁴ the absence of any intrinsic connection of God to the creature *(non producit creaturas ex necessitate naturae ut sic potentia Dei determinetur ad esse creaturae . . . Nec bonitas Dei a creaturis dependet, ut sine creaturis esse non possit).*¹⁶⁵ Indeed, this negative potentiality is reinforced. For, with respect to the intra-creaturely gradation between possible being and necessary being, it becomes clear that the expression "necessity" is really still intra-creaturely — that is, that God remains beyond even the opposition between "possible" and "necessary": *supra ordinem necessarii et contingentis, sicut est supra totum esse creaturae.*¹⁶⁶ And yet, it is precisely here that we encounter the true wonder of a potentiality that is so positive as to be the "possibility of not being possible" or "the non-necessity of being necessary":¹⁶⁷ *licet creaturae incorruptibiles ex Dei voluntate dependeant, quae potest eis esse praebere et non praebere* (the potentiality to be or not to be), *consequuntur tamen ex divina voluntate absolutam necessitatem essendi, in quantum in tali natura causantur, in qua non sit possibilitas ad non esse* (no potentiality to be or not to be).¹⁶⁸

---

163. The necessity of being attaches to other things according to their nature when the possibility of not being has been removed from their nature. *De Pot.* q. 5, a. 3, corp.

164. Simply not to be is not in itself impossible, as though it implied contradiction. *De Pot.* q. 5, a. 3, corp.

165. He does not produce creatures out of any necessity of nature, as though the power of God were determined to the being of the creature . . . Nor does the goodness of God depend upon creatures, as though without them it would be unable to exist. *De Pot.* q. 5, a. 3, corp.

166. [His will is] above the order of necessary and contingent, just as [it is] above the whole being of the creature. *De Malo* q. 16, a. 7, ad 15.

167. *Möglichkeit zu Unmöglichkeit, Nichtnotwendigkeit zu Notwendigkeit.* — Trans.

168. Although incorruptible creatures may be dependent upon the will of God, which is able either to impart or not impart being to them, still they attain to an absolute necessity of being on account of the divine will, insofar as they are caused to possess the sort of nature in which no possibility of not being inheres. *De Pot.* q. 5, a. 3, ad 12. [The reference here is to

This positivity is — fourthly — especially prominent in the problem of good and evil. By virtue of its potentiality, every creaturely "is (valid)" is *ens in potentia.* As such, on the one hand, its essential ordination is towards the "positive" of a rounding-out to perfection *(cum esse in potentia nihil aliud sit quam ordinari in actum)*[169] and is therefore in itself "good": *id quod est in potentia ex hoc ipso quod est in potentia, habet rationem boni.*[170] On the other hand, however, it is precisely this character of an *ens in potentia* that lays the ground for the possibility of evil: *malum . . . est . . . in bono, secundum quod ens in potentia dicitur bonum.*[171] For an *ens in potentia,* by virtue of its essence, is capable of falling away from essence: *cum . . . malum . . . nihil aliud sit quam privatio debitae perfectionis: privatio autem non sit nisi in ente in potentia, quia hoc privari dicimus quod natum est habere aliquid et non habet.*[172] Thus arises the paradox that the good is so much the cause of evil *(causa mali est bonum)*[173] that, in the very willing of evil, the good is willed: *nullus facit aliquod malum, nisi intendens aliquod bonum, ut sibi videtur.*[174] In that the creaturely "of itself" is "nothing," it contains within itself the possibility of that suicidal plunge into nothing which is the nihilistic characteristic of the innermost tendency of evil. But precisely here the "positive," which is stronger, triumphs: for the nihilistic itself, as such, can be willed only under a *ratio boni,* and is thus itself still sustained by the positive "is" of the Is (and in this is most decisively overcome). Even nothingness itself, as nothingness, must bear the stamp of the Is, and therefore must be subject — of service — to it: *quamvis discordet voluntas hominis a Dei voluntate quantum ad motum voluntatis, numquam tamen potest discordare*

---

created spirits, which — though they depend entirely upon God's creative will for their being — are so constituted as to be indestructible (they are simple, and only the composite can be destroyed). — Trans.]

169. Since to be in potential is nothing other than to be ordered towards act. *De Malo,* q. 1, a. 2, corp.

170. That which is in potential, precisely because it is in potential, possesses the nature [ratio] of the good. *De Malo,* q. 1, a. 2, corp.

171. Evil . . . is . . . in the good, in that being in potential is said to be good. *De Malo,* q. 1, a. 2, ad 7.

172. Since . . . evil . . . is nothing other than a privation of a destined perfection, and there can be no privation except in a being in potential, because we say something suffers privation only when it does not possess something that it is natural for it to possess. *De Malo,* q. 1, a. 2, corp.

173. *De Malo,* q. 1, a. 3, corp.

174. No one does anything evil except that he intends the good as it appears to him. *De Malo,* q. 1, a. 3, corp.

quantum ad exitum vel eventum: quia semper voluntas hominis hunc eventum sortitur, quod Deus de homine suam voluntatem implet.[175]

It is not so surprising then — finally and fifthly — that even that negative potentiality which pointed most intensely into the depths of the Is still has a positive aspect: the *potentia oboedientialis* (which is ordered towards the supernatural). To be sure, it remains a potentiality that is "beyond nature," so much so that even a knowledge of the sphere of the supernatural is "beyond nature": *(modus supernaturalis) homini notus esse non potest, cum ipsum donum gratiae cognitionem hominis excedat.*[176] For a true *naturalis appetitus,* i.e., a conscious orientation intrinsic to nature in itself, proceeds only toward a general "proximity to the divine" *(aliqua contemplatio divinorum),*[177] whereas the truly supernatural, the vision of God as Eternal Life *(vita aeterna quae consistit in visione Dei per essentiam),*[178] has as its correlate within the human being a proper and direct "being prepared by God" *(finis ad quem homo a Deo praeparatur),*[179] i.e., in our *potentia oboedientialis.* But, on the other hand — and here even this most intense negative potentiality becomes positive — this "supernatural" incorporates itself entirely into the relational edifice of the natural. It incorporates itself into the relational structure of end and means[180]: the supernatural "concerns the end itself" *(circa finem),* while the natural is "underway" to the end *(ad finem).*[181] It incorporates itself into the relational structure of how and what: in the supernatural lies the "correct mode" *(modus conveniens),* in the natural the "correct content" *(substantia actus).*[182] Logically, therefore, that which is most properly supernatural, the vision of God as Eternal Life, becomes the "ultimate perfection" of the natural: subjectively for the spirit, in that it is only here that its *naturale desiderium* finds rest;[183] objectively for creation as

---

175. Although the human will may not accord with the will of God as regards the movement of the will, still it can never fail to accord as regards its outcome or result: for the will of man always obtains this result, that God fulfills his will for man. *De Malo,* q. 6, a. 1, ad 5.

176. [The supernatural mode] cannot be known by a man, since even the gift of grace exceeds human knowledge. *De Ver.* q. 24, a. 15, corp.

177. A certain contemplation of divine things. *De Ver.* q. 27, a. 2, corp.

178. Eternal life, which consists in the vision of God through his essence. *De Ver.* q. 27, a. 2, corp.

179. The end for which man is prepared by God. *De Ver.* q. 27, a. 2, corp.

180. *Mittel.* — Trans.

181. *De Ver.* q. 14, a. 3, ad 9; a. 10, ad 3.

182. *De Ver.* q. 24, a. 12, ad 16; *De Ver.* q. 24, a. 1, ad 2; *Summa Th.* I, q. 89, a. 6, ad 3.

183. *Summa c. Gent.,* III, 50.

such, which in this perfection of the spirit arrives at the end that corresponds to its original procession from God *(reditio in Deum exitum adaequaret)*.[184]

This coinherence of "beyond nature" and "in nature" is expressed in the full character of the *potentia oboedientialis*. On the one hand, the "beyond nature" is not "against nature," because (understanding potentiality in a more negative sense) everything creaturely is more profoundly subject to the Creator than it is related — one thing to another — to itself: *inest cuilibet rei creatae naturalis subjectio ad Creatorem, multo magis quam corporibus inferioribus ad corpora coelestia*.[185] On the other hand, however, it is not simply a (more negative) "sub-jection" *(subjectio)* but precisely a (positive) "directedness towards . . ." or "readiness . . ." *(habilitas sive aptitudo ad bonum gratiae)*[186] "in the mode of a receptive capacity" *(sicut potentiae susceptivae)*,[187] which as a "natural good" *(bonum naturale)* "belongs to the spiritual nature as such" *(naturam rationalem consequitur in quantum huiusmodi)*.[188] Thus, the most incisive characteristic of the creaturely "is (valid)" is that its most extreme negative potentiality (that of the *potentia oboedientialis*) is at the same time the boldest of positive potentialities — a positive potentiality so bold as to journey into the nature of God himself. It is an "in-sufficiency from one's own ground"[189] *(naturae propriae principia non sufficient)*[190] that is nevertheless a "capacity for . . ." *(capax summi boni per visionem et fruitionem)*.[191] It is a positive display of an orientation towards the supernatural[192] that is a negative display of an "incapacity from one's own power."[193]

In this way our positive potentiality passes over into what we must call, in the true sense of the word, *"active potentiality"*: "active" wholly and utterly upon the basis of the "negative" of the negative potentiality, but nevertheless

184. The return into God is adequate to the exit from God. *De Ver.* q. 20, a. 4, corp.

185. There is in any created thing a subjection to its Creator far greater than the subjection of lower bodies to celestial bodies. *De Malo* q. 5, a. 5, ad 4.

186. *De Malo* q. 2, a. 11, ad 16.

187. *De Malo* q. 2, a. 12, corp.

188. *De Malo* q. 2, a. 12, corp.

189. *Es ist ein "Nicht-zureichen von eigenem Grund aus"*: one could also translate this as "in-sufficiency" and "not-reaching"; the *zureichen* picks up from the preceding sentence's image of a venturing into the divine nature. — Trans.

190. The principles of one's own nature are insufficient. *De Malo* q. 5, a. 1, corp.

191. A capacity for the highest good through vision and enjoyment. *De Malo* q. 5, a. 1, corp.

192. *De Ver.* q. 8, a. 1, corp.; *Summa c. Gent.*, III, 50.

193. *De Ver.* q. 8, a. 3, corp.; *Summa c. Gent.*, III, 52, 53.

in such a way that makes fully clear what the positive potentiality was meant to establish: namely, a sharp distinction from any "fusion with God" (in some passive theopanism). It becomes the active potentiality of an unlimited "service to God." One must say that this represents the decisive reversal of Aristotelianism. The Aristotelian δύναμις is in itself (despite the prius of an ἐνέργεια that enacts it) an origin (ἀρχὴ κινήσεως ἢ μεταβολῆς).[194] As such it is the opposite both of the "static" and of the "impossible"[195] — it is, that is to say, a "concentrated possibility."[196] It is by all means the prototype of Heidegger's "productive Nothing": the Nothing of pure possibility as the All *in fieri:* as "the site of all contraries in one" (ταὐτὸν τἀναντία), it is the opposite pole of the actual All, understood as the equilibrium of actualized contraries set into motion within an eternal cycle of change (κυκλοφορία). With the development of our fourfold potentiality, however, this godlike "primordial womb of the All" undergoes a thoroughgoing "twilight of the gods." It is really transformed, in every last respect, into "pure" possibility: *potentia passiva.* "Fruitful possibility" *(potentia activa)* is not a function of this *potentia passiva* in its own right; rather, it is a "free gift from above," by virtue of the nothing of "powerlessness" being summoned to "service." In this way it realizes the Augustinian notion of being liberated by God *(gratia liberatrix)*[197] for free service *(libera servitus).*[198] It becomes the wondrous peak of potentiality as a whole: at its highest point, our utterly passive potentiality (in the fourth negative potentiality) is a summons to action; far from constituting an *emancipari a Deo* — as Augustine calls Pelagianism[199] — the deed of free action is an indication of the most incisive potentiality: the distance of the servant from the Lord.

This is the crown that Thomas Aquinas places atop our entire discussion of potentiality: the doctrine of secondary causes *(causae secundae):* the doctrine that the creaturely "is (valid)" is so very much something produced *from* the divine Is (Truth, etc.) as to have its own power of operation *(prima causa ex eminentia bonitatis suae rebus aliis confert non solum quod sint, sed etiam quod causae sint).*[200] According to Thomas, this is the decisive mean, set over against

194. A beginning of movement and of change. *Met.* V, 12, 1019a, 14f.
195. *Met.* V, 12, 1019a, 22f.; 34f.
196. *Geballte Möglichkeit.* — Trans.
197. *Serm.* CLXXIV, ii, 2.
198. *In Ps.* XCIX, 7.
199. *Opus Imperf. in Jul.*
200. Out of the eminence of its goodness, the first cause gives to other things not only their existence but the power also to be causes themselves. *De Ver.* q. 11, a. 1, corp.

both theopanism (an absolute *devolutio* from above) and pantheism (an absolute *evolutio* from below), and it obtains in the realm of the ontic as well as in that of the wholly noetic.[201] This idea has three stages of intensity. Firstly, the divine Is (Truth, etc.) is the innermost efficient principle in the creaturely "is (valid)" *(Ipse Deus est propria et immediata causa uniuscuiusque rei et quodam modo magis intima cuique quam ipsum sit intimum sibi)*[202] in the sense that God's maximal proximity to the creaturely is the maximal liberation of the creaturely unto active, free self-movement *(quanto aliqua natura Deo vicinior, tanto minus ab eo inclinatur et nata est seipsam inclinare).*[203] Secondly, the divine Is (Truth, etc.) is the inexhaustible, all-giving wellspring of the creaturely "is (valid)" in the sense that, as the maximum of its giving, it imparts even the ability to give *(non solum in tantum communicat eis de sua bonitate, quod in se sint bona et perfecta, sed etiam ut aliis perfectionem largiantur)*[204] — to the point of sharing its property of being the "cause of all good" *(quod sint causa bonitatis aliorum),*[205] indeed, to the point of sharing even its providential office *(non solum quod sint provisae, sed etiam quod provideant).*[206] Thirdly, and finally, the divine Is (Truth, etc.) is the *one* immediate "necessity" of the creaturely "is (valid)," to the point that there is a complete co-relation between spirit *(mens)* and God *(immediate a Deo creatur . . . , dicitur immediate formari ab ipsa Veritate Prima . . . , immediate in Ipso sicut in fine beatificatur),*[207] in the sense that this immediacy leads to the creature's greatest possible independence — even to the creature having the property of being "self-caused" *(causa sui ipsius),*[208] indeed even to the point of the creature having the possibility of saying No to God *(aversio . . . a bono incommutabili . . . , respectu cuius se impotentem fecit)*[209] — which does not however override the *one* will of the

---

201. *De Ver.* q. 11, a. 1, corp.

202. God himself is the proper and immediate cause of everything whatsoever, and in a way more intimate to each thing than it is to itself. *De Ver.* q. 8, a. 16, ad 12.

203. The nearer any nature is to God, the less inclined it is to be moved by another and the more capable it is of moving itself. *De Ver.* q. 22, a. 4, corp.

204. He communicates his goodness to them not solely that they might be good and perfect in themselves, but also that they might give perfection to others. *De Ver.* q. 9, a. 2, corp.

205. That they might be the cause of goodness in others. *De Ver.* q. 5, a. 8, corp.

206. That they be not only provided for, but provident. *De Ver.* q. 5, a. 5, corp.

207. It is immediately created by God . . . , it is said to be formed immediately by the First Truth itself . . . , it is beatified immediately in him as its end. *De Ver.* q. 18, a. 1, ad 7.

208. *De Ver.* q. 24, a. 1, corp.

209. An aversion . . . from the changeless good . . . , in respect of which one has made oneself impotent. *De Ver.* q. 28, a. 2, corp.

one Is, but rather fulfills it *(semper voluntas hominis hunc eventum sortitur, quod Deus de homine suam voluntatem implet).*[210]

8. From the totality of these potentialities, we can read off the positive nature of our *concluding analogy,* which comprises the relation between the intra-creaturely analogy and the analogy between God and creature. We will find it most incisively expressed, however, in the three modes of our active potentiality; for with regard to each mode in question, the scope of its first part is fully elaborated in the potentialities that precede it. It is thus self-evident that this active potentiality is virtually already the formula for this concluding analogy.

The first implication of this formula is that here every last "attributive" analogy *(analogia attributionis)* reduces to an incomprehensible "suspended" analogy *(analogia proportionis).* To be sure, there is such a thing as a positive statement concerning God, but it is merely the basis of a negative statement concerning his absolute otherness: *intellectus negationis semper fundatur in aliqua affirmatione . . . : unde nisi intellectus humanus aliquid de Deo affirmative cognosceret, nihil de Deo posset negare.*[211] In this sense, our active potentiality was powerless to posit anything as ultimately irreducible as such: for it is the most proper mystery of the divine Is (Truth, etc.) that something can remain completely *from* him and yet be so little identical with him that it can even say No to Him. This mystery declares the most proper otherness of God, above and beyond every creaturely similitude. It is analogy in the strictest Aristotelian sense: beyond any commonality of quantitative calculation (κατ᾽ ἀριθμὸν in the ὕλη μία),[212] beyond any commonality of qualitative concept (κατ᾽ εἶδος in λόγος εἷς),[213] beyond any commonality in ultimate *genera* as expressed in the categories, the forms of predication as such (κατὰ γένος in the αὐτὸ σχῆμα τῆς κατηγορίας):[214] *analogy,* that is, strictly *as a relation of mutual alterity*[215] (ὡς ἄλλο πρὸς ἄλλο).[216] It is a "relation" (of God to the

---

210. The will of man always obtains this result, that God fulfills his will for man. *De Malo* q. 6, a. 1, ad 5.

211. The perception of a negation is always founded upon a certain affirmation . . . : hence, unless the human mind possessed some positive knowledge of God, it would be impossible for it to deny anything of God. *De Pot.* q. 7, a. 5, corp.

212. [Some things are one] according to number/[whose] matter is one. *Met.* V, 6, 1016b, 31, 33.

213. [One] according to species/[whose] definition is one. *Met.* V, 6, 1016b, 32, 33.

214. [One] according to genus/[to which] the same predicative figure applies. *Met.* V, 6, 1016b, 32, 33.

215. *Beziehung gegenseitigen Andersseins.* — Trans.

216. [Which is related] as a third thing to a fourth. *Met.* V, 6, 1016b, 34-35. [More liter-

creaturely, in that the creaturely is related to God as to its innermost and abiding *principium et finis*),[217] and it is a "genuine" relation (i.e., to God as genuinely God) insofar as it expresses the fundamental "alterity" of God with respect to the creaturely. At its peak, the *positivum* of "relation" reveals itself as the *negativum* of "alterity." But precisely as such the *negativum* of "alterity" is the sign of the fulfillment of the *positivum* of "relation": incomprehensibility being the sign that it is God; comprehension, the sign that it is not God: *si . . . comprehendis, non est Deus;*[218] *hoc ergo non est, si comprehendisti: si autem hoc est, non comprehendisti.*[219]

Hence, for Thomas Aquinas, the decisive analogy is essentially that of *proportio,*[220] not however *secundum convenientiam proportionis* (i.e., a mutual relation to a third),[221] but *secundum convenientiam proportionalitatis* (i.e., observing the absolute dividing line of difference).[222] Analogy thus lies between univocity *(univocatio)* and complete equivocity *(aequivocatio)*, which would also obliterate the "relation."[223] It is (as *proportio proportionalitatis*) the alterity *(diversas proportiones)* of the same *one* term that is predicated of both God and creature *(ad aliquid unum:* e.g., being, good, etc.) in God and creature *(diversas proportiones ad aliquid unum).* Thus, if the *aliquid unum* implies a similarity *(similitudo)* between God and creature, this similarity is not simply "balanced out" by the dissimilarity of the mode *(modus)* in which this same *one* is in both God and creature (like and unlike, *simile "et" dissimile).*[224] For then it would not be the divine Is (Truth, etc.) that is ultimately decisive, but instead this suspended equilibrium between God and creature. No: the positive commonality of the *ad aliquid unum* is

---

ally: as is one other thing to another other thing. That is to say, analogy here is defined as a proportion, of the purely quadratic variety (a:b::c:d). — Trans.]

217. *Summa Th.* I, q. 13, a. 7, ad 4-5.

218. If . . . you comprehend it, it is not God. Augustine, *In Ps.* LXXXV, 12.

219. This therefore is no God, if you have comprehended it: if though this is God, then you have not comprehended it. Augustine, *Serm.* LII, vi, 16.

220. *Summa Th.* I, q. 13, a. 5, corp.

221. According to an agreement of proportion. *De Ver.* q. 2, a. 11, corp.

222. According to an agreement of proportionality. *De Ver.* q. 23, a. 7, ad 9. [The distinction here is simple enough: there can be no proper proportion between the finite and the infinite, and the two cannot be comprised within a single category or defined in relation to some *tertium quid*. But they can be "proportionable" in a broader sense: that is, it is not false to say that, say, as a prince governs a city, so God governs the universe; even though in real terms there is no commensurability between the two instances. — Trans.]

223. *Summa Th.* I, q. 13, a. 5, corp.

224. *De Ver.* q. 2, a. 11, ad 1.

led beyond itself into the genuinely Areopagitic "dazzling darkness" of the *diversas proportiones* — into an "ever greater dissimilarity": *creaturae . . . quamvis aliquam Dei similitudinem gerant in seipsis, tamen maxima dissimilitudo subest.*[225] An "attributive" analogy *(analogia attributionis)* stands at the beginning only insofar as the creaturely "is (valid)" points to the divine Is (Truth, etc.) as its determinative original ground *(primo cognoscitur eius productio et efficacia).*[226] But this itself is already an incomprehensible "suspended" analogy *(analogia proportionis),* since in this relation the creaturely points beyond itself, i.e., beyond its mode *(proportio)* of the ontic and the noetic, into the wholly other mode of God, so that, here already, it remains solely a matter of the *proportionalitas* between these absolutely *diversae proportiones*: the "kind of relation" *(aliqua habitudo)* that obtains between that which is completely "derived" and him who is essentially "from himself, in himself, and to himself": *aliqua habitudine . . . , utpote ab eo effectus et ei subiectus.*[227]

No matter what is said in common of both God and creature (being, truth-goodness-beauty, etc.), it is not the case that God and creature are now related to something they have in common: *quo aliquid praedicatur de duobus per respectum ad aliquod tertium.*[228] Rather everything reduces to the ultimate irreducible *prius* of God: the creaturely (both ontic and noetic) is in every respect ordered beyond itself to God as its *prius,* without any "possibility of appeal" to a third (being, etc.); for God is the absolute *prius (cum Deo nihil sit prius, sed ipse sit prior creatura).*[229] Thus, the "summit of our knowledge" *(in fine nostrae cognitionis)*[230] is reached when this all-determining "analogy as relation of alterity" comes to full expression: in the "ever greater dissimilarity" within every "similarity, however great," and therefore in the manifestation of the divine Is (Truth, etc.) as the unknown God, *Deus tamquam ignotus (secundum hoc dicimur in fine nostrae cognitionis Deum*

---

225. Although creatures bear within themselves a certain likeness to God, there is nevertheless present the greatest unlikeness. *De Ver.* q. 1, a. 10, ad 1 in contr.

226. [God is known] primarily as his productivity and efficacity are known. *In Boeth. de Trin.* q. 1, a. 2, corp.

227. [A man stands] in a certain relation [to God] . . . , insofar as he is an effect of God and subject to God. *De Ver.* q. 23, a. 7, ad 9.

228. By which something is predicated of two things with respect to a third. *De Pot.* q. 7, a. 7, corp.

229. Since nothing is prior to God, but he is himself prior to the creature. *De Pot.* q. 7, a. 7, corp.

230. *In Boeth. de Trin.* q. 1, a. 2, ad 1.

*tamquam ignotum cognoscere, quia tunc maxime mens in Dei cognitione per-
fectissime invenitur, quando cognoscitur eius essentiam esse supra omne id
quod apprehendere potest in statu huius vitae).*[231]

With this conclusion, we have already intimated, as the deeper core of
the relation between *analogia attributionis* and *proportionis,* the classical formula for analogy from the Fourth Lateran Council: within every "similarity,
however great" is an "ever greater dissimilarity" *(inter Creatorem et
creaturam non potest tanta similitudo notari, quin inter eos maior sit
dissimilitudo notanda).*[232] This formula serves to establish universally that
even the highest supernatural participation in God — namely, participation
in the intra-divine life of the three persons (union of love in grace, *unio
caritatis in gratia*) — does not abolish the distance from what God is in himself (unity of identity in nature, *identitatis unitas in natura*), beyond everything, beyond even the most graced of creatures. Given, then, that this formula encompasses both the natural and the supernatural, which is to say
that it is at once philosophical and theological, it expresses, in yet another
step, not only something factual ("that" it holds true even at the apex of the
supernatural), but also a necessity: as truly as every relation, even the highest
relationship, concerns the relation between "Creator" and "creature," so
truly is it the case that one "cannot . . ." *(non potest).* The intrinsic ground of
this "cannot" is not, however, an objective principle that "regulates" the relation between God and creature. For then it would stand above both; that is,
it would itself be what is really divine. On the contrary, the intrinsic ground
is God as *Deus semper maior,* as Augustine says:[233] God as ever more exalted,
beyond everything creaturely, ontic or noetic.

This *analogy of ever greater dissimilarity* encompasses each of the three
moments we encountered in the course of the preceding exposition. In this
analogy we begin with the "positive relationship" of a "similarity, however
great" *(tanta similitudo).* Hence we begin with an "attributive" analogy
(analogia attributionis): insofar as the divine Is (Truth, etc.) appears as the
primordial ground from the vantage of the creaturely "is (valid)." But in this
— secondly — the "negative alterity" is made manifest: the "ever greater dis-

231. We are said, at the pinnacle of our knowledge, to know God as unknown, because
the mind is found to have entered most perfectly into the knowledge of God when it knows
his essence to be beyond everything that it is able to comprehend in the conditions of this
life. *In Boeth. de Trin.* q. 1, a. 2, ad 1.

232. One cannot note any similarity between Creator and creature, however great,
without being compelled to note an even greater dissimilarity between them. Denz., 432.

233. *In Ps.* LXII, xvi.

similarity" *(maior dissimilitudo)* in the negative sense. The "attributive" analogy *(analogia attributionis)* is thus intrinsically overcome — by virtue of the ever new above-and-beyond of God, beyond even the greatest possible proximity to him — in an illimitable "suspended" analogy *(analogia proportionis secundum convenientiam proportionalitatis).*[234] For God is only the primordial ground insofar as he is "ineffably sublime, beyond all that is external to him or all that can be thought."[235] And yet — thirdly — what is peculiar to the creaturely hereby stands out positively, against the background of the *Deus semper maior,* in its relatively distinct autonomy or proper causal agency *(causae secundae).* The illimitable "suspended" analogy *(analogia proportionis secundum convenientiam proportionalitatis)* establishes a new "attributive" analogy *(analogia attributionis),* but one that proceeds not, as in the first moment, from below to above, but rather from above to below: from the *Deus semper maior,* the creature's "realm of service" is "attributed" to it. The "ever greater dissimilarity" *(maior dissimilitudo)* here has a positive sense: that of the delimitation of a positive realm into which the creature is "sent forth" for the "performing of a service." "Sent forth" is to say that the creature receives its essential groundedness from the supereminent divine Is (Truth, etc.). To say "performing" is to underscore the active autonomy of the creature thus sent forth *(causae secundae).* To say "service" is to make clear how this active positivity is simply another and more acute form of the above-and-beyond of God (in the *maior dissimilitudo*): the mysticism of rapture is humbled by the distance between Lord and servant. This is most clearly expressed in the way that revelation portrays the perfection of Eternal Life. It is called a *visio beatifica,* indicating from this standpoint the summit of union between God and creature: "to be light in light," in the formula of the Greek Church fathers. But precisely for this reason it is called *laus Dei,* which reveals the summit of union to be an ineffable dawning of the surpassing greatness of God, to whom the profoundest adoration is owed. "Longing" (in the ascending *analogia attributionis*) becomes a "blinding rapture" (in the *analogia proportionis*), in order to become "service" (in the descending *analogia attributionis*).

It is in this sense that *analogia* is now called ***analogia entis.*** *Entis* means that the analogy is decisively located in that foundation[236] which is expressed by the principle of non-contradiction: "is (valid)" as "is not not (valid)."

---

234. Analogy of proportion according to an agreement of proportionality.
235. Vatic. sess. 3, cap. 1 — Denz. 1782.
236. *Bestand.* — Trans.

Analogy is thus identified — as follows from our entire exposition — as what is ultimately fundamental: in the ontic as well as the noetic. At the same time, therefore, it is the ultimate structure, encompassing and thoroughly shaping everything. Within the intra-creaturely it spans the abyss between being and nothingness that lies perpetually open within all becoming: *enti et non-enti aliquid secundum analogiam convenit, quia ipsum non-ens ens dicitur analogice.*[237] But it also spans the even greater distance between the divine Is, which alone, as such, is "true being" *(germanum Est),* and the creaturely "is," which in comparison with God *(secundum commensurationem)* looks like nothing *(Deo comparata, invenitur quasi nihil):*[238] given that God and creature have neither a common form nor a common genus, indeed, given that God is "outside every genus" *(extra omne genus),*[239] the "analogy of being" is certainly a bridge: *secundum aliqualem analogiam, sicut ipsum esse est commune omnibus.*[240] But precisely at this point the *analogia **entis*** is pronounced as an ***analogia** entis:* in the sense of the "ever greater dissimilarity." The "is (valid)" of the principle of non-contradiction is not stated out of any identity with itself as "is (valid)" (which would lead to the principle of identity, as we have seen). Nor does it merely state a pure facticity, which would genuinely separate it from an absolute whose being is necessary. Rather, what it decisively expresses is the "is not not (valid)." Thus, what is especially distinctive to the "is (valid)" within the principle of non-contradiction is the form of the "not": whereby the "is (valid)" is strictly expressed in the "not not." That is to say that the analogy is situated in the "is (valid)" in the sense that this "is (valid)" is an analogous "is (valid)": which is to say that the "is (valid)" of the principle of non-contradiction *is* analogy. And it is analogy in the strictest sense: as between being (God) and nothingness (the creature). Like Augustine, Thomas distinguishes here between the God who "Is" and the creature, understood as that which, ontically and noetically, (of itself) is "not." Insofar as any given "is (valid)" obtains, it not only points beyond itself to the divine Is as its everlasting and intrinsically binding origin *(utpote ab eo effectus, et ei subjectus)*[241] — an origin that is not merely "different in kind" *(diversorum*

237. Between being and non-being there is a certain agreement according to analogy, because non-being itself is called being analogously. *De Ver.* q. 2, a. 11, ad 5.

238. [A thing is compared to God] according to a common measure [and when this is done, the creature] compared to God, is found to be as nothing. *De Ver.* q. 2, a. 3, ad 18.

239. *Summa Th.* I, q. 4, a. 3, ad 2.

240. According to some kind of analogy, as being is itself common to all things. *Summa Th.* I, q. 4, a. 3, corp.

241. Insofar as he is an effect of God and subject to God. *De Ver.* q. 23, a. 7, ad 9.

generum),²⁴² but explicitly "outside every genus" *(sicut id quod est extra omne genus).*²⁴³ What is ultimate and decisive is rather that it stands out as "nothing" against the divine Is and *herein* has its authentic relation to Him: *enti et non-enti aliquid secundum analogiam convenit, quia ipsum non-ens ens dicitur analogice . . . : unde naturae distantia quae est inter creaturam et Deum, communitatem analogiae impedire non potest.*²⁴⁴ The *communitas analogiae* is thus that of the "nothing" to the "Creator out of nothing." Such is the *analogia entis* in its fundamental concept: the intra-creaturely "is (valid)" is so intrinsically (in the essence of "becoming") an "is in the not" (the Augustinian *est non est*) that, in the relation between God and creature, it is related as "nothing" to the "Creator out of nothing."

242. *Summa Th.,* I, q. 4, a. 3, ad 2.
243. *Summa Th.,* I, q. 4, a. 3, ad 2.
244. Between being and non-being there is a certain agreement according to analogy, because non-being itself is called being analogously . . . : hence the distance between the creature and God is not able to prevent their community in an analogy. *De Ver.* q. 2, a. 11, ad 5.

§7 The Scope of the Problem of the *Analogia Entis*

1. To this point, our explication of the *analogia entis* has brought us precisely as far as these two conclusions: that the *analogia entis* has its foundation in the principle of non-contradiction and that, by having such a foundation, it is distinguished from (pure) logic and dialectic. On the one hand, we have hereby certainly (despite and amid all our historical reflections) achieved the standpoint proper to a superhistorical *objective problematic*.[1] On the other hand, however, this objective problematic is still more of a negative schema, because and insofar as its determinative foundation, the principle of non-contradiction, is a "negative reductive formality." From our initial perspective, certainly, the scope of the *historical problematic* of the *analogia entis*, which follows below, would already seem to be staked out *a priori*, since the scope of the problem is grounded in the objective essence of the problem. Seen from the second perspective, however, this "negative schema" stands to be filled out with a content provided by the scope of its historical configurations. As a matter of method, therefore, it will indeed be necessary for us to feel our way forward in each case from the objective essence of the problem into its historical scope. But it will be equally necessary to maintain a lively sense of the distinctiveness of the truly historical configurations; in them the objective essence of the problem is not divided up into parts, but present as a whole in various accents and hues.

The superhistorical objective problematic made it clear how, in the *analogia entis*, practically everything refers back to the *span between "ana"* understood as "from the above and back to the above" (ἄνω) *and "ana"* in the sense of an "intrinsic order" (ἀνά). This is evident in the intra-

---

1. *Sachproblematik.* — Trans.

creaturely analogy: in the way that the span between δύναμις and ἐνέργεια glides back and forth (between an actualization fruitfully conditioned by possibility and a possibility passively directed towards actualization), it expresses the neutral correlationality of the ἀνά; but in the way that, within this span, ἐντελέχεια not only adds emphasis to ἐνέργεια but also endows it with the character of an "end towards which . . . ," the ἄνω rings out determinatively within the ἀνά as the explosive above-and-beyond of one side of the reciprocal relation. This is equally evident in the analogy between God and creature: the "transcending immanence" (of the creature towards God) puts the stress more on the in-between of a relational determination between creature and God (since God comes into view from the problem of the creature) and is thus borne by the ἀνά; in the "indwelling transcendence" (of God towards the creature), on the other hand, what rings out is, preeminently, the "above" and "from-above" and "according-to-the-above" of the sovereign movement of God — that is, the ἄνω. Thus, finally, the span between the ἀνά and the ἄνω also enters into the analogy that holds sway between the two analogies that emerged in the course of our exposition, which took us from the problem of active potentiality (negative and positive), to the *analogia attributionis* and *proportionis,* to the *tanta similitudo* and *maior dissimilitudo,* to the formal *analogia entis.* On the one hand, these spans seemed to indicate a suspended reciprocity,[2] this being the distinctive feature of the ἀνά; but, on the other hand, the ultimate sense of this dynamic suspension turned out ever again and to an ever greater degree to be the *Illum oportet crescere, me autem minui*[3] (as Augustine interprets the phrase): the above-and-beyond of God, which is to say, the excellence of the ἄνω.

2. In the background of the problematic of analogy as we find it in *Plato,* we find the same thing that we find in Aristotle: a critique of the two extremes of absolute change[4] and absolute identity[5] and, as a result of this, a fundamental emphasis upon the μέσον between them.[6] This *"middle"* is then thoroughly worked out in Plato's principal systematic formulae. "Archetype and image" (παράδειγμα — εἰκών) indeed stand in relation to one another in such a way that ultimately an "in-between" is implied: the "in-stantiation" of the archetypes in nature (which on this account is in itself dynamically

2. *Gegenseitigkeits-Verhältnis.* — Trans.
3. He must increase, but I must decrease. John 3:30.
4. *Theaetetus* 152d-183b.
5. *Parmenides* 137c-162b.
6. *Theaetetus* 180e.

stretched open) (εἴδη . . . ὥσπερ παραδείγματα ἑστάναι ἐν τῇ φύσει).[7] Inasmuch as the "archetypes" (εἴδη as παραδείγματα) are forms that impinge upon the stuff of nature, they become — according to Plato's second formula — "limits" set against the (chaotic) "limitless" (πέρας — ἄπειρον). The "middle" is thus reinforced. For in it the "limits" take effect within the "illimitable": in the formation of a "nature measured by rhythm" (ἔμμετρον καὶ ἅμα σύμμετρον).[8] Plato's other two formulae (or technical terms) could perhaps be included in this respect, though, in and of itself, the notion of the "middle" would seem to be exploded by them. The first of these terms, which is difficult to translate, is the ἐξαίφνης, the "unexpected suddenness of the moment," in which we find joined not only rest (στάσις) and movement (κίνησις), but also being (εἶναι) and arising-and-perishing, as well as the one and the many, the similar and the dissimilar, the great and the small, the equal and the contrary.[9] It is, assuredly, the "in-between" (μεταξύ) of a collision, and herein the paradox of something "beyond contraries": both at rest and in motion (ἕστηκέ τε καὶ κινεῖται),[10] neither existent nor nonexistent (οὔτε ἔστι τότε οὔτε οὐκ ἔστι),[11] neither one nor many (οὔτε ἕν ἐστιν οὔτε πολλά),[12] neither separable nor combined (οὔτε διακρίνεται οὔτε συγκρίνεται).[13] And yet, it is essentially the super-antithetical in-between within the immanence of antitheses, and herein the point of their connection — if only for the flash of a moment — in a neutralized middle. To this we may certainly add Plato's other systematic formula (term), which bears this out more fully: ἔρως, which in and of itself is a vertical breaking-through to the above. To be sure, Eros is the "hunter" who ever more thoroughly traverses all things.[14] But no less is he the "fruitfulness" actively impregnating[15] the world of becoming

7. The ideas . . . are like patterns fixed in nature. *Parmenides* 132d.
8. Measured and balanced. *Philebus* 26a.
9. *Parmenides* 156e-157b.
10. *Parmenides* 156e.
11. *Parmenides* 157a.
12. *Parmenides* 157a.
13. *Parmenides* 157a.
14. *Symposium* 203b-d.
15. *In die Werde-Welt wirkende "Fruchtbarkeit."* To translate this phrase with the word "impregnate" may be a bit of a stretch, but it is clearly implied: Eros makes the world fruitful. It also helps to capture the sense of the accusative case here, since Eros is precisely not comfortably resident in the world (in which case the dative would be appropriate), but, as a homeless hunter, is at work *in* the world (in the transitive sense) as one who is passing through and *beyond* it. Thus Eros is an image of the in-and-beyond *qua* middle that Przywara attempts to describe. — Trans.

(τῆς γεννήσεως καὶ τοῦ τόκου)[16] — so much so that this becoming is stressed over against the "purity" of the absolute (ἔστι γὰρ οὐ τοῦ καλοῦ ὁ ἔρως . . . , ἀλλὰ . . . τῆς γεννήσεως καὶ τοῦ τόκου ἐν τῷ καλῷ).[17] So much is it an "in-between" (μεταξὺ θνητοῦ καὶ ἀθανάτου)[18] that an intra-creaturely eternity is born (ἀειγενές . . . καὶ ἀθάνατον ὡς θνητῷ)[19] — namely, "eternal change."[20]

It is notable, however, that this middle is established between the extremes (of Heraclitus and Parmenides): as an "unconscious *co-incidence*" (λελήθαμεν . . . εἰς τὸ μέσον πεπτωκότες).[21] This is positively expressed in Plato's first systematic formula (archetype-image): as the "unconscious coincidence" of a "grace from above." For as much as the archetypes can be said to be "instantiated within nature," nevertheless, in its essence, the real not only goes "towards the above" but comes "from above": in the "insofar as" of its imaged mirroring of the archetypes. For the παραδείγματα are not "abstract paradigms," which first attain "figural concrete reality" in the εἰκόνες; rather, the εἰκόνες are "icons" — that is, in their figural content they are the radiance of what lies beyond the heavens: figurality (εἰκασθῆναι) as participation (μέθεξις).[22] With respect, however, to the rhythm (μέτρον) of Plato's second formula (limits and the illimitable), one must not forget a certain Pythagorean background: the inner correlation between "antitheses" and "numbers." To be sure, the ἔμμετρον καὶ ἅμα σύμμετρον "rests" "upon" the antitheses, but it is "realized" "in" the primordial relations of numbers. Thus, whereas polarity is "matter," number is "form." Number, though, is an effect of unity and, hence, comes "from above" — so much so that this rhythm, as such, is the divine,[23] and the creaturely is, in its rhythmics, a kind of "divine play" (θεοῦ τι παίγνιον).[24] The same thing is betrayed still more strikingly (in Plato's third formula) by the ἐξαίφνης, understood as the "unexpected suddenness of the moment." As "timelessness" (ἐν χρόνῳ οὐδενὶ οὖσα)[25] it is not so much the "moment" of Nietzsche: that of "ingenious harmony." Rather, we have here

16. *Symposium* 206e [see next fn.].

17. For eros is not love of the beautiful . . . , but . . . of conception and birth in the beautiful. *Symposium* 206e.

18. Between mortal and immortal. *Symposium* 202e.

19. [Procreation is] like eternity and immortality within our mortality. *Symposium* 206e.

20. *Symposium* 207d-208a.

21. We have unknowingly advanced into the middle between the two sides. *Theaetetus* 180e.

22. *Parmenides* 132d.

23. *Laws* IV, 716c-d.

24. *Laws* VII, 803c.

25. It occupies no time. *Parmenides* 156e.

something that at least "approximates" the "moment" of Kierkegaard: moment understood not as the punctiliar boundedness of the "is" between "was" and "will be" (and thus, as the point of intersection of relations, determined by their interweaving), but rather as the "incidence of eternity." It is, finally, in this light that we come to see the special features of transcendence in the formula of Eros (Plato's fourth formula): not only in the "sequence" of the "hunt" as it passes "through all concrete particulars" towards "beauty in itself" (θεώμενος ἐφεξῆς τε καὶ ὀρθῶς τὰ καλά),²⁶ but in the "attraction"²⁷ of this "beauty in itself," which first calls the hunt forth.

What is decisive in the specific case of the Platonic analogy, however, lies not only in the "ringing out" of a somehow "antecedent" ἄνω through the ἀνά, but more exactly in "how" it does so. On the one hand, the divine appears (in the formula of archetype and image) as what is primordially creative "in" the archetypes: since a relation to the archetypes is a relation to the divine (παραπλήσια ἑαυτῷ; ὅμοιον . . . τῷ παντελεῖ ζώῳ).²⁸ On the other hand, though, the activity of the divine is portrayed as a "looking to" the (antecedent) archetypes (κατὰ ταὐτὰ βλέπων; γεννετῷ παραδείγματι προσχρώμενος).²⁹ This is the vacillating mystery of the *Euthyphro:* is the It of an ideal "in itself" reducible to the He of a "living God" (παντελεῖ ζώῳ)³⁰ or is this He (as a "facticity") subject to the It (as an "ideality"): ἆρα τὸ ὅσιον ὅτι ὅσιόν ἐστιν, φιλεῖται ὑπὸ τῶν θεῶν, ἢ ὅτι φιλεῖται, ὅσιόν ἐστιν?³¹ On the one hand (in correlation with Plato's other three formulae, which are in a special sense dynamic and rhythmic), the divine is the "measure of all things" (ὁ δή θεὸς ἡμῖν πάντων χρημάτων μέτρον)³² and is thus a "friend of rhythmic movement" (μετρίῳ φίλον),³³ inasmuch as it "comprises the be-

26. Contemplating beautiful things in their correct ordering. *Symposium* 210e, f.

27. *Zug.* Przywara plays here on the multiple meanings of "Zug," in this case, as a trait or feature in things (as in the first part of the sentence) and (in this second part) as something that "draws," "attracts," or, like a train, literally "pulls." Thus the inherent span within the German word "Zug" itself exemplifies the "in-and-beyond." — Trans.

28. Resembling him [the creator]. *Timaeus* 29e. [That the cosmos might be] like . . . the perfect living being. *Timaeus* 31b.

29. Looking to them. *Timaeus* 28a. Using a pattern from that which is subject to becoming. *Timaeus* 28b.

30. *Timaeus* 31b.

31. Is that which is holy holy because the gods love it, or do the gods love it because it is holy? *Euthyphro* 10a.

32. For us, then, God should be the measure of all things. *Laws* IV, 716c-d.

33. *Laws* IV, 716c-d. [More literally, measure accords with measure, and so the "measured" man is "like" God and dear to him. — Trans.]

ginning, middle, and end of all things" (ἀρχήν τε καὶ τελευτήν καὶ μέσα τῶν ὄντων ἔχων).³⁴ But, on the other hand, as the "cause of unification" (αἰτία ξυμμίξεως) within the rhythmic interpenetration of contraries, the divine is diametrically opposed to any "cause of division" (αἰτία διακρίσεως);³⁵ its sovereign inner rhythm of "beginning, middle, and end in one" betrays itself as a correlate of the attempt of knowledge to grasp the beginning and end of what is "posited" (thereby establishing the middle between them),³⁶ and thus do away with the creatureliness of man, who "staggers towards nothingness" because he "cannot join beginning to end" (τὴν ἀρχὴν τῷ τέλει προσάψαι).³⁷

The real stress of the Platonic analogy thus falls upon that *"immortal struggle"* in which the "gods and daemons" are our "fellow combatants" but in which, at the same time, creatures are their "possessions" (μάχη δή φαμεν ἀθάνατός ἐστιν. . . . ξύμμαχοι δὲ ἡμῶν θεοί τε ἅμα καὶ δαίμονες, ἡμεῖς δ' αὖ κτήματα θεῶν καὶ δαιμόνων).³⁸ The creaturely moves between these two extremes, that of being enclosed within itself (αὐτὸν . . . στρέφειν ἑαυτὸν ἀεί)³⁹ and that of being moved by God alone (ὅλον ἀεὶ ὑπό θεοῦ στρέφεσθαι),⁴⁰ alternating between being immediately led by God (ὁ θεὸς ξυμποδηγεῖ πορευόμενον καὶ συγκυκλεῖ)⁴¹ and rapidly falling away from God (τότε δὲ ἀνῆκεν [ὁ θεός] . . . , τὸ δὲ πάλιν αὐτόματον εἰς τἀναντία περιάγεται)⁴² — without, however, supposing its cause to be some twofold (that is, both good and evil) ground of the world (δύο τινὲ θεώ).⁴³

Here we see, on the one hand, how the Platonic analogy is actually constituted in its hidden ground by the whole formal and objective fabric of the *analogia entis:* by a middle between pantheism and theopanism that is not dialectic. But, on the other hand, it is nevertheless clear that this hidden

34. *Laws* IV, 716a.
35. *Philebus* 23d; 30c, d.
36. *Republic,* VII, 533cd.
37. Alcmaeon, Diels 24, 2.
38. And this battle is undying. . . . Gods and spirits [daimons] are our allies, and moreover we are the property of these gods and spirits. *Laws* X, 906a.
39. [We may not say of the universe that] it . . . perpetually turns itself. *Statesman* 269e.
40. [We may not say] it is perpetually turned by God. *Statesman* 269e.
41. When God guides it on its path and imparts to it its revolving motion. *Statesman* 269c.
42. When [God] releases it . . . , and it then begins to turn back again on its own in the contrary direction. *Statesman* 269c.
43. [We must not say it is moved] by two gods. *Statesman* 269e.

ground is precisely nothing more than a "hidden" ground, which is to say that it is woven into the motif of "immortal struggle": what is immortal is not really God, but this struggle. From here it becomes clear how Origenism (as depicted by Thomas Aquinas) is Platonism's final and most acute expression: the hyperextension[44] of freedom's *ad diversa posse:*[45] there can be nothing "definitive," because it is freedom's nature to be ever and again capable of the opposite, even and precisely with regard to the antithesis of good and evil. To be sure, it is the freedom of *struggle,* i.e., a freedom that does not level-out the antitheses, but rather "strives upward" into the one and "falls away" into the other — and this with the intended goal of a possible "victory." But even so it remains the *freedom* of struggle (in the above Origenist sense), i.e., in which the emphasis is placed upon a constant "undulation of the in-between," and for which, logically, "victory" is only a limit concept — a concept, moreover, whose retrospective qualification of the "in-between" consists in conferring upon it the character of struggle. For struggle is struggle in view of a possible victory.

But this struggle has yet another hue, which becomes visible against the background of the four Platonic formulae (mentioned above). In light of the formula of "limit and the illimitable," the formula of "archetype and image" is properly revealed as the formula of artistic experience:[46] the "artistic idea" (παράδειγμα), which becomes "figural, flesh and blood," though ever "incomplete" (εἰκών), in that the "flow of matter" (ἄπειρον) is "delimited" (πέρας) in forms. Whereas the formula of "Eros" accentuates artistic experience in terms of "conception and birth" (τοῦ τόκου ἐν τῷ καλῷ), the formula of "the moment," the ἐξαίφνης, signals the intuitive timeless "lightning-flash" of the artistic event. Thus "immortal struggle" bears the note of *"artistic struggle."* Indeed, one could say that it is precisely by virtue of this note that the struggle is "immortal." For it is all too characteristic of artistic experience that the felicity of its intoxication lies in becoming, whereas that which has become — even when it does not "disappoint" or, at least, "fall short" — always has about it the character of something one is "done with."[47] For this reason the old formula of "ideal exemplarism" (to advert to the most properly Platonic of doctrines) is one-sided only if one recognizes in the Platonic analogy no other question than that of the "thus"

44. *Überspannung.* — Trans.
45. *De Malo,* q. 16, a. 5, corp.
46. *Künstlerisches Geschehen.* — Trans.
47. *Erledigt.* — Trans.

of essence: the *causa exemplaris.* For one certainly finds the question of existence in the "Eros" formula: "production and giving birth" as the true *causa efficiens.* For that matter, the formula for the "moment" (ἐξαίφνης) indicates the opposite of a "static relation of essence," inasmuch as it speaks of the "for now" of an "is" in the midst of a perpetual whirl. But insofar as it captures a distinctive nuance of a whole, the old formula of ideal exemplarism is correct. The "artistic" (insofar as it is contemplation and production in one: *causa exemplaris* and *causa efficiens*) implies, in contrast to the "practical and profane," a "distance of the idea" and a "tendency to posit the idea directly into reality."[48] On the one hand, this expresses the Platonic analogy's tendency towards a "predominant exemplarism": which is to say that the Platonic analogy does not actually aim at the ideal "through" the real, but at the ideal "from" the real. On the other hand, herein lies its self-correspondence between "distance" (χωρισμός) and "immortal struggle" (μάχη ἀθάνατος), since the "artistic" seeks both to "separate" itself from the "practical and profane" and at the same time to "overcome" it.

The Platonic analogy is thus, on the one hand, the basis for Thomas Aquinas's preferred metaphor for the relation between God and creature: the artist *(artifex),* the artist's idea *(idea artificis),* and the work of art *(artificiatum).* On the other hand, however, it remains *only* a basis, because it does not (as is proper to a metaphor) speak through and beyond itself. For, in Plato, the "artistic" is turned precisely into the "immortal struggle."[49] It is an analogy in which the ἄνω is fixed *within* the ἀνά, but only *as a "goad."* Consequently, it does not flow into the mystery of God, but into the mystery of the between of God and creature.

3. *Aristotle*'s understanding of analogy is already distinctive in that, whereas in Plato the term is marginal (since from the outset analogy is presented in the mode of "archetype and image"), Aristotle classifies analogy from the first as belonging to the central formal aspect of his thought: likeness in number (the same *individuum*), in species (κατ᾽ εἶδος), in genus, in "analogy."[50] Connected to this is the fact that Aristotle sees in Platonism only disconnected antitheses for which one must seek a connecting third;[51] that he criticizes this same Platonism for having only a formal and a material

48. *Distanz von der Idee aus.* — Trans.
49. *Eben in den "unsterblichen Kampf" gewendet.* — Trans.
50. *Met.* V, 6, 1016b, 32-1017a, 3.
51. *Met.* XII, 10, 1075a, 28-31.

cause (εἶδος-ὕλη), which, lacking an efficient and final cause, are lacking in movement;[52] that, for him, by contrast, the "middle" (μέσον) is in reality the actual "cause" (τὸ γὰρ μέσον αἴτιον),[53] which not only binds together all questions at a general level,[54] but logically constitutes the coordinate intersection of the "four causes":[55]

$$
\begin{array}{c}
\varepsilon\widetilde{\iota}\delta o\varsigma \\
\mid \\
\grave{\alpha}\rho\chi\acute{\eta}\ \kappa\iota\nu\acute{\eta}\sigma\varepsilon\omega\varsigma\ \begin{array}{c}\rule[0.5ex]{1em}{0.4pt}\end{array}\!\!\!+\!\!\!\begin{array}{c}\rule[0.5ex]{1em}{0.4pt}\end{array}\ \tau\acute{\varepsilon}\lambda o\varsigma \\
\mid \\
\ddot{\upsilon}\lambda\eta
\end{array}
$$

This leads to a twofold conclusion: on the one hand, he contends with Plato over the issue of the inner completeness of the world of sensible particulars,[56] since it is not "participation," but rather an "indwelling" (ἐνυπάρχοντα and καθ᾽ ὑποκείμενον)[57] — indeed, a downright "(real-) identity" — that unites idea and reality (αὐτὸ ἄρα ζῷον ἕν ἕκαστον ἔσται τῶν ἐν τοῖς ζῴοις);[58] but then, on the other hand, he nevertheless posits an inner "rhythmic oscillation" within this world, which appeared to have become static in the extreme, since the μέσον is the ἀνάλογον,[59] which is to say, a middle that oscillates between positions that share no likeness, whether of number, species, or genus.[60]

Accordingly, the principle "τὸ γὰρ ἀνάλογον μέσον" (which we may identify as the central formal aspect of Aristotelianism) denotes on the one hand a determination of the ἀνάλογον *towards the* μέσον — that is, from analogy's "oscillation beyond everything determinable" (since it lies beyond

52. *Met.* I, 6, 988a, 9-15.

53. For it is the middle that is the cause. *Post. An.* II, 12, 95a, 11-13. [Aristotle is here discussing how far any actual effect, what unites subject to predicate (or what makes the effect what it is), is an actuating middle term directed to an end: to use one of Aristotle's examples, if ice is solidified water, the middle term (absence of heat) that unites the subject (water) to the predicate (solidified) is the cause of the effect (ice). — Trans.]

54. *Met.* II, 2, 994a, 1-994b, 31.

55. *Met.* III, 2, 996b, 23.

56. *Met.* I, 6, 987a, 32-987b, 1.

57. *Met.* I, 9, 991a, 14; *Met.* VII, 6, 1031a, 18.

58. Therefore the animal in each [species] will be the one animal-in-itself. *Met.* VII, 14, 1039b, 13.

59. *Eth. Nic.* V, 4, 1131b, 11.

60. *Met.* V, 6, 1016b, 32-1017a, 3.

even a common genus) towards that "equilibrium" that is signified by μέσον in pointed contrast to Plato. Given how Aristotle develops the problematic of analogy from that of the one (ἕν) and the many (πολλά) (in that this can be extended further to the problematic of the ταὐτό-ὅμοιον-ἴσον and the ἕτερον-ἀνόμοιον-ἄνισον),[61] ἀνάλογον does not actually signify here an ultimate span between the two series (as the "relationship of alterities,"[62] as the πρός between ἄλλο and ἄλλο),[63] but rather the most extreme point of the one's self-transposition into the many. The region of the one (understood as the region of identity-similitude-equality) is here, at the same time, the region of the formal (because it is a region of "one and the same" quality). The region of the many, by contrast (understood as the region of alterity-dissimilitude-inequality), accentuates the materiality of "many" qualities. It is in this sense that ἀνάλογον is here defined as a positive "equation" (ἰσότης . . . λόγων),[64] and thus as something that develops out of a concrete comparison between *concreta* (ἀναλογία γεομετρική)[65] into an abstract proportion of numerical relations (ἀναλογία ἀριθμετική),[66] and out of an oscillating relation of different living things (ἐν . . . ἀνομοιοειδέσι . . . τὸ ἀνάλογον . . . σώζει τὴν φιλίαν)[67] into a quantitative measure that takes the place of qualitative distinctions (in the νόμισμα, the recognized "coin" of the realm).[68] In this way the ἀνάλογον indeed becomes the μέσον, which not only quantifies the plenitude of qualities, but does so to an extreme in order to bind things together as tightly as possible.

It is in this spirit that Aristotle's account of the *true* (in one of its aspects) is concentrated in syllogistics, and that all forms of the latter are seen to be deductions from a single form, namely, that of the "first figure":[69] the true is said to be in the μέσον insofar as the μέσον signifies the identifiable closed "in-herence"[70] (of all antitheses within one another).[71] It is likewise in this spirit that Aristotle's account of the *good* (in his doctrine of the vir-

---

61. Same-like-equal/other-unlike-unequal. *Met.* X, 3, 1054a, 29.

62. *Beziehung des Anders-seins.* — Trans.

63. *Met.* V, 6, 1016b, 35.

64. Equality . . . of ratios. *Eth. Nic.* V, 3, 1131a, 31.

65. Geometrical proportion. *Eth. Nic.* V, 3, 1131b, 13.

66. Arithmetical proportion. *Eth. Nic.* V, 4, 1132a, 30.

67. In [friendship] between those who are dissimilar . . . it is proportion . . . that preserves the friendship. *Eth. Nic.* IX, 1, 1163b, 32f.

68. *Eth. Nic.* V, 5, 1133a, 18f.

69. *Prior An.* I, 1, 24a, 26-28; I, 23, 41b, 3-5.

70. *Eth. Nic.* II, 6, 1106b, 5-8. [*In-Sein.* — Trans.]

71. *Prior An.* I, 4, 25b, 32-34.

tues) aims at a μέσον as formalized as possible: whereas evil is represented as "pluriform *in infinitum*" (πολλαχῶς and τοῦ ἀπείρου),[72] the good is represented as a "uniformly delimited" middle (τοῦ πεπερασμένου and μοναχῶς).[73] Finally, it is in this spirit, therefore, that Aristotle's account of the *beautiful* is reducible in its "principal essence" (μέγιστα εἴδη) to "order, symmetry, and limit" (τάξις καὶ σύμμετρον καὶ τὸ ὡρισμένον), and this expressly in the sense of a formal mathematics (ἃ μάλιστα δεικνύουσιν αἱ μαθηματικαὶ ἐπιστῆμαι).[74] In this form the noetic pleroma (true-good-beautiful) is one with the *ontic*, given that, as we have just seen, the relation between "indwelling" and "(real-) identity" (between antitheses) holds true, and given that all the "indeterminacy" of the *"in infinitum"* is hereby neutralized:[75] precisely for this reason what aims at the middle (ἐπὶ τὸ μέσον) and what proceeds from it (ἀπὸ τοῦ μέσου) cannot possibly be *"in infinitum"* (ἄπειρον).[76] Rather, the μέσον is that "within" which, as such, can be grasped, examined, and understood.[77] When its suspended character was most pronounced, analogy signified the "to" (πρός) between alterities "as" alterities (since there was not even the "within" of a common genus); here, on the other hand — because and to the degree that it is oriented towards a "pure" μέσον — analogy comes to signify a "within" that places alterities firmly within one another (καλῶ δὲ μέσον μὲν, ὅ καὶ αὐτὸ ἐν ἄλλῳ, καὶ ἄλλο ἐν τούτῳ ἐστίν).[78]

Even so, however, because analogy's character as a "relation of alterity" is not lost, the opposite sense of the principle "τὸ γὰρ ἀνάλογον μέσον" becomes manifest: as a determination of the μέσον *towards the ἀνάλογον*, that is, from a "delimited and delimiting equilibrium" towards an "oscillation beyond everything determinable." This is immediately evident if we fully consider the way in which the μέσον holds sway within the transcendentals. To be sure, syllogistics stands at the heart of Aristotle's understanding of the *true*. And yet, precisely within its extreme mathematical precision, syllogistics is manifestly a play of tensions between δέσις and λύσις, "bind-

---

72. *Prior An.* I, 4, 25b, 28-30.

73. *Prior An.* I, 4, 25b, 30, 31.

74. The principal forms [of beauty] are order, symmetry, and limit, which the mathematical sciences demonstrate exceedingly well. *Met.* XII, 3, 1078a, 36-b, 2.

75. *Aufgehoben.* — Trans.

76. *Coel.* I, 6, 273a, 7-8.

77. *Das gefaßte und befaßte und erfaßte "in."* — Trans.

78. I call "middle" that which both is itself in another and has another in itself. *Prior An.* I, 4, 25b, 35-36.

ing" and "loosing" — a play that depends upon one having assumed within oneself and retained a lively sense of the whole range of antithetical positions (τὸν ὥσπερ ἀντιδίκων καὶ ἀμφισβητούντων λόγων ἀκηκοότα πάντων).[79] It follows from this that the "sphere of the syllogistic" is besieged on either side by an *"in infinitum."* On one side, leading towards it, there is the *"in infinitum"* of the ἐπαγωγή, the "ascent" out of the fullness of concrete experience (ἐμπειρία): from a "wise fullness of experience" (πιθανώτερον καὶ σαφέστερον)[80] to a "compelling force against one's adversaries" (βιαστικώτερον καὶ πρὸς τοὺς ἀντιλογικοὺς ἐνεργέστερον).[81] The other *"in infinitum"* lies beyond the syllogistic sphere: as the "wakefulness" of "simple contemplation" ("contemplation," θεωρεῖν, understood as "waking," ἐγρήγορσις, as opposed to "knowledge," ἐπιστήμη, understood as "sleep," ὕπνος),[82] as the sphere of "mind as such" (νοῦς), which grasps that "first" and "last" that defies all demonstration,[83] the "mature eye" that sees beyond all proofs. Thus it happens that the true, which *can* be measured in the μέσον, *cannot* be measured in its presuppositions (ἀρχαί), since all "proof" rests upon the unprovable (ἀνάγκη τὴν ἀποδεικτικὴν ἐπιστήμην ἐξ ἀληθῶν τ᾿ εἶναι καὶ πρώτων καὶ ἀμέσων).[84] What is more, these presuppositions are discretely specific to each science (ἴδια ἑκάστης ἐπιστήμης) and have only an "analogous" commonality (κοινὰ δὲ κατ᾿ ἀναλογίαν),[85] such that the "stability" of the μέσον rests upon the "uncertainty" of the ἀρχαί (χαλεπὸν δ᾿ ἐστὶ τὸ γνῶναι εἰ οἶδεν ἢ μή).[86] That is to say: the μέσον of the true bears both below and above itself the most extreme "above-and-beyond" of the ἀνάλογον.

The same thing can already be found within Aristotle's account of the *good* to the extent that the good as such accentuates "striving" (ἐφίεσθαι), "end" (τέλος), and "actualization" (ἐνέργεια)[87] — and this, furthermore, in the sense of the "act that rests in itself": man's work, ἔργον τοῦ ἀνθρώπου;[88]

---

79. Having listened to all the contending arguments, as if to [forensic] disputants. *Met.* III, 1, 995b, 4.

80. More persuasive and clearer. *Top.* I, 12, 105a, 16.

81. More compelling and effective against disputants. *Top.* I, 12, 105a, 18.

82. *De Anima*, II, 1, 412a, 9-10, 25-26.

83. *Post. An.* I, 33, 88b, 36-37; *Eth. Nic.* VI, 6, 1141a, 7; *Eth. Nic.* VI, 11, 1143a, 36.

84. It is necessary that apodeictic understanding be derived from things true and primary and immediate. *Post. An.* I, 2, 71b, 20ff.

85. *Post. An.* I, 10, 76a, 38-39.

86. It is difficult to know whether one knows or not. *Post. An.* I, 9, 76a, 26ff.

87. *Eth. Nic.* I, 1, 1094a, 3-6; *Eth. Nic.* I, 7, 1097a, 20-33.

88. *Eth. Nic.* I, 7, 1097b, 27f.

life, ζωή, understood as the act of the soul, ψυχῆς ἐνέργεια;[89] the practice, πρᾶξις, of those who compete in the games, ἀγωνιζόμενοι.[90] This "energetic dynamism," for which "objects" would almost seem to be a limit concept, then finds precise expression in the μέσον itself. The analyses of virtue already show how one only rarely succeeds in achieving a clear logic of the relational field between the mean and the extremes (ἄκρα); for in all too many cases not only can the ἄκρα be described only by negation, but even the μέσον itself remains unnamable (ἀνώνυμον) — such that a determination becomes possible only in view of the whole general objective field of the virtue in question,[91] or, indeed, that the μέσον appears as nothing but a "feeling for the moment" (as with gentility, πρᾳότης: ἐν γὰρ τοῖς καθ' ἕκαστα καὶ τῇ αἰσθήσει ἡ κρίσις).[92] The mark of the μέσον thus becomes the virtue of "supple versatility"[93] proper to the "graceful freeman" whose "law is his sense of tact" (χαρίεις καὶ ἐλεύθερος . . . οἷον νόμος ὢν ἐαυτῷ):[94] as "spiritual agility" (ὥσπερ δὲ τὰ σώματα ἐκ τῶν κινήσεων κρίνεται, οὕτω καὶ τὰ ἤθη).[95] Indeed, with regard to virtue in general, the μέσον is represented, principally, as "the art of hitting the mark with a taut bow" (στοχαστική):[96] one is confronted not only by an "abyss" (of error) to the right or the left of the mark (μεσότης δὲ δύο κακιῶν),[97] nor only by an "ambiguous iridescence at its very middle" (that makes the mark appear from the right to be to the left and from the left to be to the right),[98] but also and precisely by the need to strike the mark by way of an "alternating deviation to right and left" (εἰς τοὐναντίον δ' ἑαυτοὺς ἀφέλκειν and ἀποκλίνειν ὅτε μὲν ἐπὶ τὴν ὑπερβολὴν ὁτὲ δ' ἐπὶ τὴν ἔλλειψιν).[99] It is no wonder, then, that the μέσον ultimately begins to merge into something explicitly Platonic: into the sphere of ἔρως. The "logical" becomes the "heroic," which is opposed to the abyss of the

---

89. *Eth. Nic.* I, 7, 1098a, 13.

90. *Eth. Nic.* I, 7, 1099a, 3-5.

91. E.g., *Eth. Nic.* IV, 7, 1127a, 12ff.

92. For one's decision depends upon the particular facts of the situation and one's perception of them. *Eth. Nic.* I, 5, 1126b, 3-4.

93. *Geschmeidige Gelenkigkeit.* — Trans.

94. The gracious freeman . . . is as it were a law to himself. *Eth. Nic.* I, 8, 1128a, 31-32.

95. Just as bodies are judged by their movements, so too are characters. *Eth. Nic.* I, 8, 1128a, 11-12.

96. With good aim; or, sagacious. *Eth. Nic.* II, 6, 1106b, 28.

97. The mean between two vices. *Eth. Nic.* II, 6, 1107a, 2.

98. *Eth. Nic.* II, 8, 1108b, 17-32.

99. Pulling ourselves towards the opposite extreme/but [we must] incline either towards excess or towards deficiency. *Eth. Nic.* II, 9, 1109b, 4-5, 24-25.

"bestial."[100] The "equilibrium" of the μέσον is revealed to be a "steep ascent to the summit" (an extreme, ἀκρότης),[101] so that "mean" means "elevation" (τὸ μέσον εἶναι πως ἄκρον).[102] Thus, even "cool rationality" finally disappears into the "love-borne flight" of pleasure (ἡδονή),[103] happiness (εὐδαιμονία),[104] and express friendship (φιλία).[105] The μέσον becomes nothing short of rapture into the proximity of God (θεοφιλέστατος).[106]

Finally, the nuances in the Aristotelian account of the *beautiful* indicate the same kind of "blessedly enraptured uncertainty," in that "mathematical proportion" appears to be no less a "turning between darkness and light" (περιπέτεια . . . εἰς τὸ ἐναντίον . . . μεταβολή).[107]

The *ontic* dimension, which corresponds to this noetic pleroma (true-beautiful-good), then manifests itself in the way that Aristotle — despite his (real-)identity of the ideative and the real particular — refers "definition" (ὅρισμος) and "proof" (ἀπόδειξις) exclusively to the ideative-universal (the αὐτὸ καθ' αὐτό), since what is at issue is that which is "necessary."[108] Thus, (real-)identity — understood as the most extreme symbol of a world measured according to its own inner middle — carries within itself, despite everything, the old Platonic "rift of tension" (χωρισμός): between necessity (that of the ideative-universal) and contingency (that of the real-factical).

What takes place here is, indeed, the reversal of what we saw above: the measured, serenely sated "in" of the μέσον (αὐτὸ ἐν ἄλλῳ καὶ ἄλλο ἐν τούτῳ) springs up into the "to" — "suspended in the immeasurable" — of the most acuminate ἄνω of the ἀνάλογον: into the in-between of the "away from oneself" (ὡς ἄλλο πρὸς ἄλλο understood as ἄλλο πρὸς) but "nevertheless not in the other" (ὡς ἄλλο πρὸς ἄλλο understood as πρὸς ἄλλο).

From a purely formal perspective, this relation between an emphatic ἀνά (of an ἀνάλογον oriented towards the μέσον) and an emphatic ἄνω (of a μέσον oriented towards an ἀνάλογον) could seem to represent a return to Pla-

100. *Eth. Nic.* VII, 1, 1145a, 23ff.
101. *Eth. Nic.* II, 6, 1107a, 6-8.
102. The mean is in a sense an extreme. *Eth. Nic.* II, 6, 1107a, 23.
103. *Eth. Nic.* X, 4, 1174b, 31-33; 1175a, 15-20.
104. *Eth. Nic.* X, 6-9.
105. *Eth. Nic.* VIII, 2, 1155b, 18-21.
106. Dearest to God/the gods. *Eth. Nic.* X, 9, 1179a, 30.
107. *Peripeteia* [being] a change . . . into the opposite. *Poet.* 11, 1452a, 22-23.
108. *Met.* VII, 15, 1039b, 27-31.

tonism, especially if Plato's ἀθάνατος μάχη is seen as corresponding to the ἀγωνίζεσθαι in Aristotle. But as soon as we probe the imponderables of the Aristotelian relation the difference between them becomes clear. In Platonism, as we have seen, the ἄνω turned out to be the "goad" of the ἀνά. In Aristotelianism, on the other hand, though the μέσον represents the most strenuous attempt to "master" the limitless flowing apart of things, it is nevertheless the case that, both below and above this "mastering," infinities break open. Indeed, this also agrees with the most general impression that Aristotle's writings afford: the impression of energy strained by the effort of exact "determination" (as opposed to "Platonic poetry"), an effort resulting however in the ultimate helplessness of a boundless merging into the infinite. It is an activity of "division" and "discrimination" that is ever renewed only to "flow away."[109] It turns out to be nothing less than the formalization of "movement in itself" as an end in itself. Thus, in contrast to Platonism's "immortal struggle," ἀθάνατος μάχη, we have in Aristotle an "eternal movement," ἀΐδιος κίνησις, understood as an "eternal revolution of movement," κυκλοφορία τέλειος,[110] and as "the infinite," ἄπειρον:[111] "an eternal movement in itself *in infinitum*." It is a movement synonymous not with "struggle," but with "*alternation*"[112] (κίνησις καὶ μεταβολή). According to Aristotle, to be ignorant of this is to be ignorant of nature as such (ἀναγκαῖον γὰρ ἀγνοουμένης αὐτῆς ἀγνοεῖσθαι καὶ τὴν φύσιν),[113] since the categories of being are the categories of alternating movement (κινήσεως καὶ μεταβολῆς ἐστιν εἴδη τοσαῦτα ὅσα τοῦ ὄντος).[114] Thus even the Aristotelian *true* is ultimately reducible to the "thought that we think" (νοοῖμον ὅτι νοοῦμεν)[115] and hence to the "thinking of thought" (νοήσεως νόησις).[116] Thus the Aristotelian *good* is the "autarchy"[117] of the "act of the soul in itself" (ψυχῆς ἐνέργεια . . . κατ᾽ ἀρετήν)[118] in the sense of μὴ ἄλλο τι ἔργον παρὰ τὴν ἐνέργειαν.[119] And thus, finally, the Aristotelian *beautiful* de-

---

109. *Aufspalten, Abspalten, Ablaufen.* — Trans.

110. *Coel.* II, 1, 284a, 7.

111. *Phys.* VIII, 8, 261b, 27.

112. *Umschwung,* i.e., change, but change in the sense of a sudden turnabout or revolution. — Trans.

113. For, necessarily, if this be unknown, so will be nature also. *Phys.* III, 1, 200b, 14f.

114. There are as many forms of motion and change as there are of being. *Phys.* III, 1, 201a, 8.

115. *Eth. Nic.* IX, 9, 1170a, 32.

116. *Met.* XII, 9, 1074b, 34-35.

117. *Eth. Nic.* I, 7, 1097b, 14ff.

118. An activity of the soul . . . in accord with virtue. *Eth. Nic.* I, 7, 1098a, 16.

119. [There being] no other result than the actuality. *Met.* IX, 8, 1050a, 34-35.

mands integral unity of beginning, middle, and end in a "pure event" (μίαν πρᾶξιν ὅλην καὶ τελείαν, ἔχουσαν ἀρχὴν καὶ μέσον καὶ τέλος).[120]

This "movement" is *formally* located in the actual "analogy" between possibility (δύναμις) and actualization (ἐνέργεια).[121] This is given (according to its Aristotelian specification) in three forms. In the first form, the stress is on a "concentrated possibility" "straining to discharge itself": "capable," δυνατόν — understood as ἔχον κινήσεως ἀρχὴν ἢ μεταβολῆς[122] — as opposed to "fixed," στατικόν. The "analogy" in the "movement" is here manifestly "creative from below and forward."[123] In the second form, everything lies in an "in-between" between possibility and actuality that is itself neither (οὔτ᾽ εἰς δύναμιν . . . οὔτ᾽ εἰς ἐνέργειαν ἔστι θεῖναι αὐτήν).[124] This inbetween is more precisely designated as an "incomplete actualization" (ἐνέργεια . . . ἀτελής),[125] which, seen "prospectively," is an "incompleted goal-in-itself" (ἐντελέχεια κινητοῦ ἀτελής)[126] but, seen "retrospectively," is something "seemingly limitless" (ἀόριστον τὸ δοκεῖ)[127] because it is an "incomplete possibility" (ἀτελὲς τὸ δυνατόν, οὗ ἐστὶν ἡ ἐνέργεια).[128] Finally, the third form indicates an "impulse from without," because every possibility is actualized by the already actual (ἀεὶ γὰρ ἐκ τοῦ δυνάμει ὄντος γίγνεται τὸ ἐνέργεια ὂν ὑπὸ ἐνέργεια ὄντος),[129] so much so that, ultimately, there lies at the ground of all movement not an "eternal possibility (that is infinitely explicated)," but the "eternally actual (that actualizes possibilities)" (ἔστι δ᾽ οὐθὲν δυνάμει ἀΐδιον).[130]

But then there is the *material aspect,* which by all means bears an intrinsic correspondence to this threefold formality of movement: the unresolved back-and-forth of the metaphysical structure of the world. The first formality ("possibility straining to discharge itself") works itself out in

---

120. *In-Sich-Eins.* One action whole and complete, containing a beginning, middle, and end. *Poet.* 23, 1459a, 19-20.

121. *Met.* IX, 6, 1048a, 37; b, 6-10.

122. Having a beginning of motion or change. *Met.* V, 12, 1019a, 34.

123. That is, from the efficient and material causes. — Trans.

124. [Movement] cannot be classed with potentiality or with actuality. *Met.* XI, 9, 1066a, 18-19.

125. *Phys.* III, 2, 201b, 31-32.

126. An imperfect entelechy of motion. *Phys.* VIII, 5, 257b, 8.

127. *Met.* XI, 9, 1066a, 14.

128. The possibility whereof it is the actualization is imperfect. *Phys.* III, 2, 201b, 32-33.

129. For actuality is produced from potentiality always by something actual. *Met.* IX, 8, 1049b, 24-25.

130. Nothing eternal exists in potential. *Met.* IX, 8, 1050b, 7-8.

the metaphysical formula of "eternal movement," to which the "movers" are "servants" (εἴπερ ἀνάγκη ἀεὶ κίνησιν εἶναι),[131] insofar as they constitute the sort of order among themselves (ὥσπερ στράτευμα)[132] that makes this "divine totality" possible: the κυκλοφορία τέλειος as "deathless and divine," ἀθανατόν τι καὶ θεῖον, as religious tradition would have it.[133] Logically, then, the force of the "cosmic cycle" (κυκλοφορία τέλειος) is centered in the "intellective cycle" (νοήσεως νόησις),[134] because this is where its principle is most concentrated: from itself, in itself, to itself. The metaphysical formula attending the second formality (the "in-between" as determined both backwards and forwards) is found in the intersecting midpoint of the "now" (νῦν). "Eternal time" exists by virtue of the fact that the "now" is a certain kind of middle: one in which, in each case, beginning and end are not only "simultaneous" (μεσότης τις, καὶ ἀρχὴν καὶ τελευτὴν ἔχον ἅμα, ἀρχὴν μὲν τοῦ ἐσομένου χρόνου, τελευτὴν δὲ τοῦ παρελθόντος),[135] but also diverge within their very simultaneity.[136] Thus, the same "now" is at once unification and separation (ταὐτὸ καὶ κατὰ ταὐτὸ ἡ διαίρεσις καὶ ἡ ἔνωσις).[137] Finally, the third formality (the "impulse from without") points to the metaphysical formula that Aristotle opposes to Platonism: a "first" that is above all antitheses,[138] and so above the "cycle circling into itself" that is conditioned by the play of antitheses — a cycle that, in fact, "can be set in motion" only by this "first," inasmuch as its own immanent antitheses hold it in equilibrium (οὐ γὰρ ἐστιν ἐναντίον τῷ πρώτῳ οὐθέν).[139]

This view is pointedly expressed in the problematic of one final concept, which, more than any other, distinguishes the Aristotelian from the Platonic: the καθόλου. The Latin translation of Aristotle renders this as *universale*, but this very term has such a tone of neutrality about it as to signify the general universality of the problem, prior to either Aristotelianism or Platonism. *Universale* understood as *universale in re* means καθόλου,

---

131. Since it is necessary that there always be movement. *Phys.* VIII, 257b, 25; cf. 258b, 10-259a, 9.

132. Like an army. *Met.* XII, 10, 1075a, 13.

133. *Coel.* II, 1, 284a, 3f.

134. *Met.* XII, 9, 1074b, 34.

135. A certain mediacy possessing simultaneously a beginning and an end, a beginning of time future, and an end of time past. *Phys.* VIII, 1, 251b, 20-22.

136. *Phys.* IV, 13, 222a, 10-20.

137. The division and the unification are the same and in reference to the same thing. *Phys.* IV, 13, 222a, 19-20.

138. *Übergegensätzlichkeit eines "Ersten."* — Trans.

139. For to the first there is no contrary. *Met.* XII, 10, 1075b, 11-1076a, 4.

while *universale* understood as *universale trans rem* means εἶδος. For Aristotle, however, the καθόλου means that the εἶδος is superfluous.[140] The καθόλου comprises two moments: the "in itself" (καθ᾽ αὑτό) and the "in everything" (κατὰ παντός): ὃ ἂν κατὰ παντός τε ὑπάρχῃ καὶ καθ᾽ αὑτό.[141] As the "in everything" it belongs to the problematic of whole and part, and thus, insofar as it is understood as "according to the whole" (καθ᾽ ὅλον), its opposing concept is "according to a part" (κατὰ μέρος): τὸ δὲ καθόλου ὅλον τί ἐστιν· πολλὰ γὰρ περιλαμβάνει ὡς μέρη τὸ καθόλου.[142] Insofar, however, as πᾶν and ὅλον are distinguished as "all" and "whole," and insofar as καθόλου belongs (as κατὰ παντός) to πᾶν, but (as καθ᾽ ὅλον) to ὅλον;[143] and insofar, furthermore, as καθόλου comprises both "necessity" (ἐξ ἀνάγκης)[144] and "eternity" (ἀΐδιον),[145] we can already observe a clear tension: between "all," a word whose resonances tend in the direction of "summation" — from the sense of "commonality" (κοινόν)[146] to that of "in most cases" (ἐπὶ πλειόνων),[147] and thus in the direction of the "factical" — and "whole," a word that is attuned to the "essential" and thus involves "necessity" (ἐξ ἀνάγκης).[148] This tension is then thoroughly manifest in the "in itself" (καθ᾽ αὑτά), which is the second component of the καθόλου, and which now appears downright Platonic: as an "identity in itself as itself." Consequently, the "particular instance" (καθ᾽ ἕκαστον),[149] which is here the distinctly contrary concept, can scarcely be conceived other than as "being the particular instance" of this "identity in itself": as the "individuation"[150] of the "in itself" itself (ὡς ἕκαστον ἕν, etc., ἕν ἅπαντα εἶναι ὡς ἕκαστον).[151] But even this is still equivocal. For, on the one hand, the predominant accent in this "individuation" (in the καθ᾽ ἕκαστον) is that of the καθόλου "maintaining possession of itself" within its "individuation" (because it remains "the same" "in itself": καθ᾽ αὑτά understood as ᾗ αὐτὸ ταὐτόν). But then it

---

140. *Post. An.* I, 11, 77a, 5-10.

141. That which appertains to every instance and to itself. *Post. An.* I, 4, 73b, 26-27.

142. And the universal is a kind of whole: for it comprises many things within itself as parts. *Phys.* I, 1, 184a, 25-26.

143. Cf. *Met.* V, 26, 1024a, 2ff.

144. *Post. An.* I, 4, 73a, 28.

145. *Post. An.* I, 8, 75b, 22.

146. E.g., *Phys.* III, 1, 200b, 24-25.

147. E.g., *Hermen.* 7, 17a, 39.

148. *Post. An.* I, 4, 72b, 28.

149. *Das "jeweils Jegliche,"* "each thing in its respective moment." — Trans.

150. *Jeglichung,* literally "each-ing." — Trans.

151. As each one/each and all of them are as one. *Met.* V, 26, 1023b, 28, 31.

appears equally to be the "appropriation of a neutral universal as a peculiar independent possession":[152] insofar as the καθ' ἕκαστον also means property, ἴδιον. Hence "individuation" appears, on the one hand, as a falling away from necessity towards purely practical presence and, ultimately, towards fortuity: because the καθ' ἕκαστον as such belongs to the accidental, συμβεβηκός (since it is the "just now" of the "case"),[153] while συμβεβηκός has chance, τύχη, for its cause.[154] On the other hand, however, this "individuation" is equally the actualization of something that is merely possible: because the καθόλου is related to the καθ' ἕκαστον as δύναμις to ἐνέργεια, so much so that only the καθ' ἕκαστον, and not the καθόλου, is subsistent being (οὐσία).[155]

Given, then, that the problem of the καθόλου forms the centerpiece of the Aristotelian conception of "movement" (because it concerns the innermost movement of being as such: the movement in which it comes to pass *as* being), the most poignant characteristic of this movement is the enigma of an "alternation within itself."[156] For, on the one hand, one sees here a spanning of opposites entirely of the same sort as the Platonic separation (χωρισμός): λόγος, understood as the sphere of the καθόλου (because it is eternal, ἀεί); τύχη παράλογος, unpredictable chance, understood as the sphere of the καθ' ἕκαστον (because it is accidental, κατὰ συμβεβηκός).[157] As such, the primordial movement of "individuation" is nothing short of a span of contradiction between sense and sense-less. But then again, on the other hand, both spheres are bound to a sphere of "necessary being": here there is none of that Platonic opposition between the ideative imperishability (because necessity) of the εἴδη and the perishability of factually concrete being;[158] rather, necessity is an abstraction that is represented as concretely existing in both imperishable necessary being and perishable necessary being (τῶν . . . ἐξ ἀνάγκης ὑπαρχόντων ἄμφω).[159] The concretely existing unity of both, then, is the eternal alternating movement itself, to

---

152. *In-Besitz-Nahme eines Neutral-Allgemeinen in eigenständigem Sonder-Besitz.* — Trans.

153. *Post. An.* I, 8, 75b, 21-30; I, 31, 87b, 30.

154. *Met.* XI, 8, 1065a, 30.

155. *Met.* XIII, 10, 1087a, 1-15. [*Bestehendes Sein.* — Trans.]

156. *Umschwung in sich selbst.* Both "revolution" and "sudden reversal" are implied. — Trans.

157. *Phys.* II, 4, 196a, 9-19.

158. *Met.* X, 10, 1059a, 10-11.

159. Both [perishability and imperishability] pertain necessarily. *Met.* X, 10, 1059a, 8.

which imperishable necessary being (as the "unmoved mover") is subservient (as we have just seen). That is to say, what is peculiar to this mode of "individuation" is precisely the (real)-identity of Platonism's contrary poles: necessity and perishability. Consequently, "individuation" is represented as a "span of contradiction within identical being":[160] "identical contradiction" and "contradictory identity."

The particular accent here is made clear by a further determination peculiar to the Aristotelian web of concepts. Certainly, the "movement of alternation," in its abruptly changing rhythm of "contradiction-identity," accentuates the "in-between" (μεταξύ); and this is a splendid expression: it belongs intrinsically both to "alternation" (εἰς ὅσα μεταβάλλειν ἀνάγκη πρότερον τὸ μεταβάλλον)[161] and to "opposition" (πάντα γε τὰ μεταξύ ἐστιν ἀντικειμένων τινῶν).[162] But, true to its Platonic ancestry,[163] this form of the in-between is that of a rhythmic equilibrium, and as such incompatible with the severity of "contradiction" (ἀντιφάσεως μὲν οὐκ ἔστι μεταξύ).[164] That particular in-between of which Plato has no notion and which Aristotle explicitly subsumes under his καθόλου is, rather, the κολοβόν: the "mutilated," which is to say, the "*torso*." It is at once "part" and "whole": μεριστόν τε . . . καὶ ὅλον.[165] While the Platonic rhythm is identifiable by its oscillating in-between, the in-between manifested by the Aristotelian rhythm is the "mutilation" of the "torso," that is, the remainder that is ever again left behind by the abrupt movement of alternation.

Finally, with regard to this "mutilation," there is one minor but distinctive feature that bears mentioning. The severely[166] critical ictus peculiar to Aristotle's polemic falls upon the αἰτία, understood as both κινοῦν and τέλος: in the sense of "real cause" and "real end," and hence in the sense of "sober natural-scientific explanation" and "sober practical use" — as opposed to Platonic "mysticism and aesthetics." But, then, it is precisely this Aristotelianism that, at the summit of its positive exposition, slips into that "most mystical" and "most aesthetic" aspect of Platonism — into eros: love's attraction and drive as the ultimate essence of "movement" (κινεῖ δὲ ὡς

---

160. *Widerspruch-Spanne im Selbig-Sein.* — Trans.

161. [The "between" is] that into which what changes must change first. *Met.* X, 7, 1057a, 21-22.

162. Every "between" is between certain opposites. *Met.* X, 7, 1057a, 30-31.

163. *Republic* V, 477a ff.

164. *Met.* X, 7, 1057a, 34 [contradiction has no "between"].

165. *Met.* V, 27, 1024a, 12.

166. *Ingrimmig.* Literally, ireful, wrathful. — Trans.

ἐρώμενον);[167] the "real cause" and "real end" in the "beautiful as an end in itself" (τὸ καλὸν καὶ τὸ δι' αὐτὸ αἱρετόν).[168]

What is especially distinctive to the Aristotelian analogy, then, is not merely the paradoxical unity of the enigma of "movement" (which was delineated above): a movement that is, in one respect, "from itself forward *in infinitum*," then "bound to itself in a dividing middle," but equally "posited and driven by something external to itself."[169] For, given that with the problem of the καθόλου, all of this culminates in the form of "contradiction and identity," a further distinctive mark turns out to be this "mutilation" and this *"involuntary eros for the beautiful."* This is the mark of the great enigma of Aristotelianism: on the one hand, the most developed formal doctrine of God; on the other hand, the material divine is the "eternal movement of alternation." The consequence of thus forcing God into the realm of creaturely immanence is then: "contradiction-identity," "mutilation," and "involuntary propulsion."[170] Thus, by "Aristotelian analogy" we indeed mean what we saw at the outset: an ἀνά, of the *strictest equilibrium,* within a cyclical movement closed in on itself — a cyclical movement, however, that is always breaking apart into the limitless (and this, right within its very own middle, since it is a dividing middle); moreover, a cyclical movement whose middle of contradiction-identity is occupied by something "mutilated," a "torso," though *in such a way that,* precisely here, and however *involuntarily,* the ἄνω *springs up.* The mystery of God reveals itself in the mystery of creaturely disintegration.

4. Thus, what *both the Platonic and the Aristotelian analogies* have in common is, first of all, a certain ultimate priority of the ἀνά: in the Platonic analogy it appears as the in-between of the artistic within "immortal struggle"; in the Aristotelian, as the "torso," pointing finally and involuntarily beyond itself, the "mutilation" of the "eternal alternation of movement in itself." The tendency of both is towards the greatest possible immanence of the creaturely. In Plato it is transfigured into the ideality of a "struggle" that bears the traits of immortality. In Aristotle it unmasks itself as the reality of an ultimate "torso," the countenance of finitude within the "eternal alternation of movement." These are the two basic forms of a metaphysics of imma-

167. It moves things by being loved. *Met.* XII, 7, 1072b, 3.

168. The good and in itself desirable. *Met.* XII, 7, 1072a, 34.

169. Przywara is referring to the nexus of the four causes, given graphic form above: the ἀρχή κινήσεως moves from itself forward, is bound to itself in the "dividing middle" of εἶδος and ὕλη, and is "posited and driven" by a τέλος "external to itself." — Trans.

170. *Auftrieb wider Willen.* — Trans.

nence: idealism's "progress *in infinitum*" and realism's "closed finitude," which are first intertwined in modern philosophy. In the first form, the ἄνω would appear to explode the ἀνά to such a degree that the mystery of God would have to become manifest as the defining-end of the creaturely. And yet, it turns out to be not an explosion, but rather an internal expansion: the *progressive analogy of the intra-creaturely* (progressing into a heroic idealism). For the *tanta similitudo* between God and creature is not overcome by the *maior dissimilitudo,* but instead transforms the latter into a "formal goad" that expands its enclosure. In the second form, "pure finitude" is taken seriously, including the concept of the "torso," so that one would naturally expect to find here the clearest example of something pointing-above-and-beyond-itself. As it turns out, however, it is not a positive "above-and-beyond-itself," but rather a more intense confinement of finitude, to the point that it becomes a passive "witness to disintegration": a *regressive analogy of the intra-creaturely* (regressing into tragic realism). On the one hand, the *tanta similitudo* appears to be extinguished in an exclusive *maior dissimilitudo* (of a pronounced finitude). But in that it seeks to be a "closed" finitude, the *tanta similitudo* becomes the absolute form of a negative *maior dissimilitudo* that is turned downwards: not into the greater mystery of God beyond itself, but rather into the explosive paradox of the "absoluteness of relativity," of the "infinity of finitude," of the "divinity of the creaturely" — in order to betray, within this explosion, the presence of the ἄνω.

There is, however, one other thing worth noting in these two analogies that is not reducible to what we have just described. Even this description itself already resonates with various accents and nuances that cannot be resolved into the neutrality of what one might call a "strict concept." The extent to which the (Platonic) progressive analogy appears as an expression of "heroic idealism" is a function of the Platonic (objective) μέθεξις and (subjective) ὁμοίωσις having to overcome the abyssal chasm of the χωρισμός that lies before that blessed "other shore." The (Aristotelian) regressive analogy, on the other hand, bears the stigma of "tragic realism," because it aims from the very first at the harmonious ideal of a seamlessly secure enclosure, and thus betrays itself as, at bottom, the sobriety of a "shipwrecked idealism." The "in face of death" (of Platonic idealism) and the "sobering wreck" (of Aristotelian realism) — compared with the tendency towards absolutization found in either — cannot be explained simply by saying that the two forms are ultimately intersecting forms, each with a different stress: realism → idealism (Plato), idealism → realism (Aristotle). Rather, they betray a "desperate longing" for the divine: a variously accented "delirium," reeling between intoxicated unity with the divine and defiant distance from it: Tantalus and Prometheus.

The first thing that this reveals is how closely theology and philosophy are bound together in analogy (in keeping with §4). For what is expressed in all the moments we have just delineated is the theologoumenon of *original sin and redemption*. Secondly, it is an indication of how profoundly Plato and Aristotle become "Christian" in Augustine and Thomas: as *una verissimae philosophiae disciplina*, as Augustine puts it.[171] It is a certain application of the relation between Old and New Testaments (in the spirit of Clement of Alexandria): the old is disclosed in the new, and the new lies hidden in the old: *vetus in novo patet, novum in vetere latet.* On the one hand, Augustine appears as a "Christian *Plato*," and Thomas as a "Christian *Aristotle*": because each appears to adopt the fundamental motifs of his respective philosopher. On the other hand, however, Augustine is emphatically a "*Christian* Plato," and Thomas a "*Christian* Aristotle": because it is in them that the profounder paradox of either philosopher's fundamental motifs is, for the first time, resolved. At first, therefore, the concept of analogy in Augustine and in Thomas will stand out as an emphatically "Christian" concept; we will then see, however, that it brings resolution to Plato's and Aristotle's concepts of analogy in their own right. Here we have the fundamental realization of the *non destruit, supponit, perficit,* as defining the relation between theology and philosophy (§4, 5-6): in the most formal concept of the *analogia entis.*

5. In *Augustine* analogy is characterized, on the one hand, by how the antitheses *sensibilia-intelligibilia, exterius-interius, temporale-aeternum* relate to one another; and, on the other hand, by how, in these antitheses, the soul *(animus)* or the mind *(mens)* relates to the truth-goodness-beauty, which is God. Whereas in Plato the soul is more or less the site of the antitheses *sensibilia-intelligibilia,* etc., and whereas in Aristotle, by contrast, these antitheses are ultimately traceable back to the activity of the soul (νοήσεως νόησις), in Augustine the picture proves to be multidimensional. Not only in the sense we just touched upon: that the soul itself, in which the antitheses *sensibilia-intelligibilia,* etc. intersect, is stretched further, beyond itself (in an insistent, incessant search for God). Rather, one must observe how the soul's movement "towards God" instigates a movement "away from" ("beyond" the *sensibilia, externa, temporalia*), while its provenance "from God" tends to express itself in a clarified movement "towards" ("towards" the *sensibilia,*

171. *Contra Acad.* III, xix, 42.

etc., as what is distinctly appropriate to human beings). Thus, it is not simply that the ἀνά of a middle relation (of the soul in the midst of the antitheses) is transected by an ἄνω (of the soul directed towards God); rather, this very ἄνω bears in itself the tension between an ascent ("towards God"), which overcomes[172] the self-containment of the ἀνά, and a descent ("from God"), which emphasizes the ἀνά as what is "appropriate (to the creature)." And so much is this ἄνω (in its tension) the determining form that with the question of an inner ordination[173] of the ἀνά — and of a principle of unity for such an ordination *(quid sit unum)* — we have nothing less than the concrete question of God and the soul: *cuius duplex quaestio est: una de anima, altera de Deo.*[174] It is not only that "order" (as the quintessence of ἀνά) is intrinsically turned "towards God" *(ordo est quem si tenuerimus in vita, perducet ad Deum),*[175] but that the "question concerning God and the soul" is the quintessence of "order" *(hic est ordo studiorum sapientiae, per quem fit quisque idoneus ad intelligendum ordinem rerum)*[176] — so much so that the most precise expression of the ἀνά, numerical balance *(aequalitatem illam . . . in sensibilibus numeris),*[177] has the site of its "uniformity" *(incommutabilem veritatem numerorum)*[178] in God.[179] Thus, it follows, it is *"order" by virtue of the most extreme "above-and-beyond":* knowledge of this order is knowledge in the most rigorous sense (inasmuch as it is "comprehensive in principle"), but God, in whom knowledge of this order is grounded, comes to be known only insofar as he is "not known" *(cuius nulla scientia est in anima, nisi scire quomodo eum nesciat).*[180]

The first trait distinctive to the Augustinian analogy, then, is the *emphatic motion of its "back-and-forth."* As much as the passage from the *sensibilia* to the *intelligibilia* attests to a longing for the "purely spiritual" *(penitus esse ita sensibilia fugienda),*[181] it is equally the case that the draw of

---

172. *Aufhebt.* — Trans.

173. *Zuordnung.* — Trans.

174. Whereof the question is twofold: of the soul and of God. *De Ord.* II, xviii, 47.

175. There is an ordering that, if we keep to it in this life, will lead to God. *De Ord.* I, ix, 27.

176. This is the ordering of those eager for wisdom, whereby everyone is made capable of knowing the order of things. *De Ord.* II, 18; 47.

177. That equality . . . in sensible numbers [rhythms]. *De Musica* IV, xii, 34.

178. The unchangeable truth of numbers. *De Liber. Arb.* II, xi, 30.

179. *De Liber. Arb.* II, xvi, 44.

180. Whereof there is no knowledge in the soul, except the knowledge that it does not know him. *De Ord.* II, xviii, 47.

181. Sensible things are to be utterly fled. *Solil.* I, xiv, 24.

the "appropriately human" is towards the sensible *(facilius et quasi familiarius visibilia quam intelligibilia pertractamus)*,[182] such that the spiritual is perceived within the sensible in a way that is "better adapted" *(accomodatius)*.[183] As much as the path to truth is the path inward *(noli foras ire, in teipsum redi: in interiore homine habitat veritas)*,[184] to the point of "self-presence" *(sibi praesens)* as the most incontrovertible root of "truth,"[185] this "path inward" is nevertheless negative and reflexive, the "retreat to the invincible," whereas the positive and direct[186] movement aims towards the "exterior" of the bodily sense, *sensus corporis,* and the testimony of others, *testimonium aliorum.* And as truly as one may speak (in the theoretical realm of *sapientia* and in the practical realm of holy repose, *otium sanctum*) of the primacy of the *aeternum* (i.e., a more intense "breakthrough to the immediate"), nevertheless, once again, the *temporale* of *scientia* and its just employment, *negotium iustum,* positively insinuates itself, like the interlacing of right and left hands (to use Augustine's image for the practical aspect of the question).[187]

It is similar with the relation between the *soul and God.* To be sure, everything seems to be concentrated upon the interior of the spirit, on the "inner room" of the "within yourself," *secretarium tuum* of the *intus in te.*[188] Not only does the "truth" flash decidedly in self-presence, *sibi praesens;*[189] not only does "wisdom" appear precisely as the *modus animi . . . , quo sese animus librat;*[190] not only does God appear as the one who is "beyond all being and possibility" fundamentally in the formal "ever above-and-beyond" of the movement of the spirit *(cogitatur ut aliquid quo nihil melius atque sublimius illa cogitatio conetur attingere);*[191] but, what is more, the

182. We deal more easily and more familiarly with things visible than with things intelligible. *De Trin.* XI, i, 1.

183. *De Trin.* XI, i, 1.

184. Do not go out, but return into yourself: truth dwells in the inner man. *De Ver. Relig.* XXXIX, 72.

185. *De Trin.* X, iii, 5–viii, 11.

186. *Direktive.* — Trans.

187. Cf. *De Trin.* XII, ii, 2-3; vii, 12; xiii, 21; xiv, 22–xv, 25 with *In Ps.* CXX, 8-9; CXLIII, 18; *De Civ. Dei* XIX, xix.

188. *In Jo. Tract.* XXIII, 10.

189. *De Trin.* X, iii, 5–viii,11.

190. The mode of intellect . . . whereby the intellect gives itself equilibrium. *De Beata Vita* iv, 33.

191. The thought [of those who conceive of one supreme God] strives to rise to the thought of something than which there is nothing greater or more sublime. *De Doctr. Christ.* I, 7.

most veiled mystery of God, his three Persons,[192] becomes "visible in an image" *(ex rerum notarum similitudine vel comparatione)*[193] only in *memoria sui, intellectus sui,* and *voluntas sui,* as the personal trinity of the *one* self-related spirit.[194] But this very *intus te* is, in the strictest sense, only a "step towards . . . ," as in towards the "above-and-beyond," indeed, as in "lifted up from the ground towards . . ." *(quasi gradu facto inde surgat atque attolatur):*[195] not only in the sense of "not remaining in oneself" *(cum redieris ad te, noli remanere in te),*[196] nor only in the sense of a "self-surmounting" *(transcende et te),*[197] nor only in the sense of "seeing oneself only in retrospect" to the point of "self-forgetting,"[198] but, moreover, in the sense of "intellective life not according to the intellect" *(non secundum ipsam [mentem et rationem] debet vivere),*[199] to the point of "putting oneself away from oneself" *(tolle te . . . a te).*[200] Thus, "truth" becomes so much the inner sense to which soul and spirit are referred that they not only imply, in increasing degrees, a looking away from self and into it[201] (in the succession of their functions: *animatio, sensus, ars, virtus, tranquilitas, ingressio, contemplatio),*[202] but themselves devolve[203] out of any empirical facticity into precisely the absolute here-and-now of ideative truth *(intuemus inviolabilem veritatem, ex qua perfecte quantum possumus, definiamus, non qualis sit uniuscuiusque hominis mens, sed qualis esse sempiternis rationibus debeat).*[204] Thus, God presents himself fundamen-

192. *Dreipersönlichkeit.* — Trans.

193. From a similitude of or comparison to things known. *De Trin.* VIII, v, 8.

194. *De Trin.* X, xi, 18, in its abbreviated formula.

195. Like a step taken [or stage reached] from which one rises up or is elevated. *Retract.* I, viii, 3.

196. If you would return to yourself, do not remain within yourself. *Serm.* 330, 3.

197. But transcend yourself. *Serm.* 153, 7, 9.

198. *De Liber. Arb.* III, xxv, 76.

199. [The mind] ought not live according to [mind and reason] themselves. *Retract.* I, i, 2.

200. Remove yourself . . . from yourself. *Serm.* 169, 9, 11.

201. *Das wachsende sich-verschauende Hinein in sie [die Wahrheit].* Cf. "sich verschauen" in the sense of "to fall for." — Trans.

202. Animation, sense, art, virtue, tranquility, entering [into the divine], contemplation. *De Quant. Anim.* xxxv, 79.

203. *Entwerden,* and so "devolution" not in the sense of an evolution from above, but in the sense of an undoing of what has evolved. — Trans.

204. We look to inviolable truth, from which — insofar as we are able — we perfectly define not of what kind the mind of a given man might be, but of what sort it ought to be in regard to the timeless truths of reason. *De Trin.* IX, vi, 9.

tally in the rhythm of the "ever above-and-beyond" of the rational soul,[205] in order to ascend ever higher above this rhythm, since every attempt to comprehend him is a growing experience of his in-comprehensibility *(quam sit incomprehensibile . . . , invenire),*[206] a "comprehending" of "in-com-prehensibility" *(incomprehensibile comprehendit esse quod quaerit);*[207] for whatever is "ap-prehended" is *ipso facto* not God *(hoc . . . non est, si comprehendisti: si autem hoc est, non comprehendisti).*[208] Thus, ultimately, it is not simply that the mind's *imago Trinitatis* is transected by a "dissimilitude beyond all explanation" *(quanta sit . . . dissimilitudo, quis potest explicare?),*[209] but that the mind is an *imago* only in such measure as *memoria sui, intellectus sui,* and *voluntas sui* are not *sui,* but rather *Dei,*[210] insofar as they are a "mirror in an enigma" — which is to say, a mirror "through which" one sees *(per speculum),*[211] but in such a way that one actually knows only the mirror, and not him *(in te enim quod est, potes nosse: in eo qui te fecit quod est, quidquid est, quando potes nosse?).*[212] Finally, in negative terms, the mystery of the mind (in its threefold form) already, in advance, causes one to fall silent before the greater mystery of God: *ne ineffabilis quidem dicendus est Deus, quia et hoc cum dicitur, aliquid dicitur.*[213] In positive terms, the *imago Trinitatis* implies the surrender of the mind's immanence to an infinity of incomprehensibility: *memenerim Tui, intelligam Te, diligam Te.*[214]

What we see in this pronounced movement is precisely the dynamic "in-between" of the (Platonic) progressive and (Aristotelian) regressive analogies. What is peculiar to it, however, is that its final note is not the Aristotelian "torso" (κολοβόν). The final note is, at first hearing, the *"rhythm of what is passing away."* To be sure, the creaturely is a "cascading torrent"

---

205. *De Trin.* XI, iv, 6.

206. To find how incomprehensible he is. *De Trin.* XV, ii, 2.

207. One comprehends that what one seeks is incomprehensible. *De Trin.* XV, ii, 2.

208. This . . . is not [God] if you have understood it; if, however, it is [God], you have not understood it. *Serm.* 52, 6, 16.

209. How great is . . . this dissimilitude; who can explain it? *De Trin.* XV, vii, 12.

210. *De Trin.* XIV, xii, 15.

211. *De Trin.* XV, xxiii, 44–xxiv, 44.

212. You may be able to learn what is proper to yourself: but can you ever learn what — whatever it may be — is proper to him who made you? *Serm.* 52, 10, 23.

213. God is not even to be said to be "ineffable," because when this is said something has then been said of him. *De Doctr. Christ.* I, vi.

214. [O, my God,] may I remember Thee, understand Thee, and love Thee. *De Trin.* XV, xxviii, 51.

(torrens . . . colligitur, redundat, perstrepit, currit et currendo decurrit);[215] indeed, one could even say that it only "was" or "will be," but never "is" *(antequam sint non sunt, et cum sunt fugiunt, et cum fugerint non erunt).*[216] But it is just this "passing away" that gives the "whole" its peculiar resonance: just as a spoken work of art depends upon each verse, each syllable, each letter "passing away."[217] And it is precisely the contrariety of things contending with one another (to the point of mutual extinction) that plaits them into a unity: *contrariorum oppositione saeculi pulchritudo componitur.*[218] The only appropriate posture, then, is that of "flowing with what flows" *(fateor me ex eorum numero esse conari, qui proficiendo scribunt et scribendo proficiunt),*[219] to the point of an ever more rapid "trickling away" *(si intelligentia tibi placet . . . , intellige quid non intelligas).*[220] But the final clarification of this "rhythm of what passes away" is based in this: that this rhythm is, more profoundly, a *manifestation of the mystery of God:* the God who works through and sustains this rhythm in its entirety *(Deus sub quo totum est, in quo totum est, cum quo totum est);*[221] the God who hereby joins its "nothingness" to an "is" *(Deus per quem omnia, quae per se non essent, tendunt esse. Deus qui non id quidem quod se invicem perimit, perire permittis);*[222] the God who through himself overcomes even the gravest gulf of contradiction, that between good and evil *(Deus per quem universitas etiam cum sinistra parte perfecta est. Deus a quo dissonantia usque in extremum nulla est, cum deteriora melioribus concinunt . . . Deus in quo sunt omnia, cui tamen universae creaturae nec turpitudo turpis est, nec malitia nocet, nec error errat);*[223] the God, therefore,

215. A torrent . . . is gathered, overflows, thunders, runs and in running runs off. *In Ps.* CIX, xx.

216. Before they might be they are not, and when they are they are fleeing away, and when they have fled they no longer are. *De Liber. Arb.* III, vii, 21.

217. *De Ver. Relig.* XX, 42-43.

218. Beauty is composed from the opposition of the world's contraries. *De Civ. Dei* XI, xviii.

219. I confess that I endeavor to be ranked among those who, having made some progress, write and who, through writing, continue to progress. Ep. 143, 2.

220. Since understanding is what so pleases you . . . understand what it is that you do not understand. *De Natura et Origine Animae* IV, xi, 15.

221. God beneath whom is all, within whom is all, with whom is all. *Solil.* I, i, 4.

222. God through whom all things, which of themselves would not exist, tend towards being. God who does not allow to perish even that which mutually destroys itself. *Solil.* I, i, 2.

223. God through whom the universe, even with its dark side, is perfect. God with whom there is no dissonance, even from what is most removed from you, since things that are worse exist in balance with things that are better . . . God in whom all things are, whom

who ultimately unites the mysteries in himself: in that he contains in himself what passes away *(non enim haberent vias transeundi, nisi contineres ea)*,[224] he is "beyond all things" as "innermost in all things" *(interior omni re, quia in ipso sunt omnia, et exterior omni re, quia ipse est super omnia)*,[225] and, therefore, at once that which "precedes all things" and that which "pervades all things" *(antiquior . . . omnibus, quia ipse est ante omnia, et novior omnibus, quia idem ipse post omnia)*.[226] The fundamental mutability of the creature, alternating between antitheses[227] — between the root *(ante omnia)* and the flower and fruit *(post omnia)*, between old age *(antiquior)* and youth *(novior)*, indeed, even the alternating rhythm between "standing above" *(exterior . . . , super omnia)* and "right within" *(interior . . . , in ipso . . . omnia)* — opens upon the mystery of God in the very moment of its passing over from the "positive" of its antithetical poles (*antiquum,* etc.) into the "*in infinitum*" of the "comparative" *(antiqui-or)*. The most creaturely aspect of the creature (in view of which its "analogy" to God would appear to be the severest conflict with God: intrinsic opposition versus unity, no versus yes, nothing versus Is) — precisely *this* is the site of the profoundest disclosure of God (the site, that is, of an "analogy to God" not merely in the sense of "exemplarity," but almost in the sense of "revelation").

Here we gain a sense of what is ultimate and decisive in the Augustinian analogy: its theologoumenon. This is true, first of all, at the level of formal method: the standpoint taken here is formally theological: *from God to creature.* Of course, ultimately we were obliged to note something similar in Plato and Aristotle. But there it was more of an "unconscious background" or even something "involuntary." Here, though, it is the "light that penetrates all things." For this reason, the material-theological aspect also has an explicit form: the theology of supernature, of original sin and redemption. The extent to which the theology of *supernature (consortium naturae divinae)* is the fundamental form is evident from the fact that the most characteristic mode of the Augustinian analogy is the doctrine of the *imago Trinitatis.* The *consor-*

---

nevertheless neither does any creature's disgracefulness disgrace, nor malice injure, nor error mislead. *Solil.* I, i, 2.

224. Indeed they would not even have a means of passing away did you not sustain them. *Conf.* I, vi, 10.

225. Within everything, because all things are within him, and outside of everything, because he is beyond all things. *De Gen. ad Litt.* VIII, xxvi, 48.

226. Older . . . than all things, because he is before all things, and newer than all things, because he is after all things. *De Gen. ad Litt.* VIII, xxvi, 48.

227. *Der Grund-Gegensatz-Wandel der Kreatur.* — Trans.

tium naturae divinae implies a "filiation to God" of such a sort that we are "children of the Father," "in the likeness of the Son," with "the Holy Spirit in our hearts." The doctrine of the *imago Trinitatis,* though, evinces this formal mode in the formal mode of the mind's life. The presence of the theological is almost more pervasive in the concrete theology of supernature — this being a matter of *original sin and redemption.* This is already appreciable in the final accents of what we observed above: on the one hand, an analogy whose span and dynamic are extreme enough to cause a tearing and separation; but, on the other hand, this right within a genuine "repose in the beyond," which one might take for a posture of "aesthetic distance" if one did not sense in it such "ardor." A creature is precisely, as such, the "inconstancy of change" (for even *quando ab omni languore sanabitur, mutabitur)*[228] — and yet precisely this "mutability itself" *(mutabilitas . . . rerum mutabilium)*[229] "somehow is" *(utcumque erat).*[230] Within these formal accents we can already observe the effects of what is distinctive to the Augustinian theology of original sin and redemption. It is, on the one hand, a *theology of original sin as viewed from the standpoint of redemption* (and in this respect already incompatible with Reformation theology's doctrine of the "distance of the ineradicable *homo peccator*").[231] Here the severity of original sin seems almost "exaggerated," because it is in this way that the greater mercy of redemption is revealed in its overwhelming triumph. The analogy between God and creature is portrayed precisely (in original sin) as the contradiction between *"homo mendax"* and *"Deus veritas" (quaere quid sit hominis proprium, mendacium invenies . . . Veritas enim e Deo est, mendacium abs te),*[232] because it is precisely in this way, in light of God's overflowing truth in the Father's self-revelation in the Logos, that the contradiction is made glaringly clear. But then, conversely, it is equally a *theology of redemption that takes into consideration the full realism of the world of original sin* (which utterly abolishes the distance posited by Reformation theology, inasmuch as it integrates the entire world into Christ). The grounds for this lie in the Logos himself, since all the oppositions of creaturely "togetherness" and "succession"[233] are in Him, from eternity, but

228. When it will be healed of every infirmity, still it will change. *De Trin.* XV, xxiii, 43.

229. The mutability . . . of mutable things. *Conf.* XII, vi, 6.

230. In some way was. *Conf.* XII, vi, 6.

231. *Distanz des untilgbaren Erbsünders.* That is to say, because Reformation theology sees each Christian as *simul iustus et peccator.* — Trans.

232. Seek what is proper to man, and you will find falsehood . . . For truth is of God, and falsehood comes from you. *Serm.* 32, 10.

233. As above, *Nebeneinander* and *Nacheinander.* — Trans.

"*one* life": *ubi principaliter atque incommutabiliter sunt omnia simul: non solum quae nunc sunt . . . , verum etiam quae fuerunt et futura sunt. Ibi autem nec fuerunt nec futura sunt, sed tantummodo sunt: et omnia vita sunt et omnia unum sunt, et magis unum est et una vita est.*[234] This has its intramundane reality in the *Corpus Christi mysticum:* for the incarnate God goes the way of the cross of the riddle and evil of the world not only once, but ever anew, while the world comes to share in the glory of God precisely in God's being crucified ever anew *(corpus coniunctum est capiti suo . . . et corpus in capite suo est . . . Et nos ibi sedemus, et ipse hic laborat.);*[235] for, it follows, the world participates in the glory of God to the degree that it is crucified along with the crucified God *(deformitas Christi te format . . . Hanc viam teneamus, et ad speciem perveniemus).*[236]

The word that best captures the essence of Augustinianism is therefore "night." All manner of illumination flows into it: self-knowledge and mutual understanding[237] and experience of life[238] and guidance from above (Ep. 140, 2, 3-11, 28). And yet it is night in all its ambiguity: as the dusk and the dawn of the day: between evening and morning. It is, to be more precise: the Easter vigil. The night following upon Good Friday: immersion in the absurdity — the "non-sense" — of a God put to death by his creation. The night in anticipation of Easter morning: rapture into the "super-sense"[239] of a creation redeemed by God and into God by the killing of God. It is thus the *"vigilant night" (vigilat . . . ista nocte et mundus inimicus et mundus reconciliatus).*[240] Vigilance in the negative sense: of the acutest consciousness of the abysses that have been torn open. And vigilance in the positive sense: of the night that is already day. It is the night in which the abyss of the creature *(quid est profundius hoc abysso?)*[241] and the groundlessness of God *(ut inventus*

---

234. Where all things exist in their principle and unchangingly: not only those things that now are . . . , but indeed those things that have been and will be. There, moreover, they neither have been, nor will be, but simply are: and all things are life and all things are one, or — rather — is one thing and one life. *De Trin.* IV, i, 3.

235. The body is joined to its head . . . and the body is in its head. . . . And there we rest, while here he labors. *In Ps.* LV, 3.

236. The deformity of Christ gives form to you . . . Let us hold to this path and we shall come to that beauty. *Serm.* 27, 6, 6.

237. *In Ps.* C, xii.

238. *In Ps.* LXXVI, iv.

239. *In den Über-Sinn.* — Trans.

240. Both the hostile world and the reconciled world keep vigil through that night. *Serm.* 219.

241. What is deeper than this abyss? *In Ps.* XLI, xiii.

quaeratur, immensus est)[242] are unfathomably one.[243] The word "night" thus indicates that the Augustinian analogy breaks through in both a downward and an upward direction: downward into the abyss of the creaturely, which — beyond an "ever greater dissimilarity" — is almost a "contradiction"; and upward into the immeasurability of God's incomprehensibility, into which the creature is enraptured, such that — beyond even the "so great a similarity" of "exemplarity" — one must almost speak of a "cessation into God."[244] It is the mystery of Augustine's favorite phrase from the Psalms: **adhaerere Deo.** "To be suspended in God"[245] means that the one who is suspended has only an "abyss of emptiness" beneath him. But then it means that for just this reason he is completely surrendered to Him "in" whom he is suspended. The ground whereon he stands is none other than that "wherein" he is suspended: he "stands" "beyond himself."

This makes clear how, here, the relation between ἄνω and ἀνά is precisely the reverse of their relation in Plato and Aristotle (despite the Augustinian analogy having appeared above as a synthesis of the two). It is not only that every ἀνά is determined by the ἄνω, but that the ἄνω itself is not from "below to above," but "from above to below." And even this is to be understood not merely in the sense we uncovered as we developed the *analogia entis* from the principle of non-contradiction: the sense, that is, that ultimately follows from the movement "from below to above" (since in such a relation the "above" is necessarily primary: the κινοῦν ἀκίνητον of all movement). But rather in the altogether distinct theo-logical sense: that, for the mystery of God, the creaturely is the instrument of revelation. In Plato this meant: the ἄνω was the goad within the ἀνά: its ultimate termination was the mystery of the in-between of God and creature (from the perspective of the creature). In Aristotle it meant: the ἄνω was that which sprang up involuntarily out of the most complete (and earnestly attempted) enclosure of the ἀνά: the mystery of God that is revealed in the mystery of the disintegration of the creaturely. By contrast, in Augustine it must be taken to mean: *the ἀνά as the declaration of the ἄνω:* the most nocturnal mystery[246] of the crea-

---

242. So that he who has been found might be sought, he is unending. *In Jo. Tract.* LXIII, 1.

243. It is impossible to reproduce Przywara's wordplay here in English: *Es ist Nacht, in der das Abgründige des Geschöpfes und das Grundlose Gottes unergründlich eins sind.* — Trans.

244. *Aufhören in Gott hinein.* — Trans.

245. *"Hangen in . . .":* literally, "hanging in" or "depending from" (like a picture hung upon a hook). — Trans.

246. *Nächtigste Geheimnis.* — Trans.

ture understood as the revelation of the "superluminous darkness" of God. It is Augustine's conclusion concerning the "problem of evil" in *De libero arbitrio: apparet omnia, sive cum offendunt vel offenduntur, sive cum delectant vel delectantur, unitatem insinuare atque praedicare Creatoris.*[247] From Plato to Aristotle to Augustine, this analogy would appear to sink ever more deeply into the land of "unlikeness": from the symbol of "immortal struggle" (ἀθάνατος μάχη) to that of the "torso" (κολοβόν) to that of "night" *(nox)*. But it is precisely in this "sinking into the groundless" that a "180 degree turn" is made. For what is decisive is that the night of "godforsakenness" is the night in which "God is all in all."

6. Compared to the Augustinian analogy, the concept of analogy distinctive to Thomas Aquinas presents an either-or of possible interpretations: either one understands it in abstraction from the theological as a purely formal order between creator and creature — or one understands it as that which completes the theological in anticipation of the concretely harmonious order between God and a redeemed world. The word "order," which serves as Thomas's particular systematic principle,[248] is ambiguous: on the one hand, it means the "given natural order" between God and creature — on the other hand, it means the "order restored" by redemption between God and a fallen world. This is nowhere so clear-cut as in the structure of his *Summa Theologiae*. On the one hand, it is characterized by the ancient Greek schema of the "*exitus* and *reditus* of the creature," and this (given that Thomas conceives of the "*exitus*" as a *processio Dei ad extra*) in its consummate form, the Areopagite's circle of God's self-donating love (ἐξ ἑαυτῆς καὶ δι' ἑαυτῆς καὶ ἐφ' ἑαυτῆς ἑαυτὴν ἀνακυκλοῦσα):[249] *imperfectus esset creaturarum a Deo exitus, nisi reditio in Deum exitum adaequaret.*[250] It is thus an explicitly theological schema: proceeding from the self-imparting God of our original state to the mediator-God of the redemption that leads us home. But, on the other hand, within the framework of this schema, the entire "natural relation" between creator and creature is sketched out; so much so, that the quintessence[251] of Thomas's work appears to be a formal

---

247. All things appear — whether they either offend or take offense, or delight or take delight — to suggest and assert the unity of their Creator. III, xxiii, 70.

248. *De Spir. Creat.* a 5, corp.

249. [The Good] revolves back to itself from itself and through itself and upon itself. *De div. nom.* IV, 17.

250. The procession of creatures forth from God would be imperfect if their return into God were not adequate to that procession. *De Ver.* q. 20, a. 4, corp.

251. *Inbegriff.* — Trans.

ontology — one that is distinct from Aristotle's simply because it has gone through the further development of Aristotelianism (in Jewish and Arabic philosophy) and has already been clarified with respect to — and by way of — theology. Seen from this standpoint, it is no coincidence that Aquinas's actual commentaries are devoted to these two figures: Dionysius the Areopagite and Aristotle. In fact, the symbol of Thomas's position is a spanning together of both: *"holy order"* (ἱερ-αρχία) and *"natural order"* (*ordo rerum,* or *ordo universi*): *non solum omnium Angelorum, sed etiam totius rationalis creaturae, quae sacrorum particeps esse potest, una est hierarchia.*[252] On the one hand, the Augustinian "disquiet of longing" has subsided into a "quiet transfiguration";[253] but, on the other hand, the (disintegrating) tension of the Aristotelian attempt to "encompass everything in thought"[254] is liberated into a "serene sobriety." What is at issue here comes down to this "quiet transfiguration," which appears as a "serene sobriety," and this "serene sobriety," which is disclosed in "quiet transfiguration."

Let us begin with the *objective configuration* of this unity. The principle of Thomas's method — which he poses over against the Platonic *(abstractionem universalium)* and Aristotelian *(perpetuitatem motus)* principles — is that of the *ex perfectione universi,*[255] which is accented in various ways. On the one hand, *"universi"* expresses Thomas's predominant leaning towards a *"natural order"* and hence his predilection for Aristotle *(vera philosophiae principia quae consideravit Aristoteles).*[256] This leaning, however, rests upon three moments, each conditioned by and circling into its opposite. The first moment is manifest in the *corpus* of Thomas's proofs for the existence of God, which set out from the form of the universe (understood in terms of movement, generation-and-corruption, possibility-and-actuality, gradation, governance),[257] and do so, moreover, in rejection of the Anselmian point of departure.[258] Here the universe, as the "all," is plainly opposed to the noetic act (of a "particular being"). In the second moment, however, the situation is nearly reversed in that the Aristotelian universe, which is "fash-

---

252. There is one hierarchy, not only of all the angels, but also of every rational creature capable of participating in sacred things. *Summa Th.* I, q. 108, a. 1, corp.

253. *Zur ruhenden Verklärtheit entworden.* — Trans.

254. *Umfassung im Denken.* — Trans.

255. *De Spir. Creat.* a. 5 corp.

256. The true principles of philosophy, to which Aristotle gave consideration. *De Spir. Creat.* a. 3, corp.

257. *Summa Th.,* I, q. 2, a. 3, corp.

258. *De Ver.* q. 10, a. 12, corp. and ad 2.

ioned by the grace of the intellect"[259] *(sua abstractione intellectus facit istam unitatem universalem),*[260] is opposed to the real presence of the Platonic *unum in multis* (of the web of the "universals"). Thus, an ideative universe is here opposed to a real one (insofar as what is at issue is the "how" of the form, which "resides" only in the intellect as such). In the third moment, however, there is yet another turn of the circle. As something "fashioned by the grace of the intellect," the (reflexive) universe consists "in the order of truth." Its "universal validity" can then be established in one of two ways: either (in Aristotelian terms) because the reflexively known universe "corresponds to the essence of things," which is universally the same *(ratione unitatis rei),* or (in Augustinian terms) because the order of "truth as such" guarantees that this validity is "universal" *(ratione unitatis primae lucis in omnes mentes influentis).*[261] The emphasis here (since Thomas inclines towards the first solution) is upon a universe that is as real as possible. The "universe" is opposed (in the first moment) to the noetic act (understood as part of the universe), in order to constitute itself (in the second moment) formally-reflexively in the noetic act (in the *"forma" universi*), but in such a way as to appear essentially (in the third moment) as a "real universe." Thus, what is meant by *universi* in *ex perfectione universi* is that which is ultimate within the world — that wherein world and spirit (in the human being) are bound mutually together: spirit is turned towards the world inasmuch as the world is constituted "as" world in the spirit.

But the suspendedness of this connection points beyond itself — to a *"holy order."* Thomas traces all systems that teach two antithetical cosmic principles back to this: that in their reflections they remain only at the level of isolated things *(iudicaverunt de rebus secundum quod in se considerantur tantum),*[262] or at any rate only at the level of their interrelations *(vel secundum ordinem unius rei ad aliam rem),*[263] whereas the unity is made manifest only by reference to the "whole" *(in comparatione ad totum ordinem universi).*[264] But in many ways this "whole" is not truly apparent except "from God." It is constituted as a "unity of diverse things" *(ut in*

259. *Gebilde von Gnaden des Intellektes.* — Trans.

260. The intellect fashions that universal unity by abstraction. *De An.* a. 3, ad 8.

261. By reason of the unity of the thing or by reason of the unity of the first light flowing into all minds. *De Spir. Creat.* a. 10, ad 13.

262. They judged things according as things are considered in themselves. *De Pot.* q. 3, a. 6, corp.

263. Or according to the order of one thing in relation to another. *De Pot.* q. 3, a. 6, corp.

264. In comparison to the total order of the universe. *De Pot.* q. 3, a. 6, corp.

diversitate creaturarum perfectio consisteret universi)[265] and thus immanently overcomes any disintegration into antitheses. But precisely for this reason it has its definitive ground in the essence of God, who is the essential unity of what, divided and apportioned, constitutes the manifold fullness of the creature *(hoc ipsum ad perfectam Dei unitatem pertinet, quod ea, quae sunt multipliciter et divisim in aliis, in ipso sunt simpliciter et unite. Et ex hoc contingit quod est unus re et multiplex secundum rationem).*[266] Accordingly, then, the universe is not actually an "all-unity" in an immanent and positivist sense, but rather in a transcendently relational sense — namely, by virtue of the reference of the "all" of multiplicity to the unity of God *(repraesentante universo per multiplices et varios modos creaturarum quod in divina bonitate simpliciter et indistincte praeexistit).*[267] What is more, while any particular thing within the universe can find its explanation within the universe itself *(ex ordine universi, ad quem quaelibet creatura ordinatur sicut pars ad formam totius),*[268] the explanation for the universe *(quare sit tale vel tale)*[269] leads immediately to the pure *"that it is"* of the unfathomable determination of the divine will *(nec . . . ex parte divinae potentiae quae est infinita, nec divinae bonitatis, quae rebus non indiget,* but simply *ex simplici voluntate producentis).*[270] It is, therefore, not only the case that the *perfectio* in *"ex perfectione universi"* has its determinative primordial form[271] in the *perfectio* of God (anticipating the ambiguity of Nicholas of Cusa's *coincidentia oppositorum*), but that the *tale vel tale* of this *perfectio* is itself a purely positive divine determination — one for which grounds can so little be adduced as to rule out even a "ground in God himself"[272] *(ex parte divinae potentiae* or

---

265. That the perfection of the universe should consist in the diversity of creatures. *De Pot.* q. 3, a. 16, corp.

266. It belongs to the perfect unity of God that those things that are multiple and separate in others abide in him simply and singly. And from this it follows that he is objectively one and multiple according to our reason. *Summa Th.* I, q. 13, a. 4, ad 3.

267. The universe can be represented through the multiple and various modes of creatures because it preexists simply and undifferentiatedly in the divine goodness. *De Pot.* q. 3, a. 16, corp.

268. From the order of the universe, to which every creature is ordained as a part to the form of the whole. *De Pot.* q. 3, a. 17, corp.

269. Why [the creature] should be such or such. *De Pot.* q. 3, a. 17, corp.

270. [We can derive a reason] neither . . . from the divine power, which is infinite, nor from the divine goodness, which has no need of anything/[but only from] the will of the Creator alone. *De Pot.* q. 3, a. 17, corp.

271. *Urgestalt.* — Trans.

272. *Begründung von Gott aus.* — Trans.

divinae bonitatis). Seen from this perspective, the word "universe" has such a supermundane reference that it is virtually a theological designation. It breaks through, inasmuch as it is essentially a substitute for another word: the οἰκουμένη of the οἰκονομία — that is, the universe of the order of salvation, which is but one: the *one* supernatural order of fall and redemption. For, according to Thomas, it is precisely the final enclosure of all particular things (in their togetherness) and all particular events (in their succession) into the "all-unity" (of togetherness and succession) that is the "site" of the "supernatural," which thoroughly shapes everything else: the *one* supernatural "order," which issues from the *one* supernatural "end" (the *visio beatifica*). It is not simply that the supernatural concerns the *modus*[273] or the *qualiter*[274] in general, that is, the final form that "transforms"[275] *(gratia perficit)* every material content (*substantia actus* or *quid*) into a unity, but that it does so explicitly with regard to the "end," namely, the "goal": the "natural" (the *quid* of its contents) is *ad finem,* whereas the "supernatural" (the *qualiter*) is *circa finem.*[276]

The **perfectio** in *ex perfectione universi* thus has a *double aspect:* the supernatural *perfectio* of the "perfected kingdom of God" is ever again peering through the features of a seemingly rational-natural *perfectio;* conversely, the *perfectio* of the perfected kingdom of God is expressed under the veil of a likeness in the rational and natural *perfectio.* In this respect we see in Thomas something like the complete form of the ambiguity inherent in the Pauline phrase "God all in all" (1 Cor. 15:28): it refers to the final fulfillment[277] of the supernatural kingdom of God, but in such a way as to be, at the same time, the acutest expression of the natural-rational relation between Creator and creature. Thus, it assuredly belongs to the logical form of a closed universe that "it lack nothing that is possible" *(ut non desit ei aliqua natura quam possibile sit esse);*[278] that there be an inner "seamless continuity" *(ut ab uno extremo in alterum non perveniatur nisi per media)*[279] and that, therefore, not only should whatever is highest in each lower level be in contact with what-

273. *De Ver.* q. 24, a. 13, corp.
274. *De Ver.* q. 24, a. 1, ad 2.
275. *Überformt.* — Trans.
276. *De Ver.* q. 14, a. 3, ad 9; a. 5, ad 11, 13; a. 10, ad 3.
277. *End-Vollendung.* — Trans.
278. Such that it is not lacking in any nature that is at all possible. *De Spir. Creat.* a. 5, corp.

279. That it is not possible to pass from one extreme to another save through the intermediate. *De Spir. Creat.* a. 5, corp.

ever is lowest in each higher level *(inferior natura attingit in sui supremo ad aliquid quod est proprium superioris naturae, imperfecte illud participans),*[280] but each higher level should contain each lower level in a "more eminent" way *(ut quaecumque inveniuntur in inferiori natura, inveniantur excellentius in superiori natura)*[281] and thus "actuate" it;[282] that, consequently, everything in this universe should aim at bringing the universe to representation: whether in that (as the lowest form of such representation) everything particular exists to serve the universe and its meaning *(quod bonum commune est eminentius quam bonum singulare),*[283] or whether in that (as the highest form of such representation) the particular itself, in its respective highest forms, becomes "universal," both formally *(potentia superior per se respicit universaliorem rationem)*[284] and materially *(ut in ea describatur totus ordo universi et causarum eius);*[285] yet it is also proper to the logical form of a closed universe that (since the actual parts of the universe are situated, practically speaking, in the middle between these two formal modes of representation) the universe represent a "unity of multiplicity" *(non omnia . . . aequalia; sic enim imperfectum esset universum, cui multi gradus entium deessent).*[286] The moment one peers through and beyond these features, however, one is confronted by the way that God — the God who comprehends in unitary and self-same fashion[287] all perfection in himself — pervades the All, and does so in such a way that it is his bodily expression: the "mystical body" of the incarnate God *(corpus Christi mysticum).* This is why Thomas bases the "completeness of all the stages" upon the "perfection" of the original (supernatural) state *(propter quod Gen 1 singula dicuntur bona, omnia autem simul valde bona).*[288] This is why his "connection of extremes in a given middle" *(non . . .*

---

280. The lower nature, at its highest point, touches upon something proper to the higher nature, participating in it imperfectly. *De Ver.* q. 16, a. 1, corp.

281. That whatsoever is found in an inferior nature is found more eminently in a superior nature. *De An.* a. 18, corp.

282. *De Ver.* q. 9, a. 1, corp.

283. That the common good is higher than the individual good. *De Ver.* q. 5, a. 3, corp.

284. The higher power, in itself, regards a more universal dimension. *Summa Th.* I, q. 77, a. 3, ad 4.

285. That in [the soul] the entire order of the universe and of its causes is represented. *De Ver.* q. 2, a. 2, corp.

286. Not all things [are made by God to be] equal; indeed the universe would thus be imperfect, lacking as it would the many grades of beings. *De An.* a. 7, corp.

287. *Einshaft-selbig.* — Trans.

288. For this reason, in Genesis 1, individual things are said to be good, while all things together are said to be very good. *De Spir. Creat.* a. 5, corp.

nisi per media)[289] bears the unmistakable "stigma" of Augustinian Christology: Christ as the midpoint of all of creation's antitheses. This is why his distinctive understanding of the "permeation, containment, and activation, one by another, of the levels of being" is based upon the Areopagite's "hierarchy" — a word that refers, essentially, to the sacred universe of the supernatural.[290] This is why, finally, the "unity of multiplicity" is patently a philosophical formula for the "body of many and diverse parts" of 1 Corinthians *(ut in diversitate creaturarum perfectio consisteret universi).*[291] It is, therefore, surely no interpolation to see in the *ordo partium exercitus* and its relation to God as *dux in exercitu*[292] not only a reappropriation of the Aristotelian στράτευμα metaphor[293] but, through and beyond this, the features of the "church militant." For Thomas bases the *ordo partium exercitus* upon the principle of order proper to supernature: *unde apostolus dicit Rom. 13:1: Quae a Deo sunt, ordinata sunt.*[294]

This relation is pointedly expressed by Thomas in that he uses the same word, *perfectio,* to signify both what is most proper to God and the *ordo rerum.* God as "God" is related to creatures *(ad omnes rerum essentias)* not as universality to particularity *(sicut commune ad propria),* not as the *one* to the many *(ut unitas ad numeras),* not as the center to its radii *(vel centrum ad lineas),* but rather as perfection to imperfection *(sicut perfectus actus ad imperfectos)*[295] — so much so that to be a creature means simply "the *how* of imperfection within the creature's participation in the *what* of divine perfection" *(modus imperfectus, quo a creatura participatur divina perfectio).*[296] But, on the other hand, all talk of the *ordo rerum* has no other intention than that a *perfectio* should be attained *(omnia quodammodo sunt unum perfectum)*[297] — such a *perfectio,* indeed, as almost to coincide with God's essence, inasmuch as both have the appearance of a unity of the All: *quaelibet . . . natura creata, cum sit finita, non ita perfecte repraesentat divinam*

---

289. *De Spir. Creat.* a. 5, corp.

290. *De Ver.* q. 16, corp., etc.

291. That the perfection of the universe consists in the diversity of creatures. *De Pot.* q. 3, a. 16, corp. See 1 Cor. 12:17-24.

292. *De Spir. Creat.* a. 8, corp.

293. *Met.* XII, 10, 1075a, 13f.

294. Hence the Apostle says in Romans 13:1: Those things that are from God are ordered. *De Spir. Creat.* a. 8, corp.

295. *Summa Th.* I, q. 14, a. 6, corp.

296. The imperfect mode whereby the divine perfection is participated in by the creature. *Summa Th.* I, q. 13, a. 3, ad 1.

297. All things are in a sense one perfect thing. *De Pot.* q. 3, a. 16, ad 1.

*bonitatem sicut multitudo naturarum: quia quod in multis naturis multi-pliciter continetur, comprehenditur in Deo unite; et ideo oportuit esse plures naturas in universo.*²⁹⁸

It is logical, then, that the relation of God to the **ordo rerum** should manifest itself in the same way. On the one hand, God is essentially "outside every order" because he is "beyond every order" *(cum Deus sit extra ordinem creaturae, et omnes creaturae ordinetur ad ipsum),*²⁹⁹ such that, while the immanent order of the universe exists only through the order of its transcendence *towards* God *(ordo qui est partium universi ad invicem, est per ordinem qui est totius universi ad Deum),*³⁰⁰ God does not belong "to the essence" of the creature *(causa prima quae Deus est, non intret essentiam rerum creatarum).*³⁰¹ But, on the other hand, the *ordo rerum* is so thoroughly permeated by God (to the point of constituting a "sacral universe," which is the fundamental idea of the Areopagite) that the propositions "God creates for his own sake" and "God creates for the sake of the universe" coincide: *Deus . . . creaturarum universitatem vult propter se ipsam, licet et propter se ipsum eam vult esse.*³⁰²

This then comes to a climax in the problematic of "relationality" **(relatio)**, which is the formal essence of order *(oportet . . . in ipsis rebus ordinem quemdam esse; hic autem ordo relatio quaedam est).*³⁰³ On the one hand, "relationality" is what distinguishes the creature most sharply from God: as *esse relativum* over against *esse absolutum:* while the creature is relationally constituted both within the world (in its togetherness and succession) and as related to the Creator, God is the one who is essentially "detached" from all things *(ab-solutus),* because "he is himself"³⁰⁴ — so much so that even his re-

---

298. A created nature of any sort, inasmuch as it is finite, is unable to represent the divine goodness as perfectly as can a multitude of natures: for what is contained multiply in a variety of natures is comprehended in God as a unity; and hence there ought to be a plurality of natures in the universe. *De. Spir. Creat.* a. 8, ad 17.

299. Since God is outside the order of the creature, and all creatures are ordered to him. *Summa Th.* I, q. 13, a. 7, corp.

300. The order that obtains among the various parts of the universe exists by virtue of the ordering of the whole universe to God. *De Pot.* q. 7, a. 9, corp.

301. The prime cause, which is God, does not enter into the essence of created things. *De Pot.* q. 3, a. 5, ad 1.

302. God . . . wills the universe of creatures for its own sake, although he also wills it to be for his own sake. *De Pot.* q. 5, a. 4, corp.

303. It is proper . . . that there be some order in things themselves, and this order moreover is a certain relation. *De Pot.* q. 7, a. 9, corp.

304. *Weil "Er selbst."* — Trans.

lation to the creature is only a relation of the creature to him *(cum ea ratione referatur Deus ad creaturam, qua creatura refertur ad ipsum).*[305] But, on the other hand, it is precisely this "relationality" that enters into the divine sphere, not merely in a general way, but in a privileged way, entering into its most essential mystery, the tri-personal life, since "relationality" does not contain in itself any *modus imperfectus.*[306] What is more, for Thomas (as for as Trinitarian theology in general), relationality as such is the peculiar mode of the *imago Trinitatis.* Whereas, for Augustine, the life of the mind[307] in *memoria sui, intellectus sui,* and *voluntas sui* is the site where the tri-personal life appears in the "enigma of a likeness,"[308] for Thomas, the *memoria sui* disappears (save for a few lingering traces); there is, moreover, a shift in perspective towards the formal concept of "order." The ideal image of order is the closed circle. Logically, therefore, the *imago Trinitatis* within the mind is concentrated in the *circulatio* that takes place between *intelligere* and *velle (voluntas redit in id a quo fuit principium intelligendi).*[309] But then, taken to its logical conclusion, this demands that the content of the mind finally recede entirely, and that the tri-personal life have its formal *imago* in "order as such" inasmuch as its antithetical categories are one in the tri-personal life: *singularitas-diversitas* is contracted to *unitas-pluralitas, divisio-unicitas* is contracted to *simplicitas-distinctio, disparitas-confusio* is contracted to *aequalitas-discretio, alienitas-solitudo* is contracted to *similitudo-consonantia.*[310] In this respect, Thomas represents the fulfillment of the Greek fathers (and in this, too, he stands in the closest proximity to Dionysius the Areopagite): as regards the way in which they develop the theology of the trinitarian relations in closest connection to the theology of the "Trinity in salvation history." The matrix of the formal si-

---

305. Since God is related to the creature only in that the creature is related to him. *Summa Th.* I, q. 13, a. 7, ad 5.

306. *De Pot.* q. 7, a. 8, ad 4.

307. *Geist.* — Trans.

308. The reference is to the δι' ἐσόπτρου ἐν αἰνίγματι *(per speculum in aenigmate)* of 1 Cor. 13:12. — Trans.

309. The will returns to that from which the source of its understanding came. *De Pot.* q. 9, a. 9, corp.

310. *De Pot.* q. 9, a. 8, corp. [*Gebunden zu.* While this phrase would ordinarily be translated as "bound to" or "joined to," etc., this does not fit with the immediately preceding sentence or with the reference to *De potentia.* Certainly, Przywara means that there is a relation between the pairs — since the order of antitheses somehow images the divine unity; the point here, though, is that the antitheses are unified in the divine in a way that results in a different set of terms. Thus, if the pairs are really bound together it is only *per analogiam.* — Trans.]

militude between "order as such" and the order of the tri-personal life is the material structure of salvation history, which is trinitarian: the universe, which is formally comprised in a beginning, middle, and end, is now concretely comprised in the Father, who as Creator stands at the beginning, in the Son, who as redeemer constitutes the middle, and in the Holy Spirit, who is perfection. We hereby attain the full meaning of *perfectio* in *ex perfectione universi,* since it is a translation of the Greek τελείωσις, which means at once both "perfection" and "consecration" (in the sense proper to the mysteries). In the language of the Greek fathers, the Holy Spirit is the intra-divine τελείωσις, the "seal" of "perfection" within the *mysterium mysteriorum* of the tri-personal life. The universe, on the other hand, as the "sacral universe" of the "Trinity of salvation history," attains the intrinsic completion of "perfection" in that it is "initiated" into this *mysterium mysteriorum.*

The *subjective method,* then, corresponds to this picture of the objective *ex perfectione universi.* If everything on the objective side can ultimately be summed up in *relatio* (as the formal essence of *ordo*), then, logically, subjective method is concentrated in the problematic of relational thought — i.e., *relatio* as the *act within the true* — as distinct from purely intuitive thought.[311] This relational thought presents itself, on the one hand, as a "deduction from first principles" *(ratio ex principiis secundum viam inveniendi in conclusiones pervenit, et conclusiones inventas in principia resolvendo examinat secundum viam iudicandi).*[312] But the ultimate ground of these "first principles" is in God, the *prima Veritas (a veritate intellectus divini exemplariter procedit in intellectum nostrum veritas primorum principiorum).*[313] This should not be taken to mean, however, that God is simply another name for "absolute truth," but rather that "absolute truth" refers back to God. God does not occupy the place of an "ultimate principle" in the manner of other ultimate structural principles within philosophy (such as duality, circularity, etc.). On the contrary, he is the "ultimate principle" as "breaking through all objective principles." He breaks through the principle of a graded continuum because he is immediately present to everything.[314] He breaks through the principle of an ultimate duality not only because ev-

---

311. *Rein anschauenden Denken,* purely contemplative thought. — Trans.

312. Starting from principles, reason arrives at its conclusions by way of discovery; and, through reducing the conclusions thus discovered back into their principles, examines them by way of judgment. *De Ver.* q. 10, a. 8, ad 10.

313. From the truth of the divine intellect, as the exemplar, the truth of first principles proceeds into our intellect. *De Ver.* q. 1, a. 4, ad 5.

314. Cf. *De Ver.* q. 11, a. 3, ad 10; q. 8, a. 7, corp.; q. 9, a. 1, ad 4; etc.

ery potentiality is made capable by God of supernatural actualities that transcend the proper actuality assigned to it,[315] but still more fundamentally because even the lowest potentiality *(materia prima)* comes from God.[316] He breaks through the principle of the reduction of everything real to an objective order of the ideal, because he stands above this objective order, as the *creatrix essentia* who himself creates the "pure essences" *(ipsa quidditas creari dicitur).*[317] And therefore, finally, he breaks through the "principle of all principles," that of calculable internal equilibrium. For not only is he, in the actual supernatural order, the God of *caritas,* which — in excess of all rationally measuring *prudentia* — "super-forms" all things as the *forma virtutum;*[318] nor only is he the God of *iustitia divina,* which issues not from the balancing of the common good, but directly from the personal God;[319] nor only is he the God of the *visio beatifica,* which is the "goal," and yet "beyond everything attainable from below";[320] for even in the "creature as such,"[321] there is the *potentia oboedientialis* to such an order, a positive-negative "explosiveness exceeding every natural measure."[322] Thus, as much as God is the *universale principium omnium,*[323] and hence the particular *principium* for each of the respective *genera (in omnibus generibus sicut principium generis),*[324] he is this *principium* in such a way that, essentially, he is not only *not a principium* immanently implicated within any particular *genus (quod Deus non sit in genere per reductionem ut principium),*[325] but fundamentally *extra omne genus.*[326] For this reason, too, God does not coincide with any of the *perfectiones absolute,* which reach their consummation in the

---

315. *De Ver.* q. 8, a. 3, ad 12; q. 29, a. 3, ad 3.

316. *De Ver.* q. 12, a. 4, corp.; *De Pot.* q. 3, a. 1, ad 17.

317. The quiddity itself is said to be created. *De Pot.* q. 3, a. 5, ad 2.

318. *De Ver.* q. 27, a. 5, ad 5.

319. *De Ver.* q. 28, a. 1, corp.

320. *De Ver.* q. 8, a. 3, ad 12.

321. *De Ver.* a. 4, ad 13.

322. It is perhaps necessary to lay special stress on Przywara's argument here, given a certain venerable Protestant misunderstanding of the *potentia oboedientialis.* The logic of this passage is that natural theology has no claim upon God, even as the "principle of principles," for even the creature's *capax gratiae* is not a simple property of the creature's nature, but is God acting within the creature to make it capable of "more" than its nature. — Trans.

323. *Summa Th.* I, q. 84, a. 2, ad 3.

324. [God is] in every genus as the principle of the genus. *De Pot.* q. 7, a. 8, ad 2.

325. That God is not found in any genus through reduction to its principle. *Summa Th.* I, q. 3, a. 5, corp.

326. *Summa Th.* I, q. 4, a. 3, ad 2.

transcendentals and in being as such *(haec nomina "bonus," "sapiens," et similia . . . non . . . sunt imposita ad significandam divinam naturam, sed ad significandas ipsas perfectiones absolute).*[327] Rather, transcending them, he is the final irreducibility of what is "beyond and in all things" *(aliquid . . . supra omnia existens, quod est principium omnium et remotum ab omnibus),*[328] and this in the concrete form of the *universalis rerum providentia (omnes enim loquentes de Deo hoc intendunt nominare Deum, quod habet providentiam universalem de rebus);*[329] for what is ultimately at issue here is the "simple will of the one who produces," the *simplex voluntas producentis,*[330] the irreducibility of "being-posited" over against all deductions, even those drawn from a *ratio Dei (nec . . . ex parte divinae potentiae . . . nec divinae bonitatis . . . ratio determinatae dispositionis universi sumi possit).*[331] "Thinking from first principles" is therefore, ultimately, a thinking from the absolute positivity (susceptible of no further derivation) of divine providence. For it is this that founds the "first principles" (even and precisely the principle of non-contradiction): *necessitas principiorum dictorum consequitur providentiam divinam et dispositionem.*[332] But this already expresses something formally theological, namely, the positive of a positing; consequently, there is no further reason to be surprised that, for Thomas, the *omnium providentia* belongs explicitly to theology.[333]

On the other hand, however, these same "first principles" point below themselves back to the flux of the experience of being and to the concretely empirical All. They appear as the formal innermost "nature" of thought: in a *necessitas naturalis*[334] that is prior to all learning and discovery.[335] They are therefore the internal "instrumentarium" of thought: "the first instruments

---

327. These names "good," "wise," and other similar designations . . . are not applied so as to signify the divine nature, but only to signify these perfections themselves in an absolute sense. *Summa Th.* I, q. 13, a. 9, ad 3.

328. Something . . . existing beyond all things, which is the principle of all things and removed from all things. *Summa Th.* I, q. 13, a. 8, ad 2.

329. For all who speak of "God" intend thereby to name the God that exercises universal providence over things. *Summa Th.* I, q. 13, a. 8, corp.

330. *De Pot.* q. 3, a. 17, corp.

331. On account neither of divine power . . . nor of divine goodness . . . can the reason for the particular disposition of the universe be supposed. *De Pot.* q. 3, a. 17, corp.

332. The necessity of the principles we have enunciated depends upon divine providence and disposition. *De Ver.* q. 5, a. 2, ad 7.

333. *De Ver.* q. 14, a. 9, ad 9.

334. *Summa Th.* I, q. 82, a. 1, corp.

335. *In Boeth. de Trin.* q. 6, a. 4, corp.

of the agent intellect," *prima instrumenta intellectus agentis*.[336] To the extent, however, that thought, as human thought, takes place entirely within the limits of sense experience *(tantum se nostra naturalis cognitio extendere potest, in quantum manuduci potest per sensibilia)*,[337] its "instrumentarium" — being precisely the innermost "nature" of thought — is also subject to this *tantum-quantum:* for the "first principles," sense experience is a "principle" *(principium cognitionis principiorum est ex sensu et memoria)*,[338] the limit of validity *(non ducunt nos ulterius nisi ad ea, quorum cognitionem acquirere possumus ex his quae a sensu comprehenduntur)*,[339] and the site of final reference *(quia primum principium nostrae cognitionis est sensus, oportet ad sensum quodammodo resolvere omnia de quibus iudicamus)*.[340] However much these principles are grounded, even here, *in ratione entis,* that is, in the most universal web of order of the concretely empirical All — which, for all its flux, nevertheless somehow "is," and thus implies a minimum of enduring order[341] — even this is essentially embedded in the gradual ascent "from below to above," in which the essence of "abstraction" consists. The activity of "abstraction," which presents itself as the higher and nobler agency, *superius et nobilius agens,* is essentially and intrisincially related to sense experience, and to this extent it is passive *(facit phantasmata a sensibus accepta intelligibilia in actu per modum abstractionis cuiusdam)*.[342] This also makes plain the consequence of such an ascent "from below to above": a direct relation to the below *(se extendit secundum statum praesentis vitae ad materialia sola)*;[343] an indirect relation to the above, inasmuch as the above is known only negatively, from below and by means of the below (all *immaterialia* are known only *per negationem et remotionem*);[344] and this indirectness taken to

---

336. *De Ver.* q. 12, a. 3, corp.

337. Our natural knowledge can go only so far as it is able to be led by sensible things. *Summa Th.* I, q. 12, a. 12, corp.

338. The principle of our knowledge of these principles comes from sense and memory. *In Boeth. de Trin.* q. 6, a. 4, corp.

339. They [these principles] take us no further than what we are able to know from the things comprehended by the senses. *In Boeth. de Trin.* q. 6, a. 4, corp.

340. Since the first principle of our knowledge is sense, it is necessary somehow to reduce everything concerning which we make judgments to sense. *De Ver.* q. 12, a. 3, ad 2.

341. *Summa Th.* I-II, q. 94, a. 2, corp.

342. It makes the phantasms received from the senses into things actually intelligible by way of a certain abstraction. *Summa Th.* I, q. 84, a. 6, corp.

343. In accord with the state of this present life, it extends to material things only. *Summa Th.* I, q. 88, a. 1, corp.

344. *Summa Th.* I, q. 88, a. 2, ad 2.

the point that God, as the ultimate "above," appears not only *per negationem et remotionem,* but (since he is above and beyond even the intelligible realm[345] and the knowledge that pure spirit has of him)[346] as the absolute "above and beyond" *(quod Deus est super illud quod de ipso intellectui repraesentatur).*[347] This law extends so far that even revelation and theology are subject to it, inasmuch as they speak in human terms and, hence, according to the senses: *quamvis enim per relevationem elevemur ad aliquod cognoscendum quod alias nobis esset ignotum, non tamen ad hoc quod alio modo cognoscamus nisi per sensibilia.*[348] The final, incisive expression of this is that even the mystical experience of God as a "dazzling darkness" (the ὑπέρφωτος γνόφος of the Areopagite)[349] ends up subject to the same standpoint: the "mystical night" (as the most exalted height of the supernatural) appears as the "night of failure" (of our natural powers): the God of night as the superabundance of light (ἀοράτῳ γε ὄντι διὰ τὴν ὑπερέχουσαν φανότητα)[350] presents himself to our sense-conditioned knowledge as the "unknown God" *(secundum hoc dicimur in fine nostrae cognitionis Deum tamquam ignotum cognoscere, quia tunc maxime mens in Dei cognitione perfectissime invenitur, quando cognoscitur eius essentiam esse supra omne id quod apprehendere potest).*[351]

When we considered the first aspect of thought as *relatio in actu,* i.e., as relational thought, every act of relation[352] was derived from God, because truth appeared as deriving from him as the *Veritas Prima (mens dicitur immediate formari ab ipsa Veritate Prima . . . , per modum quo exemplatum formatur ad suum exemplar immediatum).*[353] The direction of our reflec-

---

345. *Das Geistige.* — Trans.

346. *Summa Th.* I, q. 56, a. 3, ad 6. [*Die der reine Geist von Ihm hat.* That is to say, angelic intelligence, which does not know forms *per sensibilia,* but by a formal knowledge infused by God. — Trans.]

347. For God is beyond what our intellect can of itself represent. *De Ver.* q. 8, a. 1, ad 8.

348. In fact, though we may be raised by revelation to the knowledge of something that would otherwise be unknown to us; nevertheless that to which we are raised we can know in no way other than through sensible things. *In Boeth. de Trin.* q. 6, a. 3, corp.

349. Dionysius, *Myst. Theol.* I, 1.

350. Dionysius, *Ep. ad Dorotheum.*

351. We are said, at the pinnacle of our knowledge, to know God as unknown, because the mind is found to have entered most perfectly into the knowledge of God when it knows his essence to be beyond everything that it is able to comprehend. *In Boeth. de Trin.* q. 1, a. 2, ad 1.

352. *Beziehungsvollzug.* — Trans.

353. The mind is said to be fashioned immediately by the First Truth itself . . . , in the way that a copy is fashioned after its immediate exemplar. *De Ver.* q. 18, a. 1, ad 7.

tions thus took us from the "imperfect relation" (as it occurs in the creaturely realm) to the way — veiled in the night of the divine mystery — in which, within the intra-divine life of the three Persons, the relations *are* the divine Persons. Under the second aspect of relational thought, the act of relation is grounded in "abstraction," which is to say, in the way that human thought analytically and synthetically forms the data of the senses into a "pure order," which is relationally at play among these data. Thus, truth is here situated in this analytic and synthetic activity, i.e., in thought that examines relations, in the *intellectus dividens et componens*;[354] and it is situated in it, therefore, inasmuch as the intellect exercises this activity upon and within the data of the senses, such that its truth appears at the last as an *adaequatio intellectus ad rem*.[355] But this then leads in the direction of an ever greater "failure of all relation": from the independence of the intelligible from the material (such that they are *diversorum generum*)[356] to the absolute relationlessness of God to the creature (such that he is the absolute "above-and-beyond," *extra omne genus*).[357]

This theoretical view of *relatio in actu* (in the true) is then reinforced by its practical aspect (in the *good*). This practical "relation as act" is freedom. It thus presents itself, on the one hand ("from above to below"), as the freedom of the range of application of the "ultimate end," as was the case in the realm of the theoretical with respect to the "first principles" *(necesse est quod sicut intellectus ex necessitate inhaeret primis principiis, ita voluntas ex necessitate inhaereat ultimo fini, qui est beatitudo)*.[358] Freedom, in its depths, is a striving that can be satisfied only by God, because the idea of the absolutely Good lies in him *(objectum . . . proprium voluntatis est ipsum bonum absolute)*.[359] This internal necessity is the ground of freedom with regard to everything creaturely, nothing of which is sufficient to the idea of the Good *(cum . . . possibilitas voluntatis sit respectu boni universalis et perfecti, non subicitur eius possibilitas tota alicui particulari bono; et ideo non ex necessitate movetur ab illo)*.[360] Thus, freedom is here a (descending) "freedom from

354. *De Ver.* q. 1, a. 3, corp.
355. *De Ver.* q. 1, a. 1, corp.
356. *De Ver.* q. 8, a. 9, corp.
357. *Summa Th.* I, q. 4, a. 3, ad 2.
358. It must be the case that just as the intellect of necessity adheres to first principles, so must the will of necessity adhere to its final end, which is beatitude. *Summa Th.* I, q. 82, a. 1, corp.
359. The proper object of the will is the absolute Good itself. *De Ver.* q. 25, a. 1, corp.
360. Since . . . the will's capacity is a capacity with respect to the universal and perfect

God." But equally (as we just saw in the theoretical realm of the true) freedom is grounded in the essence of *ratio*, which, in its task of ordering the
manifold, is free with regard to the particular *(ratio est collativa plurium; et
ideo ex pluribus moveri potest appetitus intellectivus, scil voluntas, et non ex
uno ex necessitate).*[361] Here freedom is derived from the position of the human being as the one who imposes order within the manifold of the world.
Its intrinsic "infinity of possibilities" thus mirrors not the *infinitum actu* (of
God), as above, but rather the *infinitum potentia* (of *materia prima*). It is
thus an (ascending) "freedom through possibilities": here the absolutely
passive "unlimited possibility" of *materia prima* becomes a spontaneously
active "freedom over possibilities"; precisely as such, however, it is essentially
an "unstable infirmity"[362] and so something like the positive form of the
creature's original nothingness *(ex hoc quod aliquid est ex nihilo, sequitur
quod sit . . . vertibile).*[363] According to our first consideration, freedom was a
necessary clinging to God, and it is precisely by virtue of this clinging that it
has an independence from the creaturely and a power to preside over it.
Given that there is an immediate correlation of the rational will to God
*(voluntas rationalis creaturae soli Deo subiacet, et ipse solus in eam operari
potest),*[364] it is God himself who, in the final analysis, effects freedom, not
only in that he bestows it *(quanto aliqua natura Deo vicinior, tanto minus ab
eo inclinatur et magis nata est seipsam inclinare),*[365] but in that he himself is

---

Good, its capacity in its entirety is not subject to any particular good; and thus it is not of
necessity moved by that particular good. *Summa Th.* I, q. 82, a. 2, ad 2.

361. Reason gathers together a plurality of things; and thus the intellectual appetite —
that is to say, the will — can be moved by many things, but cannot be moved of necessity by
any one thing. *Summa Th.* I, q. 82, ad 3.

362. *Schwankende Gebrechlichkeit.* — Trans.

363. Insofar as something comes from nothing, it follows that it is . . . labile. *De Malo*
q. 16, a. 6, ad 5. [Thus freedom, for the creature, is the effect of the *analogia entis*: we become
what we are in the infinite interval of the difference between our intrinsic nothingness and
God's supereminent "no-thing-ness" (so to speak), and our very infirmity and dependence
upon God is thus both what "liberates" us from nothingness and makes us free agents. This
would not be the case if God related to us only as the highest principle or the total order of
the "all"; because he transcends all things, he gives us being freely and calls us to an end
transcending every immanent order. Far, then, from confining finite existence within a rigid
and "essentialist" taxonomy, the analogy is what emancipates us from the regime of mere
"essence" from the first. — Trans.]

364. The will of the rational creature is subject to God alone, and he alone can work
within it. *Summa Th.* I, q. 57, a. 4, corp.

365. The nearer a nature is to God, so much the less is it inclined by another and so
much the more greatly is it native to it that it incline itself. *De Ver.* q. 22, a. 4, corp.

the ultimate act within its act[366] *(sic enim Deus res movet secundum quod competit earum naturae).*[367] It is "theological freedom," as consummately expressed in Augustine's *gratia liberatrix.*[368] According to our second consideration, however, it is "creaturely freedom" in a specific sense: an active "self-determination" *(ipsa inclinatio non determinatur ei ab alio, sed a seipsa)*[369] as a passive "possibility" with regard to everything *(se habet indifferenter ad multa; et sic quoddammodo est in potentia, nisi mota per aliquid activum):*[370] as a kind of "intra-worldly *divinity*" *(sui causa),*[371] but as an "*intra-worldly* divinity" *(in potentia)*[372] — the power of determination as the powerlessness of determinability.

The logical conclusion to the foregoing, then, is provided by those few fragmentary traces that can be found in Thomas concerning the *beautiful.* With regard to the true[373] and the good,[374] the beautiful signifies that which is "complete in itself" ("modified and specified in itself," *in seipso modificatum et specificatum*) "in pure form" ("by reason of the formal cause," *de ratione causae formalis*), and so, logically bears, in a pure form, the very form we have just encountered in the true and the good. We can understand, then, on the one hand, why Thomas has a penchant for portraying God with the features of the artist *(artifex).* The words "creative" and "pure form," which are proper to the character of the beautiful, are the very words he uses to speak of God: *Creator* and *Forma Ipsa.* The theological aspect of the true and the good thus finds in the beautiful its most emphatic mode. But, on the other hand, if the world appears as a "work of art" *(artificium),* this lends equal emphasis to the creaturely aspect of the true and the good, to the point of that essential "fragility" that (in Solger's felicitous phrase) constitutes the work of art. *In that* the beautiful is in an absolute sense the *perfectio* (in *ex perfectione universi*) and thus more or less convertible with God (which is what lies at the foundation of the peculiar

---

366. Cf. Phil. 2:12-13. — Trans.

367. Thus indeed God moves things in accord with what is suitable to their nature. *Comp. Theol.* c. 129.

368. *Serm.* 174, 2, 2.

369. The inclination itself is not determined to [its object] by something else, but of itself. *De Ver.* q. 22, a. 5, corp.

370. [The human will is] indifferently determined to many [acts]; and thus, were it not moved by something actual, is in some sense only in potency. *De Ver.* q. 24, a. 14, corp.

371. *De Ver.* q. 24, a. 1, corp.

372. *De Ver.* q. 24, a. 14, corp.

373. *Summa Th.* I, q. 6, a. 4. [Given the content of this article, the accuracy of this reference seems uncertain. — Trans.]

374. *De Ver.* q. 22, a. 1, ad 12.

demonism of the beautiful), it is also the maximal expression of creaturely frailty.[375] For it constitutes itself in the "swinging back and forth of nothingness"[376] (of which music is the exemplar).

In light of all the foregoing considerations, the analogy distinctive to Thomas would seem to coincide with his understanding of (objective and subjective) relation (as follows from the *ex perfectione universi*). The Aristotelian primacy of the ἀνά thus returns, but only after having passed through Augustine and been reversed in the process: the ἀνά of the *perfectio universi* is the ἄνω, since the "sacral universe" declares itself in the "natural universe." Thus the definition of analogy as a "relation of mutual alterities" (§6, 8) is reprised in a new way: in that it is within the problem of relation (as we just unpacked it in Thomas) that "alterity" opens up. Our remaining task is now to sketch out this decisive aspect of relation.

Because it is synonymous with order *(ordo relatio quaedam est)*,[377] relation seems to aim at balance and, in the final analysis, at a formula for such balance. And yet, it is characteristic of the relation in our *perfectio universi* that every closed system of mutual relatedness is exploded by an *"above-and-beyond."*

This, then, is what characterizes the *universe as oriented "towards God."* We observe this in the realm of the immanent: in the relatedness of spirit[378] and (corporeal, sensible) nature one to the other. To be sure, according to its objective being, the spiritual soul in man is the intrinsically corresponding form of bodily life in its full scope *(anima . . . est quo corpus humanum habet esse actu)*,[379] such that this belongs to the soul's very essence *(hoc est ei essentiale, quod sit corporis forma)*,[380] and such that the soul is constituted as "this" (individually differentiated) spiritual soul only in and through the life of the body *(anima . . . individuate . . . secundum habitudinem ad materiam in qua est)*.[381] But, at the same time, it *is* this intrinsically corresponding form in that it is independently "above-and-beyond" the body *(non . . . a corpore totaliter comprehensa quasi ei immersa,*

---

375. *Hinfälligkeit.* — Trans.

376. *Im "schwingenden Nichts."* — Trans.

377. *De Ver.* q. 7, a. 9, corp.

378. *Geist.* — Trans.

379. The soul is that whereby the human body has its act of being. *De An.* a. 1, corp.

380. It is essential to it that it be the form of the body. *De Spir. Creat.* a. 9, ad 4.

381. The soul [is] . . . individuated . . . on account of its relation to the matter in which it resides. *De An.* a. 6, ad 13.

. . . sed excedat capacitatem totius materiae corporalis),[382] "exceeding" every closed correspondence *(superexcedat corporis proportionem)*[383] by virtue of its "being-beyond" *(esse elevatum supra corpus non dependens ab eo).*[384] The same holds true for subjective consciousness. Intellectual reflection[385] is, on the one hand, entirely bound to the sphere of sense experience *(tantum se nostra naturalis cognitio extendere potest, in quantum manuduci potest per sensibilia),*[386] such that every intellectual operation upon the *sensibilia* (by the *intellectus agens*) is nevertheless a receptivity with respect to them *(in potentia . . . ad similitudines quae sunt principia sentiendi),*[387] to the point of a necessary dependency *(perturbata vi sensitiva interiori de necessitate perturbatur intellectus).*[388] On the other hand, however, not only is this condition of being bound to the senses a "principle" *(principium humanae cognitionis)*[389] to which, negatively speaking, "not everything is subject," so as not to require that "everything follow from it" *(non tamen oportet quod quidquid ab homine cognoscitur, sit sensui subiectum vel per effectum sensibilem immediate cognoscatur);*[390] it is also, positively speaking, a "principle" in the sense of a point of departure to something beyond itself *(ex his quae sensus apprehendit, mens in aliqua **ulteriora** manuducatur).*[391] Just as within the subjective being of worldly immanence (between spirit and nature) the relation is a "transcending correlation"[392] (a *habitudo,* but *superexcedens*), within subjective consciousness (between thought and sense-experience) it is a relation of "departure in approach"[393] *(intellectus*

---

382. [It is] not . . . entirely comprehended by the body, as if it were immersed in the body, . . . but exceeds the capacity of all bodily matter. *De An.* a. 2, corp.

383. It surpasses the measure of the body. *De Spir. Creat.* a. 2, ad 19.

384. Being elevated above the body, it does not depend upon it. *De An.* a. 1, corp.

385. *Das geistige Denken.* — Trans.

386. Our natural knowledge can go only so far as it is able to be led by sensible things. *Summa Th.* I, q. 12, a. 12, corp.

387. [The soul] is in potency . . . with regard to those likenesses that are the principles of sensation. *Summa Th.* I, q. 84, a. 3, corp.

388. When there is a perturbation of an interior sensitive power, there is of necessity a perturbation of the intellect. *De Ver.* q. 5, a. 10, corp.

389. *De Malo* q. 6, a. 1, ad 18.

390. Nonetheless, it does not follow that whatever is known by a man is subject to sense or known immediately by way of a sensible effect. *De Malo* q. 6, a. 1, ad 18.

391. From the things the senses apprehend the mind is led on to something more. *De Ver.* q. 10, a. 6, ad 2.

392. *Überhinausgehenden Zueinander.* — Trans.

393. *"Von-weg im Hin-zu."* — Trans.

abstrahit a phantasmatibus; et tamen non intelligit nisi convertendo se ad phantasmata).[394]

We are now prepared to see how this same relation leads to the transcendent: in the relation between the creature and God. On the one hand, objectively, so entirely is God the *one* comprehensive archetype of the creature *(essentia Dei est perfecta similitudo omnium quantum ad omnia . . . sicut universale principium omnium)*[395] that he relates to the creature as unity to multiplicity *(ea quae sunt multipliciter et divisim in aliis, in ipso sunt simpliciter et unite).*[396] But, on the other hand, he is so far above-and-beyond such an archetype[397] ("the *supereminent* likeness of things," *supereminens similitudo rerum*)[398] that all commonality is exploded, since God is *extra omne genus.*[399] For this reason, to be sure, the knowledge of God begins subjectively with a positive, approximating attempt *(intellectus negationis . . . fundatur in aliqua affirmatione)*[400] to grasp God as the unity of his manifold reflection in the world *(est unus re et multiplex secundum rationem, quia intellectus noster ita multipliciter apprehendit eum, sicut res multipliciter eum repraesentant).*[401] But God is not truly recognized as God until we become aware of him not merely as that "being than which none greater can be thought" *(ens quo maius cogitari non potest),* but as that "being who is beyond anything that can be thought" *(aliquid supra id quod cogitari potest)*[402] and, hence, as the one who is known in not-being-

394. Intellect abstracts from phantasms; nevertheless, it cannot understand save by turning to phantasms. *Summa Th.* I, q. 85, a. 5, ad 2.

395. The divine essence is a perfect likeness of all things of every sort . . . as it is the principle of all things. *Summa Th.* I, q. 84, a. 2, ad 3.

396. Those things that are multiple and separate in others abide in him simply and singly. *Summa Th.* I, q. 13, a. 4, ad 3.

397. *Das Überhinaus solchen Urbildes.* — Trans.

398. *De Pot.* q. 7, a. 7, ad 5.

399. *Summa Th.* I, q. 4, a. 3, ad 2.

400. Knowledge of a negation . . . is based upon a certain affirmation. *De Pot.* q. 7, a. 5, corp.

401. He is objectively one and multiple according to our reason, because our intellect apprehends him in a multiple manner, just as things represent him in a multiple fashion. *Summa Th.* I, q. 13, a. 4, ad 3.

402. *Summa c. Gent.* I, 5. Anselm of Canterbury himself intensifies his formula: *non solum es quo maius cogitari nequit, sed es quiddam maius quam cogitari potest* (not only are you that than which a greater cannot be thought, but you are something greater than can be thought at all) (Proslog. 15).

known *(hoc est ultimum cognitionis humanae de Deo, quod sciat se Deum nescire).*[403] Precisely in that not-knowing becomes a kind of knowledge by negation[404] *(de eo quid est . . . cognoscere non possumus, nisi in quantum de eo cognoscimus quid non est),*[405] God's "not withholding himself from a formal figure of thought" *(non . . . ita quod intellectus noster secundum nullam formam intelligibilem Deo assimiletur)*[406] is realized here "below by an evasion of every formal figure in the above-and-beyond" *(Deus subterfugit formam intellectus nostri quasi omnem formam intellectus nostri excedens).*[407]

The supreme instance of this relation, then, is the span intrinsic to the supernatural "vision of God" *(visio beatifica).* As the *"actus perfectissimus intellectus,"*[408] this vision is the ultimate defining end[409] intrinsic to the spiritual life *(ultima perfectio cuiuslibet rei est, quando pertingit ad suum principium),*[410] an immediate return into God corresponding to an immediate origination from God[411] — and yet, it is a defining end as far beyond every proportion as God in himself is beyond the creature *(excedit proportionem cuiuslibet naturae creatae, soli Deo connaturalis existens).*[412] Within the spiritual creature there is a "capacity" for this vision *(capax est summi boni per visionem et fruitionem),*[413] and an "aptitude" *(habilitas . . .*

---

403. This is the ultimate human knowledge of God: to know that one does not know God. *De Pot.* q. 7, a. 5, ad 14.

404. *Abscheidung:* one should perhaps render this as "leave-taking," in keeping with the image of Moses espying only the hinder parts of God in Exodus 33:18-23 (and in keeping, one might add, with Gregory of Nyssa's gloss on this episode as an image of the soul's perpetual "pursuit" of the God who is "ever greater" and "ever beyond"). — Trans.

405. We cannot know what he is . . . except to the degree that we know what he is not. *De Ver.* q. 10, a. 12, ad 7.

406. Not . . . as though our intellect were in no intelligible way similar to him. *De Pot.* q. 7, a. 5, ad 13.

407. God eludes the form of our intellect, as he is beyond every form our intellect can conceive. *De Pot.* q. 7, a. 5, ad 13. [*"Unten durch entgehen im Über-Hinaus über alle Form-Gestalt."* — Trans.]

408. *De Pot.* q. 13, a. 4, corp.

409. *Sinnziel.* — Trans.

410. The ultimate perfection of anything comes when it reaches its principle. *De Ver.* q. 8, a. 1, corp.

411. *De Ver.* q. 8, a. 1, corp; *De Ver.* q. 20, a. 4, corp.

412. [The vision of God's essence] exceeds the measure of any created nature, being connatural to God alone. *De Ver.* q. 27, a. 2, corp.

413. It is a capacity for the highest good through vision and enjoyment. *De Malo* q. 5, a. 1, corp.

sicut potentiae susceptivae)[414] — but at the same time a complete "incapacity from one's own power" *(naturae propriae principia non sufficient)*[415] and a "need to be elevated beyond one's nature" *(ipsa natura hominis elevetur ad quandam dignitatem, secundum quam talis finis sit ei competens).*[416] There is, therefore, in the essence of spiritual being, not only a "natural inclination" towards the vision of God *(homo naturaliter inclinetur),*[417] but a "natural restless longing" *(desiderium . . . non quiescit, nisi ad summum rerum cardinem et factorem pervenerit);*[418] and yet, at the same time, not only is the "inclination" itself the work of supernatural grace *(ut homini detur aliquid, . . . per quod inclinetur eius appetitus in finem illum),*[419] but even the knowledge of the existence of such a supernatural goal is grace *(cum ipsum donum gratiae cognitionem hominis excedat).*[420] This rhythm of the "above-and-beyond in the within" is consummated in that, in the realization of this vision, one indeed sees "God through God" *(videre . . . essentiam Dei impossibile est nisi ipsa divina essentia sit forma intellectus quo intelligit)*[421] — but in such a way that he appears as the one who is more incomprehensible, beyond all comprehension on the part of the one contemplating him *(impossibile est . . . quod intellectus creatus divinam substantiam comprehendat).*[422]

And yet, at this ultimate point (since it involves God's self-communication), we can already see how our rhythm is reversed: in the way that the *universe* is construed *"from God."* When we considered the universe as directed "towards God," we saw how the ascending "above-and-beyond" effectively exploded the enclosure of reciprocal relatedness. When we con-

---

414. An aptitude [for grace on the part of a rational nature] . . . [is] like that of a receptive potency. *De Malo* q. 2, a. 12, corp.

415. The principles of [the rational creature's] nature are not sufficient [to attain to the vision and enjoyment of God]. *De Malo* q. 5, a. 1, corp.

416. [It is necessary] that man's nature itself be elevated to such a dignity that such an end might be suited to it. *De Ver.* q. 27, a. 2, corp.

417. Man naturally inclines. . . . *In Boeth. de Trin.* q. 6, a. 4, ad 5.

418. Desire . . . does not rest unless it reach the highest point of reference and maker of things. *Summa c. Gent.* III, 50.

419. [It is necessary] that something be given man . . . whereby his appetite might be inclined towards that end. *De Ver.* q. 27, a. 2, corp.

420. Since the very gift of grace surpasses man's knowledge. *De Ver.* q. 24, a. 15, corp.

421. To see . . . the essence of God is impossible but that the divine essence itself be the form of the intellect through which it understands. *Summa c. Gent.* III, 52.

422. It is impossible . . . that a created intellect should comprehend the divine substance. *Summa c. Gent.* III, 55.

sider the universe as coming "from God," on the other hand, what we see is a descending "above-and-beyond." In the first case, God "sets himself apart" as the above-and-beyond at the very moment when he might appear as the immanent unity of the universe. In the second case, the creature "sets itself apart" as a (relatively independent and self-efficacious) above-and-beyond at the very moment when it could appear as if it were God alone working within all the creature's works. This is clear from what we have just shown. The vision of God is essentially a vision of "God through God," which is to say, by all appearances, the clearest case of God alone working all things.[423] And yet the creature admitted to this vision is created in such a way that, "in its nature," it brings to it a "capacity" *(capax)*, an "aptitude" *(habilitas)*, a "natural inclination" *(naturaliter inclinetur)*, and a "natural longing" *(desiderium naturale)*. Here, the great law, which expresses the descending "above-and-beyond," becomes abundantly clear: the law of secondary causality *(causae secundae)*.

So entirely is God the creative primordial ground of all being *(a primo uno procedunt omnia una, et a primo ente omnia entia, et a primo bono omnia bona)*[424] that all being is always simply "the moment" of its directly proceeding from him *(secundum se . . . est in instanti. Unde operatio Dei, quae est per se causa quod res sit, non est alia, secundum quod facit principium essendi et essendi continuationem)*.[425] And yet this being is so entirely "set apart" from God that God is "in it" *(intra rem quamlibet)*[426] not only in that he not only does not belong to it *(non sicut pars essentiae)*,[427] but also in that he does not "enter" into its essence *(non intret essentiam rerum creatarum)*,[428] such that created being is genuinely "set-apart" by its own inner "essentiality."[429] So entirely is God the *one* who works all things *(quod Deus in omnibus intime operatur;*[430] as *propria et immediata causa . . . magis intima cuique quam*

423. *Alleinwirksamkeit.* — Trans.
424. From the first One proceed all unities, from the first Being all beings, and from the first Good all goods. *De Ver.* q. 5, a. 1, ad 7.
425. [The existence of things that endure] according to itself . . . is in an instant. Hence, the operation of God, which is by itself the cause of a thing's existence, is not distinct as, on the one hand, the principle of a thing's being and, on the other, the principle of its continuation in being. *De Pot.* q. 5, a. 1, ad 2.
426. Within everything whatsoever. *De Pot.* q. 3, a. 7, corp.
427. Not as part of its essence. *De Pot.* q. 3, a. 7, corp.
428. Does not enter into the essence of created things. *De Pot.* q. 3, a. 5, ad 1.
429. *De Ver.* q. 21, a. 5, ad 1.
430. That God operates within in all things. *Summa Th.,* I, q. 105, a. 5, corp.

292

ipsum sit intimum sibi)[431] that he exercises his most immediate operation even and precisely within the free spiritual essence of the creature: he is immediate to it in its being *(inter mentem nostram et Deum nihil cadit medium),*[432] immediate to it in its knowledge *(mens . . . dicitur immediate formari ab ipsa veritate prima),*[433] immediate to it in its will — and not only as its defining end *(ipse Deus immediate est finis humanae vitae),*[434] but as the efficient cause within it *(ipse solus imprimere potest in voluntatem nostram).*[435] And yet not only does the *one* who works all things bind his working to the distinct nature of creatures *(operatur in unoquoque secundum eius proprietatem),*[436] so much so as to cause freedom precisely "as" freedom *(voluntatem movet . . . , non ut necessitate, sed ut indeterminate se habentem ad multa),*[437] inasmuch as God's ever greater proximity to the creature is the cause of an ever greater independence on the creature's part *(quanto aliqua natura Deo vicinior, tanto minus ab eo inclinatur et magis nata est seipsam inclinare).*[438] What is more, this setting apart of the creature from God, as the most proper revelation of God's bounty *(ex eminentia bonitatis suae;*[439] *ex eius perfectissima plenitudine),*[440] happens in such a way that the creature, thus set apart, seems almost to assume the features of God: appearing as an original ground of itself *(causa sui ipsius),*[441] as a creative cause *(quod causae sint),*[442] as a generous cause *(quod aliis esse et bonitatem largiretur),*[443] and as providence for others *(non solum . . . quod sint provisae, sed etiam quod*

431. The proper and immediate cause . . . nearer to something than it is to itself in its inmost parts. *De Ver.* q. 8, a. 16, ad 12.

432. Between our mind and God no medium interposes itself. *De Ver.* q. 27, a. 1, ad 10.

433. Mind . . . is said to be immediately formed by the first Truth itself. *De Ver.* q. 18, a. 1, ad 7.

434. God himself, immediately, is the end of human life. *De Ver.* q. 5, a. 10, corp.

435. He alone is able to make an impress upon our will. *De Ver.* q. 5, a. 10, corp.

436. It operates in each thing in accord with what is proper to it. *Summa Th.* I, q. 83, a. 1, ad 3.

437. It moves the will . . . , not as by necessity, but as indeterminately inclining towards many things. *De Malo* q. 6, a. 1, corp.

438. The nearer a nature is to God, so much the less is it inclined by another and so much the more greatly is it native to it that it incline itself. *De Ver.* q. 22, a. 4, corp.

439. From the eminence of his goodness. *De Ver.* q. 11, a. 1, corp.

440. From his most perfect plenitude. *De Spir. Creat.* a. 10, ad 16.

441. The cause of itself. *De Ver.* q. 24, a. 1, corp.

442. That they might be causes. *De Ver.* q. 11, a. 1, corp.

443. That they might bestow being and goodness on other things. *De Ver.* q. 5, a. 8, corp.

provideant)[444] — even to the point that the creature is permitted to contradict God *(Deus plus amat quod est magis bonum, et ideo magis vult praesentiam magis boni quam absentiam minus mali . . . : ideo ad hoc quod aliqua bona maiora eliciantur, permittit aliquos in mala culpa cadere, quae maxime secundum genus sunt odibilia).*[445]

In the end, therefore, what distinguishes this entire approach is that it is oriented not so much by the self-sufficiency of an Aristotelian "natural universe," but explicitly by the "sacral universe" of the Areopagite: by, that is, that "most noble mode of divine imitation" *(nobilissimus modus divinae imitationis)* wherein creatures are "dispensers of perfection" *(ut aliis perfectionem largiantur)*, which is another way of saying with the Areopagite that we are "God's co-laborers (in the soul's salvation)"[446] — just as this is simply another version of Colossians 1:24: "filling up what is lacking in Christ's afflictions for the sake of his body, the church."

Accordingly, the connection between the web of relations, which was discussed earlier, and this "above-and-beyond," which both ascends (towards God) and descends (from God) is one in which the enclosure of reciprocal relatedness is exploded to ever greater degrees. There is a break within the immanent logic of the first "above-and-beyond" (of the universe towards God) just where it seems to reach its summit. For, in keeping with the fundamental concept of the second "above-and-beyond" (that of the universe coming from God), the "above-and-beyond" of the all-sovereign God who works all things becomes manifest precisely where this all-sovereign omnificence seems to be put in question: in the amplification of the creature's independence to the point of a kind of autonomy *(domina suorum actuum)*.[447] But then, the moment this independence (following the immanent logic of its concept) would seek to become absolute autonomy, the first "above-and-beyond" (going towards God) is reintroduced within the second "above-and-beyond" (precisely *because* it comes from God). It is therefore not simply the case that a general "above-and-beyond" is instantiated in two concrete instances. Nor is it simply

444. Not only . . . that they are provided for, but that they also provide. *De Ver.* q. 5, a. 5, corp.

445. God loves more the greater good — and thus more greatly wills the presence of the greater good — than he does the absence of the lesser evil . . . : thus, in order that certain greater goods might be brought forth, he permits some to fall into evil crimes, of a kind most odious. *De Ver.* q. 5, a. 5, ad 3.

446. *De Ver.* q. 9, a. 2, corp.

447. [It is characteristic of the will that it be] master over its own acts. *De Ver.* q. 22, a. 5, ad 7, in contr.

the case that the first "above-and-beyond" is oriented towards the second and fulfilled in it. It is rather the case that, to put it pointedly, the process runs repeatedly in a circle — though not in such a way as to make this circle some kind of "ultimate formula." Rather, the clearest sign of God as God is that, with respect to him, even the subtlest formulae fail. This is not only the case with the formula "within the in towards the beyond" — the *im In zum Über* — as seen in the breaking off of the first "above-and-beyond" into the second. Nor is it only the case with the formula "within the beyond towards the in" — the *im Über zum In* — as seen in the reintroduction of the first "above-and-beyond" within the second. It is rather the case even with the formula of an immanent rhythm between the "within the in towards the beyond" and the "within the beyond towards the in." For such an immanent rhythm would be possible only as an *in-between* between the creature and God. But, seen from one side, such an in-between would be a semi-divine *creature*-liness (and hence would destroy the first "above-and-beyond"); seen from the other, it would be a semi-*divine* creatureliness (and hence would destroy the second "above-and-beyond").[448] Precisely the ἀνά of such an immanent rhythm is nothing but the manifestation of the greater urgency of the ἄνω. The "relation" shows itself to be transparent — beyond the rhythm of the "above-and-beyond" — to an explicit *theologia negativa* of the *perfectio universi*. Consequently, if the analogy distinctive to Thomas is seen in the *perfectio universi*, then the *perfectio universi* in turn, and even more acutely, reveals the *analogy*.

This question of the immanent rhythm, though, implicitly raises the question of something that is in other respects peculiar to Aquinas and that, indeed, inwardly shapes his conception of the *perfectio universi:* the question of the *"middle."* The rhythm of the first (ascending) "above-and-beyond" serves to overcome the excessive enclosedness[449] of a totality. The rhythm of the second (descending) "above-and-beyond" tempers the excess of a divine agency,[450] which alone is efficacious, into the proportion[451] of a relative all-unity[452] between Divine omnificence[453] and the creature's own proper agency.

448. *Halb-Gott-**Geschöpf**-lichkeit; Halb-**Gott**-Geschöpf-lichkeit.* — Trans.
449. *Übermaß der Geschloßenheit.* — Trans.
450. *Übermaß einer göttlichen Allein-Wirksamkeit.* — Trans.
451. *Gleichmaß.* — Trans.
452. *Ganz-Einheit.* — Trans.
453. *All-Wirksamkeit.* Przywara presumably capitalizes the adjective "divine" in this instance in order to emphasize, over against his understanding of the Lutheran and Reformed traditions, that *Allwirksamkeit* and not *Alleinwirksamkeit* is properly attributed to the divine. — Trans.

And so we come to the point that this "middle" could be taken as *the* defining word for Thomas Aquinas's method: *fides . . . catholica media via incedit:*[454] applying to the fundamental, specifically philosophical question of *potentia* and *actus*,[455] as well as to the fundamental, specifically theological questions of the relation between grace and freedom,[456] and of God and man in Christ.[457] It is not without reason, however, that this middle is attributed to the *fides catholica*. Which is to say that it is the more concise — and indeed more precise — formula for the rhythm of the "above-and-beyond," as we have just seen.

Certainly, with respect to many of its features, it could seem to be an immanent middle: *within the human being*. Man's conscious life is situated, according to its formal object, in the middle between the purely material and the purely spiritual, between *forma prout in materia corporali* and *forma sine materia subsistens:* as the *medio modo* of the freely suspended *forma in materia quidem corporali . . . , non tamen prout est in tali materia*.[458] Logically, therefore, this detached suspendedness consists in an inner universality: in the "universe as it were" of the human soul, whose features are virtually those of the divine all-unity: *anima hominis fit omnia quoddamodo secundum sensum et intellectum, in quo cognitionem habentia ad Dei similitudinem quoddamodo appropinquant, in quo omnia praeexistunt*.[459] It is a characteristic of this middle, however, that it seems from below to be what is highest *(tota operatio inferioris naturae terminatur ad hominem sicut perfectissimum)*,[460] but seems from above to be what is lowest *(inter substantias intellectuales secundum naturae ordinem infimas esse animas humanas)*.[461] The human being, as "middle," thus becomes a "border as transition"[462] *(in confinio corporalium et*

454. The Catholic faith takes the middle way. *De Ver.* q. 24, a. 12, corp.

455. *De Ver.* q. 11, a. 1, corp.

456. *De Ver.* q. 24, a. 12, corp.

457. *Summa Th.* III, q. 2, a. 6, corp.

458. [There is] form as existing in corporeal matter . . . / [the object of angelic knowledge is] form subsisting without material . . . / [human intellect occupies] a middle modality . . . / [thus it is proper to it to know] form that does in fact exist in corporeal matter . . . / not as existing in such matter. *Summa Th.* I, q. 85, a. 1, corp.

459. The human soul in a sense becomes all things, according to sense and intellect, whereby all things having knowledge approach the likeness of God, in Whom all things preexist. *Summa Th.* I, q. 80, a. 1, corp.

460. The whole operation of lower nature terminates with man as that which is most perfect. *De An.* a. 8, corp.

461. Among intellectual substances, according to the order of nature, human souls are the lowest. *Summa Th.* III, q. 89, a. 1, corp.

462. *Grenze als Übergang.* — Trans.

separatarum substantiarum).[463] But it is a "border as transition" in the stricter sense of "intersection as divergence."[464] For the corporeal and the spiritual are distinguished not only by kind, but also by genus: *res . . . materiales et intelligibiles sunt omnino diversorum generum.*[465] As a result, they are distinguished to the point of a divergence of "directions" that, when reversed, again converge: in the case of the corporeal, the direction is toward the lowest level of imperfection as what is "primary" *(in substantiis . . . materialibus attenduntur diversi gradus speciem diversificantes in ordine ad primum principium quod est materia);*[466] in the case of the spiritual it is towards the highest level of perfection as what is "primary" *(in substantiis . . . immaterialibus ordo graduum diversorum specierum attenditur . . . secundum comparationem ad primum agens quod oportet esse perfectissimum).*[467] For this reason, however, as a final determination, the second orientation receives so preponderant an emphasis that the first orientation becomes its function: the corporeal is primarily preexistent in the spiritual *(omnia materialia in ipsis Angelis praeexistunt simplicius . . . et immaterialius quam in ipsis rebus),*[468] since it is proper to pure spirit that it knows the corporeal from the vantage of God's creative knowledge *(dicitur . . . Angelus accepisse in Verbo cognitionem ipsius [rei] ut fiendae).*[469] And thus it is from this vantage that the whole order of things is realized: as the structure[470] produced by the working of the purely spiritual (in its three "hierarchies") upon the whole: from the "ideas in God" *(rationes rerum in Deo)* as the "goal" *(consideratio finis),* to the "universal causes" *(in causis universalibus)* as "that which disposes" *(dispositio universalis de agendis),* to the "particular effects" *(determinationem ad speciales effectus)* as the "appli-

463. In the confines of bodies and discrete substances. *Summa Th.* III, q. 89, a. 1, corp.

464. *Eines Sich-schneidens als Sich-scheidens:* "intersection (or self-scission) as divergence (or self-divorce, departure, severance)"; at a crossroads, the point of convergence is also the point of divergence. — Trans.

465. Material and intelligible objects are of entirely different genera. *De Ver.* q. 8, a. 9, corp.

466. In material substances one observes that the diverse grades diversifying the species are ordered towards the first principle, which is matter. *De An.* a. 7, corp.

467. In immaterial substances one observes an order of the grades of diverse species . . . according to its relative position with regard to the first agency, which must needs be the most perfect. *De An.* a. 7, corp.

468. In the angels themselves, all material things preexist more simply . . . and in a more immaterial fashion than they exist themselves. *Summa Th.* I, q. 57, a. 1, corp.

469. The angel is said to receive knowledge in the Word of (the thing) itself as of something yet to be made. *De Pot.* q. 4, a. 2, ad 12.

470. *Gliederung.* — Trans.

cation" thereof *(applicatio dispositionis ad effectum, quae est operis executio)*.[471] The human being, as "middle," thus becomes the "passageway of the above to the below": permeable in its spiritual life to the pure spirits[472] who govern the corporeal *(omnia corporalia regentur per Angelos)*.[473]

So, logically, now *pure spirit* appears to be the connecting middle. The above of God and the below of the sub-spiritual make contact in the being of pure spirit: *ea quae sunt infra Angelum et ea quae sunt supra ipsum sunt quodam modo in substantia eius*.[474] Its knowledge is effectively a middle *(media inter . . .)* between a receptive *(cognitione quae est a rebus accepta)* and a productive *(cognitione quae sit causa rerum)* mode of knowledge.[475] Its freedom preserves the middle *(medium locum tenet)* between the immutable freedom of God and the vacillating freedom of the human being *(participans aliqualiter cum utroque extremorum)*.[476] Thus, what turned out to be the defining end of the human being *(finem ultimum hominis)* proves to be more truly the definition of pure spirit: the "bearing of the all within itself" *(ut in ea describatur totus ordo universi et causarum eius)*,[477] since its own form of being is that of "an all unto itself" *(substantiae intellectuales . . . redeunt ad essentiam suam reditione completa)*.[478] But precisely here, where pure spirit could be mistaken for God himself *(intellectus Angeli est deiformis)*,[479] they are once again sharply separated: the *ut in ea . . . totus ordo universi et causarum eius* is simply a provisional similitude[480] of that which

---

471. [The highest hierarchy (of angels) contemplates] the reasons of things in God . . . / [to this first hierarchy belongs] consideration of the end . . . / [the second contemplates them] in the universal causes . . . / [to this middle hierarchy belongs] the universal disposition of that which is to be done . . . / [the third contemplates their] determination to particular effects . . . / [to this last hierarchy belongs] the application of this disposition to the effect, which is the execution of the work. *Summa Th.* I, q. 108, a. 6, corp.

472. *Summa Th.* I, q. 111.

473. All things material are governed by angels. *Summa Th.* I, q. 110, a. 1, corp.

474. Those things that are below an angel and those things that are above him are, in a certain manner, immanent to his substance. *Summa Th.* I, q. 55, a. 1, ad 3.

475. [An angel's knowledge is] a mean between . . . / the knowledge that is the cause of things / [and] the knowledge that is received from things. *De Pot.* q. 3, a. 4, ad 13.

476. Participating equally in the extremes found in either direction. *De Ver.*, q. 24, a. 2, corp.

477. That in it might be represented the order of the universe and of its causes. *De Ver.* q. 2, a. 2, corp.

478. Intellectual substances . . . return to their essence with a complete return. *De Ver.* q. 1, a. 9, corp. [*"Zu einem All in sich Geschlossensein."* — Trans.]

479. The intellect of an angel is deiform. *De Malo* q. 7, a. 9, ad 1.

480. *Vordeutendes Gleichnis.* — Trans.

takes place in, from, and through God alone — in the supernatural vision of God, in which the all opens up before the visionary in God: *in visione Dei . . . quid est quod non videant qui Videntem omnia vident.*[481] For all its participation in the creative knowledge of God, pure spirit — as the opposite pole to the corporeal — is still confined within the universe *(licet creaturae corporales et spirituales sint disparatae secundum proprias naturas, tamen sunt connexae secundum ordinem universi),*[482] so much so that its confinement within the universe directly undercuts[483] its universal supervision, since this supervision, despite its *a priori* character *(cognitionem . . . ut fiendae),* grasps merely what happens to exist, but not the future.[484] In this respect pure spirit is itself mutable *(ipsi Angeli creaturae sunt),*[485] an "evening" intellection joined to an "evening" being *(esse rerum in intelligentia angelica comprehenditur sub vespertina cognitione, sicut et esse rerum in propria natura).*[486] Consequently, humanity and pure spirit now come together in this *genus logicum* of mutability *(cum earum quidditas non sit earum esse),*[487] whereas between God and pure spirit there is set an "infinite distance" *(Deus in infinitum distat ab Angelo).*[488]

Thus it is *God* who is the "middle": as the one in whom alone all multiplicity and all correlated antitheses are one *(hoc ipsum ad perfectam Dei unitatem pertinet quod ea quae sunt multipliciter et divisim in aliis, in ipso*

481. [The ultimate end of man consists] in the vision of God, [for, in the words of Gregory,] "What is there that they do not see who see him who sees all things?" (Gregory the Great, *Dialogues* IV, 33). *De Ver.* q. 2, a. 2, corp.

482. Though corporeal and spiritual creatures may be disparate according to their proper natures, they are connected according to the order of the universe. *De Pot.* q. 3, a. 18, ad 16.

483. Literally, "cuts right through," *mitten hindurch schneidet.* — Trans.

484. *Summa Th.* I, q. 57, a. 3, ad 3.

485. The angels are themselves creatures. *Summa Th.* I, q. 58, a. 6, ad 3.

486. The being of things is comprehended within angelic knowledge under a vesperal knowledge, as also the being of things in their proper nature. *Summa Th.* I, q. 58, a. 6, ad 3. [According to Thomas, angels can be said to possess both "morning knowledge" (that is, the knowledge of things as contemplated in the Logos) and "evening knowledge" (that is, a knowledge of things in their own being), which — while not separate — are distinct. In either case, such knowledge is infused in the angelic intellect by God, and so all angelic knowledge is always complete and *in actu*; nevertheless, angelic intellect still contains potential (in that God might impart to it special revelations) and is still finite (in that its knowledge of creatures is multiple and successive). — Trans.]

487. Since their essence is not their existence. *Summa Th.* I, q. 88, a. 2, ad 4.

488. God is infinitely distant from the angel. *Summa Th.* I, q. 56, a. 3, ad 2.

sunt simpliciter et unite).[489] Thus (passing over man as middle and spirit as middle), the Aristotelian middle passes over into the middle of the Areopagite: *quod in inferioribus continetur deficienter et partialiter et multipliciter, in superioribus continetur eminenter et per quandam totalitatem et simplicitatem.*[490] It is a middle "from above, descending to the antithetical" *(quod in inferioribus . . . , in superioribus),* and only as such (and "to this extent") is it an (Aristotelian) "middle between antitheses." It is a middle as a "unity-in-itself vis-à-vis the manifold" *(quod deficienter et partialiter et multipliciter . . . , eminenter et per quandam totalitatem et simplicitatem),* and only as such (and "to this extent") is it an (Aristotelian) "middle of equilibrium." Finally, it is a middle as (objectively) "antecedent" *(in superioribus continetur . . . per quandam totalitatem et simplicitatem),* and only as such (and "to this extent") is it an (Aristotelian) "consequent middle." It is a middle in which the "above-and-beyond" has gone from being the "above-and-beyond of a given instance" to that of a wholly sovereign "antecedent above-and-beyond." It is therefore not a middle that (of itself) so closely approximates God as to become a "middle as God" (as is the tendency of a pure Aristotelianism); rather, within the creaturely realm, this middle is the highest possible name for God: *in Deo, sicut in summo rerum vertice, omnia supersubstantialiter praeexistunt secundum ipsum suum simplex esse, ut Dionysius dicit.*[491]

From this middle, understood as "antecedently above-and-beyond," two things follow, whose relation to one another displays a still more precise concept of this middle. On the one hand, all creaturely forms of a middle[492] appear as the (descending) revelation of God as the middle. This is the case with spirit as middle: insofar as in spirit the universe of being[493] is found (objectively) "in advance" in the unity of consciousness (which participates in God's creative knowledge): *ista perfectio ad Angelos quidem derivatur, secundum quod omnia sunt in eorum cognitione, quae sunt a Deo producta per*

---

489. It belongs to the perfect unity of God that those things that are multiple and separate in others abide in him simply and singly. *Summa Th.* I, q. 13, a. 4, ad 3.

490. Whatever is contained in lower beings deficiently and partially and multiply is contained in higher beings eminently and in a certain kind of fullness and simplicity. *Summa Th.* I, q. 57, a. 1, corp.

491. In God, as in the highest summit of things, all things supersubstantially preexist according to his simple being in itself, as Dionysius says (*Divine Names* I, 5). *Summa Th.* I, q. 57, a. 1, corp.

492. *Mitte-Bildungen.* — Trans.

493. *Seins-All.* — Trans.

*formas diversas.*⁴⁹⁴ It is the case with man as middle: insofar as man is, according to his being, all aspects of being in one⁴⁹⁵ and, as such, himself an "all": *ad hominem vero derivatur, . . .* (in that he) *est ex rebus omnibus quodammodo compositus . . . Et propter hoc homo dicitur minor mundus, quia omnes creaturae mundi quodammodo inveniuntur in eo.*⁴⁹⁶ On the other hand, however, all of these revelations of God as middle fall short of the *personal* revelation of God as middle in "the mediator." Christ appears as *the* reality of the way in which God-the-middle takes up the All: as the "infinity that assumes" *(infinita virtus assumentis)*⁴⁹⁷ he is the unifying head of everything from the invisible to the visible,⁴⁹⁸ not only of all persons of every age,⁴⁹⁹ but also of pure spirits.⁵⁰⁰ The nearest likeness to this headship would be the way that man *(huius . . . unionis exemplum in rebus creatis nullum est propinquius quam unio animae rationalis ad corpus)*⁵⁰¹ was seen to be a world *(minor mundus)* and an All *(quodammodo omnia).* The likeness would be stronger still if one were to conceive of the governance of the corporeal world by the purely spiritual as the operation of a single world soul within the *one* world *(esset . . . adhuc similius si fingamus, sicut plerique volunt, esse in mundo animam generalem).*⁵⁰² But these likenesses merely illustrate more clearly not only how the mode of the personal revelation of God as middle in God the mediator is formally beyond all creaturely forms of a middle *(singularis supra omnes modos . . . nobis notos),*⁵⁰³ but how the form of its uniqueness⁵⁰⁴ is the uniqueness of God himself: the "All in one" of the mediator figuring as the immediate visibility of the oneness of God *(sicut . . . Deus*

494. To the angels is imparted this perfection, inasmuch as within their knowledge are all things that are produced by God through diverse forms. *Summa Th.* I, q. 91, a. 1, corp.

495. *Seins-All in Eins.* — Trans.

496. To man however [this perfection] is imparted . . . [in that he] in a certain manner is composed of all things . . . and for this reason man is said to be a little world, since all the creatures in the world are in a certain way found in him. *Summa Th.* I, q. 91, a. 1, corp.

497. The infinite virtue of the one assuming. *De Un. Verbi Incarn.* a. 2, ad 15.

498. *Summa Th.* III, q. 8, a. 6.

499. *Summa Th.* III, q. 8, a. 3, corp.

500. *Summa Th.* III, q. 8, a. 4, corp.

501. Of this . . . union there is among things created no likeness more proximate than that of the union of the rational soul with the body. *De Un. Verbi Incarn.* a. 1, corp.

502. It might be . . . a yet better likeness if we were to suppose, as a great many wish to do, that there is a universal soul in the world. *De Un. Verbi Incarn.* a. 1, corp.

503. The singular beyond all modes . . . known to us. *De Un. Verbi Incarn.* a. 1, corp.

504. *Einzigkeit.* The word *Einzigkeit* here would seem to share the ambiguity of the word "one" that one finds in translations of the Shema (Deut. 6:4), where "one" can signify both oneness (or unicity) and uniqueness. — Trans.

*. . . est ipsa unitas per essentiam, . . . potuit facere novum modum unionis . . . ,
quamvis ad hoc in creaturis nullum sufficiens exemplum inveniretur).*[505] For
this reason the mediacy of the mediator is grounded in the "infinite above-
and-beyond" of God *(infinitus excessus):*[506] not in such a way that God is
comprised within the creature, nor even in such a way that he "enters into a
relation" with it "by extension" *(ut . . . [natura humana] secundum aliquam
proportionem certam a persona verbi excedatur);*[507] nor even in such a way
that God, going beyond himself, lowers himself to the creature *(persona
verbi comprehenditur sub natura verbi nec potest se ad aliquid ultra
extendere);*[508] but rather in such a way that the "below" of the creature is assumed *(magis accipit quod est infra)*[509] into personal unity with the "infinite
above-and-beyond" *(infinitus excessus non excludit quin quodam ineffabili
modo persona Dei humanam naturam sibi copulaverit in unitatem
hypostasis).*[510] But then, accordingly, far from being bound to the highest
possible manifestation of the creaturely, this media-cy[511] of the mediator appears not merely as a human being (rather than pure spirit), but as the expiation for sin (rather than some neutral "crown of creation" independent
thereof).[512] Hence, what is meant by the concrete form that "God as middle"
assumes in the mediator is: a "oneness with the infinite above-and-beyond"
(the *unitas hypostasis* united to the *infinitus excessus* of the *persona Dei*) as a
"oneness with (through the vicarious bearing of) the nothingness of sin."

At this summit of the formality of the middle (and thus the formality
of analogy) as understood by Thomas Aquinas, three conclusive formulae
of his thought become especially clear. As we have just seen, the formality
of the middle takes shape in such a way that, while it "appears" to rise gradually from the creaturely towards God (in the movement of the "universe

505. As . . . God . . . is unity itself by essence, . . . he was able to create a new mode of
union . . . , though to this mode no adequate likeness can be found among creatures. *De Un.
Verbi Incarn.* a. 1, corp.

506. *De Un. Verbi Incarn.* a. 2, ad 15.

507. That . . . [human nature] is exceeded by the Person of the Word by a certain fixed
proportion. *De Un. Verbi Incarn.* a. 2, ad 15.

508. The Person of the Word is comprehended under the nature of the Word, nor can
he extend himself to anything "beyond" that nature. *De Un. Verbi Incarn.* a. 1, ad 14.

509. The greater assumes what is below it. *De Un. Verbi Incarn.* a. 1, ad 14.

510. Infinite excess did not prevent the Person of the Word — by some ineffable mode
— from joining human nature to himself in the unity of his hypostasis. *De Un. Verbi Incarn.*
a. 2, ad 18.

511. *Mitte-tum.* — Trans.

512. *Summa Th.* III, q. 1, a. 3, corp.; *De Ver.* q. 29, a. 4, ad 3.

towards God"), it "exists"[513] in God and therefore derives its existence from God (in the movement of the "universe out of God"). Here we see the imprint of the analogy peculiar to Thomas as it applies to the most important determinations: *ens et bonum et huiusmodi*.[514] There is the *prius* of an ascending analogy of "positive naming," rising from the creature to God (*prius fuerunt creaturis imposita, et ex his ad divinam praedicationem translata*),[515] but it is subject to the *prius* of a descending analogy of "antecedent validity (that can only be discovered)," descending from God to the creature (*quamvis esse et bonum prius inveniantur in Deo*).[516] Secondly, our formality of the middle shows this relation to consist, specifically and concretely, in the connection between its "natural" mode of ascent (from man to the angels) to God and the "supernatural" mode of descent from God (in the "mediator"). Here we see the concrete form of the analogy peculiar to Thomas, as stated in the familiar maxim, which has its basis in his thought: *gratia (fides) non destruit, sed supponit et perficit naturam (rationem)*.[517] The form of this maxim hangs on the double sense of **perficit.** On the one hand, the word *perficit* would suggest that *gratia (fides)* is the "final form": that *natura* and *ratio* exist simply and solely within the one and, in fact, only order, the supernatural order of redemption, which "super-forms"[518] all things through the incarnation. But, on the other hand, this same word *perficit* also implies that *gratia (fides)*, far from being an exclusive "final form" (*non destruit*), is the frame within which *natura (ratio)* not only leads positively (beyond itself) to grace (*supponit*), but also "fulfills" (*perficit*) itself in grace. It is by virtue of the descending supernatural analogy (in which the creature is "found" in "the form of God":[519] *in illius inveniamur forma, in quo tecum est nostra substantia*)[520] that an ascending natural anal-

---

513. *Besteht.* — Trans.

514. [Such names as] "being" and "good" and so on. . . . *De Ver.* q. 4, a. 1, corp.

515. . . . Are applied first to creatures, and from creatures are then translated into divine predication. . . . *De Ver.* q. 4, a. 1, corp.

516. . . . Although being and the good are found first in God. *De Ver.* q. 4, a. 1, corp.

517. Grace [faith] does not destroy, but presupposes and perfects nature [reason]. Cf. *De Ver.* q. 14, a. 10, ad 9; *Summa Th.* I, q. 1, a. 8, ad 2; *Summa Th.* I, q. 2, a. 2, ad 1.

518. *Über-formend.* — Trans.

519. Przywara writes: *in der das Geschöpf in "die Form Gottes" hinein "erfunden" wird.* The use of *erfunden wird*, rather than *gefunden wird*, to render *inveniamur*, as well as the accusative construction *in die*, rather than the dative *in der*, cleverly exploits the dual connotation of *invenire*, but defies seamless translation. — Trans.

520. May we be found in his form, in Whom with Thee is our substance. Postcommunion for the first Christmas Mass.

ogy of *natura (ratio)* is brought to fulfillment, reaching its own perfection in the perfection of God.

Thirdly, it was in the course of our gradual unfolding of the formality of the middle that the decisive and pivotal point was at last laid bare: at the point where the notion of spirit as middle was superseded — *aufgehoben* — by the recognition of God as middle. Here we saw that humanity and pure spirit still belong together within a single *genus logicum* that is pervaded by an "infinite distance" from God.[521] This *genus logicum* is the unity-in-tension[522] of essence *(quidditas)* and existence *(esse):* which is to say that, in the creature, there is a unity of existing essence and "essencing" existence,[523] but as a unity of difference *(cum earum quidditas non sit earum esse);*[524] whereas God alone is the essential unity of "essence as existence" *(sua . . . essentia est suum esse)*[525] and "existence as essence" *(quod non sit aliud in eo essentia quam suum esse).*[526] This grounds the essential relation between God and not-God. Firstly, we see here the sovereign "beyond" of God (in that he, being an essential unity of *essentia* and *esse,* is who he is through himself, in himself, and to himself) within the intimate "in" of God (in that the essence and existence of the creature, and the ever new factical unity of the two, come from him, so that he is "more intimate" to the creature than the creature is to itself).[527] But, secondly, this is to be understood in such a way that the creature's being (in its unity of essence and existence) possesses a true independence, as regards both its essence *(Deus . . . non intret essentiam rerum creatarum)*[528] and its existence *(cuilibet creaturae dat proprium modum essendi).*[529] Thus, thirdly, the creature, in the "I am" of the (factical) unity of its being, bears a true likeness to the "I Am" of the essential unity of divine being *(res Deo similis . . . in esse).*[530] But, then, this is also the fulcrum of the concrete relation between God and not God: in that the mystery of the supernatural incarnation reaches its critical climax in the question concerning the being of Christ: for, on the one hand, the *one* divine Person, as

---

521. *Summa Th.* I, q. 88, a. 2, ad 4; q. 56, a. 3, ad 2.

522. *Spannungs-Eins.* — Trans.

523. *Das Eins daseinden Soseins und soseinden Dasein.* — Trans.

524. Since their essence is not their existence. *Summa Th.* I, q. 88, a. 2, ad 4.

525. His . . . essence is his existence. *Summa Th.* I, q. 3, a. 4, corp.

526. Because there in him essence is nothing other than existence. *Summa Th.* I, q. 3, a. 4, corp.

527. *De Ver.* q. 8, a. 16, ad 12.

528. God . . . does not enter into the essence of created things. *De Pot.* q. 3, a. 5, ad 1.

529. He gives to each creature its own mode of existing. *De Ver.* q. 10, a. 11, ad 8.

530. A thing is like God . . . in its being. *De Pot.* q. 3, a. 7, corp.

one substance, also stipulates the *one* divine *esse* of Christ (*unum esse simpliciter propter unum esse aeternum suppositi*);[531] but, on the other hand, the reality of Christ's humanity at the same time includes the *being* of his humanity as an *esse secundarium,* though not *accidentale,*[532] in the mode of a *nova habitudo esse personalis praeexistentis ad naturam humanam.*[533] It thus becomes evident how, even and precisely in its distinctiveness, the analogy proper to Thomas Aquinas's thought culminates in the **analogia entis**: the *entis* signifies so great a separation between God and creature that there is no common *genus* whatsoever between them (*si . . . non in genere . . .* , then *secundum aliqualem analogiam sicut ipsum esse est commune omnibus*)[534] — but even so, it is precisely here that, at the root, a radically positive unity is declared (*illa quae sunt a Deo, assimilantur ei, in quantum sunt entia, ut primo et universali principio totius esse*).[535]

The *analogia entis,* in the distinct form in which we encounter it in Thomas Aquinas, is characterized here by the inner relation between two terms that he uses when referring to humanity and the world: he speaks of humanity as the border (*in confinio*) between nature and spirit[536] and of the world as a *perfectio (universi).*[537] Whereas for Plato it was ultimately a matter of the "immortal struggle" (ἀθάνατος μάχη); and for Aristotle, the "torso" (κολοβόν); and for Augustine, the "vigilant night" (*vigilat ista nocte . . .*), for Thomas it is a matter of the *"perfecting border"*[538] (*confinium* as *perfectio*). The phenomenon of the "border" signifies in each case a "going beyond": from man as middle to spirit as middle to God as middle. But it is precisely this that makes it the phenomenon of "perfection," since the "middle of creation" is constituted by God in the God-man, and this not merely as a human middle, but rather (in the "scandal of the cross") as a human middle within the all-too-human, and as such — in this way — a middle that brings all things to perfection.

---

531. One simple being on account of the one eternal being of the suppositum. *De Un. Verbi Incarn.* a. 4, corp.

532. *De Un. Verbi Incarn.* a. 4, corp.

533. A new relation of the preexistent personal being to human nature. *Summa Th.* III, q. 17, a. 12.

534. If . . . [an agency is] not in any genus . . . , [then the likeness is only] according to a certain analogy, inasmuch as being is itself common to all. *Summa Th.* I, q. 4, a. 3, corp.

535. Those things that come from God, inasmuch as they are beings, are likened to him as to the first and universal principle of all being. *Summa Th.* I, q. 4, a. 3, corp.

536. *De An.* a. 1, corp.

537. *De Spir. Creat.* a. 5, corp.

538. *Vollendende Grenze.* — Trans.

This connects two terms that, from the first, we have noted as properly belonging to Thomas's thought: *sanctificatio* (in the "sacral universe") and *perfectio* (in the "natural universe"). To the degree that everything is "consecrated by separation" from all things and from itself unto God (*sanctificatio* understood as *ab operibus in ipso Deo . . . quiescamus*),[539] it receives the "consecration of participation" in the God who reposes complete within himself (*sanctificatio* as *sicut Deus a rebus conditis in se ipso . . . sufficientiam habens*).[540] In that the order of the incarnation (understood as the *one* factical universe) is perfection in the sense of the "ending" of the end (*perfectio* as "the ultimate": *non enim legi evangelicae aliud status succedit, quae ad perfectum adduxit*),[541] it is perfection in the sense of the positive "duration" of the "perfect" (in the "perfect God") *(verba . . . quae videntur in Scripturis . . . pertinere . . . ad finis propinquitatem . . . sunt . . . referenda . . . ad status mundi dispositionem).*[542]

It is clear here why the problematic of the *analogia entis* is so thoroughly concluded with Thomas Aquinas that it generally goes by his name: because in this version the ἀνά and the ἄνω interpenetrate even in perfection: *proportio* (ἀνά) and *excedens* (ἄνω) as both *proportio* **excedens** and **proportio** *excedens*. As such, it is an ἀνά *of the* ἄνω, in which the ἀνά and the ἄνω are nevertheless preserved, each in its proper essence.

---

539. We are to rest . . . from works in God. *De Pot.* q. 4, a. 2, ad 5.

540. As God [rests] from the things he has made in himself . . . having his sufficiency in himself. *De Pot.* q. 4, a. 2, ad 5.

541. For no other state will succeed that of the law of the gospel, which has brought things to their perfection. *De Pot.* q. 5, a. 6, ad 9.

542. Words . . . that seem in scripture . . . to pertain . . . to the nearness of the end . . . are to be referred . . . to a particular disposition of the state of the world. *De Pot.* q. 5, a. 6, ad 9.

§8 The *Analogia Entis* as a Principle

At this point we have yet to draw the explicit conclusion from the co-implication of the first and second sections. For in reality we have already seen *that* the *analogia entis* is the form of the principle demanded by metaphysics "as such," and, likewise, *how* the *analogia entis* can be understood as such a principle. Our task here is expressly to formulate this "that" and this "how" that have already, in fact, emerged.

1. That *the analogia entis is the actual principle of metaphysics-as-such* is evident from the way that our fundamental reflections concerning a formal principle for metaphysics-as-such (§1-4) and our historical analysis of the original tradition with respect to its formal principle (§7) converged in the *analogia entis,* as it decisively figured in the problematic of the principle of non-contradiction (§6). The formal principle of metaphysics as such was shown to be one that — in the form[1] of the relation between essence and existence — comprises the entire problematic, including the problematic at play between philosophy and theology (§4, 5f.). The problematic of the "relation" was fulfilled in the problematic of the *analogia entis* as *analogia:* from its relative universal form (§5-6) to the concrete range of oscillation within it between ἀνά and ἄνω (§7); from the relatively positive framework of its structure (between the intra-creaturely analogy and the analogy between God and creature: §6, 5-6) to a "relationship of mutual alterity" (§6, 8), to the play — even here — among its various accentuations (§7). On the other hand, the problematic obtaining "between essence and existence" developed into the problematic of the *analogia* as *entis:* from an "order of being in thought" (§5), to the "is (valid)" as essentially "analogous" (§6, 5), to the ex-

---

1. *Formgestalt.* — Trans.

plicit avowal that the span between essence *(essentia)* and existence *(esse)* constitutes the essence of analogy (§7, conclusion). Finally, as for the problematic "including . . . philosophy and theology," we discovered the more exact foundation of this problematic in the way that the fully developed *analogia entis* — in its problematic of potentiality — arranged the relationship that was previously demanded between the two (§6, 7), and in the way in which, in the classical systems, the concrete forms of analogy exhibited the unity of their distinctness (§7). But, beyond all this, we discovered the still more decisive foundation of the entire principle: in the principle of non-contradiction (§6).

We then found a correlative supplement to this in the way that our historical analysis of the original tradition yielded the same result. For, on the one hand, in this original tradition (from the antithesis between Heraclitus and Parmenides, to the interplay of emphases[2] between Plato and Aristotle, and to the further interplay of Platonic and Aristotelian emphases between Augustine and Thomas), we repeatedly encountered the formal structure of metaphysics as such, as it was objectively developed (§1-4), and therein also the fundamental form of analogy (§5-6); but, on the other hand, we discovered a wealth of possibilities proper to this formal structure and this fundamental form of analogy, which showed, for the first time, their full range of variation: from Plato's "immortal struggle" (the ἄνω as the goad of the ἀνά) to the Aristotelian "torso of alternation" (the ἀνά in its enclosure bursting upwards into the ἄνω) to the "vigilant night" of Augustine (the ἀνά as the declaration of the ἄνω) to the "perfecting border" of Thomas Aquinas (the ἀνά of the ἄνω). Even here, though, the practical purpose of this exposition was decisively to confirm the way that the *analogia entis* was manifest within the principle of non-contradiction: not as within a "principle from which . . . ," but rather as within a "negative reductive formality" — that is, as "the basis of movement."[3] For the historical systems belonging to this original tradition are not "construed out of" the *analogia entis;* rather, the *analogia entis* proved to be the rhythm of this tradition's inner movement. The way "that" the *analogia entis* is grounded as a principle in the principle of non-contradiction is that the mode of the latter as a "negative reductive formality" and as a "basis of movement" (which is itself the "commencing of movement") is expressed in the *analogia entis.*

2. But, within this mode of the "that," the *"how" of the analogia entis as*

2. *Akzent-Ineinander.* — Trans.
3. *Vide supra* p. 206, n. 56. — Trans.

a principle is already revealed. In that the *analogia entis* is grounded in the principle of non-contradiction, it shows itself to be the most radical of principles. In that precisely here, however, the *analogia entis* shares in the principle of non-contradiction's mode of a "negative reductive formality" and a "movement in *actu primo*," it shows itself to be the most open of principles. With respect to the former aspect, therefore, it is a "maximal principle" (since what "is [valid]" includes every "is [valid]"); with respect to the second, however, it is a "minimal principle" (since it consists in the commencement of a "movement *in infinitum*"). The first "how" answers the question of the *"starting point."*[4] The succession of historical systems is characterized, fundamentally, by a tendency to secure, in each case, an ever more original starting point. For the natural philosophers of antiquity, this more original starting point appeared to be the primordial elements; for Anaxagoras, it was the mind[5] by which these elements were ordered; for Plato, this mind's object (the εἴδη); for Aristotle, the subjective act of this same mind (the νόησις); for Descartes, consequently, the being-unto-itself of the mental act (in the enclosure of the *cogito*); for Kant, the form of the act as such (the transcendental); for Hegel, the *dynamis* [*sic*] of this form of the act (in his ternary); for Husserl, the ultimate irreducibility of the objective and intentional forms of the mental act (*noema-noesis* as the form of transcendental subjectivity). The critique implicit in this succession consists in the reduction undertaken to something regarded, in each instance, as still more original. Yet all such attempts are subject to the same critique: to wit, that how one establishes what, in each instance, is to be elected as the more original starting point is itself already determined by this starting point. This gives rise to a fatal either-or: either the starting point is "posited" (in the manner of a decree) or the attempt to establish it ends up in a "circle." Clearly, from this perspective, the most promising starting point will be one that occurs, firstly, within what is most formal and elementary to the movement of thought, and therefore, secondly, entails only such "being-posited" or "circularity" as is inevitable for what is most formal and elementary (and thus, in practical terms, cancels itself out). But this is undeniably the case with the "*analogia entis* in the principle of non-contradiction." For, as our investigation showed (§5-6), the *analogia entis* is simply nothing other than the "genuine form" of the principle of non-contradiction, while all the other starting points — though they themselves are rooted in the principle of non-

4. *Ansatz.* — Trans.
5. *Geist.* — Trans.

contradiction (even if unconsciously) — "interpret" it in a certain direction, thereby demonstrating that their foundation is in themselves and not in it. Since the *analogia entis* merely "expresses" the principle of non-contradiction without interpreting it, it is a starting point by virtue of *being* the starting point, and thus a starting point in the most radical sense. Thus *"analogia entis"* signifies a starting point inasmuch as thought itself is its own starting point.

And yet, precisely here, the contrary is also implied: that the starting point for thought as thought consists in analogy, and hence in analogy as we repeatedly encountered it. We first encountered it implicitly in our discussion of the formal principle of metaphysics as such (§1-4): as a suspended relation that points not only ever beyond itself, but — through and beyond its positive expression — to the *quid non est.* Then, in the objective problematic of the *analogia entis* itself (§5-6): as a middle within a moving equilibrium that tended ever more beyond itself, to the point of appearing precisely — and emphatically — as an *(analogia) entis* within the nothing. Finally, the *analogia entis* was implicit in the historical problematic (§7): as the range of oscillation proper to its varying emphases (between ἀνά and ἄνω) — but one that passes over (in the interrelation of these varying emphases, from Plato to Thomas) into a structure of differentiations, to the point of the unsystematizable surd left behind by the plenitude of historical configurations. In this respect, the *analogia entis* shows itself to be — in the strongest sense — a *"creaturely principle"* and, thus, as consisting in the illimitable openness of the movement of becoming. Were it something like *the* formula of the creaturely (and so, logically, of the relation between God and creature), it would constitute the most absolute starting point for an absolute metaphysics: from which everything could be deduced, even the profoundest of theological mysteries. As it is, however, it is merely an expression for how the uttermost potentiality of the creaturely (including the *potentia obedientialis*) is at work within the starting point of thought as thought. It is not a principle that makes the creaturely comprehensible and thus manipulable, but one in which the creaturely oscillates unhindered in its utter potentiality. It is the principle of a metaphysics that measures out the "all" of the creaturely: not because this metaphysics deduces the all from this principle, but because it opens itself to the all in this principle. It is the principle of a metaphysics that sees the all as ordered to God as its origin and defining end: not because it takes this principle to comprehend the all from the vantage of God, but because its openness allows it to experience the all as pointing through and beyond itself to God. It is, finally, the principle of a philosophical-theological metaphysics: not because it is a metaphysics that can deduce even the mysteries of theology from this principle, nor even because it can resolve them by reducing them to this principle, but because the depth of this principle is the very *potentia oboedientialis* that stands in immediate relation to the God of supernature *(in potentia ad illa quae supra naturam Deus in eo potest facere)*.[6]

We thus find the best formulation of this "creatureliness" in the very same *Thomas Aquinas*. There is here, to be sure, a *cogito ergo sum*, like that of Descartes's formula: thought's "complete circular return into itself" *(reditio completa)*[7] in its reflection upon itself, within which truth as such flashes out *(secundum hoc cognoscit veritatem intellectus, quod supra seipsum reflectitur)*,[8] and within which the intellect is actively in-and-to itself *(nihil aliud [reditio] dicitur nisi subsistentia rei in seipsa)*.[9] But this is not simply a reflection, a turning-back-into-itself of the act that — in its in-tention, its forward motion — is underway towards its object.[10] Nor is it simply a reflection that reveals — in "addition to" a knowledge of the act — the relation of the act to its object *(non solum secundum quod cognoscit actum suum, sed secundum quod cognoscit proportionem eius ad rem)*.[11] Rather, it is decidedly a kind of reflection in which the intention towards objects is recognized to be the essential nature of the act *(cognoscit actum suum . . . quod quidem cognosci non potest nisi cognita natura ipsius actus; quae cognosci non potest nisi cognoscatur natura principii activi, quod est ipse intellectus, in cuius natura est ut rebus conformetur)*,[12] and not merely towards an object immanent to this act (towards the *noema* of the *noesis*), but explicitly towards an existing "thing" *(ut rebus conformetur)*. But if this radical *cogito* hereby reveals a more radical creatureliness (that of a general dependency and specific

---

6. [A thing can be in merely obediential potency, which is to say that it is] in potency regarding those things beyond its nature that God can bring to pass within it. *De Ver.* q. 8, a. 4, ad 13.

7. *De Ver.* q. 1, a. 9, corp.

8. Thus the intellect knows truth because it reflects upon itself. *De Ver.* q. 1, a. 9, corp.

9. [In *The Book of Causes,* this (return) to one's own essence] is said to be nothing other than the subsistence of a thing in itself. *De Ver.* q. 2, a. 2, ad 2.

10. *Summa Th.* I, q. 87, a. 3, corp.

11. [The intellect reflects upon its own act] not only insofar as it knows its act, but insofar as it knows the proportion of its act to the thing. *De Ver.* q. 1, a. 9, corp.

12. It knows its act . . . which indeed cannot be known unless the nature of this act is itself known; which in turn cannot be known unless the nature of its active principle be known, which is to say the intellect itself, to whose nature it is proper that it be conformed to things. *De Ver.* q. 1, a. 9, corp.

ordering of creaturely beings one to another[13] — i.e., that of their member-ship in a world), then the final consequence is that even the truth that flashes out within this *cogito* does so "transparently":[14] not as an eternal immutable truth "in the *cogito*," but in-and-beyond the becoming of the creaturely cor-relation of consciousness and being *(si accipiamus veritatem pro veritate creatorum verorum eis inhaerente, quam invenimus in rebus et in intellectu creato, sic veritas non est aeterna, nec rerum, nec enuntiabilium).*[15]

It was in this sense, then, that we also discovered *analogia* as a princi-ple within the *cogito*. It came into view not as something formal from which objects could be derived, but as the formality of movement[16] towards an ob-ject. This is how it was implied within the problematic of metaphysics as such (§1-4): within the broadest possible unencumbered consideration of the objective problems residing in metaphysics as such. This is also what emerged when we considered it as an objective problematic in its own right (§5-6): from the least misconstrued[17] self-manifestation of logos and the principle of non-contradiction. Thus it broadened into its historical prob-lematic (§7): in the most comprehensive view of all possible sides of the rele-vant systems, as the rhythm of this span. This also implies the second aspect[18]: the formal "never finished *in infinitum*" of this movement: the *creatura mutabilis* of St. Augustine. It is not that the *analogia entis*, as a prin-ciple, spares one the necessity of undertaking ever new and unprejudiced ex-aminations of objective facts. But rather the opposite: it enables one to un-dertake such examinations, and indeed compels one to do so. Nor is it the case that the *analogia entis*, as a principle, is grounds to be satisfied with a system that is once and for all finished. Rather the opposite: it enables one to see through and beyond everything that seems to be finished into what is ever new *(invenitur quaerendum)*. Thus one could say that the *analogia entis* not only represents what is genuine in both phenomenological and aporetic methods, each individually, but also binds them together into a unity.

---

13. Or perhaps "the subordination of creaturely beings within genera and their ar-rangement into species." — Trans.

14. *"Transparierend."* — Trans.

15. If we understand truth to mean the truth that inheres in true created things, which we find within things and within the created intellect, then truth is not eternal, neither the truth of things nor the truth of statements. *De Ver.* q. 1, a. 5, corp.

16. *Formales der Bewegung.* — Trans.

17. *Möglichst unverdeutet.* — Trans.

18. The reference here seems to be to the second aspect of the "how" of the *analogia entis* at the beginning of this section. — Trans.

The statement drafted by the *Vatican Council* on the unity of *fides* and *ratio*[19] is therefore especially relevant to the *analogia entis* as a principle. This unity is expressed negatively, from below, in terms of an "above-and-beyond": *etsi fides sit supra rationem, nulla tamen unquam inter fidem et rationem vera dissensio esse potest.*[20] It is only from above that it appears in the form of an identity: *Deus . . . negare se ipsum non possit nec verum vero unquam contradicere.*[21] But even within this form of identity from above, the form of the "above-and-beyond" — formulated negatively, from below — continues to apply: not only because the identity of truth *(verum vero)* rests in the identity of God *(Deus . . . se ipsum),* who is "ineffably exalted above all things that exist or can be conceived alongside him,"[22] but also because it rests in him as he appears in the difference between nature and supernature, in the similitude of creaturely non-unity *(cum idem Deus, qui mysteria revelat et fidem infundit, animo humano rationis lumen indiderit);*[23] but then (more emphatically), because this identity is itself expressed negatively in God himself *(Deus . . . negare se ipsum non possit)* and therefore in the truth *(nec verum vero unquam contradicere).* On the one hand, it is such a movement of the ever "above-and-beyond" that even this unity of faith and reason continues to be expressed according to the forms of this movement. On the other hand, it is a unity of such a kind that the "above-and-beyond" is already borne by it *(idem Deus . . . mysteria revelat et fidem infundit, animo humano rationis lumen indiderit).* It is the "unity in the movement" between truth and truth: between its first commencing in the principle of non-contradiction (τὴν ἀντίφασιν ἀδύνατον ἀληθεύειν κατὰ τοῦ αὐτοῦ)[24] and its fulfillment in God *(Deus . . . negare se ipsum non possit nec verum vero unquam contradicere).* Its inexorable "ever above-and-beyond" is conditioned, in its first commencing, precisely by this fulfillment: *ut inventus quaeratur immensus*

19. Verum etsi fides sit supra rationem, nulla tamen unquam inter fidem et rationem vera dissensio esse potest: cum idem Deus, qui mysteria revelat et fidem infundit, animo humano rationis lumen indiderit, Deus autem negare se ipsum non possit, nec verum vero unquam contradicere. Denz. 1797.

20. Although faith is higher than reason, nevertheless there can never be any true discord between faith and reason.

21. God . . . cannot negate himself nor ever contradict one truth with another.

22. Denz. 3001.

23. For the same God who reveals mysteries and infuses faith has also imparted the light of reason to the human soul.

24. It is impossible to make contradictory true assertions regarding the same thing. *Met.* XI, 5, 1061b, 36–1062a, 19-20.

est.[25] But for just this reason it is an "ever above-and-beyond" "within order." Firstly, insofar as it does not go on *"in infinitum"* in order to be an infinity in itself, but because it is "subordinate" to that which is in itself infinite. Secondly, because it is therefore not the destructive demonism of a negative boundlessness, but rather a movement within the "limits" that are "set" by that which is in itself infinite. Thirdly, and finally, because it does not have the infinite in itself simply as a limit idea "beyond itself," but as an effective principle already "within itself" — in itself as "beyond itself." Thus we see once again how the *analogia entis,* as a principle, consists in the unity of its ἀνά and ἄνω: the ἄνω of the ever "above-and-beyond" and yet — and therefore — the ἀνά of "inner order." It is a "principle" insofar as He alone is called *principium et finis,* i.e., the principle from whom and to whom are all things: *idem Deus.* This "insofar" is its measure: the nothing before the Creator out of nothing.

In no way, however, is it a "principle," if one supposes this to mean something originally static, "from which" everything else could be deduced or "to which" everything else could be reduced. On the contrary, it is essentially the primordial dynamic: defining the swaying of the intra-creaturely, the in-between-God-and-the-creaturely, and the intra-divine itself, the hyper-transcendent expression of which is the theologoumenon of the intra-divine "relations" *(relationes),* which *are* the Father, Son, and Holy Spirit. The "being" — *Sein* — which all philosophies take to be the primordial question and primordial datum with respect to everything else, does not (subsequently) "have" analogy as an attribute or as something developing from it; rather analogy *is* being, and thus thought *is* (noetically) analogy. As this primordial dynamic, analogy is a rhythm — just as, according to Pythagoras, the cosmos vibrates with a "resonant rhythm," and just as, according to Plato, God is the "measure of all things and all actions."[26] Only in the sense of such a rhythm and such a measure is analogy a "principle." Ontically as being and noetically as thought, it is "principally" the mystery of the primordial music of this rhythm — as with the fugues in Bach's "Art of Fugue," which, interweaving one another, pass beyond themselves into "great silence." The "resonant analogy" is fulfilled in this "silent analogy."

---

25. So that he who has been found might be sought, he is unending. Augustine, *In Jo. Tract.* 63, 1.

26. *Laws* IV, 716c-d.

PART II

Universal Rhythm

1 Philosophies of Essence and Existence

1939

1. A *philosophy of existence* can be contrasted with a *philosophy of essence* in two respects. Firstly, from the standpoint of the formal *object* of knowledge (that is, noematically). The formal object of knowledge of a philosophy of essence would then be the ideal essence in the full scope of its historical manifestations: the Platonic εἶδος (ideal being in itself), the Aristotelian μορφή (the ideal shape within things), the scholastic universal (the universal essence that, in one way or another, resides within individual things), the material or formal "forms" and "laws" of modern philosophy. As its counterpart, a philosophy of existence would be concerned precisely with the very thing that, in a noematic essentialist philosophy, was "disregarded" or that, at the very least, constituted merely its "background": real being (as opposed to εἶδος), concrete things (as opposed to μορφή), the unique individual (as opposed to the universal), the flow of life (as opposed to "forms" and "laws"). But then this very existence would nevertheless become the object of a philosophy whose method tends towards "abstraction" and "formulation" in concepts, and which to this extent necessarily transfers its object — and so too existence itself, considered as an object — to the level of essence. In this case, a noematic philosophy of existence would turn out to be an extreme instance of a philosophy of essence: that is, an essentialization even of existence.

The problem thus shifts of itself to the level of the cognitive *act* (into, that is, the sphere of the noetic). The formal act of a philosophy of essence would then be precisely this "essentializing" of all the objects it intends: be it

---

This essay first appeared in *Scholastik* (1939).

an objective essentialization (in that it elevates everything real to the level of ideal being, as in ancient philosophy) — or a formal essentialization (in that it lays hold of the flux of things by way of immutable concepts, as in scholastic philosophy) — or a methodological essentialization (in that it beholds the whole of creaturely becoming in absolute truth, as in modern philosophy). As its counterpart, a philosophy of existence would consist in an act whereby, under all three of these aspects, the peculiarity of creaturely existence-in-becoming would rise untouched to the level of philosophical reflection. This is not, therefore, a kind of existentialization, in parallel to an essentialization (understood as the formal act of an essentialist philosophy). For this would be a noetic act of creation: the positing-into-existence of an ideal being. Nor can it be an "illumination of existence"[1] (as Karl Jaspers formulates it). For "illumination" implies the clarity of ideal being or of clear concepts or of pure truth, and is thus a form of essentialization. Rather, the formal act of a philosophy of existence would consist, on the one hand, in the sort of conception of existence — as (the conception of) existence — that would leave the particularity of existence untouched; on the other hand, in such a conception of existence — as the conception (of existence) — that it is precisely this particularity that stands out in its peculiar distinctiveness over against everything essential.

This could be understood, firstly, in an objective fashion: as a self-giving of real, concrete things (in contrast to an objective essentialization). Secondly, it would be possible in a subjective sense: as the comprehension achieved through the concrete life of the man who comprehends (in contrast to a subjective essentialization). Thirdly, and finally, it could be elaborated in terms of how the method proper to knowledge itself intrinsically takes shape — and thus in terms of the correlation between object and subject — through the particularity of existence as such: not, that is, as the unity of object and subject in the identity of absolute truth (as in the case of a methodological essentialization), but as a tension in conflict, as is proper to the world's real existents. The first case, that of an objective philosophy of existence (in the manner of a *"Lebensphilosophie"*), would certainly assure the maximum of objectivity, but its subjective mode of comprehension would remain unclarified and unexamined. The second case, that of a subjective philosophy of existence (like Heidegger's), would certainly include within itself the examination and clarification thus lacking, but to take the concrete life of the human being as the form of such a philosophy leads to an anthropolo-

---

1. *Existenz-Erhellung.* — Trans.

gization of things. The third case, that of a methodological philosophy of existence (like Bergson's, Grisebach's, Jaspers's, and Heyse's), certainly preserves the tension of difference between the man who comprehends and the world that is comprehended. But logically this very tension of difference, as such, does away with all knowledge: because all knowledge rests upon a relation of being that depends on some kind of equivalence.[2] But if, instead of taking this tension of difference as the formal structure of one's philosophy, one posits the content that sustains this relationship — object and subject, that is — the question swings back to that of the choice between an objective or a subjective philosophy of existence. What would thus remain would be only whatever results from each instance of this differential tension: an "electric spark" (as Baader, for example, views the philosophical process). But this is clearly more a case of a religio-mystical process, a *cogitor* (as Baader logically puts it), not a philosophically reflexive act, and, consequently, not a *cogito*. The problem at issue between a philosophy of essence and a philosophy of existence thus leads to the question at issue between them: between a philosophically reflexive *cogito* and a religio-mystical *cogitor*.

2. The governing problem here is therefore best viewed from the perspective of the concrete *historical origins* of both a philosophy of essence and a philosophy of existence. The historical source of all philosophies that explicitly call themselves philosophies of existence is found in the correlation between Hegel and Kierkegaard. On the one hand, in that *Hegel* conceives ideal being itself as dialectical becoming, we find in the sphere of essence itself the highest approximation to a philosophy of existence: in that the Idea is grasped existentially, in its development into existence — in the play of antitheses, as is commensurate with concrete being. But, on the other hand, in that Hegel seeks equally to comprehend the sphere of existence on the basis of the dialectic of ideal being, he lays the ground for the most extreme form of a philosophy of essence: the essentialization even of existence. It is in *Kierkegaard,* by contrast, that a genuine philosophy of existence emerges. Its object is existence in itself, but "according to the individual,"[3] as an object of the "utmost interest" to the "one who exists,"[4] and as the "sole reality" — in the sense of what is "properly ethical" — for the "one who exists."[5] Existence is equally the act of the philosophy of existence, but only as the act of "un-

2. *Gleichung.* — Trans.
3. Journals, Haecker II, 128.
4. Works, Schrempf VII, 13.
5. Works, Schrempf VII, 15.

derstanding . . . oneself as existing"[6] on the part of the human being who "exists for himself"[7] — such that "to think existence and to exist go together" and "one who exists is one who thinks."[8] Equally, however, the thinker of existence "understands"[9] not only how "to instantiate his abstract humanity in the concrete and thus to be *this* individual existing human being"; he or she also understands that "actual subjectivity is subjectivity that exists ethically,"[10] and that "one's greatest possible immersion in existence" is concretely "consciousness that consists essentially in guilt."[11]

The philosophy of existence thus sees itself doubly opposed to that most extreme form of the philosophy of essence that we find in Hegel. It is, firstly, a *metaphysical opposition:* existence in itself is posed against every mode of essence. At a material metaphysical level, a concrete existential philosophy of anxiety, guilt, and death is posed against an abstract essentialist philosophy of the sphere of the ideal: the concrete versus the abstract, the pessimistically real versus the optimistically ideal, the affective versus the intellectual. Correspondingly, at the formal metaphysical level, a form of "self-understanding from existence" is posed against the disregard or bracketing of existence; likewise, dynamically evolving thought is advanced against systematic thought; finally, dialogical thought (in address and conversation) is posed against monological thought (understood as the pure development of one's own thought). But hidden more deeply behind this is the *religious opposition:* broken existence as opposed to a self-assured existence (which, for just this reason, comprehends itself in the repose of an ideal sphere). The theologoumenon of Hegel's essentialist philosophy is the Trinitarian life of the Godhead understood as the creature's principle of movement. In Kierkegaard, by stark contrast, the theologoumenon is the riven disquiet of the man of original sin. Thus the depth of the material metaphysics here is the enduring guilt of the world of original sin awaiting redemption. And the depth of the formal metaphysics is the actual consciousness of original sin in distance and flight and defiance — which stands to be sublated[12] in a moment into the omnificence of love.

6. Works, Schrempf VII, 49.

7. Works, Schrempf VI, 265.

8. Works, Schrempf VII, 13.

9. *Versteht,* which is an altogether ordinary German word, but here in the sense of understanding from a properly relocated standpoint. — Trans.

10. Works, Schrempf VII, 15.

11. Works, Schrempf VII, 215.

12. *Aufgehoben.* — Trans.

3. Its counter-image is found in the historical sources of an explicit *philosophy of essence:* in its objectively present[13] form stemming from Parmenides; in its subjective-active[14] form, stemming from Descartes. In both cases, an equation is made between being (Parmenides: εἶναι; Descartes: *sum*) and the noetic (Parmenides: νοεῖν; Descartes: *cogito*): and thus between essence as ontic "nature" — "*Wesen*" — and essence as a noetic "defining concept" — "*Inbegriff.*" In the tradition, specifically, of *Parmenides,* a philosophy of essence aims at an objectively present noetic as the determinative ground of objectively present being (in contrast to the physical cosmological principles of Ionian philosophy: fire, water, etc.). The "It" of "thought in itself" (νοεῖν) appears as the ground of "being in itself" (εἶναι), and so the luminosity of a thought-shaped "defining concept" appears to be "just what being is": "indeed, thought is precisely the same as being" (τὸ γὰρ αὐτὸ νοεῖν ἐστίν τε καὶ εἶναι). Conversely, in the tradition of *Descartes,* a philosophy of essence seeks to establish subjectively active being by way of a subjectively active noetic (as a certification of being within the "I" — in contrast to the objective certainty of being in itself, such as one finds in scholastic philosophy). Within the I of "I think" *(cogito),* the I of "I am" *(sum)* appears indubitable, and so the luminosity of the being of consciousness (as being "made certain") appears as the inner consequence of an I that thinks itself: "I think, therefore I am" *(cogito ergo sum).* To be sure, Parmenides and Descartes would appear to be one in their "noeticization" of being (which is the common tendency of a philosophy of essence): "The defining concept of being" as "being within the defining concept." But they are distinguished in that in the case of Parmenides there is an "onticization" of the noetic into the principles of being. In Descartes, on the other hand, there is a noeticization of the ontic into the ground of consciousness. In Parmenides it is a de-noeticizing noeticization,[15] inasmuch as the noetic is transformed into being's principle as such. In Descartes it is an en-noeticizing noeticization,[16] inasmuch as the ontic strictly bears the form of the noetic.

In any case, the *total problematic of a philosophy of essence* develops from both Parmenides and Descartes. In the Cartesian tradition, its objectively present form is interpreted with respect both to its material content (as a noematic noeticization) and to its formal act (as a noetic

---

13. *Objektiv-gegenstandshaft.* — Trans.
14. *Subjektiv-akthaft.* — Trans.
15. *Ent-noëtisierende Noëtisierung.* — Trans.
16. *Ein-noëtisierende Noëtisierung.* — Trans.

noeticization). In the tradition of Parmenides, Plato takes the fundamental principle to be the noematic *eide;* for Aristotle, on the other hand, it is the dynamic noetic movement of "thought thinking itself" (νόησις νοήσεως). Similarly, in the Cartesian tradition, whereas Descartes himself interprets the *cogito* noetically (as a kind of thought), Husserl interprets it (in the final analysis) noematically (as a world of transcendental essences). This twofold form in the formal method is then reflected in the content of the two forms of a philosophy of essence as well: appearing both as predominantly anthropological and as predominantly cosmological. In the Parmenidean tradition, for Plato the content is predominantly anthropological (centering upon the ψυχή), whereas for Aristotle it is predominantly cosmological (centering upon the κόσμος). In the Cartesian tradition, it is anthropological for Kant and Fichte (in the transcendental subject), but cosmological for Schelling and Hegel (in the world-shaped Spirit).[17] We then come full circle in a return to formal method, inasmuch as the nous of the noeticization appears within the scope of the transcendentals (the true, good, beautiful). In the Parmenidean tradition we see an intellectual noeticization in Plato, Aristotle, and Thomas, but an ethical noeticization in Arabian and Franciscan scholasticism. In the Cartesian tradition we see an intellectual noeticization in Descartes, Hegel, and Husserl; an ethical noeticization in Kant and Fichte; and an aesthetic noeticization in Schelling.

In the end, though, what is more obviously expressed within this entire problematic is the fundamental *difference* between the "de-noeticized noeticization" of Parmenides and the "en-noeticized noeticization" of Descartes. And so it is with regard to material content: whereas Plato's *eidos* and Aristotle's "thought thinking itself" are conceived as material-substantial[18] being, Descartes's *cogito* and Husserl's essentiality possess only the being of consciousness. Thus in the tension between the anthropological and the cosmological in Plato and Aristotle we see the span of a metaphysics of being; in the tension between Descartes, Kant, and Fichte (on the one hand) and Schelling and Hegel (on the other) we see the span of an immanent metaphysics of consciousness. And as regards the problem of an ultimate transcendentality, whereas in Plato-Aristotle-Thomas, as well as in Arabian and Franciscan scholasticism, it is a question of primacy among transcendental orientations of being, in Descartes-Hegel-Husserl, Kant-Fichte, and Schelling, it is a question of primacy among transcendental ori-

17. *Im welt-förmigen Geist.* — Trans.
18. *Material-inhaltliches Sein.* — Trans.

entations of consciousness. It is here, however, that the religious problem breaks through. The "de-noeticized noeticization" that originates with Parmenides sees the properly divine in the existing[19] Logos or Nous, or in the hierarchy of the Ideas, or in "thought thinking itself" — leading up to the medieval disputations concerning whether God is, most properly speaking, intellect or will, truth or love. In the case of the "en-noeticized noeticization" that originates with Descartes, on the other hand, the interior certainty proper to the Reformation is powerfully at work: the certainty of possessing the divine, understood as that which alone is efficacious, within the absolute orientations of consciousness, in which alone being is certain and, to this extent, is being at all. In other words, even the philosophy of essence is ultimately determined by a theologoumenon, namely, that of the *identity of the creaturely with the divine,* whereas the determining theologoumenon of the philosophy of existence is that of tragic distance (that of original sin).

4. But then, in philosophies both of existence and of essence, what we ultimately have is an *opposition proper to existence:* the existence of the creature within the finite, and the existence of the creature within the "ideative-ideal"; finite existence and ideal existence. But inasmuch as, in the final analysis, finite existence conceives of itself as the (tragic) divinity of pure finitude, while ideal existence conceives of itself as a manifestation of divine ideality, both (for all their opposition one to the other) have the form of an *identity of essence and existence,* and hence the form of God: pure existence (which, insofar as it is "purely" for and to and in itself, constitutes its own "essence"), and pure essence (which, insofar as it is "purely" for and to and in itself, constitutes its own "existence").

Thus the way to a solution lies in a double reflection: on the one hand, from the standpoint of *the relation between existence and essence* and, on the other hand, from that of *the relation between tragic distance and ideal identity.*

*   *   *

The *objective philosophical problem* posed by the differences between a philosophy of essence and a philosophy of existence can be elaborated in three steps, by way of an explication of the very word "philosophy." First, taking essence and existence as formally methodological modes intrinsic to the concept of philosophy as such. Second, taking essence and existence as for-

---

19. *Seinshaften.* — Trans.

mally methodological modes within that formally methodological mode proper to the general being and standpoint[20] of philosophy as such. Third, taking essence and existence as formally methodological modes of philosophy. We are thus led gradually from the implicit to the explicit problem.[21]

Fundamentally, our problem is implied in the *literal meaning of the word "philosophy,"* as it bears reference to *sophia* and *philein*. While the concept of *sophia* prefigures objective possibilities, the concept of *philein* provides these objective possibilities with their corresponding subjective standpoints. Seen in terms of this correspondence, it then becomes possible to discern — within the subsequent problem of the being and standpoint of philosophy — the first explicit features of the field of tension that lies between philosophies of essence and philosophies of existence.

The *"sophia"* in *"(philo-)sophy"* declares these fundamental objective possibilities at three levels. *Sophia* (σοφία) is, firstly, *wisdom,* in the sense of the *form of the act* that corresponds to life as objectivity. As such, wisdom stands on the one hand "opposed" to life: as the ideal stability of an eternally immutable wisdom in contrast to the mutability of real life. But, on the other hand, as the form of the act, it must also correspond to real life as objectivity; that is, it must be a life-wisdom, a wisdom "of" life itself, and thus an internal maturation that takes place "within" life: as something eternal that is immanent to the becoming of life itself. Thus, whereas in "*eternal wisdom* as distinct from life," we see the form of essence, in "*life-wisdom* within life itself" we see the form of existence. But this gives rise, secondly, to a *distinction* intrinsic to "*sophia*" itself between *wisdom* (σοφία, sapientia) and (over against it) *science* (ἐπιστήμη, scientia). Accordingly, "wisdom" means the vision of a self-manifesting region of ideas, connections, or essences. "Science," by contrast, means a view of reality rendered by way of reality itself: by way of experience, experiment, and practical proof (understood as either praxis or technology). Thus, in wisdom we see more clearly the mode of ideal essence; in science, that of real existence. But since wisdom, understood as life-wisdom, is conditioned by its orientation towards life itself (and thus towards the realm of science), and since, conversely, as a form of thought, science aims at the ideative, which is to say at theory (and thus at

---

20. *Des allgemeinen Seins- und Standpunktshaften.* — Trans.

21. The only adjectives we employ here are "essential (existential)": in the sense of an intrinsic essential (existential) quality. Heidegger's distinction between existential and *existentiell* is a matter of standpoint: because for him existence is its own essence. Accordingly, existential signifies the materially essential [*Essentiale*] in this existence, whereas *existentiell* signifies its formal existence.

the realm of wisdom), the most proper problematic intrinsic to *sophia* is —
thirdly — the *tension between two directions of movement within the correlation between wisdom and science*. The one direction of movement proceeds
from the "above" of the realm of (ideal) wisdom to the "below" of the realm
of (real) science: following an *a priori method* of deduction from first principles, whereby reality is known. The other direction of movement ascends
from the "below" of (real) science to the "above" of (ideal) wisdom: following an *a posteriori method* of induction, whereby the ultimate essential
grounds might be disclosed. But, then, within the *a priori* the form of ideal
essence is ultimately revealed to be a movement towards real existence
(which precisely hereby shows itself to be an *essential existence*), while,
within the *a posteriori*, the form of real existence is revealed to be a movement towards ideal essence (which precisely hereby shows itself to be *existential essence*).[22]

By contrast, the *"philein"* in "philo(-sophy),"* understood as an intentional relating to *sophia*, signifies the range of formal positions one might
assume in regard to *sophia*'s objective possibilities. This range of positions
lies between the word's two meanings: φιλεῖν in the sense of "to love" and
φιλεῖν in the sense of "to seek." The former thus has the form of unity, the

---

22. Nicolai Hartmann likes to think of ideality-reality as distinct from essence-
existence: "Ideal being has its own essence *and* existence. . . . And real being has its own existence *and* essence" (*Grundlegung der Ontologie,* Berlin 1935, p. 114). But Hartmann's break
from classical tradition is conditioned by a particular standpoint. In making ideal constructs
independent — making them, that is, into an "ideal being" with its own essence-existence —
one sees (in spite of all his struggle against it) the continuing aftereffects of the standpoint of
phenomenology: which concerns the realm of objective essences. To bind existence and essence to pure "moments of being" of what is identically real, however, is to posit one's own
standpoint — that of the immanently absolute finitude of "ontic becoming" — over against
the distinction between (absolute) being (= God) and (relative) becoming (= creation)
(*Möglichkeit und Wirklichkeit,* Berlin 1938, pp. 133ff., 151ff.), since the divine identity of
essence-existence is now the form of the "whole of the world" as "continually delayed identity" (*Grundlegung* . . . p. 133), in keeping with "ontic becoming." What is nevertheless possible — at the heart of Hartmann's distinctions — is the formal hypothetical conception of
"ideal being" (to which then corresponds real being's factical, non-necessary unity of
existence-essence). Ideal being is then, in truth, "subsistent essence," whereas real being is
"essential existence [*soseiendes Dasein*]." But the "subsistence" of ideal being is hypothetical:
to the point that it merges with the problem of real spiritual being [*Geist-Seins*], and thus
with the existence-essence problem of real being. Furthermore, real being's unity of
existence-essence is a purely practical becoming (as is therefore also the case with the "whole
of the world"), ultimately pointing to an absolute Is as its source, and so to an actual *ens
necessarium* for the ideality of existence and essence.

latter that of distance. "Philo(-sophy)," as *the love of wisdom* and so having the form of unity, thus means a disposition towards *union with the objective possibilities contained within sophia.* On the one hand, this disposition towards union can take the form of a unity with one of these objective possibilities, as distinct from all others: in the mode, that is, of a *direct philosophy,* in which in each case a single objective possibility is advanced "against all others" and "through all others" *(di-),* straight on *(regere)* to the very end. But then this very directness is formally differentiated within itself, corresponding to the objective possibilities: as a directness with regard to principles or experience (corresponding to eternal wisdom) and as life-wisdom (corresponding to wisdom and science); as an *a priori* or *a posteriori* directness (corresponding to a particular direction of movement, either wisdom → science or science → wisdom). On the other hand, this disposition towards union can be conceived as a union with the totality of objective possibilities, and thus as a union with the matter-of-fact relation of tension that obtains among them, and so finally as a union with the ever new alternation between them: in the mode of an *objective dialectical philosophy,* whereby the "between" — that of the opposition and correlation between these objective possibilities (διά-) — is expressed in its proper order (λέγειν). Consequently, this objective dialectic appears as, so to speak, the self-realization of the entire web of these objective possibilities and their actual occurrence; but equally, therefore, in the most formal sense, as the objective back-and-forth between them, and therefore as the manifestation of a formal objective aporetics of the objective relation between them. So, whereas a direct philosophy realizes the internal structure of only one of the objective possibilities, an objective dialectical philosophy realizes the structure that obtains between them.

At the same time, however, "philo(-sophy)" means *"the seeking of wisdom"* and so signifies the form of a *distance between wisdom* — understood as objectively ever beyond any attainable union — *and the seeking of it* — understood as subjectively ever distant from any union perfectly attained: the objective distance (of wisdom), the subjective distance (of seeking). From this arise two final forms. In the case of the objective distance (of wisdom), *philein* aims away from itself and towards union with objective existence,[23] which is to say, with that web of objective possibilities contained in *sophia* as it was purely expressed in objective dialectical philosophy. As an "aiming at," however, *philein* does not proceed towards this union from the

---

23. *Bestand.* — Trans.

objectively existent (in the sense of a self-manifestation of this existence, as is the case in an objective dialectical philosophy), but proceeds rather towards union with the objectively existent. It thus aims at achieving a balance between the possibilities of the objectively existent, to be accomplished through and in *philein.* Consequently (since it arises actively from the subject), it is a *subjective dialectical philosophy:* wherein the objective opposition and correlation of these objective possibilities are verbally formed (λέγειν) into a consciously ordered (λόγος) "in-between" (διά). The objective distance (of wisdom) becomes manifest in precisely this way: since the subjective dialectic, as the formulation of the in-between, allows one to see that the inner objective unity of wisdom itself is above-and-beyond every subjective union with it (in "aiming towards"). At the same time, its counterpart, the form of subjective distance (of seeking), arises in the same way. For this is the corresponding movement that answers to the ever new and ever greater above-and-beyond of the inner objective unity "of" wisdom in itself, beyond every subjective union (through seeking) "with" it, whether aspired to or attained. *Philein* thus becomes a "pure seeking" that stands apart critically — at the greatest possible "pure distance" — from any union subjectively attained: critical at once towards every passively subjective union (in direct and objective dialectical philosophy) and towards every actively subjective union (in subjective dialectical philosophy). As such, it is a *formal-critical philosophy of distance:* it is the distance of separation and differentiation (κρίνειν) from every stable attainment of unity (in all three of the forms mentioned above) and hence is so formally — standing, that is, not upon any particular content (neither upon any one of the objective possibilities taken by itself, nor upon the interweaving of these possibilities, nor upon some actively subjective balance that might be achieved between them), but rather solely upon the "form" of a "distinctly discriminating"[24] (critical) "standing in the gap" *(di-stare).*

It is evident here that the very word *philein* expresses a distinct *mode of essence and existence.* In general, *sophia* and *philein* appear to be correlated in such a way that *philein* has the character of a positing-in-existence of those possibilities — objectively ideal and hence having the form of essences[25] — that are contained within *sophia.* But then, within these possibilities that have the form of essences, there exists (on the one hand) an internal relation between essence and existence and (on the other) an inner relation of the vari-

24. *Scheidend unterscheidenden.* — Trans.
25. *Essenz-förmig.* — Trans.

ous forms of *philein* — which have the form of existence[26] — to these various possibilities. Hence this positing-in-existence, understood as the general mode of *philein*, is not simply the form of existence in relation to *sophia*, understood as the form of essence, but is rather existence as intrinsically corresponding to itself. Consequently, direct philosophy and objective dialectical philosophy, as forms of union with *sophia*, also appear as forms of *sophia's immanent existence* — that is, for its objective possibilities, which have the form of essences; whereas subjective dialectical philosophy and the formal-critical philosophy of distance, as forms of the distance from *sophia*, also express the form of a *distant existence*. Just as, within the possibilities contained in *sophia*, there appeared in each case an opposition between the form of ideal essence and the form of real existence, one that was gradually elucidated in terms of the opposition of the forms of unity proper to each — an opposition between the movement from ideal essence towards essential existence (in the case of the *a priori*) and the movement of real existence towards existential essence (in the case of the *a posteriori*) — so now, in *philein*, these objective forms of essence-existence enter themselves into a new relationship of essence-and-existence, one derived from the subjectively active practice of philosophy. In the case of the immanent existence of *philein*, the form that *sophia* assumes is predominantly that of *"essence-and-existence"*: which in the case of direct philosophy places the emphasis upon essence (since direct philosophy is a process of intrinsic logical deduction from a basic ideative principle), while in the case of objective dialectical philosophy the emphasis is placed upon existence (since the formal movement of objective dialectic itself has the form of existence). In the case of the existence-at-a-distance of *philein*, however, *sophia* is translated to the level of *"existence-and-essence"*: in which case subjective dialectical philosophy underscores essence (since there is still an internal movement of balancing that takes place among those possibilities in *sophia* that have the form of essence), whereas the formal-critical philosophy of distance places its emphasis upon existence (since there remains only a critical "standpoint over against," from which *sophia* is first posited in existence).

     5. What emerges, then, within the internal problematic of philosophy — between *sophia* and *philein* — is the most formal aspect of being: the "standpoint" within it. *"Standpoint"* means, on the one hand, the most formal aspect of "content": the "being" of the standpoint's content and thus the "esse" in "essence." But then, equally, "standpoint" also means the act of po-

26. *Existenz-förmig.* — Trans.

sitioning at its most formal: the "stance" of the standpoint and thus the *sistere* of existence. Everything that belonged to (the content) of *sophia* is thus contained in the standpoint, understood as "being," whereas the standpoint, understood as "stance," contains everything that appeared in (active) *philein*. But it is in the correlation of these two that the general kinds of standpoint are revealed in their full range: a range, that is, implicit in the fundamental orientations of a philosophy of essence and of existence.

Thus, one can consider the question of standpoint first — in its correlation of (objective) being and (subjective) stance — from the vantage of (objective) being: as, that is, the standpoint of this being itself, such that the (subjective) stance is the stance *of* this being, i.e., an *objective standpoint*. Logically, then, the "being" of this objective standpoint is the "pure being" of "pure" *sophia:* the pure being of eternal wisdom as opposed to "life-wisdom," wisdom as opposed to science, the *a priori* as opposed to the *a posteriori*. Accordingly, the "stance" of this objective standpoint is that of an immediate unity with this "pure being": *philein* as the co-enactment of *sophia's* objective possibilities. Thus, with regard to content, this objective standpoint establishes a *philosophy of eternity* (since it is a philosophy of "pure being"); with regard to the act, it establishes a *philosophy of identity* (since, as a form of stance, it is a philosophy of "immediate unity"). In the problematic of *philein,* on the other hand, the unity proved to be twofold: a unity, in each case, with one of the objective possibilities of *sophia* (in direct philosophy) and also a unity with the ever new alternation between these possibilities (in objective dialectical philosophy). This establishes a twofold form for the philosophy of eternity and of identity: that of the "eternal" within the eternality of a pure "Is" *(ipsum esse),* and that of the "eternal" within the eternality of the rhythm of pure change *(ipsum fieri)*. Direct philosophy thus establishes the *Parmenidean* type of philosophy: a stance within the pure being of the pure Is. Objective dialectical philosophy, on the other hand, takes the shape of the *Heraclitean* type of philosophy: a stance within the pure being of the rhythm of pure change.

But a standpoint can also be developed from a (subjective) stance. This stance is presented as something specifically distinct from a "pure being": i.e., as a standing of the concrete human being within concrete space and concrete time. For this stance, therefore, (objective) being also appears as the being of the concrete world. What is determinative here is the subject as human being in the world. That is to say, it is a *subjective standpoint*. The "being" of this subjective standpoint is, consequently, that of an intra-worldly *sophia:* in the sense of life-wisdom as opposed to eternal wisdom, science as opposed to wisdom, the *a posteriori* as opposed to the *a priori*. Accordingly, the "stance" of this subjective standpoint is characterized as a mutable *philein*, i.e., as a "seeking of . . . ," as is proper to mutable being, which can be seen in the mutability of life-wisdom, etc. For this reason, this subjective standpoint can be characterized, with regard to its content, as a *philosophy of the world* (since it is a philosophy of finite "being in becoming") and, with regard to its act, as a *philosophy of distinction* (since, as the form of "stance," it is a philosophy of the distance in a "seeking of . . ."). But, then again, in the problematic of *philein*, the distance of the seeking was twofold: it was at once a way towards achieving a balance between the objective possibilities of *sophia* (in subjective dialectical philosophy), and formally a way in itself (in the formal-critical philosophy of distance). This gives rise to a twofold form for a worldly philosophy of distinction[27]: one in which every (active) "distinction" subserves a "world picture" that is balanced (throughout its oppositions), and so underway towards the being of an order within (finite) becoming itself, i.e., underway towards a "cosmic system" *(esse in fiendo)*: another, however, in which the ever new (active) event of the "distinction" is itself the actual world, i.e., as the being of (finite) becoming, which has its corresponding consciousness in the human being's ever renewed "seeking of . . ." and thus has the form of the "anthropological aporia" *(fieri)*. Subjective dialectical philosophy thus establishes the *Aristotelian* type of philosophy: a stance oriented towards the shaping of an enclosed (finite) world. Formal-critical philosophy, on the other hand, takes the shape of the *Platonic* type of philosophy: the stance as (finite) becoming.

6. What arises out of this relation between being and stance within the "standpoint" and is now seen to be ultimate is the explicit problematic of *existence and essence in the act of philosophy*. The four types of philosophy we named above — the Parmenidean, Heraclitean, Aristotelian, and Platonic — yield corresponding types of philosophies of essence and existence. For whereas essence was prefigured in the objective content of the "being" of the "standpoint," existence was prefigured in the subjective act of the "stance."

By the *Parmenidean type* of philosophy — understood as the type of direct philosophy — we mean an act of philosophy in which objective substantial[28] "being" appears "in its subsistence as true," that is to say, as existent only insofar as the essence of ideal being is its own ideal existence. Accordingly, to philosophize means to engage in an act in which the true ideal

---

27. *Welt- und Distinktions-Philosophie.* — Trans.
28. *Inhaltlich.* — Trans.

world of "eternal being" becomes manifest through the foreground of the real world — whereby, it is supposed, one first comes to perceive and understand the movement of the *a posteriori* of real worldly being within the peaceful *a priori* of this eternal being: within eternal essence existing in itself. This is the type of *apriorism* that one finds in a pure *philosophy of ideal identity*[29] of the kind *German rationalism* strove to realize. It is thus a type of a pure philosophy of essence, understood as a *philosophy of essence-and-existence* (that is, one in which essence is taken to be its own existence).

By the *Heraclitean type* of philosophy, understood as the type of objective dialectical philosophy, we mean an act of philosophy in which objective substantial "being" is seen in terms of an immanent movement — a movement that, as "immanent," remains within the region of ideal being, but as "movement" is the movement in which the real world is ever coming to be and passing away, such that the essence of ideal being always exists as tending towards a real being. Accordingly, to philosophize means to engage in an act in which the foreground of the real world's arising and passing away is revealed to be the ideal movement of "eternal being" — whereby, it is supposed, one first discerns and understands the *a posteriori* movement of real worldly being within the *a priori* movement of this eternal being: in the movement-into-existence[30] of eternal essence. We thus see here the type of *apriorism* proper to a pure *philosophy of rhythmic identity,* such as Hegel intended. It is a type of an *essential philosophy of existence* (that is, one in which existence appears as the immanent movement of essence).

By the *Aristotelian type* of philosophy, understood as the type of subjective dialectical philosophy, we mean an act of philosophy in which objective substantial "being" makes itself known in the enclosed region of a subjective active "stance," which is to say, in the real world of a real human being, and through the taxonomic knowledge of this real human being concerning a real world. Objective "being" is understood as the being of the real world, inasmuch as the really existing human being investigates the real existent world, right down to its ultimate forms, structures, laws, and relations — that is, down to its real essence. Accordingly, to philosophize means to engage in an act in which, within the enclosure of a real world, the immanent ideal structure of this real world reveals itself — whereby, it is supposed, one first discerns and understands the *a posteriori* movement of real worldly being in its ordination to this immanent ideal structure: in the movement-to-

---

29. *Idee-Identitäts-Philosophie.* — Trans.
30. *Existenz-Bewegung.* — Trans.

essence[31] of real existence. It is thus (as a direct anti-type to Hegel) a type of the *a posteriori* that one finds in a pure *philosophy of the world through its distinction,*[32] as was the goal of the *critical realism* that the natural sciences advanced in the nineteenth century against German rationalism and Hegelian speculation alike. We thus see here a type of an *existential philosophy of essence* (that is, one in which essence manifests itself in the immanent movement of existence).

The *Platonic type* of philosophy, finally, understood as the type of a formal-critical philosophy of distance, includes within it an act of philosophy in which objective substantial "being" — even when understood as immanent within the world — is absorbed into the subjective active "stance," so as then to appear only as the inner instance[33] of the "position" of this "stance" at any given moment and as, therefore, the inner (formal) "being" of this active "stance" — that is, as the immanent essence of formal subjective existence. To philosophize, accordingly, means to engage in an act in which the real world declares its essence in the human being's ever renewed formal "seeking of . . ." (this being understood as true philosophizing) — whereby, it is supposed, one first comes to perceive and understand the self-contained *a posteriori* movement of real worldly being in this act and as this act: in finite real existence, understood as its own essence. The act of philosophizing, understood as conscious-being,[34] is thus the act in which the act of finite real existence (in its unique, mutable, matter-of-fact occurrence) comes to perceive and understand this existence as its essence. As such, it is a formal-critical, ever distant "seeking of . . . ," since the only ultimate "being" is precisely this "seeking of . . ." itself: no longer "in distinction" from a "world" (as in critical realism), but rather "distinction" as "world": the real finite world unveiled in its essence as formally real finite existence; for in the act of philosophizing, as a conscious act of existence, the act of existence perceives and understands itself as its own essence. It is, consequently (as the most direct anti-type to German Rationalism), a type of the pure (i.e., active, formal) *a posteriori* of a *philosophy of distinction as world,*[35] the basis for which one finds in *Kant's pure criticism,* and which has since become the conscious method of today's *pure philosophy of existence.*

31. *Essenz-Bewegung.* — Trans.
32. *Welt-Distinktions-Philosophie.* — Trans.
33. *Jeweils.* — Trans.
34. *Bewußt-sein.* — Trans.
35. *Distinktions-Welt-Philosophie.* — Trans.

But just as Kant, looking backwards, still stands in the tracks of German Rational-ism (and so stands within the last aftereffects of a pure philosophy of essence) and, looking ahead, lays the ground for both Hegel (an essential philosophy of existence) and critical realism (an existential philosophy of essence), so it is with today's pure philosophy of existence, which captures these same nuances in its span. The "tran-scending" of existence in Karl Jaspers, which comes to pass under the *chiffre* of "fail-ure," discloses the features of a region of ideal being, which is desired but denied: here one sees a tragic existentialism under the secret standard of a pure philosophy of essence. In Nicolai Hartmann, the aporetic stratification of the world of an iden-tity of existence-and-essence still betrays the de-idealized rhythm of Hegel's objec-tive ideal dialectic, which has been hardened into intrinsically necessary existence: here one sees a tragic existentialism that stands under the hidden standard of an es-sential philosophy of existence. Finally, in Martin Heidegger, one sees how, on the one hand, the hidden being of finite (and hence "concerned, caring" — *sorgend besorgend*) existence opens into the unconcealment (of truth) and how, on the other hand, precisely man, as demiurge, is projected into the ever new nothingness of the world: this existentialism of the human being in the world clearly betrays the features of critical realism, its creativity and worldly minded sobriety, and thus stands as an emphatically tragic existentialism under the secret standard of an exis-tential philosophy of essence.

A pure philosophy of existence can be characterized, therefore, in its entirety, as a *philosophy of existence-and-essence* (i.e., a philosophy in which existence grasps itself as its own essence). As such, it stands, on the one hand, in sharp-est contrast to German Rationalism, understood as a philosophy of essence-and-existence (i.e., a philosophy in which essence grasped itself as its own existence). But, on the other hand, it is such an antithesis within one and the same formality: that of the identity between essence and existence. For, within existentialism, the most extreme distinction, that of the "pure stance," turns out once again to be the most extreme identity: since pure ex-istence is its own essence.

The origins of an explicit philosophy of essence and of existence in our four types of philosophy — the Parmenidean, Heraclitean, Aristotelian, and Platonic — thus stand under the defining mark of this identity; whereas, in its origin, this identity was the sign of a titanic idealism, at its conclusion it proves to be the sign of an erupted tragedy. It is a creative identity that usurped the place of the creator God: in the pure essentialism of its origin, it did so under the aspect of an "ideal" God; in the pure existentialism of its conclusion, under the aspect of a "tragic" God. It is the form of identity that has its religious origin in the Reformation, and then became a rational formula in post-Reformation philosophy: an internally contradictory identity that signifies at once the ideal and exclusive agency of God in the human being and the divine form of the human being who is eternally tragic.

Thus, from within the objective philosophical problem, a view of the deeper religious problem opens up. In this respect, philosophies of essence and existence were previously seen in terms of the opposition between ideal identity and tragic distance. It became clear, however, that tragic distance was simply an internal inversion of ideal identity. Thus, as the inner form even of tragic distance, identity turns out to be the authentic religious face of philosophies of essence and existence.

*   *   *

7. Logically, therefore, the *religious problem* proper to philosophies of essence and existence lies precisely in the connections we have just explicated: inasmuch as the Christianity of the Reformation gives rise to that form of tragedy which, as tragic distance, is simply the inner inversion of ideal identity — since this identity is its inner form. Consequently, the problem lies, firstly, in the *relation of the tragic to Christianity* and, secondly, in the *relation* of this relation *to the problem of essence and existence*.

What we mean by the *tragic* can best be gleaned from tragedy itself. For just as art in general translates the practical forms of life into a "pure style," tragedy shows us the style of the tragic. It is significant, therefore, that tragedy arose twice out of a religious *mysterium:* first in the transformation of the ancient cult of Dionysus (in its mixture of Greek and oriental elements) into classical Greek tragedy; then in the birth of mediaeval and modern tragedy out of the dramatic retelling of Christ's passion during the church's Good Friday liturgy (which is already "dramatic" insofar as it is divided among three readers). Indeed, what we find at the birth of tragedy and of the "pure style" of the tragic is a confrontation[36] between the "Dionysian passion" (which consists in the mutilation and resurrection of the God of lust for life) and the "Christian Passion" (which consists in the cross and resurrection of the God of self-giving love) — a confrontation that Nietzsche reinterprets as a rebirth of the Dionysian (as the affirmation of life over against a Christian denial of life).

The cultic *mimos* of the god Dionysus, who reconstitutes himself amid ecstatic mutilation, is transformed in the development of *Greek tragedy* from Aeschylus to Sopho-

---

36. *Das Aug im Aug.* — Trans.

cles to Euripides. In the tragedy of Aeschylus it is still a matter of the human being's struggle with the divine (hence the prevalence of the choir, with its sacral, ceremonial function). Already in the tragedy of Sophocles, however, the divine (now cosmologized) is replaced by the objective world of fate (hence the reconfiguration of the choir to reflect the "language of the objective").[37] Finally, in the tragedy of Euripides, fate (now anthropologized) appears as human character (hence the prevalence of individual "scenes"). One thus sees the increasing secularization of something originally sacral. The sacrality that is secularized, though, is that of the "lower gods": the chthonic dimension of life's elementary drives (in its brute "creative cruelty"), which increasingly appears sublimated as world and soul. What would appear to be a degrading secularization of the sacral is in reality an elevating sublimation of the vital: because the governing sacrality is in this case the sacrality of the vital.

Christian tragedy stands, first of all, directly under the sign of the sacrifice of the Mass: as the "respective now"[38] of the saving passion of the incarnate God, who is both "Spirit" and "Logos." Hence, Christian tragedy is, before all else, a "Passion play": which is to say, a dramatic expression and portrayal of Christ's passion. But, since this is essentially the passion of Christ as the "*one* Christ, head and body," it gives rise just as directly to the "sacrament plays" and "tragedies of the martyrs and saints" of the Baroque period (in Calderón, Lope de Vega, and the poets of the Jesuit stage). The Reformation, however, destroyed the form of representation that implicitly held sway here, in order to replace it with the (temporally irresolvable) contradiction between a distant divinity that works all things alone (in the metaphysical distance of the wrathful *Deus absconditus* and in the historical distance of the redeeming *Deus revelatus* in the purely unique historical Christ) and an immanent (and God-defying) sphere of the profane. As a result, the secularization of the sacred that one finds in various forms in antiquity returns, albeit at a different level. The defiant agon with God in (Aeschylean) tragedy lives on in the Faust motif, whose influence upon modern tragedy is ubiquitous: as a secularization of the struggle of Christ and of the Christian (as a "member of Christ") with the will of the Father. The prevailing fate that one sees in (Sophoclean) tragedy is the secret form of the "objective entanglement"[39] of Shakespeare's tragedy: understood as a secularization of the succumbing of Christ and of the Christian in the "night of the Cross." In Hebbel's more psychological and Paul Ernst's more mythical tragedy of "the purely human," one sees a resurrection of the (Euripidean) tragedy of "fate as character" in the principle of an "internal tragic necessity": understood as a secularization of Christ's and the Christian's own descent into the "form of a man like any other."

The form of ancient tragedy — understood as an elevating sublimation of the vital — is thus renewed to the extent that the Christian mystery of suffering-

---

37. *Sprache des Objektiven.* — Trans.
38. *Je-Jetzt.* — Trans.
39. *Objektive Verwicklung.* — Trans.

redeeming love is secularized (in keeping with the original impulse of the Reformation) in terms of the tragedy that unfolds between a God of abyssal darkness and a humanity both defiant and helpless. The mystery of redemption is first displaced by the "tragic passion" (as in the almost bourgeois, anthropocentric style of Bach's passions), and is finally altogether absorbed into "cosmic tragedy" (in Schopenhauer's tragic life-will, for example, which gives rise, in the form of a vitalized "Passion play," to Richard Wagner's "Parsifal," but equally — though in "hostile friendship" — to Nietzsche's myth of Dionysus). In the process of this displacement, the God of Christianity is finally displaced by a chthonic divinity of the hoariest antiquity: the life-drive (as is prefigured in the unleashing of vital passion during the Reformation's precipitate and passionate battle against the Catholic devotion to representation). The Christian mystery of a "God who spares not even his Son, whom he sacrifices on our behalf" (and hence the mystery of the "ferocity[40] of God's creative love"), is replaced by that most ancient mystery of nature, the "creative ferocity" of the life-drive. The secularization of "Christian tragedy" is thus a function of an original secularizing transformation of Christianity into a Dionysian vitalism (just as the tragic in Schopenhauer and Nietzsche is simply a formulaic reflection of a movement that broke out objectively in Luther). Modern tragedy is a rebirth of ancient tragedy, insofar as the Christian devolves back into the Dionysian. This secularization is, firstly (objectively), something that occurs within the sacred itself: the descent of the Passion of God incarnate is secularized into the ascent of the Dionysian passion of "divine life" (a "passion of god-like flesh"). In a second (objective) step, secularized tragedy comes about as the self-development of this Dionysian passion: from cosmic fate (in Shakespeare) to anthropological fate (in Hebbel) to a mythical fate of character (in Paul Ernst). In other words, the form of Dionysian sacrality, contrary to what happened in antiquity, is not unveiled until the end.

We can now glean from this historical account the following *systematic* structure. What is first apparent is the contrast between sacral tragedy (in both the original Dionysian and the later Christian *passio Dei*) and profane tragedy (in ancient and modern tragedies of fate and character). It is therefore logically connected to the tension between representational tragedy (in the Dionysian *mimos* and in Christian plays about the sacraments and the martyrs: *repraesentare Deum*) and the tragedy of the autonomous agent (as seen in the tragic "self-assertion"[41] of ancient and modern tragedies of fate). It then merges into the broad interval between a tragedy of conflict (with God or world: in Aeschylean and Faustian tragedy) and a tragedy of immanence (the tragic understood as fate within character: in ancient and

---

40. *Grausamkeit.* — Trans.
41. *Sichdurchsetzen.* — Trans.

modern tragedies of character). The tragic is thus governed by a movement between two absolute forms of identity with the divine: a passive identity ("living the part of the tragic God") and an active ("living like God and thus tragically"). We see "pure tragedy" to the degree that we see this absolutism. Accordingly, the "you shall be like God" of original sin is at play in the style of the tragic, but it is a "like God" that is in the grip of passion: just as the words "tragic" and "tragedy" signify — etymologically — a "high and magisterial tone" (that of "tragic pathos"), but in the deeper, vital sense the tone of an "aggressive rearing up" that is nevertheless a "fruitless shooting up" and merely a "bad odor" (the "fatted goat" of the tragic: τραγάω, τράγος).

Since the "style" of original sin continues to be at work in the tragic, the tragic thus stands in direct confrontation with *Christianity,* understood as salvation from original sin. This is already evident from the contrast between the meaning of the word "Christian" and the meaning of the word "tragic": the "chrism" of "Christ" as the Anointed in the anointing of the Holy Spirit, who is the love of God, which for the sake of redemption empties itself out into nothingness and for nothing.[42] What we mean by Christianity is, firstly, *redemption from original sin,* the sin in which man wanted to be "like God, knowing the difference between good and evil." "The tragic" — which faces a "tragic guilt" understood as a "guiltless fate," and shakes its fist at the ultimate fatedness of a singularly divine judgment concerning good and evil, only to stand in this ultimate position itself and be "like God" — is therefore the "tragic" of original sin. Christianity, accordingly, is redemption from the tragic, and every *factum* of tragedy expresses the conflict between redemption from original sin and original sin's resistance to redemption. Christianity is redemption from original sin, secondly, as the *"wonder of exchange" (admirabile commercium)* between God and man: for God became man in order that we through our participation in a single human nature (as members of his visible body) might again receive a share in the divine nature, which was lost in the "like God" of original sin. Staged between God and humanity — on the one hand, actively resisting the satisfactory denouement of man into God and, on the other hand, deifying humanity's ultimate darkness — the tragic is that of original sin set over against the "wonder of exchange": the self-enclosing of the human against the self-

---

42. *Ins Nichts und Umsonst.* This last word can connote either gratuity ("for free") or futility ("in vain"); both meanings could be at work here, inasmuch as the self-emptying of love, which is freely given, reaches its extreme in the "in vain" of love's rejection. — Trans.

donating of God; a "god-like" struggle against the service of God. Christianity is thus redemption from *this* tragic, and every *factum* of tragedy expresses the conflict between a redemptive participation in God through participation in his authentic human nature and the "like God" of original sin, which resists this participation. But, thirdly, Christianity is this "wonder of exchange" *in the mystery of the cross.* The humanity in which God participates by virtue of this "exchange" is that of the new covenant, which betrays, denies, and flees from this God as its "head"; it is that of the old covenant, which on charges of blasphemy condemns this God, as its "messiah," to death on a cross "outside the preserve of the covenant"; and it is that of the pagan world, which as the instrument of the old covenant nails to "the wood of the curse" the very God who gathers it in. The Godhead, however, that gives itself to human beings in this "exchange" is the Godhead of the Father, "who spares not his own Son, but gives him up for us all" in his "love for the world"; it is the Godhead of the Son, who "loves me and gave himself up for me"; and is the Godhead of the Holy Spirit, who is "the divine weakness" and the "divine foolishness" of the "breadth and length and height and depth" of the "consuming fire" of this love. The spectacle of the greatest tragedy (in the ordinary sense of the term) is thus, within Christianity, the spectacle of the most divine God as the God of love: the cross as the glory of this love. The tragic — which stands at the cross of insoluble crossings-over, not only as the cross of mute rebellion against a "good God," but as the cross of a likeness to an obscure divine fate — is therefore that of original sin set over against the "glory of the cross." As intra-creaturely tragic, it is a belittling rebellion that downplays the greater darkness of the cross of God's own self-abandonment into the godforsakenness of God. As absolute, it is a rebellion that shuts out the greater, all-surpassing glory of love in the greatest darkness of the cross. Accordingly, the Christian is redemption from the tragic, as we have just now described it, and every *factum* of tragedy expresses the conflict between the redemptive love of God in the cross of God and the "final tragedy" of original sin, which resists this "love in the cross."

The tragic and the Christian are thus related in the way that Romans 8 views the world — a world that is redeemed, but redeemed in that it cooperates with redemption in the sign of the Cross: there are the "groaning of all creation" and the "firstfruits of the Spirit," indeed the "groaning of the Spirit" itself in the "intercessory bearing of our weakness" (Rom. 8:20-26), but this is understood at the same time in terms of the jubilation of being "in all things more than conquerors for the sake of him who loved us" (8:31-39), but precisely for this reason in the defining form of an "awaiting in patient perseverence" (8:25). This is the form that connects the span between the *Christian tragic* and the *tragically Christian*: the Christian tragic of an atoning patience, in which man bears up his own tragedy of original sin in and into the power of God's redeeming love; the tragically Christian of a co-redemptive patience, in which man cooperates in bearing the tragedy of the cross of God's incomprehensible love into the tragic world of original sin. Here, however, the word "tragic" fades away before the truer correlation between the *patience of* (atoning) *man* and the *patience of* (the redeeming) *God* (in co-redeeming man). Instead of the tragic, with its active or passive identity with God, there is, decidedly, the earthly, peaceful, positive distance of this patience. For, since this patience includes what is ultimately insoluble in the patience of man (who participates in God) and what is ultimately insoluble in the patience of the (incarnate) God, it is here that what is most divine in God appears within what is most human in man: love in a "patience of patience": patience itself as the form of unity between the patience of God and the patience of man.

8. The most general relation between God and the creature has now come into view — precisely by way of the question of the relation between the "tragic" of original sin and the "tragic" of redemption, that is, between (tragic) identity and the (Christian) distance (of patience). Now, in the same way (though in the reverse order of sections 1 to 7 above), the truly *crucial demarcations between essentialism and existentialism* also come into view. They appear, quite logically, to accord with the law that, for Thomas Aquinas, governs the relationship between nature and supernature: nature as a factical "presupposition" *(gratia supponit naturam)* and supernature as the factical "final form that fulfills it" *(gratia perficit naturam)*. For essence-existence constitutes the innermost nature of the creature as such, whereas original-sin-and-redemption (as the determining element within the opposition between tragic identity and the Christian distance of patience) is the final, factically concrete form of the one supernatural order of salvation in which creator and creature factically stand. On the one hand, the opposition of the tragic and the Christian cannot be derived from the relation between essence and existence: for supernature cannot be derived "essentially" from nature. But, on the other hand, the relation between essence and existence first appears in its concreteness under the form of the opposition between the tragic and the Christian: for factically concrete nature "exists" *as* factically concrete only under the final form of supernature (original-sin-and-redemption). The mutual underivability and existential unity of the tragic-and-Christian and essence-and-existence are thus themselves a final

representation of the true relation between essence and existence: against identity (understood as the form of all absolutizations). But it is just as clear how the (supernatural) tragic-and-Christian "appears" "within" this form of the relation between essence and existence (since it is a quality given to the creature), without "arising" "from" this form (as if it were a quality that resulted from the creature).

(a) On the one hand, the basic lines of the opposition between the tragic and the Christian appear in and are "presupposed" by the relation between essence and existence itself: the *objective problem of essence-and-existence as a "presupposition" of the religious problem of the tragic-and-Christian*. We thus attain the objective problem of essence-and-existence (in the sense of a basic form, according to sections 1-7) as a factical *ontology intrinsic to the religious problem of the tragic-and-Christian* (a merely factical ontology in keeping with its essential underivability, but nevertheless an "intrinsic" ontology in keeping with the existential unity of the remaining problems).

Creaturely existence is *becoming*. This becoming can be interpreted *essentially or existentially:* as the actualization of the "thus" — *So* — (essential becoming); or as the "there" — *Da* — of this actualization in itself (existential becoming); as the "thus" to which the "there" happens to occur, making it into an existential essence *(essentia, cui accidit esse);* or as the "there" that happens to be limited to a given "thus" (as the form which it receives and gives it expression), making it into an essential existence *(esse, quod recipitur in essentia).* In both cases, within becoming, something *supercreaturely* becomes manifest *in its real distinction from the creaturely.* In essential becoming it is the eternity and immutability of the "pure idea" whose actualization is always an accidental occurrence (creatureliness in the sense of an ever-accidental actualization): the idealism of essence. In existential becoming it is the infinity of "pure being" that is always received by and expressed in the "thus" of the delimiting forms (creatureliness in the sense of ever delimiting expression): the realism of existence. In both cases, therefore, the relation between the supercreaturely and the creaturely is ambiguous: whether *as a tension produced by creaturely striving* (spontaneous ethical becoming) or *as a tension produced by a given supercreaturely participation* (mystical passive becoming).[43] Essential becoming, accordingly, appears either as the tension of a striving towards the pure idea (the spontaneous ethical idealism of an essential developmental becoming: like, in metaphysical terms, the *rationes*

---

43. *Teilgabe-Spannung vom Übergeschöpflichen her.* — Trans.

seminales of Stoicism or, in empirical-scientific terms, the *Anlage* of La-marckianism) — or as the tension produced by a given participation in the pure idea (the mystical passive idealism of an essential emanative becoming: such as that, in metaphysical terms, of Plotinus or, in empirical-scientific terms, of Edgar Dacqué). Accordingly, existential becoming appears either as a tension of becoming that develops out of its own particular form into universal being,[44] in order to be man, world, earth, and being as such (the spontaneous ethical realism of an existential developmental becoming: like that, in metaphysical terms, of voluntaristic nominalism or, in empirical-scientific terms, of Darwinism's drive towards existence from the first particular forms into the universal plenitude of forms) — or as a tension produced by a given participation in pure being (the mystical passive realism of an existential emanative becoming: like that, in metaphysical terms, of Averroism or, in empirical-scientific terms, of Bergsonianism's self-differentiating *élan vital*).

What is *formative* in both cases, therefore, and for both kinds of tension, is the *absolutum,* which corresponds to what is supercreaturely in either, *of an identity of essence and existence:* as the passive goal providing the outer limit of the tension of striving, and as the active origin providing the limit of the tension of participation. The idealism of the essential becoming of an existential essence is subordinate to the determining limit of *essence-*and-existence as an *absolutum* (God as *Ipsa Forma:* the "existing ideal as such"): as the passive goal providing the outer limit of a spontaneous ethical idealism (striving towards the goal of an "ideal in existence" *in infinitum*) — as the active origin providing the limit of a mystical passive idealism (in order to reveal the "existent ideal" *in infinitum*). On the other hand, the realism of the existential becoming of an essential existence is subordinate to the determining limit of *existence-*and-essence as an *absolutum* (God as *Ipsum Esse:* "pure being as such"): as the passive goal providing the outer limit of a spontaneous ethical realism (striving towards the goal of "existence as such" *in infinitum*),[45] as the active origin that provides the limit of a mystical passive realism (to reveal "pure existence" *in infinitum*). By the same token, however, the creaturely itself comes to be an *in infinitum,* for which the *absolutum* provides the respective measure; yet, precisely on this account, it is also unfulfillable and therefore "tragic." This form of the *tragic* — that of a *shipwrecking upon the measure of the absolute* — follows from the form of a dynamic identity with the absolute. The active dynamic identity, which re-

44. *All-Sein.* — Trans.
45. *Eines Existierens schlechthin.* — Trans.

sides within the mode of the tension of striving, results in an ethical "tragicism": a striving for the absolute that, in each case, is shipwrecked upon it. The passive dynamic identity, on the other hand, which is implied in the mode of the tension of participation, produces a mystical "tragicism": the imparting of the absolute becomes the process of the absolute's own coming to wreck (into the relative).

In this dual form of an inner tragicism, we can now recognize our two perspectives upon becoming: *idealism and realism*. Since the measure for the idealism of the essential becoming of an existential essence is the absolute of *essence*-and-existence, it is intrinsically an *ideative tragicism* (as in "the tragic of the idea"): it is ethically ideative insofar as it is the active shipwreck of the tension of striving (proper to a spontaneous ethical idealism) upon the absolute of the "ideal in existence"; it is mystically ideative insofar as it is the passive shipwreck of the tension of participation in the absolute of an "existent ideal" (as in a mystical passive idealism). On the other hand, since the measure of the realism of the existential becoming of an essential existence is the absolute of *existence*-and-essence, it is intrinsically a *realistic tragicism* (as in "the tragic of being"): it is ethically real insofar as it is the active shipwreck of the tension of striving (proper to a spontaneous ethical realism) upon the absolute of an "absolute existence"; it is mystically real insofar as it is the passive shipwreck of the tension of participation in the absolute of a "pure existence" (in a mystical passive realism).

9. Thus the inner *correlation between* the form of the *tragic* (8) *and* the forms proper to the *philosophies of essence and existence* (5-7) becomes manifest. For our survey of the forms of creaturely becoming now transfers from the ontic to the noetic so as to apply to a survey of the forms proper to philosophies of essence and existence: a pure philosophy of essence now appears within the same range of forms that stretches between the extreme poles of *essence*-and-existence (corresponding to a pure philosophy of essence) and *existence*-and-essence (corresponding to a pure philosophy of existence); and it appears as well within the mediate possibilities of existential essence (corresponding to an existential philosophy of essence) and essential existence (corresponding to an existential philosophy of existence).[46]

46. The difference is simply that the earlier, noetic approach (5-7) centered around the (noetic) act, whereas the current approach is an immediate analysis of the (ontic) object. The distribution of the range of forms among various historical philosophies is thus in each case reversed. Viewed from the vantage of the noetic, Platonism is an existentialism: because it is situated noetically and methodologically, as a formal-critical philosophy of distance, in the formal existence of the thinker. Viewed from the vantage of the ontic, however, it is an

Equally, however, identity appears as the formal principle within this entire range of forms; and thus what appears is precisely the tragic that was proper to the previous range: the range stretching between the active and passive forms of the tragic (8) now appears as stretching between ethical and mystical tragicism. But, as such, this identity is the "presupposition" for the tragic of original sin: as the "like God," which precipitates the Fall and is represented in the concrete supernatural order (as the locus of original sin) at the level of participation in the divine nature. The pure form of this "like God" that precipitates the Fall (as the pure form of the tragic) is the universal "natural" form, but it is a "natural" form that is qualified at the level of participation in the divine nature: as a seizing of the God who has shared himself beyond all measure. It is also logical, therefore, that the explicit forms of a philosophy of essence and existence erupt from the Reformation, since in its fundamental impulse the Reformation directly took the absolute God as its measure (in the Lutheran interpretation of the first commandment), and hence could view the human being only as essentially failed and shipwrecked (and thus as tragic). Here, in the realm of the sacred, original sin's form of absolutism-tragicism thus broke out anew (in keeping with the Reformation's doctrine of the indelibility of original sin), and it is precisely this impulse that is at work — as the logical secularization of the Reformation's fundamental form — in the explicit range of forms proper to essentialism and existentialism.[47]

---

essentialism: for, by virtue of its standing within the formal existence of the thinker, it is situated objectively in the world of pure ideas as idealism. Likewise, viewed from the vantage of the noetic, Aristotelianism is an essentialism: because it is, as the subjective dialectical philosophy of a cosmic system, noetically and methodologically objective thought. Viewed from the vantage of the ontic, however, it is precisely on this account an existentialism: because it is situated objectively in the world of existences, as realism, by virtue of its noetic orientation towards the (noetic) objective. The usual typology of essentialism-and-existentialism is thus an inadmissible simplification. And even what we have just set forth is still an unsatisfying abridgement: because what was actually meant by "Platonism-and-Aristotelianism" was "Parmenides-Heraclitus-Plato-Aristotle" (6-7). But the essence of the matter is clear: that the tragic proper to "absolute" philosophy consists not only in its absolutism, but in the internal contradiction of each of two absolutisms: a noetic existentialism that is, ontically, an essentialism; a noetic essentialism that is, ontically, an existentialism.

47. In this respect, however, the Reformation is simply the form in which the most formal form of all heresies became manifest. This is implicit in the two words for heresy — *Häresie* and *Ketzerei* — themselves. *Heresy,* which comes from αἵρεσις, signifies one's own personal choice, in which everything objective stands as something relatively selectable over against the selecting will, understood as the site and instrument of the absolute: choice over against the objective, and not service within the objective. The one who chooses absolutely

Precisely for this reason, therefore, the entire range of forms proper to essentialism and existentialism cannot provide the "presupposition" of the Christian. For this range of forms is that of the always tragic alternation between different identities (the identity of absolute essence as *essence*-and-existence — or the identity of absolute existence as *existence*-and-essence). Countering the "impatience" of these rending absolutizations, there is the "patience" of *standing within the genuinely creaturely interval between* creaturely essence and creaturely existence. Nothing creaturely, nothing within the creature by its contrast to something else, constitutes a specifically "divine" reality: neither a divine ideality of essence (understood as "exemplary identity" with God), nor a divine dynamism of existence (understood as "rhythmic identity" with God). Rather, authentic creaturely becoming, which is immediately related to the creator, is just this becoming itself, rather than any sort of derivation from an essence or an existence. The underivable now of each moment of becoming stands in an immediate relation to the eternal moment of the creator *(in praesenti aeternitatis)*.[48] Creaturely becoming is not even an (always tragic) interval *between;* rather, it is, so to speak, a *potentia oboedientialis* understood as the more profound form of the factical creaturely correlation (one, though, that is neither necessary nor a matter of mutual derivation) between creaturely essence and creaturely existence: the innermost relation to the creator as a letting be of the actualization that is given by him.[49] Neither essence nor existence, nor

thus takes up a position over against the objective — as a "tragic individual." *Ketzerei,* on the other hand, which comes from καθαρός, signifies the orientation to an "absolute purity" (which God alone possesses and is) in contrast to every "human admixture." It is a separating of oneself from the humanity of human forms for the sake of an immediacy to the "absolutely pure." Whereas *Häresie* signifies the act, *Ketzerei* signifies the corresponding object. It is precisely here, therefore, that we see the formal form of original sin. Its "like-God" is found at the level of its act in *Häresie* understood as absolute choice; and at the level of its object in *Ketzerei* understood as the absolutely pure: an absolute orientation to the Absolute. Its "knowledge of good and evil" is found at the level of its act in *Häresie* understood as reflexively conscious choice; at the level of its object, in *Ketzerei* understood as the content that is purified by examination. And in this sense it is also the "biting of the apple": the "tragic" of a fall from the divine sphere of the "absolutely pure" into naturalism, since an unfettered naturalistic passion was already the more profound dimension within "absolute choice." For precisely this reason all forms of heresy are in the final analysis not a breaking away from a given particular Christian content, but rather a breaking with the Christian as such, and with God as such — the logical conclusion of which is that it assumes the form of a pure naturalism and of the Dionysian.

48. Thomas Aquinas, *De Pot.* q. 1, a. 5, ad 2.

49. *Ein Vollziehenlassen des Vollzugs von ihm her.* — Trans.

any derivation between them, nor any "for itself" on the part of the interval of the between as such, can provide the form for an authentically creaturely philosophy: it can be provided, rather, only by what is implicit in becoming: *analogy* (as the relation to the "ever beyond" of the creator) *and being at disposal* (as the "ever now" of the letting be of the actualization that comes from him). In this sense, it is the true "presupposition" of what is Christian: as the preservation of what is distinctive to the creaturely, which God assumes in the incarnation, in order that we, in the form of the creature that God assumed, might again have a share in his divinity.[50]

(b) This grants us a view of the other side of the matter: it shows how the *Christian*[51] is the factical inner *"fulfillment"* of creaturely becoming as we have thus far presented it *(gratia perficit naturam)*. The religious problem of the overcoming[52] of the tragic (of original sin) in the Christian (in accord with section 8 above) appears as the factical *theology intrinsic to the objective problem of the overcoming of essentialism-existentialism in the form of analogy and being at disposal* (a merely factical theology as accords with its essential underivability, but nevertheless an "intrinsic" theology as accords with the existential unity of the remaining problems). This theology therefore comprises two things: the "fulfillment," on the one hand, of the (negative) overcoming of the absolutisms and (consequently) tragicisms of the forms proper to essence-existence; the "fulfillment," on the other hand, of the (positive) preservation of creaturely becoming (in analogy and disposal). The negative occurs by way of the positive: in that God appears in becoming man, and in that, on the other hand, what is distinctive to the creaturely appears through God and is confirmed in God himself, the tragic absolutisms (in which the creaturely either deifies itself in an active pantheistic fashion, or dissolves itself, as God's effluence, in a passive theopanistic fashion) vanish.

Seen in light of these connections what is specifically Christian is fundamentally the *making visible of the invisible God* (John 1:18): over against the world of original sin, which has made the creaturely into God (whether it be creaturely "nature" or creaturely "righteousness": Rom. 1–4), God appears as the one who alone is absolute, in the utter absoluteness of the freedom of his will in judgment and love (Rom. 8–11), so that, precisely thus, the presumptuous absoluteness of the creaturely is unmasked as the human clay

---

50. Cf. in this regard *Analogia Entis* Part I; *Deus semper maior* I-III, 1938-39 (Freiburg: Herder 1938) and the next essay, on the scope of analogy as a fundamental Catholic form.
51. *Das Christliche.* — Trans.
52. *Aufhebung.* — Trans.

of the earth and the sin and falsehood of man (Rom. 1–4; 9–11). This "ful-fills" the envisioned overcoming of the spontaneous-ethical tragic absolut-ism that we discovered within the essential and existential tension of striv-ing: the tragic, absolute striving towards the "ideal within existence" *(Ipsa Forma)* or towards an "absolute existing" *(Ipsum Esse)* is redeemed in the *pa-tience of humility*.[53] The patience of humility becomes the fundamental Christian form *(perficit)* of genuine creaturely becoming.

Secondly, however, what is specifically Christian is the making visible of the invisible God *in "the form of a man like any other"* (Phil. 2:7): over against the drive of the world of original sin to be "like God," the God who alone is "wholly God" appears as "wholly man,"[54] and "wholly Christ" precisely as "head and body,"[55] i.e., in the visibility of an earthly, human church "of mere men of mere earth," so that in precisely this way the creature, who wants to be like God, might learn simply to be a "man upon the earth": *Cum Deus esset, homo factus est, ut se homo hominem cognosceret.*[56] This "fulfills" the envi-sioned overcoming of the mystical passive tragic absolutism that we discov-ered within the essential and existential tension of participation: the tragically absolute imparting of the "existent ideal" or of "pure existence" is redeemed in the *patience of human ordinariness*. What remains here of the tragic — the un-masking of the presumption to be God as human falsehood — is also resolved; for even this underscoring of human falsehood fades away into the inconspic-uousness of a "man like any other." The patience of resting in the ordinary is therefore the more complete form of the patience of humility, and, as such, the Christian form *(perficit)* of genuine creaturely becoming.

Finally, however — and thirdly — what is specifically Christian is the making visible of the invisible God not simply in "the form [*schema*] of a man like any other," but *in the "form of a slave,"* as the "worm" that was crushed in the "scandal" of "death on a cross" (Phil. 2:7-10; Ps. 22:6; 1 Cor. 1:23): in contrast to the drive of the world of original sin, which seeks funda-mentally to overcome the limitation of the creaturely in an unlimited form *(Forma Ipsa)* and an unlimited being *(Ipsum Esse)*, he who alone is unlim-ited in form and being (essence and existence) appears in the patience of the longsuffering of the most extreme limitation — in the "deformed" form[57] of

53. *Demütigung.* — Trans.

54. Augustine, *Serm.* 293, 7.

55. Augustine, *In Ps.* 56, 1.

56. While being God, he was made man, in order that man should know himself to be only man. Augustine, *Serm.* 77, 7, 11.

57. Augustine, *Serm.* 27, 6.

the crucified slave and of the worm crushed in the non-being of death — so that in the continuation of this form and this being within a deformed church, which as the body of his members is "dying" ever anew,[58] the patience of creaturely limitation might render service to this redemptive patience of God. This fulfills the most decisive overcoming of tragic absolutism: the tragically absolute tension — which is at work within the spontaneous ethical tension of striving and the mystical passive tension of participation — is redeemed in the *patience of service*. What remains of the tragic — a submission to the ordinary — is redeemed in this: that every personal suffering from personal limitation disappears[59] in the members' office of service to the patience of God himself in his uttermost limitation. Service thus becomes the mystery of the profounder unity of distance and identity (which in the case of the tragic had the form of a contradictory explosiveness): service to the patience of God occurs as a representation of this patience (and thus in an *"identity of service"*); at the same time, though, it occurs as the realization of the posture proper to the creature as such (and thus in "service as distance"). The patience of this service to the patience of God (as the inner overcoming of an ultimate "patience with God") is thus the perfected form of the patience of resting in the ordinary, and, as such, the fully Christian form *(perficit)* of genuine creaturely becoming.

58. Augustine, *Serm.* 27, 6.
59. *Untergeht.* — Trans.

2 The Scope of Analogy as a Fundamental Catholic Form

1940

"Analogy" was not called a "fundamental Catholic form" prior to the dispute in whose course it was formulated as such.[1] It was a dispute that took in a complex assemblage of questions, representing the incipient German Newman movement, the neo-Augustinianism of Hessen, Scheler's phenomenology of nature and revelation, and Karl Adam's analysis of faith. Throughout this dispute, what was really at issue was the unity between nature and supernature, philosophy and theology, a unity to be found within a basic and underivative concept of "the religious." Initially, these circles were inspired by the way that Rudolf Otto's "numinous" and Scheler's "feeling of value" had transposed the older attempts in this direction — on the parts of Jacobi and Schleiermacher, as well as of English and French modernism — from the subjective plane (that of a fundamental "religious need") to the objective plane (that of a fundamental "religious value"). By contrast, the *"analogia entis"* seemed to provide the desired form of unity intrinsic to Catholicism.[2] This first stage was immediately followed by a second: the *analogia entis* as a Catholic response to Protestant theology's own fundamental form, as most consistently set forth by Karl Barth.[3] But since one could already descry the ranks of modern philosophy in general ranged just behind the front lines of the Protestant position,[4] it was

1. "Gottesfahrung und Gottesbeweis," *Stimmen der Zeit* 104 (October 1922): 12-19.
2. "Gott in uns oder Gott über uns?" *Stimmen der Zeit* 105 (October-November 1922; May-June, September 1923): 343-62; *Religionsbegründung,* 1923; *Gottgeheimnis der Welt,* 1923; repr. in *Schriften,* vol. 2, 1962.
3. *Stimmen der Zeit* (August 1923).
4. *Gottgeheimnis der Welt,* 1923 (*Schriften,* vol. 2, 1962).

This essay first appeared in *Scholastik* (1940).

self-evident from the outset that a third stage would be necessary: the *analogia entis* presented as a Catholic response to modern thought since Descartes. This, at the same time, laid the ground for the fourth and final stage, which first came to the forefront in the course of the debate with Maréchal: the *analogia entis* as a response to the way in which Franco-Belgian Thomism (and soon thereafter, following in its wake, the new German Thomism) attempted to "transpose" modern thought onto a foundation of scholasticism.[5] In these four stages, the *analogia entis* was presented as the "fundamental Catholic form" whose formulation by the Fourth Lateran Council in 1215 is valid, with regard both to content and method, for the inner unity of nature and supernature, philosophy and theology.[6]

From the beginning, with regard to all of this, similar forms were proposed, but forms that were, whether consciously or unconsciously, fundamentally opposed to the *analogia entis*. The *opposition* proposed by *Romano Guardini* (1926) preserves a tension between antitheses — to the point, on the one hand, of creating a structure that ultimately oscillates only within itself; and does so in such a way, on the other hand, that supernature and theology threaten to become but one side (the personalistic) of the antithesis. *Heidegger's* method of a fundamentally finite philosophy (1929)[7] shares my emphasis upon creatureliness as a form of thought, but for Heidegger it is a pure finitude. *Karl Barth* has constructed his dogmatics (since 1927) according to the method of a suspended middle between antitheses, but for him this is a (purely theopanistic) *"analogia fidei"* as opposed to the *analogia entis* (which he characterizes as "anti-Christian"). *Theodor Haecker* developed an anthropology that carries analogy, understood as "similitude," as far as an *analogia Trinitatis*, but precisely in order to portray the finitude of man as a fall.[8] *Karl Adam* aims, on the one hand, at the most extreme kind of Thomism, for which nature and philosophy no longer have their own ground of existence, but then, on the other hand, he aims at a kind of Thom-

---

5. *Philosophisches Jahrbuch* (1929).

6. *Gottgeheimnis der Welt*, 1923; *Gott*, 1926; *Religionsphilosophie katholischer Theologie*, 1926; now reprinted in *Religionsphilosophische Schriften, Schriften*, vol. 2, 1962; "Neue Theologie," in *Stimmen der Zeit* (August-September, 1926); "Das katholische Kirchenprinzip, in *Zwischen den Zeiten* (July 1929). Cf., as a systematic complement, the corpus of the (unpublished) Whylen Lectures on philosophy and theology from 1924 to 1927, as well as that of the Salzburg lectures on the method of theology from August 1931; see also *Analogia Entis* I.

7. *Kant und das Problem der Metaphysik* (Frankfurt: Klosterman, 1951).

8. *Was ist der Mensch* (Leipzig: Hegner, 1933); *Schöpfer und Geschöpf* (Leipzig: Hegner, 1934); etc.

ism behind which one detects the stronger influence of a Scotism of the personal irrational in the flux of history (1939).[9]

All of this was then radicalized by a younger generation. The *Gnosis des Christentums* (1939) of *Georg Koepgen* is symptomatic of the most extreme fissure of contradiction. On the one hand, one sees the supertemporal Gnosis of the Christian East: in the attempts to formulate a "traditional theology" whose extreme prototype is Greek Orthodox theology with its principle of the "pneumatico-sophiological tradition." On the other hand, one sees a Western personalism: in the attempts to make Ferdinand Ebner a founding figure, who could take over the leading role previously assigned to Pascal and Newman, and to formulate a dynamically actual "theology of proclamation" — whose extreme prototype is the theology of the Reformation, with its principle of "actualistic proclamation": interpreted in a more subjective and psychological fashion by Schleiermacher (according to the formal principle of "being seized"[10] as a "being affected," and according to the material principle of an immediate relation with the person of Christ); but interpreted in an objective fashion by Barth (as the here-and-now of the God who speaks in the word of preaching).

The counterpart to this is found in the philosophy of a Catholic Heidegger school, which attempts to unite Maréchal and Heidegger. All efforts in this direction proceed from the point of view I laid out in my own work, from *Religionsphilosophie katholischer Theologie* to the first volume of *Analogia Entis*: that, namely, of the metaphysics of Thomas Aquinas, understood as a metaphysics of "analogy," distinguished both from a metaphysics of the infinite and from a metaphysics of the finite. But it is precisely this analogy that is done away with in order to posit in its place an immediate dynamic between the infinite and the finite: whereas the systematic principle of Maréchal's Thomism is a dynamic infinity, that of Heidegger's phenomenology is a dynamic finitude. *Max Müller* has given the clearest formulation of this synthesis.[11] At the level of content, the issue is the "unity of existential finitude and essential infinity."[12] Formally, therefore, what is at issue is a style of thought in which spirit and truth are identical: "spirit coming to itself . . . , insofar as spirit recognizes itself as the truth, the truth of all reality."[13] There is a certain

---

9. "Von dem angeblichen Zirkel im katholischen Lehrsystem oder von dem einen Weg der Theologie," *Wissenschaft und Weisheit* 6 (1939).

10. *Ergriffenheit.* — Trans.

11. *Realität und Rationalität*, Dissertation, University of Freiburg, 1938.

12. *Realität und Rationalität*, p. 3.

13. *Realität und Rationalität*, p. 5.

identity contained within this formula as regards both content and act: the identity of "essential infinity" between God and creature; the identity of "truth" and "reality" in divine and creaturely spirit. The final direction taken by this school is thus a transposition of Thomas onto Hegel. *Johannes B. Lotz* still sees the common element of this new school in keeping with the original and measured view of Maréchal: creaturely movement (in being and consciousness) as a "reenactment of the original divine act," but only insofar as "divine Being" "discloses" and "reveals" itself in "universal being as such."[14] Conversely, *Karl Rahner* — following the predominant tendency of Heidegger's thought — gives "essential infinity" a decisive orientation towards "existential finitude": in that the *abstractio* (as Maréchal says) is fulfilled in the *imaginatio* (as Heidegger says): the "spirit" in the "world."[15] Finally, *Gustav Siewerth* takes Max Müller's formula of the double identity to its logical conclusion.[16] The fundamental relation between God and creature is one of "exemplary (ideal) identity,"[17] to the point that finite being bears "necessity, absoluteness, divinity" as the "seal of its birth."[18] Accordingly, truth and reality are (formally) identical in spirit: since reason "out of the depth of its divine birth, beholds being in its contemplation of beings, and looks into the very ground of being. Its actuality is the actuality of truth."[19] Thus, on the one hand,[20] the "self-emptying of God" appears as the essence of the natural creation,[21] and participation in the tri-personal life as a natural "divine birth" of reason.[22] On the other hand, however, the "knowledge of the relation between God and world . . . sways undecidedly, in a self-contradictory border zone, between 'deistic difference' and 'pantheistic identity.'"[23]

Over against this entire group, *Hans Urs von Balthasar*[24] essentially employs a complete method of "analogy" and opposes it to the form of "contradiction-identity" in virtually the same way as I do in my work. Here

---

14. *Sein und Wert I* (Paderborn: Schöning, 1938).

15. *Geist in Welt. Zur Metaphysik der endlichen Erkenntnis bei Thomas von Aquin* (München: Kösel, 1964; originally 1939).

16. *Der Thomismus als Identitätssystem* (Frankfurt: Schulte-Bulmke, 1939).

17. *Der Thomismus als Identitätssystem*, pp. 5ff. [*Exemplarische (ideele) Identität.* — Trans.]

18. *Der Thomismus als Identitätssystem*, p. 33.

19. *Der Thomismus als Identitätssystem*, p. 208 to the end.

20. *Der Thomismus als Identitätssystem*, pp. 75, 134.

21. *Der Thomismus als Identitätssystem*, p. 33.

22. *Der Thomismus als Identitätssystem*, pp. 205ff.

23. *Der Thomismus als Identitätssystem*, p. 52.

24. *Apokalypse der Seele I-III* (Salzburg-Leipzig: Pustet, 1937/39).

too the deeper form of analogy — which is the mystery of the Cross — holds sway: to ascend into the "similarity, however great" only to fall into the "ever greater dissimilarity," though it is in just this way that one first comes to participate in the majesty of God. In all of this, however, from the first volume of his *Apokalypse* onward, one hears a double emphasis: on the one hand, the (existential) emphasis upon a "flowing with the flow of the world"; on the other hand, the (essential) emphasis upon a "suspension of the image"[25]: the first being a subdued version of the Dionysian; the second, a subdued version of the mythical, though the mythical (as suspended) is ultimately subordinated to the Dionysian. As it happens, this yields a position comparable to the formula of Max Müller and Gustav Siewerth: an existential infinity (of a subdued Dionysianism, in Paul Claudel's sense) and an essential finitude (of the mythical), and thus a rhythmic identity with God (because it is an existential infinity). Balthasar therefore, logically, says no to the Origen of pneumatic ascent (and to the dissolution of the earthly form of the image into pure spirit), but he says yes to the Origen of the Dionysian vitality of an earthly "life in fire."

Thus, as alternatives to "analogy," the contemporary situation presents us with two formulae: exemplary and rhythmic "identity." Of course, on the face of it, "existential finitude and essential infinity" within "exemplary identity" expresses the primacy of the Maréchalian progress towards "pure ideal being" (as the rebirth, by way of the spirit of German Idealism, of the exemplarism of the early Middle Ages); but in this respect it is the Gnosis and pneuma of a positive "spiritualization *in infinitum*"[26] and thus, ultimately, something peculiarly Eastern. On the other hand, the formula of "existential infinity and essential finitude" within a rhythmic identity with God aims at the kind of Dionysianism and mythicality proper to a positive "vitalization *in finitum*,"[27] and precisely thus at something peculiarly Western. The ultimate imprecisions in Guardini, Heidegger, Barth, Haecker, Adam become clear when contrasted with these two formulae: in the philosophical dispute between a suspended dynamism of existence and a suspended ideality of pure essences; in the theological dispute between a theology of personal history and a theology of pneumatic Gnosis; in the practical religious dispute between a mystical ascesis that expresses a personal vision of value and an ascetic mysticism of cultic initiation.

25. *Schweben des Bildes.* — Trans.
26. *Vergeistigung ins Unendliche.* — Trans.
27. *Verlebendigung ins Endliche.* — Trans.

In all of these controversies, we see a new and more acute version of the old opposition between Thomism and Scotism, and, beneath this, the old debate between the Alexandrian and Antiochene schools; and, at the foundation of it all, the opposition between Eastern thought — which, when made absolute, becomes a supernaturalistic theopanism — and Western thought — which, when made absolute, eventuates in a naturalistic pantheism. We thus have here the opposition that was the objective presupposition for "analogy." Viewed historically, however, it also represents the return of a situation similar to that found in the chapter of the Fourth Lateran Council denouncing Joachim of Fiore, which resulted in the classical formulation of "analogy": given that the extreme West and the extreme East were united in Joachim's Gnostic mysticism and mystical Gnosis. Thus, once again, our task is to elaborate the entire scope of this analogy as a fundamental Catholic form: from the perspective of its historical and its objective presuppositions.

I. The Meaning of Analogy in View of Its Historical Presuppositions

1. The classical formula of analogy is stated in the second chapter of the Fourth Lateran Council, where it is presented as the council's internal response to *Abbot Joachim of Fiore's doctrine of the Trinity*.[28] In its response, the council adopted Peter Lombard's doctrine of the Trinity as its own — the very doctrine that Joachim of Fiore had censured as implying a "quaternity in God" ("the three Persons and their common essence as a virtual fourth") — and at the conclusion of its decision developed "analogy" as the internal ground of its decision.

Abbot Joachim's doctrine of the Trinity regards the unity of the Three Divine Persons as identical with the form of unity that is the church, insofar as it is one with the Father and the Son in the Holy Spirit. For this reason, he affirms that "Father and Son and Holy Spirit are one essence, one substance, and one nature,"[29] but not in the sense of "a true and proper *(veram et propriam)* unity," but rather in the sense of a "collective and by similitude *(quasi collectivam et similitudinariam),* just as many persons are called one people, and many believers one church."[30] "To support his doctrine he relies mainly on the word Christ spoke in the Gospel concerning the faithful: 'I

---

28. Denz. 431-32.
29. Denz. 431.
30. Denz. 431.

will, Father, that they be one in us as we are one, that they may be perfectly one' (Jn 17:22ff.). This is how he argues: Christ's believers are one not as *one single thing* common to all *(quaedam una res)*, but they are one, namely, in the way that they are one church on account of the unity of the Catholic faith, and ultimately one kingdom on account of the unity of indissoluble charity."[31]

Against this identity — between the tri-personal "unity of God" and "unity with (the tri-personal) God" — the council posits the sharpest of distinctions. *Firstly,* while the one true God is, as such, the mystery of the Three Persons, he is not therefore, as the one and only God, that which *results* from the Three Persons, but is rather the "true and proper" self-identity of "one essence, one substance and one nature." For this reason, the church's confession in the word of faith and the practices of religious life (as a participation that comes from God and goes towards God) is addressed not to the Three Persons and their, as it were, consequent and resultant unity, but rather, conversely, to the *one* and *only* God, who as such is the mystery of the Three Persons: "We therefore, with the approval of the Sacred Council, believe and confess with Peter the Lombard that there is One Highest Something *(una quaedam summa res),* incomprehensible and ineffable, which is truly Father, Son, and Holy Spirit."[32] *Secondly,* and for this reason, the "unity of God," understood as the "unity of identity in nature," is essentially contrasted with "unity with God," understood as a "union of charity in grace." "When then he who is the Truth prays to the Father for his faithful 'that they may be one in us as we also are one' (Jn 17:22), the word 'one' as applied to the disciples is to be taken in the sense of a union of charity in grace, while in the case of the divine Persons it is to be taken in the sense of a unity of identity in nature. In the same way, on another occasion the Truth says: 'you must be perfect as your heavenly Father is perfect' (Mt 5:48), as though he were saying more explicitly: 'you must be perfect' in the perfection of grace 'as your heavenly Father is perfect' in the perfection of nature — that is, each in the way proper to each."

Thirdly, however, because the ineradicable difference between God and creature is manifested precisely in such supreme concepts as "one" *(unum)* and "perfection" *(perfectio),* the mystery of unity with and in the tri-personal God (as the greatest and most profound mystery of the supernatural and of redemption) becomes the site of the most formal manifestation of

31. Denz. 431.
32. Denz. 431. [*Ein Höchstes Etwas.* — Trans.]

the distance between God, the creator, and the creature. Whereas the council had previously opposed the intimacy of the tri-personal life — understood in almost matter-of-fact terms as the impersonal officiality of the "One Highest Something" — to the indifferentiation between the "unity of God" and "unity with God," even to the point of contrasting God as a silent, majestic "thing"[33] *(res)* with the "personal," it now determines explicitly, at the conclusion of the verdict, that the "reason" *(quia)* for this verdict is the "ever greater" distance between "creator" and "creature." Through the mystery, "however great," of personal life with and in the tri-personal God, there appears the "ever greater" realism of the matter-of-fact relation between "creator" and "creature." Within this relation itself there is, furthermore, through and beyond every unity of similarity between creator and creature, "however great," the "ever greater" distance of "dissimilarity": as it was inexorably manifested in the relation between the creaturely "unity of plurality" *(unitatem . . . collectivam)* and the mystery of that most exalted unity, the divine "One, Highest, Incomprehensible, and Ineffable Something" *(una quaedam summa res incomprehensibilis et ineffabilis).* "Each (perfection) in the way proper to each: because one cannot note any similarity between creator and creature, however great, without being compelled to observe an ever greater dissimilarity between them."[34]

The point of departure for the council's verdict is thus the greatest, most profound, and most intimate mystery of revelation: the mystery of deification through "participation in the divine nature," as children of the Father, con-formed[35] to the Son, in the Spirit of the Holy Spirit; the mystery of redemption as that of the "unity" of the church as a unity with the Father who sends, in unity with the Son who is sent, and thus in unity with the Holy Spirit as the unity of the Father and the Son; and hence the most proper mystery of God as the mystery of the self-communication of the tri-personal life in the personal life of the "children of God" as "members of the church." And yet this is precisely the point of departure into the "ever greater" mystery of the "ever greater dissimilarity" between the "creator" — understood as the "Incomprehensible and Ineffable One Highest Something" (whose intimacy to itself is that of "Father, Son, and Holy Spirit") — and the "creature," which in itself is "one people of many persons, and one church of many believers."

33. *Sache.* — Trans.
34. Denz. 431.
35. *Mit-förmig.* — Trans.

2. The significance of the Fourth Lateran Council's taking a stand with Peter Lombard (who marks the beginning of classical scholasticism) against Joachim of Fiore becomes clearer in light of *Joachim's full doctrine*.[36]

Firstly, as the council describes it, his doctrine of the Trinity is a kind of "tritheism." The unity of the Father, Son, and Holy Spirit is not the "true and proper" unity of *"one* essence, *one* substance, and *one* nature," but, "so to speak, a collective" unity that results from the Persons and is contained in them. It consists solely in the dynamic succession of the tri-personal life: from the Father to the Son to the Holy Spirit as the unity of both. As a result, Father, Son, and Holy Spirit are not "equal," as it were; on the contrary, the Holy Spirit is in his essence the reentry of the Son to the Father. He is therefore, as "Spirit," the spiritual stage, as it were, of the unity of the Father and the Son — a unity that would objectively precede the procession of the Son from the Father. He is thus, as the "spirituality"[37] of this "fatherhood," most properly the "Spirit of the Father," and thus possesses the distinction of "proceeding from the Father." But precisely on this account he proceeds "through" the Son or "in" the Son, inasmuch as the original fatherhood already implies the Son; hence the "spirituality" of the concluding unity of the Son in the Father in the Spirit objectively presupposes the Son standing opposite the Father. The inner form of Joachim's "tritheism" is thus that of an intra-divine circulation between a "vitality" (that of the original "fatherhood" of the unity of the Son in the Father) and a concluding "spirituality" (that of the restored unity of the Son in the Father in "the Spirit of the Father"). Joachim's "tritheism" thus stands in an essential relationship to the trinitarian doctrine of the Greek Orthodox East, for which the Holy Spirit is essentially the "Spirit of the Father" — certainly "through" and "in the Son," but not as the "Spirit of the Father and the Son" and, hence, "proceeding from the Father *and* the Son" *(ex Patre Filioque)*. By the same token, therefore, it is essentially connected to the Gnostic Sophiology of the Greek Orthodox East, as the ultimate consequence of its trinitarian doctrine: the Son appears as the "antithesis" between the proper divinity of "fatherhood" and the proper divinity of "spirituality" and therefore, ultimately (in a theopanistic and tragic rendering of the incarnation), as the moment of the tragic fall of the divine life into the world.[38] God is thus the intra-divine process between the "thesis" of an

---

36. The best illustrations are given by H. Denifle, "Das Evangelium aeternum und die Commission zu Anagni," *Archiv für Literatur und Kirchengeschichte* 1 (1885): 49-142; E. Jordan, *Dict. Th. Cath.* VIII, 1425ff.; and E. Benz, *Ecclesia spiritualis* (Stuttgart: Kohlhammer, 1934); "Joachim-Studien II: Die Excerptsätze der Pariser Professoren aus dem Evangelium Aeternum," in *Zeitschrift für Kirchengeschichte* 51 (1933): 415-55; and "Joachim-Studien III: Thomas von Aquin und Joachim de Fiore," in *Zeitschrift für Kirchengeschichte* 52 (1934): 52-116.

37. *Geistigkeit.* — Trans.

38. Notwithstanding its merit, Przywara's reading of Russian Sophiology would seem

"original fatherhood" (of the original unity of the Son in the Father) *and* the "synthesis" of a *"final spirituality"* (of the restored unity of the Son in the Father in the Spirit) by way of the tragic antithesis of a "fall" and "contradiction" that takes place in God through the generation of the world in the Son. Therefore, seen in this context, it is only logical that the Second Council of Lyons — for the same reason that the Fourth Lateran Council decided against Joachim — should direct its charges against the "Greeks": since Michael Palaeologus is enjoined to declare himself both for the *Filioque* and against "tritheism": confessing the Holy Spirit as "fully, perfectly, and truly God, proceeding from the Father and the Son" and thus affirming that the "Holy Trinity is not three gods, but one God, the only God, almighty, eternal, invisible, and immutable."[39] Joachim and the Greek Orthodox East thus appear under the common ensign of a single "terminal spirituality,"[40] understood as the actual unity sealing God within God, whereas the church asserts, to the contrary, the "One and Only Highest Something,"[41] understood as the "One and Only God":[42] the "Incomprehensible and Ineffable" God[43] rather than the "Spirit."

There are yet further perspectives on the matter. For — *secondly* — when we consider all the connections of Joachim's doctrine of the Trinity, he stands in the history of ideas, on the one hand, between the spiritualism of Origen (understood as the original Christian father of the East) and the trinitarian gnosis of the modern Russian Sophiologists; at the same time, however, he is the father of the mystical spiritualism of the West (which, for this reason, is simply termed "Joachimism": from the Franciscan "spirituals" to the Reformation and Jansenism, which fashion "pure spirit" into an explicit heresy). This "tritheism" — which culminates specifically in "Spirit as goal and end" — is for Joachim the principle of the Trinity of God (that is, of the super-economic Trinity), since the *Trinity is the principle of creation* (as economic Trinity). The Spirit is the goal and end and completion in God, since the Spirit is the goal and end and completion of creation. Three ages thus correspond to the Father, Son, and Holy Spirit: the Old Covenant as the age of the Father, the New Covenant as the age of the Son, and the termination of the New Covenant in an age of the Holy Spirit. The Old Covenant, as the age of the Father, is the age of the "ancients" and of the "married," the age of "life according to the flesh," under the "law" and thus in "slavish service" and hence in "fear": corresponding therefore to a "fatherhood" that is not yet "spirit." The New Covenant, as the age of the Son in the visible church, is the age of "youths" and "clerics," the age of "life according to the

---

to apply more to its (Joachimite-)Schellingian roots than to its late flowering in Bulgakov. — Trans.

39. Denz. 463.
40. *End-Geistigkeit.* — Trans.
41. Denz. 432.
42. Denz. 463.
43. Denz. 432.

flesh and the spirit" and, as such, in "grace," but in the "obedience of the Son" and therefore in "faith": corresponding therefore to the "Son," who is the "middle" within the intra-divine life and who, in keeping with the mystery of his incarnation, lives on in a church that is no longer the Old Covenant, but as "church" is not yet "pure spirit." The third age, that of completion, is therefore the age of the world peculiar to the Holy Spirit: the age of "children" and "monks" (beginning with St. Benedict as the first "spiritual man"),[44] the age of pure "life in the Spirit" and, as such, in the "overflowing of grace" and in "freedom" and so in "love": thus corresponding to the Holy Spirit as the one in whom sonship (and so too the church, understood as the visibility of sonship) passes over into a unity of "spiritual fatherhood" and "spiritual sonship" (as prefigured in the monastery of "children" and "monks"). Corresponding to the succession from the "married" to "clerics" to "spiritual monks," the direction of the three ages of the world is that of an increasing worldlessness and timelessness: under the sign, that is, of an explicit eschatologism, and thus always under the sign of the "Antichrist" (so that each new age of the world contends with the age that has just elapsed as with the "Antichrist": just as the "spirituals," and after them the Reformers and Jansenists, viewed the church as "Antichrist"). Corresponding to the succession from "flesh (law, slavery, fear)" to "spirit (grace, overflowing, freedom, love)," the direction taken is one of increasing spiritualization: under this sign, that is, of a growing spiritualism or pneumaticism (which, to be sure, retains revelation and, in particular, the gospel: not, though, in the "form of the church," but rather in the transfigured form of "eternity" and, therefore, as the "eternal Gospel" — and this in the form of the "Spirit" and therefore in "spiritual, pneumatic exegesis" and so, finally, in a theology of the Spirit over against the "hypertrophy of the scholastic discipline of the schools").

Viewed from one side, this entire matter appears to stand between Origenism and modern Russian trinitarian gnosis (which was founded in the middle of the nineteenth century). Joachimism is a development of Origenism: since, for Origen, the way of salvation is one of increasing spiritualization — even to the point of an ideal dissolution of the visible forms of the New Covenant into "pure spirit,"[45] though as of yet without the explicit distinction of the three stages proposed by Joachim. Conversely, modern Russian trinitarian gnosis is a development of Joachimism: since Joachim depicts his tritheism, as the principle of history, simply as a matter of fact, whereas in the case of modern Russian trinitarian gnosis it amounts

44. Cf. the way in which Odo Casel has recently constructed a pneumatic "theology of the tradition" upon the basis of "Benedict of Nursia as a Pneumatic" ("Benedikt von Nursia als Pneumatiker" in Casel, *Heilige Überlieferung* [Münster: Aschendorff, 1938]), even though the Rule of St. Benedict counters the pneumaticism of eastern monasticism with the "toil of obedience" (prologue) and the "common life" (chapter 1) of a "school of service to the Lord" (prologue).

45. Cf. the study of A. Lieske, *Die Theologie der Logosmystik bei Origenes* (Münster: Aschendorff, 1938).

to a fundamentally speculative theory that conceives of the Trinity — basically — merely as the principle of a "divine history." Within this continuum, Abbot Joachim represents a definite midpoint in the peculiar development of the *"Eastern."* Seen thus, it is a theopanistic, cosmological *pneumaticism.* The Holy Spirit appears as the divine principle of the world, of nature, and of history and, therefore, as "Pneuma," i.e., as that "divine quality" whose "process" *is* world, nature, and history. Viewed from the other side, however, this same Joachimism stands essentially within the history of Western "spiritualism,"[46] which is similarly rooted in Origen, but in an Origen whose path to salvation, as one of spiritualization, is interpreted in personalistic fashion and thus points to the Augustinian *imago Trinitatis* within personal spirit *(memoria, intellectus, voluntas).*[47] From this perspective we see the rise of the Franciscan spirituals and the trinitarian spiritualism of Meister Eckhart: indeed, even their two orders, the Franciscans and the Dominicans, were perceived at the time of their inception (1210 and 1216) as the "spiritual monks" of Joachim (†1201). The internal conflict of the Franciscan order, therefore, was one between the "spiritual church" of a "pure Gospel" (as in the case of the Franciscan spirituals) and the visible church (in the authentic spirit of St. Francis). And on behalf of the Dominican order, even Thomas Aquinas had to furnish energetic proof that this order could not be construed as a form of "Joachimism." From the Spirituals and Meister Eckhart, however, this radical development continues on unimpeded to the Reformation, to Jansenism, and to German Idealism: from the religious "spiritual man" (in the case of the Reformation and Jansenism) to the secularized "spiritual man" (in the case of German Idealism). Abbot Joachim thus appears from this perspective as the turning point in the particular development of the *"Western."* It is, in this respect, a pantheistic, personalistic *spiritualism.* The Holy Spirit becomes the intrinsic divinity of the personal spirit and is therefore *"spiritus"* in like terms. But it is Baader, Schelling, and Hegel who represent the most authentic unleashing of "Joachimism." For in each of them the trinitarian dialectic of the personal spirit is at the same time, matter-of-factly, the trinitarian dialectic of cosmic history: which is why Schelling, quite logically, baptizes Joachim's third age of the world with the name that from that time on became generally accepted: that of the Johannine Christianity of the Spirit and of love — as contrasted with the Old Covenant which, as Petrine Christianity, represents the stage of the fatherly discipline of the "Roman church," and the New Covenant, which, as Pauline Christianity, represents the stage of the filial faith of the Reformation. By the same token, however, historically it is also the case that in Baader, Schelling, and Hegel Eastern pneumaticism and Western spiritualism enter upon a new middle path: not only because they definitively absolutize the self-

46. Cf. above all, E. Benz *(Ecclesia spiritualis),* for whom Joachimism signifies *the* position contrary to the Catholic position (leading up, therefore, to the Reformation, etc.).
47. This Origenism has been demonstrated above all by W. Völker. See his *Vollkommenheitsideal des Origenes* (Tübingen: Mohr, 1931).

containment of the personal "spirit" that one finds in Western spiritualism; but also because, for Eastern pneumaticism, they give rise to the secularized form of the absolute, the cosmic trinitarian Gnosis of the modern Russians (leading to Berdyaev, Bulgakov, etc.). In them, therefore, Joachimism appears in its most formal form: as the *unity of the Western and Eastern* in their absolute form: both a spiritualism of the trinitarian person and a pneumaticism of the trinitarian cosmos as the extreme consequence of the identification established by Abbot Joachim between divine and creaturely tritheism. In the word that for Schelling and Hegel is precisely *the* word, Joachimism achieves its most precise formula: *identity* between God and creature.

Now, it is when set over against all these forms of Joachimism, that we see — *thirdly* — the full significance of the Fourth Lateran Council's decision, but now in its agreement with the later, corresponding position of Thomas Aquinas.[48] Over against a trinitarian identity between God and creature, the council asserts the inexorable *distance* of the "one highest, incomprehensible, and ineffable reality." It is Thomas Aquinas who completes this move by first expounding — over against the trinitarianism of history — the ultimacy of the New Covenant of the visible church,[49] in order then — from this perspective — to dissolve the entire trinitarian structure of history: "the Old Law was not only that of the Father, but also that of the Son, because Christ was prefigured in the Old Law; for this reason the Lord says: 'If you believed Moses, you would also believe me; for he wrote about me.' Likewise, too, the New Law is not only the law of Christ, but also that of the Holy Spirit, according to the expression: the law of the Spirit of life in Christ Jesus";[50] "and for this reason the idle talk of certain persons — that one is to expect yet another age of the Holy Spirit — is ruled out of consideration."[51] Such trinitarianism is therefore nullified not only at the material level, by the indissoluble correlation of the twinship of Old and New Covenants, but also at the formal level — insofar as its "form" is one of "identity" — by an emphasis upon the "law" in both, and even indeed upon the "law of the Spirit," and hence by an emphasis upon distance. Correspondingly, something similar also occurs in Thomas's treatment of the trinitarianism of the person. In the final books of *De Trinitate*,[52] even Augustine had keenly emphasized the

---

48. For a very good elucidation of Thomas's position vis-à-vis Joachim's trinitarianism of history, see E. Benz, *Joachim-Studien III*, pp. 52-116.

49. *Summa Th.* II, 1, q. 106.

50. *Summa Th.* II, 1, q. 106, a. 4, ad 3.

51. *Summa Th.* II, 1, q. 106, a. 4, ad 2.

52. XV, 20, 39.

"dissimilarity, however great" within the similarity of the *imago Trinitatis* to its archetype, to the point that he could say, almost in the words of the future council, that even in the condition of eternal beatitude, "that which is made changeless by grace does not attain to equality with that which is immutable by nature; for the creature does not attain to equality with the creator."[53] Indeed, Sermon LII goes so far as to treat the *imago Trinitatis* not even as an "analogy," but as an *"argumentum ad hominem"*: "Believe then in what is *there* [i.e., in the Trinitarian archetype] . . . if you have heard, seen, and grasped it in what is *here* [i.e., in the *imago Trinitatis* within you]. What is within you, you can know; but what is within him who created you . . . , when can you know that? And, even if you will be able one day to know it, you cannot know it yet. Moreover, even when you can know it, will you be able then to know God as God knows himself?"[54] Now Thomas Aquinas — in a way that parallels his disposing of the trinitarianism of history — first tacitly drops the *memoria* in the *imago Trinitatis* and then examines in the two moments that remain, *intellectus* and *voluntas,* only the *circulatio,* the internal circulation of "will into the origin of understanding."[55] This *circulatio* is not in itself the *imago Trinitatis;* rather, it is the *imago Trinitatis* only insofar as it contains within itself — as a movement — the general abstract form of order that obtains between unity and multiplicity, etc.: which is to say, the categories of relation that come to be applied whenever one thinks about the Trinity.[56] Thus, just as Thomas subordinates the gnostic identity of the trinitarianism of history to the distance of the law, here he subordinates the mystical identity of the trinitarianism of the person to the distance of order.

Implied in this, however, is the Fourth Lateran Council's fundamental agreement with Thomas: in the posing of the formula of "analogy" over against Joachimite "identity" in general. The council bases its rejection of an identical trinitarianism between God and creature upon the fundamental law of the "ever greater dissimilarity" that is always to be observed between "creator" and "creature" as such: *"because* one *cannot* note any similarity between creator and creature, however great, without being compelled to observe an ever greater dissimilarity between them." For his part, accordingly, Thomas roots this "cannot" and this "compelled" in being

53. XV, 23, 43.
54. Sermon 52, 10, 23.
55. *De Pot.* q. 9, a. 9, corp.
56. *De Pot.* q. 9, a. 8, corp.

as such. God is "being by his essence" *(ens per essentiam)*, whereas the creature is being only "by participation" *(per participationem)*, and hence there is "no similarity between God and creatures by virtue of any agreement in form *(convenientiam in forma)*": that is, there is a similarity neither in the form of essence (as the "exemplary identity" of the Eastern "life as spirit" would have it), nor in the form of existence (as the "rhythmic identity" of the Western "spirit as life" would have it), "but rather only according to analogy."[57] That is to say, with utter exactitude, that every "limited similarity" *(aliqualem similitudinem)* is transected by the "greatest dissimilarity" *(maxima dissimilitudo)*.[58] Analogy is the "being other" of the "same" predication spoken of both God and creature (as *proportio proportionalitatis*).[59] Indeed, at the end of the day, it is precisely the reverse. The "distance" now appears as what is natural to the relation between creator and creature, and the "analogy" as what mitigates that distance: "the distance of nature that obtains between creature and God cannot preclude that which they have in common within the analogy."[60]

Thus, at the critical heart of the entire question, there stand, on the one side, the Joachimism of the West and East and, on the other, the Fourth Lateran Council and Thomas Aquinas: in the former case, gnostic or mystic, exemplary or rhythmic identity as the fundamental principle of theopanism or pantheism (understood as the basic forms of the absolutized Eastern or Western) — in the latter, analogy as the utterly fundamental principle of Catholicism, because analogy is the utterly fundamental principle obtaining between God and creature.[61]

---

57. *Summa Th.* I, q. 4, a. 3.

58. *De Ver.* q. 1, a. 10, ad 1 in contr.

59. *De Ver.* q. 23, a. 7, ad 9.

60. *De Ver.* q. 2, a. 11, ad 5.

61. Regarding this opposition, it is not insignificant that Abbot Joachim is venerated as blessed, just as Origen died as a martyr, whereas the decision of the church, which alone is true, is not infrequently rendered by human instruments who cannot compete, in enthusiasm and sanctity, with the founders of a central heresy, but who are nevertheless entirely the representatives of the church, servants occupying an office. For this reason, according to the liturgy, it is incumbent upon the bishop who rescinds the suspension of a cleric to use this formula: *"ego, licet peccator, tamen episcopus,"* "I, though a sinner, am nevertheless bishop." So too in the liturgical *"Ordo ad synodum"* the ecclesial synod prays: "Here we are, Lord, Holy Spirit, here we are — in the chains of immense sin *(peccati immanitate detenti)* — nevertheless specially gathered in your name." The "spirit" that stands against the church is a pseudo-spirit, even though it appear in a saint, whereas the Spirit who speaks through the official church is alone the true Holy Spirit, even if sinful tongues are his instruments. In-

II. The Meaning of Analogy in View of Its Objective Presuppositions

The objective extent of the Fourth Lateran Council's decision is reflected in its historical context. In affirming Peter Lombard against Abbot Joachim, the council also affirmed that third epoch of theology that was about to commence: the epoch, that is, of classical scholasticism, whose central compendium was Peter Lombard's *Sentences*. The council was convened under Innocent III, the most powerful pope of the Middle Ages, but also the pope under whose governance the Franciscan and Dominican orders arose — orders that are taken to represent that spiritual monasticism of the age of the Holy Spirit (of which Joachim had spoken), whose effect was the inauguration of modernity (in the Franciscan Ockham and the Dominican Meister Eckhart), and the emergence of the greatest spectrum of theological schools. In this respect, the council — with its emphasis, over against various trinitarian speculations, upon our distance from the "One Highest Something" — is an acute symptom of the opposition between the aristocratic sobriety of the juridicality of the church and the progressive sapiential intuition or scientific logic that one finds in the theological schools.

All the objective questions are summed up and contained in this central point. For what stands out in the council's advocacy of the commencing age of classical scholasticism (as compared to the previous theology of the church Fathers) is the objective structure of theological movements: from the theology of the Greek fathers to that of Augustine to that of scholasticism. The fact that the language of the council stresses distance (leading to the language of "greater dissimilarity") raises the question of the relation between a "theology of the church" and theological movements in general. In finally posing the relation of "creator" to "creature" over against a genuinely supernatural reality (that of "participation" between God and man, and this within the realm of the genuinely trinitarian), the council delineates everything that concerns the relation between nature and supernature, knowledge and faith. The first objective question (concerning the differences among theological movements) is directly stated in the conciliar text, inasmuch as the text defends the scholasticism that is about to commence against the continuing effects of earlier theological movements. The second objective question (concerning theological movements and the theology of the church as such) is contained, as it were, in the style of the conciliar text, inasmuch as it poses a strictly juridical understanding of the faith over against all possible interpretations of the faith. The third objective question, finally (that concerning nature and supernature, etc.), simply remains to be found within the objective perspective provided by the formula of analogy, inasmuch as the essential relationship between nature and supernature, etc. is included and expressed within the

---

deed, as a logical consequence of our redemption by God, who "bore the sins of the world," the one who confesses himself to be under "immense sin" is the most adequate instrument of the true purity of the Holy Spirit.

formula's "cannot" and "compelled." In this way, "analogy," in the fullest sense of the word, turns out to be a fundamental Catholic form.

3. Inasmuch as the council affirms Peter Lombard over against Abbot Joachim, and logically counters every indistinct trinitarian "unity" with the distance between "Creator" and "creature," we are able to discern the *structural principle of possible objective theologies*.[62] This structural principle is found in the complete formula of analogy as such. It is a formula that proceeds from a word of revelation — a word that expresses the heart and consummation of the mystery of supernatural "participation in the divine nature," and of supernatural incarnation and redemption, in terms of trinitarian unity: "that they may be one in us, as we are one" (John 17:22). The formula then goes on to emphasize that, within this twofold supernatural mystery, the natural relationship between "Creator" and "creature" is not only not abrogated, but remains both the measure and the rule: "*because* one *cannot* . . . without being *compelled*. . . ." The formula of analogy thus contains the *three components of the **one** factical economy of salvation: natural creatureliness, supernatural participation in the divine nature, supernatural redemption*.[63] These components appear in the formula within a definite

---

62. This part of my argument corresponds to the view expressed in my *Religionsphilosophie katholischer Theologie* of 1926 (second edition in *Schriften*, vol. 2, 1962).

63. For the language of Holy Scripture, which views the *one* factical economy of salvation in terms of its properly concrete form and thus in terms of the contrast between original sin and redemption, the word "grace" is central, as a kind of short form for redemption. The language of the Greek fathers distinguishes this "grace" from a universal "gracious condescension" of God: the "grace" of "participation in the divine nature," which was lost through original sin and restored, freely and mercifully, through redemption, understood as that of "God's participation in human nature." For just this reason, finally, the language of more recent theology is wont to call this distinct grace "supernature." One may, as the conclusion of this development, deduce an objective structure: "grace" and "supernaturality" have the distinction of expressing the formal aspect of the *one* order of salvation. Whereas "participation in the divine nature" and redemption, understood in terms of "God's participation in human nature," express its content, the phrase "grace of God" expresses the general and formal free condescension of God to the creature, which appears within the purely natural order as "God's assistance"; within the supernatural order, however, it is "grace as God." "Supernaturality" thus expresses the formal aspect of this "grace as God": not only is there a universal self-condescension of God to the creature here, but God himself "is" the "grace" within the "participation in nature" between God and creature, and is thus "beyond" every obligation and every claim and every expectation proper to the "nature" of the creature — and hence is "supernatural." This formal supernaturality, as the "participation in nature" between God and creature, is concrete within the content of the *one* economy of salva-

structure: they appear in *three propositions from which the formal principles of all three possible objective theologies arise* (for while these objective theologies contain all three components, they do so in such a way that each theology is subject to one of these components, which then serves as the formal principle of the other two components). Objectively speaking, each of these formal principles is first of all an ontic principle of being (in the essence of the order that objectively, factically exists between God and man); temporally speaking, however, each is first of all a practical principle of orientation (in the lived conscious-ness[64] of religious life), and only subsequently, by abstraction, a theoretical principle of method (in the reflected consciousness of theological doctrine).

The first principle takes the text of John (17:22) in the sense of a *supernatural "participation in the Divine nature,"* which was freely given to man "in the first moment of creation," which man freely lost in original sin, and which God freely restored in redemption. This supernatural "deification" (θείωσις) is, in its innermost essence, what is described in the Gospel's "one in us, as we are one": "Participation" in the Father because one is a "child of the Father"; "participation" in the Son because one is "conformed to the Son"; and thus "participation" in the Holy Spirit, as the unity of Father and Son, because one is a "holy-spiritual man" (πνευματικός).[65] Since this supernatural deification is imparted to man "in the first moment of creation" and is thus the one content both lost in original sin and restored in redemption, it is here that creation appears in its actual concrete content. Within this relation of "participation in the divine nature," the relation between Creator and creature is made factically concrete. For even the distinctiveness

---

tion: as participation of the creature in God in the "participation in the Divine nature"; and as the participation of God in the creature in "God's participation in human nature" in redemption. But then, viewed in light of this concrete content, the formal terms "grace" and "supernaturality" are each fulfilled in one of the components of this content. "Supernaturality" is fulfilled specifically in "participation in the Divine nature" (and this is why recent theology, in accord with the Greek fathers, also employs it as a synonym for "deification"): because the particular form of what is "beyond" creaturely nature is to be found in the "participation (of the creature) in the Divine nature." "Grace" is fulfilled specifically in redemption understood as the "participation of God in human nature" (and is thus used in Holy Scripture as a synonym for redemption): because the most explicit form of God's universal self-condescension to the creature is found in a "participation in the descent (of God)," just as the most extreme form of the graciousness of a freely bestowed mercy is found in a redemption that consists in God's vicarious atonement.

64. *Bewußt-sein.* — Trans.
65. *Heilig-Geist-Mensch.* — Trans.

of redemption is comprised within this content: insofar as redemption appears (from the particular perspective of the Alexandrian school) as the "assumption of human nature" in Christ into the form of a divine person and thus also, logically, the assumption of the "members of Christ" into participation in this "assumption." Thus "participation in the divine nature" becomes precisely a "participation in the divine person," thereby showing the "deification" to be complete. It is the point of view that originates with Irenaeus and lives on above all in the *Greek fathers:* such that "being in Christ" appears essentially as "being in God." Accordingly, it is from this perspective that Irenaeus sums up the incarnation: "Jesus Christ, our Lord, who . . . became what we are in order to perfect us, to be that which he is."[66] So too (at the zenith of this development) Cyril of Alexandria considers "officiating as God"[67] to be the very essence of the order of redemption: "Though we are human beings according to nature, we officiate as God — as those who are in Christ; for Christ is God."[68]

The path of the practical Christian life is therefore, as definitively developed by Clement of Alexandria and Origen, one of the growth of the Christian as a "God in becoming and thus already likened unto God" (ἐσόμενος καὶ δὴ ἐξομοιούμενος θεός).[69] And, of course, since "deification" is essentially restored and completed in Christ, the path of this growth appears essentially in the form of Christ — but of Christ as essentially a divine person and thus as the "Logos"; and of Christ as the one who is essentially *the* "Christ," the "anointed," with the Holy Spirit as the unction, and whose work is thus fulfilled in the outpouring of the Holy Spirit as the "Pneuma." The growth proper to "deification" thus occurs as growth in the sign of the "Logos" and the "Pneuma," and thus as an increasing "spiritualization": to the point that, in Origen, the visibility and sacramentality of the church appear as provisional to a breakthrough to "pure Spirit" (this being the foundation of Joachim's "*Ecclesia spiritualis*" and of the entire Joachimite tradition).

The formal content of the theology that develops from this point on is therefore this "*participation in God's nature and person.*" And since this "deification" is at the same time a "pure spiritualization," the formal act of this theology, i.e., its proper method, is a spiritually conscious "participation" in and thus anticipation of the *eternal vision (visio beatifica)* in that "gnosis" that is

---

66. *Adversus haereses* V, Pref.
67. *Amten als Gott.* — Trans.
68. *Thes. de trin.*, ass. 33.
69. Clement, *Stromateis*, VII, 1.

implied in "faith," as faith's form: "gnosis is believing; belief, however, is gnostic."[70] Accordingly, just as "deification" is the formal content of theology, "gnosis" is its formal act. The objectively ontic "participation" is known in the subjectively noetic "participation." Just as the theological object is a "co-enactment"[71] of the Being of God's "nature" and "person," so too, logically, the theological act is a "co-enactment" of God's consciousness: a receiving of God's self-expression in faith that becomes a self-unveiling of this self-expression in gnosis. Theology occurs as this self-unveiling of what has been handed down by God, and precisely for this reason it occurs in his Son, as his "Logos," and in the Holy Spirit, as his "Pneuma." Just as man's natural being appears in ontic "participation and co-enactment" simply as the *"potentia oboedientialis"* — the "let-it-be-done-unto-me"[72] — so also natural human consciousness (that of logical thought) appears within noetic "participation and co-enactment" simply as the corresponding noetic *"potentia oboedientialis"* —that is, as a harkening, obedient concurrence with[73] the "Logos" and "Pneuma" of the "divine tradition." Theology is theology of the tradition in Logos and Pneuma.

The *second principle* contained in the full formula of analogy takes the verse from John concerning trinitarian unity in the specific sense of *supernatural redemption in the incarnation of God.* "Participation in the divine nature" achieves its full concreteness only in the "fullness of time," when it is restored by God's "participation in human nature": inasmuch as the incarnation of God, as history's ultimate point, is also logically what determines the goal of God's plan: "He chose us (in Christ) before the foundation of the world" (Eph. 1:4). Even the "assumption of human nature," in Christ, into the form of the divine person (the specifically Alexandrian view of the incarnation) comes to pass essentially in the form of "God's descent into flesh, earth, and world," understood as the goal of God's plan (the Antiochene school's view of the matter). In this way, the full meaning of the verse from John is unveiled: Father, Son, and Holy Spirit appear essentially — in Christ's high-priestly prayer — *within* the mystery of a "mission into the world." This is not a direct revelation of God's trinitarian life in itself; rather, it is a revelation insofar as the mystery of the sending of the Son by the Father, and of the Holy Spirit by the Father and the Son (as one finds

---

70. Clement, *Stromateis*, II, 4; etc.
71. *Mitvollzug.* — Trans.
72. *An-sich-geschehen-Lassens.* — Trans.
73. *Mitgehen im.*

throughout the Lord's valedictory discourses) becomes transparent to the mystery of the trinitarian life. Thus, logically, the "one in us" of which Christ speaks is a unity with the trinitarian life, which is bestowed by union with the mission of the Son and the Holy Spirit. "Deification" as "participation in the divine nature and person" comes about essentially by "participation in God's mission," that is, by participation in God's "incarnation," and this to the point of the abasement and emptiness of the powerlessness of the flesh in the scandal of the cross (1 Cor. 1; Phil. 2:7ff.). This perspective has its basis above all in *Augustine*. Participation in the purely spiritual God is bestowed by participation in the church, understood as his earthly, sensible "body."[74] Participation in the unity and uniqueness of God is bestowed by participation as a "member" in this "body" that consists in manifold difference and in the varying oppositions of its "many members."[75] Participation in God, understood as "pure form," is bestowed by participation in the "deformed" Christ in the "deformed" church.[76] Such is the clear opposition between redemption and original sin: the "as any other man" of God versus the "like God" of the first man. Thus the full law of "deification" reads: As Christ is essentially the descending God, so too the ascent of our "participation in God" occurs solely through participation in God's descent. The glory of God (the core of deification) is found within the scandal of the cross (the core of redemption).

Thus, logically, the practical Christian life is the living out of this descent. The sacramental life is one of increasing "incorporation" into the corporate form of the church of "many members."[77] And for this reason, one's personal ascetical-mystical life is not merely the life of a "member within the body," but a life lived in an emphatic submitting of oneself and giving of oneself to the real concreteness of this body: "Bear with the tares, if you are wheat; bear with the chaff, if you are grain; bear with the bad fish in the net, if you are a good fish."[78] And therefore it is a life that is fulfilled in the knowledge of one's own nothingness. Just as the entire greatness of God appears in the "nothingness" of Christ (Phil. 2:7ff.), and just as the full holiness of God appears in Christ as the "lamb . . . bearing the sins of the world," the proper Christian face of "deification" and "spiritualization" is seen in the opposition between the nothingness of the human being and the All of God, between the sin of man and the mercy of God: "such is . . . the greatest knowledge, that man

74. *In Ps.*, 130, 13.
75. *In Ps.*, 6; 99, 12ff.
76. *Serm.* 27, 6.
77. *Serm.* 272.
78. *In Ps.*, 40, 8.

should know that he is *per se* nothing; and, whatever he is, he is of God and on account of God."[79]

The content of the theology that corresponds to this second principle is therefore that of this "descent between antitheses": God's Spirithood (and our participation in it) in his flesh; God's kingdom (and our participation in it) in his poverty; God's holiness (and our participation in it) in his "bearing the sins of the world"; God's glory (and our participation in it) in his scandal of shame.[80] Precisely for this reason, though, even this theology's formal method of reflection does not amount to a "gnosis" of direct ascent into a divine spiritual realm, but rather consists in the "noetic" mystery of a "descent between antitheses": an antithetical thinking within the ultimate mystery (which is, indeed, the essence of Augustine's language). It is thus a *"theologia crucis,"* a "theology of the cross" in the fullest sense of the term: its content is the crossing between God's All and God's nothingness[81] within a self-crossing thinking;[82] but, precisely as such, its content is the inviolate mystery of God within a thinking that is itself mysterious;[83] and, precisely as such, a thinking within the true Logos and Pneuma, since it takes place within Christ, who is the "Logos of the cross" (1 Cor. 1:18), and within the Holy Spirit, who is the Spirit of the "wisdom of the cross" (1 Cor. 2:2-16).

These two principles are the formal principles, respectively, for a theology of divine tradition and a theology of the cross; and to these the Fourth Lateran Council adds a *third* principle concerning the relation between "creator" and "creature": a principle that follows from the council's earlier assertion, against tritheism, of our distance from the "One Highest Something," and from the emphasis the council placed — within Trinitarian theology — on the difference between the creature's "union of love in grace" and the creator's "unity of identity by nature": between, that is, the "perfection of grace" within the creature and the "perfection of nature" within the creator. That is to say, however, that supernatural participation in God and supernatural redemption are essentially *endowments of the "creature"* and thus not only do not negate the essential "nature" of the creature but, as Thomas later formulates it, are added as a "quality" *(qualiter agere)* to its "what" *(quid agere)* and

79. *In Ps.*, 70, 1, 4.
80. *Serm.* 191, etc.
81. Ep. 140, 25, 62ff. [*Sich-Kreuzen zwischen Gottes All und Nichts.* — Trans.]
82. *Sich-kreuzenden Denken.* — Trans.
83. *Serm.* 52, 6, 16.

as a "mode" *(modum agendi)* to its "substance" *(substantiam actus)*.[84] As much as the actually existing creature first appears in its actual "final form" within the mystery of supernatural participation in God and supernatural redemption, it is nevertheless the case that both this participation and this redemption are given to it precisely as creaturely endowments, which, as such, neither stand in "contradiction" to the "nature" of creatureliness, nor "negate" it, but rather presuppose "certain similarities" within it and therefore, "in fact complete" it.[85] Moreover, in keeping with this ontological relation,[86] even God's revelation speaks in a creaturely way, indeed "in likenesses taken from the data of the senses,"[87] and precisely for this reason faith "presupposes natural knowledge, as does grace nature, and perfection that which is perfected."[88] Thus the ultimate and conclusive view of the matter is that of the ontically and noetically *"completed nature"* of the *"creature"*: because the whole of the creature's growth into more and more of its supernatural endowments constitutes precisely not any "progress on God's part," but rather a progress of the creature: certainly, it is a progress that goes beyond every "natural" possibility or ability or claim proper to the creature, but it is still a progress that "can" happen to the "creature" through the "creator" (since, in its *"potentia oboedientialis,"* precisely as a "creature," it is absolutely in the hands of the creator),[89] and as such is truly a "progress" of the creature towards "perfection." Such is the view of *classical scholasticism,* as represented — in its basic outlines — in the Fourth Lateran Council's affirmation of Peter Lombard over against Abbot Joachim: however intimate God's self-revelation in supernatural "participation" and "redemption" may be, God is nevertheless and precisely the "One Highest Incomprehensible and Ineffable Something"; and man, however great his supernatural elevation to the status of a "child of God" and a "member of Christ" may be, is nevertheless and precisely the "creature" of the "Creator" — "very similar" to his Creator, of course, but still "ever more dissimilar."

In keeping with its content *(secundum substantiam actus),* practical religious life thus turns out to be the authentic life of the creature, while its "supernaturality" consists merely in its formal "mode of action": "insofar as the human being is guided by the

---

84. Thomas Aquinas, *De Ver.* q. 24, a. 1, ad 2; q. 24, a. 13, corp.
85. *In Boeth. de Trin.* q. 2, a. 3, corp.
86. *Seinsverhältnis.* — Trans.
87. *In Boeth. de Trin.* q. 6, a. 3, corp.
88. *Summa Th.* I, q. 2, a. 2, ad 1.
89. *De Ver.* q. 8, a. 12, ad 4.

love that makes the spirit of man one with God."⁹⁰ And even this love (understood as the epitome of the supernaturality proper to a "child of God" and "member of Christ") is a "mode" of "natural love": "for to love God above all and to love oneself for the sake of God, insofar as this constitutes the natural good of all creatures, is incumbent by nature not only upon the rationally endowed creature, but even upon common animals and soulless bodies, insofar as they participate in a natural love for the Highest Good."⁹¹ Practical religious life is thus an increasing practical affirmation of this "naturality" of the creature. For it is precisely in this affirmation that genuine "supernaturality" is fulfilled: because it is in the creature's "participation in God's nature and person" that we see God's affirmation of his creature; indeed, in the incarnation of God, God himself becomes this affirmation, in that he becomes a creature as a "man like any other." Thus, "creatureliness," "naturality," "natural rationality" *(creatura, natura, ratio)* — these basic terms of classical scholasticism — signify precisely a maturation in the theological understanding of supernaturality that commenced with the Greek fathers and Augustine.

In this sense, then, scholastic theology is a "rational speculative theology": thoroughly and in every respect a theology of the one supernatural order of redemption, but with particular attention paid to (ontic) *natura* and (noetic) *ratio.* What is proper to the trinitarian God appears under the "natural" categories proper to the "One Highest Incomprehensible and Ineffable Something" as the "creator," and precisely for this reason under the categories of being, intellect, and will. The content of the trinitarian order of the world appears under the "natural" categories of the "origin" and ultimate "goal" of the "universe" as "creation," and precisely for this reason under the categories of the natural order of being, from matter up to spirit (within the gradations of which order Thomas, for one, consistently includes everything, even the "most supernatural" of questions). This is the *one* content that thoroughly informs everything between "creator" and "creature," and precisely for this reason "causality" is its fundamental category. This is especially so with regard to "efficient causality" *(causa efficiens),* since this form of causality most decisively manifests the "ever greater" difference between the "creator," who alone is sovereign, and the "creature," who is created (which is why the church later, with good reason, emphasized "cause and effect" as the relation between God and creature, contrary to every "modernism").⁹² The basic content of this "causality,"

90. *De Ver.* q. 24, a. 13, corp.
91. *De Malo* q. 16, a. 4, ad 15.
92. Denz. 2145.

therefore, finds its corresponding act in "causal thought," including even the strict form of such thought, the syllogism. Just as God's revelation speaks in "likenesses taken from the data of the senses," and thus in the natural mode of creatureliness,[93] so all the more must the theologian — who is a creature — receive and grasp and transmit this revelation in a creaturely way: that is to say, within genuinely human thought, which reflects upon these data in their interrelations, and thus in terms of the fundamental connection between "cause and effect," i.e., in a "causal" way. It is in this way that thought first matures into the actuality of a theology of the "Logos" and "Pneuma": for the self-impartation of the truly divine Logos and Pneuma is the "action of God *ad extra*," which is to say that it is a self-impartation to creation and, as such, one that occurs in a genuinely creaturely form. Just as the "excellence" of God, according to Thomas, is declared precisely in his creation of creatures who possess their own proper actuality and their own proper efficacy,[94] so too his true Logos and true Pneuma reveal themselves precisely by taking the sound logic of the rational human intellect as their instrument: just as Christ too, precisely in his incarnation, did not manifest himself exclusively as the divine Logos, but as a corporeal man possessing a human intellect.

From this perspective — fourthly — we can now clearly see the *entire span* of possibilities included in and illuminated by the Fourth Lateran Council's formula. By moving the discussion from supernatural trinitarianism to the natural relation between creator and creature — and this with particular emphasis upon the "ever greater dissimilarity" — the council assumes a critical position over against the tendency of the theology of the Greeks and Augustine to think in terms only of God's sole and exclusive agency.[95] To conceive of God in such "sole and exclusive" terms leads to identity with God, as is evident in the case of Joachimism. When the theology of the Greek fathers becomes the "sole and exclusive" factor, then one has Greek Orthodox theology: a supranaturalistic theopanism of Logos and Pneuma within gnosis. When the theology of Augustine, on the other hand,

93. *In Boeth. de Trin.* q. 6, a. 3, corp.

94. *De Ver.* q. 11, a. 1, corp. etc.

95. This "sole and exclusive" [*Allein und Ausschließlich*] also has repercussions for the way in which, here and hereafter, particular orientations of thought are represented. In the historical fullness of their vitality, they explode the limits of the strict form they are given in this exposition. But, on the other hand, it is this strict form that first illumines what is distinctive about their intentions. For the sake of clarification, therefore, a certain amount of hyperbole is unavoidable.

becomes the "sole and exclusive" factor, one has the theology of the Reformation (which leads to Jansenism and the immanentist theology of German Idealism): the supranaturalistic theopanism of the divine dialectic or divine tragedy of the paradox of the cross.

On closer examination, however, this turns out to be a conception of God's identity in terms of what is lower: just as the council depicts Joachimism as construing the trinity of God as a human society of three persons. When the theology of the Greek fathers becomes the "sole and exclusive" factor, it appears to dissolve the nature of the creature into a purely passive cooperation "with"; but precisely thus the theology of "participation" secretly becomes a purely natural philosophism of the principle of participation as such: to the point of becoming a naturalistic pantheism that understands "nature as participation between non-being and being," which is to say a Parmenidean Platonism. Equally, when the theology of Augustine becomes the "sole and exclusive" factor, it seems to condemn the nature of the creature as a rebellious or impotent nothing; but precisely thus the theology of "dialectic" secretly becomes a purely natural philosophism of dialectic as such: to the point of becoming a naturalistic pantheism that understands "nature as a dialectic between antitheses," which is to say, a Heraclitean Platonism. In view of the fate of such theology, which treats supernature in exclusive terms, scholastic theology stands justified. One is presented with an either-or: either one recognizes the creatureliness within everything supernatural (as scholastic theology does) or one is compelled secretly to naturalize the supernatural.

By the same token, however, this marks out the critical limits of scholastic theology itself, though from the reverse direction: inasmuch as the "ever greater dissimilarity" truly appears "within" the "similarity, however great"; and inasmuch as the natural relation between Creator and creature appears "within" supernatural trinitarian unity. "Rational speculative" theology is only genuine theology insofar as its object is the fullness of actual revelation, and insofar as the origin, measure, and defining goal of its act is found within the fullness of actual faith: its object being the "causal connections" as such proper to the supernatural creation, which comprises both participation and redemption; its act being "causal thought" as such, which is a reflective supernatural faith. Thus, scholastic theology is genuine theology in that it represents the ripening of the theology of the Greek fathers and Augustine. To treat *natura* and *ratio* as "sole and exclusive," however, would lead directly to the "natural theology" of the Enlightenment and of rationalism, which is to say, to a pantheism of "pure nature" and "pure reason." Even as regards its "rational speculative" character, the authenticity of scholastic theology depends upon its roots in the theology of the Greek fathers and Augustine. For "nature" and "reason" can be understood only as concrete, supernaturally elevated, and redeemed nature and reason. Every other "nature" or "reason" is a lifeless "abstraction." Thus, to treat the "rational speculative" as "sole and exclusive" would lead to the unreality of nature and reason themselves. It would constitute the inversion of (though one intrinsically corresponding to) the curse of the Enlightenment and of rationalism: the abstract theopanism of a purely conceptual "nature in itself" and "reason in itself."

Consequently, nature, supernatural participation in God, and supernatural redemption depend — in their true relation to one another — upon the back-and-forth of "analogy." This means, on the one hand, that for any supernaturality, "however great," the naturality of the relation between creator and creature constitutes the decisive "because" *(quia);* and within this relation itself the "ever greater dissimilarity" constitutes the determinative "cannot" *(non potest . . . notari)* and "compelled" *(sit . . . notanda)* of the "similarity, however great." But this means, on the other hand, that the naturality of the relation between creator and creature appears factically only "within" supernaturality, "however great" (the supernaturality of the *one* factical historical order of supernatural participation and redemption); and within the relation between creator and creature the "ever greater dissimilarity" appears essentially only "within" the "similarity, however great." According to the council, this "analogy" is the form of the object and the act of the only possible theology.

4. In both the context and the style of the entire second chapter of the Fourth Lateran Council — which is directed against Abbot Joachim — "analogy" appears not so much as a principle or as the form of a new theological possibility, but rather as the *self-expression of the position of the church* as regards all possible theologies.[96] It constitutes something like "ecclesial discretion." The council does not emphasize the natural relation between creator and creature and the "ever greater dissimilarity" in order to identify itself with any single possible theology; rather, the language proper to the mind of the church is one of an aristocratic and sober distance from the "enthusiasms" of Charismatics, Pneumatics, and so on: in this case, a distance from the enthusiasm of Abbot Joachim — the same distance expressed by the Council of Trent's rejection of the Reformation, by the church's edicts

---

96. Cf. the view expressed in "Neue Theologie" in *Ringen der Gegenwart* (Augsburg: Filser, 1929), vol. 2, 669ff.

against Jansenism, by the Vatican Council's rejection of Romanticism, and by the church's edicts against modernism. Insofar as classical scholasticism, with its sober emphasis upon *creature* and *nature,* is to a special degree in accord with this "ecclesial discretion," it is certainly no coincidence that the Fourth Lateran Council explicitly sides with Peter Lombard; here is the inner reason for Thomas Aquinas — and no one else — becoming the formative theologian and philosopher of the church: it was by virtue of his aristocratic distance. But precisely here we see clearly that "analogy," as the council understands it, is neither a principle nor a form in and of itself, but is something like the explicit form of the distance of the church's discretion.

Seen from the perspective of objective principles, all possibilities are exhausted in the three that were considered by the council.[97] For supernatural participation in God, supernatural redemption, and (participating and redeemed) nature are the three components proper to the *one* order of supernatural redemption; and the development of theology from the Greek fathers to Augustine to scholasticism represents the shift of the church's emphasis from one of these components to another.[98] Hence a theology of "analogy" cannot be added to these three as yet a fourth; rather, it concerns the rhythm that obtains among these three theologies. Implicit in this "rhythm," however, is a posture of distance from these theologies themselves. There is, consequently, an either-or. Either one conceives of this rhythm itself as an autonomous formal principle, or one conceives of it as the expression of an existing and living instance. If it is taken to be a formal principle, however, then as such a principle it signifies what is properly absolute over against these three theologies, and, consequently, theology as such is dissolved into the rationalism of an absolute principle. If, on the other hand, it is the expression of an existing and living instantiation, it is this expression — inasmuch as it concerns the *one* order of God *in* Christ *in* the church — solely as the authoritative self-expression of this *one* reality: God *in* Christ *in* the church. In this way it also corresponds to the formula of analogy itself, as enunciated in the second chapter of the council. Just as the council inexorably subordinates all pneumatic Trinitarianism to the majestic distance of the "One Highest Incomprehensible and Ineffable Something," so too it subordinates these three theologies to the "ever greater dissimilarity." That is to say, what is at issue in this "ever greater dissimilarity" is the sovereignty of the divine majesty itself: not some rhythm between these three components — participation in God,

97. Cf. Part I, 3.
98. Cf. Part I, 3.

redemption, and nature — and thus between similarity and dissimilarity, but rather the ever greater sovereignty of the living God in himself. Since what is at issue, however, is the God of the *one* order of redemption, it is essentially a matter of God *in* Christ *in* the church, and thus a matter of the sovereignty of God in a truly sovereign church — which is to say, in a sovereign pope. Thus, inasmuch as it made its decision against Abbot Joachim, the father of absolute pneumaticism, under Innocent III, the most powerful pope of the Middle Ages, the council marks the definitive inauguration of the question concerning the *inner form of any theology whatsoever.*

As both Thomas Aquinas[99] and the Vatican Council[100] stress — in almost the same words — participation in God, redemption, and nature are one in God, their *one* author. It is one and the same God from whom they are derived, and so, too, therefore, it is only through God himself that their unity is apparent to consciousness. Such is, in the genuine sense of the word, *Theo*-logy: a word that comes from God concerning everything that comes from God. Theological authority, in its essence, is God. The "invisible" God appears as this authority in the visible Christ, understood as his "exegesis" (John 1:18): the "Word who comes from God" appears in the "Word that became flesh"; the "Logos" of the logic of this Word in the "Logos that became flesh." And since this Christ is none other than "*one* Christ, head and body" (Augustine), the church alone constitutes the concreteness of God in Christ: just as the first chapter of the letter to the Ephesians begins with "the mystery of the will of God in Christ," understood as the mystery of the "at-oneness of heaven and earth," in order then to provide a vision of its consummation in the "church," understood as "his body, the fullness of him who fills all in all": the infinite God as *the* fullness, and the church as the "fullness of the one who fills all in all." Here we see an inexorable confrontation, whose history begins with the situation faced by the Fourth Lateran Council and reaches completion in that faced by the Vatican Council: does the "fullness" of the church consist in the official sovereignty of its authority (and thus in its infallible teaching authority, and so — at its apex — in an infallible pope) — or does it consist in a non-binding and fluctuating "fullness" of the "Spirit" in its "members"? Whose authority is valid, that of Innocence III or that of Abbot Joachim? To be sure, the formula of "God in Christ in the church" essentially contains three components, but as regards the question of genuine theological authority there is only a single either-or:

99. *In Boeth. de Trin.* q. 2, a. 3, corp.
100. Denz. 1797.

between God in an authoritative church and an absolute pneumaticism that is really a naturalism, because in any such pneumaticism one or another human movement posits itself as absolute.

We can cast some light on this matter — *firstly* — by viewing it *in relation to the three theologies* derived from the objective components of the *one* order of redemption.

According to its own logic, the *theology of the Greek fathers,* understood as a theology of "participation in the divine nature and person," tends to see formal theological authority as residing immediately in God himself: since, for this theology, everything creaturely — including Christ and the church — appears in terms of the greatest possible "rapture into God"[101] *(assumpta natura)* and thus in terms of a rapture into a spiritual existence in God as eternal, immutable Spirit. Taken by itself, therefore, this theology is oriented towards the formal *"theological" authority* of an "immutable divine tradition in the Spirit." This is not an earthly, visible church, assisted by the Holy Spirit; on the contrary, this is the "holy eternal immutable Pneuma" itself *as* church. That is to say, its ultimate consequence is the standpoint of the Greek Orthodox Church: the "pneumatic tradition" as theological authority. The mystery of the incarnation is retracted into a pure pneumaticism, and the authority of a living God is objectified in a "divine tradition."

According to its own terms as a theology of "redemption in God's descent," *Augustine's theology* is likewise directed from within itself toward a corresponding formal theological authority, but one vested emphatically in Christ, understood as "*one* Christ, head and body": this is so, on the one hand, because the infinity of God is made manifest by having-become-flesh within the internal unity-in-opposition of the "body of many members"; but also, on the other hand, because the church is essentially constituted as this one *"totus Christus"* in the extension of Christ as "head and body" through space and time. Accordingly, taken by itself, this theology is oriented towards the formal theological authority of this *"totus Christus."* This *"Christological" authority* then contains three moments. First, the absolutely definitive authority of the *"original Christ"* and thus the authority of "original Christianity" understood as "radical authority." Second, the authority of this same Christ, but in the whole of his living presence across space and time, and thus the authority of the "ecumenical" understood as "collective authority." Third, the authority of this same Christ, but as "vital here and now," and thus the authority of a "contemporary proclamation" understood as "actual authority."[102] To be sure, it is the authority of "God in Christ," but it is an authority that is purely "in the Spirit," understood as the

---

101. *Hinauf-entnommen in Gott hinein.* — Trans.

102. *Aktuale Autorität.* Przywara seems to mean authority here in the sense of actualism, i.e., an authority that is not enduring but consists merely on a momentary basis, as it were, "in the event" of proclamation. — Trans.

"Spirit of the origin," the "Spirit of the All," and the "Spirit today." It is not the authority of the personal God as it extends to the personal authority of the church understood as the authoritative and visible "Spirit of Christ"; rather, the church consists solely in the "original" and "ecumenical" and "actual" Spirit of Christ himself. In other words, the ultimate consequence of this theology is the standpoint of the Reformation: the "Spirit of Christ" as theological authority. Here too, therefore, the mystery of the incarnation is retracted into a pure pneumaticism, and the authority of a living God is objectified in a "Christian Spirit."

Scholastic theology, by contrast, understood as a theology of "(elevated and redeemed) nature," tends distinctly, in and of itself, towards the form of a genuine visible authority of the incarnate God: in that the authority of God, being that of a *sovereign* will, can visibly declare itself only in the genuinely human authority of a *sovereign* will, and thus solely in an authoritative church, whose authority is without any higher instantiation in a "Spirit of Christ" or a "divine tradition"; rather, the true "Spirit of Christ" and the true "divine tradition" are represented precisely in this authority's "inappellability." But, on the other hand, it is also and precisely in scholastic theology that revelation tends to be represented in rational categories, which leads to the authority of the "theological school" and thus to the authority of whichever fundamental concept is proper to any given school. Certainly, these fundamental concepts are originally "theological": God as Being (and thus Being figuring as the fundamental concept); God as Intelligence or Idea (and thus Intelligence or the Idea figuring as the fundamental concept); God as Will (and thus Will figuring as the fundamental concept). Given, however, the peculiar authority of *ratio*, there is at least the "danger" of a reversal: namely, the danger that Being or Intelligence or Idea or Will may be taken for God (as happens in the founding absolutisms of modern philosophy). The actual situation of scholastic theology is thus that of an in-between. In Thomas, certainly, this is given a definite form, inasmuch as he conceives of the "articles of faith" as the "principles" from which all "speculation" proceeds and from which it receives its measure and orientation.[103] To be sure, to judge from scholasticism's later development, the question would seem rather undecided: on the one hand, there is the increasing tendency towards a "positive theology," which is to say a theology of positive decisions (in the church's authoritative explication of the word of revelation); on the other hand, there is the multiplicity of "theological schools," which are distinguished from one another by the fundamental rational principle peculiar to each. But the peculiar *"ecclesiological"* authority of scholastic theology is revealed precisely in this in-between. For in its essence even the "theological school" is not the "Spirit blowing where it will," but a "school" and a "school of the church," which is to say, subject to the form of the church's authoritative discipline. And with regard to the "theological schools," it is not insignificant that, for the most part, they arise originally out of the great orders of the church; hence the *ratio* that is at work

---

103. *Summa Th.* I, q. 1, a. 2, ad 8.

within them intrinsically bears the form of obedience — an obedience, moreover, explicitly to "Christ the King" within the authoritative sovereignty of his church, as St. Benedict declares at the beginning of his *Rule,* in anticipation of all future orders: "Serving the Lord, Christ the King, in war, you will take in hand all the power and majesty of the weapons of obedience." This fundamental attitude toward the Divine Majesty is what we see in Christ as Redeemer in contrast to the disobedience of original sin; and we continue to find this fundamental concrete Christian attitude in the in-between of scholastic theology: theological, Christological authority made concrete in the ecclesiological authority of the "church of authoritative obedience." In this respect, as the theology of the Fourth Lateran Council, scholastic theology is the first to take a decisive stand against all forms of pneumaticism whatsoever — including Joachimism, which is the central representative of all pneumaticisms.

Secondly, now that we have discovered within these three objective tendencies of theology the definitive formal tendency of theology as such — albeit in an unexplicated form — the theological significance of the development that runs *from the Fourth Lateran Council to the present* becomes clear. What is at issue is the formal site of God's absoluteness on earth in the incarnation. The Fourth Lateran Council pronounces its verdict against the absolute Pneuma of Joachimism. The Vatican Council pronounces its verdict in favor of the infallibility of the pope. Our theme is thus framed by this beginning and this conclusion. What is at issue here is the exact *meaning of the ecclesiological.* Certainly, the Fourth Lateran Council itself lays the foundation, since (as we showed at the outset) what is ultimate within the formula of analogy is "ecclesial discretion": the "ever greater" distance of the sovereignty of the "One and Only Highest Incomprehensible and Ineffable Something" within the *sovereign* church, in the midst of every unity, "however great," of theological wisdom with Divine Wisdom. And yet, from this point onward, right up to the Vatican Council and the edicts against modernism that represented the council's final consequences, it is precisely this more concrete version of "analogy" that has become the subject of the greatest contention.

The opposing positions implicit within each of *theology's three objective tendencies* — when taken as "sole and exclusive" — now become genuinely explicit. Over against the authority of the sovereign church we now see posed the *principle of authority proper to an absolute Greek theology* — that of the "Divine Tradition" — as was made obvious in the course of the attempts at reunion with the Greek Orthodox Church in the centuries before the Reformation, and as we discover in our own day in the infiltrations of

Greek Orthodox thought. In this "Divine Tradition" there is an "identity" between immutable Divine Wisdom and human formulae: in the symbol of the icon, understood as a static intratemporal eternity. By contrast, the authority of the church — in the development towards the definition of papal infallibility — manifests itself as the "ever greater" of the distant sovereignty in the moment of living history: there is no supertemporal Divine Tradition in itself, which could be said to stand over against the church as a higher court; rather, the living, sovereign, deciding church is itself the "tradition *in actu*": as logically follows, since there is no higher court — no idea or principle or wisdom "in itself" — that stands over against God; rather, all of these things come essentially from him who is the *one* sovereignty. Within the order of the incarnation, the "site" of Divine Sovereignty is provided neither by an Eternal Theology nor by an Eternal Liturgy, but solely by the Infallible Magisterium, which stands always in the present moment of its historical decision — a decision that is derivable neither from the eternal fact of a tradition nor from the Magisterium's earlier decisions, but that stands strictly in the present moment of an actual definition. For, in this way, it serves as a logical representation: the representation of the will of the Father in the Son whom the Father has sent, in the church that the Son has sent (John 20:21).

But this same authority to decide is also contested by the *principle of authority proper to an absolute Augustinian theology:* that of the "Spirit" of the *"totus Christus."* In this case, in contrast to the "Divine Tradition," the intention is to preserve the genuine historicity of the order of the incarnation. At a minimum, this comes to pass in the principle of authority provided by the "original Christ": in the unique historicity of Christ and hence in an "original Christianity," taken as an absolute norm. This "original Christianity" then constitutes a kind of "history as ideal" and aims, consequently, at the "ideal church of the original Christians." The "it-ness" of "Divine Tradition" remains, but is transformed into a historical it-ness. Thus we find here the fundamental form of the spiritual Franciscans, the Reformation, and Jansenism: theological authority understood as the "spiritual church" of the "original Christians" of the "original Spirit of Christ."

Where the principle of authority is the "ecumenical Christ," one finds a stronger emphasis on historicity, i.e., upon the historical continuity of Christ in the whole of his extension in space and time; thus "collective Christianity" is here the absolute norm. This "collective Christianity" is, then, either (in the spatial sense of "collective") the integration of all the members of the body of Christ: just as conciliar theory connects the infallibility of the church strictly to "majority decision"; and just as Jansenism sees the formal seat of authority as residing in the purely collective church of the "mystical body of Christ," from which the church's official authority is only a secondary derivative; and just as modern "world Protestantism" and the "evangelical catholicity" of Söderblom and Heiler would establish — as "ecumenical authority" — a "world church" (that is, an internal balance struck among all of humanity's [denominational] tendencies). But, similarly, "collective Christianity" appears (in the temporal sense of "collective") in the mode of a dynamic integration of the entire process of historical development: just as modernism proposes the dynamic of history itself as the site of authority, one whose only law is that of "fruitful development." In this, however, we see a transition to the most radical form of historicity, that of "the actual Christ"[104] as the principle of authority: Christ ever here and now in the "event" of "proclamation": which is the basic theory behind Protestantism's notion of "the word alone" (the clearest expression of which is found in Karl Barth).[105] On the one hand, the principle at work here is the modernist principle of "fruitful development"; on the other hand, however, this very principle stands to be overcome by the principle of an "absoluteness here and now," since it is Christ himself — as the Divine Word, in the immediate working of the Holy Spirit — who is the "event" in the here and now of proclamation. Consequently, the most radically historical theory thus reverts to the Eternal Tradition of Greek Orthodoxy: for that which is eternally divine appears immediately within the particular historical moment. The meaning of the development of the church's decrees stands in particularly sharp contrast to this whole development (from the "original" to the "collective" to the "actual" Christ). The infallibility of the pope stands, on the one hand, as a sovereign, living, actual decision over against every "ideality" and "collectivity": so much so that the ecclesiology of Möhler and Newman inevitably had to pass through the fire of the Vatican Council's definition, in order to be purged of any lingering residue of the "original" and "collective Christ." But, on the other hand, this "sovereign, living, actual decision" is not the actuality of a purely historical "now"; rather, it is always the given "now" of God's decision, understood as the decision of the Immutable Truth *within* the decision of the Infallible Magisterium: so much so that Newman's theology of history had to be tried precisely in the inexorable fire of the church's decrees against modernism and distinguish itself from the latter's fundamentally mutable truth.[106]

104. As previously noted, Przywara means by this term (as here applied to Barth) that Christ is present "in the event" of proclamation; this is the most radical form of historicity inasmuch as Christ is present not continuously in the church as his body, but only in the historical "moment" of one's hearing the Word. — Trans.

105. If a Catholic "theology of proclamation" is to be pursued, in the manner of certain recent attempts, it will thus have to distinguish itself clearly, at the level of method, over against this original Protestant position.

106. From this perspective, the opposition between the *Vaticanum* and nineteenth-century thought becomes clear. One sees this, for example, in the way that Möhler's first

But this same development also brings clarification to *scholastic theology's* own *formal principle of authority*. On the one hand, in contrast to the other two theological tendencies, one sees here a kind of positivism of purely material historical facts. On the other hand, however, there is a need to give this theology of facts a final form: either by incorporating this pure materiality of facts within the *ratio* of a closed speculative system (in which case, however, there is the danger that theological authority will be replaced by pure *ratio*) — or by subsuming it within an unconscious theory of an ultimate theological positivism of history as such. This either-or is clarified in light of the ultimate significance of the development of the church's decrees. The positivity of the theological consists essentially in the positivity of the *infallible* decision of that church in which the *one sovereign* God speaks who allowed his Logos to become man and, what is more, to become incarnate in the church, and who gave to the church the internal assistance of his Pneuma: the "Logos," in whom the "invisible God," in his full depth, "represents and interprets himself" (John 1:18); the "Pneuma" who "searches the depths of God" (1 Cor. 2:10). The positivism of the sovereign decision of the

---

work poses the "organic church" as the church of the "mystical body of Christ" over against papal primacy, and only gradually attempts to illuminate the latter by way of this fundamental concept of the "organic church"; and in the way that Newman affirms papal infallibility, but does so only negatively as an "antidote" to the hubris of human reason — in all of this one sees how nineteenth-century thought, even that of its most profound theologians, remains fixed in the opposition between an "organic church," understood as the church of the "mystical body of Christ," and the "organized church," understood as a purely profane, juridical structure, which is at best an "indispensable earthly necessity." That is to say, the supernatural aspect of the church is seen in terms of the purely natural opposition between Romanticism and Enlightenment: organism versus organization, life versus law, love versus *ratio*, etc. By contrast, the *Vaticanum* emphasizes not organization and law, but what is decidedly supernatural about the church: the mystery of the incarnation, understood as the "mystery of the divine will" within the church (Eph. 1:9-23) and therefore, in the most formal sense, within a *sovereign ecclesial* will in a supernaturally *sovereign pope*: since the incarnational mystery of God's redemptive obedience stands directly opposed to man's disobedience in original sin (Rom. 5:19; Phil. 2:5-10; Heb. 5:1-10), and, as such, essentially in representation of the Father who sends, in the obedience of the Son who is sent, and in the united obedience of the apostles who are sent by the Son (John 12:44-50; 17:4-21; 20:21). It is, therefore, only insofar as the church is the church of rightful apostolic succession that the mystical body of Christ is the true church of God and not an apotheosis of the principle of organism. And it is only insofar as the church is the "juridical church" of a *sovereign will* and an unconditional obedience that the "church of love" [*Liebes-Kirche*] is the true church of God and not an apotheosis of collective love [*Liebes-Kollektiv*]. Every attempt to play the "mystical body of Christ" and the "church of love" against the "juridical church" is an obstinate adherence to nineteenth-century thought in preference to the *Vaticanum*.

church is therefore not that of the positivism of historical contingencies, but the positivism of the sovereign majesty of the God who is *infinite* yet *one.* This underscores what is enduringly true and authentic in both Greek patristic and Augustinian theology: their insight concerning the inner objective connections among the sovereign decisions of the church. For though the ecclesiology of the one theological authority stands upon the inappellability of an infallible decision, this decision is nevertheless the decision of the church wherein the *one* revelation lives on as the *one* tradition (as Greek theology perceives), and the decision of the church that is "one Christ, head and body" (as Augustinian theology perceives).

But in this way, *thirdly,* the features of "analogy" become apparent within "ecclesiology." On the one hand, within every "however great" of an "immanent ecclesiology" (such as one finds in Greek patristic and Augustinian theology, inasmuch as they view the church as the living divine Truth and as the living incarnate Truth in the body of the Christ of many members) — within this "however great" the distance of "dissimilarity" is "ever greater" with regard to the inappellable and decisive will of God *within* the decisive will of the church's definition of dogma. On the other hand, however, this very definition is pronounced within the precincts of the church of the living divine Truth incarnate in Christ, and precisely for this reason the incisive moment of "dissimilarity" in its underivative pronouncement truly appears "within" the genuine "similarity, however great" proper to a theological "wisdom" (even if it necessarily "stands open" to the future) of the inner connections among the church's decrees (grasped at the ideative level in an ideal theology of tradition; and at the historical level in a historical theology of the living "*one* Christ, head and body"). — Hence the *theology of the "ecclesial analogy"* herein constitutes on the one hand (as accords with the "similarity, however great"), a kind of theology that maximally manifests something like an inner rhythm proper to the church's decisions (grasped at the ideative level as the inner structure of the church's dogma and thus of revelation as such; and at the level of historical theology as the inner law of historical development): just as, say, Christology takes shape (materially) through the mutual determinations of the Alexandrian and Antiochene schools, etc. On the other hand, however, it is a theology whose formal authority cannot reside in this rhythm, but can reside only (as accords with the "ever greater dissimilarity") in each underivable and inappellable decision of the church; and thus it must stand open not only "to the future," but even in regard to the structure it had previously possessed. Thus we have, for the first time (formally speaking), *Theo*-logy: that is, something completely at the disposal of the *sovereign divine will*. Thus we have, for the first time (formally speaking), *Christo*-logical theology: that is, something completely at the disposal of the visibility of this *sovereign divine will* in Christ, understood as its representation. Thus we have, for the first time, *ecclesio*-logical Christological theology: that is, something completely at the disposal of the authoritative here-and-now of this representation of God in Christ, namely, the here-and-now of a church that makes infallible decisions. Thus we see, for the first time, the divinely living Holy Spirit, who "searches the depths of God": neither the "objective Spirit" of the "pneumatic tradition" of the theology of the Greek fathers in its absolute form, nor the "historical Spirit" of the theology of Augustine in its absolute form, nor the "pure Spirit" of scholastic theology in its absolute form, but rather the actual Spirit of the Father and the Son, the creative sovereignty of the will of the Divine Majesty blowing where it will. Only the authentic "church" guarantees the authentic "Pneuma," over against the Pseudo-Pneuma of the various pneumaticisms.

5. This, however, raises a final question, *the question as to whether this ecclesiology itself has an inner "metaphysical structure."* This question is in fact a circular set of questions. First, the "analogy" appears as a form in itself: as the "rhythm" that obtains among the three objective theologies (section 3). Then its concrete form is unveiled as "ecclesial discretion," which is condensed into an "ecclesial theology" (section 4). And now, once again, the question is posed concerning a possible "analogy in itself."[107] For in its transition from trinitarian theology to a theology of the relation between Creator and creature, the formula of analogy promulgated by the Fourth Lateran Council contains the law governing the rhythm that obtains among the three possible objective theologies (section 3). Nor, in placing so particular an emphasis upon the distance of submission (as distinct from identity with the Pneuma), does the formula contain the law of relation between a (solely authoritative) "ecclesial theology" and an (always provisional) "theological wisdom" (as represented by the three possible objective theologies) merely in order thereby to provide an answer to the question concerning theology's proper formal principle. Rather, in all of this, there is a good reason why the council's formula of analogy carries within itself a strict "because" and "cannot" and "compelled." The properly (and formally) supernatural character of genuine "trinitarian unity" is established by the formula's "because" — and this on the basis of the fundamental relation between Creator and creature: "because between Creator and creature. . . ." Moreover, even this fundamental and, in this respect, "natural" relation between Creator and creature appears — in itself — not as a simple facticity, but rather within a strict structure of necessity: "because . . . cannot . . . without being . . . compelled." To be sure, this "because"

107. This part corresponds to the particular point of view of *Analogia Entis* I.

and "cannot" and "compelled" are derived fundamentally from the nature of the Creator: from that decisive distance in which he stands as the "One Highest Incomprehensible and Ineffable Something" over against every attempt to grasp and comprehend him in terms of identity. But even so, in passing from its emphasis upon this distance to its enunciation of the actual formula of analogy, the council nevertheless allows this distance to appear precisely and decisively within the "in-between of Creator and creature." Thus, the ultimate factor hidden within the council's decision is the fundamental question that carries over into the church's battle with modernism: that of the relation between (formal) *supernature* (as in supernatural deification and redemption) *and nature.*

What makes this question so acute is legible right within the council's formula of analogy. Is it the case that "nature" does not appear as factically concrete except within supernature (as would accord with the pride of place the supernatural "trinitarian unity" enjoys within the formula of analogy, and with the way in which the structure of the natural relation "between Creator and creature" is subsequently made clear in terms of the true structure of this unity)? Or is it the case that it is precisely "nature" that determines the law and the limit of supernature (as would accord with the way in which, within the very sequence of words in the formula of analogy, the natural relation "between Creator and creature" is emphasized as the "because" upon which the true structure of the supernatural "trinitarian unity" is predicated)? But, then, is it clearly the case that, within this "nature" that determines law and limit, it is the "nature" of the "Creator" — understood as the "One Highest Incomprehensible and Ineffable Something" — that, given its necessary distance ("cannot," "compelled"), determines this law and this limit for every possible supernature (as would accord with the way in which, within the text of the council, the explicit formula of analogy is the result of the earlier emphasis upon the divine distance)? Or is it the case, on the contrary, that the "nature" of the relation "between Creator and creature" and, logically, the "nature" of the "creature as such" possesses within itself the law and the limit of every possible supernature (as would accord with the way in which, right within the text of the council, the earlier emphasis upon precisely this divine distance is given its foundation by the explicit formulation of analogy)?

The strictness of the inner logic of these questions becomes clearer when they are seen — *firstly* — *in view of our three objective theologies.*

In *Greek patristic theology,* for which everything comes down to "participation in God's nature and person," nature simply is this form of participation: nature is not understood, properly speaking, as a potency in itself, but only as a *"potentia oboedientialis";* and even this *potentia oboedientialis* is not understood, properly speaking, as prior to its actualization (at least at the objective level); rather, it is understood simply as the dimension of becoming proper to participation in God. It was given its first definitive formulation by Irenaeus: "God is distinguished from human beings in this, that God acts, but man happens";[108] "as much as God is in need of nothing, so much does the human being need the fellowship of God."[109] Thus, logically, supernatural participation in God is the *one* content diversified in all the areas of practical and theoretical life (logic, ethics, aesthetics, culture, science, politics). By "natural," here, all that is meant is becoming the form proper to what "happens" through God and in "need of fellowship with God." Nature is (formally speaking) nothing but the becoming of supernature (wherein the only content is to be found).

In the *theology of Augustine,* which centers everything upon the "cross" — understood as redemption's very form — nature appears under the form of contrariety that this implies: not only in terms of the opposition between original sin and redemption — between the "like God" of Adam's human nature and the "man like any other" of Christ's divine nature — but also in terms of the opposition between the creaturely nothing that seeks in Adam to be the divine All and the divine All that in Christ pours itself out and freely becomes nothing (Phil. 2:7). In Adam, human nature appears within the paradox of oppositions proper to original sin; in Christ, human nature appears within the paradox of oppositions proper to redemption. But then nature as such is presented under this general form of a "paradox of oppositions." And so it is with the "natural" side of the manifestation of the supernatural mystery of the relation between original sin and redemption. Thus, on the one hand, this "natural" side is certainly not the neutral "becoming" of a *potentia oboedientialis,"* as is the case in Greek patristic theology; rather it is, in Adam, the "natural" side of the manifestation of the impotence — puffed up by sin — of the man who seeks to be God; whereas in Christ it is the "natural" side of the manifestation of the atoning, impotent omnipotence of the incarnate God. From this perspective, all the realms of practical and theoretical life are seen in terms of a final contradiction between an absolutized "pure naturality" (corresponding to the form of Adam) and an important supernaturality within the natural (corresponding to the form of Christ) — between faithless nature and natureless supernature. But then, on the other hand, a general form of opposition holds sway precisely within these concrete paradoxes, so as to become in its own right a "neutral" form, as "becoming" was for the Greeks; indeed, it becomes almost a "harmonic form," as Augustine himself admits that "the beauty of the world" lies "in the opposition of contraries";[110] for God declares himself to be ever greater — within every opposition between original

108. Irenaeus, *Adv. haer.* IV, 11, 2. [Trans.: *der Mensch aber geschieht.*]
109. Irenaeus, *Adv. haer.* IV, 14, 1.
110. Augustine, *De Civ. Dei* XI, 18.

sin and redemption — as the "beauty that is ever new and ever ancient,"[111] "with whom" not only "is there no dissonance, even in what is most remote from [him], since the worse and the better harmonize with one another,"[112] but who himself reveals his infinity within the interplay of the things of creation (as Augustine develops this theme in his doctrine of God). Logically, therefore, the realms of practical and theoretical life appear — throughout the formal contradiction between faithless nature and natureless supernature — in the form of this "beauty of oppositions." To be sure, this is essentially, in the highest sense, a "supernatural beauty": since it is *God* who appears — throughout the mystery of original sin and redemption — under the likeness of opposition. But then, on the other hand, this "opposition of contraries" *(contrariorum oppositio)*, which is taken to constitute the "beauty of the world," is nevertheless a property of this beauty's "nature." Thus, on the one hand, all the realms of practical and theoretical life bear the marks of an almost transcendent divine form (inasmuch as they express the manifestation *of God* within opposition); on the other hand, however, they possess the form of an "opposition of contrary to contrary" *(contraria contrariis opposita)*, which is taken to constitute the "beauty of speech."[113] On the one hand, this leads to an almost transcendent divine world and culture and science and politics, and so on; but, on the other hand, their "natural form" is that of an antithetics or polarity. Antithetics or polarity appears, on the one hand, as the most extreme form of "theological" reflection and activity when it is reflection and activity in light of the superiority of God (in and beyond all antitheses) — only to appear, on the other hand, as the most profound or most subtle or ultimate form of "natural" creatureliness itself.

From this perspective it becomes immediately apparent in what sense *scholastic theology* is a theology of (supernaturally elevated and redeemed) nature. On the one hand, it contains within itself the influences of the Greek patristic and Augustinian theologies: at its beginning stands the Augustinianism of Anselm of Canterbury, and at its end the Augustinianism of Duns Scotus; but in its definitive middle we find Thomas Aquinas, whose thought is borne along by the thought of the Areopagite, the very quintessence of Greek theology. On the other hand, in contrast to the Greek and Augustinian theologies, scholastic theology seeks especially to grasp "nature" within the *one* supernatural order: for instance, we see the beginning of scholastic method in Peter Lombard's emphasis on the distance between Creator and creature, and we see that method reach its apex when Albert the Great and Thomas Aquinas incorporate Aristotelianism's closed natural order into the *one* supernatural

111. Augustine, *Conf.* X, 27, 38.
112. Augustine, *Solil.* I, 1, 2.
113. Augustine, *De Civ. Dei* XI, 18.

order of the Areopagite and Augustine. Thus the formal "order of the universe," which is common to all of the classical scholastics, is on the one hand (in the constitutive tradition) the natural form by which an essentially supernatural universe of participation in God and in redemption is made manifest: including the typical medieval form in which all the realms of practical and theoretical life are to be understood: that of the *"Civitas Dei"* — diversified into the natural, practical, and theoretical — of the *"Sacrum Imperium"* of the One Holy church. On the other hand, however, this same formal "order of the universe" is intended to be a "pure natural order" in contrast both to (freely adventitious) supernature and to (deviant) unnature: this includes all the paths that "pure nature" and "pure humanity" and "pure reason" will take in the future, in all the realms of practical and theoretical life: that of a "pure *Civitas*" diversified into all the human realms, including those of "natural religion" and "natural theology" (from humanism to the Renaissance to the Enlightenment to Idealism). It is thus neither a nature of purely passive potentiality (as in the theology of the Greek fathers), nor a nature of pure antithetics or polarity (as in the theology of Augustine), but a nature of active potency (as Thomas Aquinas formulates it): it is, of course, an active potency whose ultimate depth is the *"potentia oboedientialis"* and which in this respect appears as an extension (into nature) of the activity of supernature; but, nonetheless, it is an active potency that remains and acts within all the realms of nature precisely as nature whole and undiminished (as a truly substantial cause[114] and so also, in consciousness, as causal thought: as ontically and noetically causal). The whole of supernatural participation in God and redemption subsists and works within all the realms of practical and theoretical life as the whole of an active naturality.

Thus — *secondly* — it is peculiar to all three of our objective theologies that, taken by themselves, they tend to take nature, in keeping with a *radical "supernaturalism,"* merely as the visible aspect of supernature; but that, on the other hand, when completely thought through to their conclusions, they nevertheless end up with a "pure nature," to the point that the *resulting "naturalism"* peculiar to each could be seen as an expression of the historical situation of the given period.

Taken solely and exclusively by itself, the *theology of the Greek fathers* sees nature as that side of supernature that is *in fieri*,[115] thus leading to the theopanism of "deifica-

---

114. *Seinshafte Ursache.* — Trans.
115. *Werde-Seite der Übernatur.* — Trans.

tion." In just this way, however, a form of purely passive "participation" becomes nature's inner form, and "deification" is naturalized into nature's inner essence: creaturely existence appears, essentially, as a passive growing participation[116] in a divine ideality. Thus, beneath the gilding of theopanistic "deification," one sees the natural form of an absolute (and consequently pantheistic) essentialism: the being of the creature as a growing participation in the Divine form; the becoming and agency of the creature as a growing participation in Divine virtue.[117] Here we see what "nature" historically means in the *East,* and so also the theology specific to the East in its Greek Orthodox form. Thus, wherever they should appear, a *theology of participation* and *essentialism* — the latter understood as the definitive Eastern philosophoumenon — represent an apotheosis of what is distinctive to the East.

Taken solely and exclusively by itself, the *theology of Augustine* sees nature as the *drama* of the antitheses of concrete supernature (the opposition between original sin and redemption) and thus regards it ultimately as the drama of the mystery of God in these antitheses, thus leading to the theopanism of the "mystery of God within opposition." In just this way, however, the form of "opposition" becomes nature's inner form, and the "mystery of God within opposition" is naturalized into nature's inner essence: creaturely existence appears essentially as the drama of divine movement between antitheses. Thus, beneath the gilding of a theopanistic "mystery of God within opposition" we see the natural form of an absolute (and consequently pantheistic) existentialism: the being of the creature as the drama of divine movement; the becoming and agency of the creature as the drama of divine life. Here we see what "nature" historically means in the *"West,"* and so also the theology peculiar to the West: one and the same theology of a paradoxically "living" God — from Luther to Pascal to Nietzsche to Bergson — secularized into one and the same philosophy of a paradoxical divine becoming. Thus, wherever they should appear, a *theology of opposition* and *existentialism* — the latter understood as the definitive Western philosophoumenon — represent the apotheosis of the "West."

Taken solely and exclusively by itself, *scholastic theology* conceives of nature as a *system* of divine order within the universe of supernature (in the unity of the various lines of salvation history), thus leading to a theopanism of the "*divine* order": of, that is, a divinely intelligible principle of order (along the lines of Thomistic scholasticism) or that of a divinely voluntaristic positing of order (along the lines of Scotistic scholasticism). In just this way, however, the form of "order" is transformed into nature's inner form, and "divine order" is naturalized into nature's inner essence: creaturely existence thus appears essentially as a system of "divine order": either as the finite existence of a divinely ideal order of essentiality (in an absolutized Thomism) or as the finite essence of a divinely energetic order of existentiality (in an absolutized Scotism). Thus, beneath the gilding of theopanistic "divine order," we see

116. *Werde-Teilnahme.* — Trans.
117. *Wert.* — Trans.

the natural form of an absolute (and consequently pantheistic) inner unity of existence and essence: either as an existential essentialism, in the case of an absolute
Thomism of the "contingent" existence of "eternal" essences (that is, an "essential infinity" within a respective "finite existence," which therefore involves a self-
distribution of the divine *essence*-and-existence) — or as an essential existentialism
in the case of an absolute Scotism of the "delimitation" of the "pure Being" of eternal
existence in "limited" essences (that is, an "existential infinity" limited in each case to
a "finite essence," which thus involves a self-distribution of the divine *existence*-and-
essence). The being of the creature is then a systematization *ad extra* of divine order:
a systematization *ad extra* of divine ideality (in Thomism in its absolute form) or a
systematization *ad extra* of divine rhythm (in Scotism in its absolute form). Accordingly, the becoming and agency of the creature are a self-ordering within this divine
order: either an ideative self-ordering (in the absolute Thomism of an adequation to
the divine arche-type) or a rhythmic self-ordering (in the absolute Scotism of the reproduction of the divine arche-motion).[118] Here we see what "nature" historically
means for the "middle" between "West" and "East": just as scholasticism's historical
hour is that of the expansion of the *Sacrum Imperium* around the whole world (expanding from the middle of Europe); just as, accordingly, its formal method consists
in the conjunction of Western and Eastern philosophy; and just as its fundamental
formal problem (in scholasticism's fundamental question concerning the relation
between "existence" and "essence") consists in an inner unity between (Western) existentialism and (Eastern) essentialism.[119] Such, then, is the peculiar theology of the
"middle": from Nicholas of Cusa (who transposes scholasticism's final problematic
into a reflexive equilibrium) to Hegel: one and the same theology of the "divine middle" within the "order of antitheses," which is secularized into one and the same
philosophy of a systematic dialectic of "God as middle." Thus, wherever they should

---

118. Given that the formulae adopted by the most recent generation of Catholic
thinkers (*vide supra* the prefatory passage of this essay) seem to be formulae drawn from
Thomism and Scotism, one can see how all the confrontations that take shape between the
two, throughout their variations, remain fixed within this original confrontation. In the
most recent generation of Catholic thinkers, the confrontation between pneumaticism and
personalism attaches itself (on the personalist front) to Newman, and reaches back, on its
pneumaticist front, to the foundation of scholasticism's "divine order" in the Areopagite:
just as, prior to the war, the confrontation between Newman and neo-scholasticism developed from — as a variation of — the confrontation between Molinism and Bañezianism
(called "Thomism"): just as, in turn, the tension between Molinism and Bañezianism stems
from variously accentuated syntheses between Scotism and Thomism. Cf. *Religionsphilosophie katholischer Theologie* 1926 (= *Religionsphilosophische Schriften*, 1962); *Crucis mysterium*
(Paderborn: Schöningh, 1939), pp. 52ff., 178ff.; "Spiritualismus oder Christentum," *Stimmen
der Zeit* (June 1939).

119. As regards the entire problematic of essentialism and existentialism implicit in all
of this, see "Philosophies of Essence and Existence" above.

appear, a *theology of order* and *existentialism-essentialism* — the latter understood as the middle's definitive philosophoumenon — represent the apotheosis of the "middle."

Thus, within our three objective theologies, insofar as they stand *solely and exclusively by themselves,* what takes shape is a supernaturalism of absolute supernature that is secretly a naturalism of absolute nature — and for this reason these theologies are increasingly and ever more powerfully confronted by a fundamentally pure naturalism, which sees all supernature as merely the mask of nature. On the one hand, supernatural philosophy, morality, culture, and politics, which objectively turn out to be distinct types of natural philosophy, morality, culture, and politics — on the other hand (in response to this), a fundamentally pure rationalism, which exposes all revelation and grace as the *mythos* generated by "pure nature and reason": a fundamental anthropologism that interprets everything divine as an image of "pure humanity"; a fundamental psychologism and biologism that dilute all objective validity into the objectification of "pure life"; a fundamental pathologism that unmasks everything ideal as an illusion generated by "pure drive." In either case, the fundamental form is that of identity: on the one hand, an ideal illusion proceeding from above to below; on the other, a de-idealizing disillusionment proceeding from below to above.

But this — *thirdly* — is precisely the state of affairs that the Fourth Lateran Council's formula of analogy, in its ultimate and definitive sense, confronts: we see this in the trenchancy with which the *analogy* of "ever greater dissimilarity" is posed *over against* the "pure similarity" of *identity.* As is the case with scholastic theology, the formula's opposition to the supernaturalism of identity consists firstly in its emphasis upon the order of relation obtaining "between Creator and creature." But this order is then defined in such a way that the "dissimilarity" is seen to be "ever greater" with respect to every "similarity, however great." First, though, this "ever greater dissimilarity" is not that of the infinite horizon of a "similarity *in infinitum*" (as is the case with all three of our objective theologies taken solely in their own terms: whether as a "negative theology" of participation, or as the dynamism of antitheses, or as an order "*in infinitum*" by virtue of the "divine ever greater"); rather, the wording of the council's text defines this "ever greater dissimilarity" according to the fundamental distinction between the wholly disparate modes of God and of the creature: "each in its own mode" *(utraque in suo modo).* But, secondly, for precisely this reason, this is an "ever greater dissimilarity" wherein the creaturely "*modus*" is not opposed to the divine *"modus"* as a lesser grade or as in any way negative (as is the case with all three of our objective theologies taken solely in their own terms, by virtue of a "similarity *in infinitum*": whether as the "negative philosophy" of an "always deficient" divine ideality, or as a divine rhythm, or as a divine order by virtue of the creaturely "ever lesser"); rather, with regard to this "ever greater dissimilarity" the wording of the council's text distinguishes between positivities: between the positive unity *(unum)* of "the unity of the identity of nature" (in God) and the positive unity of the "union of love in grace" (in the creature): between the positively perfect *(perfectio)* and the "perfection of grace" (in the creature). Analogy is thus posed against identity, which "theopanizes" God and "pantheizes" the creature; the analogy portrays the unity of the creature's created being as deriving from God as Creator *(creatorem . . . creaturam)* within the positive "difference of one mode from the other" *(utraque . . . suo modo)* — and thus portrays this unity both as a genuine "in between" ("inter" creatorem, etc.) and as a genuine "and" *(creatorem "et" creaturam)*. And what this implies — over against the imperative "because" and "cannot" and "compelled" of identity in its theopanistic or pantheistic form (whether this imperative follows from an exclusive supernature or an exclusive nature) — is the objective "because" *(quia)* and "cannot" *(non potest . . . notari)* and "compelled" *(sit notanda)* of that irreducible distance that allows for freedom (the freedom both of an uncoercible and underivable supernature, as well as the freedom of a nature that — even within the supernatural, however exalted — is "presupposed" and "not destroyed" and, indeed, "perfected").

In this way the council's formula of analogy provided the decisive basis for the entire *development of the church's teaching* on the relation between nature and supernature: from the edicts against the Reformation to those against modernism: as follows from the fact that one and the same fundamental principle of identity, which appears in the Reformation as a supernatural theopanism (in which the invisible redeemer God alone works all things), is unveiled in modernism as a natural pantheism (in which the sole reality is that of visible life, whose progress is taken for the redeemer).

In this regard, against the Reformation, there is an emphasis upon the objective, official "service" of "representation" (in the *opus operatum*) and upon subjective, genuinely human "works": over against the supernaturalism of a God who alone works all things within an invisible interiority, which for this reason recognizes no service but that of "personal life," nor any common human works but those of "passive experience." We see here the determination of a positive cooperation — the "with" —

392

of nature within supernature: service is understood as a passive relation in which the positivity of God appears in the positive mode of the creature's agency; and work as an active relation in which the positivity of the creature appears as an effect of the God who positively gives.

Logically, the second step of this development is then made in the church's battle against *Jansenism and traditionalism:* for here the church emphasizes the fundamentally objective, positive "independence" of nature (in being and knowing). Thus it emphasizes that, on the one hand, nature is positively objectively "differentiated" from everything supernatural (in being and knowing) and that, on the other hand (precisely for this reason), nature is positively objectively "presupposed" for everything supernatural (in being and knowing) and positively objectively "led" to it (in being and knowing) — all of this, that is, is emphasized over against the supernaturalism of an exclusive supernature, for which "nature" (in being and knowing) means merely a sinful fall or a passive "letting happen." What we see here then is the determination of a positive and active distinctness of nature within supernature: in natural being, natural goodness, and natural religious knowledge, which are the objective presuppositions of the supernatural and also, precisely thus, the "active"[120] presuppositions implied in the church's doctrine concerning the *"praeambula fidei."*

The final, concluding step is taken by the *Vatican Council* and the edicts against *modernism:* in the gradual formulation of that really existing unity in (positively objective) "difference" that the Fourth Lateran Council's formula of analogy established. To be sure, the *one* "order" *(ordinavit)* that really exists is ordered "to the supernatural meaning and goal" of "participation in Divine goods";[121] within this order, however, there exists, positively and objectively, a theoretical and practical[122] knowledge of the true God[123] that is distinctly and "naturally human" *(naturali humanae rationis lumine),* having a genuinely positive, natural creaturely form of "causal thought" *(causam per effectum)* and formal "demonstration" *(demonstrari);*[124] and, precisely for this reason, this order is ordered towards a positive cooperation with revelation, which it interprets "within the context of the mysteries," but which it also interprets from the position of the naturally given "final goal of man" — such that both of these, this purely theological synthesis and this theological-philosophical systematics, are joined together in the form of unity peculiar to "analogy."[125] To be sure, the concreteness of this *one* really existing "supernatural order" is found in the church of the "apostolic vocation," understood as the church of the "Divine office," which as such extends to all areas of life,[126] since it represents God's au-

120. *Aktuierte.* — Trans.
121. Denz. 1786.
122. *Coll. Lac.* VII, 127, 133, 236.
123. Denz. 1785.
124. Denz. 2145.
125. Denz. 1796.
126. Denz. 1798.

thority from above and not a mystical collective from below,[127] but within this limit-less sovereignty of "God in Christ in the church" there exists a genuinely positive, distinct independence of "objective areas of culture" *(humanarum artium et disciplinarum cultura),* consisting in the "legitimate freedom" of each "distinct area operating by its own principles and methods"[128] and in the genuinely positive sover-eignty of the state and of the people and of politics, each "according to its proper right" within its own distinctive "domain," and insofar as each is genuinely the "highest of its kind."[129]

It is — *fourthly* — within this "ecclesial theology of analogy" (that is, the church's formula of analogy made actual, in each instance, by its method of "ecclesial discretion") that each of our *three objective theologies* acquires its *own proper "discretion."* For "man" as such, as God has in fact "ordained" him to be, there is only the *one* really existing order of a "supernatural defining-goal"[130] within the authoritative visible church, understood as the compre-hensive form of order;[131] for this reason, no purely natural religion, no purely natural morality, no purely natural culture, no purely natural science, and no purely natural politics really exists; rather, everything without exception (since everything belongs to this one man who is in fact "so" "ordained" by God) has as its final form — whether explicitly or implicitly, consciously or uncon-sciously, to the highest or lowest degree — the one supernatural form of "God in Christ in the church." At the level of real existence there is, without excep-tion, only an either-or: a yes or no to this *one* order. This — in light of "ecclesial discretion" — is the positive yield of our three objective theologies: *one* partic-ipation in God's nature and person, *one* mystery of the relation between origi-nal sin and redemption, *one* Divine order. But precisely because everything, within every possible "in between" existing between "Creator and creature," ultimately and definitively comes down to the "difference between the *modus* of each" within the "ever greater dissimilarity," the all-embracing unity and unicity that we have just emphasized depends precisely upon this positive dif-ference. On the one hand, the supernatural "God in Christ in the church" ap-pears essentially and decisively as the sovereignty of the Divine will within the sovereign will of the church (in the concluding condemnation of modernism); on the other hand, supernaturally elevated and redeemed nature is given

---

127. Denz. 2053, etc.
128. Denz. 1799.
129. Denz. 1866.
130. Denz. 1786.
131. Denz. 1798.

within its true, distinct, and purely natural "autonomy" *(propriis principiis et propria methodo).* And since the *one* really existing supernatural order appears precisely within the contents proper to this nature, and since the revelation of God "speaks in the likenesses of the data of the senses,"[132] and since grace is imparted in the sensible signs of the "total sacrament of the church" *(totius ecclesiae . . . sacramentum)* in its sacraments — since the whole of God *(totus Deus)* lives and lives on in the mystery of the incarnation, understood as the totality of man-like-any-other *(totus homo)* — so, too, consequently, the *one* supernatural Divine order possesses the true "form of man like any other" in the natural human forms of religion, the natural human contents of morality, natural human culture, natural human science, and natural human politics. This is how "ecclesial discretion" emancipates our three objective theologies from their various absolutisms; indeed, how it draws out and brings to perfection the positive view of the natural that develops gradually out of them: from the passive potential nature of Greek patristic theology to the formally antithetical nature of Augustinian theology to the active nature of scholastic theology. In precisely this way, then, the "church" becomes "grace" in the proper sense: grace being, according to the maxim of Thomas Aquinas, on the one hand, for "nature," the truly "final form" (as the definitive form of the *one* supernatural order), but, on the other hand, that within which "nature" is genuinely "completed": according to the double sense of the word *"perficit."*

Thus, finally, two things become clear regarding this "ecclesial theology of analogy": how it serves further to clarify scholastic theology, and why *Thomas Aquinas* is the most adequate theologian of this theology of analogy. Insofar as any particular scholastic theology seeks ultimately to comprehend the openness of the "ever greater dissimilarity" within some identical concept, it needs to clarify itself by way of this "ecclesial theology of analogy": this is so whether the identical concept in question is that of an ultimately absolute exemplarism (of the Divine idea) or of an intellectualism (of the Divine intellect) or of a voluntarism (of the Divine will) or of an ontologism (of the Divine being). Nevertheless, an "ecclesial theology of analogy" is especially compatible with scholastic theology, insofar as the latter is most definitely not an intuitive Gnosis but rather — true to its name — a discipline proper to the order of the school: for it is in this spirit that the order of the positive difference between God and creature is preserved — the difference, namely, between God's complete sovereignty and the creature's active "exercises." And, in this sense, Thomas Aquinas (as opposed to any systematic

132. Thomas Aquinas, *In Boeth de Trin.* q. 6, a. 3, corp.

"Thomism") is the special "theologian of the church": because what is for-mulated in his thought, in its properly fundamental form, is what is also as-serted in the course of the development of the "ecclesial theology of analogy" from the Fourth Lateran Council to the edicts against modernism: that God's surpassing greatness is manifest precisely in that he establishes the creature's independence from himself — endowing the creature with its own proper being, its own proper agency, and its own proper providence.[133]

Here, however — *fifthly* — we have answered the question with which we began our last investigation: Is the formula of analogy, as it is expressed in the formula of the Fourth Lateran Council, merely the expression of the structure of the supernatural aspect of the "ecclesial" (even as it includes all the various realms of the natural), or is the supernatural aspect of the "ecclesial," on the contrary, reducible to analogy, understood as a natural, creaturely metaphysical structure (even as it includes all the contents of the supernatural aspect of the "ecclesial")? The question, phrased more pre-cisely, is this: Is *analogy* a *theological form* ("in which . . .") *or a philosophical principle* ("from which . . .")? The formula of Thomas Aquinas that we have just sketched out denies that this is an either-or and affirms instead that it is a simultaneity. For, on the one hand, it is a formula that spells out the factical and pervasive structure of the one supernatural order of "God in Christ in the church": as, that is, a theological "form in which. . . ." But, on the other hand, it anchors this same structure in the true "inner essence" of the rela-tion between God and creature as such: in the manner, that is, of a philo-sophical "principle from which. . . ." In this way, then, we discover the formal aspect corresponding to the material aspect that we have unfolded in this part of our investigation: just as the one all-embracing supernatural order of "God in Christ in the church" is simultaneously accompanied by the positive difference of an autonomous nature, so too analogy as a theological form is simultaneously accompanied by analogy as philosophical principle. The "proper being and proper agency and proper providence" of the creature point, with a genuine necessity, beyond themselves to the "surpassing great-ness of God": to, that is, an "analogy directed towards the above," in the manner of a philosophical principle. At the same time, in his supernatural self-communication, "God's surpassing greatness" manifests its formal es-sence in "establishing" the creature's "independence" in its own "proper be-ing and proper agency and proper providence": in, that is, an "analogy di-rected towards the below," in the manner of a theological form. What is

---

133. *De. Ver.* q. 9, a. 2, corp.; q. 11, a. 1, corp.; etc.

essential to the "analogy directed towards the above" (in the manner of a philosophical principle) is that it points to God insofar as he is "surpassingly great"; and thus, logically, it is precisely his sovereignty that the analogy emphasizes, a sovereignty that is not derivable like a principle that one can manipulate, and from which nothing can be objectively derived. Likewise, what is essential to the "analogy directed towards the below" (in the manner of a theological form) is that it points to the creaturely insofar as the creature possesses its own "proper being and proper agency and proper providence"; and thus, logically, it is precisely the positive autonomy of the creaturely that the analogy emphasizes, an autonomy that cannot be derived from revelation and theology.[134] In this way the "in between" in the phrase "between Creator and creature" (in the council's formula of analogy) genuinely supports the "because" and "cannot" and "compelled." The analogy consists, on the one hand, in the essence of the relation "between Creator and creature," and in this respect it is truly a philosophical principle. But, just the same, it is on the other hand the formal structure of the sovereign creativity of the Creator — whether he wants a creature at all and how he should want the crea-

---

134. Thus the attempts of Barth and Söhngen to pose an *"analogia fidei"* over against an *"analogia entis"* — or, as the case may be, to supplement the latter with the former — contain their own riposte. By the phrase *"analogia fidei,"* which is taken from Rom. 12:6, what is meant — in the context of this verse and in connection with 1 Cor. 12 — is the most authoritative regulation of the personal *charisma* of "prophecy" by the "analogy of faith," as it is worked out in the unity of the *one* body through the "measure of faith" that "God has given" (12:3): "if a man's gift is prophecy, then let him use it according to the measure (analogy) of faith." This "analogy" is thus something objectively authoritative that is given by God, standing above the subjective religious experience of "prophecy": and thus it clearly points towards the "ecclesial theology of analogy," as we developed it above. It is thus not an "actual *analogia fidei*" found within the event of actual "proclamation," as Barth conceives the *"analogia fidei":* for such "actuality" is precisely the actuality of "prophecy," which is to be measured according to an objectively enduring "analogy of faith." Nor does it suffice to articulate an "objective *analogia fidei,*" understood as the whole harmonious complex of the particular truths of the faith, as Söhngen would have it: for what is ultimate in the living "body" is the living "authority" of the head, the "mystery," that is, "of the (authoritative, positing) will," which according to the letter to the Ephesians is the final form of the church. Thus only one "authoritative *analogia fidei*" remains, i.e., the form of "ecclesiological christological theological authority," as we unfolded it above. Viewed from the perspective of the Fourth Lateran Council, however, the *"analogia entis"* is regarded solely and exclusively as the "final form" of the unity of supernature and nature itself. Which goes to say that there is no duality between an *"analogia entis"* and an *"analogia fidei,"* but rather that one and the same *"analogia entis,"* directed in its double form both "above" and "below," is in the response of the Fourth Lateran Council the "metaphysical structure" of one and the same "authoritative *analogia fidei.*"

ture to be — and in this respect its form is theological. Hence analogy is, on the one hand, what is ultimate and decisive, thoroughly shaping everything in the one factical supernatural order as well as everything in every possible order, be it ever so supernatural (given that, according to the council, the analogy has the form of a "because" and "cannot" and "compelled"). But, on the other hand, it is impossible to derive anything from analogy, as follows from the sovereignty of the God who is himself underivable (given that, according to the council, analogy appears — now and always — "within" the order sovereignly decreed by God's free will).

In light — *sixthly* — of what we found to be ultimate in our three objective theologies, this can be rendered in a final, still more precise form: for what we found to be ultimate was that all of these theologies led back to some version of the relation between *essence and existence*. In the theology of the Greek fathers we saw an ultimate, pure essentialism; in the theology of Augustine, similarly, an ultimate existentialism; and in scholastic theology, a dialectic between an existential essentialism (in Thomism) and an essential existentialism (in Scotism). At the level of method, "analogy" could appear to be something similar: since it emphasizes, on the one hand, the one real existentiality of the order of "God in Christ in the church" but, on the other hand, the essential difference between an underivable supernature and an ineffaceable nature. The corresponding formula would then be: an existential unity within an essential difference.

But this is precisely what indicates the clear alternative to the formulae we discovered above in our three objective theologies. For hidden beneath this methodological formula there is the objective formula: that the form of essence-and-existence proper to God (even in his supernatural self-communication) is to be distinguished from the form of essence-and-existence genuinely proper to the creature (within every supernatural self-communication of God, "however great").[135] Thus, as far as the question of

---

135. As far as the *one* supernatural order of redemption is concerned, this is fundamentally expressed in the controversy between Thomism and Scotism: whether in Christ there is only the one "divine existence" or whether there is, in addition, a true "human existence." Logically, the former thesis comes to emphasize the form of "divine existence" as such: in keeping with a preference for the "heavenly church" and the "heavenly life" of the Christian — which is to say that it tends in the direction of the theology of the Greek fathers. The latter thesis, on the other hand, emphasizes "human existence," with the same formal logical consistency, as a decisive expression of God's true descent, to the point of being "totally human" and thus dwelling within a human "existence," which is to say that it tends in the direction of the theology of Augustine. Accordingly, to take the methodological formula

the relation between essence and existence is concerned, it is in fact "analogy" itself that proves to be the ultimate form, without analogy itself being reducible to any "necessary" form of play between essence and existence. This is the inexorable, final consequence of the council's formula of analogy: for, since the relation "between Creator and creature" as such is solely and strictly and necessarily the analogy of the "ever greater dissimilarity" within every "similarity, however great," so also and precisely with regard to essence and existence, analogy is the ultimate and definitive "because" and "cannot" and "compelled." There is no autonomous theology of essence (of the eternal tradition), nor is there an autonomous theology of existence (of actual proclamation), nor is there a form of play between them. There is no autonomous philosophy of essence (of eternal essences and truths), nor is there an autonomous philosophy of existence (of actual movement), nor is there a form of play between them. For this reason, too, there is no unity of theology and philosophy in an autonomous principle of essence or existence or in any "form of play" between them. All of that is simply the ever ancient and ever new play between theopanism and pantheism, as we have seen: the rebellion of the created spirit, which seeks to be the uncreated Pneuma, passively as an efflux of God or actively in the form of God. There is only theology (however many relative directions it might possibly take) in analogy understood as the "form in which. . . ." There is only philosophy (however many relative directions it might possibly take) in analogy understood as the "principle from which. . . ." There is only a unity of theology and philosophy in this underivable and therefore in its own right "analogous" correlation between the (theological) "analogy from above" and the (philosophical) "analogy from below." All of this is implied in the exceptionless "because" and "cannot" and "compelled" of the formula of the Fourth Lateran Council.

---

of "existential unity" as the direct expression of an identical existence would be to identify one-sidedly with the thesis of Thomism and thus with the theology of the Greek fathers. By "existential unity," then, one means the unity of "divine existence" and "human existence," which are themselves essentially distinct, in the *one* existence of Christ (and in him, by participation, in the existence of the church; and in her, by membership, in the existence of the individual Christian). And the form of this unity is itself, in the most mysterious sense of the word, analogy. For the innermost mystery of Christ is that in him deity and humanity are *one* person, but within a difference between the two that not only is not negated but, indeed, necessarily cannot be: thus within a hypostatic union that is neither abrogated nor can be, and as such *is* the analogy of "ever greater dissimilarity" that cannot be negated (*non potest*, according to the council). Cf. Chapter 4 of my *Gott: Fünf Vorträge über das religionsphilosophische Problem* (Cologne-Munich-Vienna: Oratoriums-Verlag, 1926): reprinted in *Religionsphilosophische Schriften* (Einsiedeln: Johannes-Verlag, 1962).

3 Philosophy as a Problem

1941

1. The fundamental problem of *philosophy* is implicit in its name: love (φιλεῖν) of wisdom (σοφία). Socrates and Plato interpret this love as a (distant) "seeking for . . ." (wisdom), as distinguished from an immediate "possession of . . . (wisdom)."[1] In this case philosophy tends to have the character of a general aporetics, and for this reason it is a doctrine concerning ultimate questions. By contrast, the traditional Eastern conception of philosophy is one in which the "love of . . . (wisdom)" signifies a "union with . . . (wisdom)" (as the word φιλεῖν suggests, connoting the intimacy and union of an embraced, embracing love). In this case, in this form of participation in wisdom itself, philosophy becomes a system of universal principles, and thus a doctrine concerning ultimate foundations. Both forms of philosophy, however — that of an aporetics and that of a systematics of principles — manifest themselves in terms of theoretical and practical philosophy. As theoretical philosophies, they manifest themselves in the superpersonal, objective form of a "knowledge of . . ." that is prosecuted reflexively and can be transmitted in terms of method and concepts: as an aporetics and a systematics of principles in the properly neutral sense[2] of these terms. As practical philosophies, however, they are lived out in the intrapersonal form of life of a "posture within . . ." that can be realized only in a direct fashion, and that is witnessed to by example and imitation: aporetics here being understood as the objective expression of the personal posture of the "self-abnegating sage"

1. *Phaedo* 278d.
2. *Es-Sinn.* — Trans.

This essay first appeared in *Philosophisches Jahrbuch der Görres-Gesellschaft* (1941).

(who "sees through" everything in terms of its final questionability) — while a systematics of principles is understood as the objective expression of the personal posture of the "contemplative sage" (who "surveys" everything in light of its ultimate foundations). Such are the antitheses that cut across and through the entire history of philosophy: critique versus intuition, pure knowledge versus life-knowledge.

2. The shape of philosophy can be defined more precisely in light of its *standing with regard to science and theology*. Science, according to its subject matter, has to do with particular regions of reality; these regions it then investigates, according to its method, in terms of their inner lawfulness, inner coherence, inner order, inner sense — that is, their inner "logos." Thus bio-logy is concerned with the *logos* of *bios,* i.e., vegetal life, psycho-logy, with the *logos* of *psyche,* i.e., the sensible and intellectual aspects of the life of the soul, etc. Consequently, science is conducted between two limits: at its lower limit it is in effect a gathering of purely material data (in which case, seeking the closest approximation to "positive facts," it is conducted as a "positive" science — to the point, at one extreme, of becoming a pure "positivism"); at its upper limit it aims at the pure form proper to its given area (in which case, seeking the closest approximation to its "pure idea" or "pure structure," it is conducted as a "constructive" science — to the point, at the other extreme, of becoming a pure "constructivism"). What remains common to both, however, is that in each case thought ascends from below to above: whether it be from disordered to ordered material (in the case of "positive" science) or from the material to the formal (in the case of "constructive" science).

Theology, by contrast, according to its strict concept, proceeds in the reverse direction, moving from above to below: not only as regards its subject matter — that is, its "speech" concerning the "meaning and coherence"[3] of God (theo-logy in the sense of "logia" concerning God) — but also as regards its form — that is, God himself speaking about his meaning and coherence (theo-logy as "logia" on the part of God). What goes on in theology is not a kind of research that leads from the creature to the Creator, or from the grounded to its ground, but rather a self-revelation of the Creator to the creature, or of the ground to the grounded. It is, of course, "speech" in the medium of "creaturely signs" (Thomas Aquinas), but only insofar as it is God himself who speaks. And it is, of course, a "speech" that created men labor to interpret. But they are theologians only insofar as their labor — always dependent and provisional — depends upon the sole authority of the

3. *Sinn und Zusammenhang.* — Trans.

God who speaks. Thus, since theology is a movement from above to below, it is neither a doctrine regarding the natural relationship of man to God (a philosophy of subjective religion), nor a doctrine regarding God as the ground and meaning of the world (a philosophy of objective religion), nor a doctrine regarding God solely in himself (a philosophy of the divine as such). Rather, it is a doctrine regarding the free relation of God to man (as a theology of salvation), the mysteries of God in himself (as a theology of God), and the being and history of the entire world as it derives from God (as a theology of the kingdom of God).

Right in the middle — between science, understood as a strict movement from below to above, and theology, understood as a strict movement from above to below — lies philosophy. On the one hand, seen from the standpoint of science, it is the home of those "pure ideas" or "pure structures" at which science, understood as constructive science, aims. In this respect, philosophy appears either within a movement immanent to the creature, from below to above, as an *a posteriori* "philosophy of the sciences" (since its final conclusions depict that very region of "pure structures" at which science aims), or it presents itself within a movement immanent to the creature, from above to below, as an *a priori* "pure philosophy" (inasmuch as it comprises a direct vision of those "pure ideas," proper to particular regions of science, by which scientific research is guided and towards which it strives, or at least inasmuch as it provides the "pure method," be it critical or intuitive, to which scientific research turns for guidance). One finds the mirror image of this when one views philosophy from the perspective of theology. In this respect, either philosophy — when it moves from the creature to God, from below to above — bears a special resemblance to a "natural theology," understood as a doctrine of the divine insofar as the divine appears as the ground and end *(principium et finis)* of the creaturely world;[4] or — when it moves from God to the creature, from above to below — it becomes a "theological philosophy," since it sets out from theological data, but according to a philosophical method, in order to connect the answers of theology to the questions and presentiments of philosophy, and thus to arrive at a system (as, in fact, is the practice peculiar to the *Summae* of classical scholasticism).[5]

3. A *properly Christian* perspective has the final word: for there is only one concretely existing order between God and creature in this concretely existing world: the order between original sin in Adam and redemption in

4. Thomas Aquinas, *In Boeth. de Trin.* q. 5, a. 4, corp.
5. Denz. 1796.

Christ, the crucified. The concretely existing face of philosophy (every philosophy, that is, found within the concretely existing world and its history) is not visible except from the perspective of this order (within which, as an objectively universal order, every concretely existing human being stands, whether he or she knows it or not). Consequently, the question of a "Christian philosophy" is not the question of one particular philosophy among others within the ambit of philosophy as such — rather, the question of the relation between Christianity and philosophy is the question concerning the concretely existing shape of philosophy as such (within this single, concretely existing order that obtains between original sin in Adam and redemption in Christ).

With regard to how we understand this concretely existing shape, the dual maxim that traces back to Thomas Aquinas[6] is apposite: grace (or faith) does not destroy nature (or reason), but rather presupposes it and perfects it, providing its final form. When the stress is placed upon "grace and nature," the maxim — as it pertains to our question — means that while being and history, as the object of philosophy, have the "grace" of redemption in Christ as their final form *(per-ficit)*, they are perfected in such a way that their natural shape continues to be preserved. When a corresponding stress is placed upon "faith and reason," the same maxim means that while thought — understood as the act of philosophy — has "faith" in redemption in Christ for its final form *(per-ficit)*, it is perfected in such a way that its natural lawfulness continues to be preserved.

The meaning of these maxims becomes clearer if we take a closer look at the essence of Christianity, which is the "final form," but which nevertheless does not negate the "natural form," but rather includes it. By what is Christian here we mean: the incarnation of God, redemption in the cross, and incarnation and redemption as church (since Christ is "*one* Christ, head and body"). In this way what is properly Christian is opposed to original sin: the incarnation is opposed to man's seeking to become God; redemption in the cross is opposed to man's seeking to assert himself into eternal life; the church (whose religious orders involve blind obedience) is opposed to man's seeking to be independent. Everything comes down to this *one* antithesis: whereas Adam (and in him all of humanity), by taking the path of unconditional self-affirmation, plunges into sin, death, and hell — salvation, eternal life, and heaven are opened up by the unconditional self-offering of Christ (and the offering in him of all who are redeemed by him). "Life through

---

6. Thomas Aquinas, *Summa Th.* I, 1, q. 1, a. 8, ad 2; q. 2, a. 2, ad 1.

death" (in the mystery of redemption) is opposed to "death through life" (in the mystery of original sin). This is the word of the Gospel: "Whoever seeks to save his life will lose it; but whoever loses his life for my sake will find it" (Matt. 16:25).

The consequence of this for philosophy is that, insofar as the form of the cross constitutes its ultimate form, philosophy preserves its natural form. Concretely existing philosophy occurs as genuine philosophy within the one concrete order of original sin and redemption to the degree that its operative principle is the Pauline "dying, and yet we live" (2 Cor. 6:9). The either-or of concretely existing philosophy stands between "fallen" philosophy under the sign of "original sin" and "redeemed" philosophy. A fallen philosophy is one that seeks to be absolute (it is no accident that the formula of original sin in Gen. 3:5 is that of "knowing . . . like God"), only then to succumb either to the dead absoluteness of "pure concepts" (in a "pure logic") or to the hellish absoluteness of a "pure critique" that rends everything apart (in a "pure dialectic") and thus truly progresses from sin to death to hell. A "redeemed" philosophy not only knows itself to be living before the *one* living absolute (God) in its creaturely distinction from this absolute (and hence to be living within the unfettered creaturely movement of genuine "becoming"), but also and precisely recognizes its own native tendency to fall into the death of "pure concepts" and into the hell of "pure critique" (and for this reason realizes its ever new becoming in the fashion of an ever new resurrection from an ever new death and an ever new hell, since it suffers an ever new fall into these "original sins" and through them dies into an ever new redemption).

Thus Christian philosophy, in the proper sense, consists in Christianity's transformation of "fallen" philosophy into "redeemed" philosophy, redeeming it from "philosophy as God" and *into* a "philosophy of the creature *coram Deo*" (in the "analogy" of "ever greater dissimilarity" within "a unity, however great").[7] What is at issue, therefore, is the "ensign," so to speak, that is borne by the problematic of philosophy as we developed it in the first two parts of this section. If it is the ensign of "original sin," then this problematic becomes an either-or between the contradictions that exist between mutually exclusive absolute philosophies. If, on the other hand, the ensign is that of "redemption," then this same problematic reveals itself as a tension, resulting from a genuinely creaturely movement, between the various aspects of a single whole.

Such is the position sketched out in certain corresponding proposi-

7. Denz. 432.

tions of the Vatican Council. On the one hand, the Christian moment constitutes the "final form": since "the church . . . has its right . . . and duty from
God to condemn any science, falsely so called, in order that no one be de-
ceived by philosophy and vain falsehood."[8] On the other hand, however, it is
precisely in this way that a genuinely "natural form" of philosophy arises:
since "the perpetual consensus of the Catholic Church has held and holds"
that natural knowledge and research possess their own "object" and "principle,"[9] and that "such disciplines, each in its domain, use their own principles
and their own methods."[10]

It is precisely this problem of concretely existing philosophy that
brings us to the problem of the individual *philosophical disciplines.*

4. Philosophical striving — when marked by "original sin" — attempts
to attain an *"absolutum"* within the realm of the creaturely itself, from which
one might then unfold the coherence and meaning of being and history. Almost every one of the individual philosophical disciplines one encounters in
the course of the history of philosophy appears to be such an attempt. Philosophy *qua* cosmology or the philosophy of nature is grounded in the cosmos
as an *"absolutum"* — whether static or dynamic — by which all the questions
of philosophy are resolved: as we see in the Chinese Tao, the Ionian philosophy of the elements of the world (earth, fire, water, air), the Aristotelian philosophy of the cyclical revolution, the Renaissance philosophy of the divine
cosmos. Philosophy *qua* anthropology is either grounded in "humanity" as
an *absolutum:* as we see in Enlightenment philosophy and in the contemporary philosophy of the human sciences; or it is grounded in the "totality" (of
humanity, of the folk, of community or society) as an *absolutum:* as we see in
the Enlightenment philosophy of man, the folk philosophy of Herder and Romanticism, and the recent sociology and philosophy of race. Philosophy, understood as the noetics of a cognitive philosophy or a philosophy of mind, is
grounded in "pure thought" as an *absolutum:* as we see in Eckhart and German mysticism, empirically in contemporary psychology, methodologically
in Descartes and modern phenomenology, critically in Kant, metaphysically
in Leibniz, Hegel, and German Idealism. Philosophy *qua* ethics is grounded
(at the level of the act) in the *absolutum* of a "pure desire" or (at the level of
the object) in the *absolutum* of a "pure value": as we see in Chinese Confu-
cianism, original Socratic Platonism, late medieval voluntarism, and modern

8. Denz. 1798.
9. Denz. 1795.
10. Denz. 1799.

philosophies of life, value, and existence. Philosophy *qua* aesthetics is grounded in "pure rhythm" or "pure harmony" or the "pure ideal" as an *absolutum:* as we see in the development of Platonism into neo-Platonism, Schelling's "polarity" regarded as a development of certain intimations in Kant's *Critique of Judgment,* and the tragic pessimistic or tragic Dionysian "rhythm of the world" in Schopenhauer and Nietzsche. Philosophy, understood as ontology or metaphysics, appears historically either in the forms we have delineated above (the cosmos, or man, or the true, or the good, or the beautiful, understood as "the" proper name for being) or as something under the direct guidance of theology, as a philosophy concerning creation and the creature: as we see in the philosophies of India, patristic philosophy, the scholasticism of the Middle Ages, and neo-scholasticism. These last philosophies present themselves historically either as direct "theological philosophies" (in the sense we touched upon earlier), or as philosophies that, guided by theology, assume guarded or circumspect positions with regard to the philosophies we sketched out above, with their respective *absoluta* — or as a mixture of both types.

5. From this picture of "fallen" philosophies we can now identify the features of "redeemed" philosophy: just as Romans 11:32 introduces the "mercy" of redemption in the midst of the "obstinacy of unbelief" (over to which "God has bound all men").

The redemptive de-absolutization of all fallen "absolute" philosophies allows, *firstly,* the *absoluta* that we delineated above to appear in their creaturely relativity, thus resolving the mutual contradiction and conflict between differing absolute philosophies into a tension that arises naturally from objective possibilities proper to philosophy's various aspects. Hidden within philosophy *qua* cosmology and anthropology we discover the one objective span between nature and spirit (centered in man as the midpoint of the passage between them). In philosophy *qua* noetics, ethics, and aesthetics we discover (at the level of the act) the one span of the so-called transcendentals: among the true, the good, and the beautiful. And, logically, a philosophy of the objective span (between nature and spirit) will appear under the ensign, respectively, of one of the three transcendentals; just as any "total" philosophy[11] will logically appear as a suspended correlation among these three.

But, *secondly,* it is precisely here that one comes to see in the form of suspended correlation the particular form of creatureliness in its ontological

---

11. *Gesamt-Philosophie.* — Trans.

correlation of existence and essence. For in the case of the true, the stress of this ontological correlation[12] falls on the side of a relatively pure essence; in the case of the good, on the tension of becoming between existence and essence ("become what you are"); in the case of the beautiful, on a relatively ideal existence. Thus, what emerges out of the aforementioned "total" philosophy is a philosophy of this intrinsic ontological correlation between existence and essence: an ontology or metaphysics of creaturely being.

But, *thirdly,* this ontology or metaphysics of creaturely being logically comes to completion when it envisions God: since the tension of the correlation of existence and essence (essence in-and-beyond existence) proper to the realm of the creaturely points beyond itself to an *absolutum* of existence-and-essence: to God, that is, understood as the essential identity of existence and essence, as the pure Is (*ipsum Est,* as Augustine puts it; *ipsum esse,* as Thomas Aquinas puts it).

Fourthly and finally, the intra-creaturely *absoluta* proper to "philosophies shaped by original sin," divested of their absoluteness, are transformed into just so many similitudes of this divine Is. Indeed, from the perspective of trinitarian theology (taken as the core of Christian theology), the threefold flowing[13] of the true, the good, and the beautiful within the "total" philosophy can now appear as a vestigial image of the triune flowing of the intra-divine life. If Hegel's philosophy, as an "absolute philosophy" marked by original sin, usurped the realm of the Trinitarian, and made it identical with the intrinsic form of the philosophizing mind, even this is now "redeemed": for the one true *"imago Trinitatis"* appears within concretely existing philosophy's final aspect: the beautiful is assigned to the Augustinian *memoria,* and thus to the "Father"; the true is assigned to the Augustinian *intellectus,* and thus to the "Son"; the good is assigned to the Augustinian *voluntas,* and thus to the "Holy Spirit."

We see the structure of "redeemed" philosophy in this ascent of a three-streamed *transcendental philosophy* to an *ontology of creaturely being* to an *ontology of the relation between God and creature* to a *philosophy of the imago Trinitatis* (one, however, that must first be developed from theology). In this respect, philosophy truly does lie between science and theology; it is conditioned by both, but is at the same time relatively independent of them. In this respect, equally, it bears the particular ensign of "redeemed" philosophy as its inner form: the "analogy" of "ever greater dissimilarity" in every

---

12. *Seins-Zueinander.* — Trans.
13. *Drei-Strömigkeit.* — Trans.

"unity, however great" (as opposed to "pure logic" and "pure dialectic," understood as forms of "fallen" philosophy). In the ascent from transcendental philosophy to an ontology (of creaturely being and its relation to the Creator), philosophy proceeds from the "analogy" between existence and essence to the incomparably greater analogy between the unity of existence and essence in the creature (as a tension of correlation) and the unity of existence and essence in God (as an essential identity). And, in the case of the crowning philosophy of the *imago Trinitatis* (as developed from theology), it is no longer even the kind of analogy that might open from below to the above (not even in the form of an "ever greater dissimilarity"), but is a mysterious "likeness" that becomes manifest solely through God's Word.

Such is the shape of philosophy — as it commences in the pre-Christian era, having the features of Platonic and Aristotelian philosophy (though under the form of absolutisms marked by original sin); as it is delineated by theology in the Christian era, during the patristic and scholastic periods; as it is clothed in modern philosophy (since the Renaissance and the Enlightenment) in a new absoluteness marked by original sin (as follows from the Reformation's doctrine, which stands at the inception of modern philosophy, of the ineradicability of original sin); but also as it seeks to be resurrected anew, passing through and beyond this most recent absoluteness, as a true "redeemed" philosophy, possessing its "own method" and its "own principle."[14]

14. Denz. 1799.

4 Metaphysics, Religion, Analogy

1956

Metaphysics and religion occupy a common plane "between the below and the above." For metaphysics this plane "between the below and the above" is the plane situated between those "real things" (τὰ φυσικά, in the Aristotelian sense) that we can experience and an "ultimate ground" (ἀρχαί, in the Ionian sense: water, earth, air, fire, logos, chance, and fate). For religion this plane "between the below and the above" is situated between the living creature and the living God. And it is by way of the discussion that opens up between metaphysics and religion — between these two versions of the "between the below and the above" — that we are led to the question of "analogy."

I

In the realm of *metaphysics,* this "between" is characterized by the historical opposition between *a posteriori* and *a priori* "experience": as we see in the Aristotelian opposition between "αἰσθάνεσθαι"[1] and "νοεῖν" — culminating in the modern opposition between the empirically critical metaphysics proper to a "metaphysics of the natural sciences" and "phenomenology," whether that of Husserl's *a priori* "intuition of essences" or of Scheler's "feeling of value" or of Heidegger's "understanding of Being." For its part, the critical "empiricism" of a metaphysics of the natural sciences has the sense

---

1. In the German text, this word is rendered, catachrestically, as αἰσθανεῖν. — Trans.

This essay first appeared in *Archivio di Filosofia,* Rome (1956).

etymologically of "experience," whether in Greek, Latin, or German: since the Greek "ἐμπειρία," which is connected with the verb "πειράζω," suggests an "experience resulting from practical experiment" (the chief example being a physician's experiment), just as the precise connotation of the Greek word "αἰσθάνεσθαι" is that of a "groping awareness" (through the sense of touch); and since the explicit connotation of the Latin *"experiri"* is that of a "putting to the test" (whence the word "experiment"); and since, finally, it is no coincidence that the German word *"erfahren"* signifies in its stem *"fahren"* a kind of "experience gained abroad" and thus, in the most universal sense, an "experience in all places with all the senses," being distinguished most sharply from Augustine's mystical "turn inward to where truth resides."[2] But even Aristotle, for all his critical realism, ultimately recognizes in all empirical experience a "νοῦς" within the human being that directly apprehends the "ἀρχαί,"[3] and therein the "original and ultimate limits of individual πράγματα."[4] "Among the things that appear," this "νοῦς" is what is "most divine," in that it is "unto itself . . . (as a) νόησις νοήσεως."[5] The innermost core of every (empirical) experience, however real, is a kind of "pure experience in the interior of the intellect" that cognitively experiences the "principles (ἀρχαί)" and the "beginning and end of all real things," in that it has only itself as an object (in the strict sense, a "self-thinking of thought"), thereby providing the basis not only of Descartes's *"cogito"* and the "transcendental subjectivity" of Kant's "categories," but also — explicitly — of Husserl's monadological transcendentalism (understood as an experience of the All in the pure experience of the self). Accordingly, metaphysics occurs between "experience" and "experience." On the one hand: experience in the sense of "sensing"[6] and "trial through testing" and "complete traversal" of the concrete universe of concretely individual things, wherein the "μετά" of the "φυσικά" declares itself, but does so strictly *within* the "φυσικά" (*"intra sensibilia,* says Thomas!"); which is to say (according to the etymology of "μετά"), it declares itself as that which "underlies the physical" but is nevertheless something "simultaneous and together with the physical." On the other hand: experience in the sense of a (Platonic) "τόπος νοητός" within the (Aristotelian) "νόησις νοήσεως," which is to say, experience of a "noetic world (of the origin — the *Ur* — as the beginning and end of physical

2. *De Vera Rel.* 39, 72; *In Jo. Tract.* 23, 10.
3. *Eth. Nic.* VI, 6, 1141a, 7.
4. *Eth. Nic.* VI, 12, 1143a, 36.
5. *Met.* XII, 9, 1074b, 19, 33-35.
6. *Erspüren.* — Trans.

things)" within the inner revolution of the "noetic act," which, as the revolution of a "thinking of thought," is at the same time, according to Aristotle, the innermost dynamic core of that telluric and sidereal "revolution" (κυκλοφορία τέλειος)[7] that (for Aristotle) constitutes the real physical universe. Thus, on the one hand, metaphysical experience indicates a "thoroughgoing experience" of what "underlies all physical things" ("physical" meaning everything that can be experienced by the senses), whereby that which "underlies" is nevertheless experienced strictly within the realm of "physical things" as that which is "with" the physical and "simultaneous" to it (that is, as an "indwelling transcendence").[8] On the other hand, "metaphysical experience" indicates a "turning away from everything external" and a total "turn inward to a pure interior" (as Augustine says)[9] such that, nevertheless, within the "νόησις νοήσεως" — that is to say, within the inner intellectual revolution of "I think myself thinking" — one not only experiences a "monadological world" (Husserl), but experiences this inner intellectual revolution as what, moving all things, is innermost to the real physical revolution of the external cosmos as such (Aristotle) — experiences it, that is, in terms of a "transcending immanence." Thus, "metaphysical experience" occurs within an ultimate rhythm between an "indwelling transcendence" (which is what is ultimate for a real critical metaphysics of the natural sciences) and a "transcending immanence" (which is what is ultimate for an idealist metaphysics of the immanence of consciousness). What appears to be an either-or between a realist and an idealist metaphysics is actually a dialectic between them (a dialectic in which they are always — at the point of their most extreme opposition — "ignited" by one another); and, in such a dialectic, what reveals itself as truly "ultimate," and as superordinate to and beyond the dialectical opposition itself, is the oscillating rhythm between an "indwelling transcendence" and a "transcending immanence" — a rhythm, however, that is hidden behind the revolutions of the ever renewed dialectic between absolute realism and absolute idealism, between a metaphysics of "being" (for which "consciousness" is simply the "consciousness of being") and a metaphysics of "consciousness" (for which "being" is simply "being within consciousness").

In this rhythm concealed within a manifest dialectic between realist and idealist metaphysics we discover what is ultimate "between the below and

---

7. *De caelo* II, 1, 284a, 3f.

8. *Immanierende Transzendenz.* — Trans.

9. *In Jo. Tract.* 23, 10; *De Trin.* X, iii, 5; v, 7; viii, 11; ix, 12.

the above" specific to metaphysics and "metaphysical experience." In a realist metaphysics, what is "below" are the "φυσικά," the real things, whereas what is "above" (according to the sense of "μετά" in "metaphysics") is what ultimately "underlies" the physical as "concomitant with and simultaneous to it," which is to say, a "super-real ultimate," from which real things derive, and in which they are rooted, and which itself "lives and moves and has its being" in them, while they "live and move and have their being" in It (as Paul points out on the Areopagus in Acts 17:28 regarding the relation between creation and the Divine ground from which it originally derives and in which it subsists): the original "ground from which," the *Urgrund*, and the "ground in which," the *Ingrund*, of all real things, the ground that thus appears as, so to speak, the "maternal substrate," the cosmic "womb of all things," and yet at the same time as the "cosmic revolution wherein all things revolve" (just as the ultimate cosmic principle, as Aristotle conceives it, is the "κυκλοφορία," the "revolution" that Dionysius the Areopagite unveils as the "divine cycle" ("κύκλος θεῖος") of "divine love" ("θεῖος ἔρως"). In an idealist metaphysics, on the other hand, what is "below" appears as "phenomenal consciousness," which by way of the "logia" of self-analysis explicates itself into a "phenomenological consciousness" (as is both the method and the point of all phenomenology), in which one experiences the "ideal above" of a "noumenal consciousness" (either as "absolute Spirit," following Hegel, or as a "monadological world," following Husserl). But here, too, this is experienced more profoundly as what "underlies, as 'concomitant with and simultaneous to'" (in keeping with the sense of "μετά" in "metaphysics"), since "noumenal consciousness" "lies at the ground" of "phenomenal consciousness," and is formatively at work within it as what is "concomitant with and simultaneous to" it; but here too, finally, it is experienced as a "revolution," the revolution of a "νόησις νοήσεως" within the phenomenal and phenomenological "νόησις νοήσεως," the revolution proper to an absolute Spirit, absolutely "from itself, about itself, to itself,"[10] which as the "paternal principle," as it were, "enspirits"[11] the revolution of "I think myself thinking," and vice versa (just as Husserl senses an ultimate "absolute consciousness" formatively "enspiriting" "egological" and "monadological" consciousness; and just as Hegel plainly perceives a "trinitarian absolute Spirit" in the cadence of judgment in thesis, antithesis, and synthesis — in receptive "perception"[12] and in the criti-

10. *Aus Sich, Um Sich, Zu Sich.* — Trans.
11. *Geisten.* — Trans.
12. *Vernehmen.* — Trans.

cally adjudicative "perception" of "reason," as distinguished from the penetrating self-positing and "stance" of "under-standing").[13]

II

The word *"religion"* — with its peculiar connotations — we find only in Latin. Its first syllable, "re," already reveals something essential to Roman culture: the belief that there is something primordial to which "ever again" (according to one sense of "re") a "return" is to be made (according to another sense of "re"). For the Romans this primordial reality — *Urhafte* — was not a "private personal God" proper to a "private personal piety" (with the desired goal of a "private personal revelation," or at least "private or personal intuitions"). Rather, its primordiality was that of something divine as represented within the institutional order of a "cult," and hence in the "institution of the cult," and hence in the ordered institution of the family and the state. Whether the word *"religio"* is derived, as by Cicero,[14] from *"re-legere"* (understood as a "reading one's way back") or, as by Lactantius[15] and Augustine,[16] from *"re-ligare"* (understood as a "binding back"), in either interpretation it is a "return ever again" to an origin: to the original "letter" of sacred tradition or to the original sacred "bond" (in the sense that, for the Romans, cultic institution, the family, and the state together constitute a single *"religio"*). The corresponding Greek word "εὐσέβεια" signifies an explicit comportment before the primordial as such: just as Greek culture stands nearer to that of Asia, for which cultic institution, the family, and the state are at best (secondary) "manifestations" of what is primordial, whereas for Roman culture what is primordial has its decisive "embodiment" in them (in keeping with the authentically juridical nature of the West). In this sense "εὐσέβεια" signifies the "εὖ" of the "σεβάζεσθαι" of "σέβας." The "σεβάζεσθαι" of "σέβας" is the primordial Greek feeling, the fundamental feeling that predominates in — above all — the tragedies of Aeschylus: the primordial "awe" of Homer before the abysses of being, which leads to a primordial "shyness" before them, and hence to that "adoration" that, as a kind of "fearful veneration," continues to betray the traces of Asiatic "προσκύνησις": that "helpless surrender of one

13. *Verstand.* — Trans.
14. Cicero, *De natura deorum* II, 28.
15. Lactantius, *Divinae institutiones* IV, 28.
16. Augustine, *Retract.* I, 13.

struck down and hurled to the earth, overpowered in something overpowering," and this captured (according to the stem "κύνησις") in the symbol of the "dog before and turned to its master" (the "πρός" attitude proper to a "dog"). To be sure, the prefix "εὖ," attached to the "σεβάζεσθαι" of "σέβας," indicates (to the Greek sensibility) an emphasis upon what is humanly "good, just, happy, and fair": just as the ultimately divine countenance of parents and fatherland (though not of the state in the strict Roman legal sense of the term) is, as it were, the "human countenance" of a divine primordiality. But, as is shown by the word "εὐσέβεια" in the precise sense Aeschylus gives it in his tragedies, this properly human "εὖ," in the final analysis, merely rustles like a "gentle veil" over the "σεβάζεσθαι" of "σέβας"; and what peers through that veil is the "sublimely uncanny, which provokes awe": the primordial "εἱμαρμένη" of "μοῖρα," the ultimate "sovereign allotment of fate." In the language of the Old Testament, on the basis of which alone the New can be understood, "religion" arises solely and exclusively out of the "covenant," understood as "God's marriage with Israel" — not only in the "cult and offering of the temple," but in the sense of the injunction "be ye holy, as I am holy" (in Leviticus's original rendering of the Ten Commandments), which is to say, in the sense that the entire life of the people is to be a "cultic action," extending even to the most trivial and profane (as ordained in the giving of the law at Sinai, and as later interpreted, in a manner going beyond mere fidelity to the letter, by the immense work of the Talmud). Moreover, even the so-called "prophetic piety" that modern Protestantism has long loved and still loves to pose over against such "priestly piety" (so as to root the Reformation already in the Old Testament, as it were) is actually, on the contrary, a movement within this single "religion" of a "cultic marriage enacted in all aspects of life." The so-called "classical loci" of prophetic piety show this clearly in their actual context. Yes, Psalm 51 [50] poses the sacrifice of a "broken spirit and contrite heart" against "blood offerings, gifts, and burnt offerings," but ultimately in the sense of an internal purification that leads to "a burnt offering and a perfect offering upon Your altar." Yes, the prophet Jeremiah contrasts a "new spirit in a heart of flesh" in "My Spirit" with the "heart of stone" and "stiff neck" of Israel, understood as the "house of contradiction," but he does not go so far as to propound a "religion of the heart" or a "religion of the spirit"; rather he goes so far as to speak of the "new Jerusalem" of the "new temple," understood as the only place of which one can say "Here He is." Yes, over against the sacrilegious audacity of saying "Surely the Lord is with us! No harm shall come upon us" (Micah 3:11) — over against, that is, what would seem to be an "interior personal religion" — the prophet Micah announces the simple (and almost naturally religious) message: "He has told you, O mortal, what is good; and what does the Lord require of you but to do justice, and to love kindness, and to walk humbly with your God?" (6:8); but even this is stated in terms of a new covenantal reality between the "shepherd" and his flock: "Shepherd your people with your staff, the flock that belongs to you" (7:14); "Show faithfulness to Jacob and unswerving loyalty to Abraham, as you have sworn to our ancestors from the days of old" (7:20). Even in the case of an apparent "religion of *agape* between human beings," in the Johannine sense of a "pure humanity" — as one could read the proper message of the New Covenant in contradistinction to the "burden of the law" of the Old Covenant — the ultimate symbol for this message is not that of an "apocalyptic, purely Johannine spirituality," but rather (to use the precise language of the Apocalypse) the "New Jerusalem" of the "marriage of the lamb" and the "wedding feast of the lamb," understood cosmically as a "new heaven and new earth." Finally, even the root word *fromm* — "pious" — in the German word *Frömmigkeit* — "piety" — (understood in the sense of a seemingly "purely personal piety of the heart") bespeaks the particular virtue of "allegiance" — *Gefolgschaft* — to a "sovereign" — *Fürst,* and so clearly suggests the "benefit" — *"Nutz und Frommen"* — of being "pliant and brave" — *fügsam und tapfer* — that etymologically it can be tied directly to the word *"Fürst."*

There is, to be sure, a genuine tension between the meaning of *"religio"* in Augustine and Thomas Aquinas — one strikingly parallel to the tension between "idealist metaphysics" (stemming from Augustine) and "realist metaphysics" (stemming from Thomas). In *De vera religione* Augustine seems to ground religion immediately between "the One Omnipotent God" and "our spiritual sense," in an immediacy without mediator, as was later taken to its extreme by Meister Eckhart: "May religion bind us back ever and again to the One Omnipotent God: for no creature is placed between our spiritual sense *(mens),* by which we have insight into the Father, and the truth, i.e., the inner light, by which we see him."[17] Thomas Aquinas's *Quaestiones* concerning "religion" seem to emphasize precisely the opposite: "Religion is . . . that virtue whereby one offers something to the service and cult of God," just as service and cult are "rendered up to the supereminence of God, to whom reverence is owed"; and just as, accordingly, the fundamental act of religion is that of *"protestari divinam excellentiam et subjectionem sui ad Deum"* — that of "testifying to the divine excellence and to one's own

---

17. Augustine, *De Vera Rel.* 55, 113.

submission to God" — "rendering *(exhibere)* something to him or also receiving *(assumere)* something divine"; and just as, for this reason (as what is ultimate in such religion) "not only are men called holy, but also the temple and the vessels, etc., inasmuch as they are devoted to the divine cult."[18] If, for Augustine, religion takes place in the "inner light" "without the mediation of any creature" between "God" and "our spiritual sense" — and if, by contrast, Thomas defines religion as a visible "service and cult" directed to "God's supereminence," the two would seem to be sharply opposed to one another: on the one hand, an inner religion enacted between the Spirit of God and the human spirit "in the inner light" in an ultimate, internal immediacy; on the other hand, an external religion of "service and cult" enacted between "God's supereminence" and "(human) submission": here we see the foundation of the opposition between, on the one hand, the religion of German mysticism and the Reformation (leading to the various forms of European Idealism) and, on the other hand, the religion of medieval Catholicism (leading to Tridentine and post-Tridentine Catholicism). Augustinian "religion," then, would be the, so to speak, "ultimate religious interior" of the idealist type of metaphysics (from Aristotle's "νόησις νοήσεως," to Descartes's *"cogito,"* to Kant's "transcendental ego," to Hegel's "Spirit of Spirit," to Husserl's "monadological world-ego"); similarly, Thomistic "religion" would be the "ultimate religious interior" of a realist metaphysics (from the Aristotelianism of "real forms," to the cosmicism advanced by the Jewish and Islamic Aristotelians, to the *"ordo universi"* of high scholasticism, to the "empirically critical metaphysics" of neo-scholasticism). But, if we consider the Augustinian view in its entirety, we find that the inner contact between the "One Omnipotent God" and our "spiritual sense" *(mens)* — which occurs precisely in the *"imago Trinitatis"* in *"memoria, intellectus, voluntas"* — is the root of the "surrender" *(transilire)* of precisely this "godlike spirit" to that real Tri-personal God, who as the "economic Trinity" (that is, the Trinity in the economy of salvation) is the fundamental real structure of the real cosmos: the God who essentially, in the end, represents himself not only as the totality of the "One Christ, head and body," but explicitly in the form of the *"Civitas Dei,"* which is to say, in a real political structure. And likewise, conversely, for Thomas "service, cult, burnt offering, the sanctuary," as well as the "rendering *(exhibere)*" and "receiving *(assumere)*" corresponding to these things, are grounded in the innermost "utter hanging upon God *(inhaereat),*" and thus in that "hanging, hanging onto, hanging upon"

---

18. Thomas Aquinas, *Summa Th.* II-II, q. 81, a. 3, ad 2; a. 8, corp.

(haerere, cohaerere, inhaerere) that is, in fact, the original form of Augustine's "immediate contact between God and our spiritual sense in the inner light." Augustinian religion in its complete form thus consists in a kind of "immanence between God and the human spirit" that exalts (by virtue of the *"transilire"* in *"haerere, cohaerere, inhaerere"*) the ever greater "transcendence between God and the human spirit": in that, in keeping with the mature Augustine's view, it is precisely the *"imago Trinitatis"* in *"memoria, intellectus, voluntas"* that ultimately points to the ever greater "speechless submission" of a "little one, like a little chick" beneath the "wings" of the "ever greater God," within the real cosmos of "God's body" and "God's city" (given that, for this "little one, like a little chick," one's own spiritual life in *"memoria, intellectus, voluntas"* is already an impenetrable mystery).[19] Thomistic religion in its complete form, on the other hand, consists in an interval of "transcendence between God's *excellentia* and the *subjectio* of man in service and cult and universal obedience and sacrifice,"[20] which is nevertheless interiorly grounded in an "application of the spiritual sense *(mens)* to God . . . as the ultimate goal and primal ground" in "immovability"[21] and, hence, in a fundamental "hanging upon God as the perfection of man"[22] and, hence, in an "ordering of all virtues towards the divine goodness."[23]

For precisely this reason the complete form of Augustinian religion can be characterized as a "transcending immanence" between God and human beings, whereas the complete form of Thomistic religion can be characterized as an "indwelling transcendence" between God and human beings. Thus, Augustinian religion in its complete form is not only classifiable as an idealist metaphysics of transcending immanence, but is in fact the ultimate "religious depth" of this metaphysics: to the point that an idealist metaphysics of transcending immanence could be seen as a "secularization" of Augustinian religion in its complete form (as in Hegel, for instance); just as, conversely, such a metaphysics could be seen as a religious *"intellectus"* appropriate to the religious *"fides"* of Augustinian religion in its complete form (as in the *"fides quaerens intellectum"* of Anselm of Canterbury, whom Hegel — reasonably enough — regarded as his "doctor of the church"). And, by the same token, Thomistic religion in its complete form is not only

---

19. Cf. *Serm.* 52, 10, 23; *De Trin.* XV, 9, 16; 7, 11f.; 11, 20; 20, 39; 22, 42; *In Ps.* 85, 12; *Serm.* 52, 6, 16; *In Ps.* 62, 16.

20. Cf. *Summa Th.* II-II, q. 81, a. 3, ad 2; q. 186, a. 1, corp.; a. 5, ad 1.

21. *Summa Th.* II-II, q. 81, a. 8, corp.

22. *Summa Th.* II-II, q. 186, a. 1, corp.

23. *Summa Th.* II-II, q. 81, a. 1, ad 1.

classifiable as a realist metaphysics of indwelling transcendence, but is in fact the ultimate "religious depth" of such a metaphysics: to the point that a realist metaphysics of indwelling transcendence could be portrayed as a "secularization" of Thomistic religion in its complete form (as is the case with Nicolai Hartmann, whose stratified realism can be interpreted as an atheistic version of Thomas's *"ordo universi"*; and as is even the case with dialectical materialism, whose positive core the Roman Jesuit Gustav Wetter has shown to be an Aristotelian-Thomistic realism);[24] just as, conversely, according to high and neo-scholasticism, an Aristotelian realism (in the form of the *"intellectus"*) belongs to the religious *"fides"* of Thomistic religion in its complete form (in the way that the "speculative theology" typical of scholasticism takes the world of revelation proper to a strict theology of revelation — understood as *"Sacra Scriptura"* — and translates it into an Aristotelian ontology of the real[25] as the *"intellectus"* of the revealed *"fides"*: *"fides [thomisto-catholica] quaerens intellectum [aristotelicum]"*). In view of these connections it is not simply the case that metaphysics and religion occupy the same level "between the above and the below" of a "transcending immanence" and an "indwelling transcendence." Rather, the ultimate oscillation between these oscillating rhythms — seen as what is ultimate in metaphysics and metaphysical experience (and thus as the "primordial metaphysics") — is, on the one hand, the "foreshadowing" of a philosophical "searching" that is realized in the "bodily reality" of religion's rhythmic oscillation between its intrinsic oscillating structures of "transcending immanence" and "indwelling transcendence"; but then, on the other hand, religion (understood as *"fides"*) should discover its corresponding *"intellectus"* in precisely such a primordial metaphysics of "oscillation between oscillating structures," given that "religion" in its "origin" (as, so to speak, a "primordial religion") is itself an "oscillation between oscillating structures." In that metaphysics and religion exhibit the same structures of oscillation — Augustinian "transcending immanence" and Thomistic "indwelling transcendence" — and in that they reveal, by virtue of their reciprocal oscillation, the "ultimate oscillation," we are brought at last to the "primordial rhythm" in metaphysics and religion. This primordial oscillation between structures that are (themselves) oscillating is itself the primordial rhythm within the rhythm between metaphysics and religion: it

24. Gustav A. Wetter, *Der dialektische Materialismus* (Freiburg: Herder, 1952), pp. 310ff.

25. *Real-Ontologie.* — Trans.

applies both to the injunction "understand in order that you might believe" (*"intellige ut credas"*), which is but the metaphysical "shadow" of the "bodily reality" of religion — as well as to the injunction "believe in order that you might understand" (*"crede ut intelligas"*), as is proper to a religious reality, which leads to a "metaphysical conception of the world" corollary and congenial to it.

III

This primordial structure of an ultimate rhythm oscillating between an (Augustinian) "transcending immanence" and a (Thomistic) "indwelling transcendence," to which we were led by our structural analysis of metaphysics and religion, is nothing other than *"analogy."* Thus, historically speaking, "analogy" appears as what is primordially ultimate in both historical metaphysics and historical religion.

As far as historical *metaphysics* is concerned, "analogy" is Aristotle's most fundamental term, the term he posits as genuinely conclusive, as opposed to all previous attempts at a fundamental term. As I demonstrated in *Analogia Entis* Part I,[26] for Aristotle the radical opposition between the immediately identical "ταὐτόν" of Parmenides and the "ἐναντία" of Heraclitus — understood as an opposition between a metaphysics of eternal identity and a metaphysics of the back-and-forth oscillation of antitheses — is essentially resolved in his analysis of the principle of non-contradiction, in such a way that analogy finds its ground in this principle. No wonder, then, that for him the fundamental principle of metaphysics is: "τὸ γὰρ ἀνάλογον μέσον," "the analogy is the middle."[27] For both Parmenides and Heraclitus there is neither anything "analogical" nor any "middle": because for Parmenides everything is eternal identity; and, for Heraclitus, everything is oscillating antitheses (hence his "logos" is, at bottom, merely the *"chiffre"* of an incomprehensible rhythm of antitheses). Of course, Plato stresses the "μέσον," the "middle,"[28] but he stresses it as something purely rhythmical (ἔμμετρον καὶ ἅμα σύμμετρον)[29] proper to the "unexpected suddenness of the moment" (ἐξαίφνης)[30] in an "unconscious co-incidence" (λελήθαμεν . . . εἰς τὸ μέσον

26. §6.
27. §6, 3.
28. *Theaetetus* 180e.
29. *Philebus* 26a-b.
30. *Parmenides* 156e.

πεπτωκότες)³¹ in the "in between" (μεταξύ)³² of an "immortal struggle" (μάχη ἀθάνατος)³³ situated in the "distance" that abides between "antitheses" (χωρισμός); moreover, this for him is the "divine play" (Θεοῦ τι παίγνιον)³⁴ of "birth in the beautiful," understood as the birth of the mystery of "Eros,"³⁵ not only "in the interval between mortals and immortals,"³⁶ but ultimately between being "led and circumscribed by God" and "slipping suddenly away from God" into the "opposite" (ξυμποδηγεῖ πορευόμενον καὶ συγκυκλεῖ . . . τότε δὲ ἀνῆκεν . . . , τὸ δὲ πάλιν αὐτόματον εἰς τἀναντία περιάγεται).³⁷ It is against this Platonic "μέσον," understood as the "contingent middle" within the "immortal struggle of antitheses," that Aristotle poses his "ἀνάλογον μέσον," "the analogous as the middle."³⁸ This "analogy" is distinguished sharply both from a Platonic "similitude consisting in the image and its copy" (the "παράδειγμα" of a "θεο-ειδές") and from a Heraclitean "purely dissimilar contrariety."³⁹ Over against Plato's "similitude consisting in image and copy" Aristotle poses "analogy" in the sense of "ἄλλο πρὸς ἄλλο," beyond every commonality in "species, genus, number": which is to say, strictly speaking, in the sense of a correlation between two X's, each of which stands in relation to the other as the "wholly other." Over against Heraclitus's "pure dissimilarity of antitheses one to the other," on the other hand, Aristotle stresses the positive aspect of the "πρὸς" between these two X's, the *analogia proportionis* of the classical Thomistic-Bañezian school. "The *analogous* as middle" underscores the element of "dissimilarity" and thus makes the "middle" into something unidentifiable. "The analogous as *middle*," on the other hand, stresses the element of "*proportio*," the oscillating "πρὸς," as a "rhythmic middle" and thus — but only thus — as something positive. The "analogy as middle," for Aristotle, is "primordial": it is the "*Ur*" (ἀρχή) in all being (just as fire, earth, air, logos, and rhythm were the "ἀρχαί" of the philosophers before him); and this same "analogy as

---

31. *Theaetetus* 180e.
32. *Parmenides* 156e.
33. *Laws* X, 906b-c.
34. *Laws* VII, 803c.
35. *Symp.* 203b-d; 206e.
36. *Symp.* 202e.
37. [God] guides it on its path and imparts to it its revolving motion . . . when he releases it . . . , and it then begins to turn back again on its own in the contrary direction. *Statesman* 269c-e.
38. *Eth. Nic.* V, 7, 1131b, 11.
39. Cf. Heraclitus, Diels 22b, 67.

ἀρχή" (which is also to say "being as analogy") is "analogy as a relation (πρὸς) of mutual alterity (ἄλλο . . . ἄλλο)": "ὡς ἄλλο πρὸς ἄλλο," beyond all commonality.[40]

This "analogy as ἀρχή," understood as "being as analogy," is the final aspect of metaphysics in both of its forms, that of "transcending immanence" (in Augustinian "ideal metaphysics") and that of "indwelling transcendence" (in Thomistic "real metaphysics"). A metaphysics of "transcending immanence" fathoms the space of the immanence of consciousness, passing through everything comprehensible, until it encounters that which is absolutely incomprehensible to it (its own immanent "ἄλλο"); at which point, precisely in this "ἄλλο," it encounters the "wholly other" of reality, the reality that is not merely experienced as the "wholly other" (and thus in its "resistance" to all consciousness, as Scheler formulates it), but that ultimately leads to an experience of the absolute incomprehensibility of this reality itself (in its own "ἄλλο"). Conversely, a metaphysics of "indwelling transcendence" delves into the space of real actuality, passing through everything comprehensible, until it encounters what is absolutely incomprehensible to it (its ultimate "ἄλλο"); at which point it is forced back through and out of all real "causes" (in the sense given that word by the natural sciences) to a "primordiality of the spirit," which is present and is experienced solely in the "spiritual immanence" of consciousness, but increasingly leads towards the absolute incomprehensibility of this "primordiality of the spirit" itself (in its own "ἄλλο"). In the final analysis, however, these two orientations of metaphysics are themselves related to one another in the manner of "ἄλλο πρὸς ἄλλο" (but taken to a higher degree). On the one hand, a metaphysics of "transcending immanence" and a metaphysics of "indwelling transcendence" are themselves related, each to the other, as something "wholly other" (which is why the "typical" state of relations between the systems that have, through the course of history, embodied these two metaphysics has always been one of hostile alienation from one another) — and, on the other hand, they are so "related" to one another (in the "πρὸς") that their correlation is what first gives us a genuine and complete metaphysics. "Analogy" as "ἄλλο πρὸς ἄλλο" is not only the formal principle within each of the two orientations of metaphysics; rather, it is ultimately the formal principle of the essential relation between them, in which they are — "in" their condition of being essentially "wholly other to one another" — integrated into *one* metaphysics. The "analogy between analogy and analogy"

---

40. *Met.* V, 6, 1016b, 31-35.

(in which the "ἄλλο πρὸς ἄλλο" is made complete) is the ultimate formal principle of "metaphysics as such." The consequence of this for "metaphysical experience" is clear. If "analogy" (in its essential form as "ἄλλο πρὸς ἄλλο") is the formal principle of each of these two forms of metaphysics and also, ultimately, of their integration into a *single* metaphysics, then there is no such thing as "direct metaphysical experience," either in the space of consciousness (for an "ideal metaphysics" of transcending immanence), or in the space of reality (for a "real metaphysics" of indwelling transcendence), or even for a metaphysics that integrates the two orientations. There is only the experience of the "ἄλλο πρὸς ἄλλο," which is to say, the experience of an "oscillating relation" ("πρὸς") between "wholly other" and "wholly other." There is no progress "ever more into the light" (as though each new system brought greater resolution than its predecessor), but really only a "wandering from darkness to darkness" (within the "πρὸς" between "ἄλλο" and "ἄλλο"). There is only an ever greater *reductio in mysterium* (which is how I designated such a method in *"Analogia Entis* I," in contradistinction to both deduction and induction),[41] which is to say, an ever greater return back through every seeming "illumination" to a "deepening darkness," so that one discovers the "light" solely in the "darkness of mystery." Just as Dionysius the Areopagite experiences the "overflowing light" of God "beyond being" as "γνόφος," which is to say, as "darkness in a whirlwind," so too authentic "metaphysical experience" occurs in a final "darkness" (of all "brilliant solutions") "in the whirlwind" (of a "vortex of problems").

The correlate of analogy in metaphysics is the *analogy in religion:* as formulated by the Fourth Lateran Council (1215) in the second chapter of its decrees. Whereas the Aristotelian analogy posits the "ἄλλο πρὸς ἄλλο," the proportion between two X's, as the form of every metaphysics, the Lateran analogy, as the form of any religion, posits a *"maior dissimilitudo,"* an "ever greater dissimilarity," arising out of every *"tanta similitudo,"* every "similarity, however great," for every conceivable "interval between God and creature."[42] Just as, in the case of the Aristotelian metaphysical analogy, all commonality in "genus, species, and number" is merely the horizon of the final dawn of the "ἄλλο πρὸς ἄλλο" — of, that is, the "wholly other" as what is ultimate in all "similarities" — so too, in the case of the Lateran religious analogy, the "wholly other" of an "ever greater dissimilarity" holds true in the midst of "every similarity, however great" between "Creator and creature" as

41. §4, 5.
42. Denz. 432.

such. What is decisive for the Lateran religious analogy is that it is defined precisely with regard to the most extreme case of "similarity" — indeed, almost "identity" or at least "unity" — between Creator and creature: with regard, that is, to the unity between the unity of the Three Divine Persons and the unity of the Three Divine Persons with the human being who "participates in the divine nature." At issue is the most extreme possible reading of the words of Christ's high-priestly prayer: "that they may be one as We are one" — ". . . that they may all be one. As you, Father, are in me and I in you, may they be one in Us!" (John 17:11, 21f.). For the council's definition is concerned explicitly with this word of revelation: in order to clarify the "unity, however great (proper to the greatest 'similarity')," which is expressed in this revealed word, and in order to purify it of all dreams of identity (as the council encountered in Abbot Joachim of Fiore's vision of the "three kingdoms" with the Father, Son, and Spirit as their respective forms), it asserted the "ever greater dissimilarity" between a "unity of identity in nature" (*identitatis unitas in natura:* in the unity of the Divine Persons) and a "unity of love in grace" (*unio caritatis in gratia:* in the unity of the Divine Persons with regard to and in "those who believe"). This most extreme case of similarity and unity "between Creator and creature" is taken up by the council in order, with respect to it, to define a "general law" for the "interval between Creator and creature": the law, namely, that "between Creator and creature no similarity can be noted, however great, without being compelled to observe a greater dissimilarity between them." This "cannot" and this "compelled" — understood as an essentially corresponding *"quia,"* which is to say, a "because" grounded in the nature of the Creator and the nature of creatures as such — are defined by the council in reference to the most extreme positive instance in the economy of salvation of the relation between a "unity in God" and a "unity of God in the unity of believers among themselves." In this sense, an "ever greater dissimilarity within a similarity, however great" is the "essence" of the "being" of and between "Creator and creature": in that even and precisely here — within the highest instance of a supernatural "unity between Creator and creature" — this dissimilarity is not only preserved as "natural being," but is declared precisely as (according to the council's decree) the "ultimate aspect" of this supernatural "unity" as well. The "analogy of ever greater dissimilarity" is the essence of the being of and between "Creator and creature" as such. This "being" — by which we mean nothing other than "Creator and creature" as such — is an "analogy of ever greater dissimilarity within every similarity, however great." It is the *"analogia entis,"* because "being *qua* being" (ὄν ᾗ ὄν, as Aristotle says) is this "analogy." There is no other "being *qua* being" than the "analogy" of "ever greater dissimilarity within every similarity, however great."

If this, and this alone, is the objective essence of the relation between "Creator and creature" — that is, religion in the sense of *"religare"* (a continual "binding back" of the creature to the Creator) — then even if one takes religion in the senses of *"relegere"* and *"religere"* — that is, as a continual conscious "reading oneself back"[43] and a continual voluntary living out of the "choice to return"[44] — the Lateran "analogy" alone can be said to constitute religion's formal law. For conscious and voluntarily lived-out religion is neither a "free phenomenon of value" (as in the Baden philosophy of value, from Rickert to Hessen), nor an "anthropological type" (as it is for the tradition running from Dilthey to Spranger), but rather a "consciousness of being," the conscious and voluntarily lived-out "being" of religion as the being of the "interval between Creator and creature," which is none other than the "analogy of ever greater dissimilarity within every similarity, however great." In precisely this sense, "analogy" — as the essence of objective religion — is the formal law of "religious experience" between the living God and the living human being. That is to say, with absolute rigor: there is no "revelation" (understood as a "religious experience coming from God") and no "mysticism" (understood as a "religious experience arising in man") in which the experience of the "ever greater dissimilarity" within "every similarity, however great" (in "likeness" and "image" and "word," etc.), would not be what is ultimate and highest. For this reason it holds true that God can be "seen, heard, beheld, and touched" solely in and as the "incarnate Christ," who is *"totus homo"* as *"totus Deus"*: a man wholly circumscribed in his humanity, in whose humanity there is nothing visible, audible, scrutable, or tangible that would immediately suggest divinity, but who is simply "wholly man," and as such is "wholly God." For this reason it holds true, furthermore, that this Christ alone, as "wholly man, wholly God" throughout the entire span of his life — his conception, birth, life, passion, death, resurrection, ascension, session at the right hand of the Father, and coming again at the end of the world — is and remains the sole and exclusive "revelation" and "intuition" of God, and that he is such solely and exclusively as *"one* Christ, head and body (of the church)." Thus every revelation and intuition of God originates solely with him (in the "type" of the Old Covenant) and with him completely closes (in his "apostles"); and thus all so-called "private revelations" are strictly classi-

43. *Je und je Sich-Zurück-lesen.* — Trans.
44. *Je und je Zurück-erwählen.* — Trans.

fied as private personal "experience," which (as John of the Cross and many others emphasize), inasmuch as it involves a new "seeing, hearing, viewing, and touching" of God (even of God in Christ), is rightly deemed "suspicious" so long as the intoxication of some "similarity, however great" (that of "vision, audition, etc."), is not thoroughly sobered by a "dark faith *(obscuritas fidei)*," leading to the "ever greater dissimilarity" (of all "images, words, etc." with regard to the "God, who dwells in inaccessible light," as St. Paul himself stresses towards the end of his life). For this reason one may speak of authentic "religious experience" only insofar as what is ultimate in this experience is the distance of "ever greater dissimilarity" — and insofar as it thus bears within itself the "form of Christ," the "form of the wholly human" that reveals the wholly divine only as the wholly human, and, what is more (as the *"Adoro Te"* tells us), not only in the "hiddenness of his divinity in the cross" but in the "hiddenness even of his humanity" beneath the wholly sensible signs of the sacrament, such that (according to Thomas) the only "appearance of Christ" is the "second coming." Consequently, in keeping with this complete formal law of religion subjectively lived out, all three practical forms of "religious experience" are essentially situated within the "analogy of ever greater dissimilarity within every similarity, however great." Every *"mysterium"* of the liturgy is a genuine form of religious experience to the extent that in it all "proximity to the holy" flows into the ever greater distance of the "service of adoration." Every "sacrifice" and every ascetic "discipline" is a genuine form of religious experience to the extent that in it the "however great" of a self-overcoming will flows into the "ever greater" of a complete "surrender to the free decree of God's most holy will." Every life of prayer (including mysticism and precisely as leading to mysticism) is a genuine form of religious experience to the extent that all proximity, even the experience of "love," becomes sober by passing into an "ever greater" reverence and an "ever greater" distance: such that every "holy intoxication and dream" — even that of the "spiritual senses" — and all "mystical certainties and mandates and missions" are increasingly darkened and dissipated in the "holy chill" of an eyeless, earless, senseless "Thy will be done" — of, that is, an "ever greater dissimilarity" with respect to all "intuition."[45]

This *analogy* of "ever greater dissimilarity" is the final word *for the two basic forms* of religion as such: for an Augustinian religion of "transcending immanence" and a Thomistic religion of "indwelling transcendence." In an (Augustinian) religion of "transcending immanence" the "however great" of

45. *Innewerden.* — Trans.

the "similarity" between God and the human being is located in what Augustine calls an immediacy *(nulla interposita creatura)* between the "One Omnipotent God" and our "spiritual sense *(mens)*" "in the inner light" — to the point that, in the *"imago Trinitatis,"* the Divine Trinity and the intrinsically trinitarian spirit almost interpenetrate: in the *"Deus interior intimis meis,"* "God more inward than my inmost parts." But precisely here, within this greatest proximity, the "ever greater dissimilarity" comes into play: since (for Augustine at his most mature) an unfathomable mystery of the "inward" itself (the mystery of the *"imago Trinitatis"*) directs all "intuition" beyond itself: into the still more unfathomable mystery of God himself, understood as the mystery of the "ever greater." Conversely, in a (Thomistic) religion of "indwelling transcendence," the "however great" of the similarity between God and human beings is located in an almost indiscriminate fusing together of the "universe" — in the *"perfectio universi"* — and the "universal God."[46] But even this greatest (real) proximity, wherein man seems to be as rooted in God, as it were, as he is rooted in the palpable universe (as incorporated into God as he is incorporated into the world),[47] reveals itself to be, more profoundly, an "inherence" or a "hanging in" (as we see in the phrase *"Deo inhaereat,"* understood as Thomas's final definition of religion), which is to say, a "hanging in infinite space." In that man, who belongs to the "macrocosm" of the "universe," experiences himself inwardly as the *"quodammodo omnia"* — as "in some measure an All" — of a "microcosm,"[48] both "cosmic space" and "spiritual space" come to be for him "ever more transcendent" as they give way to the "ever greater dissimilarity" of "heights and depths," understood as the "super-heights and un-depths"[49] of the absolutely incomprehensible "universal God" in whose "super-space" and "un-space"[50] man simply "hangs." "To hang within the ever greater God" is "religion as analogy," for Augustinian as well as for Thomistic religion: in that in Augustinian religion an "ever greater God" explodes all "interior rootedness" into the "ever greater" — whereas in Thomistic religion a radical, pure "hanging in God" uproots, to an ever greater degree, every fixed "rootedness in the universe," leaving it "suspended between heaven and earth in the incomprehensible God."

Finally, then, this analogy of "ever greater dissimilarity" is also the final

46. *De Pot.* q. 3, a. 16, corp.; a. 17, corp.
47. *Eingegöttlicht als eingeweltigt.* — Trans.
48. *Summa Th.* I, q. 80, a. 1, corp.
49. *Über-Höhen und Un-Tiefen.* — Trans.
50. *Über-Raum und Un-Raum.* — Trans.

word concerning the correlation between religion and metaphysics. The inner analogy of Augustinian religion is the innermost aspect of Augustinian metaphysics, just as the inner analogy of Thomistic religion reveals itself to be the innermost aspect of Thomistic metaphysics (as became obvious in the course of our earlier investigations). But "analogy as religion" (in both forms) is "innermost" to "analogy as metaphysics" (in both forms) in such a way as itself to have the form of an "analogy": for "analogy as metaphysics" and "analogy as religion" are related to one another by a "similarity, however great" (to the point that every age exhibits forms of "religious metaphysics" and "metaphysical religion") in such a way that the "ever greater dissimilarity" nevertheless proves to be ultimate: in the "ever greater God," who explodes the limits of every metaphysics as such, and even within the realm of religion itself uproots every "rootedness," leaving it in a condition of "pure hanging." But, finally, one must still characterize even the correlation between Augustinian metaphysics and religion on the one hand, and Thomistic metaphysics and religion on the other, as essentially an "analogy of ever greater dissimilarity within a similarity, however great." For, despite its "transcendence" towards the "ever greater God," an Augustinian correlation of metaphysics and religion is nevertheless situated within the "similarity, however great" of a "God more inward than my inmost parts" (understood as a "similarity, however great" between "my inmost" and "God more inward"). A Thomistic correlation between metaphysics and religion, on the other hand, stands emphatically within the "ever greater dissimilarity": not only because in this case God is the transcendent "unity of the antitheses" of the universe, which already within the universe itself constitutes something incomprehensible,[51] but also because here the only thing that is "inmost" is pure "hanging in God (as in the incomprehensible)." Even when viewed in terms of "analogy," an Augustinian (analogous) correlation between metaphysics and religion is emphatically the site of a "similarity, however great," which passes over into a Thomistic (analogous) correlation between metaphysics and religion that, notwithstanding its emphasis upon analogy in the fullest sense of the term, is still the special site of the "ever greater dissimilarity." Insofar as this *one* (Aristotelian and Lateran) analogy is not only the ultimate formal principle of metaphysics and religion; and not only the ultimate formal principle of the correlation between metaphysics and religion; and not only the ultimate formal principle in Augustinian and Thomistic metaphysics and religion; and not only the ultimate formal principle of the

---

51. *Summa Th.* I, q. 13, a. 4.

Augustinian and Thomistic correlations between metaphysics and religion, but fully obtains in the ultimate relation between these two particular correlations (Augustinian and Thomistic) of metaphysics and religion — insofar, that is, that all of this is true, the Aristotelian and Lateran "analogy" appears as the exclusive and all-inclusive "formal principle as such": *forma sola universalis.*

This "analogy" excludes all systems that exclusively assert the "similarity, however great": from early Augustinianism, which sees the world as a direct "image and likeness" of the divine (the kind of Augustinianism that today Alois Dempf's school would like to revive, as is especially evident in his disciple Lakebrink's "analectics" of "similar dissimilarity") to the Suarezianism of an *"analogia attributionis,"* for which an *"ens qua tale"* or *"ens ut sic"* — that is to say, an (at least negatively) univocal being — is prior to any pure analogy. By the same token, however, this "analogy" also excludes all systems that exclusively assert the "ever greater dissimilarity": as in the case of Thomistic-Bañezianism, in which a genuine *"analogia proportionis"* (one in which the "πρὸς" of the "proportion" proves to be what is ultimate) ultimately seeks to anchor itself in a God of the *"praemotio physica":* which is to say, in a palpable — if incomprehensible — guidance by an unambiguous providence, which sublates every "hanging between possibilities" into the "straight line" of a (purely transcendent) God who alone determines all things; this we find in a stricter and stylistically purer form, however, in the directions taken by Reformation thought, from Luther to Hegel to Kierkegaard to Karl Barth, for which what is ultimate is a "dialectic of contradiction" between a "God of judgment" — who for precisely this reason is not "known" — and a "God of grace" — who for precisely this reason surpasses all possible understanding.

Finally, the one sole analogy of "ever greater dissimilarity within every similarity, however great" appears as a "rhythmical middle" within this either-or between systems of "similarity, however great" and systems of "ever greater dissimilarity"; this being so, all such "attempted escapes" from the analogy as have been made since the appearance of my *Analogia Entis* (1932) are, at the last, frustrated. The escape attempted by Karl Barth, who described analogy as the "invention of Antichrist" so as to flee into a pure "biblical Christianity," is to no avail: because for him this biblical Christianity came, in fact, to assume the shape of a system of "ever greater dissimilarity," which is to say it fell under the spell of the very analogy he sought to flee. Nor is any aid provided by the attempts of Gottlieb Söhngen and Theodor Haecker to construct — on top of the allegedly purely metaphysical *"analogia entis"* — an *"analogia fidei"* or *"analogia Trinitatis"* that is "higher and nearer to God": for the Fourth Lateran Council made it clear that its "analogy" applied precisely to the domain of the supernatural at its highest — even to Trinitarian doctrine. Nor is any aid provided by the attempted escape implicit within all of these attempts: the attempt to take "analogy" as something somehow penultimate, in order somehow, nevertheless, to "resolve" it in some "principle" of resolution: for it is precisely in the analogy, understood as the "analogy of ever greater dissimilarity," that God is mighty and declares himself — the God who, "if you comprehend him, is not God,"[52] and the God therefore whom we "encounter" solely in the "free hanging" of the "free suspendedness" of "analogy," which for both metaphysics and religion is what is "ultimate."[53]

---

52. Augustine, *Serm.* 117, 3, 3.
53. Cf. the second essay of Part II, above, on the scope of analogy.

5 Image, Likeness, Symbol, Mythos, Mysterium, Logos

1956

1. The question implied in this title is the actual question posed not only by the relation between Eastern and Western philosophies, but also by the relation between the two fundamental orientations within Western philosophy itself: between a "philosophy of the pure concept"[1] (which reaches its climax in the tradition running from Descartes to Hegel) and a "philosophy of the pure image"[2] (as found in the early Augustinianism of the Victorines and developed more thoroughly by the Romantics, above all, by Baader).[3] Eastern philosophy is so thoroughly a *"philosophy of the pure image"* that it is in no sense a philosophy guided by method; rather, it is an ultimate "wisdom" that is either objectively contained within a pure "image as likeness" or subjectively discerned by the "sage" in an enduring "image as likeness" and then interpreted for his disciples. Western philosophy, in its most extreme form (from Descartes to Hegel), is so thoroughly a *"philosophy of the pure concept"* that all "images" are seen as belonging to that same sensible world that (for Descartes) must be doubted with a radical, total doubt, in order to be "rationalized"[4] (ultimately, indeed, "technicized")[5] within the pure cogito alone, by way of the rational "τέχνη" of the "ἄνθρωπος τεχνικός," who "techni-

1. *Philosophie im reinen Begriff.* — Trans.
2. *Philosophie im reinen Bild.* — Trans.
3. Indeed, one might go so far as to say that an image-based transcendentalism, of the kind that Klages opposed to the conceptual transcendentalism of European idealism, is only an aftereffect of Baader's thought.
4. *Er-rationalisiert.* — Trans.
5. *Er-technisiert.* — Trans.

This essay first appeared in *Archivio di Filosofia*, Rome (1956).

cizes" a mere *"res extensa,"* or so that (in Hegel's, in this respect, milder form) the sensible world of image-like "phaenomena" might be (both negatively and positively) sublated in "pure Spirit" into a purely "noumenal" "world of the Spirit," one, however, that is fundamentally nothing other than a single objectification of judgment's formal ternary of thesis, antithesis, and synthesis (inasmuch as Hegel conceives of political history, the history of the Spirit, and the history of religion as, at bottom, merely the "paradigma" of the ternary of judgment).

Between the two extreme antitheses of a "philosophy of the pure image" (for which the sequence "image, likeness, symbol, *mythos, mysterium*" is and remains what is — ontically, noetically, and practically — "real," and which is itself merely "transparent" to a hidden and — in the end — permanently hidden "Logos")[6] and a "philosophy of the pure concept" (for which this whole sequence, "image, likeness, symbol, *mythos, mysterium,*" is a sequence of purely "provisional," "purely sensible phenomena," which have at best a "popular pedagogical" purpose for the common man, who is not yet capable of "Spirit," but who nevertheless has a vocation completely to "enlighten" and clarify himself into the purely "noumenal" realm of the "Spirit") — between, that is, these two extreme antitheses stands the actual position of Thomas Aquinas, as most fully and precisely formulated in his commentary *In Boethium de Trinitate:* not only *"intelligibilia per sensibilia,"* and not only *"intelligibilia in sensibilibus,"* but even *"intelligibilia intra sensibilia":* which is to say that what is "sensible" (in, that is, "image, likeness, symbol, *mythos, mysterium*") is not only the *"per,"* i.e., the necessary passage to the intelligible world of the "Logos" — nor only the *"in,"* i.e., the necessary site wherein alone this intelligible world can be experienced — but also the *"intra,"* that delimited realm within which alone any knowledge of the intelligible world is possible: which is to say, possible not in any intuitive or direct or positive way, but only discursively (within the "perimeters" of the sensible world) and negatively (which means that one can only say in terms of an "apophatic negative philosophy," as a prelude to an ultimate "apophatic negative theology," what the intelligible world "is not"). And even this properly Thomistic position remains subject to the stricter law of the *Lateran* "analogy of ever greater dissimilarity within every similarity,

---

6. Although the words "mythos" and "mysterium" are not capitalized here, in view of traditional transliterations, as well as the philosophical and theological import of the term, the word "logos" has generally been capitalized throughout — as also accords, though more arbitrarily, with the standard capitalization of nouns in German. — Trans.

however great" (as we have more closely interpreted it in the previous essay, "Metaphysics, Religion, Analogy"). That is to say, to the degree that the "intelligible world of the Logos" is to be comprehended in its ultimate and divine ground, even the "discursive, indirect, and negative" knowledge of it ("from" and "in" and "within" the phenomenal realm) is always a knowledge attained first within the realm of "a similarity, however great," which must still be crossed through by the "ever greater dissimilarity." The simple "transparency" of the "sensible phenomenal world," which points within itself beyond itself to an "intelligible noumenal world" (in accord with that ultimate rhythm of the "in-and-beyond"), is in the final analysis simply an intra-creaturely transparency (consisting in the "in-and-beyond" of the relation between "sensible phenomenal existence" and "intelligible noumenal essence": in the intra-creaturely "in-and-beyond" obtaining between existence and essence). As such, inasmuch as the ultimate divine ground is concerned, this intra-creaturely transparency must itself be understood as a "transparency of a transparency": just as the absolutely transcendent-immanent God first becomes "transparent" only by way of the totality of the creature, in the transparency of the relation between existence and essence. The "discursive, indirect, and negative" knowledge of the "intelligible world of the Logos" "through and in and within" the "sensible world" thus becomes — as this "transparency of a transparency" indicates — the "ὑπέρ" proper to its status (as that prefix is used by Dionysius the Areopagite, following Paul and the Cappadocians, to describe the divine realm and our knowledge of it: "God beyond being" for "eyeless eyes" and "unknowing knowledge"). It becomes a knowledge that is "hyper-discursive, hyper-indirect, hyper-negative." And in a double sense: Firstly, in the sense that the knower must "ever more" thoroughly "traverse" the whole of the sensible world and the whole of the creaturely world (as is implied in "ὑπέρ," "supra," and "discurrere"). Secondly, in the sense that one should experience within the "however great" of concrete intra-worldly experience — with all its plenitude and fullness of color — the "ever greater dissimilarity" of its Divine Ground: the "ὑπέρφωτος γνόφος" of the divine in the fullness of the "πολυποίκιλος κόσμος" (to use the complementary expressions of Paul and the Areopagite), the "ever greater dissimilarity" of the divine "superluminous darkness of a stormy night"[7] within the "similarity, however great," of the "multicolored splendor of the cosmos."

With regard to a "philosophy of the pure concept" and its relation to a

---

7. *Überlichten Sturmnacht-Finsternis.* — Trans.

"philosophy of the pure image," it is clear — given this "transparency of the transparency" — that in both cases the pure "pure" should fundamentally be replaced by this "transparency of the transparency." That is to say, in neither philosophy is "identity" possible in any sense that would correspond to this word "pure": neither "identity" in a "concept" that is "identical" with the thing (such as European idealism sought in the "absolute concept") nor identity in an "image" that is "identical" with the thing (in the archaic magical sense in which Romanticism conceived of the "image": as an image into which the real thing is "conjured" and "charmed," which means that there is a power of "conjuration" intrinsic to the image itself). In other words, the formal ground of the "transparency of the transparency," as opposed to either rational or magical identity (understood as the formal ground both of a "philosophy of the pure concept" and of a "philosophy of the pure image"), is the *analogy of analogy*" (as I expounded it above in "Metaphysics, Religion, Analogy"). The "analogy of ever greater dissimilarity within every similarity, however great" is, first of all, the formal ground of the simple transparency between the *"mundus intelligibilis"* and the *"mundus sensibilis,"* between the "world of pure essences" and the "world of real existence": "(ideal) essence in-and-beyond (really existing) existence." But if — and insofar as — what is at issue in this simple analogy is an ultimate divine ground, ultimately this analogy is crossed through by the "analogy of ever greater dissimilarity within every similarity, however great" that obtains between the creature as such (which is an "essence in-and-beyond existence") and God as such (who is related to the creature as essence-existence or existence-essence "in-and-beyond" the creaturely "essence in-and-beyond existence").[8] By virtue of this "analogy (between God and creature) of the (intra-creaturely) analogy (between ideal essence and really existing existence)" every "pure" absolutization of "concept" or "image" is pulled up at the root: which means that it is impossible to produce a "pure concept" or "pure image" even of this sort of ultimate "analogy of analogy" (which would involve the titanism of an "ultimate formula of the world," which is something in excess even of the audacity of a "pure concept" or "pure image"); rather, the knowing creature itself can ultimately only live out the "suspendedness" of the "analogy of analogy" — and even then not as if this "suspendedness" were itself "ultimate," but only insofar as this "suspendedness" is seen as a mere "cipher" for the sole sovereignty of the God who is "within and beyond all things" (which is what is properly "ulti-

8. Cf. Part I above.

mate," and around which the theology of Augustine and of Gregory the Great almost hymnically turns).[9]

2. Now, inasmuch as the opposition between a "philosophy of the pure concept" and a "philosophy of the pure image" is overcome — in the *one* "suspendedness" of an analogical philosophy (in terms of its act) of the analogy of analogy (in terms of content) — we are able to assign the proper meaning to the sequence of words in our title — *"Image, Likeness, Symbol, Mythos, Mysterium, Logos"*: it means the, so to speak, *rhythmical expression* of such an *"analogical philosophy of the analogy-of-analogy."* But since, as a matter of fact, every positive aspect of either a "philosophy of the pure concept" or a "philosophy of the pure image" is positively sublated in this *one* philosophy (just as their "absolutization" is negatively sublated by a fundamental "analogy," as opposed to all "identity"), both of these philosophies — antithetical to one another in their origins — enter into the rhythm of *"Image, Likeness, Symbol, Mythos, Mysterium, Logos"* as "distinct rhythmizations" (of the *one* "analogical philosophy of analogy") by virtue of this positive and negative "sublation" (in Hegel's sense of the word). The positive aspect of a "philosophy of the concept," then, has its analogue in a *"progressive rhythm,"* which "ascends" from the "image," by way of "likeness, symbol, *mythos, mysterium,"* to "Logos" (which is more or less the original impetus of European idealism). Conversely, the positive aspect of a "philosophy of the image" has its analogue in a *"regressive rhythm,"* which "descends" from a relatively pure "Logos" (whose "purity" borders on the fruitless "ice of abstraction"), through *"mysterium, mythos,* symbol, likeness," into the "fruitful bathos" of the "image" (as we see in that "regress" to the "maternal" "origins" that is the basic demand and achievement of Romanticism). For just this reason, however, this double rhythmization itself (taken as something ultimate) appears within the individual elements of the sequence, "image, likeness, symbol, *mythos, mysterium,* Logos." If, in the final analysis, the linguistic and historical etymology of these six words should force us to affirm that there is a mysterious rhythm within them, then this rhythm, whose existence to this point we have only suspected, will disclose itself in the measure that we discern the meaning of these words from the context of their twofold sequence, when each word has its respective "place" as an intersecting point of passage within this progressive (from "image" to "Logos") and regressive (from "Logos" to "image") rhythm — a "place" that precisely for this reason is no "static" place (indicating a static

9. Augustine, *De Gen. ad Litt.* VIII, 26, 48; Gregory, *Hom.* 17 *in Ezekiel.*

"univocity"), but solely the site of a "passive dynamic" (indicating a suspended "ambiguity").

In order to do this, we will be obliged to carry out a kind of *phenomenology of the words* "*image, likeness, symbol, mythos, mysterium, Logos*," i.e., to lay bare the meaning of these words, both in terms of their proper etymology (judging from the structure of the words) as well as their history (judging from their use).

3. The Greek word for "image," "εἰκών," comes from the verb "εἴκω." "Εἴκω" lies in the span between a simple (ontic) "likeness" and a practical "being owed" (in the sense that I am "owed a place" among "those of my kind"); both meanings, however (in keeping with the derivation of εἴκω from εἴδω), have the sense of "appearance" — *Erscheinung* — understood as that through which one "experiences" and "recognizes" and "knows" something, but in the form of a "semblance" — *Schein* — that is, nevertheless, an immediate appearance to the eyes, an *Augenschein* (as one sees in the Latin "*video*," which derives etymologically from the Greek "εἴδω"). The word "εἰκών" thus implies an ambiguity: between an image that is simply "like" its real object and thus "represents" it (i.e., makes it in each case present), so that the image is owed the position and the honor of its object (just as the ancient statues of the emperor carried an imperial dignity, and were thus to be venerated like the emperor, and just as the "icon" of the Eastern Church is precisely the "sacramental presence" of its subject) — and an image that is, in the final analysis, only something that "appears to the eyes," i.e., appears only for the sphere of the senses and thus, in the final analysis, in contrast to noumenal, intelligible "spiritual presence," is only "mere appearance," which one must "see through" in order to behold the "pure idea" or the "pure concept."

"Image," from the Latin word "*imago*," comes from the verb "*imo*" or "*imor*," the root of the word "*imitor*," which suggests "an imitative representation," but one that carries the special acceptation of those wax masks of one's ancestors that were borne as life-sized "*imagines*" in funeral processions by bearers dressed in appropriate attire and marked with appropriate insignias; or that stood enshrined as ancestral images adorned with laurel wreaths in a case in the atrium. Thus, in this word, we see another tension: between "image" in the sense of a "representation" of the ontic succession of one's ancestors (from which meaning psychoanalysis has constructed its concept of the "*imago*": the presence of an "archetype" within some corresponding "complex": the maternal bond as "Oedipus complex," etc.) — and "image" as "model" (just as, for Walter Otto, Greek thought is properly understood in terms of the "figure," which is a "model" in the sense of being a "mediator of the archetype," in comparison with which every "law" is merely a subsequent rational interpretation).[10] Finally, the German word for "image," *Bild*, is based upon the Germanic root word "bil," which signifies a "wonderful power" — *Wunderkraft* — both super-typical and a-typical; hence the original meaning of *"Bild"* is that of a "miraculous sign" — *Wunderzeichen* — implying the presence of the "miracle" of an "(ontic) essence" — *Wesen*. It thus carries, at the same time, the sense of the Eastern "icon" and the Greek sense (according to Otto) of the "(divine) archetype in the model as figure" — while the other meaning of *"Bild,"* i.e., a "reconstructed copy" *(Abbild in Nachbildung),* is a strictly secondary meaning, a rationalization, as it were, of the original "presence of the miraculous God-archetype in the image, understood as a miraculous sign." Accordingly, the tension in this "image as the presence of the Divine in the miraculous sign" is a manifest expression of the original tension between the constructions *"biliden"* (in the sense of "giving shape and essence to something") and *"bilidon"* (in the sense of "reconstructing a figure on the basis of a given model" (according to the Kluge-Goetz etymological dictionary): that is, a tension between what is properly "of the creator" ("giving shape and essence") and what is properly "of the creature" ("reproducing a figure according to a given model"); hence the "image" is the site where something creaturely appears simultaneously as "creator" and "creature," which endues the "image" with divinity, but only as an "appearance," behind which is concealed the purely "artisanal work" of "imitation."

A *"philosophy of the image"* is therefore essentially located within this whole span of ambiguity among such words as "εἰκών," *"imago,"* and *"Bild."* It is, on the one hand (within this ambiguous span), primordial[11] for any "creaturely philosophy": since "creator" and "creature" intersect in the same "image" and thus in the ultimate transparency of the divine "archetype" in the "model" to the figure as its "representation."[12] But, on the other hand, this primordiality, which is metaphysical and indeed religious (since, according to Genesis and the sense of the Hebrew, man is created "in the image of God after God's likeness"[13]) — this primordiality stands equi-primordially under the sign of a "(mere) appearance" or at least a "first appearance" that remains to be examined critically and rationally and thus

---

10. Walter F. Otto, *Die Gestalt und das Sein* (Düsseldorf and Cologne: Eugen Diederichs Verlag, 1955), pp. 25-90.

11. *Das Urhafte.* — Trans.

12. *Urbild, Vorbild, Nachbild.* — Trans.

13. *Im Bild Gottes zu Gleichnis.* — Trans.

translated from the status of a mere "phaenomenon" to the more proper status of a "noumenon." A "philosophy of the image" is thus, simultaneously, the *terminus ad quem* of a "regressive philosophy," which strives backwards out of the mere ideativity of a "world of (mere) Logos" towards the "primordiality" of the situation of creatureliness — and the *terminus a quo* of a "progressive philosophy," which strives ahead, out of the phenomenal realm of the senses, which is always "just an image" and thus mere "appearance," and into the "essential" realm of the ideal noumena of the Logos.

Given, however, that "image" (in a philosophy of the image) and "Logos" (in a philosophy of the Logos) intrinsically condition one another — a movement "towards" (in progressive philosophy) and a movement "back" (in regressive philosophy) — it is only natural to understand the series that lies "between" them ("likeness, symbol, *mythos, mysterium*") as variously accented grades within this movement back and forth (whether the accent should fall on progress or regress). Viewed from the vantage of the "image" (proper to a philosophy of the image), these same grades appear (speaking in terms of progress) as an ascent to the "Logos" and thus as an increasing accentuation of the "Logos" (moving progressively from image to symbol to *mythos* to *mysterium*). Viewed from the vantage of the "Logos" (proper to a philosophy of the Logos), however, these same grades appear in reverse order as a (regenerative) descent back to the "image" and thus as an increasing reappearance of the "image" (moving regressively from *mysterium* to *mythos* to symbol to likeness). But even within this intermediate series there turns out to be a distinct ordering, which could equally be regarded as subject to different accents of "progress" or of "regress." Accordingly, one will reckon "likeness" and "symbol" as being more proximate in meaning to "image," as the "immanent dynamic transcending" of the "image": from a sensible image that rests primarily in itself (image as "pure figure" in Otto's sense) to a "symbol"[14] that points beyond itself (in the direction of what Otto calls the "intelligible" "model").[15] By contrast, one would have to regard *"mythos"* and *"mysterium"* precisely as the "womb" of the "Logos" and thus as the "genesis of the Logos" (just as in antiquity "authentic wisdom" was expressed in the *mythos,* so that it might be communicated in the *"mysterium,"* understood as an "initiation," whereby alone, according to Plato, as the "wisdom of the initiate," it might become an explicit "philosophy of the Logos" — this being a kind of *praeambulum* to the way in

14. *Sinnbild.* — Trans.
15. *Vorbild.* — Trans.

which Christianity initially appears in the form of an "evangelium," especially in Matthew's Gospel, in order then to become, in the story of the Passion, a *mysterium* in the sense of an initiation, and thus finally to become, in John's Gospel, a participation in the "Logos" himself, who according to Justin Martyr and Clement of Alexandria comprises in himself all philosophies, however pagan they may be, as "σπέρματα τοῦ λόγου"). But this ordering of our terms according to the logic of "progress" also conditions their corresponding ordering according to the logic of "regress." If the "Logos" is not merely some dry "formula of the world," it is to the extent that it always lives anew as the "Logos in *mysterium* and *mythos*" (as we see with Plato, who allows that the "pure εἴδη" can be attained by way of *mysterium* and *mythos* in the mystic state of the philosopher as "initiate";[16] and as we see in Christianity for which, corresponding to this *"praeambulum,"* the *one* true "Logos" is essentially "Jesus Christ in the flesh" in the mystery of "exchange" [καταλλαγή understood as *commercium*], such that the Christian receives and possesses "wisdom in the Spirit," understood as participation in the *one* "Logos," only insofar as he lives ever anew with the "Logos made flesh" in the mystery of the "communion of his flesh and blood"). And *"mysterium"* and *"mythos"* have this power to "regenerate" the "Logos" as long as they are not taken (following the Enlightenment) as pure "exemplifications" of what belongs to the "pure Logos," but rather live ever anew as realizations of a genuine "symbol" and "likeness" (just as a genuine philosophical "initiation," which receives the *"mythos"* within the *"mysterium"* wherein the "Logos" reveals itself, requires an openness to "symbol" and "likeness"; and just as this in turn is "preambulatory" to a Christianity in which the Logos Jesus Christ "speaks only in parables, and never without them" and, in the course of the Last Supper, initially communicates himself in the "symbol" of bread and wine in order then, having passed *through* this "participation in the symbol," to communicate *himself* as the "Logos" — in the valedictory discourses of John's Gospel in the *"logia"* that disclose his mystery as "Logos").

But then, in the final analysis, this rhythmic ordering of our terms, which is itself differentiated between a progressive and a regressive rhythm, is little more than a "geometric schema" (like the geometric engravings of Dürer, Altdorfer, etc.) whose "color" appears only by virtue of the particular "colors" of the concrete members of this intermediate series of terms, "likeness, symbol, *mythos, mysterium.*"

4. From the parables of Asian philosophy (like Chuang-Tse's in China,

16. *Zuständlichen "Mysten"-tum des Philosophen.* — Trans.

438

but even more so in the style of that secret Islamic philosophy found in the *Thousand-and-One Nights*) to the parables of the Gospel (which constitute the basic form of the gospel: Matthew 13), *"likeness"* does not simply have the meaning of "ὁμοίωμα" (which suggests merely the formal quality of "being-like," and can be found even in the "image" considered in itself); rather, its essential meaning is that of "παρα-βολή," *"parable."* On the one hand, when the rhythmic ordering of our terms is of the progressive kind, it is in the form of the parable that "likeness" takes its first step beyond the mere "image": since the parable takes the simple image resting in itself and transforms it not only by giving it the animation of a "history," but by changing it into something accessible only discursively and always elliptically, which makes the parable's elliptical and circuitous nature the formal style — the mathematical form — intrinsic to it. On the other hand, when that rhythmic ordering is of the regressive kind, the parable is the site, as it were, where the discursive circularity of the "Logos" as "νόησις νοήσεως" appears for one last spin, in the whirling "trajectory" of the "circling" of the parable, only thereby to sink down again into the peace of the "image" that rests in itself and that always constitutes the "Antaean earth" of an ever renewed progress. In this sense "likeness" essentially means "parable," and parable in the sense of the span between "παρά" and "βολή." Taken by itself, "παρά" has a persistent ambiguity itself: it has the connotation of "passing alongside," but also of "towards," but then again also of "against and opposed to" — so far, indeed, as to mean "outside of" — but then again also of "while" and "through" and "on account of": that is, it is precisely a play of contradiction among antithetical possibilities, and in this respect it approximates that "dialectic" in which, for Heraclitus, the secret "Logos" has its seat, and which, for Hegel, is the immediate inner dynamic of the "Logos." As opposed to a "dialectical Logos," however, the dialectic proper to the "παρά" of parable consists decidedly in the second syllable "βολή," which comes from "βάλλειν" and so means a "throw." The apparent dialectic of the parable is really the "free throw," in which "history" "pro-jects" itself in the parable, wherein it is freely thrown apart (in the foliation of the parable's history) and freely thrown together, such that the parable is, in the highest degree, the "throw" of a natural formation, in stark contrast to any "dialectical Logos" in the sense of a logically strict and artificial construct. Precisely for this reason what the Lord says in the Gospel about his "speaking in parables" applies to the parable as such: "The reason I speak to them in parables is that 'in seeing they do not perceive, and hearing they do not listen, nor in understanding do they understand'" (Matt. 13:14). Whereas the defining goal of a "dialectical Logos" is the most refined kind of logical reasoning, namely, the "ratio of the (apparently) irrational," the parable seeks to "strike open" (ἐρεύξομαι) the crypts of "things hidden from the foundations (of the world)" (κεκρυμμένα ἀπὸ καταβολῆς) — an opening that occurs only because "I will open my mouth in parables" (Matt. 13:35), i.e., in an "unconcealing concealing of what is concealed,"[17] as is proper to nature, which "discloses" itself in the outgrowth from its roots, but in such a way that, ultimately, these outgrowths nevertheless remain "hidden" again in their roots (which is why Heidegger's method of a "concealing disclosure" is the method of a *philosophy in parables*," which betrays his native Black-Forest-ness in that, as a poet of dialectic parables, he feels an affinity for Johann Peter Hebel, figuring as a "third," as it were, next to Gellert and Hebel — but being precisely a "third," his poems are not those of a moralistic human parabolics like Gellert's, nor those of a natural-peasant-like parabolics like Hebel's, but rather those of a philosophical parabolics, which therefore reproduce the circularity of the geometric parable in their style).

5. But if the "likeness as parable" dynamizes the simple, inert "image" (into the "free dynamic" of freely revolving history), this itself leads directly to a "counter-movement" in the *"symbol"* as a form of crystallization. At a purely semantic level, the word "symbol" is already intimately related to the word "parable." Both have the same second syllable, "βολ": that is, a "throw." Whereas the first syllable of the word "parable" designates (among its other senses of "alongside" and "toward" and "against" and "whereas") the throwing into opposition and confusion[18] of antithetical relations, the first syllable of the word "symbol" designates the same thing as the first syllable of the word synthesis: namely, that however much dynamic of movement is set loose between antitheses, it is nevertheless posited within a "perfecting togetherness in accord"[19] (which is the range of meaning suggested by the Greek syllable "σύν"). To the extent that the intrinsically static "image," the "thesis" (so to speak), was dynamized into the "antithesis" (so to speak) of the "parable" — and thus into the juxtaposition and disorder of antithetical relations — the "perfecting togetherness in accord" in the "symbol" binds this dynamic into the "synthesis" (so to speak) of a "higher image." But then, conversely, seen in terms of the regression from "Logos" back to "image," the "symbol" appears as the form in which the intelligible,

17. *Entbergen des Verborgenen als Verbergen.* — Trans.
18. *Gegen- und Durcheinander-schießen.* — Trans.
19. *Vollendendes Zusammen im Miteinander.* — Trans.

self-contained Logos shines through one last time: it shines out from the institutional *"mysterium"* to the *"mythos"* (understood as the "image" intrinsic to the *mysterium*), and then once again in the "image" internal to the "symbol" (understood as the "Logos in the image," as it were); at which point the Logos immediately disappears in the freely revolving "parable," which circles back finally to the "image" in which it has its synthesis. We thus see in this movement of regression a reverse "synthesis": proceeding from the purely intelligible "thesis" of the "Logos," through the "antithesis" of a real, living *"mysterium"* and *"mythos,"* to the "synthesis" of the "symbol." By virtue of this intersection between progress (from the "image" to the "Logos") and regress (from the "Logos" to the "image"), the "symbol" is not simply the site of transition (whether of the transition beyond the sensible sphere of the "image" into the initial sphere of the "Logos," namely, the "immanent Logos of *mythos*"; or whether of the transition from the purely intelligible sphere of the "Logos" — commencing already with the immanent *"mythos* of Logos" — back to the sensible sphere of the "image," whose first stage, once again, resides in the "symbol"). Rather, as the site simultaneously of a progressive passage beyond and a regressive journey back, the "symbol" is precisely a transition with two faces: one looks over and beyond (in the movement of "progress") into the intelligible sphere of the "Logos," while the other, at the same time, looks downward (in the movement of "regress") into the sensible sphere of the "image." This is precisely what is expressed, already at a purely etymological level, in the very word "symbol." The syllables "sym" and "bol" do not mean, as a naïve etymology always tended to suggest, that the symbol as an instrumental reality (a piece of money or even of metal or wood) was broken in order to be divided between two persons, so that these persons, each possessing a half, might then "recognize" "each other" by way of the "belonging together" of the separated halves. For the reality of the symbol is a totality in itself, like those animals, for instance, that serve as the symbols of various kingdoms, or those heroes who serve as symbols of various peoples. In truth, the "symbol" is the "sign" in its entirety: originally it had the sense of an omen[20] (in the sense of the Latin *"omen"* or *"portentum"*: a "sign of the gods" and a "sign of fortune" and precisely as a "solemn custom"; or in the double sense of *"portentum,"* which means simultaneously a "miraculous sign" and also a "freak" or "monstrosity"); only thereafter did it come to mean a "recognizable mark" or "seal" for the purpose of "certification";

20. *Wahrzeichen.* — Trans.

and, finally, a "sealed contract between peoples," what Aristotle calls the "κοινωνία τῶν σύμβολων."[21] The "divided manifold" that a naïve etymology reads into the reality of the symbol is therefore, in fact, located in the "symbolized reality" (between the one who "certifies" and that which is "certified," between peoples, etc.). Thus the "symbol" belongs to that intermediate realm between "ideal reality" (the reality of the symbol) and "actual manifold reality" (reality symbolized). By virtue of its relation to the symbolized, manifold, and antithetical reality, the symbol remains "sensible" (and thus points, by way of the "parable," back towards the realm of the "image"). By virtue, however, of its "ideal reality in itself," the "symbol" (the reality of the symbol) points (through and beyond *mythos* and *mysterium*, in which it is transformed from a "dead object" into a "living reality," which in the *mythos* possesses the "life of the word," and in *mysterium* the "life of action") to the "Logos," in whose realm the "ideal in itself" exists in the form either of the Platonic "τόπος νοητός" or of the Aristotelian "νόησις νοήσεως." Thus, the "symbol" moves essentially and distinctively between the *"mundus sensibilis"* of manifold, polychromatic (πολυποίκιλος) "matter" (in the broad sense given the term in ancient philosophy) and the *"mundus intelligibilis"* of the pure "εἴδη" or "forms." A *"philosophy of the symbol"*[22] could thus be classified in terms of *"imaginatio"* or *"phantasma,"* in whose domain and by virtue of which, according to Thomas Aquinas, the manifold of the *"mundus sensibilis"* in all its color is transferred by the *"intellectus abstractionis"* into the "ideal realm" of the *"universalia,"* which are "abstracted" from the individually diversified, sensible, real *"universum."* Viewed historically, therefore, in the context of the medieval debate concerning universals, a "philosophy of the symbol" would constitute a suspended middle: between the *"universalia in re"* of early Augustinianism (which attributes existence in the proper sense to the "ideal world" of the pure "εἴδη" or "forms" or *"universalia"*) and the *"universalia in flatu vocis"* of nominalism (which attributes existence in the proper sense to the "real sensible world," in contrast to which the *"universalia"* are either purely instrumental "concepts" or simply "words," which subserve the organization of a "formal order"). On the one hand, a "philosophy of the symbol" makes its historical appearance in the religious philosophy of the Victorines, who took all reality merely as "sensible symbols" (as symbols, that is, of the incarnation or the Trinity). The philosophy of "symbolic things," on the other

21. *Politics* III, 1; 6.
22. *Philosophie im Symbol.* — Trans.

442

hand, developed (unconsciously) by Ernst Jünger and, even more so, by Friedrich Georg Jünger, would appear to be just the opposite: for it arises out of rational reflection as the overcoming, as it were, of the Kantian philosophy of the "categories" and the Hegelian philosophy of "dialectic," and as the ultimate form of that "philosophy of value" — developing from Lotze to the Southern German Kant school to Eucken to Scheler to Nicolai Hartmann — that posited and posits "material values" in place of Kant's purely formal "categories" and "postulates."

A "philosophy of the symbol," at its fullest, would thus be situated between these two historical constructs. The symbolizing construct of early Augustinianism, on the one hand, bears the stigma of a pre-reflexive naïveté; on the other hand, it is genuinely rooted in the *one "Mysterium Christi"* — the mystery of Christ as the "head of that reality *in* which heaven and earth and all things taken together are *one*" (the reality declared in the first chapter of Ephesians and the first and second chapters of Colossians to be the "quintessence of the world" and thus, in the fullest sense of the word, "revelation," i.e., the "exposition" of all "things hidden" in the "depths of the riches and the wisdom" of the "unsearchable judgments and inscrutable ways" of God, "from whom, through whom, for whom, and in whom are all things" [Rom. 11:33, 36]). In contrast to early Augustinianism, the construct of the Jüngerian "philosophy of the symbol" (which is also the actual basis of Romano Guardini's philosophy) arises, on the one hand, as a reflexive tendency, which attempts to overcome both Kantian and Hegelian rationalism as well as practical technicism; on the other hand, however, it seeks either (in the case of the two Jüngers) to construct a freely suspended "symbolic world" or (in the case of Romano Guardini) to "gild" the real world of the incarnation, with its "scandal" and "foolish madness" (σκάνδαλον, μωρία: 1 Cor. 1:18ff.), with the "world of the glory of the symbols of the liturgy" (to the point of an *"evacuatio crucis"* of the cross as the structure of the world, as Augustine saw it, and its rendering into a "historical accident" attributable to the Jews, whose "no" to Christ prevented the immediate inauguration of the eschatological glory of "God's pure kingdom" and practically caused the inter-vention of a church). Understood thus, however, a "philosophy of the symbol" realizes the proper position of the "symbol" as the specific point of intersection between "progress" (of "image" to "Logos") and "regress" (of "Logos" to "image"). For its part, the early Augustinian "philosophy of the symbol" stands within the movement of progress: from a "naïve symbol," to the "conscious concept" of Aristotelian scholasticism, up to the "pure Logos" one finds in the "categories" of Kant, the "monads" of Leibniz, the "world-dialectic" of Hegel, and, ultimately, the Husserlian world of the primordial correlation between *"noesis"* and *"noema"* in a "noological monadology." The other "philosophy of the symbol," which sounds the final note of the philosophy of the West, and which constitutes the peculiar philosophy of the two Jüngers and Romano Guardini, is situated within the movement of regress: from a purely "logical" or "technical" world back to the "concrete image," but in such a way that this regress remains within the suspendedness of the "intelligible and sensible symbol" and thus lives ultimately in a "world of unrestrained fantasy," which seeks to be "free," both from the "logical necessity" of the "world of the Logos" as well as from the "real necessity" of a "world of an all-too-real sensible reality."[23]

6. But then *"mythos"* and *"mysterium"* become the critical stage for a "philosophy of the symbol": both in its progressive, early Augustinian form and in its contemporary form. To the degree that it strives toward the "Logos," the progressive, early Augustinian form of "philosophy of the symbol" remains tied to its maternal ground in *mythos* and *mysterium* (*"manere in lacte matris,"* as Augustine puts it); and, precisely to this extent, it never evolves into some "world of free fantasy" (as one finds in no small measure in Romantic philosophy, whose own "philosophy of the symbol" is largely a resuscitation of early Augustinianism). Likewise, to the extent that a regressive, contemporary "philosophy of the symbol" (as one finds in the two Jüngers and in Romano Guardini) seeks to live not in some "freely symbolic world," but rather in the fruitful suspense *between,* on the one hand, a realistic *mythos* and *mysterium* of "resurrection in death, power in impotence, plenty in nothing, glory in disgrace, honor in scandal, wisdom in folly and madness" *and,* on the other, the sensible reality, to which it wholly corre-

---

23. As of today, the only genuine attempt at a "philosophy of the symbol" is that of Siegfried Behn — the author of a "metaphysics" in the spirit of Nicholas of Cusa (*Einleitung in die Metaphysik* [Freiburg: Herder, 1933]) and an aesthetics that sees the "beautiful" in relation to "magic" (in *Schönheit und Magie* [Münich: Kösel und Pustet, 1932]) — in his little-known but definitive treatise, "Zauber, Sinnbild und Geheimnis," in *Der Weg zur Seele* 2 (1950): 3-17. On the one hand, he posits the "symbol" in close proximity to *mythos* and *mysterium:* "The one who acts symbolically is one who hopes, by means of signs, to attain to an intimate contact with active powers, which otherwise can be sensed only through disclosure, revelation, and miracle" (p. 5). On the other hand, he posits the "symbol" in direct confrontation with the "Logos": for he not only translates symbol as "sensible image" [*Sinnbild*] (so that it constitutes a middle term, as it were, between "image" and "sense as Logos"), but opposes a "world of symbols" (which includes magic and the mantic) to the "world of critical and technical *ratio*": the former being the genuinely fruitful bathos of everything rational and technical.

sponds, of the world of Heraclitus's "imagery" of "strife and war" and "consuming fire" and "rubbish" — held, that is, to this strict measure, a regressive, contemporary "philosophy of the symbol" avoids becoming a "flight into the glorifications of fantasy," in which case, it would truly have to "unmask" itself (psychoanalytically, as it were) as doubly fugitive: fleeing both the realistic *mythos* and *mysterium* of "resurrection in death, etc." and the corresponding all-too-realistic reality of "strife, fire, rubbish."

The Enlightenment, which presumed that it had attained a "pure Logos," rejected *mythos* and *mysterium* as a stage of "primitive fables" and "primitive magic" — to the point that, to this day, even Catholic theology and the Catholic study of religion ultimately see *mythos*, understood as pagan fantasy, as being at odds with "sober revelation," and have condemned the *"mysterium"* theology of Maria-Laach (as founded by Odo Casel, who was himself, admittedly, too dependent upon Reitzenstein) for confusing the liturgical cultus with a "mystery rite." But, given that *mythos* and *mysterium* belong to humanity as primordial religious forms, and given that God became incarnate as *"totus homo,"* it stands to reason that the Divine should enter into these forms (in the way that the Heraclitean "Logos" is transformed into the "λόγος σάρξ" of the Gospel of John). In even more radical fashion, Harnack and, more recently, Bultmann, sought to do away with the offensive *"mysterium"* (Harnack) and the offensive *"mythos"* (Bultmann), in order to attain a "pure" Christianity (which is to say, a Christianity free of mystery and de-mythologized), which consists henceforth solely in the "trust one places in God as Father" (Harnack) or in the struggle of "the caring man who is full of cares" (Bultmann). To be sure, the Romanticism of Josef Görres (in his history of myths) and Franz von Baader practically saw in *mythos* a self-revelation of the ultimate "origins." And, certainly, in our own day, Simone Weil has undertaken to show that the *one* "resurrection in death" is implied in all the myths and mysteries of all peoples: the *one* Christian evangel of death and resurrection is the "true mythos" implied in all the stammering anticipations of the myths of all peoples. The first two scholars to recognize the fundamental structure underlying *mysterium* and *mythos*, however, were *Arnold Gehlen*[24] and (definitively, as it were) *Walter F. Otto.*[25] According to Gehlen, far from being the "free fabulations" of the poetic, *"mythos"* expresses "the consciousness of an authentic epoch in the weightiest sense of the term" — in the sense of "a transformation and elevation of

24. *Urmensch und Spätkultur* (Bonn: Athenäum-Verlag, 1956).
25. *Die Gestalt und das Sein* (Düsseldorf-Cologne: Eugen Diederichs Verlag, 1955).

445

existence, which *mythos* declares to be definitive."[26] *Mythos* and rite (cult and *mysterium*) intrinsically belong to one another: "whereas rite has been primary from primordial times, *mythos* is its self-interpretation":[27] "one cannot exalt the divine in a concept,[28] but only in a story; the essentials can in no way be stripped . . . of their relation to ritual."[29] In this sense, "*mythos* is itself Logos,"[30] to the point that "the primacy of ritual begins to be reversed," in that the rite is presented "as a dramatic performance of the *mythos*."[31] This, then, is precisely where we begin to see the perversion of the correlation between rite and *mythos:* when both are "instrumentalized" and turned into "magic," both the magic of ritual action and the magic of the "*mythos* as word," whereas genuine ritual and genuine *mythos* are "ends in themselves"[32] by virtue of the end-in-itself of the primordial reality that is "celebrated" in them (whether in rite or cult or *mysterium*) and that "expresses itself" (in the myth) — which is ultimately to say by virtue of the "end-in-itself of the divine" (though, admittedly, Gehlen does not say this, but only implies it).[33]

According to the findings of *Walter F. Otto,* who completes the masterful scholarship of Wilamowitz-Möllendorf and Werner Jaeger (since he takes the "humane" in both to its properly "divine" depth), *mythos,* cult, and *mysterium* constitute a unity whereby "the thing itself"[34] declares itself as a "self-revelation of being"[35] in the "primordial phenomenon of the origin":[36] in a kind of "exchange" between the divine and the human that involves a "humanization of the divine" (especially in *mythos*) and a "divinization of the human" (especially in cult and *mysterium*) and shows primal Greek thought (whether Otto consciously intended this or not) to possess features of the primal Christian concept of "*commercium*" (between God and man in Christ);[37] but, even more profoundly, the divine ultimately appears here in a trinitarian form (having also, however unconsciously, the form "from God,

26. *Urmensch und Spätkultur,* p. 244.
27. *Urmensch und Spätkultur,* p. 246.
28. *In den Begriff heben.* — Trans.
29. *Urmensch und Spätkultur,* p. 248.
30. *Urmensch und Spätkultur,* p. 250.
31. *Urmensch und Spätkultur,* p. 215.
32. *Selbstzwecklich.* — Trans.
33. *Urmensch und Spätkultur,* pp. 260-72.
34. *Die Gestalt und das Sein,* p. 68. [*Die Sache selbst.* — Trans.]
35. *Die Gestalt und das Sein,* p. 71.
36. *Die Gestalt und das Sein,* p. 17.
37. *Die Gestalt und das Sein,* p. 254.

through God, and in God" of Rom. 11:36): "in the past the ancient eternal God, in the future the God who comes with infinity before him, in the present the peering through of the God beyond time,"[38] such that "in the encounters with them . . . man becomes aware of being . . . and, simultaneously, of his own essence" as an "answer."[39] Whether consciously or *de facto* suppressing it, it is this broad conception of *mythos* that Heidegger (whether following or inspiring Bultmann's "demythologizing") ascribes to authentic "thought": understood as a "self-disclosure of concealed being" in "truth" as (ontic) unconcealment (ἀ-λήθεια). For Otto, *mythos* is originally a "self-revelation of being," which "does not distinguish between word and being,"[40] since *mythos* is the "appearance of being and event in the word."[41] As both "word and thing,"[42] it is precisely *mythos* that is "the thing itself,"[43] whereas the Logos signifies that which (at a distance) is "deliberated and calculated."[44] So *mythos* is "the true archetype," "since things fundamentally are as *mythos* has conceived them."[45]

It follows, then, that as a "humanization of the divine" (in *mythos*) and a "divinization of the human being" (in the cult), *mythos* and cult (and, by implication, *mysterium*) are fundamentally a single reality, such that just as "no cult is without its *mythos*," conversely, "*mythos* calls for the cult."[46] Just as *mythos* is a self-revelation of primordial being in the "word," "cultic action" is a "revelation of the divine and its very presence" in the "form of human action"; it is not a "reconstruction," but a "repetition of a primordial divine event"[47] — even if this repetition be a "necessary response of man to the presence of the divine" in a "voluntary human action," in the cultic action of the folding of hands, etc. It thus has the form of unity-in-difference, the fulfillment of which is found in the cultic mystery of Christianity, which is the pure "(objective) *memoria*" and "(objective) *praesentia*" of the divine in Christ (in the sense, therefore, of "*totus Deus*"), but consisting nevertheless in a sensible, spontaneous action on the part of man (in the sense, there-

38. *Die Gestalt und das Sein*, p. 23.
39. *Die Gestalt und das Sein*, p. 71.
40. *Die Gestalt und das Sein*, p. 71.
41. *Die Gestalt und das Sein*, p. 72.
42. *Die Gestalt und das Sein*, p. 69.
43. *Die Gestalt und das Sein*, p. 72.
44. *Die Gestalt und das Sein*, p. 68.
45. *Die Gestalt und das Sein*, pp. 88f.
46. *Die Gestalt und das Sein*, p. 76.
47. *Die Gestalt und das Sein*, p. 80.

fore, of *"totus homo")*. In this way, then, *"mythos* is a kind of cult" and "cult
... a kind of *mythos,"* in that "in the cult the human being is lifted up to the
divine and, to some extent, acts with the divine, whereas in *mythos* the divine
descends, embodies itself as word in a human form or in a related form, and
acts in a quasi-human way"[48] — just as Christianity presupposes the objective incarnation of "God the Word in the flesh" in order that in the cultic
mystery the human (under the symbols of bread and wine) might be
"transubstantiated" into the divinity of "God the Word in the flesh."

But precisely this is the site of *mysterium,* as Otto demonstrates in his
analysis of the Eleusinian mysteries. In its unity with *mythos,* the cult is essentially already *mysterium:* in view of the transformation that takes place within
it between God and man, and which Otto ultimately inscribes directly into
the style of the mysteries: "since God himself emerges as perfect presence and
casts aside the reality of all things like a veil," and since, in corresponding
fashion, "man too" casts aside the "veil."[49] Such is the formal aspect of
mysterium: a *memoria* and *praesentia* of the divine understood as a "repetition of a primordial divine event,"[50] but for the sake of a "veiling" of the "unveiled human being" (from whom everything earthly has been stripped
away), in the "divine" that "unveils" itself to him, as he is led with "mouth"
and "eyes" "closed" (in the sense of the "μυ" in μυστήριον, which comes from
the verb μύω) into that which is "closed" within the divine itself — which, as
the "primordial phenomenon of the origin,"[51] necessarily "dwells," as Paul
says of it, "in unapproachable light" (1 Tim. 6:16), in the "depths" of God,
which no one "searches" but "the Spirit of God" (1 Cor. 2:10f.). The content of
mysterium, however, is already prefigured in its formal structure. All the historical "mystery" religions (both those of Greece and those of the East) are
connected with an explicit or implicit Manichean dualism: between a "divine
good" and a "divine evil," between a "divine light" and a "divine darkness."
Accordingly, they seek to "advance through" or "battle through" or "suffer
through" and hence, finally, to "die through" the "kingdom of evil" so as to
enter the "kingdom of the good," to pass through the "kingdom of darkness"
into the "kingdom of light" and, hence, through the "kingdom of death" into
the "kingdom of eternal life" — but in such a way that this "advancing
through" or "battling through" or "suffering through," as ultimately "a dying

48. *Die Gestalt und das Sein,* pp. 86f.
49. *Die Gestalt und das Sein,* p. 22.
50. *Die Gestalt und das Sein,* p. 80.
51. *Die Gestalt und das Sein,* p. 17.

through," is understood to be the "(objective) *memoria*" and "(objective) *praesentia*" of a "primordial divine occurrence."[52] For Otto, this is precisely what one finds in its classical form in the Eleusinian mysteries. Given that they "celebrate" the descent of the daughter of Mother Earth, Demeter, into the underworld and her ascent once again to the light of life (ultimately dividing her existence between an existence in the underworld and an existence in the light of life) — and this upon the background of that "most intimate alliance"[53] between Hecate (the original goddess of the underworld) and Demeter herself — the actual mystery that is celebrated is a genuine "resurrection from the dead": "death" as a "prerequisite of the growth of grain"[54] and for fruitfulness as such: "the fruitfulness, upon which man depends, he receives from the hand of death," because he receives it from the hand of the "queen of the kingdom of death,"[55] from which Otto draws the conclusion that "death is already active . . . in birth, in the act of generation."[56] Here the Eleusinian mysteries come together with the Dionysian mysteries[57] — in the sudden twinkling of an eye of "resurrection from death": in the Eleusinian mysteries in the symbol of the "suddenness" of the "increase of the grain as it grows and ripens" "from the hand of death"; in the Dionysian mysteries, in the way in which during the "Dionysian festival of intoxication" "the vine, which grows up in only a few hours," shoots up from Dionysus, who has been "mauled" by the Maenads.[58] In this correlation between the Eleusinian "increase of grain" and the Dionysian "vine" we thus see an inner *"praeambulum"* of the *one* Christian mystery in which "bread (from the increase of grain)" and "wine (from the grapevine)" constitute *one* symbol of the "body that is given" and the "blood that is poured out" of the *one* "God in Christ," who is the "grain of wheat, which bears much fruit" and the "vine, which

52. *Die Gestalt und das Sein*, p. 80.
53. *Die Gestalt und das Sein*, p. 318.
54. *Die Gestalt und das Sein*, p. 322.
55. *Die Gestalt und das Sein*, p. 323.
56. *Die Gestalt und das Sein*, p. 323.
57. One finds an authentic expression of the Dionysian mysteries in the *"Dionysiaca"* of Nonnos (ed. Scheffer; Bremen: Schünemann, 1955), above all in the first hymn, in which all mythical transactions between the divine and the human show the "Dionysian" to be the "sphere of mediation," as though it were the "inner rhythm" of these transactions. Accordingly, the final note of the *Dionysiaca* is the intrinsic correlation between the Eleusinian and Dionysian mysteries: "And they venerated the God (Dionysus) together with the son of Persephone" (Hymn 48, pp. 960ff.). Thassilo von Scheffer infers this correlation precisely from this final note.
58. *Die Gestalt und das Sein*, p. 329.

bears much fruit." But what is implied here, in the Eleusinian-Dionysian *"praeambulum,"* as well as in the "bodily reality" of Christianity, is the *one* *"mysterium* of God himself" (understood as a genuine theological *mysterium*): a *oneness* of "the most terrifying and the most refulgent"[59] that is prefigured in the Eleusinian-Dionysian *"praeambulum"* and is fulfilled in the "seen and heard and touched" of the "God who has never been seen," understood as the God of "wrathful judgment" and of the "love that has always been" in the "face of Christ" (as the "living bread" and the "uncovered vine"), in the "curse" of whose "abandonment by God" the "love of God" is "poured forth" (1 John 1:1; John 1:18; 1 Sam. 2:6; Deut. 32:39; Wis. 16:13; 2 Cor. 4:6; John 6:41; 15:1; Matt. 27:46; Gal. 3:13; Rom. 5:5).

In view of the foregoing, it is clear that *mythos* and *mysterium* constitute, in each case, a decisive "turning point": both for the progress from "image" to "Logos," as well as for the regress from "Logos" to "image." Compared to *mythos* and *mysterium,* image, likeness (in the sense of parable), and symbol appear as something provisional that has yet to descend — and enter into — the "depths"[60] of *mythos* and *mysterium;* for it is in depths that one first experiences that "absolute Being" whose ultimate expression is found in the "Logos," which for just this reason constitutes the "extreme limit" of our series. Conversely, whenever "Logos" is "exaggerated,"[61] and thus withers away in the desert of "pure abstraction" (as in the case of Hegel's Logos, but also of Aristotle's anti-mythical *logia*), it is critical that the Logos sink again beneath the "secure folds of the concept" in a regression into the "unmasterable" "ungrounded" depths of *mythos* and *mysterium* — which had seemed to have been "mastered" definitively; and that it descend from an idealist "identity of concepts" into the ungrounded and unfathomable opposition that one finds in *mythos* and *mysterium* between the "depths of God" and the "deep things of Satan" (1 Cor. 2:10; Rev. 2:24), in order to be "reborn": to return, in a state of complete helplessness that such rebirth entails, from an "outgrown maturity"[62] of the "sage" (whose "wisdom," as depicted in Gautama Buddha, seeks to be "above all things") to the "fruitful childhood" whose "mother's milk" (as Augustine has it) is found in "image, likeness, and symbol."[63] In fact, seen thus, there can be no *"philosophy in*

---

59. *Die Gestalt und das Sein,* p. 324.

60. *Ungründe.* — Trans.

61. *Verstiegenen,* which also bears connotations of fanciful or out of touch with reality. — Trans.

62. *Entwachsenen Erwachsenheit.* — Trans.

63. *In Ps.* 57, 5; 130, 13.

mythos and mysterium": since *mythos* and *mysterium* are either, in the movement of progress from image to Logos, the site of a (passive) "birth into" the
sphere of the Logos or, in the movement of regress, the site of a (passive) "rebirth" of an "exaggerated Logos" back into the sphere of "image, likeness
(parable), symbol" — just as, according to Aristotle, it is "not proper for the
initiate to learn something; rather he must suffer and be seized."[64] To be
sure, the style that one finds in the *Bhagavad Gita* and the *Tao Te Ching* appears to be that of a cosmic philosophy in *mythos* and *mysterium;* nevertheless, it is a philosophy in which, from the first, everything mythical and mystical appears in its ultimate Logos, even if this Logos appears as a
"paradoxical Logos" (as it does above all in the *Tao Te Ching*). To be sure, the
style of the pre-Socratics is almost that of prophetic oracles; but this is only
because their sayings concern the cosmic *"archai,"* the primordial origin, the
Ur of the cosmos, which lends itself to mythological language. To be sure,
one could call the writings of Dionysius the Areopagite a kind of "mystical
theology" (as he himself calls one of them); but ultimately even this would
have to be understood in terms of a "philosophical theology" whose method
is apophatic and negative. To be sure, the philosophy of Romanticism (especially in Franz von Baader) strives so radically away from an "ideative Logos"
into "mythical origins" that it becomes directly "mystagogical": that is, it
points towards the sphere of *mythos* and *mysterium;* but even this occurs
precisely within the space of a Logos, dialectical though it be (so much so
that in Baader, the director of the Bavarian mining industry, it takes the
form of "geometric thought"). To be sure, it was the most cherished dream
of the German "liturgical movement" to replace "speculative theology"
(stemming from Thomas Aquinas) with a "mystery theology" (stemming
from the Alexandrines); but this dream could not be realized in anything
other than a "meditated liturgy" after the manner of Benedictine thought,
whose home is the *"ora"* of a simply "enacted liturgy" and in the *"labora"* of
"land and field," i.e., in the unity of "cult" and "(agri-) culture," whose symbol is found in the Latin synonymy of *"colere, cultus, cultura"* (thus the great
"Benedictine culture" stands and falls with the "choir" and the "earth").
Nothing remains, therefore, but to *"philosophize out of mythos* and
mysterium," which was Plato's original idea: that the "philosopher" is obliged
not only to let go of "pleasure and grief" in the "self-recollection" of the
"soul,"[65] but also (entirely in the sense of the ancient Greek mysteries) to

64. Fragment 15, quoted in Otto, *Die Gestalt und das Sein*, p. 328.
65. *Phaedo* 82e-83e.

take the place of an Orphic and Dionysian initiate,[66] who "in imitation of one dying"[67] "sings prophetically of Hades like the death swan of Apollo"[68] and in this way enters "into the race of gods,"[69] "initiated into the consecration of perfection"[70] as one "inspired by God."[71] In this respect, *mythos* and *mysterium* appear (positively) as the all-decisive step toward the "Logos" of "philosophy": in that they announce "resurrection out of death and in death," which is the ultimate meaning of the mysteries (and which today has been secularized in the phenomenological "epochē"), as the origin of "genuine philosophizing." But precisely on this account (negatively) *mythos* and *mysterium* do not themselves appear as "philosophy." Admittedly, even Aristotle himself, that fierce opponent of myth, characterizes the "philosophos" as "philomythos" (so that there is a "love of wisdom" insofar as there is a "love of myth").[72] For the same Aristotle, however, the initiate (of *mythos* and *mysterium*) is not concerned with a (theoretical) "learning," but only with a (practical and religious) condition of "suffering" and "being seized."[73]

7. Seen in light of these connections, *Logos*[74] is therefore properly located within the space of *mythos* and *mysterium* — whether this be the Logos of a metaphysical "τόπος νοητός" within the material "εἴδη" (as in the material idealism of Plato that reaches its fulfillment in phenomenology) or that of a formal and functional "νόησις νοήσεως" (as in the formal and functional idealism of Aristotle that is developed to its extreme in the tradition running from Descartes to Kant to Hegel). If, following Otto, it is in fact the case that *mythos* and *mysterium* are in themselves not only a "movement with the primordial powers,"[75] but are, in an absolute sense, a "self-revelation of being,"[76] then they are "implicit Logos"[77] and, conversely,

66. *Phaedo* 69c-d.

67. *Phaedo* 61d, 65a.

68. *Phaedo* 85b.

69. *Phaedo* 82c.

70. *Phaedrus* 249e.

71. *Phaedrus* 249d.

72. *Met.* I, 2, 982b, 18.

73. Fragment 15.

74. Cf. besides *Analogia Entis* Part I: *Christentum gemäß Johannes* (1954), pp. 32ff. and 313ff.; *In und Gegen* (1955), pp. 281-93. Cf. the opposing position of Heidegger in his *Vorträge und Aufsätze* (1954), pp. 207-30, 257-82.

75. Otto, *Die Gestalt und das Sein*, p. 74.

76. *Die Gestalt und das Sein*, p. 71.

77. *Impliziter Logos*. — Trans.

Logos is an "explication of *mythos* and *mysterium*." In this case *mythos*, *mysterium*, and Logos properly constitute a "suspended unity": between a maximal implication of Logos in *mythos* and *mysterium*, bounded by the limit concept of an "a-logical" or at least "pre-logical" "pure *mythos* and *mysterium*" — and a maximally "explicit Logos" that appears to be "abstracted" from *mythos* and *mysterium* (in the full sense of "*abs-trahere*"), bounded by the limit concept of a "pure Logos" that is "anti-mythical" or at least "free of myth." The difference between Platonism and Aristotelianism is symbolic of this: In Plato the Logos develops consciously out of *mythos* and *mysterium* (in the way, for example, that the Logos of the cosmos develops out of the myth of the demiurge in the *Timaeus;* or that the Logos of the "εἴδη" develops out of the *mythos* of the "cave"; or that the Logos of the *Republic* develops out of the *mythos* of Atlantis); in Aristotle, on the other hand, one sees a passionate, critical, indeed ironic shedding of all "(Platonic) myths" for the sake of a Logos of pure "ἀπόδειξις" as a rational "showing" in "demonstration" — though, admittedly, he oddly retains the Platonic myth of Eros to serve as the ultimate principle of cosmic "revolution," understood as a "movement between lovers" (κινεῖ δὲ ὡς ἐρώμενον).[78] The true "Logos" thus moves between a "Logos within *mythos* and *mysterium*" and a "Logos beyond *mythos* and *mysterium*." Just as creaturely being is the movement of "essence in-and-beyond existence," so too the creaturely Logos is the movement of "Logos in-and-beyond *mythos* and *mysterium*." But this means that, just as there is no creaturely being other than "analogy as being" (which consists in the "in-and-beyond" of essence and existence), so too there is no creaturely Logos other than "analogy as Logos" (which consists in the "in-and-beyond" of Logos with regard to *mythos* and *mysterium*). It is for this reason that in Heraclitus, the original philosopher of the Logos, the Logos resides within the "universal flux" of the "changing back-and-forth" of "contraries"[79] — even if the Logos is such a sovereign "criterion and critical judge of truth"[80] that, within this "universal flux" between "antitheses" (ἐναντία), it is what is "common to all (κοινόν)" and "divine (θεῖον),"[81] as opposed to "αἴσθησις," which is regarded as "untrustworthy" (ἄπιστον).[82]

As distinguished from *mythos* and *mysterium*, "Logos" thus has to do with what is "deliberated and calculated," following Otto, who distinguishes

---

78. *Met.* XII, 7, 1072b, 3.
79. Diels 74b, 80; 88.
80. Diels 59a, 16.
81. Diels 59a, 16.
82. Diels 59a, 16.

it sharply from *mythos* (and *mysterium*), in which what is "actual and factual" declares itself as "history," such that *mythos* is "the thing in its expression, the truth of being and of [its] event in the word."[83] What Heidegger calls "(logical) truth" — namely, "being disclosed in unconcealedness (ἀ-λήθια)" — is precisely what, according to Otto, properly characterizes *mythos* and *mysterium*. And as for Heidegger's interpretation of "Logos" — by way of parabolic etymological digressions — as the "selective laying out"[84] of a "collection," which supposedly declares an "ἕν-πάντα," an "all-unity" to this interpretation, which seeks to exclude from Logos such meanings as "word" and "sense," Otto, the master of classical philology, remarks: "One cannot help but marvel at this often repeated claim that the original concept is that of a gathering."[85]

In truth, "Logos" stands in contrast to the prefix "μυ" in μῦθος and μυστήριον. The "μυ" in μῦθος and μυστήριον comes from the verb "μύω" in the sense of a "closing and shutting of eye and mouth": just as the initiate, the "μύστης," of the mysteries enters mute and blind into that formal, original mystery (which is implied in the particular mysteries) of "light suddenly in the midst of darkness" and "life suddenly in the midst of death" (as was evidently celebrated in the Mithraic, Eleusinian, and Dionysian mysteries). The "μυ" in μῦθος and μυστήριον thus signifies not only a passive event (a "suffering" and "being seized," according to Aristotle), but also a passive event with "eyes and mouth closed." It is under the heavy "veil" of this sealing up of every visual perception and every "verbal expression of the mouth" that the "perfecting initiation" takes place (τελευτή understood in the sense of the τέλειος of τελεῖσθαι, since these words do not signify a "moral completion or perfection," but rather initiation into the divine, which is the "τέλος" in an absolute sense, i.e., the "extreme limit, in the sense of goal and meaning and end," and, as such, the creature's "end").[86] It is a "perfecting initiation" into the extreme *qua* "end" (in the sense of the "*reditus creaturarum*" into God, as one finds in Origen and Thomas Aquinas), and precisely for this reason it is an initiation, with "eyes and mouth closed," into that darkness from which the light suddenly breaks forth (which for Paul too properly belongs to Christianity: "For it is the God who said, 'Let light shine out of darkness,' who has shone in our hearts to give the light . . . in the face

83. *Die Gestalt und das Sein*, pp. 68f.
84. *Legende Lese.* — Trans.
85. *Die Gestalt und das Sein*, p. 68.
86. *Ausgang.* — Trans.

of Christ" (2 Cor. 4:6); and, what is more, it is an initiation, with "eyes and mouth closed," into the night of death from which life is suddenly resurrected (just as the resurrection of the crucified Christ occurs with "suddenness": "Behold, there was a great earthquake" and "lightning" — Matt. 28:2-3). This single "μυ" is the original form in *mythos* and *mysterium*, just as these, according to Otto, together form a single indivisible unity. If it were philologically possible to derive the second syllable "θος" in μῦθος from the verb "θέσθαι," and the second syllable in μυστήριον from the verb "τηρεῖν" (which is something we must leave to the experts), then it might be possible to note a difference between the "μυ" in μῦθος and the "μυ" in μυστήριον. The difference would be that μῦθος would indicate an objective "fixed standing" of the "μυ" (from "θέσθαι" and "τίθεσθαι," in the sense of "to set"), wherein what is "enclosed" within the "primal word" originally "stood" — whereas the stress in μυστήριον would be upon the connotation of "custody" in "μυ" (from "τη-ρεῖν" in the sense of "keeping, preserving") — "custody" both in the sense of the walls enclosing the temple and also in the sense of that fixed rite in whose impenetrable "custody" one is initiated, with "eyes and mouth closed," into "light from darkness" and "life from death." Thus, what we find in Heidegger's characteristic ternary, which he takes as the form of his "truth in the Logos in thought"[87] — the ternary of the "concealed," its "unconcealment," and its return into a final "concealment" (that is lifted only with the advent of "Being's arrival") — are in fact the features of the "μυ" in μῦθος and μυστήριον. That Heidegger is determined to take these features as the features of his "truth in the Logos in thought" is avenged from the very first, but especially in the final phase of his thought, in that it presents not a thinking dedicated to a "philosophy of the Logos," but an attempt at a "new *mythos* and *mysterium*," into which he "initiates" his disciples in the role of a real "mystagogue" — whereby Bultmann's "demythologization" of the "Christian *mythos*" should be seen as a subsequent "initiation" into the "new Heideggerean *mythos* and *mysterium*," which for Bultmann is "pure Christianity free of myth": a pure Christianity in which there is only the one "light out of darkness" and the one "resurrection from death" that Heidegger's "new *mythos* and *mysterium*" provides: the light of "truth through technology" and the resurrection of the "(herein) caring man of cares,"[88] in both cases from "nothing" and in "nothing."

---

87. *Wahrheit im Logos im Denken.* — Trans.

88. *Sorgend besorgenden.* On the face of it, it seems odd indeed to associate Heidegger and (modern) technology in this way, given Heidegger's well-known critique of the latter. It

In contrast to the "μυ" in μῦθος and μυστήριον, "Logos" does not signify, as Heidegger would have it, a functional and instrumental "laying out of a selection" from the multiplicity of the phenomenal universe, which adumbrates that ultimate *metaphysicum*, the "ἕν-πάντα," the "all as one" (since a functional and instrumental "laying out of a selection" already implies, in the very form of its enactment, the "sense" of a "unity of all things"). On the contrary, according to Otto, the original sense of "Logos" is not that of a "collection," but of something "deliberated and calculated" in the sense of "having regard for, or taking into account or consideration."[89] In contrast to the essentially passive reception of the *mythos*, which is "received," and of the *mysterium*, which is "suffered," "Logos" thus implies the distance, indeed the critique — and thus the spontaneity — proper to something "deliberated and calculated" in a "having regard for, or a taking into account or consideration."

Of course, the "λέγειν" in "λόγος" also signifies a "collection" and "selection," but one that takes place by way of "counting and recounting," and as such by way of "deliberation" — as invigorated by a critical faculty of "interrogative reason," and by a critical faculty of understanding that "stands in its midst." According to Otto, the word "Logos" comes from "understanding and taking into account or consideration"; as such, it is distinguished both from "ἔπος," in the sense of a "word spoken with one's voice," and from "μῦθος," in the sense of a "word of direct testimony to what was, is, and will be" (thus corresponding to the divine "Was, Is, and Will be") and thus in the sense of a "self-revelation of being."[90] "Logos" thus implies the "consideration," "reflection," and "understanding" that is proper to a distant, critical "understanding," which stands genuinely over against "being," the "essence" of which it considers, reflects upon, and understands; and that is proper, furthermore, to a reflexive "reason" that, in "running back and forth" (the *"discurrere"* of "discursive" thought) receptively "ap-prehends" — *ver-nimmt* — this "essence," but only insofar as it "interrogates" it juridically (in the legal sense of the word *"Vernehmung"*). To be sure, in its etymological derivation from "λέγειν," "λόγος" signifies a "selective gathering," in the same sense as one "gathers" flowers, fruits, and stones — but this always occurs through a process of "selection" whose practical "meaning and purpose" (whether that

is consistent, however, with what Przywara says elsewhere about the (perhaps unwitting) technological aspect of Heidegger's philosophy as a form of secularized, immanentized, apophatic mysticism. See *In und Gegen: Stellungnahmen zur Zeit* (Nürnberg: Glock und Lutz, 1955). — Trans.

89. *Die Gestalt und das Sein*, p. 68.
90. *Die Gestalt und das Sein*, p. 71.

of a bouquet of flowers, or of a bowl of fruit for a fruit dish, or of whatever "use" might be made of stones) is at the very least the "guiding meaning" of this "gathering" — such that this functional "gathering" is already the *"in fieri"* of the realization and actuality of this "meaning and purpose." Certainly, inasmuch as it comes from "λέγειν" in the sense of "reading" (a book or a letter), "λόγος" signifies the "reading" together of letters; but this, of course, is for the sake of a "reading-oneself-into"[91] (the book or letter), such that the "meaning" of the individual words, etc. might be "understood" and "perceived" — indeed, such that even in a primitive "spelling out of letters" this "meaning" already constitutes its *"in fieri"* (since in such a spelling out of letters and the lexical elements of a word, it is the "whole" of the word that constitutes the "guiding measure").

Thus, "Logos" is not, as Heidegger would have it, a functional "laying out of a selection," in which the *metaphysicum* of a cosmic "ἓν καὶ πᾶν," an "all-unity," is immediately and objectively apparent (in the way that "primordial being" appeared in *mythos*). On the contrary, in sharp contrast to such a *"mythos"* of scholasticism's *"veritas ontologica,"* i.e., of "being itself as truth" (which is the real guiding intuition of Heidegger, the quondam neo-scholastic), Logos properly belongs to scholasticism's *"veritas in intellectu,"* and is thus "Logos" as found in "understanding" and "reason." It is Logos, therefore, in a sense almost "synonymous" with real "σοφία" (here we see the correspondence between the Old Testament "σοφία" of the Wisdom books and the New Testament "λόγος" of John's Gospel). Just as, according to its most ancient acceptation, "σοφία" simply means "bodily agility," and only by derivation comes to mean "skill" in art, science, governance, and thus something like an "essentially innate" specialized "understanding" and "rationality," so the particular accent of "Logos" is upon a reflective distance: either one in which, in the case of "logical thought," the "logos" of any given reality is set forth (in the way that in scholasticism the *"intellectus agens" qua "intellectus abstractionis"* "abstracts" the ideative "universale" from the real concrete particular); or one in which this distant reflection itself assumes the status of a *metaphysicum,* in the form of a "hypostatized Logos": in the sense, that is, either of an ontic "Logos that is the ultimate form within being's antitheses" (as with Heraclitus), or of a "Logos within a dialectically conceived divinity" (as, ultimately, with Philo), or of a "Logos God by whom all things are made" (as in the Gospel of John) and thus of a "Logos that takes the place of the Platonic ideas" (as with Thomas Aquinas).

91. *Sich-hinein-lesen.* — Trans.

Of course, "Logos" also means "word" (though, admittedly, not in the sense of a living "sound," as in the words "φωνεῖν" and *verbum*," nor in the sense of a "declaration," as in "εἰπεῖν," nor in the sense of a "conversation," as in "λαλεῖν," but rather in the sense of a "meaningful word," which is to say, an "intelligible word," in keeping with the sense of "Logos within understanding and reason"); it is this sense of Logos as "meaningful word" that reveals the ultimate span of its meaning. On the one hand, Logos means that "creative, intelligible, meaningful Word" "through which all things are made," and hence "the actual realization of the words" of the Logos as the Creator (just as, according to Genesis, heaven and earth were "shaped out of" a prior formlessness into a *mundus distinctionis,*" a world of distinct forms of being; and just as, according to Colossians, Christ, as the *"one Logos,"* is the "ἀρχή," the "absolute origin"). On the other hand, Logos means "creative, intelligible, meaningful word" in a re-creative[92] sense, as in the case of "understanding and reason" (or, at least, in the case of that "inner word" peculiar to both as essentially modes of verbal thought). Here the sensibly present, real reality is "pronounced" for the sake of abstracting and highlighting its "ontic intelligible meaning," i.e., so that in the "verbal expression" of understanding and reason, "which interrogates with the understanding," one might see — "abstracted" and "pronounced" — an "ontic logos of the forms of being." The archetypal ground for scholastic philosophy's distinction among *"ideae in Deo," "ideae in rebus,"* and *"ideae in mente"* is to be found (following Thomas's maxim that we have "the *one* divine Logos in place of Plato's ideas") in this threefold form of the "Logos": in God the creative Logos, in real things an ontic logos, and in man the re-creative, constructive, re-productive logos of the understanding (which "abstracts" the ontic logos from things) and of reason (which "interrogates" the ontic logos thus abstracted from things).

For this reason — firstly — there can be no such thing as a *"philosophy in the Logos"* in the sense of a "philosophy *of* the Logos." Inasmuch as Plato and Aristotle attribute "σοφία" to the gods, but to human beings merely "φιλο-σοφία," i.e., a "seeking and loving that is directed towards σοφία" and characterized by creaturely becoming, this "seeking and loving *towards . . .*" cannot, as a "philosophy *of* the Logos," place itself above the Logos by taking the Logos as its object. To be sure, one might very well suspect that Hegel attempted this, since his philosophy appears to make the Logos comprehensible as the dialectic of formal judgment; in point of fact, however, the Hegeli-

92. *Nachschöpferisch.* — Trans.

an dialectical Logos of "thesis, antithesis, synthesis" is ultimately the opposite: the omnipresence and omnificence (and, indeed, in the true spirit of the Reformation, the sole activity) of "absolute *Geist*" within the creaturely *Geist*, including the form of its judgment. In fact, Hegelian philosophy is for this reason the most extreme case of a "philosophy *in* the Logos": a "theosophy of the divine dialectical Logos within the creaturely logos" (theosophy in the strict sense, whose subject is no longer man "seeking and loving *toward*" — i.e., a "philo-sophizing" man — but "God as wisdom" and "wisdom as God" himself). It is rather modern logistics (in the tradition of Carnap) that attempts to take the Logos in itself as its object: a purely formal logistics, which moves within itself and takes itself as the sole *metaphysicum*, such that all questions about what is "real" and *a fortiori* about the divine are "set aside as meaningless." But we also see this in Husserl's phenomenology, which increasingly came to regard the Logos immanent to the *cogito* — a Logos whose logical form is that of "noema and noesis" — as the only Logos. And we also see this in Heidegger's phenomenology, at least in *Sein und Zeit*, which, despite all its "bracketing out of consideration," comprised everything divine within the enclosure of "being's self-understanding in the existing human being," with the result that whatever theology might then remain could be nothing more than a subsequent "theological application" of this essentially anthropological phenomenology of being (which Bultmann then duly prosecuted). As for a genuine "philosophy in the Logos," therefore, one may conclude — secondly — that it moves between the extremes of a (theopanistic) "theosophy of the Logos" (as represented by Hegel) and a "philosophy of the (formally logistical) Logos" (whose method is formally pantheistic). Since a "philosophy in the Logos," understood as "*philo-sophia*," is essentially creaturely and human, it cannot set itself up as any kind of *absolutum:* neither as the *absolutum* of a manifestation (however "methodical") of the divine (as with Hegel's theosophy of the Logos), nor as the *absolutum* of a *cogito* of the "pure logia"[93] (as a pure logistics, as a radical philosophy of "the" Logos, would have it).

For this reason — thirdly — a genuine "philosophy in the Logos," understood as an essentially creaturely philosophy, is bound to creatureliness; this is evident from the way in which, for such a philosophy, the concepts of the "purely material" and the "divine and purely spiritual" are limit concepts (equally exclusive of an evolutionary dialectical materialism and an emanative dialectical idealism). To be sure, the word "in" in the phrase "phi-

93. *Logien.* — Trans.

losophy in the Logos" indicates an ultimate "In" within a divine and absolute Logos (which is both the positive element in Hegelian idealism and the import of a Christian "philosophy in the Logos" that would, so to speak, "work out the philosophy" inherent in the Johannine and Pauline understanding of the "cosmos as from and in and to Christ the Logos"). But, even so, this still belongs to a creaturely and human *"philo-sophia,"* which is to be distinguished from divine *"sophia"* — just as these are distinguished by Plato and Aristotle, and as they are distinguished when the Wisdom books of the Old Testament and the Johannine and Pauline texts of the New Testament proclaim "σοφία" to be "God's counselor and craftsman," and thus "God's wisdom hidden away in a mystery" (which, as the *"Pneuma* that comes from God," is "freely bestowed by grace" alone). Of course, conversely, a "Logos of being,"[94] understood as that which is most "intelligible," is nevertheless given solely according to the fundamental law of human knowledge and thought — i.e., "in the sensible, through the sensible, within the sensible" (as Thomas Aquinas stresses), and thus in a true sense as a "Logos within matter" (which is why August Wetter has been able to identify a genuine link between scholastic realism and dialectical materialism). But even in the case of dialectical materialism, one is presented not with a doctrine of "matter as Logos," but with an ultimate dualism of Logos and matter, which merely emphasizes that matter (in the concrete sense of "economic conditions") is the presupposition and condition for every "logy"[95] (of science and philosophy), whose development (and so the development of the "logos of being" within developing "logia")[96] is bound to "material conditions." Thus, even here one is only a step away from a true apriorism of the "Logos" within every aposteriorism of "matter," however great, as the neo-scholastic approach of critical realism would have it: an *"a priori* Logos in-and-beyond *a posteriori* matter." What is more, this philosophical structure could be regarded as a genuine, objective "praeambulum" to the inexorable Johannine declaration of the "Logos with God" and of "God as the Logos" — namely, as the "λόγος σάρξ" who is "Christ in the flesh" (John 1:1, 14; 2 John 7).

Now, in conclusion, we are in a position to see what "Logos" means in a creaturely, human "philosophy in the Logos." It means — firstly — "Logos in analogy," as in the Lateran analogy of an "ever greater dissimilarity within every similarity between Creator and creature, however great." In

94. *Logos des Seins.* — Trans.
95. *Logie.* — Trans.
96. *Logie.* — Trans.

this sense, "being" and "Logos" are in the final analysis "analogy." To be sure, creaturely being and creaturely Logos are situated within a "similarity, however great" to "God as Being" and "God as Logos," but precisely in this respect (at the very moment when this "similarity, however great" might seek to become an "identity") they are situated ultimately and decisively within the "ever greater dissimilarity" that obtains between divine Being and Logos, on the one hand, and creaturely being and Logos, on the other. The *absolutum* of being and Logos is apparent solely within this "analogy of ever greater dissimilarity" with regard to creaturely being and Logos. What is "ultimate," therefore, in the progression of a philosophy from "image" to "likeness (or parable)" to "symbol" to "*mythos* and *mysterium*" is not a "pure Logos," but only "Logos in analogy." But given that the "analogy" stresses precisely the "ever greater dissimilarity" as its ultimate and decisive form, what the "Logos in analogy" expressly demands, right at the pinnacle of its progression from "image" to "Logos," is a corresponding regression: always back to the level at which the creature stands as the "ἄλλο," the "wholly other" (in Aristotle's formula for analogy) in a relation of "ever greater dissimilarity" to the "ἄλλο," the "Wholly Other," of the God of "ever greater dissimilarity." Accordingly, the creaturely logos realizes the "inaccessibility" of the "βάθη θεοῦ," the "depths of God" (which the Spirit of God alone "searches") to the degree that it returns ever anew, in an ever new regress, back into the creaturely, "fruitful βάθος of (sensible) experience" (Kant), which is grounded in the "image." This is why in ancient Greek "Logos" means precisely "proportion, analogy": betraying the unconscious insight that what dawns at the summit of the "Logos" (understood as the crowning dream of all philosophy) is precisely the "ever greater dissimilarity" "as" the (creaturely) Logos — which is to say that the "Logos," as the goal of the progression from "image" to "likeness (parable)" to "symbol" to "*mythos* and *mysterium*" to "Logos," is immediately, simultaneously, and indeed almost identically the "Logos" at the beginning of (and compelling) the regression from "*mythos* and *mysterium*" to "symbol" to "likeness (parable)" to "image." Consequently, just as — secondly — in the movement of progression (from "image" to "Logos") the "Logos" was immediately apparent on the basis of "*mythos* and *mysterium*," distinguishing itself from them while nevertheless establishing itself in them, so too "Logos in analogy" (as at once the goal of the progression and the beginning of the regression) means a relative "Logos beyond *mythos-mysterium*" that appears within the movement of regression (from "Logos" to "image") as, decisively, a "Logos in *mythos* and *mysterium*" (just as in Christianity the "Logos with God and as God" appears strictly as the "Logos made flesh": in the law of the *Gestalt* of Christ, and in the law of the *Gestalt* of the church as the "visible body," and of the Christian as a "visible member"). The progression (from "image" to "Logos") and the regression (from "Logos" to "image") are grounded, then, in this "in-and-beyond" between "Logos" and "*mythos and mysterium.*" But this means that they oscillate within the "analogy" (which is expressed in the "in-and-beyond") between "Logos" and "*mythos and mysterium.*" The progress (from "image" to "Logos") is the ascending movement of a "similarity, however great" to a "Logos with God and as God," which of itself would seek to super-elevate the "Logos beyond *mythos and mysterium*" to the pure Logos of an "identity between the divine Logos and the human logos. But, since the "analogy" emerges precisely within this progressive movement of the Logos, in its pressing ever above-and-beyond, it is here that the descending movement of the "ever greater dissimilarity," as the fundamental point of departure, decisively commences — whereby the Logos" sinks anew, as it were, into the "maternal ground" of "*mythos and mysterium,*" appearing emphatically as the "Logos in *mythos* and *mysterium*" (just as, all "spirituality" notwithstanding, Augustine demands that, within the Christian life, one never cease to "*manere in lacte matris,*" and that the church and the individual Christian be ever mindful of the novelty that "Christ as God" is genuinely "Christ as man" — and just as authentic Christian theology requires that every flight of "speculative theology" commencing with the "Logos" of revelation descend ever anew, along with the essentially "descending Christ," into the "fruitful βάθος" of a "positive theology" of the simple world of revelation).

But this means, definitively, that every movement proper to a "philosophy of the image," and to a "philosophy of likeness," and to a "philosophy of the symbol," and to a "philosophy of *mythos* and *mysterium,*" and to a "philosophy of the Logos" is not only a *single,* uniform movement between an ever ascending progression and an ever descending regression — but in this the *one* movement of a single "analogical philosophy of analogy." This one "analogical philosophy of analogy," understood as a "philosophical working out," so to speak, of the Lateran definition, is the "μέτρον ἁπάντων," the "universal measure and meter" for every movement of every possible philosophy.

6 Phenomenology, Realogy, Relationology

1957

These three words indicate three possibilities for philosophy. On the one hand, each of these possibilities has a tendency to understand itself in exclusive terms; but of course, on the other hand, they point to one another and reciprocally require one another simply in order to fulfill the peculiar meaning of each, such that only in their relatedness to one another do they first present a "true philosophy." There is thus a twofold requirement. First, each of the three possibilities must be recognized as an intrinsically self-contained philosophy: as distinguished from the procedure, customary in the schools, of beginning from a so-called "epistemology," which proceeds from "pure consciousness" (from, that is, the site within which a phenomenology encloses itself), in order subsequently to take up the question of reality (of, that is, what a realogy[1] would have as its own enclosed domain), and then to consummate the whole process in a "cosmology" that sees all individual realities within a common framework[2] (in an Aristotelian "cycle of change," or in a Thomist *"ordo universi,"* or in a Cusanist *"coincidentia oppositorum,"* . . . and thus according to what a relationology[3] claims exclusively for itself). But then these three possibilities need to be viewed in such a way that, while each is self-contained, their distinction becomes, at the very least, transparent to a total philosophy that these same three possibilities initially make possible. The history of philosophy, which gives the strong impression that there is a law of succession among these three possi-

1. *Realogie.* — Trans.
2. *Beziehungsfeld.* — Trans.
3. *Relationologie.* — Trans.

This essay first appeared in *Archivio di Filosofia,* Rome (1957).

bilities (in the way, for instance, that Plato's eidological phenomenology is succeeded by Aristotle's morphological realogy, and in the way that this, in turn, issues in a cosmological relationology), cannot help but transpose this law of succession to the superhistorical level of an objective law: for only in this way is it converted from a "material report" concerning particular historical philosophies (which is, methodologically, wholly indistinguishable from a "material history") into a genuine philosophical discipline, one no longer concerned with a material "reporting," but rather with a true understanding of the superhistorical structure of meaning that governs the succession of historical philosophies. As it happens, only Hegel, Dilthey, and Georg Simmel have pursued this line of thought: Hegel, who sought to comprehend the history of philosophy from the dynamic of his ternary (thesis, antithesis, synthesis); Dilthey, who set it upon the foundation of a "rhythmics" of archetypes; Georg Simmel, who saw it as the free rhythmics of life as such, between a "free flowing" and the respective "forms" into which it crystallizes, and which themselves, in turn, dissolve back into life. For all three thinkers, however, it is a line of thought that increasingly reveals itself to be a pure relationology, in which the "pure ideas" (εἴδη) of a phenomenology and the "actual realities" of a realogy are resolved into the pristine rhythmics of their relations, back and forth, with one another. In contrast to this, we shall here attempt to understand each of the three possibilities from its distinctive point of departure; this will lead us into its peculiar problematic, which breaks open immanently into each of the other points of departure, with their different problematics. Phenomenology, realogy, and relationology are possibilities that always indicate the whole of a given philosophy, but in such a fashion that their succession contains a very definite rhythm — one in which the truly "complete philosophy"[4] is played out for the first time.

1

Phenomenology is historically situated within the opposition between Hegel's emphatically noetic phenomenology and Husserl's emphatically noematic phenomenology. *Hegel's noetic phenomenology* (from his *Phenomenology of Spirit* on) concerns the inner "logy" of the whole range of Spirit's "forms of appearance," as constituted fundamentally in the Ur-dialectic of

4. *Ganze Philosophie.* — Trans.

the act of judgment: thesis, antithesis, synthesis. On the other hand, however, Hegel's various material[5] philosophies (of history in general, of the history of philosophy and of religion) represent a kind of "noematicization" of this original noetic reality[6] of Spirit: inasmuch as they translate the objective "appearances" (φαινόμενα) out of pure materiality into "forms of meaning" (and thus into the noumenal, in which the "meaning" of all real things and events first shines forth); while, conversely, it is this objective noumenality that first provides the noetic reality[7] of the Ur-dialectic of Spirit (as the "Phenomenology of Spirit") with its, so to speak, "worldly form," whereby it is transformed from a "law (or structure or dynamic) of the Spirit" into a "law (or structure or dynamic) of the world." Consequently, given that Hegel's seemingly pure noetic phenomenology is, in the full sense of the term, a *noetic-noematic phenomenology*, it forms the basis of a development that can be viewed in two different ways.

If its noematic aspect is taken as a pure objectivation of the noetic, this gives rise to a dialectical formalism of the formal Ur-dialectic of thesis, antithesis, synthesis, as is peculiar to the "orthodox Hegelians." Ultimately, this leads to a dialectical formalization of economics and of matter (in dialectical materialism), whereby the inner, dynamic dialectic of Spirit is transformed into the inner dynamic of matter. The result, strictly speaking, is that Spirit is then the "Spirit of matter," while matter is the "matter of Spirit" (leading to Lenin's mystically opaque "bi-unity":[8] Spirit in matter and matter in Spirit); until, in a final twist, the materially real is seen to be the ever new realization of the dialectic of Spirit within it, while Spirit proves to be nothing but the Ur-dialectic of matter and the material (which is to say that it leads to a "phenomenology of matter," in contrast to Hegel's noetic "phenomenology of Spirit," but in such a way that Hegel's noetic phenomenology of Spirit remains the formally creative element within it). In a reversal of emphases, this is then contrasted with a *noematic-noetic phenomenology* in which the rhythm of the noetic is transformed into a pure "method," whereby the noematic of a "world of meaning" is abstracted from a pure "world of facts": which leads to the various forms of those "philosophies of meaning" or "philosophies of types" that Dilthey, Simmel, Spranger, and Litt (though also, if differently, Nicolai Hartmann)

5. *Inhaltlichen.* — Trans.
6. *Ur-Noetischen.* — Trans.
7. *Das Noetische.* — Trans.
8. *Zwei-Eins.* — Trans.

attempted, as a "softer form of Hegelianism," until, in a fusion of Dilthey and Husserl, Heidegger sought to establish "being" itself as the "meaning of the ontic" (which is to say, in our present context, as an ontic noematic-noetic phenomenology).

As an alternative to this biformation of Hegel's noetic phenomenology, Husserl's phenomenology would appear to be a *noematic phenomenology* (as Husserl sketched out his initial position in his *Logical Investigations*). In contrast to philosophies based upon the natural sciences and the human sciences, the noematic appears here as a purely eidological sphere, which is superempirical and superhistorical and, therefore, *"a priori"* to everything empirical and historical; and, over against these other philosophies, it alone counts as "rigorous philosophy," since it first provides other "sciences" with their objects in the form of "regional phenomenologies." Equally, insofar as this purely eidological sphere can be grasped only in an "intuition of essences," which admits of no "system," it is opposed to every form of "pure speculation." As such a purely "noematic phenomenology" (one could even say, a *noematic-noematic phenomenology*), it became the defining prototype of the kind of phenomenology that shaped almost all philosophy between the first and second world wars, and that was developed above all by Max Scheler — though in his case in the form of an objective phenomenology of value.

Husserl himself, however, strides (along the path leading from the *Ideas Pertaining to a Pure Phenomenology,* to the *Formal and Transcendental Logic,* to the *Cartesian Meditations*) towards a shift of emphasis from pure noema to pure noesis, in which phenomenology is fundamentally constituted as "egology," though in a monadological sense (according to which a transcendental ego, in Kant's sense, is ultimately represented in terms of a transcendental "world of egos,"[9] in a kind of retrogression from Kant to Leibniz — though without this having a final, realogical sense, as Leibniz and even, at bottom, Kant understood their monadologies). Even this phenomenology of Husserl's last period remains a noematic phenomenology; but by virtue of the shift of emphasis from noema to noesis, it is a *noematic phenomenology as a noetic phenomenology:* because the *a priori* of the noemata (the contents of perception) has its original ground in the *a priori* of the egological-monadological noesis. To be sure, even in this last form, there remains an opposition to philosophies of the natural sciences, philosophies of the human sciences, and speculative philosophy (as well as to every

9. *Welt der Iche.* — Trans.

form of realogy, inasmuch as for Husserl the real remains "in brackets"). But an egological, monadological, noetic phenomenology nevertheless comes very near to the fundamentally noetic phenomenology of Hegel, in which all contents (those of nature, man, history, and religion) appear as reduced to an inner dialectic of the *one* noesis of "Spirit." If Hegel's noetic phenomenology could be said to globalize Descartes's *"cogito"* into a "world," then it is no accident that the late Husserl goes (in his *Cartesian Meditations*) back through Hegel, Kant, and Leibniz to precisely this *"cogito,"* in order to find within a transcendental ego (which he directly opposes to Descartes's path to reality) a purely *a priori*-eidetic version of Descartes's, Leibniz's, Kant's, and Hegel's "world" (which is why it remains highly significant that, for the late Husserl, Descartes alone is of interest, while Kant, Leibniz, and Hegel play no role at all).

The positive core basic to both forms of phenomenology, however (Hegel's as well as Husserl's), is what in the tradition of *Plato* could be called *eidology.* Following the fundamental tendencies of Plato's dialogues, eidology means prescinding the pure *"eide,"* i.e., "pure pictures," from an inviolate reality in which they are fixed as *"paradeigmata,"* i.e., "primordial exemplars," and in which the whole of reality has its form and order (εἴδη . . . ὥσπερ παραδείγματα ἑστάναι ἐν τῇ φύσει — *Parmenides* 132d). This is why in Plato these informing "eide" pass over seamlessly into the fundamental tensions of a real cosmos (almost in the tradition of Heraclitus), even into the "μάχη ἀθάνατος," the "immortal struggle" of real oppositions, one with another (*Laws* X, 906bc). As much as this kind of eidology seems to abstract an "ideal order" from a real cosmos, which for Heraclitus is an "unquenchable fire" and a "heap of rubbish" (a kind of eidology that we later see in Thomas Aquinas, who, aided by the primacy he accords to the *"universalia,"* illuminates such a cosmos — shining through even the most particular realities of the concrete world — as a *"perfectio universi"* in an *"ordo universi"*), it is nevertheless an eidology that is ultimately instrumental to a penetrating vision of a real cosmos. Eidology thus changes imperceptibly from something concerned with a particular content (the ideal, pure *eide*) to something formal (concerned with the "pure gaze of the pure eye" into an unveiled reality — as the Platonic Augustine later put it: *"oculus simplex"*).

As much as Descartes's "pure method" implies a real contrast between a pure *"cogito"* and a pure *"massa extensa,"* between, that is, a real "engineer" and a real "machine" — as much as Kant from the outset rejects every "pure consciousness" (solipsism), in order to posit an immediacy with regard to real things as the premise for a "categorization" of the real — as much as Leibniz's seemingly "pure monadology" signifies nothing other than the "spiritual kernel" of cosmic reality — as much as Hegel's noetic phenomenology, in this same tradition, strives ultimately to grasp the reality of a dialectically changing absolute Spirit by means of his ternary — as much as Husserl's noematic phenomenology maintains to the end merely a methodological "epochē" (abstention) vis-à-vis reality, as a "bracketing out" of reality: still this entire tradition of noetic and noematic phenomenology never flows out into a true realogy so intrinsically as it does, at the beginning, in the eidology of Plato. While such an eidology seems to be concerned with the original noematic content[10] of a "τόπος νοητός," an "ideal, pure world" (and so, as a *noematic eidology*, would seem to be the origin of all possible noematic phenomenologies), it is nevertheless an eidology in which the emphasis upon the noematic content of a "τόπος νοητός" undeniably mutates from within into the noetic emphasis upon a "pure vision" by a "pure eye," moreover, in such a way that it is impossible for this "noetic" to become formally, in itself, a transcendental (as with the phenomenologies from Descartes to Husserl); instead it functions solely to train an "eye open upon reality," which is to say that it is not even oriented toward a noetic eidology as the origin of a noetic phenomenology, but rather toward an *"instrumental eidology,"* whose aim is no longer "eidos," in the sense of an ideal content, but simply *"idein,"* in the sense of a pure seeing (of a really realistic reality).

By repatriating all possible phenomenologies in Platonic eidology, as their place of origin, the transcendentalism ubiquitously inherent in them is overcome: that transcendentalism that, at the very least, "brackets out" everything real from every philosophy (as is also the case with a strict Thomism, which treats the concretely real individual only "numerically," *"de ratione materiae,"* and so is forced to represent itself as a phenomenological transcendentalism of the *"universalia"*). If phenomenology is to be the methodological path to a realogy, this is the path it must take, to which the originally noematic eidology of Plato leads: that of the "instrumental eidology" of the "pure gaze" of the "eye open upon reality" into which the originally noematic eidology of Plato flows. The word "phenomenology" then no longer signifies the path from "realities as pure appearance" to the ideal or transcendental *"noumena,"* taken as "pure being" (a negative φαίνειν), but rather the manner in which the realities themselves increasingly "shine forth" (a positive φαίνειν) for a "pure, open eye."

---

10. *Das ursprünglich Noematische.* — Trans.

2

But the spoken or unspoken intention of all phenomenologies (including Plato's eidology) is to attain "actual being"[11] through really existent, concrete being. Even if a given phenomenological method intends merely to "prescind from" this concrete reality, or to "abstract" "actual being" from it ("prescind from" in the case of the Husserlian *"epochē,"* "abstract" in the case of the Thomistic *"abstractio"*), in both cases the formal object of such phenomenologies is not really existent, concrete being, but rather "ideal actual being." Leibniz was the first to reveal the reason for this: namely, that there can be no genuine *"vérité des faits,"* but only a *"vérité de raison."* In other words, because "truth" (as the concern of a given philosophy) is something "absolute," its content must also be something "absolute" and never something concretely factual. The form, "absolute truth," and the content, "absolute objects," intrinsically correspond to one another, as more or less the primordial correlation of philosophy as such. For this reason the whole of modern philosophy is defined by the attainment of an "ideal world" (be it a world of "ideal monads," or of "ideal categories," or of an "ideal dialectic"). For this reason, too, the object of classical Thomism is not the concrete, individuated world, but rather the "ideal universals" (plant in itself, animal in itself, human being in itself). And even Aristotle, who rejects the "pure eide" of Platonism in order to focus upon the "forms within matter" (μορφή), understands these forms ultimately as a kind of "ideal reality" embedded in the pure motion and pure potentiality (κίνητον of δύναμις) of "matter" (ὕλη), which, as such, cannot be the object of any philosophy. Something similar can be said even of the Scotism and nominalism of the late middle ages, which would take all "eide" and *"universalia"* as nothing but "words," indeed, as nothing but the "exhalation of words" *(flatus vocis),* in order to grasp the singularity of the unique concrete thing, in the unique moment within the universal flux; for here this dynamic itself is taken as an absolute — a dynamic that is operative solely in the unique *concretum,* such that here too an "absolute truth" corresponds to an "absolute object": to, that is, an "absolute movement." The immanent *realogy of a phenomenology* is thus, at its most extreme, a phenomenology as realogy: inasmuch as the contents of a given phenomenology are posited as the "actual reality" of concretely individual reality (in the sense of Plato's and Aristotle's "ὄντως ὄν"). The matter is essentially no different for the school of philosophy founded by Christian

---

11. *Eigentliches Sein.* — Trans.

Wolff. For even if this philosophy begins with a so-called "epistemology" and goes through the "qualities of sensation" in order to provide evidence — right within the enclosure of pure consciousness — for an actual reality, this reality nevertheless remains determined by the categories of a "pure, self-contained consciousness." To be sure, it is not a reality in the strict sense of a realogy of a phenomenology, as above, but it is still more or less in the "style of phenomenology"; for it does not discuss the peculiar nature of "reality," but simply endues its phenomenological contents with the "quality of the real" without further discussion. This is what is proper to all phenomenologies (from Platonic eidology, to Aristotelian morphology, to medieval universo-logy, to modern ideo-logy): that is, the inevitable style of directness and uniformity, the style of the "system."

This is fundamentally contrasted with a *realogical existentialism*, which posits, in Kierkegaard, the concrete "individual"; in Sartre, the dynamic situation; in Heidegger, the caring caretaking[12] human being as "existing [*Seienden*]," as opposed to a systematic "being [*Sein*] in itself." In the case of Kierkegaard and Sartre, however, this existentialism of the "ever concrete *existentiell*," which arises from a passionate hostility to every "in itself," is in fact a practical ethics, ultimately in the genealogy of the French moralists of the eighteenth century (just as Nietzsche's expressly "moral philosophy" is the inner connection between the two). It is not a realogy, but a *realistic ethics* (for which there is no problem between phenomenology and realogy in the first place). And as much as Heidegger's philosophy wants to be an ontology, or indeed, in the words of Scheler, precisely an ontics in which "truth" is understood as the objective self-disclosure of real being itself (in a rather curious appropriation of the scholastic *"veritas ontologica"*) — in point of fact even this ontics of the real[13] is a realistic ethics, or at the very least a practical anthropology: for ultimately it concerns (as is increasingly clear from Heidegger's studies of Hölderlin and his philosophy of technology, and even more so from his most recent encounter with Zen-Buddhism) a "human comportment" (as was definitively introduced in *Sein und Zeit* with his analysis of being as "care").

In contrast to both of these *apparent* realogies, the phenomenological and the existential, an *authentic realogy* strives to grasp that distinct particularity that, in sharp contrast to the contents of consciousness, is peculiar to the real. This is — firstly — essentially what Max Scheler was the first to call

12. *Sorgend besorgend.* — Trans.
13. *Real-Ontik.* — Trans.

the *"resistancy of the real."* Phenomenology is, in one way or another, idealism, whereby human beings and the world are brought into accord with one another, indeed into a coinherence of each in the other. Heraclitus's "oppositions," indeed his "contradictions," have no place here. Its prototype is the "singing harmony" of Pythagoras's mathematical world. Accordingly, everything remains within the pure relational thinking of a pure ratio, so much so that even a dialectic like Hegel's remains a purely ideal dialectic, whose calculus is "exactly worked out" — as is also the case with dialectical materialism, which, for all its emphasis upon real economy, etc., is "exactly worked out," in order to subject the genuinely real to "ideology" (leading to idealized economic plans and "leader-icons"). But the genuinely real is not an idealistic "oscillation within itself" of a poetically thinking consciousness; rather, it is that which resists my "pure thought" and that which I simply "run up against," and so does not "work out" according to my "calculation." If so-called negative theology views God as the "wholly other" (as the *"supra omne, quod cogitari potest"*), and if this "wholly other" also figures as the "negative relation" between human beings, as Eberhard Grisebach already stressed, (contradicting in advance the proclamation of Ferdinand Ebner's I-thou mysticism on the part of such contemporaries as Buber, Brunner, and Guardini) — then this "negative relation" of the "wholly other" is ultimately valid for the relation between phenomenological consciousness and genuinely realogical reality as such. This goes to say that "resistancy" (to every attempted "mastery" of the real by way of "non-contradictory concepts") does not ultimately mean that independent reality is a "limit concept" for "pure consciousness" (which, as a concept, would remain something intra-phenomenological) — rather, "resistancy" means the "wholly other" of the genuinely real over against all possible conceptualizations. So too, therefore, "resistancy" does not mean the *"quantité négligeable"* of a "remainder" (which the experimental natural sciences take into account in their investigations); rather, it is the *positivum* of the genuinely real and, as such, genuinely distinct from the phenomenological ideality in which consciousness resides.

There is then a threefold gradation to this "resistancy": from the "wholly other" of the real as such, to the "wholly other" between one human being and another, to the "wholly other" between the creature and God. Every systematization[14] of the real that would incorporate it into phenomenological consciousness, every systematization of the always unique relation

14. *Ein-Systematisierung.* — Trans.

of "human being to human being" that would incorporate this relation into an idealistically uniform anthropology, and every systematization of the absolute "wholly other" of God that would incorporate God into an idealistically uniform cosmology is confronted, according to the above gradation, by a true *"reductio in mysterium"* of the real, the human, and the divine. Whereas a "pure phenomenology" always seeks "to clear up" every "mystery" peculiar to this (graded) "wholly other" and resolve it into a "system of pure concepts" or a "structure of regional phenomenologies" (a Husserlian phenomenological monadology), an authentic realogy takes exactly the opposite path: it increasingly lets all "pure concepts," "pure structures," and "pure ideas" "run up against" a final "resistancy" of the genuinely real, in order that, in proportion to the degree of this collision, the "mystery of the real" might be experienced as inexperienceable (as the Areopagite says with regard to the knowledge of God). The corresponding prototype, then, for such a realogy, which consists in the "resistancy of the real," is the kind of revelation we find in the Old and New Testaments (but also, similarly, in all extra-Christian myths), which are in no sense a "system in clear concepts," nor can they even be translated into such terms, but are rather the jagged, imposing mountains of the truly real (as is expressed even in the symbol of Israel as the "house of resistance" and "a stubborn and stiff-necked people"), such that it is first in these "resisting mountains" that the real God of "anger and love" becomes comprehensible in his real incomprehensibility.

But what we find within this resistancy of the genuinely real is — secondly — an implicit *"contradictoriness."* It is the picture of the real that Heraclitus opposes to every concordant and univocal ideal: "opposition is what gathers together, the loveliest harmony is composed of things at variance, and the whole of things comes to be in accordance with strife" (Diels 63B, 8). This "contradictoriness as harmony" extends so far that the opposites, as opposites, ultimately coincide: such that, on the one hand, death is life and life death ("immortal mortals, mortal immortals, living each other's death and dying each other's life": 70B, 62); and such that, on the other, the divine is the very coincidence of the opposites ("God is day-night, winter-summer, war-peace, satiety-hunger": 71B, 67). It is, finally, by virtue of this maximal, tension-filled unity of opposites that the "cosmos" is indeed an "ever-living fire" (66B, 30), but also, as such, what an ideal phenomenology holds as its central concept: "Logos" as the "criterion and judge of truth" (59A, 16) and, as such, "what is universally common and divine" (61B, 1). In this entire philosophy of opposition (whether in Augustine, Nicholas of Cusa, Pascal, or Newman), whose ancestry goes back to Heraclitus, we thus see the historical form of an authentic realogy for which the resistancy of the real reveals an inner contradictoriness in the real itself — a contradictoriness that flows finally into a "coincidence of opposites" *(coincidentia oppositorum)*, in which the universe (as a "turning into one": *uni-versum*) almost merges into the divine (as with Nicholas of Cusa), which (for Thomas Aquinas) is that "supereminence of totality and simplicity" that appears in the creature "deficiently, partially, and in a manifold way,"[15] inasmuch as "the perfection of the universe consists in the contrasting variety of creatures." Consequently, this entire philosophy of opposition does not occupy a "balanced" position between contrasting phenomenologies, since this would tend rather in the direction of a rational "solution" according to a progressive conceptualization. Rather it is the logical step towards the "resistancy" of the real in a genuine realogy — the step that leads from a purely factual resistancy of the real to an inner structure of the real: to the structure of a final coincidence of opposites as opposites, which can lead to no "solution" whatsoever (as logically follows from the resistancy of the real); for the plane of an intra-cosmic co-in-cidence — *In-Eins-Fall* — already merges with the plane of the divine, which is, according to our threefold gradation of the resistancy of the real, the "wholly other" that surpasses absolutely everything. Thus, here too, as an opposition-philosophy of resistancy, realogy has its prototype (and its fulfillment) in the revelation of the Old and New Testaments (as well as in all extra-Christian myths), which Luther places under the sign of the *"absconditum sub contrario"* and *"per antithesin,"* of what is "hidden (from all) under opposition and contradiction."[16] In these depths, and as a philosophy of opposition, realogy bespeaks a mutual crossing in the cross of the crucifixion, as the "real of the real" (in quite incisive opposition to the reconciling luminosity in all phenomenologies). Realogy, under the sign of this cross as the origin and end of the real, is, from resistancy to contradictoriness, concretely a "philosophy of the cross," in the sense of the "Logos of the cross as curse."

Along these lines, however, as it develops into a philosophy of opposition on the way from resistancy to contradictoriness, a genuine realogy also reaches its greatest opposition to every phenomenology. Whereas a genuine phenomenology finds the meaning at which it aims either in the "system" (as with Hegel), or, in one or another sense, in a structure of ideal categories (as with Kant), or at least in a transcendental ego as its lucid medium (as with

---

15. *Summa Th.* I, q. 57, a. 1, corp.
16. *WA*, XV, III, 782; *WA*, XLVI, 392.

Husserl), a genuine realogy simply goes "to infinity." We see in a realogy of resistancy and contradictoriness, finally, a realization of what Thomas Aquinas designates as the primal ground of creaturely reality:[17] the *"infinitum potentia,"* which is so singularly related to God's *"infinitum actu"* as its ultimate counterpart that, far from being comprehensible within an "infinitesimal calculation" of the real (at least by way of an "ideal limit-concept"), it is, on the contrary, essentially an *"in instanti"* within this immediacy between an *"infinitum potentia"* and an *"infinitum actu."*[18] That is to say: the "to infinity" of creaturely reality stands not at the end of a realogy, but is rather from the outset its form "in the moment" as such. The specific "to infinity" of the real (for a genuine realogy) is the *"in instanti"* of the creature in relation to the God, who, as the *"infinitum actu,"* is the *"intra rem quamlibet,"* the "interior of everything real."[19] So it is not simply that what is ultimate in the "contradictoriness" of the real turns out to be this "tension of opposites unto infinity" (in contrast to an ideal "system" sought by the various phenomenologies); rather, every particular "real moment" bears in itself the opposition between the *"infinitum potentia"* and the *"infinitum actu"* as its "most interior interior" — and thus not only as the final meaning (τέλος) of dynamically oscillating contrarieties, but as the dynamic origin (ἀρχή) of every real "moment." As a philosophy of opposition, a realogy is a true "dynamism" not only by virtue of a necessarily dynamic tension of opposites, but also by virtue of the dynamism between the *"infinitum potentia"* and the *"infinitum actu"* in every real *"in instanti."* Such a realogy represents the full realization of the dynamics of Heraclitus, just as the supra-dynamic, ideal "coherence"[20] of phenomenology is a logical development of the ideal statics of Parmenides. The proper prototype (and fulfillment) of this kind of "dynamic realogy" is therefore the innermost rhythm of revelation in the Old and New Testaments (as well as in all extra-Christian myths): in their form as a truly "momentary opening to infinity," inasmuch as, on the one hand, all divine manifestation in the world is a "momentary opening to infinity," an unforeseeable "flash of lightning that opens new worlds," such that, on the other hand, this fulgurant form of divine revelation "explodes" all secure reality "into unlimited perspectives." The "consuming fire" of this "revelatory lightning," which is proclaimed by the Old (Deuteronomy) and New (Hebrews)

---

17. *Real Geschöpflichen.* — Trans.
18. *De Ver.* q. 6, a. 1, ad 2.
19. *De Ver.* q. 3, a. 7, corp.
20. *Zusammenhang.* — Trans.

Testaments as the final mystery lying between divine and creaturely reality, is thus the most proper prototype (and fulfillment) of what the original realogy of Heraclitus's "ever-living fire" designates as the origin of cosmic reality[21] (in curious accord with the Persian Avesta's "divine fire"). As such, it constitutes the most extreme antithesis of what any phenomenology, from Plotinus's onward, regards as its ideal origin: the self-emanating, unitary "light" (of "intelligibility"). Just as "evidence" is the fundamental form of any phenomenology (from Descartes's *"clarté"* to Husserl's "evidence in the intuition of essences"), the basic form of a genuine realogy is found in the "stormy night and non-ground"[22] that Dionysius the Areopagite calls "an outpouring of light" (γνόφος as φωτοχύσια): such a nocturnal overshadowing of all ideal evidence in the "non-ground" of warring opposites that the acme of such a "stormy night" is the "ever living (ἀεί ζωόν) and consuming (ἀναλίσκον) fire" of "revelatory lightning," in which the real "ὄντως ὄν," the "being of beings," stands "open" as "known as unknown," albeit in *"mythos, mysterium, apokalypsis"* — which is to say, unveiled as veiled.

3

Here we have reached the most acute antithesis between phenomenology and realogy. And yet, precisely thus we have attained the plane whereon they essentially encounter one another. It is the plane stretching between (ideal) essence and (real) existence. All phenomenologies aim at abstracting ideal *"essentiae"* from existent reality. Conversely, all realogies have this existent reality as their object (though this is to be distinguished from the various "existentialisms" whose concern is, whether in anthropological or moral terms, "the existing human being"). The antithesis between phenomenology and realogy is thus grounded in the distinction between *"essentia"* and *"existentia"* that stands at the center of ancient, medieval, and modern philosophy. In ancient and modern philosophy this distinction is "objectively present": since both attempt to abstract a coherent order of ideal essences directly from existing, concrete reality, without tackling the explicit problem between essence and existence. In medieval philosophy, certainly, the problem is central (inasmuch as it determines what differentiates Thomism, Scotism, and Molinism from one another). But in this philosophy the prob-

21. *Des Real-Kosmischen.* — Trans.
22. *Sturmnacht-Ungrund.* — Trans.

lem between essence and existence is not only a "singular" problem" specific to *"philosophia prima"* or "ontology"; rather, at the level of method, this *"philosophia prima"* or "ontology" is ultimately taken for a pure phenomenology — to be sure, one that straightaway presupposes the real, but without posing the question of a realogy proper, as essentially distinct from phenomenology (a question that could, of course, be posed only after the phenomenological philosophy of German idealism had reached its climax). Thus, once one has first set forth the essential difference between phenomenology and realogy (as we have done), it becomes possible to trace the problem between phenomenology and realogy back to the problem between "(ideal) *essentia*" and "(real) *existentia.*" The methodological problem between phenomenology and realogy is rooted in this metaphysical problem between *"essentia"* and *"existentia"* — and, conversely, it is first by rooting the methodological problem in the metaphysical problem that the metaphysical problem achieves its complete centrality in anything properly called philosophy. The problem between a phenomenology of *"essentiae"* and a realogy of *"existentia"* is thus the problem of the relation between *"essentiae"* and *"existentia."* It is the problem, in short, of a *"relationology"*: as the bridging "third," between a phenomenology (of *essentia*) and a realogy (of *existentia*). The medieval scholastic systems of Thomism, Scotism, and Molinism were in fact right to make the relation between essence and existence their chief point of contention with one another. But, methodologically, they debated without an express relationology, which can first arise only out of a conscious distinction between phenomenological and realogical methods. Certainly Thomism stresses a *"realis distinctio"* between essence and existence, but with the intention of abstracting *(abstractio)* the "pure essences" from "existence." Scotism, conversely, places the accent upon a "conceptual identity" between essence and existence, one that stresses the "dynamism" of existence, which in Occamism turns into "voluntarism" (and which then, in Luther, who explicitly admits belonging to the *"factio occamistica,"* turns into a theonomic voluntarism of a God who alone works all things). Finally, Molinism, which (like Thomistic Bañezianism) attempts a synthesis between (original) Thomism and Scotism, posits a *"distinctio rationis"* between essence and existence, leading, however, to a picture of the world as "rational being" — not indeed to a rebirth of the "ideal order" that one finds in the early Augustine and Thomas, but rather to an existing world as grasped purely by reason (which ultimately developed into European rationalism, principally in Christian Wolff, whose rationalism is not only the premise of Kant's thought, but also a preeminent source for later neo-

scholasticism). In none of the three schools, therefore, is it a matter of a genuine "relation" (σχήσις, *relatio*) between essence and existence; rather, it is,
fundamentally, always a matter of deciding among them: whether a pure essence, a pure existence, or an essentialized existence should serve as the
foundation of a given metaphysics or ontology. The reason for this is that
none of the three schools consciously undertook to distinguish between
phenomenology and realogy; rather, each begins from a kind of "phenomenology of the real" and, precisely for this reason (explicitly in the case of
neo-scholasticism), constructs first a certain phenomenology of consciousness (in the spirit of Descartes's), which leads to the real, but does so without
an actual, distinct "logy" of the real — that is to say, without at least discussing a genuine realogy.

On the other hand, the positive aspect of the three schools is that they
place the stronger accent, respectively, either upon *"essentia"* (in Thomism)
or upon *"existentia"* (in Scotism and Molinism), without, certainly, consciously or more deeply establishing this accentuation. But as much as they
are ignorant of any real relationology (as overarching phenomenology and
realogy), their differing accentuation (of either *"essentia"* or *"existentia"*)
nonetheless leads to what is qualitatively peculiar to a relationology — a
qualitative peculiarity that is intimated in that Thomism stresses the *"realis
distinctio"* between *"essentia"* and *"existentia,"* and Scotism the identity of
both, whereas Molinism strives after a median between "real distinction"
and "real identity," precisely as a "suspended middle." Whereas Thomism,
with its *"realis distinctio,"* aims at the "over"[23] of *"essentia"* over *"existentia,"*
Scotism emphasizes the "in" of *"essentia"* in *"existentia."* But a "suspended
middle" posited between the Thomistic "over" and the Scotist "in" is nothing other than the "analogy" (as we thoroughly laid it out in *Analogia Entis*
I), which — from its Aristotelian to its full form, as formulated by the
Fourth Lateran Council — has "in-over" for its structure. What is qualitatively peculiar to a relationology is thus an analogology (and not an "analectics" in the sense of an early Augustinian doctrine of similarity, as Lakebrink,
an exponent of the Dempf school, wants to construct). The (unfortunate)
expression "analectics" betrays its early Augustinian origin in that, just as an
interpretive reading of the "eternal archetypes" in their "temporal images" is
characteristic of early Augustinianism (this being the fundamental intention
of the Dempf school), "lectic" speaks of the "reading" of supra-real
exemplarities (in the *"ano"* of *"ana"*).

---

23. *Über.* — Trans.

It is precisely a genuine analogology, however, as what is qualitatively peculiar to a relationology, that also turns out to be the bridging "third" between phenomenology and realogy (taken as the original antithesis). Whereas phenomenology is distinguished by a pure "content," realogy places the stress upon an ultimate "form" (e.g., "resistancy," "contradictoriness," and "to infinity"). All true philosophies of content will of necessity be phenomenologies (as Husserl rightly emphasized in his noematic period). But then this "pure content" must consciously assume the "form" of the "real," as is only worked out in a genuine realogy. Inasmuch, however, as phenomenology, which is oriented to a content, occupies the level of *"essentia"* by virtue of this content, it stands within the "over," where *"essentia"* stands in relation to *"existentia."* Conversely, it is in a genuine realogy that the "over" of "pure contents" is first lowered from the "supercelestial site of the ideal" (which would otherwise claim its rapt attention) to the level of the realistically real of "resistancy," "contradictoriness," and "to infinity," i.e., to the emphatic "in" of *"essentia* in *existentia."* But then again, it is precisely through such lowering of "pure contents" that this level of the distinctly real (precisely in its "to infinity") becomes the site of a final, definitive "over." For its part, a phenomenology of content always stands in danger of "iconology": that is, of taking its contents as "ultimate idealities" (in emphasizing a "pure similarity" between "archetype" and "image": just as Eastern Christian icons are held to be the immediate presence of the "saints" that are represented). It is a strict realogy (with its emphasis upon the "antitheses to infinity") that first introduces the inexorable distance of an "ever greater unlikeness" between "ideal archetype" and "real image." If the "over" (of *essentia* over *existentia*) is the "over" of an "ideal zone" (such as that of the Platonic "τόπος νοητός"), then this final "over," which mounts up out of a realogy of real "antitheses to infinity," is the first decisive "surmounting": a surmounting of the ideal (of a given phenomenology's "pure *essentia*") and of the real (of "antitheses to infinity"), leading into the primordial mystery of a super- and in-comprehensible identity between the super-ideal and the super-real. This, as an identity of "essence as existence" and "existence as essence," is the Divine in its "ever greater dissimilarity" to the creature (as the language of the Fourth Lateran Council has it) — a creature that, in and of itself, stands in a relation of "such great similarity" to the Divine by virtue of being, as "essence over-in existence" (in the succession from phenomenology to realogy) and "existence in-over essence" (in the final "over" of a realogy "to infinity"), the greatest similitude *(tanta similitudo)* to the Divine.

In this respect, relationology as analogology, in its rhythmic binding together of phenomenology and realogy, provides the decisive basis for a *theo-analogology* (which is the positive element of what one till now has called theodicy or *theologia naturalis,* though both terms are purely historically conditioned: theodicy as an "apology for God" in the unbelieving age of the encyclopedia, *theologia naturalis* as the attempt to balance out the oppositions between "warring Christian confessions" at the level of "natural religion"). By contrast, a theo-analogology (which proved to be what is ultimate in relationology and analogology) has its most definitive prototype (and fulfillment) in the fundamental rhythm of revelation in the Old and New Testaments (and adumbratively in the extra-Christian myths), whose "*analogia fidei*" (between all contents, however antithetical) leads to an analogy drawn from the economy of salvation, between the "*Deus irae*" and the "*Deus misericordiae*" — such that in the ultimate depths of this analogy it not only stands in a relation of analogy to the intra-divine "mystery of relation" (of Father, Son, and Spirit), but, what is more, indicates, albeit in "greatest dissimilarity" as "ever greater dissimilarity," a "mystery of rhythm" within this intra-divine "mystery of relation," one in which a creaturely relationology, as analogology, might have a presentiment of its "all-surpassing" archetype.

7 Man, World, God, Symbol

1958

I

The *question of the relationship between humanism and symbolism* always bears reference to the turning point of a given age. Such was the case with Rome and its epochal turn[1] from the austerity of the *"Res Publica"* to the Augustan humanism of Horace, Ovid, Propertius, Catullus, *et al.* Whereas in the *"Res Publica"* the individual was merely the vehicle and instrument of the impersonal[2] "mission" of Rome, impersonally symbolized on the Capitoline and upon the ensigns of its legions, under the sun of the *"Pax Augustana"* an explicit culture of the individual person takes shape: a culture that, on the one hand, feels secure under the protection of a military empire but that, on the other, is witness to an increasing laxity and gradual softening of that original Roman *"disciplina"* upon which such a military empire must either stand or fall. Such was also the case in the Middle Ages, as it turned from an age of great symbols, which the individual was obliged to serve as a "vassal of Christ" (to employ St. Benedict's phrase) in "service to the crown" and "service to the *infula* and *tiara,"* into the age of the Renaissance, which remains in force even for us today as the revolt — the awakening — of a humanism for which "man is the highest value." The Middle Ages stood so utterly under the sign of the symbol that everything individual, national, and historical appeared simply as the cultic *"praesentia et memoria"* of the revealed symbols of

1. *Zeiten-Wende.* — Trans.
2. *Es-haft.* — Trans.

This essay first appeared in *Archivio di Filosofia*, Rome (1958).

the Old and New Testaments, as well as of the symbols of the great saints (regardless of whatever concrete humanity these saints themselves actually possessed) — which is to say, they appeared as the "presence and (objective) memorial" of Abraham, Isaac, Jacob, the prophets, and the apostles (a view maintained even through the Reformation, precisely on account of the latter's use of biblical names — especially Old Testament names — to designate both persons and events). For the Renaissance, in sharp contrast, man is himself the "great wonder," and all other symbols, however venerable they be, are valid only to the degree that they constitute a, so to speak, superficial "sensible image of 'the' pure (intelligible) human being." The humanism of the Renaissance then culminates in the humanism of modernity, whereby man not only becomes the *"cogito"* invested with dominion over everything else (thus establishing man as a *demiourgos technikos*) but — as in the case of Humboldt (who represents the pinnacle of European humanism) — begins explicitly to assume features at once human and divine, since an objective Christ now becomes the "messianic form" of man as such. The epochal turn of our own day, which began after the First World War as a programmatic "movement" and "turn" (towards the "community," the "object," the "cosmic," the "cultic," or *"mythos"*), finally opposes the anthropologism and anthropocentrism of the analytic eighteenth and nineteenth centuries with something one finds already in the Romanticism of the Creuzers, Herder, Baader, Adam Müller, and in the political theory of the Spaniard Donoso Cortés, and whose prophetic eruption lasted into the middle of the nineteenth century: the primacy of objective being versus the (modern) primacy of critical knowledge; the primacy of membership in community versus "free individuality," which had been thought to constitute the "greatest happiness" for the children of the earth; the primacy of *mythos* and *mysterium* versus a "moral kingdom," which was Kant's highest vision; the primacy of a mythical, authoritarian state versus the *"contrat social,"* which always arises out of an agreement of free individuals and always renews itself in the same fashion (according to what is, essentially, the democracy of "majority decision"); and thus, finally, the primacy of the great symbols (whether these be the "hammer and sickle," the "fasces," the "star-spangled banner," etc.), the service of which endows every man with the dignity and glory of one who is "sworn in," versus a "civilization" that understands itself as the sanctuary of "man, who is an end unto himself," for whom all symbols are merely (as with Hegel) primitive and "quasi-sensible," and so must be "clarified" and "thoroughly spiritualized" into absolute "knowledge" in the movement of "judgment."

Seen in light of these historical paradigms, humanism and symbolism stand opposed to one another as, on the one hand, something personal and intramundane over against something impersonal[3] and supramundane. Each seeks to make the other subject to itself, or even to "clarify" the other into itself. A consistent humanism, for example (like that of Kant, but also like that of Hegel and Schelling, and now of Heidegger), will explain all objective symbols as objectifications of the "purely human," according to the deepest sense of transcendentalism, for which the "noumenal man" (and thus "man in the symbol") is the "defining goal *in infinitum*," almost in fact a kind of "limit concept" that lies "beyond" the "phenomenal and empirical" man as a kind of "immanent beyond," which appears to animate empirical humanity (including everything "all-too-human") and draw it onward by a "progress *in infinitum*" — almost in the same way that the empirical man "looks up" to authentic and objective symbols and allows himself to be "drawn along" by them. In this respect, humanism — in the medium of a "*transcendental* humanism" — becomes a "symbolic humanism," even though everything symbolic continues to be "anthropologized": transformed not, of course, into a vulgar and "static humanism" (that of "bourgeois humanity") but into, precisely, a heroic and "dynamic humanism," of the sort best exemplified by Nietzsche's "overman" — who is the "self-overcoming" and "self-overvaulting" of the "human" as such — whereas Goethe's humanism (with its conscious "self-contentment") stands firmly on the border of a "static humanism." A consistent symbolism, on the other hand (classically represented in the ritual order of China's "heavenly empire," in the *Ordo Romanus* of the *Imperium Romanum*, in the Byzantine empire, in the "Holy Roman empire" of the Middle Ages, and in the modern tendency towards an absolute authoritarian State — visible in the various Bolshevisms and fascisms, but also present secretly in the deepest impulses of an imperial America — all of which seek "order in the symbol"), regards the "humane" merely as "service rendered to the symbol" and a "realization of the symbol," even to the point of "sacrifice for the symbol." Thus, for example, in Soviet Russia the "humane" is supposed to be — and seeks to be — the presence and representation of a mythical "dialectical materialism," beneath which one is of course to perceive the presence and representation of the "native soil of Russia" itself with all of its earthly and antithetical passions. So, too, in America what is meant by the "humane" is that "explosive utopian humanism" that was announced by Walt Whitman and Thomas Wolfe as the humane presence and representation of a Niagaran and Missis-

3. *Es-haftes.* — Trans.

sippian "American Cosmos," whose *"mythos"* (and accompanying "symbol")
America's foremost political scientist, MacIver, has investigated, but was actually already at work at the inception of the USA, like the sacral *mythos* of
Calvin's *"Cité de Dieu,"* which the "pilgrim fathers" brought with them in the
Mayflower: the notion that America, which they thought of as the "new
earth" in the Bible's "new heaven and a new earth," is truly "God's own land,"
subject to a quintessentially Calvinistic God, who freely predestines to either
"damnation or beatitude," and who is thus the biblical God of the ever new
"turning" between "wrath" and "love." This God is the "mythical symbol"
that is then "symbolically expressed" in the "cataractic American" as God's
"elect": on the one hand, in that this American lives out his entire predes-
tined life according to the biblical-Calvinist "symbol of America," which
subjects him to the arbitrary determinations of Calvin's God, who casts him
where he will; but, on the other hand, in that this "indentured American"
can do nothing but himself give shape in his own personal life to the incomprehensible sovereignty of the American God and his Kingdom America, in
presence and representation, as is ultimately captured in the farcical image
of the "rough-elbowed, child-like American."

In view of these examples of humanism and symbolism crossing over
into one another — whereby a pure style of humanism is replaced by a
"symbolic humanism" and a pure style of symbolism is replaced by a *"humanistic symbolism"* — it becomes clear how the "personal," with its intramundane quality, invariably tends towards the supramundane "imperson-
ality" of the "symbol," and, equally, how the latter invariably tends towards
the personal and "intramundane" quality of the "humane." On the one
hand, a humanism of the inner universe of the individual "personality" (as
one finds in Thomas's view of man as a *"parvus mundus,"* or in Nicholas of
Cusa's view of man as a "microcosm") does not achieve its proper dynamic
unless the "symbol of man" becomes the "limit idea" toward which it strives,
making it a humanism of "progress *in infinitum*" and so an "asymptotic humanism." On the other hand, a symbolism is a living symbolism only to the
degree that its symbols, though they stand above life (as points of reference),
are nevertheless ever renewed "within" life (as "entelechies," as it were); and
to the degree that it takes human beings not merely as "bearers" of symbols
(in the way that in·the Communist East but also in America they are mere
"placard-bearers" for the "images of the leader" and various "slogans," etc.),
but springs up ever anew from living humanity itself: rising from a "symbol
in life" to a "symbol above life," from a "symbol of life" to a "symbol for life,"
from "life as the ground of the symbol's development" to "life as service ren-

dered to the symbol." A purely subjective empirical humanism (of an "ego" that "plays out its own life"[4] within its own internal contradictoriness amid the chaos of mutually contradictory "egos") is just as unrealizable as a kind of "humanism" as a purely objective ideative symbolism: of an "ὄντως ὄν," "that which truly has being," an impersonal, objective, ideal region — whether of the Platonic "εἴδη," or of the "exemplars" of early medieval thought, or of the Eastern Church's "icons," or of modern "ideas" or "essences" or "values" — over against the "μὴ ὄν," the "actual non-existence," of sensible human reality. The only thing that is real and realizable is the dynamically rhythmic oscillation of a movement back and forth between an intrinsically "symbolic humanism" and a "humanistic symbolism," for which a pure style of humanism and a pure style of symbolism are simply dynamic "limit concepts," providing an orientation for the movement "above-and-beyond" of the humane towards the symbol that lies "above" it, or for the "descent" of the symbol "into" the humane that lies "below it." The movement of humanism and symbolism toward one another takes place according to a rhythmic "in-and-beyond" — the same rhythm that oscillates *de facto* in the thought of Plato, and that Georg Simmel has consciously proposed as the ultimate rhythm of being: the rhythm of an *"analogia proportionalitatis proportionis."*[5]

II

At a material level, the question of the relation between humanism and symbolism thus becomes concrete in the relation between a "symbolic humanism" and a "humanistic symbolism"; and, at a formal level, in an "in-and-beyond" that obtains between the "life (of man)" and the "symbol (beyond and for man)." But not only do the rhythms implied in such an "in-and-beyond" — the rhythms of a "self-transcendence (of man to the symbol)" and a "descent-into (of the symbol to man)" — cross into one another, and condition one another, as "progress" (from the concrete human being to the symbol) and "regress" (from the symbol into the "fruitful βάθος" of the human); they are also maintained in a perpetually renewed movement (in, that is, a dynamic and fruitful "circular revolution"); and for this reason, with respect to the real concrete space of a real concrete humanity, a pure style of

---

4. *Eines sich-auslebenden Ich.* — Trans.
5. Cf. *Analogia Entis I* and the preceding essays 4-6.

humanism and a pure style of symbolism turn out to be, in light of this dynamic of progress and regress, nothing but limit-ideas, limit-concepts, and limit-forces. On the one hand, the humanity of man, universally understood, will express itself not only in terms of a concrete reality that itself stands within a qualitative "in-and-beyond" (in the "in-and-beyond" that exists between the human as man and the human as woman), but, in a way that transcends a personal humanity, in terms of an "in-and-beyond" with regard to the world *qua* humanity and the world *qua* universe (according to the law of the "world in-and-beyond the human being") — and this, finally, *qua* creatureliness (in and together with the world), and thus according to an ultimate "analogy of ever greater dissimilarity within every similarity, however great" (in the mode of "God in-and-beyond the creature as such"). On the other hand, at the "upper limit" of this threefold "in-and-beyond" that defines concrete reality (the rhythm of which progresses from the "in-and-beyond" between man and woman to the rhythm of a higher "in-and-beyond" between world and man, and, finally, to the rhythm of the highest "in-and-beyond" between the divine and the creaturely), one can begin to descry a "region of symbols," as it were, which comes into view as, so to speak, the "glory of something superpersonal"[6] (that of Thomas's *"Deus tanquam ignotus"* and Meister Eckhart's "pathless desert" of *"Deitas"*). Conversely, this impersonal "region of glory," which is intimated only through limit ideas and limit concepts (and in whose divine *gloria* the whole creaturely "glory of symbols" participates: from the "glory of the 'great man'" to the "glory of empire and nation" to the "glory of the world" to the "glory of artwork"), must continually renew its life from the "Antaean earth," so to speak, of the corresponding concrete realities (man, world, God), as the "glory of their reality." The question of the relation between humanism and symbolism thus reduces to a kind of phenomenology of this "reality" — one that would ultimately lead to the possibility of a phenomenology of this reality's "glory in the symbol." One may answer the question of the relation between humanism and symbolism definitively, then, by way of *a phenomenology that gradually proceeds from "man" to "world" to "God" to "symbol."*

The word *man* — and this is true of the Greek word "ἄνθρωπος" and the Latin word *"homo"* (and its derivatives in the Romance tongues, *"uomo," "homme,"* and *"hombre"*), as well as the German word *"Mensch"* (and its derivative the English word "man") — signifies not some universal "human es-

---

6. *Über-persönlich Eshaften.* — Trans.

sence," but "man" — "*Mann*" — in all his concrete diversity. "Man as woman"[7] is included in this inasmuch as in Genesis it is the man, Adam, who gives every living thing its "name"; and so to the one whom God derives from him, who is "the (objective) home built" (ᾠκοδόμησεν) for him and "conceived as an adequate counterpart (to Adam)" (βοηθὸς ὅμοιος αὐτῷ), he initially gives a name corresponding to "man" — "woman," "*Männin*" (*ischscha* from *isch*), before he names her "Eve," i.e., the "mother of the living" (*hawwa* from *hai*), thereby indicating her relation to the world of the living as the "womb (of life)" who in "bearing fruit" is to "fill" the earth, just as the man Adam is summoned to "rule throughout the earth" in the "office of the original head" of creation (Gen. 1:28; 2:19-23). Thus, if the word "man" — ἄνθρωπος, *homo, Mensch* — refers originally to *the* man — *Mann* — then it refers to him as one to whom the woman is so "joined" (as is even indicated by the meaning of her first name, "woman" or "*Männin*") that he is, conversely, for all his "office of lordship," essentially ordered to her "fruitfulness" and her "filling of the earth"; indeed, he himself, in his "office as lord," is essentially ordered "to" the woman — not simply in the sense that she becomes "one flesh" with him (as though simply "taken into possession" by him), but in precisely the reverse sense that he, the man, who "rules and officiates," "leaves his father and mother" (i.e., his ancestral "home") and cleaves to his wife, in order that together they might become one flesh (i.e., might be "made a single home," which is the very sign under which the woman came from the man). To be sure, the concrete sense of *the* "man" — "*Mann*" — in the word "man" — "*Mensch*" — (ἄνθρωπος, *homo*) includes the woman who comes from the man as "bone of my bone and flesh of my flesh," and thus as "name of my name" (in her original name, "woman" or "*Männin*"), but nevertheless in such a way that this secondary origin of the woman (from the primary origin of the man) truly "redeems" the man from his "loneliness," inasmuch as the woman is an "understanding counterpart" to him, and thus "completes" him in his essence and in his existence. What is more, inasmuch as the woman's secondary origin (as related to the primacy of the man's origin) redeems the man from his "loneliness" and completes him as an "understanding counterpart," such that the two become "one body" and "one house," the woman is included in the sense of the word

---

7. "*Mensch als Frau.*" Obviously, though, the point of this passage is the prior conceptual and philological synonymy of "*Mensch*" and "*Mann*" — understood as this "real concrete man" apart from any abstractions regarding the "human as such" — and this synonymy is then construed in terms of the priority of Adam. — Trans.

"man" in such a way that, though the primacy of origin belongs to the man, the primacy of completion belongs to the woman. One could say that they are related to one another in such a way that these two principles — that "the man is for the woman" and "the woman is for the man" ("γυνὴ διὰ τὸν ἄνδρα" and "ἀνὴρ διὰ τῆς γυναικός") (1 Cor. 11:9,12) — oscillate dynamically and rhythmically within a genuine "circular revolution" (κυκλοφορία of the κύκλος), as do the "ἀρχή" and "τέλος," the "origin" and "end and goal and meaning" of the universe, in obedience to the "domestic lawfulness" — the "οἰκονομία" — of the universe's "domestic nature." Indeed, they are related to one another in such a way that in them the universe, which is "always turned *(versum)* towards *one (uni),*" continually renews its living origin and roots: in the unity of an "understanding counterpart," and the unity of "one body," and the unity of "one house"; in such a way, finally, that this threefold unity of man and woman (though "wholly other" one to the other) becomes a dynamic and cyclical "exchange" of "authority," respectively, of the one over the other, in which "the wife does not have authority over her own body, but the husband does; likewise the husband does not have authority over his own body, but the wife does" (1 Cor. 7:4) — fully corresponding to the fact that the "universe" itself, as what is "ever turned toward *one,*" realizes this *"-versum"* of an ever new "turning" as an exchange between its antitheses: in an ever renewed unity of antitheses in "the concord of opposites" (τὸ ἀντίξουν συμφέρον) and in "the discord of the most beautiful harmony" (ἐκ τῶν διαφερόντων καλλίστην ἁρμονίαν) — ultimately, indeed, in "concord *as* discord" (συμφερόμενον διαφερόμενον), which is to say, in the rhythm of the universe as unveiled by Heraclitus.[8]

Thus, from a preliminary characterization of "man" — *Mensch* — as "man" — *Mann* — "man," understood as the subject and τέλος of any "humanism," we discover that man is, more profoundly, a "unity of opposites," a unity struck between man the "wholly other" and woman the "wholly other," a unity immediately transparent to a universe that is itself a "unity of opposites." Indeed, ultimately, so much is the universe a "coincidence of opposites" (a *coincidentia oppositorum,* following Nicholas of Cusa) and a "perfection within the diversity and difference of creatures" (*in diversitate creaturarum . . . perfectio universi,* following Thomas)[9] that the divine appears within it in an almost immediate fashion, as the "simplicity and unity" of the creaturely world, "which is multiple and diversely divided" (*quod*

8. Diels 22: 8, 10.
9. *De Pot.* q. 3, a. 16, corp.

multipliciter et divisim in aliis . . . , *in Ipso* . . . *simpliciter et unite,* again following Thomas).[10] In other words, a phenomenology of "man" — *Mensch*
— reveals "man" to be such a unity of opposites — the unity, that is, of "man
as the head (who rules and officiates)" and of "woman as the body (who
bears fruit and fills)," to the point of a "co-dependence and coinherence" and
an "exchange of opposites" — that this complete unity of opposites, which
"man" *is,* not only intrinsically "prefigures" the nature of "world" and
"God"; it does so also in such a way that all three realities — man, world, and
God — appear in terms of one and the same symbol: the symbol of "marriage," which (as the research of Josef Winthuis has shown) is both the primordial religious symbol of primitive cultures and the primordial symbol of
revelation found in the Old and New Testaments (extending from the centrality of the marriage between God and Israel in the prophets and in the
Song of Songs, to the centrality of the marriage of God in Christ to the
world, and then to the centrality of the "marriage of the lamb who is slain to
the New Jerusalem," understood as the formal mystery of the "new heaven
and new earth"). The inner coherence, then, of this entire sequence, "man,
world, God," is already to be found in its first term. The fact that any "humanism" of the "human being" is revealed to be a *"nuptial humanism"* (from
the relation between man as "wholly other" and woman as "wholly other," to
that of a dynamic, cyclical "exchange" between "head" and "body") makes
this very "nuptial humanism," in its transparency to the cosmic dimension
of the universe, a *"cosmic humanism"* of *"man in the cosmos,"* which, in turn,
points to a *"cosmism"*[11] *of the "cosmos beyond man"* — such that this cosmism of the "cosmos beyond . . ." almost coincides with the *"theism" of a*
"God . . . who is ineffably, super-sublimely beyond all things outside himself
and all that can be conceived,"[12] as we see in Thomas, who speaks almost interchangeably of the *propter quod*[13] of the universe and the *Propter Quod*[14]
of God.[15] What overarches this progression — from a nuptial humanism to
a cosmic humanism to theism — is the *one* symbol of "marriage": from
"nuptial humanity" to the "nuptial cosmos" (in the sense, ultimately, of

10. *Summa Th.* I, q. 13, a. 4, ad 5.

11. *Kosmismus.* — Trans.

12. Vatican Council, ch. 1. [In keeping with his own idiom and presumably to underscore the teaching of Vatican I, Przywara translates *excelsus* not simply as *"erhaben"* —
"lofty," "sublime," or "exalted" — but as *"über-erhaben."* — Trans.]

13. *Umseinetwillen.* — Trans.

14. *Um-Seinet-willen.* — Trans.

15. *De Pot.* q. 5, a. 4, corp.

Heraclitus's "harmony of opposites") to the "Divine Marriage" (which the inner bond between Old and New Testaments ultimately reveals to be "*agape as God*," i.e., within the medium of an oscillating "encounter and response" that is realized between God and man in Christ and as Christ — which is why John is ultimately able to say [1 John 4:8]: "God *is* [this] agape"). Seen in light of its intrinsic transcendence towards the cosmic and the divine (and thus in light of an increasing transcendence), it becomes manifest that a truly genuine humanism is "energetically" and "entelechically" guided, as it were, by the "*symbol of the agape of marriage*," the symbol that is the crown of all other symbols, however glorious — and thus to be guided by an equally genuine symbolism.

All of these connections are confirmed and deepened when viewed within a phenomenological investigation of what we mean by the word "*world*." Seen in connection with the verb "κοσμέω," the Greek word "κόσμος" has the connotation of something "well arranged" and "ordered," and thus, on the one hand, something "under control" but also, on the other hand, something placed "in the adornment (of order)." Accordingly, the word "κόσμος," taken as a word for world and universe, means "the entire universe, seen in light of the wonderful arrangement of the world and all its parts" (following I. G. Schneider's etymology). Thus, when one speaks of the world as "κόσμος" one means, so to speak, the face of day and the masculine face of the world:[16] its order being seen from the perspective of a "head" that imposes order, but seen also as the "order in its totality." The Latin word "*mundus*," on the other hand, likewise depicts the world as an "order" (especially in its patriarchal Roman usage), but it depicts this order as one arising "out of the elemental powers of nature"[17] in the form of "telluric powers":[18] since the Roman-Latin "*mundus*" is originally an Etruscan word for a "vaulted well" that stood at the center of every Etruscan city and represented its "connection to the underworld."[19] Whereas for the Greek cosmos, the (masculine) "order" of "arrangement" (symbolized by the Olympian god Zeus) is overlaid with the "luster of ornament" (properly symbolized by the vernal god Aphrodite, who emerges out of the foam of the seabed), the Roman-Latin "*mundus*" (whence the Romance words "*monde*" and "*mondo*"), designating a world of Roman order, springs principally from the "fount of the underworld" — this being the *one*

16. *Das Tag- und Mannes-Gesicht der Welt.* — Trans.
17. S. Cles-Reden, *Das versunkene Volk* (Innsbruck: Rohrer, 1948), p. 55.
18. Cles-Reden, *Das versunkene Volk*, p. 55.
19. Cles-Reden, *Das versunkene Volk*, p. 58.

symbol of Rome's maternal, chthonic Etruscanism, which is the mother soil (according to Cles-Reden) hidden beneath Rome's culture, its religion, and all its institutions. In the case either of the Greek "κόσμος" or of the Roman-Latin *"mundus,"* the world explicitly bears the features of the "human being" as existing "between man and woman": whereas in the case of the Greek "κόσμος" we see the features of a masculine order that is beautified by the feminine[20] (as symbolized by "Olympian Zeus in the grace of Aphrodite"), in the case of the Roman-Latin *"mundus"* we see a marked emphasis upon the masculine that is conscious of its origin in the maternal chthonic "fount of the underworld" — an origin that it therefore seeks to the utmost to subject to the masculine:[21] to drown out its chthonic Etruscan mother in the authority "over life and death" of the *"pater familias,"* to transform entirely the Etruscan form of government of the *"matres conscriptae"* into the Roman form of government of the *"patres conscriptae"* (whose symbol is no longer any kind of personal symbol, but only the impersonal symbol of *"virtus,"* according at least to Curtius, who sees Roman religion as the cult of this *"virtus,"* expressed principally in *"constantia,"* which suggests an almost static "endurance" and which, as such, stands in the sharpest possible contrast to Etruscan "intoxication" and "dance"). In comparison to the obviously masculine and feminine characteristics of the Greek "κόσμος" and the Roman-Latin *"mundus,"* the German *"Welt,"* together with the English "world," would seem to suggest a purely masculine form of the world: since *"Welt"* can be traced back to the old high German *"wer-alt"* — *"wer"* meaning a man "at arms" and *"alt"* (like the English "old") meaning the same thing as the Latin *"saeculum,"* in the sense of a particular "age," which is to say, positively, a particular period of world history that is rounded out into a "pure form" but also, at the same time, negatively, a period that is overshadowed by historical "transience." The Germanic word *"Welt"* thus oscillates between a "protective" masculinity (that would seek to "eternalize" its specific "age" and thus protect it "with arms" against every threat of destruction) and a dark consciousness of the perpetual historical change of "ages," such that — in keeping with the law "die and become!"[22] — the passing of every "age" not only gives rise to a "new age," but shows the deepest meaning of the passing of every "old age" to be the rise of the "new age": the death-pangs of every "old age" as simultaneously the birth-pangs of a "new age" (which accounts for the liturgy's confession of God's supertemporal eternity in intratemporal terms:

20. *Weiblich über-schönten Männlichen.* — Trans.
21. *Zu über-männlichen.* — Trans.
22. *Stirb und Werde!* From Goethe's poem *"Selige Sehnsucht."* — Trans.

as that which is *"per omnia saecula saeculorum,"* as that which sovereignly passes "through and beyond" all ages in their ever renewed change).

And yet, precisely in its foregrounding of a world that seems purely masculine (the "world-at-arms" of the "man-at-arms"), the span of the German word *"Welt,"* like the Greek word "κόσμος" and the Roman Latin word *"mundus,"* likewise implies an opposition between man and woman. The opposition, at its most basic, is contained in the syllable *"wer"* found in *"Welt"* (from *"wer-alt"*), which on its face means a "man-at-arms" (a *"Wehrmann"*). More fundamentally, however, implicit in this syllable *"wer"* is the additional connotation of that primitive Germanic "camaraderie" between man and woman: as is expressed, at the human level, by the custom of women also participating in battle, guarding the "wagon-barricade" while the men stood in open combat; and, at the mythological level, by the way in which this "camaraderie" is envisaged precisely as a "guardianship and comradeship-in-arms," inasmuch as the female "Valkyries" are sent by Wotan to assist the male warriors as "heavenly female co-combatants," as *"Wal-küren,"* which is to say, as heavenly powers that "decide" [*küren*] the victory on the "battlefield" [*Wal-statt*]; and since even "fate," *Schicksal,* which is what is "ultimate," i.e., primordially divine in Germanic (as well as in Greek and Roman) culture, rests in the hands of the female "Norns." Indeed, so little is the Germanic *"Welt"* a "man's world" that it is grounded ultimately in these female figures who command both victory and fate. Moreover, the implicit meaning of the syllable *"alt"* in *"Welt"* (in the sense, namely, of *"wer-alt"*) spans the difference between *"alt"* in the positive sense of "age" in its full meaning as a kind of "pure form" (corresponding to the sense of the ancient Roman *"saeculum"*) and *"alt"* in the negative sense of historical "transience" (corresponding to the ancient Christian understanding of *"saeculum"* as temporality in change and decline, which the book of Qoheleth depicts as "vanity of vanities" [Eccl. 1:2]). In the first, the positive and active sense, it is the "age" to which the "man-at-arms" commits himself in combat, in "service" to its ideal and its glory. In the second, the negative and passive sense, however, it is the age of the "pains of transience," understood as "birth-pangs," the pains that the eighth chapter of Romans reveals as the sign "of this age," whose peculiar sign is that of the woman who "endures the pangs of child-birth": death-pangs as birth-pangs. In this sense of the *"alt"* in *"wer-alt,"* man and woman stand together in the world *"in articulo mortis,"* in order to serve the world with "death before their eyes." But, whereas for the man it is specifically a "death in active struggle" as the sign of his engagement on behalf of the "age," *"Zeit-Alter,"* for the woman death is the "wholly other," a "death within a passive birth" and, as such, the sign not only of her bearing of the "child" in the "grief (of death)" (John 16:21) but, more profoundly, in her "rising in death" of her co-bearing and re-bearing of the "age."

But then — in passing from the Greek "κόσμος" and the Roman Latin *"mundus"* to the Germanic *"Welt"* — "nuptial humanism" passes over into a *"synergistic cosmism"*: one, that is, of the "syn-ergy," the "co-operation," of man and woman. Here the masculine appears as the foreground (in "κόσμος" insofar as it means "order"; in the patriarchal overtones of *"mundus"*; in the "world-at-arms" of the "man-at-arms" in *Welt*); whereas the feminine constitutes the profounder "back-ground" and "under-ground," or even the "fulfillment" (in "κόσμος" it appears as "the radiance of ornament"; in *"mundus"* as the primal "mother-soil"; in the "world-at-arms" of *Welt* as "holding the office of guardianship at the rear of battle," as "holding the power of victory in battle," and finally as "holding the office of fate" in every life and every pursuit and every battle). Whereas a "nuptial humanism," in its transcendent orientation to the cosmic and the divine, received its "energy" and "entelechy" from the "symbol of marital agape," a "cosmic humanism," in the sense of an explicit "cosmism," is manifestly determined by the *"symbol of marriage and the family."* In this symbol, the masculine and the feminine signify a single "authority," one that entails an alternating precedence of each in regard to the other — an alternating function and primacy of the "ἀρχή" and "origin" and "primal domain" proper to the patri-arch-al and matri-arch-al "authority" of "fatherhood" (πατρι-ἀρχή) and "motherhood" (ματρι-ἀρχή). And, finally, in this co-operative structure of a world that is both masculine and feminine — and in, precisely, the word "marriage," *"Ehe"* in the sense of "eternal," *"ewe"* — we see a revelation of the eternity of the divine itself (to the point that Old and New Testament revelation alike explicitly call "God's covenant with his people" a "marital covenant" between God, the "husband," and the people and the world, his "wife" (Hos. 2:4-18). The symbolism of a "cosmic marriage in God" is thus intrinsic to a "cosmic humanism" *qua* "cosmism," providing it with its proper energy and entelechy.

Thus far we have seen how, transcending itself, a personal "nuptial humanism" leads to the cosmic level of "cosmic marriage." We have also seen how, within a "cosmic humanism" *qua* "cosmism," the "eternity" of the divine is almost immediately manifest within the *"ewe"* of the world *qua* "cosmic marriage" (as accords with Nicholas of Cusa, for whom the universe, as a *"coincidentia oppositorum,"* immediately gives rise to a notion of the divine as the "simplicity and uniformity" of what, in the creaturely realm, presents itself as "multiple, separate, and diverse," even to the point that for him God and world are related to one another as *"implicatio"* and *"explicatio")*. But if this is so — if, in transcending itself, a "nuptial humanism" leads to the divine, and if the divine also manifests itself within a "cosmic humanism" *qua* "cosmism" — then what is ultimate must be a kind of phenomenology of the divine: a "theo-phenomenology," to which an anthropo-phenomenology and a cosmo-phenomenology lead, and in which both are fulfilled (as was already prefigured by an immanent consideration of anthropo-phenomenology and cosmo-phenomenology).

According to the comparative linguistic "research" of the unjustly forgotten Muys (who traces Western languages to their Sanskrit and Semitic roots), the German word *"Gott"* (in English "God"), like the Greek word "Θεός" and the Roman-Latin word *"Deus"* (which leads in the Romance languages to *"Dio," "Dieu,"* and *"Dios"*), does not mean "god" in the sense of something "good"; nor does it mean what is suggested by the connection of the words "θεός" and *"Deus"* to the verb "θεᾶσθαι," the "pure gaze" of Platonic contemplation, a "pure visibility," and thus, as it were, the "archetypal εἶδος" of Plato's "pure εἴδη"; it means, rather, "spirit," *"Geist."* Accordingly, "God" as "spirit" is included within the full range of meanings proper to the word "spirit"; and in this respect certain languages are decisive. From the beginning of Genesis, the Hebrew word for "spirit," *"ruach,"* stands in the utmost proximity to the words *"rechem"* and *"racha,"* which mean, respectively, "womb" and "to brood": "at the beginning of creation, the Spirit of God hovered over the chaos of the waters' deeps," revealing thereby — through the correlation of *"ruach," "rechem,"* and *"rachaph"* — that the "Spirit of God" (πνεῦμα Θεοῦ) is the mystery of the birth of this creation; we see this same "hovering" of the "Spirit of God" over Mary, which is announced by the angel as the effective basis of the incarnation — through the "Holy Spirit" "coming upon" her, and through her being "overshadowed" by the "power of the Most High" (Luke 1:35) — all of which expresses the mystery of the birth of the "new creation in Christ"; we see this same "hovering" of the "Holy Spirit" over the Lord in the Jordan, where sinners are baptized, signifying that the mystery of the birth of this "new creation in Christ" is a messianic creation, which remains under the sign of the "lamb, who bears the sins of the world" (and thus, of the "lamb who is slain" — Matt. 3:16f.; John 1:29-33); so too, therefore, the Holy Spirit's "coming upon" the apostles in order that all might be "filled with the Holy Spirit" (Acts 1:8; 2:4) announces the final mystery of the birth of the messianic "new creation in

Christ": from the "groaning" "correspondence"[23] of the "Spirit" (of God and Christ) to the "groaning" of the "labor pains" of the "entire creation" to the "new heaven and new earth" of the "freedom of the glory of the children of God" (Rom. 8:18-26). The word "πνεῦμα," therefore, which is used in the Septuagint to translate the Hebrew "ruach," includes not only the sense of a sudden "inrush" (as in John 3:8: "The Spirit blows [like a storm] wherever it wills"), but also and precisely the sense of "gasping," which complements the sense of a "blowing storm" with the additional connotation of the "groaning induced by labor pains." For its part, the Roman-Latin word "spiritus" (which, in the Romance languages, evolves into "esprit," "espiritu," and the English word "spirit") underscores the sovereign "freedom of the Spirit" (cf. 2 Cor. 3:17) as conveyed in the image of a "freely blowing wind" (as John 3:8 says — of both the "wind" and the "Holy Spirit" — "you know not whence it comes nor whither it goes"). The final meaning of the word "spirit" is then found within a particular nuance of the German word "Geist," which first emerges in the English word "ghost": namely, that the positively sovereign "spiriting" of the "Spirit," and the "filling" with the "Spirit," become uncannily indistinguishable from the "spiriting about" of "spirits," i.e., a "haunting" by "ghosts" (as the English word "ghost" suggests). As a result, the sovereign "freedom of the Spirit," which most clearly indicates a genuine "divine sovereignty," enters into a twilight of meaning, conveying the sense of something "uncanny" that befalls one in a "surprising" way and, at the same time, the sense of something that is "intangible" like "empty air."

"God" as "Spirit" thus expresses the entire range of meanings, which the words for "spirit" in all the critical languages variously attempt to grasp (as when Christ says of his Father in John 4:24 that "God is Spirit" [πνεῦμα ὁ θεός]; or when Luke 4:18 says that the "χρῖσμα" of Christ, his "anointing" as the messiah or the "anointed one," is the Holy Spirit himself; or when 2 Corinthians 3:17 says of Christ himself that "the Lord is Spirit"). Certainly, God is "Spirit" in the sense meant by the Greek and, likewise, the Pauline "νοῦς": namely, spirit in the sense of "mind,"[24] which constitutes a highest point beyond both theoretical "νόησις" (active "thought") and practical "φρόνησις" ("the right sense about life"). On the one hand, "mind" is personal, as in Romans 11:34, where Paul speaks of the "mind" of a God whose judgments are unsearchable; and in 1 Corinthians 2:16, where, throughout his discourse on the "foolish madness" and "scandal" of the mystery of the Cross, he de-

23. *Mit-Entgegnen.* — Trans.
24. *Geist-Sinn.* — Trans.

clares this "mind of the Lord" to be the "mind of Christ." On the other hand, "mind" has an ideal, impersonal[25] sense, in the way that Plato conceives of this "mind" as a "τόπος νοητός," as the "site" of the ideas; or in the way that classical scholasticism regards God as the site of the eternal *"ideae rerum,"* the original ideas of all things; or, then again, in the way that Kant sees God as the *"intellectus archetypus"* of the "transcendental ego"; or, finally, in the way that Hegel conceives of God as "absolute *Geist*," which "dialecticizes" itself into everything creaturely and in everything creaturely. But "God" is equally "Spirit" in a sense peculiar to the revelation of the Old and New Testaments: in the sense, that is, of the ineffable mystery of "divine fruitfulness," whereby "God in Christ," "in the Spirit of God and Christ," is the original source of the "power[26] to become children of God" (John 1:12) — a "fruitfulness" that comes from our "being overshadowed by the Holy Spirit" and from the "labor pains" we suffer along with the "whole creation," as the "first fruits of the Spirit" who "intercedes" with "groans" [on our behalf]" (Rom. 8:18-26).

Within the phrase "Spirit is God" we thus discover a span of meanings that is adumbrated in the creaturely-human span between an ideative, masculine spirituality and a vital-fruitful, feminine spirituality; and this latter span may be regarded as a genuine transparency to the former span in that God himself, in his revelation, reveals himself both as a "father" and as a "mother." But this span within "the spiritual," considered in its properly "intelligible" aspect, is intersected by another span that concerns the "spiritual" in its, so to speak, "energetic" aspect. Without question, "God" is "(energetic) Spirit" in the sense revealed by the image of the "wind blowing where it will" (as we see in πνεῦμα and *spiritus* and in the *Geist* that "spirits about like the wind"): thus the word "Spirit" expresses that absolutely *sovereign* freedom upon which God's divinity, in the sense of his "measureless majesty," stands or falls: as we see above all in the book of Job and the first eleven chapters of Romans, which hymnically declare all things to be determined by this sovereignty, which is absolute and, precisely for this reason, "unsearchable and inscrutable": "from him and to him and for him are all things: To him be the glory [forever]" (Rom. 11:36). But this is precisely what leads to the most incisive and downright "scandalous" expression of God's absolute sovereignty (in the sense of the "σκάνδαλον": "an offense that leads either to life or to death"), which is hinted at in the etymological proximity

---

25. *Es-hafter.* — Trans.
26. *Seins-Vollmacht.* — Trans.

of the German word *Geist* to *Geistern* (the uncanny "haunting" of something *Geisterhaft*, "ghostly") and expressed in the English distinction, indeed, confusion between "spirit" and "ghost." Traversing every opposition between "good spirit" and "evil spirit," between "God-Spirit" and "God-Ghost," it ultimately pervades the revelation of the Old and New Testaments (it is there in Moses' valedictory song, in Mary's Magnificat, in Romans, and in all the fundamental rhythms of the book of Revelation) as a stupendous and earth-shaking, primordial apocalypse: the shocking confession of a God who "kills and makes alive, who leads [souls] into the underworld and back again" (Deut. 32:39; Tob. 13:2; Wis. 16:13, etc.), to the point that God appears (tyrannically and disturbingly) "arbitrary and unjust" (Rom. 9:14).

The mystery expressed in the phrase "Spirit is God" is thus adumbrated by this double opposition — an opposition that is crossed through in the form of a "pneumatic cross," as it were: in the form of a *"coincidentia oppositorum,"* which is like the "curtain before the Holy of Holies" itself, drawn before the mystery of God. In this regard it is most fitting to say with Augustine: "If you comprehend it, it is not God."[27] If our investigations of the connotations of the words "man" and "world" yielded, respectively, notions of "nuptial agape" (proper to a "nuptial humanism") and of "marital covenant" (proper to a "synergetic cosmo-humanism"), and if each of these, in turn, was shown to be a medium transparent to the divine, then this transcending movement reaches its completion in the double opposition we find in the meaning of the word "spirit." For whereas "spirit" in the active and personal sense implies a "spiritual spontaneity" that, in the creaturely realm, characterizes "the spirit of the man," "spirit" in the sense of the "fruitfulness of labor pains" signifies something distinctive to "the spirit of the woman." Correspondingly, whereas in the creaturely realm the "spirit of lordly sovereignty" expresses something characteristic of "the spirit of the man," the abrupt dialectical antithesis of a "spirit who kills and makes alive" seems to convey something of "the spirit of the woman," which seems to show itself within the creaturely realm as an "abrupt, incalculable transformation." As a result, one is presented with a paradox: that, although the "spirit" cannot be other than "supra-sexual," the qualitatively positive reality of sexual difference is nevertheless the medium in which the essence of "spirit" is incomprehensibly and comprehensibly manifest. And this paradox, which is proper to "spirit" in and of itself, is intensified by the paradox of "God as Spirit," which we find in the revelation of the Old and New Covenants. Ac-

27. *Serm.* 117, 3, 5.

cording to this paradox, the God "whom no one has ever seen" (John 1:18) and "who dwells in unapproachable light" (1 Tim. 6:16), such that he "is not God, if you comprehend Him," this God, that is, who is "super-sublimely beyond all things outside himself and all that can be conceived" (as the Vatican Council defines it), this God of complete incomprehensibility — who is essentially "incomprehensible Spirit" (John 3:8) — is apparent in the features of the difference between the "spirit of the man" and the "spirit of the woman": thus, in the language of revelation, he is referred to not only as "Father," but also as a "mother" who "comforts and cares for [her] children" (Isa. 66:13); similarly, he appears not only as the "Lord of the house, [with power] over life and death" (cf. Isa. 45:7), but also in the "labor pains" suffered by the "mother of the house," as the "mother of all life" (cf. Rom. 8:19-27). If a "nuptial humanism" (proper to "man") stood under the sign of the "marital agape (between bridegroom and bride)," and if a "synergetic cosmic humanism" *qua* "cosmism" falls under the higher sign of the "marital covenant," then the summit of a genuine theism, to which a "nuptial humanism" and a "synergetic cosmism" transcendently point, is to be found in the highest sign of all, a "creativity at once paternal and maternal." Thus the "pneumatic cross" of a double opposition, both within "spirit" and within "God as Spirit," reveals itself to be the "tree of life" in the highest sense (just as the old legends and hymns salute the gift of the "tree of life" restored in the "tree of the Cross": *"haec est arbor dignissima in paradisi medio situata"*).[28]

But whereas both our "nuptial humanism" and our "synergetic cosmism" were guided by their symbols (whether the symbol of "marital *agape*" or of "marital covenant"), such that each received its energy and its entelechy from these symbols, in the case of the double opposition of the paternal and maternal within the very essence of "spirit," it is only in its initial appearing that one can approach it as a "symbol pointing to the divine"; for the very "opening" of this symbol is itself a direct "opening" upon the "βάθη τοῦ θεοῦ," the "depths of the unsearchable and inscrutable God," which "the Spirit of God" alone "searches and finds out" (Rom. 11:33; 1 Cor. 2:10-12). To say that a "symbol points to the divine" is to say that the "similarity" in such a symbol, "however great," is abruptly crossed through by an "ever greater dissimilarity" — between every "symbol, no matter how similar to the divine," and God, the *"ens realissimum,"* who is so truly the "reality of realities" that he is "super-sublimely beyond all things outside himself and all that can

---

28. This is that noble tree, planted in the midst of paradise. — Trans.

be conceived."[29] A "symbol pointing to the divine" is essentially a "symbol pointing to the infinite and incomprehensible." Here, however, it is quite the reverse: far from it being the case that theism *qua* "paternal-maternal theism" is "guided" by the symbol of a "paternal spirit and a maternal spirit," as though it received its proper energy and entelechy from this symbol, it is rather that in its deepest essence this supreme symbol appears as something "bestowed" out of the "depths of God"[30] himself (as is clearly stressed in the revelation of the Old and New Testaments: in God's freely bestowing the "power to become children of God" — John 1:12). Not only that, but — what is more — this supreme symbol, precisely as the highest thing that may be said of the "Most High," signifies what is "thrown (-bol)" "together (sym-)" into the "depths of God" himself: into the "depths" of his paternal and maternal, creative and parturient "Spirit," who "comes you know not whence and goes you know not whither," and who alone "searches and fathoms the deep things of God."

This automatically brings us to the meaning of the word *"symbol."*[31] Symbol does not mean (as the usual interpretations would have it) the "coming together" of two parts of some object that, in being united, allow two persons, each of whom possesses one of those parts, to recognize one another as "legitimate." Nor does "symbol" mean a sensible reality that, taken in its entirety, is transparent to a spiritually intelligible reality (as one finds in Hegel, Schleiermacher, and the Catholic "modernism" that developed out of them, inasmuch as they take every objective sensible aspect, whether of extra-Christian *mythos* or revealed Christianity, to be nothing but a "mythological symbol" for a spiritual posture of the human being). On the contrary, "symbol" signifies the "co-" (sym-) in the "co-incidence" (-bol, in the sense of "βάλλω") of a reality and its indwelling "meaning": such that, on the one hand, the reality itself, by expressing this meaning, seems to exist completely

29. Vatican Council, ch. 1.

30. *Ungründen Gottes.* — Trans.

31. For a more precise concept of "symbol," see my discussion above in "Image, Likeness, Symbol, Mythos, Mysterium, Logos." No one has developed the central meaning of "symbol" more convincingly than the great German scholar of Rome, Ludwig Curtius, in his *Das Antike Rom* (1944), where he first brings to light what is properly distinctive to the *"religio Romana"* (as opposed to what is otherwise borrowed from the Etruscans and Greeks): the *"religio"* of the great Roman symbols of virtue — from *"virtus"* to *"pietas"* to *"concordia"* to *"aequitas"* to *"constantia"* — which constitutes the *"Genius populi Romani."* Cf. the rich posthumous collection *Torso*, collected and edited by Joachim Moras (Stuttgart: Deutsche Verlagsanstalt, 1957), pp. 114-18.

for the sake of this "meaning" (hence, etymologically, "σύμβολον" carries the sense of "ensign," i.e., that in which a divine mandate or mission is announced; or the sense of a "mark of identification" or "seal," given in pledge of an eventual encounter or as the guarantee of a treaty concluded between nations); but, on the other hand, however much it may dwell "in" the reality as a "symbolic reality," the "symbol in itself" nevertheless transcends this reality, so as to constitute that reality's "entelechy," as it were, in order, by virtue of its transcending of this reality, to "dynamize" this reality with a power to transcend itself. In other words, the "symbol" is neither exhausted in the "symbolic reality," nor is it something purely "ideative in itself." Rather, the relationship between "symbol" and "symbolic reality" is that of the "analogy" of the Fourth Lateran Council: the analogy of an "ever greater dissimilarity" in every "similarity, however great."[32] On the one hand, the "symbol" appears to be almost identical with the "symbolic reality": this is its "similarity, however great." On the other hand, every "symbolic reality" is always only asymptotically "underway" beyond itself toward the "pure symbol in itself": this is that "ever greater dissimilarity" between the "symbolic reality" and the "pure symbol in itself."

In this sense, the "agape of marriage" is the "pure symbol" towards which every humanism (understood as an essentially "nuptial humanism") is perpetually "striving," as towards its "ideal sense *in infinitum.*" Likewise, the "marital covenant" is the "pure symbol" toward which every cosmic humanism or cosmism (as an essentially "synergetic cosmism") is underway, as toward its "ideal sense *in infinitum.*" The case is different, however, with regard to the divine, which is distinguished by signifying, on the one hand, complete *"perfectio"* — i.e., the essentially changeless "Is" and the "whole" — but also, on the other hand, that which is incomprehensibly infinite — i.e., that which, according to Augustine, "is always sought anew even when it is found, because it is infinite."[33] Consequently, for this divine "perfection *qua* infinity," the order of "symbol" and "symbolic reality" is reversed (as accords with the "complete otherness" that obtains between Creator and creature). On the one hand, the divine reveals itself to human beings always and exclusively in "symbols" (in the symbolic myths one finds outside of Christianity, as well as in the "images" and "likenesses" and "parables" that one finds within Christianity; such is the language of the prophets, and in fact of Christ himself,

32. See above, "Metaphysics, Religion, Analogy" and "Phenomenology, Realogy, Relationology."

33. *In Jo. Tract.* LXIII, 1.

who not only employs such language himself, but who, in Matthew 13:10ff., 34ff., declares it to be a principle: a principle that quite logically culminates, in 1 Corinthians 13:12, in the statement that "now we see as in a glass [riddle] darkly"). On the other hand, however, even the most exalted revelations (in which the "images" and "likenesses" and "parables" appear to pass over into a supersensible meaning to which they have been "opened") are never more than an advance into ever more impenetrable veils of *"mysterium"* (such is even the case with the simple *mysterium* of the "Father, Son, and Holy Spirit," which not only becomes transparent to the complete incomprehensibility of the *"relationis oppositio"* — as the Council of Florence of 1441 phrased it — but even becomes transparent through, over, and beyond this to the "night" of the *"Mysterium Mysteriorum"* as such, which John of the Cross hymnically proclaims as the ultimate). The energizing *telos* of any humanism and any cosmism is to be found in the "symbol" of a humanistic and cosmic symbolism. A true theism of "God as Spirit," on the other hand, will certainly employ a theistic symbolism as the language of its manifestations and revelations "to that which is below," but ultimately, since the "depths of God" reside within these manifestations and revelations, it will also use such language to speak "towards that which is above," in an "ever greater" transparency to an "ever greater God," to the *"Mysterium Mysteriorum"* that lies through, over, and beyond even his greatest manifestations and revelations. In this sense, one could venture to say that what is signified by the word "symbol" attains its highest fulfillment or, better, its highest origin, in just such a divine *Mysterium Mysteriorum*: since the in-and-beyond of the "symbol" is immediately transparent to the in-and-beyond of the Divine *Mysterium Mysteriorum* that resides in-and-beyond all divine manifestations and revelations, however great. But if the in-and-beyond of the "symbol" is rooted in "humanity" and the "world" as their "upper limit," the *Mysterium Mysteriorum* is even more rooted in the reality of God as the *"ens realissimum,"* whereat and wherein it appears as unapparent — not in the form of a "God-symbol," nor even in the form of "God in the symbol," but as a "symbol" in the sense of the "babbling of a babe," according to 1 Corinthians 13:11 — the babbling of the *Mysterium Mysteriorum.*

8 The Religious Gnoseology of St. Augustine

1958

1. What is meant in German by an *"Erkenntnis-Theorie"* — a "theory of knowledge" — or what the Romance peoples mean by "gnoseology" can assume four distinct forms.

Its most well-known form is the one that can be traced back to Descartes, from whom it was passed down by way of European rationalism (above all in Christian Wolff), and thereafter by way of neo-scholasticism and critical realism (which goes back to Külpe and concludes with Wenzel). In this case, a "theory of knowledge" or "gnoseology" figures as a *preamble* to *"philosophia prima,"* as we see in Descartes, who arrives by way of his "universal, methodical doubt" at the *"cogito ergo sum,"* and thus at what is indubitably "fundamental." With Descartes, this foundation then becomes the critical starting point for a philosophy that exalts a sovereign *"cogito"* (proper to a strictly mathematical way of thinking) above the reality of a pure *"massa extensa."* To be sure, this latter reality is genuine; but it is a reality that is grounded by the *"cogito,"* to which, consequently, it is subject — subject, that is, as "matter" (even plants and animals being understood as "mechanisms") to the *"cogito,"* understood as a determinative formal principle, the formal principle of an "engineer and technician" who shapes out of "passive matter" a rational-technical world, the very world that today threatens to become the whole of reality (displacing the autonomously real "cosmos" that incorporates spirit and man within itself, as fellow members along with matter, plants, and animals). Admittedly, European rationalism, neo-scholasticism, and critical realism do not entertain this ultimate conclusion

This essay first appeared in *Augustinus, Rivista trimestrial,* Madrid (1958).

(which makes Descartes, in a direct sense, the true "father" of the omnivorous technology of our day), but construct a theory of knowledge that begins explicitly with "methodical doubt," in order thereby, on the basis of this *minimum* of "self-consciousness," to penetrate through the essential intentionality of "sense-consciousness" to a reality that is independent of consciousness — a reality that would then constitute the object of a "philosophy of the regions of being" (from a metaphysics of being as such to a metaphysics of vegetal life to a metaphysics of sentient life to a metaphysics of man to a metaphysics of the divine).

The problem with a preambulatory *"prima philosophia"* of this sort, however, is that, properly speaking, it does not authentically preserve what is meant by the terms "theory of knowledge" and "gnoseology": since this kind of philosophy functions merely as a transition to "philosophy proper," which is concerned with reality. According to the literal meaning of the phrase, a "theory of knowledge" means an inner contemplation ("θεωρία" coming from "θεωρεῖν," in the sense of "pure vision") of "knowledge in itself," which is undertaken for its own sake and ultimately leads to a doctrine of the "structure" of "consciousness in itself." Similarly, according to its proper etymology, "gnoseology" means an investigation of the inner "logos" of "gnosis" according to its inner *"logy,"* i.e., an "investigation into the meaning" of the "inner sense of knowledge as such." This basic type of an *autonomous theory of knowledge* or *gnoseology* can be seen in Kant's three *Critiques*, above all in *The Critique of Pure Reason*, which explicitly presupposes the existence of a genuine reality, but only in order to undertake a strict investigation of the conditions for a "knowledge of reality." This is the same kind of theory of knowledge or gnoseology that the early Husserl intended in proposing a "regional phenomenology of knowledge" through a "bracketing of reality" (from the perspective of an "ἐποχή" or method of initial "arrest").

Such "regional phenomenology of consciousness in itself," however (as can be found in Hegel's *Phenomenology of Spirit* as well as in the late Husserl's "phenomenology of egological monadological consciousness"), continually exhibits an almost innate tendency to posit itself as absolute in the form of a speculative idealism: one in which consciousness and knowledge are no longer intentionally directed toward a reality independent of consciousness, but rather understand themselves as the "sole" reality, or at least as reality in the "proper" sense, the reality of "ideal being's" own "ὄντως ὄν" over against the "μὴ ὄν" of sensible "real being" (thus reprising the guiding logic of Plato's thought). For this kind of speculative idealism, which takes the form of an *absolute theory of knowledge* (or *gnoseology*), the internal universe of consciousness — or, more specifically, the internal material-noematic and formal-noetic universe of consciousness — is understood as, in an immediate sense, the "universe in itself" (whether in its noematic structures, as Husserl intended, or in the noetic act proper to it, which Hegel conceived in terms of his rhythmic dialectical "ternary" of judgment: thesis to antithesis to synthesis). For this kind of *ideal* "universe in itself," a *real* "universe in itself" is at best the "apparent reality of the senses" — a reality that remains fundamentally "bracketed out" (as in the late Husserl), or is regarded as the "self-alienation" of the "Spirit of a spiritual universe," i.e., as the "fall" from which this same "Spirit" must redeem itself by means of an ascetical spiritual detachment, whereby it is sublated again into its primordial being as Spirit: into "absolute knowledge" of "absolute Spirit" (as is vividly displayed in the successive stages of Hegel's *Phenomenology of Spirit*: passing from the "phenomenal realm of the senses" to the "noumenal realm of the Spirit").

This self-referential theory of knowledge or gnoseology[1] represents a particular extreme (which purports to be in and of itself the only philosophy and metaphysics), and it stands in the sharpest possible contrast to any theory of knowledge concerned solely with the proper "method" necessary for an accurate knowledge of the objectively real in its ultimate foundations. This sort of *methodological theory of knowledge* or *gnoseology* lies at the basis of what is called, in East Asia, "wisdom" — a wisdom available only by way of a particular "path" (hence, in East Asia, such "wisdom" is itself called a "path" or "way" or "vehicle": as one sees, for example, in classical China, in the ancient text of the *I Ching*, in the *Tao-Te-Ching* of Lao-Tzu, and in the dialogues of Chuang-Tzu; or, in classical India, in the *Vedas* and in the discourses of Gautama Buddha). Here we have the various "doctrines of stages," concerning an increasing detachment from the senses and — still more — an increasing detachment from the self, which then enters into Western moral, ascetical, and mystical works by way of the School of Alexandria. But this sort of method is familiar to us, also, from the Old Testament wisdom literature: thus, for example, "living according to the law" is the way by which one comes to participate in "Divine Wisdom." Even the strict emphasis upon the "μωρία" (literally, the "folly") of God that one finds in 1 Corinthians terminates precisely in an emphasis upon a "wisdom of God veiled in a mystery," a wisdom that is accessible not to the "man of the flesh," who is inclined to "jealousy and quarreling," but solely to the "spiritual man" in

---

1. *Selbstzwecklich.* — Trans.

words "taught by the (Holy) Spirit" (1 Cor. 1:21–3:3). On these foundations, Clement of Alexandria goes on to develop the "way" of a "faithful gnosis" and a "gnostic faith,"[2] one defined, on the one hand, by a negative "dispassion" (ἀπάθεια)[3] and, on the other, by a positive "mutual and reciprocal love" (ἀγάπη),[4] to the point that *"gnosis"* and *"agape"* not only pass over into the "vision of God" (θεωρία),[5] but constitute, as it were, its "anticipation" (πρόληψις).[6] From here, the development of this particular methodology of knowledge not only passes (by way of Augustine and Anselm of Canterbury) to Thomas Aquinas,[7] but branches off, from the seventeenth century onward, towards Nietzsche, in a "moral methodology" for which the distinct forms of human disposition are the preconditions of genuine knowledge — to the point that the great Romantic Franz von Baader could categorically posit "wonder" and "eros" against Descartes's "universal doubt" as the decisive starting point for philosophy; this was a genuine renewal of the thought of Plato, who made "wonder" (θαυμάζειν),[8] detachment from pleasure and grief,[9] and even an induction "by way of dying" into the mysteries[10] a condition for the vision of truth. This entire development then reaches its classic conclusion in Cardinal Newman's method of a real knowledge of the real in his *Grammar of Assent* (as a doctrine of those internal "dispositions" whereby truth and reality can alone be grasped). Finally, this ascetical religious method of knowledge (from the *I Ching* to Baader to Newman) can be found in its secularized form in contemporary phenomenology: thus Husserl demands a "self-abstention from empirical reality" (ἐποχή) for the sake of authentic knowledge; so too, along the same lines, Max Scheler makes a point of "holding oneself open"; and even Heidegger's method of "destruction,"[11] which seeks to penetrate through all the conventions of *"das Man"* to something primordial, can be understood in these terms. Even the radical logicism of Carnap's school, though it regards a purely mathematical logic as the only valid philosophy and dismisses all

2. *Stromateis* II, 4; V, 1; VII, 10.
3. *Stromateis* VI, 9; IV, 23.
4. *Stromateis* IV, 18; VII, 2, 10, 11.
5. *Stromateis* IV, 6; κτλ.
6. *Stromateis* VI, 9.
7. Cf. *De Ver.* q. 14, a. 10.
8. *Theatetus* 155c-d.
9. *Phaedo* 82e-83e.
10. *Phaedo* 61d, 64a, etc.
11. *Destruierung.* — Trans.

metaphysical questions as so much nonsense, nevertheless carries within itself, consciously or not, and despite itself, the ancient tradition of a methodological theory of knowledge: since, in its pure mathematicism, it is still only a secularization of "pure number" and is thus bound to the cosmic vision of Pythagorean metaphysics.

Each of the four forms of a theory of knowledge (or gnoseology), however, bears within it a distinctly *religious substrate,* the very existence of which contradicts the claim each makes to being philosophy's methodological starting point, from which the question of the divine would emerge only as something ultimate. In point of fact, in keeping with the positive meaning of the so-called "ontological proof of God's existence" (from its origins in Augustine to its more explicit formulation in Anselm of Canterbury and Malebranche and others), the "ultimacy" of the divine is already implied in the "primacy" of any theory of knowledge — and implied in such a way that one could almost see it as the immanent *a priori* within the various starting points for a theory of knowledge.

In the case of the *Cartesian epistemology of the pure "cogito,"* as the preamble to a *"philosophia prima,"* this is betrayed by the immediate manifestation of the divine (in genuine continuity with the tradition of the ontological proof) within the *"sum"* of the *"cogito,"* wherein the divine appears as primordial being — *Ur-Seiendes* — and as the starting point for any advance to cosmic reality. The divine, which is simultaneously regarded as the "original truth" and the "original spiritual reality," is found to be the "innermost interiority" of the *"cogito ergo sum."* As such, the divine is what it was for German mysticism: a radical Augustinian *"Deus interior"* (but one that abolishes the properly Augustinian dialectic between the *"Deus interior"* and the *"Deus exterior"*).[12] Thus the philosophical "interiority" of a philosophy rooted in the *"cogito,"* understood as the "interior of the interior," is grounded in the *a priori* of a religious "interiority" wherein alone the "original interiority" of the human being is to be found: in the "God who is more inward than I am to myself" (as Augustine also prays: *"Tu interior intimis meis"*).[13]

The *a priori* assumption of a religious "interiority of the interior" — an interiority, that is to say, that is grounded "in God as the 'interior of the interior'" — is even more constitutive in the cases both of an *autonomous* and of an *absolute theory of knowledge* (or gnoseology): thus Hegel (in his *History of Philosophy*) presents the "new philosophy" (running from Descartes to

---

12. Cf. *De. Gen. ad Litt.* VIII, 26, 48.
13. *In Ps.* 118, 22, 6.

Leibniz to Kant to its culmination in Hegel himself) as the "philosophical working out," so to speak, of the Reformation's "religion of interiority" (and, in point of fact, Luther opposed a free, autonomous "interiority" to the "exteriority" of Catholicism). Whereas St. Thomas Aquinas's cosmic realism is ultimately rooted religiously — *a priori,* as it were — in the cosmic realism of a visible church with visible sacraments, an absolute "philosophy of the Spirit" (whether it be relatively or radically absolute), being a "philosophy of interiority" and thus an "idealism" (whether a material idealism as in Leibniz, Hegel, and Husserl, or a formal and functional idealism as in Descartes, Kant, and Fichte), is grounded in the "interiority" of the "afflicted-and-consoled conscience" in the "pure Spirit" of a "wrathful-and-merciful God" — an interiority that the Reformation opposed in the name of an "interior, spiritual Christianity" to the visible hierarchy and visible offices of an institutional church.

As for the religious substrate that defines a *methodological theory of knowledge (or gnoseology),* it already emerged as we were elaborating the structure proper to such a theory. This religious substrate presents a clear contrast to the religious substrate in each of the previous three theories of knowledge: the Cartesian preambulatory theory of knowledge, the autonomous theory of knowledge, and the absolute theory of knowledge. In each of these three forms there was a merging of the *"Deus interior"* with the creaturely "interior," almost to the point of a sort of "two-faced identity": on the one hand, the "creaturely face" of the creature's spiritual interiority; on the other hand, the face of a spiritual interiority that is divine. In the case of a methodological theory of knowledge, however, the religious substrate is an almost archetypal representation of the relation between "Creator and creature" that was defined by the Fourth Lateran Council as an essential span between a "similarity, however great" and an "ever greater dissimilarity."[14] In the first three forms of a theory of knowledge, this aspect of a "similarity, however great" (between a creaturely interiority and a divine interiority) is taken so far that it ultimately becomes a two-faced identity (between interior and interior, spirit and Spirit), leading to the Hegelian form of identity: a self-dialectic of the divine within every intra-creaturely dialectic. But, whereas these theories of knowledge are all forms of a philosophy of identity, the methodological theory of knowledge proves to be a perfect realization of what the word "method" literally means: inasmuch as "ὁδός" means "way," which logically underscores the distinction between something's point of departure and the "endpoint" towards which it aims — a "way"

14. Denz. 432.

that, as this distinction between something's "whence" and its "whither" implies, must be "followed *after*" (in the sense of the "μετά" in "ὁδός"). Of
course, to speak of the "whither" proper to this "following after the way" is
also to suggest an increasing approximation to the way's defining endpoint.
Nevertheless, in the midst of this approximation, the difference (and hence
"distance") remains between this "whither" and the original point of departure, the "whence." What remains is essentially that "distinction of place":
"God is in heaven, and you are on earth," as the sober diction of the book of
Ecclesiastes expresses it (Eccl. 5:2). The fundamental religious structure of a
methodological theory of knowledge is, consequently, the "analogy of ever
greater dissimilarity" (that of an above-and-beyond even with regard to the
"Deus interior" who lies beyond the interiority of the creature) within a
"similarity, however great" (that of the *"Deus interior intimo meo,"* i.e., the
"interior of my interior"). Thus, seen in light of its religious substrate, a
methodological theory of knowledge is essentially an *"analogical theory of
knowledge."* The rhythm of the Aristotelian analogy, understood as an oscillating "proportion between other and other" ("ἄλλο πρὸς ἄλλο"),[15] within
the rhythm of analogy as formulated by the Fourth Lateran Council (as an
"ever greater dissimilarity" within every "similarity, however great") constitutes the total rhythm of "analogy," to which everything can be referred
without itself being referred to anything else, consisting as it does in a genuine *"reductio in mysterium."* This total rhythm of analogy, which is the original rhythm for any authentic theory of knowledge (or gnoseology), lies at
the base of each of the forms of the methodological theory of knowledge
outlined above: from the rhythm proper to the "stages" (in Asian wisdom
and earliest Christianity) to the rhythm proper to "wonder," "ever greater ascetical preparation," "initiation by dying," and "eros" (in Platonism and Romanticism, right up through Newman). It is the rhythm that Augustine
most profoundly expressed when he wrote: "Let us seek Him (in creation
and in Himself) in order to find Him; let us seek Him upon finding Him.
That one might seek Him, He is hidden; that, having found Him, one might
continue to seek Him, He is measureless."[16]

2. On the one hand, it has been *Augustine's* fate to be regarded as the true father of the autonomous theory of knowledge (or gnoseology) that had its

---

15. *Met.* V, 6, 1016b, 34-35.
16. *In Jo. Tract.* 63, 1. *Quaeramus inveniendum, quaeramus inventum. Ut inveniendus
quaeratur, occultus est; ut inventus quaeratur, immensus est.*

origin in Descartes and its culmination and conclusion in Husserl: to the point that he is even regarded as the progenitor of the absolute theory of knowledge (or gnoseology) in the form given it by his disciple Anselm of Canterbury; but, on the other hand (as the passage above shows), the rhythm internal to a methodological theory of knowledge properly leads back to him as well. This is because when one treats the "Augustinian" theory of knowledge one tends to consider only the path laid out in his early anti-Manichean, Plotinian writings, the path of his dialogues, which extends even into the books of *De Trinitate*. It is true, of course, that Augustine does not pose or discuss the problem of an explicit theory of knowledge (or gnoseology) except in these writings. But Augustine's posing and explicit discussion of this problem is — firstly — subordinate at the most formal level to his renunciation of the Manichean dualism between a primordial light and a primordial darkness, and to his corresponding turn towards the Christian Platonism of a single primordial principle: that of the primordial divine light *as* the primordial truth. Secondly, the theory of knowledge (or gnoseology) of the early Augustine is, in the final analysis, a genuine methodological theory of knowledge — one that figures as the "noesis" (in the sense given this term by the early Husserl), corresponding to the "noema" of a Christian and Plotinian "idealism of truth." As such, it is but "one" methodological theory of knowledge, and merely the "first," among those other equally methodological theories of knowledge (or gnoseologies) that correspond to the "noematic" themes of Augustine's middle writings (such as *Civitate Dei*, the *Enarrationes in Psalmos*, and the *Tractatus in Joannem*), his anti-Donatist writings (above all the *Enarrationes in Psalmos*), and his anti-Pelagian writings (the *Opera in Julianum*). Augustine's "theory of knowledge" (or gnoseology) is not, therefore, something peculiar to the early Augustine, but is expressed differently in the various periods of his production; and it is only in view of its four different instantiations that one can begin to sense, albeit in a genuinely asymptotic way, how it could be configured out of the tensions among them. In this regard, Augustine is actually unsurpassed and unsurpassable: in that, in his writings, he himself is a "thinker in transition," who thinks "in view of" the various periods through which he has passed, whose thought therefore consists in the internal dialectic among his various periods, and who, precisely for this reason, is the dialectical origin of the entire dialectic of Western theology and philosophy.[17]

---

17. This is what I sought to demonstrate in my *Augustinus, Gestalt als Gefüge* (Leipzig: Hegner, 1934).

The theory of knowledge (or gnoseology) of the early Augustine (the only one that he expressly developed) consists in a reduction of everything "dubitable" to the primal datum "I know that I live,"[18] whereby "truth" as such flashes out immediately within this "I know that I live"; moreover, such that it is precisely within "doubt" as such that "truth" indubitably shows itself: "Whosoever knows himself to doubt most assuredly knows something true: to wit, that he doubts. . . . Whosoever, therefore, doubts that there is any such thing as truth precisely in this way possesses knowledge of something he cannot doubt. . . . Accordingly, no one who is able to harbor doubts of all kinds can doubt that there is truth."[19] This correlation between the indubitable "I know that I live" and the still more indubitable "truth within doubt itself" provides the proper basis for the (Christian and Plotinian) *idealism of the early Augustine*, as he formulates it in the *Soliloquies*: "You must flee from sensible things entirely . . . if we wish to fly from this darkness to the light above, which does not condescend to show itself to men so long as they remain immured in this cave"[20] (a passage wholly faithful to Plato's allegory of the cave). But it is a dialectical idealism. Inasmuch as it is a theory of knowledge grounded in so indubitable a principle as "I know that I live" — concretely embodied in "life" as "memory," "understanding," and "will" within "knowing" and "judging"[21] — it is specifically, with respect to this foundation, a *subjective functional idealism*: just as Thomas grounds everything in the *"veritas in intellectu"*; and just as, for Descartes, everything is rooted in the *"sum"* of the *"cogito"*; and just as, finally, for Hegel, the dynamic ternary of the "world of absolute Spirit" arises from within the functional ternary of consciousness. On the other hand, however, for Augustine, "truth itself" is essential. It appears directly within "doubt" as the "noema," so to speak, that is ultimately determinative of the "noetic" realm ("I know that I live"), virtually revealing itself as a divine absolute, as the "intelligible light" that alone is divine, as opposed to the deity of Manicheism, which is a dialectic between "light" and "darkness": "Behold before you, truth itself: embrace it . . . and drink joy in the Lord. . . . If, then, there is anything more sublime, it is none but He, God himself: but if not, then truth itself *is* God."[22] On the one hand, then, we have a subjective functional idealism of "I know (and think and judge) that I live" in the three forms of *memoria, intellectus,*

18. *De Trinitate* XV, 12, 21.
19. *De Vera Rel.* 39, 73.
20. *Soliloquies* I, 14, 24.
21. *De Trin.* X, 10, 14.
22. *De Lib. Arb.* II, 13, 35.

voluntas; on the other hand, we have an *objective theonomic idealism* of "immutable truth" understood as that "light wonderfully hidden and revealed":[23] truth as light and light as truth, both of which are either "God himself" or the place within which God directly appears, in the midst of the immanence of his truth and light, as "transcending" them, as "yet more sublime" (obviously drawing upon the ὑπερ-φῶς, the "superluminous" light of the divine "superunitary" One of Plotinus).[24] This ambiguous *correlation between a subjective and an objective idealism* (which modernity will later split into two) is the authentic face of idealism, arising from Augustine's first and only explicit theory of knowledge, which was conceived as an overcoming of the irreconcilable dialectic of Manicheism — a dialectic that rests fundamentally, therefore, upon the "restlessness of doubt," a dialectic between light (truth) and darkness (falsehood) understood as a dialectic between "God" and "Anti-God." Seen from this perspective, the kind of doubt proper to Augustine's theory of knowledge is no philosophical "methodological" doubt; rather, it is, concretely, the fundamental spiritual condition of Manicheism, in which everything, from the objectively metaphysical to the subjectively internal, is eternally "in doubt" — since everything exists within a state of perpetual twilight between divine light (truth) and divine darkness (falsehood).

This is why Augustine goes on to take a third, concluding step. Just as the subjective functional principle "I know that I live" is seen to point beyond itself to an objective "immutable truth" that transcends it, Augustine finally comes to see within this subjective, functional act of "knowing that I live" — specifically, within its threefold form of *"memoria, intellectus, voluntas"* and its three orientations of *"memoria sui* (remembering oneself in being present to oneself), *intellectus sui* ("self-consciousness"), and *voluntas sui* (affirmation of oneself) — an ultimate "image *(imago),"* which could be said to disclose something archetypal within the divinity of "truth and light." Of course, such disclosure takes place strictly within the light of the grace of divine self-revelation: the *mysterium* of the original, divine "light and truth" is no longer simply that of an "impersonal divinity" (in the way that the words "light" and "truth" are impersonal); nor is it simply that of a "divine I" (as would correspond to a philosophical concept of the "one and only God," or even to an "ultimate correlation" between a "divine I" and a "creaturely thou" or vice versa); rather, this *mysterium* appears as

---

23. *De Lib. Arb.* II, 12, 33.
24. Cf. *De Lib. Arb.* II, 13, 35.

the mysterious, rhythmic interpenetration of a divine *"Memoria Sui"* (as it appears in the "Father" as the spiritually "abiding origin"), a divine *"Intellectus Sui"* (corresponding to the "Son," understood as "Logos"), and a divine *"Voluntas Sui"* (in which and as which the "Holy Spirit" constitutes the divine "self-affirmation in love"). In other words, seen in the full context of Augustine's idealism, the Augustinian theologoumenon of an *"imago Trinitatis"* within the fundamental orientations of the life of the mind appears as the concluding synthesis between his functional idealism (seen in the "I know that I live") and his objective theonomic idealism (of "immutable truth"). What Hegel conceived in terms of his trinitarian dialectic of spiritual judgment[25] — the dialectic, that is, of a (paternal) "thesis," a (filial) "antithesis," and a (spiritual) "synthesis" — is thus an unconscious and titanic appropriation of Augustine's idealism (whereby he falls victim to the vanity of formal abstraction); even so, however, we see in Hegel the actual face of this idealism in its original form, as it appears at the very outset of Augustine's theory of knowledge: a subjective functional idealism (grounded in "I know that I live") that connects to an objective theonomic idealism (grounded in "immutable truth" disclosed in the midst of original doubt), one that connects both to one another within an ultimate *trinitarian idealism,* in which the *"memoria sui, intellectus sui, voluntas sui"* of "I know that I live" reveal themselves to be the "image" of the "archetype" of a divine *"Memoria Sui, Intellectus Sui, Voluntas Sui"* — this being the innermost communal vitality[26] inherent in the innermost *mysterium* of "immutable truth," understood as the "hidden and manifest light" of the God who is "truth and light."[27]

Over against this unilinear idealism of truth and spirit (which, going beyond the correlation between consciousness and truth, concludes in a purely positive understanding of the *"imago Trinitatis,"* which Augustine subjects to critique only in his late works); over against the "spiritualism" of the resemblance between the creaturely spirit and the divine Spirit in regard to their primordial function (a spiritualism that was not "noematicized," so to speak, until the Augustinianism of the early Middle Ages, when it was transformed into the material spiritualism of a spiritual world of "symbols"); over against this idealism of the spiritual as such, one confronts in the texts of *De Civitate Dei,* the *Enarrationes in Psalmos,* and the *Tractatus in*

---

25. *Geist-Urteil-Dialektik.* — Trans.
26. *Wir-Lebendigkeit.* — Trans.
27. Cf. my *Augustinus* (1934), pp. 8-14, 261-66.

Joannem the emphatic *realism of the corporate "head and body, One Christ."* Whereas the early Augustine understands the specifically Christian doctrine of the "incarnate Logos," essentially, only in the sense of "I am the truth," and thus, for the most part, not so much as a real "revelation in flesh and blood" (as would follow from the Johannine principle of making "Christ in the flesh" the strict criterion by which to condemn a demonic spiritualism and docetism: 2 John 7), but rather as a "revelation in spirit and truth," consistent with the correlation between the creaturely spirit and the divine Spirit: in contrast to *this* Christian spiritualism, the accent now falls upon the Christian realism of a Christ of flesh and blood, who, "in that he assumed human nature," is the only "way" to that "fixed truth" that "even the philosophers of this world" recognized as the defining goal of all searching.[28] As opposed to a Christian idealism defined by a human rejection of all sensible reality and a perfect ascent into the ideal, intelligible realm of "pure truth," one is now presented with the Christian realism of God himself, who in a Christ of flesh and blood became a way at once earthly, human, and accommodated to the senses: "the Son of God, who in the Father has always been truth and life" (corresponding to the relation between "I know that I live" and "immutable truth" found at the epistemological starting point of a human idealism), became "the way" by assuming human nature: "it is through him that you advance, to him that you advance."[29] This tension proper to the Christ of flesh and blood, understood as the "way who *is* the truth" — "through Christ . . . to Christ, through Christ the man to Christ who is God: through the Word that became flesh, to the Word that was in the beginning with God"[30] — is thus the specific way of knowledge (and, as this implies, the "theory of knowledge") proper to the corporate realism of the "head and body, One Christ."

If the path of knowledge proper to a Christian idealism started from an indubitable "I know that I live" and proceeded to a still more indubitable "immutable truth," the path of knowledge proper to a Christian realism is traveled within the span of Christ, who, as the ideal, divine "truth," is also the real, human "way." The very "flesh and blood" from which — according to the approach of a Christian idealism — one must "whole-heartedly flee" (*penitus esse ista sensibilia fugienda*)[31] are now — in the form of the "truth,

---

28. *Serm.* 141, 1-4.
29. *Serm.* 141, 4.
30. *In Jo. Tract.* 13, 14.
31. *Soliloquia* I, 14, 24.

which is life, incarnate in flesh and blood" — the definitive point of entry into the real world: the real world understood *as* the universe of the real and sensible "head and body, One Christ."

The "ascent" or "surrection"[32] out of the "darkness" of the "cave" of the real,[33] which characterizes a Christian idealism, now occurs in a diametrically opposed fashion: as an "ascent" within the real and through the real, which is none other than Christ himself as "flesh and blood" (thus taking the form of a radical "descent" or "de-rection"[34] from an unreal ideal into the "totally real"). It occurs, furthermore, in such a way that the "genuine ideality" of "real truth" is given only within this "downwards and below" (in a humbling of all intellectual pride), in a real "ascent" within the reality of the real Christ. "May Christ raise you up through his humanity" (*Erigat te Christus per id quod homo est*).[35] But then this "ascent" or "sur-rection," which takes place within the divine-human reality of Christ, is at the same time a "di-rection,"[36] as it were, into the whole span of the real, stretching between a real God and a real man. "May he lead you through the truth that God is man" (*ducat te per id quod Deus homo est*). And it is only by way of this "ascent" or "surrection" into the (de-super-idealized)[37] reality of Christ as *"totus homo"* — this radical, total, and universal "di-rection" through the sensible universe lying between a real God and a real man; this "di-rection," understood (according to Newman's formula) as a radical and total "realization," which is to say an active and practical "taking for real of this (de-super-idealized) reality"; this radical, total, and universal "di-rection" through a radical, total, and universal reality — it is only thus that the dream of Christian idealism is finally realized: a "trans-rection"[38] into the "truth, which is God," which takes place within the "I am the truth" of Christ as God. As Augustine says, "May he lead you through to that which is God" (*perducat te ad id quod Deus*).

Therefore, given that the path of knowledge proper to a Christian realism is one that "proceeds through Christ and in Christ towards Christ," who is the "way that is the truth";[39] given, moreover, that this path consists in a

---

32. *Aufrichtung.* — Trans.
33. *Soliloquia* I, 14, 24.
34. *Hinab-Richtung.* — Trans.
35. *In Jo. Tract.* 23, 6.
36. *Hinein-Richtung.* — Trans.
37. *Un-über-idealisiert.* — Trans.
38. *Hinüber-Richtung.* — Trans.
39. *In Jo. Tract.* 13, 4; *Serm.* 293, 7.

completely radical "conversion" (μετάνοια) of one's sensibility and a "dying-to": a dying to one's "own understanding and sensibilities" that leads to a "re-birth" into none other than the "mind of Christ" (νοῦς Χριστοῦ: 1 Cor. 2:16) and into a sense of what is found in Christ (φρονεῖτε ἐν ἡμῖν ὃ καὶ ἐν Χριστῷ Ἰησοῦ: Phil. 2:5); and given that this path is to be understood as consisting in a law of knowledge and a rhythmic "knowledge by stages," it is *not* to be understood as a "knowledge consisting in analysis and synthesis" or in "critique and construction" (which an idealist theory of knowledge requires as its path to "certain truth"). Rather, the path one must affirm is that taken by Augustine, which he appropriates from Clement of Alexandria and then develops, the same path handed down by way of Anselm of Canterbury to Thomas Aquinas, the *path from "credere" to "intellegere" to "videre"* in the medium of *"caritas":* the path of a "leaping beyond" (*transilire,* as Augustine loves to put it) all "self-evidence" into the "blindness and darkness of faith," in order that, by such faith, one might receive "evidence of Christ," wherein alone one can "perceive" the real universe as the universe of the "head and body, One Christ," and therein perceive also the "real truth," from which one comes to the meaning of "vision": "faith is the first thing that submits the soul to the yoke of God . . . , then come the commandments of (practical) life, the keeping of which confirms our hope, nourishes our love, and causes that which formerly one merely believed to begin to shine forth."[40] Thus this path of knowledge — leading from *"credere"* to *"intellegere"* to *"videre"* — is the "noeticization," as it were, of the "ontically real"[41] way that leads "through Christ, in Christ, and into Christ." As Augustine says, "Whoever believes in me . . . enters into me; and whoever enters into me, has me" *(Qui ergo credit in me . . . it in me; et qui it in me, habet me).*[42] And in this way, conversely, the "eyes . . . of faith" are transformed into the "knowing eyes" of God (in the real Christ): thus one can "see what God sees";[43] and thus, as Augustine suggests, in the terms proper to his genuinely cosmic Christology, one can see the "universe of Christ" "with the eyes of God, understood as the eyes of Christ": to see it, namely, as a *"coincidentia oppositorum"* of all ontically real antitheses in Christ, the "Head and Quintessence," the "Origin and End," the "First and Last," in Whom "all things hold together." In this respect, Augustine is not only the first, but the only theologian to have "drawn

---

40. *De Agone Christ.* 13, 14.
41. *Ontisch-real.* — Trans.
42. *In Jo. Tract.* 26, 10.
43. *In Ps.* 36, 2, 2.

out" the great implications of Pauline Christology into a comprehensive vision of the cosmos and of universal history.[44]

When taken together with its corollary theory of knowledge as a "surrection" patterned upon Christ, i.e., as an ascent from *"credere"* to *"intelligere"* to *"videre"* (from "Christ as man" in "Christ as God-man" to "Christ as God"), the realism in this vision of a corporate "head and body, One Christ"[45] is thus a "Christo-realism" based upon a "Christo-gnoseology." But, ultimately, within this very realism there is an abyssal depth on account of what we just called a coincidence in Christ of all the universe's antitheses — the *"coincidentia oppositorum"* (to use the phrase of Augustine's most brilliant disciple, Nicholas of Cusa). It is that acute realism that Augustine unveiled — almost as his final "testament" — in the course of his battle against the Donatists and Pelagians: against, that is, the ideative unilinearity that made both parties unwilling to entertain any notion of a "tension of antitheses." In the case of Donatism, one sees the impetuous zeal of "the orthodox and the saints," who claimed their erstwhile persecution as a mandate precipitously to cast away all the "rotten fish" from the *one* fishnet of Christ, and to rip out all the "tares" from the *one* field of Christ prior to the harvest (hence Augustine's emphasis upon these gospel parables in his arguments against a fanaticism that ultimately devolved into murder and incendiary actions against a "deformed church").[46] In the case of Pelagianism, one sees the fanaticism of "good will" and "progress in virtue" and "aristocratic manhood," which seeks to obliterate the "embarrassing" antinomy between *homo peccator,* ever again sinning, and the ever greater "mercy of the God of grace" (what is more, it seeks to do away with the mystery enunciated by Paul in Rom. 11:32: that "God has imprisoned all in disobedience so that he may be merciful to all"); it seeks instead the "respectable" unilinearity of "progress in the good," for which "free will," by itself, constitutes the only "grace." Both Donatism and Pelagianism show themselves to be forms of "integralism": in the case of Donatism, the "theonomic integralism" of an "integrated kingdom of God"; in the case of Pelagianism, the "anthroponomic integralism" of an "integrated good will." Augustine's distaste for theonomic integralism is obvious as early as the hymnody of the *Soliloquies,* even if there his early idealism rings out as a sort of "underlying *basso continuo.*" "God, through

---

44. Cf. my *Augustinus: Die Gestalt als Gefüge* (Leipzig: Hegner-Verlag, 1934), Nr. 271-517.

45. *In Ps.* 54, 3.

46. *In Ps.* 40, 8; 99, 9-12.

whom the universe, even with its sinister part, is perfect. God, from whom there is no ultimate disharmony, since the better harmonizes with the worse" (*Deus per quem universitas etiam cum sinistra parte perfecta est. Deus a quo dissonantia usque in extremum nulla est, cum deteriora melioribus concinunt*).[47] On the other hand, in opposition to anthroponomic integralism, the law posited in *De Civitate Dei* as fundamental to its view of the world is not the law of constant linear progress (the law inherited by the Anglo-Saxon ideology of progress, as a kind of "ancestral birthright" from its "father," the British monk Pelagius!); instead, *De Civitate Dei* posits the truly universal, human, and historical law of an "opposition of antitheses," an "opposition of one antithesis to another," as what constitutes the true "beauty of the world."[48] For Augustine what is ultimate, and what *ipso facto* stands opposed to every theonomic and anthroponomic integralism, is a fundamental *realism of antitheses.* If the idealism of the early Augustine represented the *negative* overcoming of his original Manicheism and its doctrine of primordial intra-divine antitheses (between a God of light and God of darkness), and if, for precisely this reason, his own idealism was in danger of degenerating into an integralism of pure "truth in the spirit" (of the kind that developed in Western integral spiritualism into a mystical counterpart to the Western Pelagianism of moral progress), then Augustine's realism of antitheses can be seen, by contrast, as a *positive* overcoming of his original Manicheism, redeeming the positive core that Manicheism had turned into an absolute. Moreover, this came about in the course of his struggles with two different kinds of integralism and with a mentality for which Augustine himself, during the period of his idealism, had an affinity. (For Augustine, the way in which these two "fronts" so to speak "interlocked" in his own person led him to the insight that the "catholic" nature of "truth" could be brought to light only if sought from the perspective of these "divisive spirits,"[49] whom he viewed as truly "great men.")[50] As this makes plain, however, the gnoseological presupposition for such an antithetical realism is a "thinking in opposites," which Augustine himself requires for his view of the world as an "opposition of antitheses." We see this in the way that he grounds the ontically real "opposition of antitheses" in a certain "style of language," in the "beauty of speech," but thereby also grounds it in a certain "style of

47. *Soliloquia* I, 1, 2.
48. *De Civ. Dei* XI, 18.
49. *Spaltgeister.* — Trans.
50. *In Ps.* 54, 22; *In Ps.* 124, 5; *De Vera Rel.* 8, 15; *Serm.* 46, 8, 18.

thought," which is proper to a "*logos* in antitheses" and is merely "expressed" in this style of language: "Just as the contraposition of contraries constitutes the beauty of speech, so too the beauty of the world is joined together in a contraposition of contraries — in an eloquence not of words, but of things."[51] In other words, the gnoseological presupposition of St. Augustine's antithetical realism is the *style of thought proper to a logos of contraries within a logia of contraries.*

At an even deeper level, however, this realism of contraries, which is grounded in a gnoseology of contrariety, becomes a, so to speak, *abyssal realism* — a realism understood as a "night" of "abysses." This is the realism that the late Augustine opposed to Pelagianism's "progressive optimism." At the same time, it is this kind of realism that stands in sharpest contrast to Augustine's own early idealism. And so it is in this form of realism that the positive core of Manicheism comes to light, which was the real temptation for the pre-Christian Augustine and which he therefore opposed in his early Christian period with all the force of a passionate idealism. This abyssal realism is grounded, however, precisely in Augustine's realism of the "head and body, One Christ": in that, in his struggle against Donatist integralism, his portrayal of the concrete "head and body, One Christ" underscores the features of the "scandal and folly and weakness" of the mystery of the Cross, the features of "*Christus deformis*": "You are formed by the disfigured deformity of Christ. . . . We bear on our foreheads the sign of this disfigured deformity."[52] Understood in such terms — as, namely, the body of this "*Christus deformis*" — the real "body of Christ" is therefore the "*Ecclesia deformis*": it contains "tares among the wheat," it is the fishnet containing "good and bad fish," and it is the wedding banquet to which the king expressly invites both the "good and the bad" and the "vagabonds along the highways" in place of the recalcitrant "sons of the household."[53] It is, accordingly, precisely in view of this abyss[54] of the "disfigured deformity" of the real "head and body, One Christ" that the ultimate correlation between "*homo abyssus*" and "*Deus abyssus*" becomes manifest (this being, so to speak, the profoundest mode in which Christ is the "image of the invisible God," such that "whoever has seen me has seen the Father," the "invisible God" who can be seen only in "*Christus deformis*," the Christ who is not Christ save as "the Crucified," in

---

51. *De Civ. Dei* XI, 18.
52. *Serm.* 27, 6.
53. Cf. *Ep.* 208, 2ff.; *In Ps.* 40, 8; *In Ps.* 99, 9-13.
54. *Abgründigkeit.* — Trans.

"disfigured deformity"). Man as such (whether man as understood by idealism or man as understood by realism) is an "unfathomability" — an unfathomability that is "so great" that it is "hidden from man himself, in whom it is found."[55] As such an "unfathomability," he is an utter "abyss," "more unfathomable" than "the depth of the sea."[56] And, as such an "abyss," he is ultimately a "mighty deep" *(grande profundum)*[57] characterized by "great solitude."[58] Corresponding to this *"homo abyssus,"* but greater still, is the *"Deus abyssus"* who inscrutably guides the economy of salvation, in which he seemingly allows "Babylon" and "Jerusalem" to intermingle, without any possibility of discrimination,[59] and indeed allows the "wicked to flourish and the good to live in toil."[60] And yet: "Do you seek to go beyond this profundity (of God)? Seek not to leap off from the wood of Christ!"[61] For it is the "profundity" of the *"Christus deformis"* that reveals the "profundity of the riches" of God himself.[62]

The final mystery of this abyssal realism is therefore "night." Man, humanity, and world are all ultimately "night":[63] "It is night because error comes from the whole human race."[64] It is "night," moreover, because Christ's "My God, my God, why hast Thou forsaken me?" is the cry of the *"totus Christus,"* of Christ as "head" as well as of us who are his "body and fullness." In this respect, "night," understood as the night of life and the night of a God apparently "abandoned to the night,"[65] constitutes the real "grace of the New Covenant," in contrast to the "fleshly plenitude" of the Old Covenant: for it is precisely in the "however great" of the earthly "night," and ultimately in the "however great" of a "night through God and with God" (as is the case in the "night of Christ"), that the "ever greater" "glory" is revealed, a glory that is revealed solely in the mystery of the Cross, the mystery of which is no longer merely that of a "disfigured figure," but that of a "day shrouded in darkness" (which is how Augustine proclaims the *"gratia*

55. *In Ps.* 41, 13.
56. *In Ps.* 76, 18.
57. *Conf.* IV, 14, 22.
58. *Serm.* 47, 14, 23.
59. *In Ps.* 136, 3f.; *In Ps.* 51, 6.
60. *In Ps.* 91, 8.
61. *In Ps.* 91, 8.
62. *Serm.* 27, 6.
63. *In Ps.* 100, 12.
64. *In Ps.* 138, 16.
65. *Hingenachtet.* — Trans.

Novi Testamenti" in his 140th letter). It is the "night" proclaimed by Dionysius the Areopagite as the "abyss of a stormy night," which is nevertheless a "superabundant outpouring of light," "γνόφος" as the "φωτοχυσία" of the "θεῖος σκότος."⁶⁶ It is "night" in the sense enunciated by John of the Cross, in keeping with the tradition of Augustine and the Areopagite, when he speaks in his hymns of "God's nuptials" (the concept central to both Old and New Testaments) as a *"noche oscura,"* a "dark night."

But then, implicit within this correlation between an "abyssal night" of man and an "abyssal night" of God, there is a corresponding *"gnoseology of night."* It is based upon the realization that the same "consciousness" that produced Augustine's idealist gnoseology is, in its profoundest aspect, precisely an "abyss": "You wish [to search out] the depths of the sea, but what is more unfathomable than human consciousness?"⁶⁷ In this respect, the idealist "interiority within consciousness" is simply a "great solitude."⁶⁸ This is why a true interpretation of "consciousness" (which is the goal of a gnoseology), far from being an idealist "ascending interpretation"⁶⁹ that ascends out of the noetic "I" up to the noematic "τόπος νοητός" of an "ideal world," is a "descending interpretation,"⁷⁰ which descends from a "luminous consciousness" into the "unfathomability" of (its own) "abyss," down into its "night." In fact, it is this "descent" that first constitutes the decisive "ascent" up out of the "fatal abyss that is man" into the "blessed abyss that is God," out of an "unholy night" into the "truly blessed night": in the ultimate symbol of Christ, who "descended into the lower parts of the earth" in order to "ascend far above all the heavens" (Eph. 4:10).

66. *Mystical Theology,* etc.
67. *In Ps.* 76, 18.
68. *Serm.* 47, 23.
69. *Hinauf-Deutung.* — Trans.
70. *Hinunter-Deutung.* — Trans.

9 Between Metaphysics and Christianity

1958

The philosophical work of Hedwig Conrad-Martius is centered upon her "Ontology of the Real,"[1] as this is developed in her *Metaphysical Dialogues* (1921). In contrast to her mentor Husserl, whose "methodological" phenomenology was transformed into a fundamental "transcendental" phenomenology (that is to say, an egological-monadological phenomenology), she conceives of methodological phenomenology in such rigorous terms that it is, from the very outset, regarded as a pure method by which to lay bare the real and "ultimate foundations of being."[2] In contrast to Husserl, for whom every metaphysics of the real remains "bracketed out," she envisages a natural path from phenomenology to metaphysics: "simple analysis," she says, will "ultimately drive us entirely into the arms of metaphysics."[3] What is more, in still greater contrast to Husserl (for whom God and, above all, revelation are "bracketed out"), she consciously develops her metaphysics with a view to the claims of Christian revelation: "the truly essential limits are nowhere preserved as purely as they are here [in revelation]."[4] Accordingly, her metaphysics rests upon certain defining points of Christian revelation, such as the doctrine of the fall of the angels, or that of the original *"status integritatis"* of man, or that of God's redemption of human beings "out of the depths of their nothingness," or that of the "threefold lumi-

1. Hedwig Conrad-Martius, *Realontologie I* (Halle: Niemeyer, 1924).
2. *Gespräche*, p. 4.
3. *Gespräche*, p. 114.
4. *Gespräche*, p. 63.

This essay first appeared in *Festschrift* for Hedwig Conrad-Martius, *Philosophisches Jahrbuch* (1958).

nosity"[5] of the Father, Son, and Spirit, and so on.[6] Equally, however, this metaphysics is inwardly sustained by the "arcane" tradition of Meister Eckhart's "birth of God in the innermost part of the soul" and by Jacob Böhme's and Franz von Baader's doctrine of the ultimate polarity between spirit and body (according to which "spiritual life" and "bodily life"[7] are understood in terms of a *single* rhythm between "exhalation" and "inhalation," between "a fullness that is interiorized" and "a fullness that is expressed");[8] this extends even to "Jacob Böhme's wisdom" regarding a God who "gives birth to himself from eternity to eternity."[9] The metaphysics of Hedwig Conrad-Martius thus moves between the poles of a methodological phenomenological metaphysics and an immanent metaphysics of Christian revelation; moreover, this latter is undertaken in constant confrontation with a "Christian Gnosis," since Jacob Böhme and Franz von Baader are not so much theologians as theosophists. Consequently, the central question raised by the work of Hedwig Conrad-Martius, whom we celebrate in this jubilee year, is the relationship between metaphysics and Christianity. In this sense we will look first toward Christianity from the perspective of metaphysics and then back, in the opposite direction, from Christianity toward metaphysics.

1. The word *metaphysics* was originally a bibliographical designation for those of Aristotle's works that were composed — and stand — "after" his writings on the "φύσικα." If we translate it into objective terms, however, we find that the essence of metaphysics is grounded, as the word suggests, in the relation between "meta" and "physics." The "φύσικα," according to Aristotle, are all the regions of real being situated between matter and spirit, insofar as they concern the "φύσις" of "φύειν," which is to say, the nature of whatever has "come to exist, been created, been generated, come to be," on the model of "vegetal growth." Thus, the "φύσικα" are the whole of things, understood as "creaturely": from what immanently "grows" to what is transcendentally "created," from an organic "begetting in the womb" to an imperial "*fiat* of creation." With regard to this span of reality, which is proper to the universe of entities, a "meta-physics" seeks what (to adopt the felicitous phrasing of Hugo Dingler) is *hintergründlich, untergründlich, obergründlich,* and, at the same time, *ingründlich.* It seeks, that is, what is "ultimate," which grounds

5. *Dreifaltigen Lichtkraft.* — Trans.
6. *Gespräche,* pp. 63ff., 125ff.; pp. 62, 68; pp. 183-84.
7. *Geisten und Leiben.* — Trans.
8. *Gespräche,* cf. pp. 62, 68, 101, 140f.
9. *Gespräche,* p. 140.

this reality by being at once "behind," "beneath," "above," and, at the same time, "interior to" it — just as "meta" means "with" in the sense of "beneath" and "in" and "before." This sense of "meta" in "meta-physics," which is almost "prefigured in (the etymology of) the word," is immediately apparent from what Gregory the Great, expanding on the tradition of Augustinian dialectic, says about God: "*Ipse est interior et exterior, ipse inferior et superior: regendo superior, portando inferior, replendo interior, circumdando exterior. Sicque est intus ut extra sit, sic circumdat ut penetret, sic praesidet ut portet, sic portat ut praesidet.*"[10] Just as, in formally grammatical terms, the μετά in "metaphysics" signifies at once an "above" and a "below," a "with" and an "in," so too, in his real divine form, God is "the one who is within and without, the one who is below and above: above in governing, below in upholding, within in filling, without in encompassing. Thus he is within in such a way that he is without; thus he encompasses in such a way that he penetrates; thus he presides in such a way that he upholds; thus he upholds in such a way that he presides." The metaphysics in the μετά — in this dialectic of cosmic and super-cosmic dimensions between "above" and "below," "interior" and "exterior" — indicates simultaneously an "ultimate rhythm" (fulfilling what Jacob Böhme and Franz von Baader meant in supposing that "God comes into being ever anew") and an "incomprehensible profundity" (like Dionysius the Areopagite's vision of God as "γνόφος," as an "abyssal, stormy night").[11]

Such is the "metaphysical" dimension in all great philosophies: in the "nothingness of plenitude" of Lao-Tzu and in the "musical rhythm" of Confucius; in the symbols of "fire, water, earth, and air" used by the Ionian philosophers (who are unjustly regarded as mere "cosmo-logists"), as well as in the tension between Heraclitus's antithetical dialectic and Parmenides' mystically self-identical being; in Plato's dialogues, whose "logical dialectic" serves merely as the foreground of the great myths, the mystery of which this dialectic should reveal, but which remains nevertheless all the more profoundly veiled; indeed, even in Aristotle, who, though his writings seem hostile to myths, nevertheless describes the "φιλόσοφος" as essentially a "φιλόμυφος," and ultimately grounds his noetic-cosmic "universal motion" in "Eros." It is the "metaphysical" correlation between an ultimate, dynamic "*coincidentia oppositorum*" and a Divine Night that presents itself only to a "*docta ignorantia,*" as one finds in Nicholas of Cusa, whose thought leads al-

10. *Hom.* 17 *In Ezech.*
11. *Mystical Theol.* II.

most directly to Hegel and the pinnacle of Western philosophy (in Hegel's audacious conception of a "trinitarian dialectic" that is immanent to *ratio* and to the cosmos). But this "metaphysical" dimension is also found in seemingly anti-metaphysical thinkers: like Kant, who, in keeping with the real connections among his "Critiques," destroys the "rationalistic order" of the Enlightenment in reality only in order to unveil, in the midst of its downfall, a mysterious "kingdom of spirits" centered upon the "highest good"; hence, what is properly divine in Kant's thought stands within a dialectic of "downfall and resurrection," i.e., within that original Lutheran dialectic of "wrath" and "mercy." Kant, seemingly the original anti-metaphysician, is thus the original prototype for two contemporary "anti-metaphysical" schools, whose style and whose tone of fervent hymnody already betray their more original metaphysical character: the "transcending" Dionysianism of Nietzsche (who seeks the God of "night and fire," the God of Heraclitus and Dionysius the Areopagite, amid the débris of a demolished Melanchthonism) and the revolutionary Dionysianism of Bakunin (for whom "fruitful destruction" is the *primum movens* and who thus bears the religious stamp of something peculiarly Russian: the abyss of consuming fire and ecstasy depicted in "icons").

This "metaphysical" dimension, which is manifest in the great philosophical systems, is not, therefore, an "ultimate conclusion" at which one arrives on the basis of the empirical sciences; it is, on the contrary, more like their *a priori*: since it is already manifest, at a formal level, in the relation between "μετά" and "φυσικά" — indeed, since "experiment" itself, understood as the organon and method of the empirical sciences, already implies a distinct "theory" (as Hugo Dingler showed in his *Experiment*).[12] Rather, as with the great Chinese and Ionian philosophers, "metaphysics" is properly a matter of contemplation for that "penetrating gaze"[13] which is the function and fruit of an examined life. In Plato, accordingly, it is the object of "ἐπιστήμη," i.e., of an "understanding" situated in the "confrontation" between the most intense proximity and a greater distance — this being the site at which the mystery of myth begins to dawn. Something similar applies even to Aristotle's "ἀπόδειξις." For, however much it would appear to be (*contra* Plato) a kind of "exact demonstration" of the sort proper to the natural sciences, as an "illustration from" — that is, an "illustration on the basis of the arche-

---

12. Hugo Dingler, *Das Experiment: Sein Wesen und seine Geschichte* (München: Reinhardt, 1928).

13. *Durchschauen.* — Trans.

type in the image" (for "δείκνυμι" means an artistic representation) — it nevertheless betrays that "immediate contact between archetype and image" in which the "knowledge" of the artist (or of the truly "inspired philosopher")[14] consists. Nor is it without reason that Thomas distinguishes between the *"intus legere"* of *"intellectus"* and the *"ratiocinari"* of *"ratio"*: between, that is, a "reading [from] within the interior of things" and a "calculative ordering." According to this distinction, *"intellectus"* is concerned with the "principles of things," while *"ratio"* is concerned instead with "calculable connections." This then develops into the tradition that one can trace not only into the thought of Nicholas of Cusa, but — from him — into the whole of modern philosophy: in that, for Kant, the moral and the artistic are the window onto ultimate being; in that, in Hegel, Schelling, and Baader it is in the "contemplation"[15] of an intuitive "vision" that the ultimate ground is disclosed; and in that the "contemplative vision of Romanticism," as mediated by Franz Brentano, is unquestionably the tradition ultimately informing both Husserl's *"Wesenschau"* and (even more so) Scheler's *"Wertfühlen."* Such is the ultimate consequence of the objective correlation between the "formal form" of "meta" (understood in terms of its inner span) and the formally theological "meta" of the divine (following the formulae of Gregory the Great and Dionysius the Areopagite). Just as, objectively, the formal "meta" and the formally theological "meta" imply a pluriform distance with regard to the "φυσικά" (that of the creaturely regions of being), so too a correspondingly subjective method will have this "meta" as its form: the form, that is, of a "beyond" and "over" and "under" and "into" in regard to these "φυσικά" — inasmuch as "like is [known] only by like" (in keeping with the strict hierarchical ordering of knowledge in Plato). The only thing that properly corresponds to an objectively distant "meta" is a "method peculiar to meta itself." It is what all methods of the religious life describe as a distancing or abstention, etc.: i.e., a solitary comportment with regard to all empirical "φυσικά," ultimately "overcoming" and "leaping over" them (*"transilire,"* in the language of Augustine). As a kind of "religiousness intrinsic to secular knowledge," it constitutes the ultimate ground of Romanticism's "contemplative vision" and of, last but not least, the "epochē" of "bracketing abstention" in Husserl's *"Wesensschau"* (this being the ultimate "religious inspiration" of his philosophy).

The following, then, are correlated: first, an objectively formal "meta"

14. *Der wahrhaft musische Philosoph.* — Trans.
15. *Kontemplativität.* — Trans.

(which can be found at the origin of every metaphysics); second, an objective, formally theological "Meta" (in which the former "meta" finds its fulfillment in the divine); and, third, conformed to each of these, a "method intrinsic to the meta itself." This correlation directly points to a *span within metaphysics* whose tension runs through all of metaphysics' possible forms.

This span lies between the "limit forms" peculiar to *a priori* metaphysics and those peculiar to *a posteriori* metaphysics. To be sure, an *a priori* metaphysics, of the sort that was the ideal of the Enlightenment (since "truth" can only be "absolute" and, hence, only a *"vérité de raison,"* never a *"vérité de faits"*) met its end in Kant's critical philosophy: since a *"vérité de raison"* can never touch upon the real, in the sense presumed by Enlightenment rationalism; rather, the real could be conceived only within an *"a priori* synthetic judgment," which is to say, within a "judgment" that would achieve a synthesis between *a priori* "absolute truth" and *a posteriori* "relative fact." An *a priori* absolute truth remains a formalism, but a metaphysics of real facts is no metaphysics of absolute truth. Accordingly, there can be no such thing as a strictly *a posteriori* metaphysics (of the kind that "critical realism" — understood as a metaphysics of ultimate conclusions — seeks to develop out of the results achieved by the empirical sciences). For these ultimate conclusions are either genuine and reached in the context of empirical evidence — in which case they intrinsically belong within the limits of the empirical sciences themselves — or they are taken as representing an authentic "leap" to a new, genuinely metaphysical level — which would demand a formally "metaphysical approach" essentially distinct from the approach of the empirical sciences. As a result, *a priori* and *a posteriori* metaphysics simply raise the obviously perplexing question asked by Kant: "How are synthetic judgments *a priori* possible?"

At base, however, this perplexity, situated between two impossibilities (which are nevertheless necessities), is a symbol: for it points through this "impossibility as necessity" to a possible medium between the two extremes of *a priori* and *a posteriori* metaphysics. In contrast to every constructive, "transcending" metaphysics, in which the "meta" proper to both of these (impossible) limit forms is purely "transcending" — whether this be a "leap" from a super-factical *a priori* into the *a posteriori* of the facts themselves, or a "leap" beyond these *a posteriori* facts into something ultimate and super-factical with an *a priori* validity — the correlation we noted above (among an objectively formal "meta" with regard to all the "φυσικά," an objective, formally theological "Meta" proper to the divine in which the former "meta" has its fulfillment, and the "method within the meta" that is conformed to

UNIVERSAL RHYTHM

both) implies a different approach: that of a metaphysics developed from within the "φυσικά," as their "interior as exterior" and their "above as below," and following a method that, corresponding to this "interior as exterior" and "above as below," proceeds precisely by means of a "passage through the world of facts," arriving through and beyond them at what is "ultimate" — since it is precisely this "ultimate" that is not simply "transcendent" but "transcendent as immanent." For this reason there can be only this *one metaphysics of "analogy"* (the analogy being implied in the tension between transcendent and immanent), for which Aristotle laid the groundwork with his definition of analogy as "ἄλλο πρὸς ἄλλο" (i.e., as an ultimate proportion between other and other) and to which the Fourth Lateran Council lent a theological form with its definition of an "ever greater dissimilarity within every similarity, however great."

Both of the impossible possibilities with regard to a metaphysics — the *a priori* and the *a posteriori* — are based upon one and the same "identitarian linear thinking" (which represents the "*in actu*," as it were, of the "principle of identity," and which lies at the basis of almost all systems). Obedient to such "linear thought," an *a priori* metaphysics seeks to deduce the *a posteriori* of the real from its *a priori*; likewise, an *a posteriori* metaphysics seeks to derive the *a priori* from its *a posteriori*. Even Hegel's solution of making the internal contradiction between the *a priori* and the *a posteriori* itself into a "metaphysical method" of "antithetical synthesis" turns out to be simply a more refined "linearity" — one in which the dialectical apriorism (among thesis, antithesis, and synthesis, in the *a priori* form of "judgment") is simply identified with the "real dialectic" found within every realm of the real universe. In contrast to this linearity (in the "*in actu*" of the "principle of identity"), "analogy as being" and "analogy as method" (i.e., *ontic* and *noetic analogy*) indicate precisely the same thing we discovered above within our threefold correlation (the correlation, that is, of an objectively formal "meta," an objective, formally theological "Meta," and a "method within the meta"). By an objectively formal "meta" we mean a μετά that is at once within and without, above and below the (entire range of the) φυσικά: i.e., the "meta" of a fundamental "in-and-beyond" that holds sway between the region of the φυσικά and the region of the μετά: in short, "meta" in the sense of "analogy." By an objective, formally theological "Meta," which represents the fulfillment of this objectively formal "meta," we mean three things: an "interiority" of the divine within the creature precisely *as* an "exteriority"; a divine "encompassing (of the creature)" precisely *as* an "indwelling"; and a divine "subtending (as the root of the creature)" pre-

526

cisely *as* a (freely sovereign) "superiority (over the creature)": that is, we mean the "Meta" of a still more radical "in-and-beyond" of the divine (understood as the content of the "Meta") with regard to the creaturely φυσικά — i.e., we mean, once again, "Meta" *as* "analogy." And then, corresponding to this twofold, objective "meta and Meta," there is a metaphysical "method within the meta," whereby — precisely within the profoundest and most penetrating investigation of the φυσικά — one becomes conscious of what grounds the φυσικά from "above" and "below" them (that is, their *"Untergrund"* and *"Obergrund"*), just as — within the most comprehensive encompassing of the φυσικά — one is conscious of the φυσικά in their inmost interior: which is to say that the metaphysical method, which "meta" implies, consists in a methodological "in-and-beyond": it consists, that is, in "analogy as method."

If "analogy as being" spans the distance between its foothold (within the formal relation between μετά and φυσικά) and its fulfillment in the divine, then to speak of "analogy as method" is to speak of conforming our method to the entire span of "analogy as being." "Analogy as method" (understood here as *the* "metaphysical method") signifies a penetration of and dwelling in and resonating with the φυσικά (in their full compass) of such a sort that, precisely in this respect, one becomes conscious of what is beneath, what is above, what is within, and what encompasses the φυσικά; precisely for this reason, however, it does not lead to a static "con-cept," but rather remains within the "rhythm" that begins ever anew as soon as the "analogy" is "attained": such that, within the resonance between the "other and other" of the φυσικά, one might discover the ultimate "proportion," which is experienced as impossible to experience (according to the Aristotelian analogy) — and such that, within "even the greatest approximation"[16] to the rhythm of this proportion, one might have a presentiment of the divine "proportion of this proportion" upon the infinite horizon of *its* "ever greater dissimilarity" (according to the Fourth Lateran Council's definition of analogy).

Precisely for this reason, however, a genuine metaphysics is possible only in the form of an *abidingly differential, immanent metaphysics* of the "other and other" of the various distinct regions of being proper to the "φυσικά": as an immanent metaphysics of matter, vegetal life, animal life, spiritual life, and human life; of knowledge, of morality, and of art. In this sense, metaphysics is methodologically "polymorphous" — indeed, "polymorphous *in infinitum*" (just as, for Thomas Aquinas, the creaturely is an

---

16. *Noch so großer Einähnlichung.* — Trans.

"*infinitum potentia*"[17]). It is only in the form of such a polymorphous metaphysics (in keeping with the "other and other" that obtains among the various regions of being proper to the "φυσικά") that this metaphysics becomes the ultimate "organon" for the "Meta" of the divine — that which, according to Thomas, can be experienced only as what is "*simpliciter et uniformiter*" with regard to the antithetical polymorphousness of the creaturely universe, and which for this reason is experienced within the medium of a cosmic "*coincidentia oppositorum*," as Nicholas of Cusa ultimately concludes from Aquinas's principle. In the past, there has been a reluctance to produce a polymorphous metaphysics of this sort; the various metaphysical systems that have historically arisen are distinguishable from one another in that almost every one of them is primarily a metaphysics of one particular region of being: thus, in Descartes one has an immanent metaphysics of knowledge; in Kant, an immanent metaphysics of morals; in Schelling, an immanent metaphysics of art; in Baader, an immanent metaphysics of sex; in Hegel, an immanent metaphysics of history. But it is only by way of a methodological de-absolutization of these different metaphysics into relative and different parts of *one* polymorphous metaphysics that a path is opened to an actual polymorphous metaphysics. When each particular region of being is translated out of the domain of its empirical "φυσικά" into its differential immanent "meta," a view opens upon the formally theological, abidingly differential "Meta" of the divine: i.e., the differentially immanent "God-aspect" within the material realm, the vegetal realm, the animal realm, the spiritual realm, the human realm, and the realms of knowledge, morality, and beauty. A so-called "*theologia naturalis*" or "theodicy" or "philosophy of religion," then, does not constitute some kind of ultimate consideration set apart from an ultimate metaphysics of the regions of creaturely being; rather, it is in each case what is ultimate for each region of being: it is the differential, formally theological "Meta" in-and-beyond their intrinsic "meta." In this way, finally, an ascending hierarchy of the regions of being (from matter to plant to animal to spirit to man to the dimensions of knowledge, morality, and art) becomes a medium — likewise characterized by an ever increasing ascent — transparent to the ever surmounting "Meta" of the divine. To use the language of Thomas: the "*infinitum potentia*," the "*in infinitum*" of the creaturely, becomes a medium transparent to the "*infinitum actu*," which is to say, to the ever more incomprehensible actual infinity of God who, precisely for this reason, "is

17. *Potentia* is in the ablative. — Trans.

sought in order to be found, and is found in order to be sought" (which Augustine sees as the most proper way to the divine).

Admittedly, such a *polymorphous dynamic metaphysics* would seem to be adumbrated in the development from John Scotus Eriugena to Paracelsus to Jacob Böhme to Franz von Baader. But the kind of metaphysics we mean here is neither a cosmological metaphysics (of the kind Baader attempted with his doctrine of an interpenetration of nature and God: between the elemental powers and the arcanum of God, which manifests itself in their opposition and correlation), nor a metaphysics of a God who gives "birth" to himself ever anew out of his own internal dialectic (as one sees in the dynamistic theosophy of Paracelsus and Jacob Böhme: in that, for them, it is in the most proper sense God himself who primordially "grounds" and "ungrounds" the "ground" and "abyss"[18] of the world, all within an ever-renewed alternation between the "fire of wrath" and the "fire of love"). Nor do we mean the metaphysics of Cusa's *"coincidentia oppositorum,"* taken in an absolute sense, such as would directly identify the cosmic *coincidentia* with God as *Coincidentia*. For, in the final analysis, what all these forms of metaphysics have in common — however much they may resemble a genuinely polymorphous dynamic metaphysics — is that the "principle of identity" is powerfully at work within them: the principle that so often misrepresents the "principle of non-contradiction," in which, in reality, the *one* "analogy" definitively appears (not as a principle, but as a rhythm). In fact, however, as its structure suggests, a polymorphous dynamic metaphysics is simply a self-manifestation of this "analogy" that governs all things: the analogy of the "proportion between other and other" intrinsic to the relation of the regions of being one to another, and within which the analogy of an "ever greater dissimilarity in every similarity, however great" — taken as, so to speak, the "proportion of the (intra-creaturely) proportion" between the divine and the totality of creaturely being — opens up: as a "vertical analogy" (between the divine and the creaturely) in-and-beyond the "horizontal analogy" (within the domain of the creature). A "metaphysics in analogy" is thus characterized by *three stages:*

1. An immanent metaphysics of the different regions of being (with the goal of discerning the "image of God" immanent to each of the regions of being, understood as the "Meta" of its "meta");
2. A metaphysics of the *"coincidentia oppositorum"* of these different

18. *"Grund"* und *"Ungrund."* — Trans.

metaphysics concerning the different regions of being (with the goal of discerning — as immanent to this cosmic *"coincidentia oppositorum"* — a universal, intra-cosmic "image of God," as the higher "Meta" of the first "Meta");

3. An explicit theo-metaphysics that is in-and-beyond this (second) metaphysics of the *coincidentia* (in which case the "similarity, however great" of a metaphysics of the *coincidentia* becomes vertically transparent to the Metaphysicum, which is "ever more dissimilar," of God in himself).

As such, a "metaphysics in analogy" (that is, a metaphysics consisting in a vertical analogy in-and-beyond a horizontal analogy) is a theo-metaphysics in a double sense. It is a theo-metaphysics, firstly, with respect to the formal minimum of the question *"an est Deus"* (as Thomas formulates it), that is, "whether" and "that" there is a "God as such," leading to the idea of God (of the *"divinum"* or the *"absolutum"*) that, according to Thomas, is shared by Christians and non-Christians alike as a "formality of the divine," which the Christian sees realized in the Trinity and the pagan in his "idol."[19] Secondly, however, it is a theo-metaphysics with respect to the material maximum of *"quid est Deus"* — that is, "what God is" — inasmuch as all statements of revelation, however exalted (not only those proper to the Christian sphere, but also those outside of it), ultimately converge upon the *"quid"* of the utterly *incomprehensible* mystery God, of whom "I can only say what he is not" (in the words of Augustine), since he is utterly *"Supra"* and, as such, the *"Deus tanquam ignotus"* (according to Anselm of Canterbury and Thomas), the one who is "beyond everything external to himself and everything that can be conceived," the one who is "ineffably super-sublime" (according to the Vatican Council [I]).[20] With regard to the formal minimum of *"an est Deus,"* the *one* "metaphysics in analogy" is a formal theo-metaphysics that constitutes, as it were, the basis[21] for all religions and revelations; at the same time, with regard to the material maximum of *"quid est Deus,"* the *one* "metaphysics in analogy" constitutes a kind of ultimate material theo-metaphysics, in that it is also theologically ultimate in regard to Christian revelation, which in the final analysis makes its most exalted material contents transparent to the "measureless depths" of the "God . . . who dwells in unapproachable light, whom

---

19. *Summa Th.* I, q. 13, a. 10, ad 5.
20. Denz. 1782.
21. *Das Unterhalb.* — Trans.

no one has ever seen or can see" (Rom. 11:33; 1 Cor. 2:10; 1 Tim. 6:16). A "metaphysics in analogy" is so radically and totally situated within its analogy (that of a vertical analogy in-and-beyond a horizontal analogy) that this analogy is at once what is lowest and what is highest: lowest in the formal analogy intrinsic to a formal theo-metaphysics (as is proper to the formal minimum of *"an est Deus"*); highest (inasmuch as this is conceivable) in the material analogy, as the Fourth Lateran Council formulates it precisely with regard to what, in Christianity, is "most supernatural," namely, the Trinity: that in "every similarity, however great (that of an indwelling of the Trinity in human beings)" what is ultimate is the "ever greater dissimilarity" (of the inaccessible mystery beyond human beings) — so much so that for Thomas, as regards God's proper *"quid est,"* God remains the "unknown God" even within his greatest self-revelation.

Having set out *from metaphysics,* we thus arrive at the point where an *internal encounter* takes place *between metaphysics and Christianity:* because the formal theo-metaphysics of *"an est Deus"* is the *"naturam supponit,"*[22] the objective presupposition, for all revealed doctrines, including those of Christianity — in such a way, however, that even the revealed doctrines of Christianity ultimately converge upon a material theo-metaphysics of *"Deus tanquam ignotus."* Thus, on the one hand, a material theo-metaphysics represents a kind of *"perficit naturam"* or crowning fulfillment; on the other hand, to the extent that this formula *"Deus tanquam ignotus"* has the appearance of a self-renunciation of a genuine *"quid est Deus,"* it is almost indistinguishable from the pure *"an est Deus"* asked by a formal theo-metaphysics. It is not simply that both a formal and a material theo-metaphysics stand, each respectively, "in analogy," but that they themselves stand in a relation of analogy to one another. *However much* a formal theo-metaphysics is fulfilled in the "however great" proper to material revelations regarding God — even to the point of a genuine *"quid est Deus"* — the only abiding *"quid est Deus"* is the "ever greater" of the Augustinian *"quid non est Deus."* In other words, what is ultimate in "what God is" is "what God is not." This entails not only the "above-and-beyond" of the actual *"quid est Deus,"* above every revelation, however exalted, but also, in the midst of this, precisely a "descent" to the poverty of a formal *"an est Deus."* For not only is every *"quid est Deus,"* however exalted and plenteous, at the end of the day the *"quid"* of the *"Deus tanquam ignotus,"* the unknown God (which is how

---

22. The reference is to the Thomistic maxim: *gratia non destruit, sed supponit et perficit naturam. Vide supra,* pp. 169f. — Trans.

Thomas sums up his entire theology in his commentary on Boethius' *De Trinitate*), but Thomas takes this so far that even the most exalted revelation remains *within* the poverty of the *"an est Deus,"* by virtue of the "ever greater dissimilarity between creator and creature," which is to say, by virtue of the *one* "analogy."

2. Having reached this conclusion, we have more or less sketched out the parameters within which the *encounter between Christianity and metaphysics* can now be seen from the opposite direction, namely, *from the perspective of Christianity:* in the patristic period it took the form of an engagement with Plotinian Platonism; in the scholastic period, with Arabic and Jewish Aristotelianism; in the past century, in Hermes, Günther, and Deutinger, with Hegelianism; and around the turn of the century, in the case of so-called "modernism" (under Loisy and Tyrrell), with [the philosophy] of Bergson. In all of these cases, however, the encounter was purely a matter of circumstance, and not based in reflection upon the fundamental principle of an encounter between Christianity and metaphysics as such. The principle of such an encounter, as seen from metaphysics, is grounded in the opposition between the minimum of *"an est Deus"* within a formal theo-metaphysics and the maximum of *"quid est Deus"* within a material theo-metaphysics.

For a formal theo-metaphysics of *"an est Deus,"* Christianity would seem to provide the requisite answer to the question *"quid est Deus?"* For, according to the Johannine and Pauline writings, Christ appears as the "what" of the "invisible God": as the "Logos," "icon," "mirror," "reflection," "image," "exegesis" of the "God whom no one has seen"[23] — not to mention the utterly incisive words of Christ himself: "Whoever has seen me has seen the Father" (John 14:9). The ultimate "essence of Christianity" is therefore this *one* (in the strict sense) "theological" asseveration: that, on the one hand, the question *"quid est Deus?"* (to which a formal theo-metaphysics of *"an est Deus"* automatically leads) is adequately answered in the "seeing of the invisible God in the seeing of Christ" (in a "self-expression" of God himself, whereby the "meaning of God is illumined by God":[24] in accordance with the twofold acceptation of "λόγος" as both "word" and "meaning") — such that, on the other hand, all human theology (as "λέγειν" concerning this *"quid est Deus"*) is practically nothing but the "interpretation" (*"exegesis"*) of the received self-expression of the meaning of God in Christ, i.e., a partici-

---

23. John 1:1; Col. 1:15; Wis. 7:26; Heb. 1:3; John 1:18.
24. *Selbst Aufleuchten des Sinn Gottes.* — Trans.

patory reenactment and comprehension of the "theology of God himself" (in his "self-expression in Christ") as the "Christological theology of God himself."

To "see" Christ, then, is to "see the invisible God"; this same Christ stands out — as the word "seen" already suggests, and as he appears throughout the Gospels, and as Christian theology from the outset conceived him — as the "incarnate Word" possessed of a complete human nature (John 1:14). Thus he appears precisely as "eternal life with the Father and to the Father," but at the same time precisely "as eternal life . . . which has appeared among us": so fully human that he is "heard (with ears), seen with eyes, beheld (as one beholds a play), and touched with hands"; precisely thus is he the "Logos of life" (1 John 1:1-2). For this reason (according to Augustine), he is *"Totus Deus totus homo,"* totally God, totally man — so much so that (according to Gelasius I) he is *"totus Deus homo et totus homo Deus,"* "totally God as man and totally man as God," whereby the "total man persists in what is God and the total God persists in what is man" (Denz. 168). It is therefore not the case that Christ is a pure manifestation of the *"quid est Deus"*: either in the way he was taken to be by the early Christian Docetists, who saw Christ's humanity as the mere "appearance" of "pure Deity," or in the way he was taken to be by the Alexandrians (and even by certain Catholic schools of theology today), for whom Christ's existence was understood as being purely a "glory-existence." Rather, everything in this Christ "in whom one sees God" is completely man in flesh and blood and spirit, according to the "common schema of man" (ἐν ὁμοιώματι ἀνθρώπων καὶ σχήματι . . . ὡς ἄνθρωπος — Phil. 2:7). Neither is it the case, on the other hand, that the "figure and form of God" in Christ (Phil. 2:6) is simply "God's glory shining through" a mere man: in the way that the early-Christian Antiochenes (and their remainder today in liberal Protestant theology, in the tradition of Schleiermacher, Ritschl, and Harnack) took Christ's existence as simply the existence of a "completed man," in whose "probation as man" God shines through, resulting in a merely symbolic "God in Christ"; rather, everything in this Christ whom one has "heard with ears, seen with eyes, touched with hands" is completely the "presence of God," even to the point of one's "hearing, seeing, and touching" the God whom "one cannot see," who dwells "in unapproachable light" (John 1:18; 1 Tim. 6:16). Thus, a *"quid est Deus,"* understood as the fulfillment of the metaphysical *"an est Deus,"* does not appear in Christ except in this way: that this Christian *"quid est Deus"* is revealed solely in "Christ the *paradox*," as the "paradox of paradoxes," and so it is but the *"quid"* of a *"Deus paradoxos."* If a formal theo-metaphysics of *"an est Deus"* reaches its highest peak in the negative material theo-metaphysics of *"quid non est Deus,"* then the "Christological theo-logy" of the positive, material *"quid est Deus"* — which is the desideratum of all theo-metaphysics — must be understood solely as the "Christological theo-paradoxo-logy" of a *"Deus Paradoxos in Christo paradoxo"* (as follows from a thorough consideration of the patristic maxim that the incarnation is the "παράδοξον παραδόξων").

This is fulfilled in the kind of encounter that takes place between a *material theo-metaphysics* of *"quid est Deus"* (by which we mean, in fact, a negative, material theo-metaphysics of *"quid Deus non est"*) and authentic Christianity. God in Christ does not simply constitute the paradox of the incarnation (in which case the appearance of a totally ideal or spiritual God *as* a totally ideal or spiritual man would still allow for the possibility of a true, positive *"quid est Deus"*). Nor is God in Christ a "paradox" in the sense of a linear ascent "above-and-beyond" all human form, however paradoxical (for, while this would disallow a positive *"quid est Deus,"* since such a God would be "beyond everything," beyond even his own human form, one could nevertheless mistake the actual *"quid"* of God, along the lines of a cataphatic *"theologia eminentiae,"* for a linear "above-and-beyond" of God). On the contrary, God in Christ is something above and beyond even "paradox"; it is what the first letter to the Corinthians, with particularly sharp emphasis, calls the "scandal" of a "foolish madness" of a "divine foolishness" and a "divine weakness" in the "scandal" and "foolish madness" of Christ, understood as the one who is (essentially!) the "crucified" (1:21-25: taken in the full sense of *"skandalon"* and *"moron"*) — whereby the crucified is to be understood, moreover, according to an ultimate realism, as one who was "made sin" and a "curse," and who was "expelled from the preserve of the covenant" as one "forsaken by God" in ultimate "messianic disgrace" (2 Cor. 5:21; Gal. 3:13; Heb. 13:12f.; Matt. 27:46) — to the point, moreover, that the "fullness of the body of Christ" is not the "body of Christ" unless this same "scandal and foolish madness" of the "cross" is at work in its "members" and, not only this, but to the point that these members have precisely the task "to fill out what is lacking in [these] afflictions" (Gal. 2:19; 1 Cor. 4:9-13; Col. 1:24). In reality there is no other "paradox of God in the paradox of the incarnation" but that which is incomparably surpassed by the "scandal and the foolish madness" of God in the crucified Christ, since it is only by virtue of the "blood" that Christ is the "head and consummation of all things, all things in heaven and all things on earth," from "before the foundation of the world," as "the lamb slain before the foundation of the world" (Eph. 1:4-14;

Rev. 13:8). Any "glory of God in the glory of Christ" consists *in* the "scandal and foolish madness" of this all-deciding *Mysterium Crucis,* and in this alone: inasmuch as there is no glory but the "glory of the cross" (Gal. 6:14). So little is it possible to secularize this *Mysterium Crucis* as a "historical accident" (as some contemporary Christian circles have sought to do, following Peterson and Guardini) that Paul, "with tears," denounces such "emptying of the cross" as "enmity toward the cross of Christ" (1 Cor. 1:17; Phil. 3:18).

This Christianity (which is the only real one) can certainly be seen as fulfilling the *"quid Deus non est"* of a material theo-metaphysics: insofar as in it the supreme inconceivability of God himself is revealed. But if the "paradox of God in the paradox of the incarnation" already downright exploded the (negatively eminent) *"quid"* of a philosophical *"Divinum"* or *"Absolutum,"* then the "scandal and foolish madness" of God in the "cross of Christ" turns out to be nothing less than the "scandal and foolish madness" of a "contradiction" of everything that can be imagined or conceived under the word "God." For in this "scandal and foolish madness" of the Christian God, the answer that is given to a material theo-metaphysics of a *"quid Deus est"* is not only that of a "contradictory God," but nothing less than a "contradiction in regard to the divine as such." Nor is it possible to resolve the "contradiction in regard to the divine as such" in such a way that one turns this contradiction into a "metaphysicum" proper to God himself: in the way that the theosophy of Jacob Böhme tries to make the *Mysterium Crucis* transparent to an intra-divine dialectic between an "abyss of wrath" and a "ground of love" within God himself, in which God, so to speak, "crucifies himself" in a "crossing" between a "God of darkness" (who darkly appears in the cross of Christ) and a "God of light" (who is reflected in the resurrection of Christ). For this would be to take what is most incomprehensible in God and conceptualize it into a comprehensible dialectic. It would constitute the worst kind of "enmity toward the cross of Christ," precisely because it is an enmity that is disguised: since in the case of this kind of reduction, the "paradoxical, scandalous, foolish, mad" reality that the "cross of Christ" *is* has been dissolved into a dialectical cosmo-theo-sophy — which actually, precisely "at Golgotha," renews the very situation of the first and original sin, the desire "to know as God knows" and thus "to be like God." The only thing that remains for us to affirm is that it is precisely in the unresolved and irresoluble *Mysterium Crucis* in the Crucified Christ that we see *the* "Logos" and "icon" and "mirror" and "reflection" and "image" and "appearance and exegesis" of the God "whom no one has ever seen or can see" (1 Tim. 6:16). When fully grasped, the words of Christ, "Whoever has seen me, has seen the Father," mean: "Whoever has seen me as the Crucified, saw in this scandal and fool-ish madness the Father," who is the "true Father" in that "he did not spare his only-begotten Son, but delivered him for us all (into the scandal and foolish madness of the cross)" (Rom. 8:32), into which Christ "gave himself up" (Gal. 2:20).

What this implies is, firstly: an internal opposition between the "para-dox (of the incarnation)" and the "scandal and foolish madness (of redemp-tion in the *Mysterium Crucis*)." But while the form of the "scandal and fool-ish madness" goes above-and-beyond the form of the "paradox," it is nevertheless the innermost form of the "paradox": since there is no other (real) incarnation than one that stands from the beginning under the form of the *Mysterium Crucis*. This "in-and-beyond" between the "scandal and foolish madness (of redemption in the *Mysterium Crucis*)" and the "paradox (of the incarnation)" is the "analogy" internal to a Christian "Christological theology." Secondly, this intra-Christian analogy, taken as a whole, is — sec-ondly — the intrinsic answer to the whole intra-metaphysical analogy be-tween a formal theo-metaphysics of *"an est Deus"* and a negative-material theo-metaphysics of *"quid Deus non est."* But — thirdly — inasmuch as the intra-Christian analogy (between God in the paradox and God in the scan-dal and foolish madness), as the intrinsic answer to the intra-metaphysical analogy (between a formal *"an est Deus"* and a negative *"quid Deus non est"*), is incomprehensibly above-and-beyond every "possible theo-metaphysics" — the relation between every possible theo-metaphysics and the only possi-ble Christianity itself consists in an ultimate "analogy." This analogy, which incomprehensibly surpasses every intra-metaphysical analogy, is an "anal-ogy" in which what is truly ultimate, above-and-beyond every similarity, however great (in the relationship between theo-metaphysics and Christian-ity), is the "ever greater dissimilarity" of the true *"Divinum"* and *"Absolutum"* in the "paradox" and "scandal and foolish madness" that Chris-tianity proclaims: the Christian "Meta" as the "Meta" of every theo-metaphysical "Meta," and thus the "Meta of the Meta" of every metaphysics of the "meta."

10 Beautiful, Sacred, Christian

1957

The only way to get to the bottom of the problem of Christian art and, specifically, Christian ecclesial art — and the only way to determine any guidelines that might apply to it — is by way of the connection among the three words in our title. On the one hand, sacred art and Christian art develop essentially out of the objective possibilities that are proper to the "beautiful." On the other hand, if these objective artistic possibilities should develop into sacred or Christian art, they are then subject to those objective necessities immanent to the sacred and the Christian. And within the realm of the sacred and the Christian, whereas Christian art is possible solely on the basis of the sacred, the sacred itself achieves its concrete form only within the realm of the Christian. On the one hand, it is impossible to develop any sacred or Christian art that is not objectively "beautiful" — which is to say, that is not really "art." But, on the other hand, it is impossible to derive what is sacred and Christian (in Christian sacred art) from what is "beautiful" in genuine "art." On the one hand, for sacred and Christian art, there can be no such thing as *"l'art pour l'art"* according to exclusively artistic criteria (still less the "gamble" of "artistic experiments"). On the other hand, it is equally impossible that the genuinely "beautiful" proper to authentic "art" should stand under the dictatorship of practical, sacred-Christian "utility." Thus, the above sequence, "beautiful, sacred, Christian," is the essential basis of our investigation.

To borrow Thomas's terms, the authentically "beautiful" in real "art" is the *"natura,"* which is unavoidably "presupposed by" *("supponit")* the *"gra-*

This essay first appeared in *Archivio di Filosofia,* Rome (1957).

tia" of the sacred and the Christian. Equally, however, the sacred (in sacred art) is suspended in the unreal free-floating air of the ideal so long as it is not envisioned in concrete terms, as is the case with Christianity (which represents the fulfillment and hence concrescence of all the sacred forms of all peoples of all times). This is by no means to say that sacred and Christian art could be developed immanently out of the genuinely "beautiful" of real "art" (as one sees in the construction of most churches today, which are intentionally modeled on the abstract technologies of today's secular buildings, without the slightest regard for what is proper to the sacred and the Christian, so that there is scarcely any discernible difference between modern churches and modern factories). But neither, on the other hand, can it be said that the sacred and the Christian constitute their own "artistic style" (which for the most part ends up in a naïve "edifying kitsch" whose only distinction from authentic art is its artistic inferiority). Our task, accordingly, is to disclose the entire range of possibilities proper to what is "beautiful" in real "art," in order then to contrast this range of possibilities with the same range of possibilities in the realm of the sacred and the Christian.

1

The range of possibilities inherent in the *"beautiful"* (in real art) is most properly revealed by the meanings of the words used to describe it: the Greek "καλόν," the Latin *"pulchrum,"* and the German *"schön."*

The Greek "καλόν" flickers between the sense of practical "utility" and that of purely evaluative "nobility." Taken in the sense of something practically "useful," "καλόν" sinks to the level of a practical form of deft evasiveness in human intercourse: "καλόν" in the sense of "That will do," the phrase by which one politely dismisses something. Taken in the sense of "noble," on the other hand, "καλόν" rises to the level of the Greeks' highest human ideal, "καλοκἀγαθόν": "noble" (καλόν), to the point of exalted astonishment (which is what ἀγαθόν actually means). In this respect, when "καλόν" is taken to mean "useful" and "polite in one's dealings," the measure of the beautiful is the "κοινόν" of what is "made common," to the point of signifying the "common taste" (and even a "common sense" art based upon "reasonable human judgment"). The measure of the beautiful in the sense of "καλόν" as "καλοκἀγαθόν," on the other hand, is the "ἐπέκεινα," the "above-and-beyond," which Plato associates with the "ἀγαθόν" beyond the "εἴδη," which virtually coincides with the divine (such that one can speak of an art of "divine genius," which precisely on this account shares with the divine its quality of being "anti-κοινόν," "surpassing all understanding," to the point that it is "rejected by the crowd"). If "καλόν" in the sense of "καλοκἀγαθόν" resides at the level of a "ὁμοίωσις τῷ θεῷ," an approximation to the "image of God," then "καλόν" in the sense of the "κοινόν," of utility in dealings with other people, ultimately implies a "ὁμοίωσις τῷ ὄχλῳ," that is, an approximation to the "image of the masses." If, then, the art of "καλόν" in the sense of "κοινόν" aims ultimately at the "ideal advertisement" of plebian democracy (the kind of "art everyone understands"), then the aim of "καλόν" in the sense of "καλοκἀγαθόν" is what we find in the icon of Byzantium, Ravenna, and the Eastern Church (but also of Giotto), which seek to portray man as an idea in God. The span of possibilities contained in "καλόν" oscillates between these two extreme poles. Since both of these poles are legitimate, there is no single possibility in which both poles would not have an effect, and in which therefore, in their influence, each would not cross over into and intertwine with the other. "Καλόν," taken in the sense of an approximation to the "image of God," will always be an approximation in an earthly, human form and, at least to this extent, is on its way to approaching the image of what is "common, earthly, and human." Conversely, an approximation to the image of what is common, earthly, and human — insofar as it is an approximation and a pictorial image — will (in however small a measure) be an "idealization of the really realistic": in the sense that even what is otherwise nothing but a "poster" nevertheless has a "style," which either makes an "essentializing simplification" of the empirically real or "translates it into a symbol" (as one sees in, say, the portrait-placards of the communist East, whose derivation from Eastern icons is undeniable). Without question, what the poster — "καλόν" as "κοινόν — and the icon — "καλόν" as "καλοκἀγαθόν" — have in common is a stylization of the real. And both share in this same "stylization of the real" when they are considered under their "mathematical and geometrical" aspect, though they differ in their characteristics: the poster — "καλόν" as "κοινόν" — is characterized by a technical mathematics (a technical mathematics in which the concrete reality is stripped down to a naked skeleton of intersecting lines, such as one sees in modern functional construction and today's ecclesial architecture); while the icon — "καλόν" as "καλοκἀγαθόν" — is characterized by a "sacred mathematics," which is, so to speak, a *"metaphysikoumenon"* that shines through, or can at least be sensed through the sensible chromaticism of artistic reality (as is also the case for someone like Dürer, whose underlying mathematical and geometrical framework can be glimpsed through the chromatic body of his paintings). Thus "καλόν," oscillating between "καλο-κἀγαθόν" and "κοινόν," oscillates here between the extreme poles of a bare mathematics (of which the poster-style of the Communist East and the poster-style of the contemporary Western world are diluted forms, but which one also sees in what Cubism and "abstract art" and modern functional architecture all seek to achieve) and a veiled mathematics, which — as a secret "measure, number, and weight" — is the ultimate mystery of the "stylization of the real" in any given work of art. Whereas the technical, naked mathematics of the "καλόν" as "κοινόν" is the ultimate consequence of the rationalized world of Descartes, the sacred, veiled mathematics stems from the deepest grounds of Pythagoras's cosmic, musical mathematics of the "divinely sacred number." What constitutes the "stylized reality" in the work of art — for all the possibilities of "καλόν" lying between the "καλοκἀγαθόν" of the icon and the "κοινόν" of the poster — is manifestly nothing other than that mathematical aspect of the genuinely "beautiful" that resides within it, which Thomas calls its *"ratio causae formalis,"*[1] the "pure form" that is abstracted from the real and, as such, is properly characterized by *"integritas, proportio debita et claritas."*[2] That is to say, what constitutes the "stylized reality" in the work of art is its essentiality, which (being opposed to what is too much or too little) consists in an oscillating proportion and clarity, understood as the splendor of this internal proportion — in other words, as the quality of Pythagoreanism's "musical number." In the technical sense of "καλόν" as "κοινόν," this "pure form" is not the abstracted "form of something real," but is rather the linear or paradoxical or exotic formalism of a "formal form in itself" that effectively has a life of its own; in the case of the (immanent) sacred "καλόν" of the "καλοκ-ἀγαθόν," on the other hand, the "pure form" accentuates the "essential" aspect of the real, which — inasmuch as it is "essential" — is there at the origin of its creation and at the end of its completion: that is to say, within the mysterious "adequation" of *"exitus"* and *"reditus."*[3] The full range of possibilities embraced by "καλόν" thus lies between this protological[4] and eschatological, historically original and historically ultimate "καλόν," and the "καλόν" of the "κοινόν," which would maintain a neutral, intrahistorical "tempered midpoint," accessible to "common human understanding," seeking to avoid every "menacing background" for the sake of an empirical "universal humanity." If, at one extreme, the "καλόν" of "καλοκ-ἀγαθόν" runs the risk of being a purely "metaphysical art," in which

---

1. *Summa Th.* I, q. 5, a. 4, ad 1.
2. *Summa Th.* I, q. 39, a. 8, corp.; *Summa Th.* I, q. 145, a. 2, corp.; *Summa Th.* I, q. 180, a. 2, ad 3.
3. *De Ver.* q. 20, a. 4, corp.
4. *Archaische* (in the sense of *archē*). — Trans.

the protological and eschatological backgrounds tend to stand out unveiled (as is more or less the case in the art of Hieronymous Bosch, Matthias Grünewald, the late Goya, van Gogh, and Gauguin), at the other extreme the "καλόν" of the "κοινόν" runs the risk of bourgeois accessibility (as in the art of the last decades of the nineteenth century) or purely empirical impressionism (a border situation that one sees, for example, in Liebermann, but also in Renoir). The authentic "καλόν" is a dynamic venture undertaken between the risks of these extremes.

The Latin-Roman notion of the beautiful is constituted by the *span between "pulchrum" and "bellum."* The word "pulchrum" is borrowed from the Greek, "πολύχροον." "Πολύχροον" signifies the "πολύ" of the "χρόα," which is to say, the pluriformity of skin, flesh, and body, as they are fundamentally experienced by our sense of touch. Accordingly, *"pulchrum"* signifies the polychromatic visibility of the shape of persons and things as such, to the point of signifying a magnificent glory. Whereas the Greek word "καλόν," on account of its form — *"de ratione formae"* — was for Plato and Plotinus an almost divine μονοειδής, the divine "simplicity of the ideal figure," the Latin word *"pulchrum"* consists precisely in a "polychromatic plenitude" — as we see, for example, in the manner in which the gods are depicted in the Palatine art of the Augustan age; but as we also see in the way that Titian and Rubens take the voluptuous, scintillating magnificence of the body as the concrete measure of the beautiful; or in the way that Baroque structures properly strive to achieve the magnificent sensory "πολύ" of an architectonic corporeal plenitude, of the sort that also governs the figures in Michelangelo's art and the intoxicating sonic fullness of Beethoven's music. Seen from this perspective, the Latin *"pulchrum"* is not merely the artistic symbol of the "πολύ" of the decidedly multiethnic *Imperium Romanum* (represented sacrally by the Roman pantheon, with its manifold gods belonging to its various peoples); rather, formally considered, it also expresses the "proud glory" of Rome — but (in keeping with the meaning it had among the original Latin peasantry) as the tangible beauty of "skin and flesh and body." Thus, if one understands "καλόν" as "pure form in itself," then *"pulchrum"* is the form it assumes in "skin and flesh and body." Whereas ancient Greek temples and sculptures look like "blowing spirit" captured in a "pure image," the defining aim of the *"pulchrum"* in Roman art is its, so to speak, humanization — indeed, superhumanization[5] — of the "Latin earth" of fields and livestock (just as the word *"cultura,"* derived from the Latin *"colere,"* simulta-

---

5. *Übermenschlichung.* — Trans.

neously means cult, culture, and agriculture). *"Bellum,"* on the other hand, means that which is beautiful in the sense of something "pretty, delightful, enchanting, fine, vivacious, pleasant, or precious." In and of itself it is not a word that suits the Roman essence (as it is expressed in *"pulchrum"*); and yet it is not without reason that it lies at the origin of the French, Italian, and even English words for the beautiful: *beau, belle, bello,* beauty, etc.). On the other hand, *"bellum"* reminds us not only of the playful luxuriance of the Roman imperial age or of the intrinsic "charm" of the "smooth radiance" of Raphael's paintings, but even to some extent — looking farther back — of the "gracile" terracottas of ancient Greece. Whereas the architectural expression of *"pulchrum"* can be seen in churches like St. Peter's and the *Gesù,* and still more in the Bavarian Baroque, *"bellum"* truly breathes in the light-winged Rococo, which is most properly expressed in the structures of the French Rococo. In fact, one could almost say that *"bellum"* became the inner form of the French and the Italian as such (and even of the English as such, to the extent that it derives from the French), while *"pulchrum"* expresses what is properly Roman, in its tension between express "glory" and earthly "corporeality." Whereas the musical expression of *"pulchrum"* is heard in the courtly pomp of Gluck and Handel (both of whom belonged to "imperial courts" in the Roman fashion: the one to imperial Vienna, the other to imperial England), *"bellum"* swings and plays and laughs (and "flirts") in the music of Haydn and Mozart — ultimately, however, under the aspect of the "καλόν" of the *"de ratione formae,"* in the sense of the pure fluttering of pure form, by which we mean neither "glory" nor "body," but rather that which is genuinely beautiful in itself, "αὐτὸ καθ' αὑτό," pure beauty as such, as an end in itself (which is how Kant and Goethe both understood the beautiful): the "Muse-ical,"[6] which is, according to Walter F. Otto, the *Urgrund* of the Hellenic as such.[7]

"Was aber schön ist, selig scheint es in ihm selbst" (Mörike).[8] In this we see, throughout all of these etymologies, that the span between *"pulchrum"* and *"bellum"* is one between the beautiful understood as "the glory of abundance and magnificence" and the beautiful understood as that which reso-

6. *Das Musische.* — Trans.
7. *Theophania,* 1956, p. 30, *inter alia.*
8. The famous last line from *"Auf eine Lampe."* The phrasing is ambiguous and can be taken to mean either "Whatever is beautiful shines blessedly within itself" or "Whatever is beautiful seems to be blessed in itself"; there have been many debates regarding which is the better reading (if one must choose), most famously that between Martin Heidegger (who preferred the former) and Emil Staiger (who preferred the latter). — Trans.

nates in itself as an end unto itself. Accordingly, whereas the beautiful understood as *"pulchrum"* is realized especially in sculpture and architecture, whose purpose has long been one of glory (both as a powerful symbol of the glory of the divine, as well as the symbol of the glory of a great people and nation), the beautiful understood as *"bellum"* is realized especially in the "pure resonance" of music, understood as that which is muse-ical (so much so that "program music," which is to say music made for a specific purpose, is repugnant to the spirit of genuine music). Inasmuch as both signify a corporeal beauty, however, *"pulchrum"* and *"bellum"* both stand opposed to the ideal beauty of "καλόν" (in its own proper span between "καλόν" understood as "καλοκἀγαθόν" and "καλόν" in the sense of the "κοινόν"). Whereas the beautiful in the sense of "καλόν" is the "μονο-ειδής" of Platonic-Plotinian tradition and, precisely to this extent, an ideal monochromaticism, beauty understood as *"pulchrum"* and *"bellum"* not only emphasizes "skin, flesh, and body," but emphasizes them expressly as "πολυειδής," as a "polychromatic" splendor. If one were to describe a possible synthesis between "καλόν" and *"pulchrum-bellum,"* the "monochromatic ideal" of "καλόν" would, on the one hand, constitute the transcendent ideality for the corporeality of *"pulchrum-bellum"* (as is organically represented in Eastern icons, but technically "organized" in today's "idealized posters" — just as also, in the realm of music, the great works of Liszt resonate with a dynamic transcendence that takes one "ever beyond" all the chromaticisms of his music). On the other hand, however, the "πολυ-ειδής" of *"pulchrum-bellum"* would seem to provide the required embodiment for the ideal and spiritual in "καλόν" (in the way that the corporeal massiveness of Michelangelo's works immediately represents the power of their idea, or in the way that Mozart's resonantly muse-ical — yet at the same time primordially powerful — music is immediately a "kingdom of the spirit"). Without the *"pulchrum-bellum,"* the "καλόν" runs the risk of becoming a spiritualistic beauty, culminating in the icily shimmering "pure kingdom" of Swedenborg, as Balzac eerily and captivatingly described it in his *Seraphita*. In the absence of the "καλόν," on the other hand, the *"pulchrum-bellum"* runs the risk of becoming a materialistic beauty (the opulence of "skin, flesh, and body," approximated by the art of Titian and by Flemish art in general, but made a reality in the long-drawn-out and indulgent sensory intoxications of Wagner's music).

The German word *"schön"* basically means that which is "fine looking" *(das Ansehnliche)*. On the one hand, it is something that is "there to be seen" in its radiance, but can be seen only when it is an object of particular attention, examination, and understanding; on the other hand, it is a kind of seeing that is simultaneously a *"Schonen,"* a "caring for" (in the sense of "treating something nicely," which is to say, treating it with care and with an eye to protecting it). Accordingly, purely in its connection with vision, the German *"schön"* means what Greek antiquity meant by "θεωρία," in the sense of what is presented to the "θεωρεῖν" of the "ἄνθρωπος θεωρετικός": that is, the pure vision granted to the purposeless gaze of the musing, simply perceiving human being, who lives by seeing, whose proper corresponding object is therefore the Platonic "εἴδη" in the sense of the "παραδείγματα" of the real, the inherently luminous archetypes, taken as the exemplars of real being. In its connection to *Schonen*, on the other hand, the German *schön* can be seen as providing an etymological foundation for what Solger calls the essential "fragility" of the beautiful: that most elevated, almost breath-like beauty, which, on the one hand, demands a straining of attention in order to be noticed and understood, but, on the other hand, not in a kind of "grasping," but only "with a light hand," as one would handle a fine and precious crystal or a fine and precious fabric that is always about to "break apart" and that is therefore experienced mostly in its subtlety, inasmuch as it is experienced essentially as something "easily broken." The German *"schön"* thus lies within this antithetical unity between an almost spiritual εἶδος and a material fragility. In this antithetical unity, eternity (that of the radiance of pure εἶδος) and transience (that of the fragility of almost spiritual matter) are joined. Whereas, by virtue of its form *(de ratione formae)*, the Greek "καλόν" aims at something like an existentiality of "pure forms" resting in themselves — at, that is, the immanent reality of an ideal form (the "existence *of* essence," as it were, or, more precisely, "essence *as* existence": just as, according to Walter F. Otto, the "pure figures" of the Greek images of the gods are the immediate presence of an "eternal being"); and whereas, conversely, the Latin *"pulchrum-bellum"* allows an ideal "καλόν" to shimmer through the opulent radiance or gracefulness of a reality rooted in itself (tending, that is, towards an "essence *of* existence" or, more precisely, "existence *as* essence"); in contrast to both "καλόν" and *"pulchrum-bellum,"* which here designate the beautiful in terms of an identity: that of an existential essence or an essential existence (and thus tend precisely to take the beautiful more or less as the divine, in which alone essence and existence are identical) — in contrast, that is, to the "beautiful as divine" in both "καλόν" and *"pulchrum-bellum"* — what we see in the German *"schön,"* in its internal antithetical unity of ideal vision and fragility, is the primordial phenomenon of the beautiful as an utmost proximity to the divine (in the moment of ideal vision), in which the ultimate event is precisely the harsh and melancholy experience of difference from the divine: the fragility of earthly, human transience. In this respect the German *"schön"* shows itself to be the genuinely "metaphysical beautiful" (that is, the beautiful in which the ultimate *"metaphysikoumenon"* of the beautiful as such presents itself: an ultimate suspension between ideal essence and fragile, transitory existence), whereas the Greek "καλόν," in identitarian fashion, takes essence as existence, and the Latin *"pulchrum-bellum"* along the same lines takes existence as essence. Whereas the Greek "καλόν" takes the Platonic-Augustinian *"ipsa forma"* of God to be the profoundest determination of the beautiful, the Latin *"pulchrum-bellum"* in like manner takes the Aristotelian-Thomistic *"ipsum esse"* of God to be the profoundest determination of being (such that ancient Greek sculpture and architecture are, as it were, "hovering spirit," while Roman sculpture and architecture are an "upheaval of the earth"). In contrast to these forms of identity, the "site" of the German *"schön"* is precisely the "analogy" of the Fourth Lateran Council: certainly there is a *"tanta similitudo"* (the greatest similarity, almost to the point of identity) between creator and creature; but this itself is ultimately situated within the *"maior dissimilitudo,"* that is, within the "ever greater dissimilarity" (and thus within the distance between the eternal and the transitory). Thus, whereas the Greek "καλόν" and the Latin *"pulchrum-bellum"* remain a "transcendental beauty" (both in the sense of the objective transcendentals of scholasticism — truth, goodness, beauty — and in the sense of their functionalization in German idealism) — the Greek "καλόν" as an "ideative transcendental," the Latin *"pulchrum-bellum"* as, so to speak, a "real transcendental" — it is in the German *"schön"* that, for the first time, the fragile creatureliness in the Greek "καλόν" and the Latin *"pulchrum-bellum"* acquires explicit form. Every form of "pure transcendentalism," however, replaces the incomprehensible "dynamic suspension" of "analogy" with something like a static *"tertium quid"* between the eternity of the divine and the fragility of the creature. Seen from this perspective, both "essence as existence" (the implicit meaning of the Greek "καλόν") and "existence as essence" (the implicit meaning of the Latin *"pulchrum-bellum"*) can be seen only as the most extreme formal limits of the "essence in-and-beyond existence" of analogy — which is the defining root of the German *"schön"* in its suspended antithetical unity between "pure vision," in its proximity to God, and creaturely "fragility." At the same time, however, the German *"schön"* cannot be "suspended in itself"; on the contrary, it receives its very dynamism from its oscillation back and forth between the most extreme formal limits of the beautiful, as represented by the

Greek "καλόν" and the Latin "*pulchrum-bellum*" (just as, according to the
Lateran formula, the "*tanta similitudo*" and the "*maior dissimilitudo*" oscillate back and forth, each into the other). The art proper to this German
"*schön*" is thus one of maximal risk, precisely because it has to be a suspension between eternity and transience. If it emphasizes the pole of fragile
transience, then it can give rise to the early Romanesque, which intimates
the abyss[9] of the divine within the abyss of the creaturely — at the same
time, however, it can also give rise to a consciously primitive and exotic
shapelessness, such as one sees in contemporary trends in art, which give the
appearance of a, so to speak, godlike "fruitful chaos." If, on the other hand,
the art of the German "*schön*" places a similar emphasis on the pole of the
"vision of the eternal," it can certainly turn into the kind of "eternal art" that
is embodied in ancient Egyptian art, but also in the art of the Aztecs and Incas, in which the Eternal Itself appears as present; equally, however, it can
evolve into the kind of art that one sees in the imposing "towers of Babel" of
today's latest architecture, in which the imperial mass of contemporary humanity presents itself as the *only* and massively imposing divinity. Quite
possibly, the only place where we see the authentic suspension of the German "*schön*," between eternity and the fragility of transience, is in the original Gothic cathedral (which communicates the heavenly breath of eternity,
but at the same time does this by making hard stones so subtle that they are
not only as fragile as a "breath," but downright close to "blowing away") —
and in the essence of classical polyphony, from Palestrina to Bach (whose
native sonority would seem to be an "eternity in itself," but which at the
same time achieves this through the extreme fragility of incessantly intersecting fugal passages; this, then, is the reason why Bach's *Art of Fugue* is virtually "analogy resounding in itself," the "beauty" that resounds between
"καλόν" and "*pulchrum-bellum*").

2

There is plainly an immanent religious quality in this last, analogical understanding of the beautiful: whether in the objective sense of a manifestation
of the divine within the beautiful (a "*religatio Dei*"), or in the subjective
sense of a turning towards the divine (a "*religatio in Deum*"). It is that [ele-
ment of] "consecration" that is inherent in the beautiful: whether objectively

9. *Ungrund.* — Trans.

explicit in the "religious work of art" (in the way that Rembrandt's biblical scenes are "religious"), or functionally implicit in the "metaphysical work of art" (in the way that Handel's and Gluck's music — even their "profane music" — is implicitly "religious"). This immanent religious dimension of genuine art is to be distinguished, however, from what is properly *sacred* (though indeed the immanent religious dimension of Vivaldi's *Four Seasons* or Gluck's *Orpheus and Eurydice* could plausibly be described as an immanence of the "sacred").

The word "sacred" comprises the tension between *"sacer"* and *"sanctus."* *"Sacer"* refers not only to something explicitly "consecrated to God" but also, contradictorily, to something that is at the same time "consecrated to death," even "cursed," and indeed "godless." "Sacred" in the sense of "consecrated to God" means that something that is essentially creaturely is removed from the circle of creaturely things so as to become the "property of God."[10] This proprietary transfer from the creaturely into the divine realm necessarily involves a dying[11] in the medium of death (this being proper to the creature) into the realm of the divine — a realm of such supracreaturely life that, to the creaturely-human realm, this "life out of death" seems "uncanny" and set under the omen of "impending death": just as, in the Old Testament, "to see God" means "death" (Exod. 19:18-24; 33:20). "Sacred" in the sense of *"sacer"* thus means, in the most precise sense, the "oblation" as *"sacri-ficium"* — not simply in the sense of an "offering" (in the way that the German word *"Opfer"* comes from the Latin *"offerre,"* that is, to offer), but rather in the concrete sense of "making something creaturely and profane into a *sacrum*" (*"sacrum facere"*), but by way of a passage through death, which is to say, through the "blood" of a holocaust[12] (cf. Heb. 9:22). This does not mean merely a "death-offering consecrated to the subterranean gods" (as the standard interpretation has it). Rather, in keeping with the sense of the word *"sacer"* (in *"sacri-ficium"*), one must preserve the ultimate unity of its internal contradiction between something both "consecrated" and "cursed," "sublime" and "appalling," "consecrated to God" and "godless" — to the point, therefore, of the genuinely abyssal dialectic of "consecration in the curse," "the sublime in the atrocious," "consecration to God in godlessness." In its mythical function, "sacred" in the sense of *"sacer"* mysteriously bears within itself what is fulfilled in Christ, understood as the highest

---

10. *"Zum Eigen Gottes."* — Trans.
11. *Umsterben.* — Trans.
12. *Vernichtung.* — Trans.

Sacrum: since he who became accursed is the blessing of God — since he who became abhorrent and scandalous is the glory of God — since he, as one forsaken by God, is the fullness of God and the face of God.

It is only by way of the sacred as *"sacer"* that we arrive at the genuine meaning of the sacred as *"sanctum":* *"sanctum"* both in the sense of the "venerability" and therefore "inviolability" of that which is *"sacrum,"* and also in the sense of the "morally holy (in the sense of virtue)," which has its original measure not in any purely human virtue, but in the Augustinian *"virtus est Deus":* that is, in such a consecration unto God that it appears (only after the fact) to be a human and "saintly virtue" (in sharp contrast to Buddhism and Stoicism and all Western ascetical semi-Buddhisms and semi-Stoicisms, which bear within themselves, consciously or not, the guiding image of a "godlike virtue"). In this regard, the sacred as *"sacer"* and *"sanctum"* points us back to the corresponding Greek words "ὅσιον" and "ἅγιον": whereas "ὅσιον" signifies the expressly objective, institutional character of something officially consecrated as the "seat of God on earth," "ἅγιον" emphasizes the "irreproachability" and "venerability" that derives therefrom (and is subsequently to be extended to all the servants and votaries of the "ὅσιον"). The same relation finally makes its way into the German word *"heilig,"* whose meaning comprises a tension between "consecrated as God's own" (just like *"sacer"* and "ὅσιον") and *"heil,"* "whole," in the sense of "unscathed" and "fortunate," which is an inherently human quality (just like *"sanctum"* and "ἅγιον").

Seen in light of these connections, the fundamental criterion of *sacred art* is the "ἱερόν," in the sense of *"templum"* and *"fanum,"* which is to say, that which is "divinely consecrated to God" (ἱερόν), indeed the "house of God" (the ναός, the point of confluence — from νάω — wherein all paths meet), a "space carved out" (*templum* as derived from "τέμνω") as a sanctuary, in the sense of a "seat of God" *(fanum),* and thus as something distinct from the *"delubrum,"* which is the place of expiation and purification. In the "ἱερόν" and "ναός" (in the sense of *"templum"* as *"fanum"*) this divine characteristic of being "distinguished from everything else" (*re et essentia a mundo distinctus . . . , super omnia, quae praeter Ipsum sunt et concipi possunt, ineffabiliter excelsus,* in the words of Vatican I)[13] — this intra-divine "absolute separateness" — is posited in a, so to speak, intra-earthly way, as an intra-earthly "divine site." Thus, the sacred nature of "ἱερόν" and "ναός" (in the sense of *"templum"* as *"fanum"*) is founded primarily upon the positive

---

13. Denz. 1782.

fact of its being a "seat of God," and only secondarily, and in consequence of this, upon the negative fact of its "godlike separation from everything else." The sacred is "sacred" primarily in the sense that it signifies a genuine "seat of God." The fact of its separation from everything around it (from which we get the word *"pro-fanum,"* i.e., the space before the *"fanum"*) is not in itself any positive quality, but is rather a prohibitive effect of this one positive quality that it is a "seat of God": just as, say, Moses demarcated Mount Sinai as the "seat of God" over against the people (Exod. 19:12). In its primary sense, therefore, the sacred nature of the "ἱερόν" of the "ναός" (understood as the *"templum"* of *"fanum"*) is defined not by the community, which "holds its divine worship" at a given demarcated location, much less by an I who becomes "conscious of God" at a particular place (even less so when the "site of the experience of God" is the separated "interiority" of this I). Rather, on the contrary, both the "chosen community" and the "chosen individual" are defined by an objectively chosen "seat of God": just as Israel is set apart as a "people of (God's) possession," as a "holy people" and a "kingdom of priests," only because — from the burning bush to Sinai to the tabernacle to the temple of Zion (cf. 1 Kings 8:17ff.; Ezek. 48:35) — God has "his seat" in Israel; and just as this is foreshadowed in all other religions, even in Buddhism, which sees in Gautama Buddha the original model of a purely functional stance "above everything, detached from everything," and then, in consequence, reveres him as the "original temple," which is the inner root of all the innumerable Buddhist temples and monasteries. Yet herein lies the internal problematic of the sacred in "sacred art" (whether in external construction, or in interior artwork, or in the "sacred style" of "sacred rites"). On the one hand, the notion of an "intra-earthly seat of God" implies that this seat has a kind of positive "divine quality" about it. On the other hand, this seat must be "separated," in its sensible arrangement, from everything earthly, which is to say that it cannot be confused with any "earthly quality." On the one hand, therefore, any "seat of God" requires a genuinely sensible form (just as all temples and churches, all "sacred implements" and "sacred actions," have a genuinely sensible form). On the other hand (on account of the "separateness" of the sacred), among all the many historical and possible "artistic styles" there is none in particular that can claim to be "the" sacred style — neither Egyptian, nor Chinese, nor Roman, nor Romanesque, nor Gothic, nor Baroque, nor Rococo, etc. Nor can this problematic be resolved by way of today's experiments with a new sacred style of art, which (consciously or unconsciously taking its lead from Rudolf Otto's *"numinosum,"* understood as a contrast-and-harmony between the *"tremendum"* and the *"fascinosum"*) strive for a kind of "archaic primitivism" — which in no small part takes as its guiding image a Black African style, which regards not only the "paradoxical," but the terrifyingly "grotesque," as the peculiar quality of the divine, in contrast to the creaturely and human. For even such an "archaic primitivism" is a genuinely intra-earthly style, whose classical form one sees in the sacred buildings of the Aztecs and Incas, and whose most spiritual expression one sees in the sacred art of the Indians, Chinese, and Egyptians. For that matter, the new sacred style that one sees today is, at bottom, not even a true example of "archaic primitivism" conceived in a sacred way. Rather, it is the product of "pure technology," which does not simply take sacred buildings as examples of technology at work, but which also seeks, in its sacred projects, however unconsciously, to give shape to a kind of "immanent sacrality," that of today's "pure technology": the seat of a "θεὸς τεχνικός," around which the "liturgy of technology" is offered. Thus, far from bringing any resolution to the inner problematic of sacred art, today's experiments with a new sacred style have merely taken that problematic virtually to the point of absurdity — not, however, to Tertullian's *"credo quia absurdum,"* but to an evacuation of the riches contained in the objective *"credo"* (the resonances of which were still audible in the sacred styles of the past) into the *"absurdum"* of technology's "cold emptiness."

Thus there remains, as the only way out, a "sacred style" in which the internal tension between its primordial qualities is at once preserved and continually varied: the internal tension between the positive style of the "ἱερόν" of the "ναός," understood as a "seat of God," and the negative style of the *"templum"* and *"fanum,"* understood as "space carved out" over against *"profane"* space. Accordingly, a genuinely sacred style is located between an emphasis upon the "ἱερόν" and an emphasis upon the *"templum"* as *"fanum,"* but in such a way that neither emphasis is ever able to attain to what is "proper" (since every "ἱερόν" of "ναός" ultimately remains something creaturely and can become transparent to the "ἱερόν" of the divine only in its maximal expression; and since no *"templum* as *fanum"* can be absolved of its connection with the creaturely universe, but can represent itself therein only as something "set apart," from which a breath of the "inaccessible light" of the divine proceeds). Seen from this perspective, a sacred style that emphasizes the "ἱερόν" has the capacity to be a style of transcendent glory: as it lives in the sacred art of Byzantium, but likewise in the sacred art of the Egyptians, Indians, Chinese, and Incas, etc. guided by the image of a mysterious presence of the divine in a radiant "icon," whether this be the icon of the Eastern Church, the enraptured smiling stillness of the Buddha, the towering death-transcending pyramids of Egypt, or even the compelling rustic simplicity of most miracle-working images. A sacred style that emphasizes the "*templum* as *fanum*," on the other hand, will be the style of something primordial that is altogether alien, in which the divine "origin and end" can be symbolically intimated — as the style of something "divinely archaic." We see this superbly realized in the early Romanesque and, correspondingly, in Gregorian choral music, but also in Pietro della Francesca, Giotto, and Pisanello — and likewise in the veiled mystery of the divinities of Asia and Africa, with their uncanny and grotesque appearances, and in certain "primitive miracle-working images" that bear a strange resemblance to them. Since the sacred style of the "*templum*" (in the sense of "*fanum*") is its intrinsically necessary counterpart, the sacred style of the "ἱερόν" (in the sense of "ναός") cannot, therefore, be that of a Baroque glory (such as we see in Baroque churches, which are very nearly "public halls" — or in the "pure beauty for beauty's sake" of the works of Raphael, Michelangelo, Titian, Tintoretto, and so on, however much they retain their status as "religious works of art"). Conversely, since the sacred style of the ἱερόν is its intrinsically necessary counterpart, the sacred style of the "*templum* as *fanum*" cannot be one of a rugged or even consciously grotesque "archaic-eschatological primitivism," which is the aim of most of today's sacred art, but can also be found in Rembrandt, Grünewald, Baldung Grien, etc., whose art could be said to be classical forms of this sort of "archaic-eschatological primitivism." Thus, the sacred style of a glorious "ἱερόν" (of the "ναός") is determined, in its authentic sacrality, by the concomitant resonance within it of the opposing style of an "archaic-eschatological" "*templum* as *fanum*": to the point that a sacred style of glory should be the style of a "death in glory" (in the way that the authentic icon of the Eastern Church could be described by the phrase "glory as death mask"). By the same token, the sacred style of an archaic-eschatological "*templum* as *fanum*" is determined, in its authentic sacrality, by the concomitant resonance within it of the opposing style of the glorious "ἱερόν" (of the "ναός"): to the point that the sacred style of the Archaic-Eschatological should be a "resurrection in death" (in the way that one could call early Romanesque art "glory in death").

On the one hand, then, no work of art can be directly legitimated as a "work of sacred art" on the basis of its possessing "beauty for beauty's sake," no matter how intrinsically "religious" it may be. But, on the other hand, it is also the case that the intrinsic "analogy," which proved to be ultimate in the beautiful, passes over into the essence of the sacred: for the sacrality of sacred art bears within it an inner tension, in which there once again resounds, though with a "different melody," the tension of analogy between the *"tanta similitudo"* and the *"maior dissimilitudo"*: since the inner measure of the sacred style of the glory of "ἱερόν" is manifestly such a *"tanta similitudo"* between the creaturely and the divine that something creaturely can be taken as the "seat of a God in his appearing" — whereas, in the sacred style of the archaic-eschatological *"templum"* as *"fanum,"* there is an adumbration of that *"maior dissimilitudo"* in which the darkness of the origin and end (the *"signum mortis"*) of the creaturely overshadows any glory of God in the creature. The beautiful and the sacred are thus related in such a way that one must first clearly distinguish between them if one is to notice what they formally have in common: the *one* rhythm of the "analogy of ever greater dissimilarity within every similarity, however great." What follows from this *"mysterium* between the beautiful and the sacred" (as one might describe it) is the paradox intrinsic to this much-disputed fact: that even the greatest mastery on the artist's part can prove incapable of genuinely sacred art, whereas wholly anonymous and clumsy folk art turns out to be the maternal womb of that most sacred art that one sees in "miracle-working images," to which (in the extra-Christian as well as in the Christian world) one goes on pilgrimage, as to a real "seat of God," as to a place of which it is said "Here HE is"[14] — and that the task of master artists is then simply to garland these anonymous popular "miracle-working images" with the riches of their artistic talents (but not differently from the way in which village children decorate a rustic shrine with wreathes of wildflowers). Such is the ultimate *"mysterium* between the beautiful and the sacred": that what appears to the "masterly spirit" as an irresoluble paradox is "achieved" in the unconscious simplicity of the "childlike spirit." For the *one* "analogy," wherein alone the beautiful and the sacred meet, stands under the sign of that solemn praise pronounced by Christ the Lord in the gospel, in which he allots to the "wise and learned" the "hiddenness of the mystery," but only to "little children" the "unveiling of the mystery" (Matt. 11:25). This is the greatest *"maior dissimilitudo"* with regard to every *"tanta similitudo"* between the *"ars Patris"* and the *"ars hominis"*: that the *"ars Patris,"* being a divine, sacred art (art in the sense of *"ars Sacratissimi"*) does not communicate itself to the one who is "ever more accomplished" (in mastery of the beautiful), but to the one who is "ever more unaccomplished": as to the one who, "ever the lesser," is "ever the greater" (Matt. 18:1ff.).

14. *Hier ist ER.* — Trans.

3

But compared to the problem of sacred beauty, the problem of *Christian sacrality* is still more unfathomable. It is not simply a sphere in which sacred beauty is applied according to the intrinsic problematic of the beautiful, the sacred, and sacred beauty, in a way that would be the same for all religions. Rather, what is specific to Christianity constitutes an essential addition. This is — firstly — the fact that Christianity, fundamentally, would seem to exclude sacred beauty. Not only is it the case that, in cleansing the temple in John's Gospel, the Lord presents himself as the true temple, which will be "destroyed" in order to be "raised," and this as a "(messianic) sign" (2:18ff.); but in John this flows into the message to Nicodemus, in which a "(sacred) flesh" is opposed to the "free blowing of the Spirit," under the sign of a dynamic "descent" (of Christ) as an "ascent" (John 3:6ff.): and this culminating in the even more pointed message to the Samaritan woman: "the hour is coming when neither on this mountain (Gerizim) nor in Jerusalem will you worship the Father. . . . The hour is coming, and now is, when the true worshipers will worship the Father in spirit and truth," for "God is spirit" (John 4:21ff.). To be sure, the "new heaven and the new earth" to which "Christianity" is underway is described as a "new Jerusalem," the resplendently bejeweled "bride of the lamb," such as Ezekiel envisions the "new Zion" to be at the end of his prophecy; but "I saw no temple . . . for its (the holy city's) temple is the Lord God Almighty, and the Lamb" (Rev. 21:22), and this alone is the "dwelling of God . . . with men. He will dwell with them and they shall be his people" (Rev. 21:3). Seen from this perspective, the sacred beauty of Christianity is Christ himself, as the "holy temple in the Lord, in whom you also are built together for a dwelling place of God in the Spirit" (Eph. 2:20-22) — and this having as a final goal that, in this "new Jerusalem," there is no temple "to be seen," since here every "temple" (everything visibly sacred) has so thoroughly become "Spirit" (through the irrevocable demise not only of the temple of the Old Covenant but of every temple of the New Covenant as well: Matt. 24:2; John 2:18ff.) that the only temple (the only thing sacred) is "God as Spirit" in the nuptial correlation between "Spirit" and "bride" (Rev. 22:17), in which every "nuptial covenant" between God and man (as, so to speak, the *arcanum* of the temple *qua* tabernacle of the covenant) comes, through and beyond itself, to fulfillment. Thus, everything intratemporal in Christian sacred art, which has its defining center in the "churches," is from the very beginning *"aufgehoben"* in Christ, head and body, as the *one* "temple in the Spirit" that is progressively fulfilled in the "I saw no temple," which is to say, in "God almighty and the Lamb" in the eschatological nuptial correlation[15] between "(God-)Spirit" and "humanity-bride" — this being the eschatological "dwelling of God with men." Seen from this radical Christian perspective, all Christian sacred art produced within time, however "divine" it may be, is — from its root, through its development, and to its end — fundamentally destined for dissolution: in the sign of Christ who, as the original Christian temple, is "destroyed" in order to be "raised" — not into a "divine temple," but into the "God who is Spirit," as the only temple of the definitive nuptial reality between "God as Spirit" and "humanity as bride."

For this reason — secondly — the only sacred art that is genuinely "Christian," possessing what could be called a "Christian sensibility," is one that represents the unique (and consequently ever new) origin of the Christian as such: the "manger" (φάτνη) of Bethlehem (Luke 2:12), the carpenter's hut in Nazareth (Luke 1:26ff.; 2:39f., 51f.; 3:23; 4:22), the homelessness in the streets of Galilee and Judea (Matt. 8:20), the "in between heaven and earth" of Godforsakenness on the gallows of the cross in the sacrality of "being cursed outside the camp" (Heb. 13:11ff.; Gal. 3:10ff.), the early Christian church's "breaking bread" and "praising God" from "house to house" (Acts 2:46-47, etc.; 1 Cor. 11:20ff.) under the constant shadow of persecution by the Jews of the Old Covenant, and finally, under the constant shadow of persecution, the celebration of the Sabbath in pagan catacombs by the Gentiles, the very ones to whom the special "mystery of God in Christ" (Eph. 2:11ff.) was vouchsafed. Thus the "scandal of the folly of the Cross," which is plainly revealed to the senses, appears as the origin, measure, and defining goal of all Christian sacred art. It may be that Christian sacred art pours itself out in the historical succession of the dominant "church styles" — from the basilica to the Romanesque cathedral to the Gothic cathedral to the magnificence of the Baroque to the blessed playfulness of the Rococo (as each of these styles further works itself out in sacred painting, sculpture, music, etc.). It may be that, in its appeal to the senses, Christian sacred art pours out all its riches on the original "manger," the "carpenter's hut," the "nameless streets and byways," the "gallows of the cross," the "profane houses," and the "catacombs." But, "however great" this outpouring of gold and precious stone and splendid color and jubilant and worshipful music, there has to be an "ever greater" breakthrough of that mysterious, one and only primal Christian reality which comprises in itself both its origin and its defining end: that of the "scandal of the folly of God" (between the "manger of God" and the

---

15. *Endhochzeitliches Zueinander.* — Trans.

"gallows of the cross of God"). By the same token, it is then also impossible to, so to speak, "stylize" this primal Christian reality (between the "manger of God" and the "gallows of the cross") in the way that the most recent Christian sacred art plainly tries to do, with its consciously "archaic-eschatological style" (to the point that not a few "modern churches," along with their attendant pictures and fixtures, look like Flemish churches in the aftermath of the Great Iconoclasm — indeed like sacred ruins!). For here the very thing that constitutes the Christian-sacred aspect of the beautiful is abrogated: the genuinely Christian-sacred "analogy" between the "however great" of the adornments of this primal Christian reality and — victoriously breaking through these adornments — the "ever greater" of this primal Christian reality itself. Now that, in our day, the great historical Christian sacred styles (from the basilica to the Rococo) seem to have exhausted themselves, perhaps the only path that remains for Christian sacred art today is a true regression through all styles, back to the "apostolic style" of profane homes and tables. At most, what remains is a return to the style of the truly simple village church, or — as an expression of the most extreme perspective — a style in which towering sacred edifices are reduced to the "without form or comeliness" of ordinary, communally shared private rooms (which, according to the Gospel [Luke 17:20], is the authentic "style of the kingdom of God": "οὐκ . . . μετὰ παρατηρήσεως").

11 *Imago Dei:* On the Theological Message of Max Picard

1958

1

At first glance, Max Picard's work appears to be nothing but a classical physiognomy, built around his principal work, *Das Menschengesicht* (1929),[1] and its counterpart, his equally important book *Ehe*, "Marriage" (1942).[2] But his *Menschengesicht* is based upon the antithesis, which appears in the human face, between the "terrestrial" and the "sidereal" — presupposing the almost apocalyptic visions of his *Der letzte Mensch* (1921)[3] and leading to the equally apocalyptic vision of his *Hitler in uns selbst* (1946).[4] Additionally, there are the great prophetic works, his *Flucht vor Gott* (1934)[5] and his *Welt des Schweigens* (1948),[6] in which man appears as a "midpoint between . . . the divine silence above" and "the human silence below,"[7] as becoming human and "(existing) only to the degree that he takes part in this flight,"[8] such that "the interval between God and man is no longer an empty nothingness, but a nothingness that is filled-up by the flight."[9] Thus, in the dynamic antithesis of his pro-

---

1. Max Picard, *Das Menschengesicht* (Erlenbach, Zürich, Leipzig: Rentsch, 1929).
2. Max Picard, *Die unerschütterliche Ehe* (Erlenbach, Zürich: Rentsch, 1942).
3. Max Picard, *Der letzte Mensch* (Leipzig: E. T. Tal & Co., 1921).
4. Max Picard, *Hitler in uns selbst* (Erlenbach, Zürich: Rentsch, 1946).
5. Max Picard, *Die Flucht vor Gott* (Erlenbach, Zürich, Leipzig: Rentsch, 1934).
6. Max Picard, *Die Welt des Schweigens* (Erlenbach, Zürich: Rentsch, 1948).
7. *Die Welt des Schweigens*, p. 242.
8. *Die Flucht vor Gott*, p. 11.
9. *Die Flucht vor Gott*, p. 16.

This essay first appeared in *Festschrift* for Max Picard (1958).

phetic physiognomy, Picard sees the human being as existing at once in greatest similarity to God (in the "starry face") and in abyssal contradiction to God (in the "earthly face" of the "flight from God," in the symbol of the "spherical man"). He sees the human being in terms of the antithesis between the "image of God" and a "counter-image of God" — an antithesis that is finally overcome by God alone: "the more the flight takes shape and the graver the falling away, the clearer it becomes that only one is standing there: God."[10]

Picard's physiognomy thus turns out to be a foreground, pointing to the background of a truly "theological message." It is a message that reawakens a central theologoumenon, which has its roots in the beginning and end of the revelation of the Old and New Testaments: the antithesis between man, created "according to our image and likeness," as God says in inaugurating the creation of man in Genesis 1:26 (cf. Sir. 17:1; Col. 3:10), and the man of the end times, who bears the "image" and "mark" of the "beast" (Rev. 13:14-17) — an antithesis from which man can be redeemed only in Christ the God-man, who, as such, is the "image of the invisible God" (2 Cor. 4:4; Col. 1:15), into whose very image we are "transformed . . . from glory to glory, as by the Spirit of the Lord" (2 Cor. 3:18). This central theologoumenon became Christian tradition, beginning with the first church Fathers, passing over into early medieval Augustinianism, as well as into the Eastern Church's theology of icons, and then into the controversy between the Reformation and the Church. We see it today in secularized form in that central concept of depth-psychology, the "*imago*," as well as in Ludwig Klage's "transcendental image." But, in contrast to these secularizations, it is only in the immanent "theological message" of Max Picard that we see a contemporary recovery of its original form. As distinct from a "Christocentric," "Mariocentric," "Pneumatic," "cultic," "cosmocentric" Christianity (as today's Christian renewal movements call themselves), what we see in Picard's immanent theological message is a Christianity of the "image of God," which is at once a Christianity of Christian humanity and of Christian divinity: a Christianity that is based upon the original idea of the human being, but based, as such, upon the idea of the human being as originating from God. It is Christianity in the spirit of Nicholas of Cusa, in whom at once the Middle Ages are crowned and modernity is born: a Christianity of the human being as *Deus humanatus*, i.e., a Christianity of the "humanized God"[11] in the human being (as the "image of God").

---

10. *Die Flucht vor Gott*, p. 198. [. . . je mehr das Gebilde der Flucht zunimmt und je heftiger es davonstürzt, desto deutlicher steht der Eine allein da: Gott. — Trans.]

11. *Des in den Menschen . . . eingemenschten Gottes.* — Trans.

In order to take cognizance of its renewal in the physiognomy of Max Picard, it is incumbent upon us to take a closer look at this tradition of the human being as the "imago Dei" and, as such, *Deus humanatus.*"

2

In the Septuagint, the *basic text* in Genesis for a theologoumenon of the *imago Dei* reads as follows: ποιήσωμεν ἄνθρωπον κατ᾽ εἰκόνα ἡμετέραν καὶ ὁμοίωσιν (Gen. 1:26), "Let us make man according to our image and likeness." Luther translates this without the "καὶ": "... *ein Bild, das uns gleich sei.*" In the first volume of his monumental *Biblical Commentary on the Old Testament* (1878), Friedrich Keil stresses, on the basis of the Hebrew, that one cannot establish any difference between "image" and "likeness," just as one cannot distinguish in German between *"Bild"* and *"Abbild,"* or between *"Umriß"* and *"Abriß."*[12] In his *Die Genesis* (1908), Hoberg similarly remarks: "These two substantives are, objectively speaking, indistinguishable."[13] Accordingly, in his translation of the Old Testament, Rießler renders the text: "... *als Unser Bild nach Unserem Gleichnis*" ["as our image, according to our likeness"]. Buber and Rosenzweig, on the other hand, render it: "... *in Unserem Bild, nach Unserer Gestalt*" ["in Our image, according to Our form"], thus following the Septuagint (and Vulgate), but at the same time in accord with Keil's interpretation of "ὁμοίωσις" as *"Umriß"* or *"Abriß."* Its context, Genesis 1:27, plainly indicates an equivalence of "εἰκών" and "ὁμοίωσις," since there it is simply said, "So God created man in his image (κατ᾽ εἰκόνα), in the image of God he created him" (following Buber and Rosenzweig), or alternately (following Rießler), "He created man as his image, as the image of God he created him." Thus, in keeping with these connections, one is obliged to take "ὁμοίωσις" as a more precise definition of "εἰκών": as either an intensification in the sense of "image to the point of equivalence" or a qualification in the sense of "image as likeness": either in the way that "ὁμοίωσις" implies a kind of "comparison" based upon a "representation by way of a similar image" (I. G. Schneider), or in the way that "ὁμοίωσις," understood as *"similitudo,"* is used in the Lord's "parables" as synonymous with "παραβολή," that is, as an "elliptical likeness" (in the sense

12. Friedrich Keil and Franz Delitzsch, *Biblisches Commentar über das Alte Testament,* vol. 1 (Leipzig: Dörfling, 1878), p. 23.
13. Gottfried Hoberg, *Die Genesis* (Freiburg: Herder, 1908), p. 19.

of a mathematical "parabola"); either in the way that the Hebrew word, which is rendered in Greek as "ὁμοίωσις," indicates a "figure in outline and relief," in which the ambiguous likeness of the "image" is clarified into a "defined figure," in the sense of a "relief[14] of the (divine) archetype," or in the way that "ὁμοίωσις in the sense of παραβολή" not only qualifies "image" as a simple *"similitudo"* (which at least points intrinsically to a "possible *dissimilitudo*"), but qualifies it, moreover, as an "elliptical similarity" (which is what we mean by parable).

The entire context of Genesis 1:26-27 thus lends itself to these two different interpretations. On the one hand, in favor of the one interpretation (that of an intensification of "εἰκών" to "ὁμοίωσις"), there is the fact that "εἰκών as ὁμοίωσις" is immediately explained by reference to the position that God gives to man within the world as a "κύριος," as an "ἀρχή," i.e., a (sanctified) "lord" (just as God himself is the absolute "Κύριος" or "Lord"), who stands at the "head" [*Ur*] of an "office" (which is what is meant by "ἀρχή"). "Let them have dominion [ἀρχέτωσαν] over the fish of the sea, and over the birds of the air, and over the cattle, and over all the earth, and over every creeping thing that creeps upon the earth" — i.e., over heaven and earth, just as God is the Lord of heaven and earth. On the other hand, the way that Genesis 1:27 represents "εἰκών" in terms of "ἄρσεν καί θῆλυ," that is, "male and female" in the sense that applies equally to plants and animals (as distinguished from "ἀνήρ-γυνή," "man-woman," as distinctive to human beings) would seem to speak for the other interpretation, namely, that of a delimiting of "εἰκών" by "ὁμοίωσις"). For in this case "εἰκών" in the sense of "ἄρσεν-θῆλυ" indicates human beings' sharp difference from God, who as "Spirit" stands high above the plant and animal kingdoms, whereas man being "ἄρσεν-θῆλυ" stresses that man belongs intrinsically to the plant and animal realm of physical sexual difference: "So God created man in his own image, in the image of God he created him; male and female he created them" (Gen. 1:27).

The human being, then, as the "image of God," appears on the one hand — when viewed as the "ἀρχή" of a "κύριος"[15] — to be placed above creation, and on the other hand — when viewed as "ἄρσεν-θῆλυ" — to be placed right in the midst of creation. Accordingly, "ὁμοίωσις" indicates both the greatest possible similarity to God (as the "ἀρχή" of a "κύριος") and at the same time an ever greater difference from God (to the point of emphasizing

14. *Abriß.* — Trans.
15. "ἀρχή" *des* "κύριος," i.e., the headship proper to a lord. — Trans.

humanity's similarity to vegetative and animal creation, which is physically constituted by the reality of sex: in "ἄρσεν-θῆλυ"). It follows, therefore, that the "εἰκών θεοῦ," the "image of God" proper to the human being, can be understood neither in unilinear nor in antithetical terms. It cannot be understood in unilinear terms (as is the tendency of all Augustinianism) since "εἰκών," in view of the double aspect of "ὁμοίωσις," appears in almost dialectical terms (between the "above creation, in the greatest possible proximity to God" and the "in creation, in natural proximity to the vegetable and the animal kingdoms"). But neither can it be construed in antithetical terms, since the double aspect of "ὁμοίωσις" in the text of Genesis 1:26 does not negate the fact that "ὁμοίωσις" is intended here as an intrinsic attribute of "εἰκών." Just as humanity's utmost proximity to God does not negate its intrinsic proximity to the intra-creaturely realm (as "ἄρσεν-θῆλυ"), neither is humanity so exclusively woven into the vegetable and animal creation that, within this creation, the utmost proximity to God did not arise. What thus comes to light, as the intrinsic form of the human being as the *"imago Dei,"* is what, since Aristotle and the Fourth Lateran Council, is called "analogy." To say that man is the *"imago Dei"* means that he is so similar to God (in *tanta similitudo*) that he nevertheless, as a creature in the midst of creation, stands in a relation of "ever greater dissimilarity" (in *"maior dissimilitudo"*) to this same God. This *"analogia hominis"* is, as it were, the reverse of the *"analogia Dei"* as defined by the Fourth Lateran Council: between the *"tanta similitudo"* of a unity between God and humanity, and the *"maior dissimilitudo"* of the God who is above-and-beyond everything creaturely. Just as God, in his original relation to the creaturely, is the "in-and-beyond" to it (which is what is meant by analogy), so too the human being, in his original relation, between creation and God, is the "in-and-beyond": "beyond" as the "εἰκών" of a divine "ἀρχή" of a "κύριος"; "in" as woven into the "ἄρσεν-θῆλυ" of the subhuman vegetal and animal creation. Humanity's *"imago Dei"* thus means *"imago* in analogy," and this *"analogia hominis"* as the reverse of the *"analogia Dei."*

This is cast into even sharper relief by Genesis 2:7 and the way that it concretely renders this *"imago* in analogy": in that the human being, as "the man Adam," appears as one who is "formed" out of the "(windblown) dust of the ground," into whose "countenance"[16] God "implants and engenders the breath of life,"[17] and who thus becomes a "living animal creation"[18] (εἰς

---

16. *Antlitz.* — Trans.
17. *Einpflanzt und einzeugt das Wehen des Lebens.* — Trans.
18. *Geschöpf-Tier.* — Trans.

ψυχὴν ζῶσαν, i.e., a psychical-animal); and in that the human being, as "the woman Eve," who is taken from the man's "rib" (that is, from his "sturdy frame"), is "built as a house" (ᾠκοδόμεσεν) to be an "understanding counterpart of the man Adam," and is thus at once "from the man" but also a "counterpart to the man" — such that she is at once a "wo-*man*"[19] (a "part taken from the man") but at the same time "a counterpart so wholly other" that, within the "one flesh" shared between man and woman, the man leaves "father and mother and cleaves to his wife" (Gen. 2:18-24). Here we see the most extreme span of the "*imago* in analogy." The "similarity to God" appears to be heightened by an "inbreathing of God," understood as an "implanting and engendering" — such that, in Christ's genealogy, the human being is in effect nothing less than a "son of God": "Adam is from God" ("Ἀδὰμ τοῦ θεοῦ") just as "Seth is from Adam" ("Σὴθ τοῦ Ἀδὰμ") (Luke 3:38). But the "similarity" extends equally to "(subhuman) creation," through similarity to vegetal and animal creation ("ἄρσεν-θῆλυ"), all the way down to the formation of "the man Adam" from the "(windblown) dust of the ground" (that is, from the "earth," which appears in the "windblown dust" as both dynamically sublimated and in its most extreme perishability and nullity: the "vanity" of the book of Qoheleth) — and to the "construction" of the "woman Eve" from the "very bones"[20] of the "man Adam" (being a variation on the "trunk" proper to trees and the skeletal frame proper to animals). But, precisely within this process, whereby an exceedingly taut span is formed between the greatest "similarity to the divine above" and the greatest "similarity to the most perishable below," not only does the human being, who is characterized by the vegetal-animal ἄρσεν-θῆλυ, acquire the distinct and properly human form of polarity: between the man Adam — who with godlike authority gives creatures their "names" on the basis of an intimate understanding of their essences (in the way that in the beginning and throughout revelation it is God alone who "gives things their names") — and the woman Eve, who is the only "understanding counterpart" to the man Adam, who understands creation (which is what "βοηθὸς κατ' αὐτόν" [Gen. 2:18] and "βοηθὸς ὅμοιος αὐτῷ" [Gen. 2:20] actually mean), and who thus becomes for the man Adam a "house and home" ("ᾠκοδόμησεν" [Gen. 2:22]) — "προσκολληθήσεται πρὸς τὴν γυναῖκα αὐτοῦ" [Gen. 2:24]). Rather, this most properly and distinctly human form of "man and woman," as opposed to the vegetal-animal form of "male and female" (ἄρσεν-θῆλυ),

---

19. *Männin.* — Trans.
20. *Knochenphysis.* — Trans.

allows one to see in the *"imago Dei"* of man as such a glimmer of the features of a God who, as the "giver of names," fulfills the features of the man Adam, and who, as the "house and home" (of the οἰκονομία), fulfills the features of the woman Eve.

The *"imago* in analogy" thus consists in a *threefold rhythm.* The first rhythm is grounded in the double sense of "ὁμοίωσις," as indicating both a similarity to God and a similarity to (subhuman) creation (since the real subject of the *"imago"* is the vegetative animality of "ἄρσεν-θῆλυ"). The second rhythm arises from the fact that within the *"imago,"* considered in its properly human aspect as "man-woman," what is peculiar to the man oscillates between the "(windblown) dust of the ground" and the "inbreathing of God," while what is peculiar to the woman oscillates between being "a part taken from the man's nature" and being "a house and home from God." And hidden within this rhythm we discover the third rhythm: that of the "ever greater" "God as the archetype in the image man-woman" within the "however great" of the rootedness of man-woman in earthly nature as "(windblown) dust." The threefold analogy, understood as the "in-and-beyond" within this threefold rhythm, turns upon the relation between "ἄρσεν-θῆλυ" and "ἀνήρ-γυνή" within the relation between man and woman (i.e., between the vegetative animality of their intra-creaturely nature and that which is specifically human within them, which makes them into a special image of the divine). For, since the correlation between man and woman points simultaneously to the intra-creaturely and to the divine, and therefore consists in the "in-and-beyond" of analogy, it is most properly here, in this "analogy proper to man-woman," that we see the movement of the threefold rhythm of the *"imago* in analogy." Thus, the fully unveiled *"imago Dei"* in which every theologoumenon of the *"imago Dei"* is rooted, is an *"imago in the analogy"* that is rooted *in the "analogy proper to man and woman."* Just as the *"imago Dei"* in the human being cannot be taken to signify a purely spiritual, much less an immediately divine region — in comparison to which the region proper to the mystery of man and woman would be that of the purely terrestrial, or indeed the actually demonic (as is the tendency of all spiritualisms and Manichean Gnosticisms: from Manicheism, to the Androgyne tradition of Judah Leon Abravanel,[21] to Paracelsus, to Jacob Böhme, to Saint Martin, to Franz von Baader, right up to recent Russian theosophy, and even including certain perversions within Christianity itself) — neither can a true theology of the *imago Dei* be sepa-

---

21. Przywara uses the older Italian designation "Ebreo" (that is, Leone Ebreo, or Leo Hebraeus). — Trans.

rated from a genuine theology of the sexes. Indeed, far from being separable, the former can be developed only to the degree that it is dynamically centered in the latter. The *"imago Dei"* is possible only as an *"imago* in analogy," and an *"imago* in analogy" is possible only as an "analogy proper to man-woman."

3

The *"imago* in analogy," as it consists in the "analogy proper to man-woman," is not concrete, however, until we see it in terms of the *opposition between original sin* (in the "first Adam and the first Eve") *and redemption* (in the "second Adam, Christ" and the "second Eve, Mary").

As the concrete reality of the original *"imago Dei,"* this opposition begins to illuminate what is ultimate in the *"imago Dei."* For the *"imago Dei"* in the "second Adam, Christ" and in the "second Eve, Mary" has the form of a *"consortium naturae divinae"* — in the sense of "θείωσις," of becoming a "god by grace" — not only as something that is given ("freely by grace"), but as something that is given "again." Indeed, this is precisely what the ancient Christian contrast between the "first Adam (and Eve)" and the "second Adam (and Eve)" was always taken to imply, because redemption is precisely a "new creation" ("καινὴ κτίσις," 2 Cor. 5:17). In light of these connections of salvation history, we can see why the *"imago Dei"* of the "first creation" must *at the same time* be understood *as a "consortium naturae divinae"* that is, as an "image" that is at the same time an "intrinsic participation in the nature of God": as a "natural image" (on the basis of the relation between creator and creature), but at the same time as a "supernatural impartation and participation"[22] (on the basis of God's free self-disclosure and self-communication). As we concluded above, it is impossible to separate the "εἰκών" from the "ὁμοίωσις," assigning the former to the "natural image" and the latter to the "supernatural impartation and participation" (as was the inclination of the first church Fathers, who — contrary to what the context of the words indicates — tend to oppose "εἰκών" and "ὁμοίωσις" to one another).[23] On the

---

22. *Teilgabe und Teilnahme.* — Trans.

23. This interpretation derives from the Platonism of the first church Fathers, who identify the Platonic "ὁμοίωσις τῷ θεῷ" (*Theaetetus* 170a-b) — in the sense of an immediate (as opposed to a distinctly rational or ethical) "assimilation into the divine" — with the (supernatural) *consortium Dei.* In passages where Plato claims that the "φιλόσοφος" belongs to the "genus of the gods" ("τὸ τῶν θεῶν γένος," *Phaedrus* 246d), indeed is "divine as God is" ("θεὸς ὢν θεῖός ἐστιν," *Phaedrus* 249c), the first church Fathers saw an anticipation of the

contrary, as we have seen from the connections between the "first" creation
and the "new" creation, the unity of the "image, to the point of equivalence in
the likeness"[24] (as was our understanding of the relationship between
"εἰκών" and "ὁμοίωσις") is that of an actual simultaneity of the "natural image" and "supernatural impartation and participation." This actual simultaneity cannot, however, be translated into an intrinsically necessary connection: in the way that the Reformation's theology of the *"imago Dei"*
understands the "natural image" as such *as* a "supernatural impartation and
participation," so that original sin entails the total loss of the *"imago Dei,"*
which is then offset by the radical uniqueness of Christ as the "image of God"
in the reconciled (but not "redeemed") human being — or in the way that,
conversely, the Jansenist theology of the *"imago Dei"* sees the "supernatural
impartation and participation" as consisting in the essence of the "natural
image,"[25] which then has nothing "supernatural" standing over against it but
the *"sola gratia"* of Christ — or in the way that a certain kind of rationalism,
which is the culmination of this Jansenism, and which affirms a divinity of
man intrinsic to nature (by virtue of his intellect and free will), claims that
the "natural image" in itself is not only an intrinsic impartation and participation, but the only impartation and participation, and, as such, a "natural"
impartation and participation. Over against these extremes, the actual unity
of the (natural) *"imago Dei"* and the (supernatural) *"consortium Dei"* must
therefore be understood as one in which the *"consortium Dei"* appears within
the *"imago,"* though as essentially "beyond" it. In other words, it is not simply
that the concrete *"imago,"* as the "εἰκών" in the "ὁμοίωσις," consists in an
"analogy," but that this form of an *"imago in analogy"* itself consists in a relation of a higher analogy to the supernatural *"consortium Dei."* It is neither
that the *"imago"* "is" the *"consortium,"* nor that the *"consortium"* "is" the
"imago." On the contrary, as opposed to every identification of the two, there
is the *one "consortium* in-and-beyond the *imago."* This *consortium in-and-
beyond the imago* (which is itself an "analogy," being related to the ambiguity
in "ὁμοίωσις") *is* the original concrete *"imago Dei."* Concretely, *"imago Dei"*
means: the *imago* of an analogy (to *"consortium"*), which stands within an
analogy (of the double sense of "ὁμοίωσις"): *the consortium in-and-beyond*

"θείας κοινωνοὶ φύσεως," the "participants in the divine nature" of 2 Peter 1:4. Accordingly,
following their general method, they could take Plato's philosophy as a *"praeambulum"* of
revelation, as a "pagan advent."

24. *Bild zu Gleichheit im Gleichnis.* — Trans.

25. Denz. 1384-85.

the *imago in-and-beyond the* (double sense of) ὁμοίωσις. Thus the original *"imago Dei,"* which consists in the "analogy proper to man-woman" (Gen. 1:27; 5:1-2), finds its corresponding concreteness in a *"consortium in-and-beyond the imago,"* which consists logically in this same "analogy proper to man-woman" — only with the qualification that this "analogy proper to man-woman," by virtue of the *consortium Dei,* is now subject to a threefold gradation: from the vegetal and animal "ἄρσεν-θῆλυ," to the properly human "ἀνήρ-γυνή," to the "ἀνήρ-γυνή" of the *consortium Dei,* wherein it is granted an interior "deification" (θείωσις) (in fulfillment of all those myths and profounder philosophies that represent the eros between man and woman as something divine: as accords with the theological view that in man's "primal estate" the one and only *"mysterium* as sacrament" would have been the *union* of man and woman — the "children of God" being the fruit thereof).

It is only now, in view of this *"consortium* in-and-beyond the *imago,"* as it consists in the threefold gradation of the "analogy proper to man-woman," that we can see the connections proper to a theology of the *imago Dei,* from original sin to redemption.

In view of the *"consortium* in-and-beyond the *imago,"* to say that the *imago Dei* exists in a state of *original sin* and *inherited sin* means that the disobedience of Adam and Eve to God is not something merely "human," but is rather a disobedience that occurs within the *consortium* — hence the symbol of "wanting to be like God" in the "knowledge of good and evil": which is to say, "knowing as God knows": which is to say, in the way that God alone "knows" the ultimate mystery of good and evil (in contrast to any human "distinction between good and evil"). In this "disobedience of Adam (and Eve)," in which we see the original sin as an inherited sin (Rom. 5:19), the human being within the *consortium Dei* grasps at "equality with God," just as the highest of the angels (Luci-fer: that is, the "bearer of the light, which is God") "seeks equality with the Most High." For this reason, it is "Lucifer as Satan (that is, as the adversary of God)" who, as a "serpent," "encoils" the human being in this same "rebellion," understood as a "robbery of God as God." Inasmuch as he thus falls from the *consortium Dei* into a *consortium anti-Dei,* the human being ends up not merely in a "state of sin," but essentially in a state of "slavery to Satan," who, due to the fall of man — the "lord of the world" — is now the "prince of this world," indeed the "god of this world," in place of the human being who is *"Deus humanatus"* (cf. Rom. 6:17ff.; John 14:30; 2 Cor. 4:4). Within this *consortium anti-Dei,* the "analogy proper to man-woman" succumbs to the form of "slavery to the adversary": in that the man Adam is now subject to the natural cosmic adversity of "thorns and thistles," destined to work in "the sweat of your face," and to "return again to dust," while the woman Eve is not only destined to suffer the antagonism of her own body (in the adversity of the increase of the "pains of childbirth"), but also enslaved to the contradiction between the "man as ruler" and her "desire for him" (Gen. 3:16-19).[26] Just as the *consortium Dei* raised the human being up to the "eternal life" of God, the *consortium anti-Dei* plunges him, in this adversity, into "death, the wages of sin" (Rom. 6:23). And just as the *consortium Dei* immersed the human being in the "blessing" of the "blessed," the *consortium anti-Dei* buries him utterly in the "curse" (Gen. 3:17). On the one hand, it is not the case that this *consortium anti-Dei* would extinguish the *imago Dei* (for even in the *consortium anti-Dei* the human being remains human "in nature" and so, as such, the *imago Dei*). Nevertheless, on the other hand, it *is* the case that the human being becomes a contradiction between the *imago Dei*, which originates with God, and the *consortium anti-Dei*, which is subject to Satan — as distinct from the original state of an analogy between the *imago Dei* and the *consortium Dei*. This state of contradiction between the *imago Dei* and the *consortium anti-Dei* is the actual *"status lapsus,"* the "state of original sin and inherited sin" (whereas Reformation theology wants to see this state as an absolute "loss of the *imago Dei*" — and whereas Molinist theology sees it as the pure "loss of the *consortium Dei*" — all three deny the original analogy between the *imago Dei* and the *consortium Dei*).

This *status* of the "fallen human being," in his contradiction between the *imago Dei* and the *consortium anti-Dei*, conditions the opposing reality of *redemption*. Redemption does not simply mean "justification" in "reconciliation" (as central as these concepts appear to be in Romans and 2 Corinthians). For both would then be simply an action of God with regard to the human being (*"actio actualis"* as an *"actio forensis"*: as the Reformation doctrine of an actual forensic "reconciliation" would have it). Rather, redemption is "incarnation[27] as redemption" (and vice versa), and is therefore what 2 Corinthians 5:17-21 signifies by the Greek word it uses for "redemption," "καταλλαγή": that is, an exchange ("κατ'-") between two alterities ("-αλλαγή"), and this through and through — which in Irenaeus, Augus-

26. The translation of this passage cannot adequately capture the wordplay that is involved here: *Widersacher* (adversary), *Widersachertum* (adversity), *Widerstand* (antagonism), *Widerspruch* (contradiction). — Trans.

27. The standard German word for Christ's incarnation, *Menschwerdung,* means "becoming human," which much better conveys the idea of a *commercium* between the human and the divine in Christ. — Trans.

tine, and even later Luther means *"commutatio"* as *"commercium,"* which is to say, an exchange in the sense of an "exchange of goods at a slave market." Thus, redemption means that the Christ — who does not merely stand in a *consortium Dei* with God, but is in the strict sense in the *"forma Dei"* — assumes the "form of a slave" borne by the fallen human being as the "slave of Satan"; moreover, such that in the *one* Christ, who is of the *"forma Dei"* and the *"forma servi,"* the human being, having once been a "slave of Satan," becomes so thoroughly the "property of God" that this, as it were, "transacted human being" is not merely "restored" to the *consortium Dei,* but is restored precisely as a "member" of the Christ, who stands in the freedom of the *"forma Dei"* (Phil. 2:5ff.; Rom. 6:13-22). This is why the *one* Christ is not only "completely God and completely man," but "completely God *as* having become sin and a curse, to the point of being delivered into the hands of Satan as one godforsaken and subject to the power of darkness" (Luke 4:1-13; 22:53; 2 Cor. 5:21; Gal. 3:10ff.; Heb. 13:11f.). By the same token, the "fallen human being as a slave of Satan" is not merely redeemed "through" this Christ, but is essentially redeemed "into" him, such that, as a "member of Christ" — who is his very "life" and "self" (Gal. 2:20; Phil. 1:21) — he is translated out of his *consortium anti-Dei* into a *consortium Dei-hominis;* which is to say, however, into a *consortium gloriae crucis* (into being "crucified with Christ": Gal. 2:19, etc.). That Christ is "none other than the Crucified" (1 Cor. 1:23; Gal. 3:1); that he is therefore the *one* "image of the invisible God" (Col. 1:15) essentially as *"Christus deformis,"* as "Christ disfigured into deformity" (Augustine); and that, by virtue of this representation of the (unseen) "Father" in the "Son" (who is seen), the lost *"consortium Dei"* of our original estate is "restored" solely in the form of a *"consortium Dei-hominis,"* that is, as a *consortium* of the Christ who, as the Christ of the *"forma Dei,"* is none other than the *"Christus deformis"* of the *"forma servi"* — these most basic connections reveal the *"status redemptionis,"* the state of the redeemed human being as a *consortium Dei gloriae* in a *consortium Dei crucifixi,* and thus as a *consortium plenitudinis Dei* in a *consortium Dei a Deo derelicti:* the (restored) gift of participation in the divine nature as the gift of participation in a crucified and godforsaken God. In this way, the accursed contradiction in the "fallen human being" between the *imago Dei* and the *consortium anti-Dei* is *aufgehoben* (in a "superabundance" of grace beyond every "abounding of sin, however great": Rom. 5:20) into the "blessed contradiction" between an *imago Dei deformis* and a *consortium Dei deformis,* between an "image of God" and an "impartation of and participation in God" as the one who is "disfigured" (in Christ and, in him, in the Christian). The *imago Dei* (proper to human nature), which persists even through sin, however great, appears in the redeemed human being under the form of an *"ad imaginem,"* i.e., as a conformity to the *"imago Christus,"*[28] understood as the Christ of the *"forma Dei"* in the *"forma servi,"* as a "co-image" of[29] the image of Christ as the "image disfigured into deformity";[30] so, too, the original analogy between the *imago Dei* and the *consortium Dei* appears "restored" in the "blessed contradiction" of a *"consortium Dei* as a *consortium Dei a Deo derelicti,"* i.e., of an "impartation of and participation in God as (so to speak) not-God" — resulting in a more than victorious[31] contrast to the accursed contradiction between the image at creation and "fallen" humanity's participation in the *anti-God.* In view of these intertwinings, we see that the radiance of the *imago* is the radiance of the "depths of God" (1 Cor. 2:10) confronting the "depths of Satan" (Rev. 2:24).

But then the final thing to consider is the way in which the original "analogy proper to man-woman," having passed through the "contradiction between man and woman" (in the status of the "fallen human being"), is not only "restored" in "redemption as *commercium* in Christ," but restored in a new "form" (in the sense of the "new" of the New Covenant). The Christ in whom this "newness" occurs is fully concrete as "Christ, the second Adam, and Mary, the second Eve" (in the way that the original Christian tradition — from Ephraim the Syrian to Augustine to Bernard of Clairvaux to Luther — reads 1 Cor. 15:45ff. in terms of the opposition between the "first Adam" and the "last Adam," eventuating in a full-scale theology of the contrast between "Adam-and-Eve" and "Christ-and-Mary"). But the particular meaning of this contrast is then expressed in the opposition between the primordial reality of "Eve from Adam" and the redemptive reality of "Christ from Mary." Just as, in the primordial reality of the *"consortium in-and-beyond the imago,"* it is the man Adam who represents the formal subject of the "analogy proper to man-woman" (since the woman Eve is "formed" from him, and only thus is there an "analogy proper to man-woman"), so now in the same sense *Mary,* as the woman who receives Christ as her Son, is *the formal subject of the redemptive "analogy proper to Christ-Mary."* To be sure, 1 Corinthians 11:8 emphasizes the original reality of the "woman from the man," even for the state of redemption (since it corresponds to the "natural state of

28. Ambrose, *In Lucam* X, 22.
29. *Mit-Bild.* — Trans.
30. *Bild im Entbildet zu Missgestalt.* — Trans.
31. *Übersiegend,* cf. Romans 8:37. — Trans.

the human being"). Nevertheless, the complementary notion in 1 Corinthians 11:9 about the woman being created "for the sake of the man" suggests that in the state of redemption this original reality of "woman from the man" assumes an almost antithetical supernatural form[32] (in the sense of *"gratia perficit naturam"*). If, from the perspective of the original form, the external visible world stands under the form of the "man as head," in its invisible interior it bears the supernatural form of "Mary as the womb and inner form" of all redeemed life. Seen in light of the symbol of the much-disputed "veil" of 1 Corinthians 11:3ff., the external visible primacy of "man (in Christ) as head" now appears as a veil "veiling" the mystery of Mary as the "nuptial womb" (θάλαμος) of all redeemed life (in Christ, who in his humanity is conceived and born solely from Mary — the most radical formulation of which we find in Luther).[33] This, though, is what lends the "blessed contradiction" of an *imago Dei* as a *"consortium Dei gloriae crucis"* (which is how the *imago Dei* appears in the "state of redemption") its distinctive and most proper form — a form that consists not simply in that of the virgin Mary as the "nuptial womb covered by the veil," but rather: in that the *divine* mystery of *"Christus deformis"* inwardly corresponds to the purely human mystery of the *"humilitas ancillae suae,"* to the "fragile, weak lowliness" of "Mary the handmaid," to whom alone God stands "face to face," not only in "regarding" her *(respexit),* but in the nuptial "overshadowing by the Holy Spirit." Mary's glory, that of "Christ from Mary" (and thus "man from woman"), is the glory of that "weak lowliness that is covered by a veil." The original "analogy proper to man-woman" passes, through and beyond original sin's "contradiction between man and woman," into a mysterious correspondence between the Christ of "power in powerlessness, glory in shame, blessing in curse, plenitude in nothingness" and the virgin Mary, understood as the "beatitude of the lowliness of the handmaid."

Here we see the complete form of the *imago Dei:* the human being as the "image of God," inasmuch as he is the *"ad imaginem,"* the likeness to the *one* "image of God in Christ in Mary," as to an "image of glory in deformity and lowliness." The *imago Dei,* in the full sense of this term, is the human being in the symbol of the "crucified" and the "mother of seven sorrows."

32. *Über-Form.* — Trans.
33. Luther, *Werke* (ed. Weimar), vol. V, p. 549; vol. I, pp. 78-79.

12 Primal Christian Terms: Kerygma, Mysterium, Kairos, Oikonomia

1959

From its inception Paul Tillich's thought has been guided in its innermost intention by a concern with Christianity's "primal terms."[1] We see this in his engagement with Schelling, who at the end of his career was himself striving towards a genuine "philosophy of revelation," which is to say, a philosophy that does not seek to translate revelation into an ultimate philosophical "con-cept"[2] and "sum-con-cept"[3] (in the way that Hegel's philosophy fulfills ancient Jewish, Islamic, and more recent philosophy, which aim at such a philosophical "con-cept as sum-con-cept"), but reduces revelation to itself, to its own immanent concept and sum-concept. Just as Schelling stands in the tradition of Jacob Böhme and Franz von Baader, each of whom constructed this kind of immanent philosophy of revelation, Tillich is engaged in his earliest works[4] with this tradition of Böhme, Baader, and Schelling, seeking to draw from it, as a final conclusion, what could be considered an original Christian term. For Tillich this term is *"kairos,"* and it is around this term that the whole of his thought now turns.[5] We are thus compelled by

1. *Urworte.* — Trans.
2. *Be-griff.* — Trans.
3. *In-be-griff.* — Trans.
4. See *Die religionsgeschichtliche Konstruktion in Schellings positiver Philosophie* (Breslau: Fleischmann, 1910); *Mystik und Schuldbewußtsein in Schellings philosophischer Entwicklung* (1912, published in *Gesammelte Werke,* vol. 1, *Frühe Hauptwerke* (Stuttgart: Evangelisches Verlagswerk, 1959).
5. *Kairos* I, published in *Gesammelte Werke,* vol. 6, *Der Widerstreit von Raum und Zeit* (Stuttgart: Evangelisches Verlagswerk, 1963); *Kairos* II (Stuttgart: Evangelisches Verlagswerk,

This essay first appeared in an earlier translation in *Religion and Culture: Essays in Honor of Paul Tillich* (1959).

this fundamental theme of Tillich's thought to undertake a thorough investigation of "Christianity's primal terms" as such.

1. Christianity's primal terms can be understood as both material and formal. *Primal material terms* are concerned with the content of Christian revelation. They seek to refer the plenitude of individual revelations back to a kind of center, which is not to be found in these revelations and is therefore intrinsically sought by them. One such center, which we see in the period from Irenaeus to Augustine, is that of the *"admirabile commercium"* or *"commutatio"*: the *"blessed exchange" between God and man,* which takes place in Christ as the "mediator" in the sense of a dynamic "middle" — following an interpretation of the Pauline "ἀπο-κατ-αλλαγή" in Romans and 2 Corinthians as meaning in its original sense not *"reconciliatio"* or "reconciliation," but rather a "thoroughgoing change" between "other" (God) and "other" (man): whereby the "other" (ἄλλο) of the man of sin and curse and death is converted (ἀλλαγή) into participation (κοινωνία) in the "other" (ἄλλο) of the holy and blessed and immortal God, in that this God first assumes the "form" of this man in Christ, who became sin and curse and death (2 Cor. 5:21; Gal. 3:13; Rev. 1:18).[6]

The primal material term specific to the Christian Middle Ages, on the other hand (above all in Thomas Aquinas), is the *"ordo universi"* in a *"perfectio universi,"* which is to say, the *"sacral order of the universe,"* the revealed basis for which is found in the prologue of John's gospel and in the introductions of the letters to the Ephesians and Colossians: Christ, from "before the foundation of the universe" and unto the "new heaven and new earth," as the "primal origin" (ἀρχή), the "head as the summing up"[7] (ἀνακεφαλαίωσις), and the "supporting ground" (συνέστηκεν) of the "entire creature" of the "entire cosmos" of "all things taken together in heaven and on the earth." It is the primal material term that figures as, so to speak, the "defining goal" of the primal Christian notion of a "blessed exchange" — to the point of a "Christian universe as a legal order" in Christ, who is the "law's Logos," and in the Holy Spirit, who as the "παράκλητος" is the "advocate" and the "law's seal."[8]

From this perspective it is understandable that the primal material term peculiar to the Reformation is *"justification by faith alone."* In this term

---

1929). Cf. my analysis of Tillich's philosophy of religion in *Humanitas* (1952), pp. 240ff., 428f., 611ff., 728f.

6. Cf. Przywara, *Christentum gemäß Johannes* (1953), pp. 229f., and Przywara, *Logos* (1962), pp. 119ff.

7. *Inbegriff.* — Trans.

8. Cf. *Christentum gemäß Johannes,* pp. 249ff.

we see a recurrence of the circumstances of Paul's letters to the Romans and the Galatians. Just as Paul is set against the "sacral law" of a "Judaism" of "god-like righteousness," and opposes to it that "righteousness of God" which "kills and brings to life, which leads down to Sheol and raises up again" (this being the fundamental saying of the Old Testament), the Reformation is set against the static legal institutionalism of the Middle Ages and opposes to it a dynamic "justi-*fic*-ation" ["*Recht*-fertig-*ung*"] that is actualized ever anew, whereby the human being is a purely receptive "potentiality" of God's free "legal *decree*" ["*Recht*-sprech-*ung*"],[9] subject to an ultimate and inscrutable dialectic between the "verdict of judgment" and the "verdict of grace." Far, however, from signifying a kind of "legal thinking" peculiar to the Reformation (as opposed to "sacramental" or, as more recent Protestantism would have it, "charismatic" thinking), the Reformation's doctrine of "justification," as the *articulus stantis et cadentis ecclesiae,* entails precisely the uprooting of all "legality" into the primal mystery of the *Deus irae et gratiae* — this being (in the words of Romans 11:33) the "abyssal depth and height"[10] that quakes in Luther's "volcanism," that Jacob Böhme turns into the original principle of a cosmic theosophy, and that has now become especially "current" in Tillich's philosophy of religion.[11]

Precisely in our own day, however, this antithetical primal material term, "justification by faith alone," has met with a (provisionally) ultimate primal term, which in a special way has renewed our consciousness of the letter to the Hebrews with its emphasis upon the cultic: the *high-priesthood of Christ in the Holy Temple* that is "made by God and not by a man":[12] a high-priesthood not only "in the heavenly places," but "proclaimed in the *agora,*" in the midst of the marketplace of the world. Christian redemption is not simply an ontic "exchange," nor is it simply an integration into a cosmic "order," nor is it simply a resonating with a divine dialectic; rather, all of this has its determining center in "The Lord is There," which is the name given to the "new temple" at the conclusion of Ezekiel's prophecy.[13] It was along

9. The emphasis on *"fertig"* points to the reality of a righteousness already perfected and prepared and then imparted, just as the emphasis on *"sprech"* points to the reality of a righteousness imparted by a free gracious decree, over and above the demands of retributive justice. — Trans.

10. *Ungrund von Tiefe und Höhe,* as a rendering of βάθος. — Trans.

11. See his *Religionsphilosophie* (1925), published in *Gesammelte Werke,* vol. 1; and his *Das Dämonische* (1926), published in *Gesammelte Werke,* vol. 6.

12. Cf. Hebrews 9:11.

13. Ezekiel 48:35.

these lines that, within Catholicism, the so-called "liturgical movement" arose in the years following the First World War. Along the same lines, a consciously liturgical and sacramental Protestantism took shape in the years following the Second World War.[14] Ultimately, however, these Catholic and Protestant movements, which sprang up within the womb of the West, are animated by Eastern Orthodox Christianity: inasmuch as, from its beginning, the "charter" for Eastern Orthodox Christianity has been the letter to the Hebrews, with its emphasis upon the high priesthood of Christ in the new temple (Christ as the "λειτουργός of the Holy and of all the holy ones") — all of which one sees in Eastern Orthodoxy's icons, iconostases, and great liturgies, which are in themselves what the Western "sermon" seeks to achieve.

2. These material "primal Christian terms" should be distinguished from *formal "primal Christian terms,"* which are not concerned with the content of Christian revelation, at least insofar as a particular content might be thought to be the all-determining center of revelation; rather, they concern the form under which the entirety of revelation concretely appears: whether in terms of the "proclamation" *(kerygma)* or in terms of the sacramental *"mysterium"* or in terms of the historical *"kairos"* or in terms of the super-historical *"oikonomia"* — which is to say, in terms of the "order of salvation," which is pre-historical in the "counsel of God before the foundation of the world" (as the letter to the Ephesians envisions it), post-historical in the "Sabbath of the people of God" (as the Revelation of John sees it), and therefore intra-historical as the law of salvation history according to which "God has bound all in disobedience that he might show mercy to all" (as stated by Romans 9–11).[15]

The formal primal term peculiar to the prophetic office in the Old Testament and to the office of the evangelist in the New Testament is *"kerygma."* Originally, "κήρυγμα," which derives from "κηρύσσειν" and "κῆρυξ," and is rooted in "γηρύω," means "sound" (in the sense that even animals "make sounds"). In its historical sense, then, it means the kind of sound broadcast by a national, military, or sacred authority by means of a "herald" who "calls together" the people or the army or the faithful for the sake of a meeting or for training and battle or for the celebration of a sacrifice. Inasmuch as the "authority" gives notice through such a "herald," the latter comes to be a repre-

14. Cf. the program of the evangelical *Michaelsbruderschaft* in *Credo Ecclesiam*, 1954.

15. Przywara cites Romans 9:11; the correct reference, however, would seem to be Romans 11:32. — Trans.

sentative of this authority, which is to say, an "ambassador" or "envoy": As such a representative ambassador, he is therefore a "herald" in the original sense of the word, that is to say, one who "presides over the army," "governing" the army (or the public gathering or the sacrificial celebration) as a "governor," on behalf of the given "authority." "Κήρυγμα" thus means an "official message" announced in the voice of the official ambassador; and for this reason it is most intimately connected to the concept of a "kingdom": whether the "gathering" of a kingdom at peace, or the "army" of a kingdom at war, or the celebratory sacrifice of a kingdom before God. Now, if this is so, if "κήρυγμα" is the central form under which Christianity appears in the prophets, the Acts of the Apostles, and the letters of Paul — as a messianic message (cf. Is. 61:1), as a message of the Messiah in the "proclamation" of John the Baptist (Mt. 3:1), as a message of the Messiah "proclaimed in his own voice" (cf. Mt. 4:17), as a message of the Messiah proclaimed by his apostles as "ambassadors to the whole world" (cf. Mt. 10:7; Mk. 16:15), as the "folly of the message of Christ Crucified" (cf. 1 Cor. 1:21, 23) — then "κήρυγμα" stands in the closest possible relation to "βασιλεία," in the sense of the "kingdom of God" or the "kingdom of heaven": which is to say that "κήρυγμα" is the "message of a kingdom." It is in this sense, then, that this "κήρυγμα" is without qualification an "εὐαγγέλιον": an "εὐαγγέλιον," that is, in the historical sense of the word, by which one is to understand not joyful "good news," but rather a message from the Roman Caesar sent to the whole *imperium Romanum* — a message, moreover (in keeping with the character of Caesar as a deity), that in itself, *as* a message, is "salvation" (which comes from Caesar as the saving god),[16] regardless whether the content of the message be punishment or pardon (just as the whole Old Testament honors the God who "kills and brings to life"). Simply as a matter of its historical form, therefore, "εὐαγγέλιον" means the "message of a kingdom" — just as "κήρυγμα," as an "official message," is issued solely "on account of the kingdom," and therefore presupposes the "kingdom" that "officiates" in the message of the official messenger. Thus, what is ultimate within this unity of "κήρυγμα" and "εὐαγγέλιον" is (in the words of the *Te Deum*) the *"Pater immensae majestatis"*: the primal divine "majesty" that, in the "κήρυγμα" and "εὐαγγέλιον" of its "messenger," "regally extends its office into the kingdom" (just as, in Hebrew, "kingdom" is used both for the divine majesty and for the "kingdom of God on earth"). Consequently, "κήρυγμα" and "εὐαγγέλιον" are necessarily grounded in the

---

16. *Heils-Gott* — a reference, in part, to the supposed divine power of an emperor to heal with the touch of his hand. — Trans.

"Word" of God, understood as "God the Word," just as the gospel of John and the Johannine corpus refer "κήρυγμα" and "εὐαγγέλιον" back to the "Λόγος," which in its very being is the "Word of God as God the Word," in order verbally to speak the "words of God" in the "κήρυγμα" and "εὐαγγέλιον." But if this "Word of God as God the Word" is the *one* "Logos," the *one* "Word" of "κήρυγμα" and "εὐαγγέλιον," then the deepest ground of all Christian "κήρυγμα and εὐαγγέλιον" — *within* all Christian proclamation (in κήρυγμα and εὐαγγέλιον) — is the *one* "I am with you" of the Λόγος, understood as the "Word of God as God the Word."

This central form of the "kerygma" is the formal ground of the particular theology of Origen: given that for him all the words of revelation in the Old and New Testaments (following the method of the *"analogia fidei,"* i.e., the analogy of the intrinsic connection between the two Testaments) constitute a *single* "κήρυγμα" of the "Λόγος of God" — whereby the entire faith and the life of faith becomes a "participation in the Λόγος," and Christianity itself becomes "logi-form."[17] In the High Middle Ages this centrality of the "κήρυγμα of the Λόγος" then becomes the formal ground of the Dominicanism of the "order of preachers" *(ordo praedicatorum),* which, in contrast to the Benedictine centrality of the liturgy, established the centrality of the "sermon" — this being rooted, in turn, in the theological centrality of the "Λόγος" as "truth." The absolute form of this central "κήρυγμα" then appears in Calvinism: in which the worship service is essentially the sermon, and for which the sacraments and the liturgy are merely a corresponding figurative "recollection and memorial" — the sermon and the responsorial confession of the "congregation hearing the sermon"[18] being in themselves the sole and exclusive cultic *"actio."* Karl Barth's theology then provides this centrality of the "κήρυγμα" with an inner metaphysics: since for him the "κήρυγμα" is ultimately rooted in the mystery of the Trinity itself, namely, in the trinitarian dialogue of revelation.[19]

The second formal "primal Christian term," *"mysterion,"* is rooted entirely in the Pauline letters — so much so that today (following Adolf Deissmann's *Mystik des Apostels Paulus*) both the "theology of the mysteries" within Catholicism and the liturgical-sacramental movement within

17. *Logos-förmig.* — Trans.
18. *Predigt-Gemeinde.* — Trans.
19. *Offenbarungs-Gespräch.* Cf. *Kirchliche Dogmatik* I/1. For more on Przywara's understanding of Barth's theology, especially as concerns the trinitarian structure of revelation, see *Humanitas: Der Mensch Gestern und Morgen* (Nürnberg: Glock und Lutz, 1952), pp. 174f. — Trans.

Protestantism use the word *"mysterium"* to designate a new "Paulinism," as opposed to a "Pauline kerygmatics." According to its literal sense, *"mysterion"* indicates a "τηρεῖν" within "μυ," which is to say, a "keeping" of something within an "enclosure." As a group of related words indicates, this sense of "keeping within an enclosure" has, so to speak, a "telluric" and a "psychic-spiritual" side. The telluric side comprises such words as "μύλλω" (for "sexual intercourse"),[20] "μυσάρχη" (for "maid"), "μύλος" (for "mill"), "μύζω" (for "suck in"), and "μυγμός" (for "moan"), etc. The psychic-spiritual side, on the other hand, comprises the words "μύσω" (for "initiating someone into a doctrine") and, corresponding to this, "μῦθος" (understood as the "word" in which the mystery of being, its "μυ" in the sense of what is "enclosed," is so to speak "secretly whispered" into the listening ear of the "μύστης") and, corresponding to this, "μυστήριον" (understood as that which is "safeguarded in the preserve of an enclosed existence").[21] This bifurcation between a telluric and a psychic-spiritual "μυ" affords us, of itself, an insight into the inner duality of the historical mysteries. The telluric side points to those primordial mysteries brought to light by the great ethnologist Winthuis:[22] the cultic celebration of the complete integration of the sexes as the presence and representation of the divine, wherein male and female are identical. This is the mystery of the "ἱερὸς γάμος," the holy nuptials, which stands at the center of the Babylonian mysteries. The psychic-spiritual side, on the other hand, points to the correlated mysteries of Eleusis and Dionysus specific to Greek antiquity, which celebrate a metaphysico-religious "resurrection in death" (as the great classical philologist Walter F. Otto has shown in *Die Gestalt und das Sein*): in the symbol of ears of corn suddenly shooting up out of the underworld, in the Eleusinian mysteries, and in the symbol of the grapevine suddenly shooting up out of the inebriation of the dismembered Dionysus. The telluric-spiritual duality of "μυ" (as we have seen from its etymology) thus constitutes a "fruitful βάθος," pointing to an "essence of *mysterium*." In the words of Otto, a *mysterium* is "a repetition of a primordial divine event" in the "cult," in which "the human being is raised up to the divine and . . . interacts in fellowship with it,"[23] thus constituting, to employ the vocabulary of ancient Christianity, the *"memoria et praesentia"* of a divine action in a "divine

20. The word μύλλω technically means "grind" or "crush," as in a mill. — Trans.
21. *Eingewahrtwerden in das Gewahrnis eines verschlossenen Seins.* — Trans.
22. See *inter alia* J. Winthuis, *Das Zweigeschlechterwesen bei den Zentralaustraliern und anderen Völkern* (Leipzig: Hirschfeld, 1928).
23. See *Die Gestalt und das Sein*, pp. 80, 86f.

nuptials" (as this is objectively prefigured in the telluric "μυ," in however earthy a way, and as it is foretokened — as "resurrection in death" — in the psychic-spiritual "μυ").

This, however, brings us into the midst of the Christian *"mysterium."* In the gospels, certainly, the Christian sense of *mysterium* is that of "the mysteries of the kingdom of heaven" (Mt. 13:11); correspondingly, in the Pauline corpus it signifies the entire order of salvation: the "comprehensive summing up of all things in heaven and on earth under the headship of Christ" as the "mystery of his will" (Eph. 1:9-10); and then, more concretely, it means the *"mysterium Christi,"* in which the "Gentiles are fellow heirs and fellow members of the same body and fellow partakers" of this *one* heavenly-earthly "kingdom" (Eph. 3:3-6) — thus pointing ultimately to a "cosmic *mysterium*" in which everything, without exception, is comprised in the "all in all of Christ." In the celebration of the Mass, however, the vitality of this central Christian mystery is ever renewed as that which, so to speak, actualizes the church as the "spouse" and "body" and "fullness" of this *one* Christ (cf. 1 Cor. 12:12ff.; Eph. 5:25ff.) — and thus as the wedding celebration, whose life is ever renewed in the church's "members" (as the "ἐπι-χορηγούμενον" and "συμβιβαζόμενον," i.e., "the round dance of the nuptial union": Col. 2:19);[24] — and as the unity of the wedding banquet of the *"anamnesis,"* i.e., in the objective *"memoria et praesentia"* in the "bread" and the "cup" of the "body and blood of the Lord"; and this as a "universal proclamation" of "the death of the Lord" (but, in keeping with 1 Cor. 15:1-11, as a proclamation of "resurrection *in* death") in the "new covenant in my blood": as we have been "baptized all of us together in *one* Spirit, into *one* body . . . and all together have been made to drink of *one* Spirit" (1 Cor. 12:13). Here we have the *"Magna Carta"* of the Christian *mysterium,* which inspired Cyril of Jerusalem to write his *Mystagogical Catecheses* and which inspired Augustine in his homilies (in the *Tractatus in Joannem* as well as in the *Enarrationes in Psalmos*) to proclaim Christianity as a cultic *"actio"* whose vitality is ever renewed, in which the *one* *"Mysterium"* is celebrated under the signs of the *one* bread and the *one* cup, in which the "crucified-resurrected" Lord celebrates his "resurrection in death" now (in the *"memoria et praesentia"* as the nup-

---

24. Here Przywara seems to be conflating the verbs ἐπιχορηγέω and ἐπιχορεύω, perhaps tracing both words back to a more original root (he may be suggesting that "to supply" means literally "to yield over to" just as each dancer in a ring-dance "yields place to" another; or, more likely, he may be recalling that the former verb is derived originally from the office of the χορηγός, who in Attic tradition was both the leader of the solemn public chorus and also the person charged with paying its costs). — Trans.

tial union of the "many members" who are "*one* body" as "Christ": 1 Cor. 12:12). This is why Augustine calls his fellow Christians not the (people) "of Christ," but simply "Christ" (*"vos non estis Christi, sed Christus"*), and why in Augustine's own time the holy meal was given to Christians with the words *"accipite, quod estis,"* "receive what you are." Thus, the distinction between "kerygmatic Christianity" and "Christianity as *mysterium*" *ipso facto* resembles the distinction that Walter F. Otto draws between *mythos* and *mysterium* in antiquity: between "being's self-expression" and "being's enactment."[25] "Christianity as *mysterium*" is the ongoing ontic realization[26] of what "kerygmatic Christianity" expresses ever anew: just as the proclamation of the "Word" of the God-man is the "wording forth" of this ontic "Word."

Taken in isolation, however, both "kerygmatic Christianity" and "Christianity as *mysterium*" at least run the risk of making Christianity out to be something suprahistorical. In the tradition of Origen, "kerygmatic Christianity" tends to become an intelligible construct, a "system contained within the Logos": a, so to speak, Christian-Platonic "τόπος νοητός" of an *"analogia fidei,"* suspended in itself, of the revealed contents of the Old and New Testaments (just as Calvinist "preaching" combines Old and New Testaments into an ever new symbol of "moral truths"). The danger of making Christianity out to be something purely suprahistorical, which is latent in "Christianity as *mysterium*," is acutely symbolized by the fate of Eastern Orthodox Christianity, whose Platonic "τόπος νοητός" is located in the correlation between the ideal world of icons and the ideal world of a suprahistorical liturgy. In its essence, however, Christianity is a genuinely real incarnation in which the totally eternal God became a totally intrahistorical human being, in order to live on intrahistorically in a totally intrahistorical church and humanity and world: as Christ, ever the same, yesterday, today, and in every age (as one should interpret Heb. 13:8). This is the site of our *third* formal "primal Christian term," which is distinctly present at the foundation of Paul Tillich's philosophy of religion: *"Kairos."*

Christianity essentially means: eternity in time and as time, absolute (divine) eternity in relative (human) time, and therefore in the sequence of yesterday, today, and tomorrow. It consists in the correlation of three words that the Greek New Testament uses to express the mystery of historical time: χρόνος, καιρός, αἰών. "Χρόνος" means the simple "duration of time" in the "course of time." "Αἰών" means the contents of an "age" or "world age": just

25. *Seins-Vollzug.* — Trans.
26. *Das je Ontische.* — Trans.

as we use this word for antiquity, the Middle Ages, and modernity. But whereas "χρόνος" accentuates the "course of time" (so much so that it gives rise to a notion of "chronology" that is most readily associated with "fleeting transience"); and whereas "αἰών" crystallizes this "fleeting transience" into relatively "eternal structures," which is what "world ages" are (so much so that the word "αἰών" is ultimately used to signify the absolutely "eternal," as in the liturgical formula *"per omnia saecula saeculorum,"* which is to say, "from eternity to eternity"); "καιρός" — in contrast to the distinct notes of "transience" in "χρόνος" and "eternity" in "αιών" — stresses the "right time" (in the sense of the Latin *"opportunitas"*), and therefore ultimately the "opportune moment." It is "opportune" in one sense on the basis of a "prior plan." But it becomes concretely "opportune" by dint of concretely historical, fateful[27] "circumstances." It is "opportune" in one sense by virtue of an ideal "determination from above." But it is equally "opportune" by virtue of a "real situation from below." "Καιρός" is "time rightly measured"[28]: simultaneously according to a supratemporal "measure," but also in keeping with an intratemporal "measure of real circumstances."

It is in this sense that, in his parting words to the apostles (who had inquired about the "time" of the "coming kingdom"), the Lord speaks respectively of both "χρόνοι and καιροί," "which the Father has set by his own authority" (Acts 1:7). That is to say: from the Father who is the "origin without origin" *(principium sine principio)* proceed both the simple course of time (χρόνοι) and those "right moments" (καιροί) that intersect it, right through its very midst, in which the divine enters into time in ever new ways. Since this "entrance" is essentially "messianic" (from the "καιροί" of the Old Covenant, understood as a "type of the messiah," to the "καιροί" of the "fullness of time" in the messiah, to the "καιρός" of the messianic return), in the gospels the word "καιρός" refers specifically to Christ: as, say, in the gospel of John, where the Lord speaks of "my καιρός" (Jn 7:6). Finally, however, since the "messianic καιρός" stands in its essential content in opposition to Satan, as the "archon and god of this world age" (Jn 14:30; 2 Cor. 4:4), and in opposition also therefore to the "Antichrist," as his particular instrument, the word "καιρός" also designates the "time" of this opposition: as it is said of Satan that, subsequent to tempting the Lord in the wilderness, the devil "left him until the καιρός" (Lk 4:13); and as the Lord sees the "καιρός" of the opposition between God and Satan (the "anti-God," *"sātān,"* "adversary"),

27. *Schicksalhaft.* — Trans.
28. *Zeit im rechten Maß.* — Trans.

which is played out in terms of the opposition between Christ and Antichrist, as "fulfilled" in that "right moment" in which he enters the Passion: "My καιρός is at hand . . . I am going to celebrate the Passover with my disciples" (Mt. 26:18). Ultimately, therefore, the word "καιρός," which is proper to a messianic intrahistorical Christianity, does not define this intrahistoricality merely as a correlation between, on the one hand, what in any given case has been "posited by the Father" and, on the other, the "Son's entrance" into these "given circumstances" (just as Luke's gospel prefers to depict "Christ's καιρός" against a background of actual chronology); rather, "Christ's καιρός" is essentially the "καιρός of redemption," in that for original Christianity this redemption takes place within the opposition between God and Satan (as anti-God), within the opposition between Christ and Antichrist (as a "ransom" of humanity from "slavery to Satan" in Christ's selling of himself as the "price of release").

For this reason Paul Tillich seeks what is ultimate in "καιρός" by way of the tradition of Jacob Böhme, Franz von Baader, and Schelling (with an affinity to the Russian theosophy of Chaadayev, Frank, Shestov, and Berdyaev): in the divine as "ground" and "unground." In his critique of Rudolf Otto, he stresses that the "holy . . . would have to be conceived . . . precisely as a breakthrough — breaking through the realm of the senses, as their abyss and ground."[29] In his "Philosophy of Religion" (1925) he allows, more pointedly, that both theism and atheism are rooted in this divine "ground" and "unground": "every genuine theism . . . contains an abyss of atheism":[30] which is what the brilliant French writer Simone Weil (in interpreting the mystery of the Cross) calls the "presence of God" in the "absence of God," the "fullness of God" in the "godforsakenness of God by God." Indeed, in this same "Philosophy of Religion" he goes so far as to speak of a "splitting of the Holy into the divine and the demonic," whereby the "demonic" is the "the holy anti-divine."[31] Here we see the mighty influence of the old Origenist tradition, which conceives of the whole "kingdom of Satan, as the archon and god of this world age," as an ultimate antithesis to God, which — in the final "ἀποκατάστασις," the "universal restoration" (Acts 3:21) — is taken back in a, so to speak, "divine synthesis," into the "God who is all in all" (1 Cor. 15:28).

29. Tillich, "Rechtfertigung und Zweifel," in Gesammelte Werke, vol. 8: Offenbarung und Glaube (Stuttgart: Evangelisches Verlagswerk, 1970), p. 96.

30. Tillich, "Religionsphilosophie," in Gesammelte Werke VIII, p. 334.

31. Tillich, "Religionsphilosophie," pp. 338-39.

Our *fourth* and final formal "primal Christian term" provides the answer to such seductive endeavors. Transcending every antithesis within salvation history between "the kingdom of God and his Christ" and "the kingdom of the anti-God, Satan, and his anti-Christ," there is what the letter to
the Ephesians calls the "οἰκονομία τοῦ πληρώματος τῶν καιρῶν," which is
rooted in the "mystery of his (God's) will, according to his good pleasure"
(Eph. 1:8-10). Every one of the καιροί within the whole of salvation history
— between the "καιρός" of Christ as the "Alpha and Omega, the First and
Last, the Origin and End" (Rev. 22:13), and as such the "head and summing
up of all things in heaven and on earth" (Eph. 1:10) "from before the foundation of the world" (Eph. 1:4) and the "καιρός" of Christ in whom "all things
are restored" in the "handing over of the kingdom (through Christ) to God
the Father" (1 Cor. 15:24) "so that God may be all in all" (1 Cor. 15:28) — between, that is, the "ἀνακεφαλαίωσις πάντων" in Christ as the "Origin" and
"First" (πρώτη, ἀρχή) and the "ἀποκατάστασις πάντων" in the same Christ
as the "End" and "Last" — all these "καιροί" of salvation history are formed,
from beginning to end, by this "Origin and First" (of the "summing up of all
things in Christ as head") and this "End and Last" (of the "restoration of all
things" in "Christ's handing over of all things [to the Father] so that God
may be all in all"). All the "καιροί" of salvation history, precisely in the context of the opposition between "the kingdom of God and his Christ" and
"the kingdom of Satan and his anti-Christ," are grounded in, live within, and
flow into this *one* "οἰκονομία τοῦ πληρώματος τῶν καιρῶν," this "domestic
lawfulness of the plenitude of *καιροί*." It is only when we trace this "domestic
lawfulness" back to the "God and Father" who is the "lord of the house"
(οἰκοδεσπότης) of the *one* "vineyard" and the *one* "marriage" (Mt. 21:33; Lk
14:21; Mt. 20:1) that we see through it to what is truly "ultimate": the unfathomable and inscrutable βάθος of God himself, God's "groundless height and
depth" (Rom. 11:33), which only the "Pneuma," the Spirit of God himself,
"searches" (1 Cor. 2:11). To be sure, it is precisely the letter to the Romans that
portrays all of the "καιροί" under the sign of a contradiction between the
"imprisoning of all (by God) in the disobedience of unbelief" (and thus ultimately in the "Satanic") and a "mercy upon all (that is offered by God and
leads to God)"[32] (Rom. 11:32) — virtually establishing what for the Origenist
tradition from Böhme to Baader to Schelling to Tillich might appear to be
"ultimate." Yet, it is precisely here, at the point of this most extreme proximity to an ultimate dialectic between God and anti-God, that the same letter

---

32. *Durch Gott in Gott hinein.* — Trans.

to the Romans leaves no course open but a confluence into the "βάθος" of the "riches and wisdom and knowledge (γνῶσις) of God," "from whom and through whom, for whom[33] and to whom" are "all things" (Rom. 11:33, 36). All the "καιροί" of salvation history, which in our experience truly shimmer between the "kingdom of God and his Christ" and the "kingdom of the anti-God Satan and his anti-Christ" — all these ambiguous καιροί are ultimately nothing other than the appearance within salvation history of the "unfathomable counsels and unsearchable ways" of the *one* "βάθος" of the *one* "οἰκοδεσπότης" of the *one* "οἰκονομία": the sovereign householder's domestic ordering of the unfathomable and unsearchable "height and depth of the groundlessness of God."

This is why the formal "primal Christian term" οἰκονομία is the fundamental term specific to Catholicism. The hierarchical aspect within Catholicism is, in accord with the two "hierarchies" of Dionysius the Areopagite, the, so to speak, "incarnational face"[34] of the "domestic ordering" of the "Father as householder." If in the truly divine the "οἰκοδεσπότης" and the "οἰκονομία" — domestic lordship and the rule of domestic order — go together, and if God really enters into the world and into history in a real incarnation, then God cannot truly appear, live, and act in this real world and in this real history other than as a human "lord of the house" in the "rule of domestic order." The "Catholic" perspective is one that recognizes, precisely in the midst of a sober view of the contradictoriness and ambiguity of the "καιροί," this "domestic ordering" of the "lord of the house" as the genuinely ultimate "primal Christian term" — a domestic ordering that is represented in a truly human way (in keeping with a real incarnation) in the "ecclesial order" of an "ecclesial Lord." The final "note" — and last "breath" — of this divine-human "οἰκονομία" is therefore one of "majesty" and "glory."[35]

---

33. *Um Seinetwillen,* for the "ἵνα" in verse 32. — Trans.
34. *Menschwerdungs-Antlitz.* — Trans.
35. Cf. by the author, *Alter und Neuer Bund* (1956), *Gespräch zwischen den Kirchen* (1957), and, for further treatment of this whole theme, *Logos* (1962/63).

13 Time, Space, Eternity

1959

1. Arguably all great philosophies involve a correlation of *time and space:* either one that encompasses an objective world and in which that world objectively "runs its course" (beginning with Ionian philosophy and culminating in the Renaissance philosophy of Nicholas of Cusa and Giordano Bruno) — or one that, as an ultimate category, shapes all subjective human cognition (as in Kant's "transcendental aesthetic," according to which space is the "form of all the appearances of external things" and time is "the form of inner sense, i.e., of the intuition of ourselves and our inner state"). So-called "critical realism" then seeks a synthesis of these two conceptions, taking space and time as an *"ens rationis"* (following Kant), but *"cum fundamento in re"* (following pre-Kantian philosophy). But such a perspective remains in the rational foreground. For in all philosophies space and time carry a distinct pathos. An objectivism of time and space ultimately arises from a picture of the human being as a "human being within the totality of the cosmos." A subjectivism of time and space, on the other hand, is rooted in a picture of the human being as "a being of internal infinity." An objectivism of time and space, corresponding to a view of the "human being within the totality of the cosmos," will therefore take time and space as the most proximate manifestation of "God within the cosmos": just as Nicholas of Cusa sees the cosmic *"coincidentia oppositorum"* (in space and time) as an immediate manifestation of the divine infinity. A subjectivism of time and space, on the other hand, as classically represented in Kant's thought, necessarily terminates in the *"Est Deus in nobis"* of the *Opus postumum,* that is, in a god-

---

This essay first appeared in *Archivio di Filosofia,* Rome (1959).

like infinity in the "transcendental subject" — a subject that, admittedly, does not explicitly bear the form of God, but in which the form of God is imperceptibly at work.

At the most formal level, time and space thus appear "at the limit" between God and creature. On the one hand, they are what most incisively distinguish the creature from God, indicating the acutest (positive and negative) difference from God. The Greek "χρόνος" does not mean "time as such" in the sense, as it were, of a continuum of succession "to infinity."[1] Rather, it means distinct "portions of time": a "long time" or "a time of hesitant lingering," but also a "short time" and, indeed, even "a moment." Equally, the Greek "χώρα" (which Aristotle uses for "space") does not mean "space as such" in the sense of a continuum of contiguity "to infinity";[2] rather, it too means the concretely particular, in this case of "place, position, and region" or, even more concretely, "land" and "country estate" — just as the corresponding verb "χωρέω" means the "occupation" of a place or the "retreat" from a place, or finally "going" as such. The Latin *tempus* further accentuates the meaning of the Greek "χρόνος": since it comes from the Greek verb "τέμνω," which means "to cut off," and thus signifies a "section"; hence, time in the sense of *tempus* is simply a succession of segments, as opposed to any intrinsically flowing continuum. What is more, the Latin *spatium* means simply a "stretch" to be "run through" like a "course" or a "racetrack," and this in a "circuit," so that "distance" and "interval" are ultimately decisive. Thus, *"spatium,"* understood as space, can even mean a "space of time," to the point of coinciding with *"tempus,"* understood as a "segment of time" — all of which is sharply distinct from the idea of an "infinite space" "within" which the concretely real occurs. The German words *Zeit* and *Raum* merely complete the picture. *"Zeit"* comes from the Indo-Germanic "di" or "da(i)," which means "to divide" or "dissect"; thus the English "time," in its relation to the Latin *"tempus,"* objectively constitutes a kind of midpoint between *"Zeit"* (from "di") and *"tempus"* (from "τέμνω"), both of which mean "to cut off" and "section." The German *"Raum,"* on the other hand, turns out to be intimately related to the meaning of the Greek "χώρα," having the sense of an "open space" or "encampment." Thus, in view of the connection between *"Raum"* and *"Räumen"* ("to make room"), the stress falls here upon the provisionality, mutability, and transience of all creaturely "space" (perhaps reflecting the wanderings of the Germanic tribes, as represented mythologi-

---

1. *Kontinuum des Nacheinander.* — Trans.
2. *Kontinuum des Nebeneinander.* — Trans.

cally in Odin, the eternal wanderer). *"Zeit"* and *"Raum"* are thus in every respect a *signum* of creatureliness: a *signum* of "fragmentariness," "transience," "wandering," "change," "disintegration," etc.; but it is nevertheless a *signum* that is always on the verge of suggesting a godlike becoming,[3] or a godlike change, at least in the sense of an immanent "tragic divinity" or an "evolving God," transcending the limits of the creaturely (as is peculiar to German theosophy in Paracelsus, Jacob Böhme, et al.).[4]

But then, on the other hand, this creaturely form of time and space ultimately suggests a "form of God." To be sure, this stands under the sign of a *"theologia negativa":* just as, in Latin, the *"finitum"* of *"tempus"* is contrasted with the divine *"in-finitum,"* and just as the *"mensum"* (of the measurable) of *"spatium"* is contrasted with the divine *"im-mensum."* Or one might use an expression for this "divine form" that, within the creaturely, suggests an unsurveyable expanse that goes to infinity; just as the Greek "αἰώνιον" originally meant a vast age of the world or age of humanity, but then also the divine eternity for which it is the highest symbol (certainly bearing in mind that the phrase *"per saecula saeculorum"* ultimately means to express the divine in terms of a *"coincidentia"* of "aeons"). Or, finally, in view of these two ways of expressing a "form of God," there is the possibility of a synthesis, as we see in German: on the one hand, as regards space, the creaturely, the *"Meßbaren"* ("measurable"), is contrasted with the divine *"Un-ermeßlichkeit"* ("im-measurability"); on the other hand, as regards time, the word *"ewig,"* being related to the Latin words *"aevum"* and *"aeternum,"* has the same function as the Greek "αἰώνιον," in that something creaturely, namely, a vast age of the world or age of man, is taken as a boundary symbol for what we call "divine eternity."

All of this reveals the actual aporia here. On the one hand, every problematic of time and space inexorably leads us to that limit of the creature at which, in the most formal sense, the divine appears: naïvely and ecstatically, in the way that Renaissance philosophy saw in the infinite course of an infinite universe the dawning of the face of God, but equally in the way that Kant perceived the *"Deus in nobis"* in the inner infinity of the transcendentality of space and time; critically, though, in Nicholas of Cusa's unique understanding of the *"coincidentia oppositorum"* in space and time as the "veiled, open limit" to a God whose *"explicatio"* in time and space is the

3. *Gotthaftes Werden.* — Trans.
4. Cf., on this theme, the relevant chapters in Przywara, *Mensch: Typologische Anthropologie* (1959).

world's *"complicatio."* On the other hand, however, all expressions and words for time and space refer so exclusively to what is distinctive to the creaturely that there is no specific proper word (nor any corresponding proper concept) for the divine in its relation to what, in the creaturely, is called time and space.

2. This aporia, which is proper to time and space in their relation to eternity (as infinity) and immeasurability, culminates in the classical attempts to come up with a kind of proper name — a name applicable both to creaturely time and space and to the supratemporality and supraspatiality of the divine, but at the same time a name in which the difference between the creaturely and the divine reaches its highest intensity. It is the problematic of the *"hodie et nunc,"* the "today and now," a phrase whose usage in regard to the dimension of time can be traced from the ancient liturgy to Augustine to Thomas Aquinas, but, being parallel to the problematic of the "here," necessarily also applies to the realm of space.

Regarding the dimension of time, the ancient *liturgy* originally (and even today) uses the word *"hodie"* for the high feast days of Easter, Pentecost, Christmas, and Epiphany: signaling the church's intention to convey that the *"memoria"* and *"praesentia"* — the memory and presence — of the respective mysteries are celebrated "today": "Today the church is joined to her heavenly bridegroom . . ." (from the liturgy for Epiphany). It is a divine "today": because it occurs in the time and space of the supratemporal and supraspatial God. But, at the same time, it is a creaturely "today": because it is today's day and today's hour, incomprehensibly flowing between a past that is already future *(praeteritum futuri)* and a future that comes out of the past *(futurum praeteriti).*

It is plainly this usage in the ancient liturgy that then leads, in *Augustine,* to a manifest, though more factual, aporia between the divine *"hodie"* and the creaturely *"hodie."* For God it holds true: "There nothing is past, as though it no longer were; nothing is to come, as though it were not yet. . . . There is neither 'was' nor 'will be'":[5] "In the sublimity of an ever-present eternity, you precede everything past and you exceed everything future, because what is yet to come, once it has come, will be past. . . . Your 'day' is not just any day, but *'today,'* because your today does not yield to a tomorrow, nor has it followed from a yesterday. Your today is eternity"[6] — thus "our days and those of our fathers have passed during your today, and from it

5. Augustine, *En. in Ps.* 102, 27.
6. *Confessions* XI, xiii, 16.

have received their measure and the manner of their existence; and others to come will also thus pass away, and thus also receive their measure and the manner of their existence."[7] But as much as it passes through the divine to-day and thereby alone "exists," in itself the creaturely is a "today" whose symbol is a "torrent of rainwater" that "runs and, by running, runs away": "this 'in-between' makes a sound and passes away."[8] And, to take the symbol of living language, the creaturely "today" is all but dissolved: "Say, 'This hour.' Yet of this hour how much can you lay hold of? Some of its moments have already passed; and those to come have not yet arrived. Say, 'In this moment.' In which moment? Even as I pronounce its syllables, if it has two syllables, the second is not heard until the first has passed away: finally, even with a single syllable, if it is composed of two letters, the second letter is not heard until the first has passed away."[9]

Then, finally, in view of this aporia between the divine "Today" and the creaturely "today," *Thomas Aquinas* posits in place of the *"Hodie"* and the *"hodie,"* the *"Nunc"* and the *"nunc"*: time and eternity in the "now," understood as an *"in indivisibili."*[10] This "now" would seem to suggest a commonality between creaturely time and divine eternity: "these '*nuncs*' are not parts of time; for time is not composed of indivisible '*nuncs*.'"[11] But this negative, abstract commonality is intersected by the "ever greater" separation between the divine *"nunc stans"* and the creaturely *"nunc fluens,"* between the "Is as Now" of God and the "flux as now" of the creature.[12] Time and eternity are related to one another as *"nunc fluens"* and *"nunc stans"*: "Just as the apprehension of time is caused in us in that we apprehend the flow of the 'now' itself, so the apprehension of eternity is caused in us inasmuch as we apprehend the 'now' standing still."[13] On the other hand, however, there exists a relation between the two *"nuncs"*: admittedly, there is neither past nor future in the divine *"nunc stans"* (in Augustine's words, neither "was" nor "will be"); nevertheless, they are similar in that the creaturely

7. *Confessions* I, vi, 10.

8. Augustine, *En. in Ps.* 109, 20. [Przywara's elisions of Augustine's text somewhat obscure the image. The metaphor in the original is of torrents of rainwater, which flow from hidden places, swell, and then vanish into the sea, and in between emergence and disappearance there is the sound of flowing water passing away. — Trans.]

9. Augustine, *En. in Ps.* 76, 8.

10. Thomas Aquinas, *Expos. in VI Phys.* V.

11. Aquinas, *Expos. in VI Phys.* XI, 2.

12. Aquinas, *Summa Th.* I, q. 10, a. 2, ad 1; a. 4, ad 2.

13. Aquinas, *Summa Th.* I, q. 10, a. 2, ad 1.

"nunc fluens" is "indifferent to past and future,"[14] inasmuch as the *"nunc"* of the creaturely is the "end of the past and the absolute beginning of the future."[15] Finally, this mystery of the relation between the two *"nuncs"* is intensified in that Thomas renders the *"nunc"* still more incisively as *"instans"*: that is, as an utterly incomprehensible "moment," "a sudden interruption,"[16] which has "no proportion to time, because it is not a part of time,"[17] but which nevertheless, just like the creaturely *"nunc fluens,"* is the "absolute beginning of the future and the end of the past."[18] Rendered more incisively as *"instans," "nunc"* thus bears the features of a "sudden divine intervention and entry" into the continuous flow of time, even as it shares that sense of the creature's *"nunc fluens"* between past and future.[19] Thus Thomas unites the *"nunc"* and the *"instans"* into an *"instantis nunc,"*[20] which is to say, into the "now of a sudden interruption." On the one hand, in the *"instantis nunc,"* the divine *"nunc stans"* appears as a divine *"instans,"* as the divine "moment" of a "sudden interruption," but, on the other hand, in the *"nunc instantis,"* the creaturely *"nunc fluens"* likewise presents itself as a "moment" — albeit not as the divine "moment as fullness,"[21] but as the kind of moment in which the "end of the past" is immediately the "absolute beginning of the future," which is to say, not even a "transitional moment" *(transitus in instanti)* between past and future, but at most a rationally incomprehensible "moment *as* transition" *(instans tanquam transitus):* to the point that the creature is ultimately *"in instanti"* only insofar as the "working of God" accomplishes the "continuation of being" in precisely this *"instans,"* a working that is "none other" than the working of a "principle of being": the principle that a thing simply "be."[22]

In other words, the aporia of time and eternity does not consist simply in that, on the one hand, both are seen in light of a strict, final analysis to be "ever of the moment"[23] (*nunc* as *instans*), but that, on the other hand, both

14. Aquinas, *In Expos. in IV Phys.* XXXI, 4.
15. Cf. Aquinas, *Summa Contra Gentiles* II, 33.
16. *Plötzlich inmitten.* — Trans.
17. Aquinas, *Expos. in libr. Arist. de caelo et mundo* I, 12.
18. *Summa Contra Gentiles* II, 36.
19. *Und ist doch gleichsinnig zum "nunc fluens" der Kreatur zwischen Vergangen und Künftig.* There is perhaps a slight amphiboly in *gleichsinnig,* suggesting that the *instans* has the same *direction* as the *nunc fluens.* — Trans.
20. *Summa Th.* q. 46, a. 1, ad 7.
21. *Fülle als Augenblick.* — Trans.
22. *De Pot.* q. 5, a. 1, ad 2.
23. *Je des Augenblicks.* — Trans.

are separated by the "ever greater difference" between the divine "fullness *qua* moment" and the creaturely "empty moment" (since everything pertaining to this creaturely moment is the last moment of the past as the first moment of the future). Rather, the utterly incomprehensible mystery of time and eternity lies in this: that every particular "neutral" moment is both a divine "infinite moment of fullness" and a creaturely "finite moment of emptiness." Time and eternity are thus in a special sense the "τόπος θεῖος," that is, the site where, in the "moment," God and creature so nearly coincide in a, so to speak, natural "divine-human moment" that precisely herein they are distinguished by an "infinite difference."[24] The fact that German mysticism tended to reduce itself to an "instant" in which God and man become one — and the fact that Kant (the Scottish puritan of interiority) singled out time as a category of the "intuition of ourselves and our internal state" — testifies, at least implicitly, to this "τόπος θεῖος" of time's relation to eternity: in the *"hodie"* as *"nunc"* as *"instans"* as *"instantis nunc"* as "moment" as "instant."

The full mystery of time and eternity is apparent, however, only when *time and space* appear, in their correlation, in a relation of contrast to the divine.[25] *Augustine* conceived this contrasting relation as a single *"transcending immanence"*: God as the innermost "in" of space-time as well as its highest and deepest "beyond." The essentially supraspatial and supratemporal God pervades the intraspatial and intratemporal realm of the creature so thoroughly that, in relation to space, he is the one who is "both interior to all things, because all things are in him, and exterior to all things, because he is beyond all things"; and that, in relation to time, he is "both older than all things, because he is before all things, and newer than all things, because he is the same after all things."[26] Furthermore, *Gregory the Great* heightens the mystery of God's being "ever within" and "ever without" the creaturely realm by introducing the dimensions of space into this dialectical rhythm: God "is within and without, he is below and above: above in reigning, below in upholding; within in filling, without in surrounding. He is thus so interior as to be exterior; he so surrounds as to penetrate; he so presides as to uphold; he so

---

24. *Daß sie eben hierin sich zum "unendlichen Unterschied" unterscheiden.* — Trans.

25. *Gegenüber zum Göttlichen. Gegenüber* could also be translated simply as opposition or even contrast. In light of Przywara's entire argument as elaborated throughout the first and second parts of this work, however, it is clear that by *Gegenüber* he means neither a facile distinction between ultimately similar things nor an equivocal opposition, but rather a relation of otherness, which is to say, what he means by analogy as ἄλλο πρὸς ἄλλο. — Trans.

26. Augustine, *De Gen. ad Litt.* VIII, xxvi, 48.

upholds as to preside";[27] "because truly he remains within all things, outside all things, above all things, below all things . . . sustaining in presiding, presiding in sustaining, penetrating in surrounding, surrounding in penetrating; just as he presides on high, so he sustains from below; and just as he surrounds from without, so he fills from within."[28] Thus God appears as "uncircumscribed (that is, as supraspatial) Spirit," but, conversely, as the one who "contains all things in himself, which he at the same time surrounds in filling, and fills in surrounding, and transcends in sustaining, and sustains in transcending."[29] *Space* becomes the "τόπος θεῖος," the "site of the divine," in that within its dimensions of the inner and the outer, the above and the below, there appears — as something ultimately incomprehensible — a divine "ever inward, ever outward, ever above, ever below": in an immanence of what circumscribes[30] that is equally a circumscription of immanence; and in a transcending of a grounding[31] that is equally a grounding of transcendence.

But then, given these intersecting dimensions, a seemingly all-encompassing and, as it were, "infinite space" (as conceived by Thomas Aquinas in terms of the "dimensions of length, breadth, and depth")[32] reduces not merely to the tension between "infinite space," "full space," and "empty space," *spatium* as *plenum* and *spatium* as *vacuum*,[33] as one also sees in the philosophy of the Renaissance, from Nicholas of Cusa on, which tends to conceive of God's positive infinity in terms of the endlessness of space (and which Nicholas of Cusa grounds in his axiom that "the world is nothing but an appearance of the invisible God" and "God [is] nothing but the invisibility of the visible"); rather, this "infinite space," understood as the "*sensorium*" of the infinite God (as the favorite adage of Renaissance philosophy has it), finally reduces, by virtue of its incomprehensibly intersecting dimensions, to their particular "point of intersection" — a point that is likewise an "*in indivisibile*," as with "*hodie*" *qua* "*nunc*" and "*instans*" and "*instantis nunc*" in regard to "infinite time" in its oscillating dimension[34] between an ever new "*praeteritum futuri*" and "*futurum praeteriti*," between a past that is ever anew becoming future and a future that is always becoming

---

27. Gregory the Great, *Hom. in Ezech.* 17.
28. Gregory the Great, *Moralia* II, 12.
29. Gregory the Great, *Moralia* XVI, 31.
30. *Immanenz des All-ringsum.* — Trans.
31. *Transzendierende Fundierung.* — Trans.
32. See Thomas Aquinas, *Expos. in IV Phys.* III, 4.
33. Aquinas, *Expos. in III Phys.* VII, 6.
34. *In ihrer schwingenden Erstreckung.* — Trans.

past. Just as "infinite time," so to speak, is determinatively (but utterly dynamically) centered in a "now *in indivisibili,*" the determinative (but utterly dynamic) center of "infinite space," so to speak, is a "here *in indivisibili.*"

The traditional way of speaking about a *"hic et nunc,"* a "here and now," captures precisely the most proper, albeit most impenetrable, mystery of space and time: that the "infinitely large" (of "infinite space" and "infinite time") is not only opposed to the "infinitely small" (of "here and now") as its (aporetic) contrary, but is precisely grounded in it, and therein has its most precise form (as Leibniz's infinitesimal calculus established for mathematics, leading to the conclusions of modern physics, which seeks to make its way through "bodies" to the "infinitely smallest"); but then it also captures the mystery of space and time in that even the divine, under the figure of *"spatium infinitum"* and *"tempus infinitum,"* has its ultimate figure[35] — on account of the "infinitely small" of the spatial "here" and the temporal "now" — precisely in this "infinitely small" (as Nicholas of Cusa was first to conclude, when he defined God as both the "infinitely greatest" and the "infinitely smallest").

But it is not as though God's "infinite greatness" (under the figure of "infinite space" and "infinite time") then takes on his "infinite smallness" (under the figure of the "now and here") as, so to speak, an "ultimate form." Rather, precisely in keeping with the temporal-spatial dialectic of Augustine and Gregory the Great, God is the "ever greater"[36] (above and beyond all the "infinity" and "fullness" of time and space, however great) in that, within "every interiority" of space and time, he is the "ever smaller,"[37] but precisely in this way — from the "core of the interiority" (of space and time), as it were — he is the ever more encompassing "ever greater." Should one wish to use the mystical terms of Johannes von Tepl's *Ploughman of Bohemia,* which render the Augustinian *"est"* and *"non est"* as *"Ichts"* and *"Nichts,"*[38] these words apply not only to the "here and now" of space and time, but even more so, under the figure of both space and time, to God. Since, for the

---

35. *Äußerste Chiffre.* — Trans.
36. *Je immer Größere.* — Trans.
37. *Je immer Kleinere.* — Trans.
38. *Ploughman of Bohemia* XX, *"Von ichte zu nichte mussen sie werden."* "They must pass from something to nothing." The odd word *"Ichts"* is produced by the privation of the initial "n" in *"Nichts,"* thus producing an untranslatable neologism for "something." Additionally, though, it is hard not to hear the echo of the first person singular pronoun *"ich"* in *"Ichts,"* suggesting that the injunction also means you must pass from being "someone" to being "no one." — Trans.

"*Ichts*" of the "infinite greatness" of space and time, the critical point of intersection is the "infinite smallness" of the here and now *qua* "*Nichts*," it is precisely here, in this focal point, that we see the ultimate and decisive "τόπος θεῖος": in God's appearing as the "ever greater" within the "ever smaller" of his "Now and Here" within the "now and here" of space and time, and so of his "*Ichts*" within the "*Nichts*" (this viewpoint being the positive root of Hegel's speculation regarding a divine "Is" as a divine "nothing"). In the very moment that the human being, guided by the idea of demiurgic man reaching "into the infinity of time and space" (this being the idea of man today), would want to raise his "so great a similarity" to God to the point of an identity with God, in this very moment he is surpassed by the "ever greater dissimilarity" of that which is most properly divine, by the "Ever Greater" of the "*Ichts*" as the "Ever Smaller" of the "*Nichts*." Thus the human being who would wish to ascend into the eternity of the "ever greater" of the "*Ichts*" — in an attempt to overcome space and time — must descend into the "*Nichts*" of his "now and here"; for it is only in such a "nothing" of the "now and here" that he becomes conscious of this eternity — just as, in Christian theological terms, the "eternity" (of God in Christ), as a genuinely creaturely eternity, is *in* space and time as "now and here": from the "now and here" of a birth in a manger and a death on a cross to the "now and here" of a real historical church under the sign of ever new "nihilations,"[39] until the complete "nothingness" of the destruction of "the old heaven and the old earth" reveals the unveiled eternity of the "*Ichts*," certainly as something "new," but whose newness is that of a "heaven and earth" that is the "tabernacling of God with men."

3. This leads us directly to a *Christian theological* understanding of *time, space, and eternity.* At issue are the words of revelation concerning the "πάντα ἐν πᾶσιν" of God in Christ in the space of the world (above all in the Pauline epistles) and the "καιρός" of God's entry in Christ into the temporal course of the world (above all in Luke).

Christ, as the "image of the invisible God" and at the same time the "origin"[40] and "firstborn of all creation" — and thus as the unity of supraspatial, supratemporal "eternity" and a creatureliness shaped by space and time — is the one "in whom all things were created, in heaven and on earth," the one "for whom and to whom all things were created," as the one who is "before all things," whereas "in him all things exist and hold together

---

39. *Nichtungen.* — Trans.
40. *Ur.* — Trans.

(συνέστηκεν)" (Col. 1:15-18). On the one hand, therefore, transcending all the limits and differences (in cosmic space), "Christ is all in all" (Eph. 1:23) — to the point that in him "God might be all in all" (1 Cor. 15:28). On the other hand, it would seem that the course of cosmic time — between "origin" and "end" and "was, is, and will be" — is taken up into the eternity of God in Christ: since the Johannine Apocalypse has God in Christ say: "I am the Alpha and the Omega, the first and the last, the beginning and the end" (Rev. 21:6; cf. 22:13; 1:17); and since the praise before the throne is sung out to the one who is "holy, holy, holy," "the one who was and is and is to come" (Ὁ ἦν καὶ ὁ ὢν καὶ ὁ ἐρχόμενος: Rev. 4:8). The eternity (of God in Christ) is, therefore, so thoroughly the "all in all" of cosmic space that all that "stands" (ἔστηκεν) in its "place" in "space," and all that "stands together" (συν-έστηκεν) with everything creaturely as a "universe," ultimately "stands" and "stands together" only in the One Eternity (of God in Christ). Equally though, and conversely, this One Eternity (of God in Christ) is hereby assumed into the essential mutability of cosmic space in cosmic time, such that this eternity (of God in Christ) is not only its "origin" and "end," but also appears, as the "was and is and is to come," precisely within cosmic time's rhythms of past, present, and future. The philosophical problem of a quasi-infinite space and a quasi-infinite time thus turns out to be a "foreshadowing" of the *mysterium* that Teilhard de Chardin justly described as the ultimate meaning of creaturely becoming and self-unfolding: the *mysterium* of a "cosmic God" in a "cosmic Christ."

Corresponding, however, to the *"hodie, nunc, instans"* in which the philosophical problem culminates, the language of the Lucan writings locates this *mysterium* of a "cosmic God in a cosmic Christ" essentially in the "καιρός," which is to say, in the particular uniqueness of the "always opportune right time," which is why "καιρός" is used for any incisive event of revelation (for the appearance of the Messiah, for his redemptive struggle, and for the end times: cf. Luke 4:13; Acts 1:7). Thus, it is not simply that the fundamental "πάντα ἐν πᾶσιν" is, so to speak, concentrated in the καιρός as in the *"in indivisibile"* of a "moment" (whence the Vulgate's rendering of "καιρός" as *"momentum"*); rather, as an "always opportune favorable moment," it is a qualified "καιρός," extracted from the neutrality of a "moment" as such, so as to have the character of a "turning point" within the universal relation among cosmic space, cosmic time, and eternity (that of the cosmic God in the cosmic Christ). As much as this "καιρός as turning point" appears to be an ordinary *"hodie, nunc, instans"* and *"hic"* (in the sense of "here") i.e., as much as it appears to be intratemporal and intraspatial, it is nevertheless a "unique breaking-in" of the Eternal God in Christ: indeed, precisely of "God as καιρός" in "the creaturely καιρός of the 'now and here.'"

The Christian theologoumenon of time, space, and eternity thus stands within the ultimate, insoluble *mysterium* of the relation between an all-encompassing "πάντα ἐν πᾶσιν," an "all-in-all" of God in Christ, and an always incalculably in-breaking "καιρός" as the "turning point" of a "turn of God."[41] In this insoluble *mysterium,* then, there ultimately appears something like the "face of God in time and space." However much God may reveal himself as veiled in the "all in all" of time and space, or even, in the bold words of the book of Sirach (43:27), simply as "the all" (in the way that even Thomas Aquinas speaks almost interchangeably of God and the universe)[42] — and however much, on the other hand, in the sharpest possible contrast to every such "total enclosure,"[43] this same God declares himself as the Sovereign God preeminently in the "καιρός," in the breaking open of every context as the ever new turning point of an ever new turn[44] — the actual eternity of the Eternal God in Christ is the inscrutable rhythm between "πάντα ἐν πᾶσιν" and "καιρός": between a, so to speak, "God-of-the-All"[45] and a, so to speak, "God-of-the-Turn."[46] God — the eternal as *He* who is eternal — is neither the absolute All (as is the tendency of Thomism, with its understanding of the *"ordo universi"* as a *"perfectio universi,"* and as is openly stated in Spinoza's God-of-the-All as Substance and in Hegel's God-of-the-All as Spirit), nor is He an absolute Turning (as is latent in the tendencies of Scotism, with its dynamic, Sovereign God-of-the-Will,[47] and as emerges in an extreme form in Nietzsche's Dionysian God-of-the-All as the destructive and creative Turning-of-the-All, but also in no small measure in Luther's reduction of the order and structure of salvation to the sovereign, lightning-like irruptions of a "God of wrath and mercy"). Rather, given that a "God-of-the-All" is aligned with the "greatest similarity" (between the creaturely All and the God-of-the-All), while a "God-of-the-Turn" is aligned with an "ever greater dissimilarity" (in the "sovereign breaking-in" of the "καιρός" into a structured All), what ultimately holds true here is a deiform "analogy,"

---

41. *Wende Gottes.* — Trans.
42. See, for example, Thomas Aquinas, *De Pot.* q. 5, a. 4, resp.
43. *All-Geschlossenheit.* — Trans.
44. *Je neuer Wende-Punkt zu je neuer Wende.* — Trans.
45. *All-Gott.* — Trans.
46. *Wende-Gott.* — Trans.
47. *Willens-Gott.* — Trans.

understood as a rhythm — admitting of no further reduction — between the "God-of-the-All" and the "God-of-the-Turn." Corresponding to a "καιρός in-and-beyond πάντα-ἐν-πᾶσιν," there is an ultimate "in-and-beyond" between the "God-of-the-Turn" and the "God-of-the-All": the God-of-the-Turn in-and-beyond the God-of-the-All.

14 Edith Stein and Simone Weil: Two Fundamental Philosophical Themes*

1956

At first glance Edith Stein and Simone Weil do not appear to go together. For one thing, though each died in the final years of the great catastrophe (Weil in 1943, Stein in 1945), they belong to different generations. Edith Stein was born in 1891, still in the nineteenth century. Simone Weil was born in 1909,

*The following portrayal presupposes what the author has already written about these two figures in other works. See *Humanitas: Der Mensch gestern und morgen* (Nürnberg: Glock und Lutz, 1952), pp. 565ff., 725f., *inter alia.* See also *In und Gegen* (Nürnberg: Glock and Lutz, 1955), pp. 61-87. For a profound spiritual portrait of Weil, see J. M. Perrin and G. Thibon, *Simone Weil as We Knew Her* (London: Routledge and Kegan Paul, 1953). The corresponding German work by Karl Epting, *Der geistliche Weg der Simone Weil* (Stuttgart: Vorwerk, 1955), presents the stages of her philosophy, but does not see the "paradox of antitheses" as its inner form. For an account of Edith Stein's religious path, see the following three biographies: Posselt, Sister Teresia Renata de Spiritu Sancto, *Edith Stein,* trans. Cecily Hastings and Donald Nicholl (New York: Sheed & Ward, 1952); *Edith Stein par une moniale française* (Paris: Éditions du Seuil, 1954); Hilda Graef, *Leben unter dem Kreuz: eine Studie über Edith Stein* (Frankfurt am Main: Josef Knecht, 1954); trans. *The Scholar and the Cross: The Life and Works of Edith Stein* (Westminster, MD: Newman Press, 1955 & New York: Longmans, Green, 1955). For some essential corrections to this last biographical account, see my *In und Gegen,* pp. 72f. While Graef touches upon the beginnings of Stein's intellectual [*geistiger*] path, the present study attempts to describe Edith Stein's path by way of her contrast with Simone Weil. Since at the time of writing this study, the author no longer had access to Edith Stein's works on "sympathy" and the "state," or her "essays on woman" or her comparison between Husserl and Thomas Aquinas (since all the copies she dedicated to him were confiscated by the Gestapo in 1941), his references to these works in this study are based entirely on memory.

This essay, which never appeared in German, was first published in a French translation in *Les Études philosophiques* 11 (1956): 458-72. The following translation, which is based upon the original typescript from Przywara's *Nachlass,* is published here with the permission of the Archive of the German Province of the Society of Jesus. — Trans.

when the age of all-out conflict between Bolshevism and Fascism was already underway. To be sure, they have in common that they were born to upper-class Jewish families whose atmospheres tended to be liberal and atheistic (despite Edith Stein's mother being strictly observant of ancient Jewish tradition). But, however significant their shared tradition may have been, in Edith Stein's case the only thing to pass over seamlessly into the style of her thought was the classicism of nineteenth-century cultural Judaism, whereas in Simone Weil's case one sees the passionate breaking away of a social revolutionary. There was, therefore, something undoubtedly fitting about Edith Stein's monastic poverty; but one could never say the same of Simone Weil's path to the factory. Indeed, whereas the path of Edith Stein belongs to the tradition of the great Jewish thinkers, from Maimonides to Cohen to Husserl, Simone Weil's is that of a single revolution against this "classical idealism." Whereas Edith Stein's thought moves transparently in the realm of Greek antiquity and is especially concerned with its final fruits (Plato and Aristotle), Simone Weil's thought breaks away from precisely this later tradition into its primal origins — those not only of the great Ionians (Parmenides and Heraclitus), but also of myth (whose *source grecque* is only apparently Plato, but in reality Homer and the Greek tragic poets, for whom myth is vital).[1] Whereas the thought of Edith Stein is harmoniously balanced (even as it eschews, in genuinely phenomenological fashion, all systematization), Simone Weil's thought is most emphatically a thinking in terms of opposition and contradiction, so much so that it is perhaps the most incisive historical manifestation of such thinking since Heraclitus (even though she does not shy away from "ultimate formulas" that sound almost Hegelian). One might thus conclude that Edith Stein's work represents a single meditative exercise in equalizing thought:[2] first in the context of Husserl's phenomenology (whose manuscripts and sketches she often adjusted into publishable form), and then in the encounter between Husserl's phenomenology and Aquinas's metaphysics (from her phenomenological interpretation of the *Quaestio de veritate,* to her imaginary nocturnal dialogue between Husserl and Thomas, to her final working out of a Thomistic metaphysics in the spirit of Husserl in *Finite and Eternal Being*) — all of which is undertaken so objectively that any "personal thought" entirely disappears. On the other hand, all of Simone Weil's posthumous writings are illustrations of precisely what it means to speak of distinctively "personal

---

1. See Simone Weil, *La Source Grecque* (Paris: Gallimard, 1953).
2. *Ein einziges nach-denkendes Ausgleichsdenken.* — Trans.

thought," so much so that the unity of these writings consists not in any objective "system," but in Simone Weil's own personality, as a "human being with all her contradictions": the contradictions between a "mystical metaphysics" and an implacable realism of "matter" and of the "emptiness" of the "worker and the workers." Thus, as a religious seal upon her thought (as it were), Edith Stein's path leads almost directly from the "holy order" of a Torah-based Judaism to the "holy order" of the liturgy of the New Covenant. Simone Weil's path, on the other hand, leads from a passionate battle against the entire Old Covenant to a Christianity whose "official" character she was so unwilling to affirm that, in the midst of a genuinely Christian mysticism, she did not even come to simple baptism, lest she lose her connection with the "unfortunates on the outside."

1. If one looks through and beyond these empirical connections, it becomes clear that Edith Stein and Simone Weil are distinct *representatives of the intellectual antitheses*[3] *of our time.* By this I mean, firstly, the antithesis between an "essential philosophy of essence" and an "existential philosophy of existence" (as I formulated it in Davos in 1926 in a three-way conversation with Cassirer and Heidegger, and as Edith Stein herself later formulated it in *Finite and Eternal Being*). But, however much Edith Stein's path from Husserl to Thomas Aquinas led her to press beyond Husserl's transcendental idealism toward a genuine metaphysics, her method, even in her Thomistic work *Finite and Eternal Being,* genuinely remains that of an "essential philosophy of essence." For her, therefore, there are not actually any "ultimate problems" or "ultimate aporias" or "ultimate antitheses" in which a mystery of being is unveiled, in a way that in reality leads ever more deeply into being's veiledness (as one sees in Pascal's *Pensées* or, more recently, in the philosophy of Georg Simmel). Rather, Edith Stein remains — even as an interpreter of St. Thomas — the most authentic disciple, indeed the "daughter," of Husserl's "phenomenological method" (though not of his transcendental idealism). Accordingly, she transfers all real existents[4] to the level of the "essential." The world that emerges, however, is not a self-enclosed "ideal world" (whether egological or monadological, as one sees in the development of Husserl's own thought), but a "free, ideal world" — one that does not even depend upon "connections," but solely upon the given "essence" that is "intuited" in its own right. Edith Stein completely unfetters "free essences" from every systematic context in a way that is altogether comparable

---

3. *Der geistigen Gegensätze.* — Trans.
4. *Realbestände.* — Trans.

to Nikolai Hartmann's unfettering of an ideal Hegelian world from the constraints of Hegel's systematic ternary. In this respect, they intellectually correspond: just as Nikolai Hartmann is guided by the idea of a freely rhythmic world of "levels," Edith Stein is guided by a free and colorfully displayed "world of essences." Indeed, her unfettering of an "ideal world" from the constraints of systematic idealism (from Descartes to Hegel) goes beyond even Hartmann. For behind Hartmann's world of "levels" he still affirms the system of a "rhythmic divinity" of the world (while consciously excluding a real "God"), whereas Edith Stein, owing to her conscious "life in God" as a Carmelite Christian, clearly has the inner freedom also to bestow upon the "world of essences" the freedom to be "suspended" — free of every systematization — as a "free plenitude." Seen in the context of all the historical idealisms (of an essential philosophy of essence), Edith Stein's philosophy thus represents the complete unfettering of a "free, ideal world" from the constraints of all "idealist systems" (even those of a Husserlian "monadology" and a Hartmannian "rhythm of levels"). Inasmuch as she gives it the "form of freedom for the sake of a free world," Edith Stein brings about the definitive demise[5] of an essential philosophy of essence: in a *free-floating essentialism.*

In sharp contrast, Simone Weil's thought is emphatically an *existentiell* thinking at the level of the real. Indeed, her thought does not even take place at the level of the morphologically real, as with Aristotle, but precisely at the level of the real as deformed: in a way oddly similar to Augustine's way of seeing real Christianity's proper level as that of the *"Christus deformis,"* the "disfigured deformity of Christ by which alone we are formed."[6] To put it in the utterly realistic terms of today, it is the level of the "work" of the "worker": not of the increasingly "progressive worker," but of the worker who is entirely sunk in "matter"; and not a "dialectical matter" that is evolving into a "new humanity," but matter in the state of "misfortune" *(malheur)* and "emptiness" *(le vide),* for which the sole *"metaphysicum"* and *"religiosum"* is a God who (in the incarnation and the Eucharist) became "matter" in his own right, such that (in contrast to every idealism) the human being is "in God" to the extent that "with God" he becomes "matter." On this view, the God of every "ideal existence" is in the final analysis the "absent God," whereas it is only in "misfortune" and "emptiness" that he is the "present God." To be sure, as Simone Weil portrays it, this existence appears in the

---

5. *Hingang.* — Trans.
6. Augustine, *Serm.* 27, 6.

image and likeness of the myths of all peoples, tempting one to classify her philosophy along with the philosophy of Romanticism — as represented by such figures as Josef von Görres and Franz von Baader, each of whom took myths to be a self-expression of the ultimate "origins." For Simone Weil, however, the Romantic understanding of myths is still too "idealistic." Certainly, she sees in them the governing idea of the *one* "resurrection in death," but for her the myths still have to be transposed into the medium of a *single* "material existence," so that their final "glory" can disappear into the "grayness and drabness" of today's "worker's existence." It is thus in Simone Weil's philosophy that we see the first and only realization of the kind of existentialism that Jaspers, Heidegger, and Sartre, respectively, seek to achieve, since each of their existentialisms continues to have a "dynamic, progressive, transcending" character. To be sure, for Jaspers, the "cipher" (*"Chiffre"*) is a "foundering," but it is under this figure that one enters into an experience of the "Encompassing."[7] Certainly, for Heidegger, *"Dasein"* is defined by "care within the nothing,"[8] but it is also defined by the expectation of an "advent of Being." And certainly, for Sartre, the "existential" is defined by "nausea within the nothing," but it is a nausea attended by an almost militant desire for "freedom." For each of these existentialisms, with their dynamic, progressive, and transcending emphases, there is still an "essential idealism" at play in the midst of an "existentiell realism." Simone Weil, by contrast, is the first and only one to present a genuinely *"pure existentialism."* She alone divests real existence of every "progressive idealism." For her the inner "dynamic" of "existence in the midst of the misfortune and emptiness of matter" is not an "idealist dynamic"; instead, the inner dynamic of this existence is none other than that of this existence, immanently conceived. Nor is this dynamic a "progressive dynamic"; on the contrary, it is a, so to speak, "degressive dynamic," pointing not to a life that models the "ascending human being," but to a life that is lived together with the "descending God," who descends "even into the matter of misfortune and emptiness" — this "together" (the σύν of Paul's epistles) being the only (veiled) "ideal" that one has, the ideal of the God of the second chapter of the letter to the Philippians, the ideal of ever greater "enslavement" and "abnegation" and "emptying" and "dying" as a "being crucified" into the one and only "glory of the Cross." This is how Simone Weil figures in the most recent development of existential philosophy, which originated within Christianity in

7. Ins *"Umgreifende."* — Trans.
8. *"Sorge im Nichts."* — Trans.

Kierkegaard and has subsequently been transformed into an explicit atheism in Heidegger and Sartre. Simone Weil's "pure existentialism" intrinsically confronts this emergent atheism — but, properly speaking, because she is intrinsically still more engaged with the "new philosophy" of dialectical materialism, understood as the "westernizing" of the previous "existentialism." With her understanding of "existence in the midst of the misfortune and emptiness of matter," in which the "absent God" is precisely the "present God," and which yields the paradox of a "Christian materialism" and a "Christian atheism," Simone Weil is the genuine Christian alternative to the contemporary rise of atheistic, dialectical materialism.[9]

The antithesis between a "pure essentialism" (in Edith Stein) and a "pure existentialism" (in Simone Weil) is thus a symbol of the very hour in which we stand. Edith Stein's pure essentialism connects the traditions of ancient Jewish and ancient Islamic philosophy (understood in terms of a Plotinian Aristotelianism) to the tradition of Thomas Aquinas (understood in terms of the essentialism of an *ordo universi*), and it connects these to the tradition of an essential transcendentalism that begins with Descartes and comes full circle in Husserl. What dies in Edith Stein's night of Carmel and in her martyr's death — and through the night and death of this broken time — is the tradition of western idealism, which becomes the "grain of wheat that dies" leading into an uncharted future. Simone Weil's pure existentialism, on the other hand, rolls together all the "non-conformist" philosophies that stand in Heraclitus's "fire of contradictions" over against the "pure being" of "Parmenides," including within it not only all the classical paradoxes that one finds in the various philosophies of contradiction (from Nicholas of Cusa to Pascal to Julius Bahnsen to Nietzsche), but even such explicit manifestations of "protest" and "revolt" against western idealism as one finds not only in Marx's and Bakunin's inversion of Hegel, but also and precisely in Heidegger's wrathful indictment of western idealism as "nihilism." The contrast between Edith Stein's pure essentialism and Simone Weil's pure existentialism acutely symbolizes the current intellectual situation in which we find ourselves, in which the western "tradition" is engaged in a life-and-death struggle with the "creative protest of revolt" that has long been simmering in its depths. In Edith Stein's night of Carmel and in her martyr's death, the tired and flagging (and therefore self-historicizing) western tradition received, as it were, the "light" of its "night," and the "life" of its

---

9. For a more detailed discussion of this paradox in Simone Weil, see Przywara, *In und Gegen,* pp. 73-87.

"death," which allows it to die out creatively and to rise in a present-day "Behold, I make all things new" (as God says in Isaiah and Revelation). By contrast, in the (apparent) futility and failure of Simone Weil's life — a life chased from the factory to the field and, finally, into exile — there is sown into the "creative revolt" and "creative destruction" (Bakunin) of a progressive, anti-theistic, dialectical materialism the secretly transformative grain of a "Christian materialism" (of the God who became precisely matter) and a "Christian atheism" (of the God who is "present" as "absent"). It is not surprising, then, that it is precisely two women who are decisive here. For, on the one hand, it is the nonchalant — and therefore greater — radicalism of the woman, specifically of the religious woman, that first makes her capable of a pure essentialism or a pure existentialism. On the other hand, it is the mystery of "giving birth in death" that gives the woman — and here again, specifically, the religious woman — the grace to offer precisely a (real) beginning in (apparent) demise: in the "as though" and "as if" of "death" the "behold" of "life": "as dying, and behold, we live" (2 Cor. 6:9).

2. But now, finally, in view of this antithesis between a pure essentialism (in Edith Stein), which dies and rises,[10] and a pure existentialism (in Simone Weil), which is victorious in defeat,[11] it becomes clear that the antithesis between these two "purisms" ultimately points beyond itself to the mystery of the *Aristotelian and Lateran "analogy"* that is "ever more greatly" declared in the "however great" of the antithesis between them: the ἄλλο πρὸς ἄλλο, to use Aristotle's formula for what is ultimate in being (the oscillation of a "free proportion" between two X's), and the "ever greater dissimilarity within every similarity, however great," to use the formula of the Fourth Lateran Council for what is ultimate "between Creator and creature."[12] To be sure, Edith Stein herself treats the analogy of Aristotle and Thomas Aquinas in her *Eternal and Finite Being,* but she treats it from the outset as the "proper relation of finite to eternal being, which permits one to speak of 'being' on the basis of a common given reference here and there."[13] That is to say, she subsumes "analogy" from the outset under the higher concept of a "common given refer-

---

10. *Untergehend aufgehend.* — Trans.

11. *Erliegend überwindend.* — Trans.

12. *Met.* V, 6, 1016b, 34-35; Denz. 432.

13. *Endliches und Ewiges Sein. Versuch eines Aufstiegs zum Sinn des Seins* (Freiburg: Herder, 2006), p. 288; cf. *Eternal and Finite Being,* trans. Kurt Reinhardt (Washington, DC: ICS Publications, 2002), p. 335: ". . . peculiar relationship that exists between finite and eternal being and which permits us to apply the term *being* to both terms of the relationship on the basis of a common constitutive element of meaning [*gemeinsamer Sinnbestand*]."

ence."[14] Thus, notwithstanding her subsequent emphasis upon the *"analogia proportionis"* as found in Thomas — according to which an "analogical commonality" consists solely in the *proportio*," that is, in the *"pros"* of the Aristotelian analogy — she still understands "analogy," however unconsciously, under the higher form of the "common." What is decisive here is not Aristotle's formula ἄλλο πρὸς ἄλλο — that is, a double "alterity" of one to another,[15] but a proportion between "different modes of being,"[16] each of which is in itself the object of an "intuition of essence"[17] undertaken by the phenomenologist Edith Stein against the background of given essences.[18] Since the formal principle of phenomenology, regarded purely as a method, is one of "identity" — that is, an immediate, noetic encounter with a given essence — the phenomenologist Edith Stein duly investigates the given essences of "finite" and "eternal" being with regard to their specifiable differences. She takes the "ἄλλο" of finite being and the "ἄλλο" of eternal being and regards each in its own right as the object of a respective "intuition of essence," and hence regards them in purely material fashion without this "ἄλλο" entering into her method. Her method is not that of an "unknowing of the unknown" (as would correspond to the two "X's" in their "ἄλλο" to one another); rather, each given essence respectively, in its objective "otherness," is immediately and completely grasped in the *Wesensschau*. Her method is not a realization of the "πρὸς" between the "ἄλλο" and "ἄλλο," that is, of the genuinely rhythmic back-and-forth between them, which is to say, "analogy as noetic method"; rather, her method is a consistently practiced, static, and direct "intuition of essence," in which the "given essence" is made statically and directly "visible." Hence, in Edith Stein one does not find the Lateran analogy of a "similarity, however great," between finite and eternal being, intersected by an "ever greater dissimilarity" in a true "rhythm *in infinitum*"; rather, what she sees in any given case are primarily "other" (that is, "dissimilar") "given essences," which she compares with one another in order to investigate their possible "similarity." For her, therefore, analogy practically means a "relationship" between different essences, but never the singular and utterly irreducible rhythm between "yes" and "no," "in" and "beyond," "unity" and "distance" that we find in the formula of the Fourth Lateran Council, which

---

14. *Gemeinsamer Sinnbestand.* — Trans.

15. *Das zweimalige "je anders."* — Trans.

16. *Seinsweisen.* See *Endliches und Ewiges Sein*, p. 289; *Eternal and Finite Being*, p. 336. — Trans.

17. *Wesensschau.* — Trans.

18. *Wesensbestände.* — Trans.

classically formulates that ancient rhythm — which is "properly essential"[19] from the Greek fathers to Dionysius the Areopagite to Nicholas of Cusa — between an apophatically qualified positive theology and a cataphatically qualified negative theology.[20] As I undertook to show in greater detail in my *Analogia Entis*, a "pure essentialism" (as was and remained the kind of thought specific to Edith Stein) harbors as its formal principle the "identity peculiar to logic" — in contrast both to "dialectic" (as the formal principle of all antithetical philosophies) and to the "formal principle of analogy," which is grounded in the principle of non-contradiction and subsequently appears in the Lateran analogy as "ultimate being":[21] which is to say that "analogy as method" is objectively grounded in "analogy as being."[22]

From the foregoing it already follows that this "analogy" also presents a crisis[23] for Simone Weil's "pure existentialism." It is true that Simone Weil nowhere emphasizes "dialectic as a principle and method"; but it is equally true that one looks in vain in her writings for any trace of a real "analogy." Certainly, there is a "relationship," indeed a positive "similarity in the image,"[24] that forms the methodological basis of her attempt to show through all the myths the ultimate Christian motif of "resurrection in death" and "ascent as descent." But this "similarity in the image," which consists in "relationships," is simply a heuristic method by which to find and sift through any material that would present clearly, in ever new ways, what for her is "properly essential": "What the relation of opposites can do in the approach to the natural being, the unifying grasp of contradictory ideas can do in the approach to God."[25] And, most significantly, this does not consist in any "midpoint" (however dynamic), like, say, Plato's conception of the "μέσον" between the primordial antitheses as a "μέτρον," but rather in a "point of intersection," which is "the arms of the Cross."[26] Seen in terms of the Aristotelian analogy, even the "πρὸς" between "ἄλλο" and "ἄλλο," which is to say,

19. *Das "Eigentliche."* — Trans.

20. *Zwischen apophatisch positiver und kataphatisch negativer Theologie.* Unless one reads into this a possible confusion of terms, Przywara seems to mean, quite precisely, that there is no directly positive or directly negative theology, but only an analogical theology whose positive and negative moments are respectively qualified. — Trans.

21. *"Letztes Sein."* — Trans.

22. See *AE*, §§5-6, §8.

23. *Krisis*, in the sense of a point of decision. — Trans.

24. *"Ähnlichkeit im Bild."* — Trans.

25. Simone Weil, *Gravity and Grace* (Lincoln: University of Nebraska Press, 1997), p. 153.

26. Simone Weil, *Waiting for God* (New York: Harper Perennial, 2009), p. 81.

the proportion between pure alterities, is here contained within the "ἄλλο" itself. There is thus no proportion but only an "intersection" between radical alterities, which is why there is no rhythm — no "dynamic point," as it were — that obtains between them, but only the "intersection" *as* "point." We thus see here the most radical antithesis to the way that in Edith Stein's pure essentialism the positivity of the "πρὸς" as a specifiable "relationship" radiates toward the radical otherness of the two kinds of "ἄλλο," making them, so to speak, "comparable entities."[27] So, too, when seen in terms of the Lateran analogy, Simone Weil reduces the level of "similarity, however great" to the level of purely heuristic material (acquired by thinking in terms of "relationship" and a "similarity in the image"), in order to make this material transparent, as it were, to a single material presentation of the *one* and *only* "ever greater dissimilarity," in which radical alterities stand in no other proportion to one another than that of the "intersection" as a "point of intersection." If the innermost intention of Edith Stein's thought proceeds (however unconsciously) from established "dissimilarities" increasingly toward a relational network of "similarities," Simone Weil's thought proceeds according to its innermost intention (however unconsciously) in the radically opposite direction: from heuristically discovered relationships of similarity increasingly in the direction of the *one* and *only* radical "dissimilarity" (consisting in the radical "intersection" of antitheses that are finally "contradictions"). Whereas Edith Stein's pure essentialism is guided by the ideal of the *"ordo universi,"* which for Thomas as well as for Husserl is the defining goal of thought, Simone Weil's pure existentialism is guided by that a-logical existence to which Heraclitus gave the names "fire," "strife," and, indeed, even "rubbish." In the final analysis, both Edith Stein's pure essentialism and Simone Weil's pure existentialism are "pure" in that in them, after all the transformations and combinations that the philosophy of the West has undergone, we see once again the original "purity" of the antithesis between Parmenides and Heraclitus (in sharp contrast to Heidegger's altogether desperate attempt in his *Introduction to Metaphysics* to transfer the level of thought one finds in Heraclitus to that of Parmenides, which suggests something of his own intrinsically essentialist existentialism). For what ultimately drives an essential, phenomenological "intuition of essence" (as νόησις), in which the essence itself directly appears (as νόημα), is the Parmenidean identity of pure being within a single world of being and thought[28] (to the

---

27. *Vergleichbarkeiten.* — Trans.
28. *In Seins-und Denk-Welt.* — Trans.

point of a ταὐτὸν between εἶναι and νοεῖν): in thoroughgoing adherence to the law of "a similarity, however great." Equally, "existentiell experience" of the real actuality of things — from their "deepest roots" in "matter in misfortune and emptiness," and thus, most authentically, in existentiell "work, misfortune, and emptiness" — is ultimately driven by the Heraclitean immanent "Logos" of "antitheses and contradictions," which in the final analysis is simply the ineffable rhythm of the most concrete existentiell reality of "fire," "strife," and "rubbish." For it is only such radical depths of objective existence and subjective "existentiell experience" that afford a veiled revelation of a "crucified godforsaken Logos": in thoroughgoing adherence to the law of "ever greater dissimilarity."

But then this antithesis between a pure essentialism of "a similarity, however great" in Edith Stein (as a pure *Gestalt* of Parmenidean philosophy) and a pure existentialism of "ever greater dissimilarity" in Simone Weil (as a pure *Gestalt* of Heraclitus) "involuntarily"[29] becomes a clear transparency "beyond itself" to the *one* rhythm of the complete, undivided philosophy of "analogy." The philosophies of Edith Stein and Simone Weil can be understood, in light of their ultimate respective intentions, only as partial moments within the *one* rhythm of "analogy" in which they appear *aufgehoben* — in keeping with the double sense in Hegel's use of the term. Edith Stein's essentialist tendency to reduce the "ἄλλο" and "ἄλλο" to the "πρὸς" between them especially emphasizes the "similarity, however great" (within the relational connection) of the Lateran formula of analogy. On the other hand, Simone Weil's existentialist tendency to reduce the "πρὸς" to the "ἄλλο" and "ἄλλο" (according to the Aristotelian formula of analogy) especially emphasizes the "ever greater dissimilarity" (in antithesis and contradiction) of the Lateran formula of analogy. When seen in terms of the full and pure rhythm of the Aristotelian and Lateran "analogy," Edith Stein's pure essentialism and Simone Weil's pure existentialism are like "springs stretched to extremes," whose "purity" is meaningful only insofar as it is instrumental in the service of this *one* rhythm of the *one* analogy.[30]

---

29. *"Wider Willen."* — Trans.

30. The author treats this analogy in the following works: *Gott* (München: Oratoriums-Verlag, 1926); *Religionsphilosophie katholischer Theologie* (München: Oldenbourg, 1927); *Analogia Entis* (München: Kösel und Pustet, 1932); *Deus semper maior*, 3 vols. (Freiburg: Herder, 1939-41); *Christentum gemäß Johannes* (Nürnberg: Glock und Lutz, 1954); *Alter und Neuer Bund* (Wien: Herold, 1956); *In und Gegen* (Nürnberg: Glock und Lutz, 1956). See also "Die Problematik der Neu-Scholastik" in *Kant-Studien* 33 (1928): 73-98; as well as the essays in the present volume, including "Philosophies of Essence and Existence" (1939),

3. The greatest evidence for this is afforded by the only thing that Edith Stein and Simone Weil appear to have in common: that St. John of the Cross's *noche oscura* or "dark night" is for both of them the innermost and decisive factor in their thought. Edith Stein concludes her essentialism, which seeks to unify Husserl and Thomas Aquinas (for all her stress upon their differences), with a phenomenology of the mysticism of the mystical doctor in *The Science of the Cross*. Simone Weil consistently brings her existentialism of "work, misfortune, and emptiness in the slavery of matter" back to its center in the mystery of the "godforsaken God," seeing this "messianic night" as the essence of John of the Cross's teaching about the "dark night." For Edith Stein, as a phenomenologist of pure essentialism, the analysis of the various stages of the ascent of Mount Carmel in *The Science of the Cross* completes what was intended by the *"epochē"* of the phenomenological method. To be sure, according to phenomenology, *"epochē"* is simply a "bracketing" of the really existing world so that one's gaze can be directed exclusively toward the ideal world of "pure essences." And so it would seem that the *"epochē"* is simply a method by which to achieve a material *"a priori* of essence" for all the empirical sciences.[31] But the word *"epochē,"* which comes from ἐπέχω, means not only a "(hesitating) abstention"[32] (corresponding to a provisional "bracketing"), but also a positive "in-tention."[33] This corresponds to the increasing shift in the meaning of *"epochē"* in Husserl's classical phenomenology: from a "(provisional methodological) abstention" to a "(fundamental) in-tention," whereby one's gaze is directed solely to the "ideal world of pure essences," ultimately to the point that, in Husserl's lectures at the Sorbonne, the only thing that remains of the world is the monadological world of "pure essences" existing in "transcendental intersubjectivity."[34] That is to say, when *"epochē"* is fundamentally taken to mean an "in-tention," one hears an ultimate "mystical stress" that is common to the stages of all the mystics — in the Chinese mysticism of Lao-Tzu, the Indian mysticism of the Bhagavad Gita, the Greek Oriental mysticism of Plotinus, as well as the Christian neo-Platonism of Dionysius the Areopagite (who became the church father of Carmelite mysticism) — but whose abso-

---

"The Scope of Analogy as a Fundamental Catholic Form" (1940), and "Metaphysics, Religion, Analogy" (1956).

31. *Realwissenschaften.* — Trans.
32. *Anhalten,* literally "stop." — Trans.
33. *Hinhalten,* which carries the same ambivalence as the Greek ἐπέχω, since it can mean a "holding in check" as well as a "holding out toward." — Trans.
34. Husserl, *Werke*, vol. 1, p. 182; cf. Przywara, *In und Gegen*, p. 40ff.

lute form is found in Gautama Buddha's doctrine of radical "detachment."[35] For Husserl this fundamentally and ultimately mystical *"epoché"* led to the Augustinian depths of his monadological "ideal world in transcendental intersubjectivity": to the *"in te redi, in interiore homine habitat veritas,"*[36] which he twice adduces in his Sorbonne lectures in support of his own philosophy. For Edith Stein, on the other hand, who never adopted the systematic form of transcendentalism into her pure essentialism, the *"epoché"* of "bracketing" was transformed into that radical *"epoché"* of "in-tention" that one finds in the stages of John of the Cross — whereby the soul so radically and totally "extends itself"[37] into the intellectual and spiritual[38] world of a spiritually invisible God that in this "self-extending," by way of a "night of the senses," it is drawn out of the splendor of the real "world of the senses" into a "night of the spirit," and thereby ultimately into the "night of God," which according to the ancient saying of the Areopagite is an "outpouring of light" as the "darkness (γνόφος) of a stormy night."[39] Whereas in her teacher Husserl's case, the understanding of *"epoché"* as a "self-intending" toward the "divine within the inner man" was only a final, secret inflection that he gave his systematic transcendentalism, in Edith Stein's "pure essentialism" we see a true fulfillment of this ultimate depth of *"epoché"* in Carmelite "detachment":[40] leading from the "world of the senses" and the "world of the spirit" into the "night of the senses" and the "night of the spirit," in which the divine *qua* "luminous night" is experienced as the true "transcendental," experienced, that is, as what is beyond all experience[41] (as one finds at the core of John of the Cross's theoretical writings and traces back to Dionysius the Areopagite), but in a way that corresponds to the "mild clarity" proper to a "pure essentialism," and thus as a "nocturnal, mild clarity of the spirit"[42] (which is how Edith Stein describes what is "ultimate" in *The Science of the Cross*).

35. *Entwerden.* The radical aspect of this term is not sufficiently captured by "detachment." Whereas "detachment" could be considered on par with *"epoché"* in the weak sense of a "bracketing," the term *"Entwerden"* suggests nothing less than a "de-creation" in the sense of an undoing or even annihilation of being. — Trans.

36. Return within yourself, truth dwells in the inward man. Augustine, *De Ver. Rel.* XXIX, 72.

37. *Hinhält.* — Trans.

38. *Geistig-geistlich.* — Trans.

39. *Sturm-Nacht-Finsternis.* — Trans.

40. *Entwerden.* — Trans.

41. *Unerfahrsam erfahren.* — Trans.

42. *Nächtlich milde Klarheit.* — Trans.

Simone Weil, the fragmentary thinker of a "pure existentialism," is no-where concerned with John of the Cross's stages — even though "night" stands at the center of her thought, and even though, of all the fathers, teachers, and theologians of the Church, John of the Cross is the only one whom she regards as her teacher. But, on the one hand, this "night" is for her a strictly messianic night of the godforsakenness of God in Christ, which alone makes Christianity "divine," because it presents the fundamental mystery of an "emptiness" that is a "fullness," and because the "crossing of the arms of the cross" is the inner essence of the ultimate structure of the world (as a "correlation of opposites" considered as a "union of contraries"), and because archetypally in "God's experience of the night of God" in the night of Christ's godforsakenness the "absent" God is "present."[43] On the other hand, she nevertheless provides a kind of metaphysical foundation for John of the Cross's doctrine of a "self-emptying" that is completed in stages by passing from a "night of the senses" to a "night of the spirit." To be sure, this foundation is still colored by Simone Weil's fascination with Hinduism: since God, the creator of the creature, has "emptied" himself, it is incumbent upon us increasingly to "de-create" ourselves (in a "de-creation" of "creation"), which is to say, empty ourselves as much as possible of all things creaturely in order that by way of our own increasing self-emptying we might requite, as it were, the "self-emptying" of God.[44] "Night," then, in the sense of a responsive encounter[45] between divine and human self-emptying, is a responsive encounter between "God's threefold folly" in creation, incarnation, and passion, and our "threefold folly," in which we "de-create" ourselves, becoming "matter" subject to the slavery of work, in order finally to die a slave's death on a slave's cross in the night of a godforsakenness that is shared in company with the godforsaken God.[46] What in existentiell terms is most real in real earthly existence is thus "night": the "night of God" as the most extreme enshrouding[47] of his divinity in the profoundest depth of the "night of matter" — the "night of God" in which we participate to the extent that with him and in him we are seen to be sunk into this "night of matter." Shortly before Edith Stein's enslavement in the concentration camp and sentencing to the gas chamber, her doctrine of a "nocturnal, mild clarity of spirit" sinks away into the image of John of the Cross, the doctor of "night":

43. *Gravity and Grace*, pp. 28, 94, 146, 153, 162 (cf. 72).
44. *Cahiers*, vol. 1, pp. 26-27, 168.
45. *Begegnung-Entgegnung.* — Trans.
46. *Cahiers*, vol. 1, pp. 14, 33, 36-37, 41.
47. *Einnachtung.* — Trans.

into the frightful image of the saint of "night" undergoing a night of enslavement at the hands of his own order, as she depicts it with uncompromising realism (as no previous biographer of the saint had) in the concluding chapter of *The Science of the Cross.*

But this opposition between an "essentialist night" (as is the particular stress in Edith Stein) and an "existential night" (as is the particular stress in Simone Weil) is grounded in an internal opposition that one finds in John of the Cross himself. In contrast to the Pauline epistles, which emphasize the "here" in which "we walk by faith and not by sight"[48] and the "then" when alone will we "know face to face," the theoretical writings of John of the Cross plainly tend in the direction of an increasing immediacy to God (to the point of a kind of anticipation of the *"visio beatifica"*). As such, these theoretical writings (the authenticity of which has been questioned by, among others, Baruzi, whose reservations even Edith Stein, for all her caution and restraint, shared) observe the law of a genuine and increasing "emptying" of everything creaturely, resulting in an increasing "divinization" (that is not only the religious fulfillment of the phenomenological *"epoche,"* but is also implied in what Simone Weil means by "de-creation"). Here we see John of the Cross as the, so to speak, "religious essentialist": whose doctrine appeared to the eyes of an orthodox and at the same time realistic Spain to be dubiously close to an "illuminationism" that fled from the "flesh" of creation and the visible Church into an immediate relation between "pure spirituality" and "God as Spirit" (in keeping with the mysticisms of China, India, Plotinus, Dionysius the Areopagite, and Eckhart). But, juxtaposed to *this* John of the Cross, whom we see in the theoretical writings, there is the John of the Cross of the hymns and letters and short sayings *(avisos),* whose authenticity is undisputed. This John of the Cross sings in his hymns of "night" both as the night of "nuptial union with God" (freely using the extravagant images of the Song of Songs) and as the night of the Godhead's inscrutable origins (fully in keeping with the theology of the "relations" in God and thus with the image of a "flowing" in God). The flowing back-and-forth of nuptial love in encounter and response becomes transparent to the flowing back-and-forth within God himself. The night of the welling depths of nuptial love (which is the fundamental mystery of the Old and New Testaments: from the prophets to the Song of Songs to the gospel of marriage declared by the evangelists from Matthew to John, to the inwardly nuptial theology of the Pauline epistles, and right up to the "wedding and wedding feast of the Lamb" as the ultimate meaning of Revelation) — this

---

48. *In der Schau der Gestalt.* — Trans.

nuptial night of God, in which the creaturely is neither "emptied" nor "de-created," but wedded to God, is, finally, the mystery of the "economic Trinity": the revelation and communication of "God's own night" (the night of the "or-igins in God") to the cosmos, which is wedded to God in this *one* marriage of the Old and New Testaments. What we first see in the double theology of the Greek church Fathers (understood as a theology of the marriage of the Old and New Covenants and of the revelation of the "economic Trinity," which is to say, the Trinity in the order of salvation and salvation history) is expressed in the undisputedly authentic writings of John of the Cross: in the tension be-tween his nuptial hymns (*"The Dark Night"* and *"The Spiritual Canticle"*) and his Trinitarian hymn of the "threefold spring in the night."[49] What is "ulti-mate," then, in this mystic of "night" is not a complete enshrouding[50] of the sensible creation in night, but a sacramental rendering of its chromatic pleni-tude into an "image and likeness" of the *one* marriage[51] in which the totality of creaturely reality is wedded to the "God who is all in all." For this reason this "ultimate" meaning is sealed in the most bitterly real "existential night" of his life's conclusion, in which the final meaning of "marriage" is fulfilled: the mar-riage of God in the passion of the cross suffered among his creatures at the hands of his creatures, in order that, through the entirely real "passion that one undergoes at another's hands,"[52] these wholly real creatures might "fill up what is lacking in the sufferings (of God in Christ)" — just as Paul himself, as the evangelist of this *one* "marriage of the cross," had to undergo a passion at the hands of his "own brothers," and just as John of the Cross is the "mystic of the night of the marriage of the Cross" only in that his life (as a genuine "prog-ress in perfection") is a progression from his being crucified by his former con-freres (the Calced Carmelites) to his being crucified by his new spiritual sons (the Discalced Carmelites).[53] The "ever greater" image of John of the Cross, which overcomes that of him as a "religious essentialist" (who speaks of the "night of de-creation"), is thus that of him as a "religious existentialist" (who endured the "night of the Cross at the hands of his own brothers"). Accord-ingly, what is apparent in John of the Cross, the *one*, final teacher for Edith Stein's "pure essentialism" and for Simone Weil's "pure existentialism" — and

49. *"Drei-Quell in der Nacht."* The reference appears to be to John's poem "Song of the soul that rejoices in knowing God through faith." — Trans.
50. *Ein-Nachtung.* — Trans.
51. *Ein-Hochzeitung.* — Trans.
52. *"Passion durch einander."* — Trans.
53. In the original typescript the references to the "Calced" and "Discalced" Carmel-ites are reversed. — Trans.

apparent as the perfecting of the opposition internal to his understanding of "night" between an "essentialist night" and an "existentialist night" — is the *one* "analogy" to which the "pure essentialism" (of Edith Stein) and the "pure existentialism" (of Simone Weil) are (however unconsciously) instrumental. The "analogy" of an "ever greater dissimilarity" within a "similarity, however great" finally appears as an "analogy of night." The "night" of a "pure (religiously understood) essentialism" is emphatically "night as light" (leading to the "ever so great" of an increasing illumination in God, who "is light and in him there is no darkness at all" (1 John 1:5). The "night" of a "pure (religiously understood) existentialism" is emphatically "light as night" (leading to the "ever greater" of an increasing participation in[54] the "night of God's marriage on the Cross" as the night of "God being forsaken by God"). What is ultimate in "analogy" is thus not only the "night" of an "ever greater dissimilarity" with regard to the "light" of a "similarity, however great." Rather, what is really and decidedly ultimate is an "analogy of night" that itself consists in an analogy: in which the "night of God's going out into the night[55] of the most real night of the creature" (and of the creature's "participation" in this night) is what is "ever greater," passing right through the "however great" of "God's night as an excess of his light" (and of the "night of the creature's blindness in this light"): *because* the actual "Being" of God is that *"agape"* that gives "soul and life for brothers and sisters."[56]

The final episode in John of the Cross's life is a fitting symbol for this "analogy": the obscuring of his work by his "own" order. In this *one* symbol Edith Stein and Simone Weil are true daughters of this father, and disciples of this master: Edith Stein in the night of death in the gas chamber in Bohemia; Simone Weil in the night of death of her exile in England.

---

54. *Mit-Ein-Nachtung.* — Trans.
55. *Ein-Nachtung.* — Trans.
56. See 1 John 3:16; 4:7-21.

15 Husserl and Heidegger

1960

The same year, 1959, marked both the centennial birthday of Edmund Husserl and the seventieth birthday of Martin Heidegger. This same year thus commemorated the great founder of phenomenology and the one in whom phenomenology comes to its puzzling conclusion. This conclusion, which is clear from Heidegger's studies of Hölderlin and Trakl, and which is prosecuted foundationally in his *On the Way to Language,* comes with his method of language analysis and with his setting out upon the path of modern English philosophy (in Moore, Ayer, and to some extent, Russell) — which, under the defining influence of Wittgenstein, conducts philosophy henceforth strictly as (positive) linguistic analysis. At the time of Husserl's seventieth birthday Heidegger was still the editor of Husserl's *Festschrift,* though he was certainly no longer its real core. Its real core was rather Edith Stein with her surprising juxtaposition of Husserl and Thomas Aquinas (a work that was originally written as a nocturnal dialogue between Husserl and Thomas, but of which, despite its high quality, Heidegger refused approval, deeming such a form insufficiently "serious"). Heidegger is no longer represented in the current *Festschrift* commemorating Husserl's centennial birthday,[1] but in Heidegger's own *Festschrift* Johannes Baptist Lotz, S.J., the leading thinker in Catholic philosophy today, has undertaken something similar to what Edith Stein un-

---

1. *Edmund Husserl 1859-1959: Recueil commémoratif publié à l'occasion du centenaire de la naissance du philosophe* (The Hague: Martinus Nijhoff, 1959).

This essay, which was ostensibly written in 1960 but never appeared in German, was first published in a French translation in *Études philosophiques* 16 (1961): 55-62. The following translation, which is based upon the original typescript from Przywara's *Nachlass,* is published here with the permission of the Archive of the German Province of the Society of Jesus.

dertook in the *Festschrift* commemorating Husserl's seventieth birthday: for just as Edith Stein compared Husserl and Thomas, now Lotz confronts Heidegger with Thomas in a masterful analysis of the latter.[2]

The *Festschrift* for Husserl's centennial jubilee contains acknowledgments from his best students and disciples: among the older Göttingen students, Hedwig Conrad-Martius and Jean Hering; among the younger ones, Helmuth Plessner, Eugen Fink, and Hans Reiner. In the *Festschrift* for the seventy-year-old Heidegger, it is not without deeper significance that the two Jünger brothers are represented; that with Heissenbüttel's *Einsätze*[3] there is an attempt at a kind of neo-Dadaism; that it concludes with poems and pages of abstract graphics; and that Walter Jensch offers literary analyses as his philosophical contribution. This corresponds to Heidegger's own discovery of the work of art as a symbol of philosophy, leading to increasingly marked attempts at "myth *as* philosophy," as one already sees in *Being and Time,* where he took the myth of "care" as his point of departure; and as one now sees in Ernst Jünger's contribution to the *Festschrift,* in which he presents Heidegger with a mythical worldview as a prophecy that anticipates the "advent"[4] of a future world (in keeping with Heidegger's "turn" to an understanding of "Being as advent").

Clearly, with contributions from scientists and distinguished doctors, like that of Binswanger in the Husserl *Festschrift* and Heisenberg in the Heidegger *Festschrift,* each *Festschrift* stands under the same symbol: symbolizing that both Husserl's *Logical Investigations* and *Ideas* as well as Heidegger's *Being and Time* have opened paths to a new methodology for all the sciences, from philology to history to medicine to physics. When one compares the two *Festschriften,* however, the sharp differences between them become all too apparent. In Husserl's case, what proved to have a clarifying and fruitful effect upon the entire intellectual world was his concern — in opposition to empiricism, psychologism, and historicism — for the *one* "return" to the (immediate, original) "things": a concern that persists throughout all of his philosophical vacillations between "pure" and "transcendental," "egological" and "monadological" phenomenology. By contrast, the numerous "turns" in Heidegger's philosophical development (which Karl Löwith unsparingly exposed in his *Denker in dürftiger Zeit,* above all the

---

2. *Martin Heidegger zum Siebzigsten Geburtstag* (Pfullingen: Günter Neske, 1959).

3. A collection of "one-sentence" poems composed between 1957 and 1960 that were reprinted in Heidegger's *Festschrift.* — Trans.

4. *Kunft.* — Trans.

turn from "Being as God" to "God as Being") signal a descent from authentic phenomenology into a veritable "literary" approach; it is not without reason, therefore, that Heidegger's *Festschrift* concludes on a "literary" note, or that Heidegger's shorter writings show an aspiration to the rank of the Jünger brothers, and perhaps not a little affinity to Sartre, who learned crucial things from him.

All of these contrasts and comparisons between the first (original) phenomenologist, Husserl, and the last (dissolving)[5] phenomenologist, Heidegger, imply something essential, which transcends them and is uncontained by them,[6] but which comes to light precisely in and through their chaotic entanglement in the two *Festschriften*.

✳   ✳   ✳

What is essential here is already evident from the respective portrait photos of Husserl and Heidegger that are included in each *Festschrift* and illustrate the antithesis between them. Husserl's features suggest, on the one hand, an expansive gaze, directed toward an ideative universal (just as Husserl's egological transcendentalism expands, along the lines of Leibniz's monadology, into an ideative cosmology) and, on the other hand, a strict exactitude similar to a schoolmaster's (which caused him to eschew every systematization). It is an authentic portrait of the German idealist thinker: entirely rapt in contemplation of the "τόπος νοητός" of Platonism's "pure εἴδη," but nevertheless subject to vigilant — almost hyper-vigilant — Aristotelian criticism. By contrast, Heidegger's portrait almost immediately calls to mind the image of a knotted tree in the Black Forest,[7] suspicious and ingrown, for which reality is downright angular,[8] to the point that any ideative dimension (of philosophical analysis) is virtually nothing but an intensity of self-contained tension.[9] What we have here is completely and utterly the picture of the "earthen man of the earth" — constitutionally opposed, as it were, to Husserl's "bracketing of reality" for the sake of an ideative, heavenly realm of "pure essences." To be sure, Heidegger began as Husserl's student and assistant; nevertheless, the features of the two philosophers symbolically illustrate the abyssal antithesis between an idealism of "pure ideas" and a Romanticism

---

5. *Auflösenden.* — Trans.
6. *Über-zufällig Wesenhaftes.* — Trans.
7. *Schwarzwälder Baum-Knorren.* — Trans.
8. *Realität in ausgesprochendster Kantigkeit.* — Trans.
9. *Intensives Angespanntsein, aber als Eingespanntsein in sich selbst.* — Trans.

of "earthly and historical origins."[10] It is understandable that in his old age Husserl had only one wish: that the Church of St. Thomas Aquinas might be the heir of his philosophy (a wish that was symbolically fulfilled in the final work of his favorite student and assistant, Edith Stein, whose hand penned Husserl's most important manuscripts), whereas in the case of Heidegger it was surely no coincidence that he was called to reorganize the university under the National Socialist regime of "blood and soil" (even if his unsparing critique soon brought him into conflict with the cultural politics of National Socialism). The opposition between the master, Husserl, and the student and disciple, Heidegger, even reached the point that Heidegger, the National Socialist, flatly refused to offer any help to the venerable master (as a half-Jew) or to his family; that Husserl was virtually forced to leave Freiburg, which once saw him as its glory, in the "dead of night," and flee to the sisters at the convent of Saint Lioba in Günterstal; that upon his death no one came to his funeral, while his widow secretly fled to Belgium and converted to Catholicism; and that a Franciscan is now the executor of his entire *Nachlass* (symbolizing the Church receiving Husserl's work unto itself — as is most profoundly symbolized by the convert and Carmelite martyr, Edith Stein).[11] But then with the "rough-earth"[12] Heidegger something strangely similar happens: for after the war and his dismissal from Husserl's university chair, the only one who could restore the postwar pension that the occupying forces had refused to give him was archbishop Gröber of Freiburg, whom Heidegger used to assist at Mass as a genuinely Catholic altar boy; notable in this regard, too, are the efforts of Catholic philosophers belonging to the circle of the [Heidegger] "Symposium," who are hoping to find and maintain a "little Catholic shrine"[13] even amid the earthly wilderness of Heidegger's *"Holzwege"* (as he himself entitled one of his works).

*   *   *

However antithetical to one another Husserl and Heidegger may be, the antithesis that emerges from their portraits indicates what is "essential." If

10. It should be noted that the French translation from 1961, for whatever reason, does not include the rest of this section of the text, which addresses the issue of Heidegger's commitment to National Socialism and his unconscionable treatment of Husserl. — Trans.

11. In the unpublished manuscript Przywara initially added to the descriptions of Edith Stein: "and doubtless future saint." — Trans.

12. *Für den Heidegger "harter Erde."* — Trans.

13. *Ein "katholisches Bildstöckchen."* — Trans.

European Idealism (from Descartes to Kant to Hegel) reached its climax and at the same time its conclusion in Husserl (in a logical rebirth of Descartes), in Heidegger's earthy Black Forest philosophy as an "analytic of *Dasein*" we see a return in concentrated form of that tragic Gnostic philosophy of the real that leads from Jacob Böhme to Franz von Baader, and that sees the human being as the "site of ultimate contradictions." The abyssal contradiction between Husserl and Heidegger thus heralds "the final hour of German philosophy" (but therein also the "final hour of ancient Greek philosophy").[14] But this "final hour" of German philosophy (in the antithesis between Husserl and Heidegger) is not simply a final version of the opposition, which emerged radically in the eighteenth century and carried over into the nineteenth century, between a rational idealist philosophy (from Descartes to Kant to Hegel) and a Romantic philosophy of historical (maternal) "origins" (leading from Jacob Böhme to his fulfillment in Franz von Baader). Rather, what is surprising and downright uncanny is that the final version of this opposition (in Husserl and Heidegger) bears the form of an intertwining, as Eugen Fink showed in the Husserl *Festschrift* on the basis of unpublished analyses from Husserl's *Nachlass,* and as is evident from the essays by Heinrich Schlier and Ernst Jünger in the Heidegger *Festschrift*, which elaborate the *mythos* Heidegger intended with his notion of "Being as advent."

Certainly, as Eugen Fink has convincingly shown, in his late analyses Husserl goes beyond Descartes, dissolving all being (of the world and the ego) into a formal "empty schema" of abstract mathematical "possibilities" (in a radical intensification of Descartes's "universal methodological doubt"), the final effect of which is a general, formal "conception of the world" that is *a priori* with respect to any real being of the world (in a hyperphilosophical rendering,[15] as it were, of what Ephesians calls "God's will before the foundation of the world"). But it is precisely this "empty schema" that secretly communicates the "third" aspect, which for Husserl completes the "first" (the "transcendental ego") and the "second" (the "transcendental monadology" as a "transcendental world"). In his analyses of time and time consciousness, the late Husserl strikes upon the "concept of transcendental presence" as a "now 'between' before and after."[16] Just as Augustine and

14. In the original typescript Przywara then adds, but crosses out: "Thus, in this hour of death that is about to commence we see standing above the contradiction between Husserl and Heidegger the figure of 'mother church' — with the 'viaticum' [*zur 'Wegzehrung'*]." — Trans.

15. *Über-Philosophierung,* which also carries the sense here of a "philosophical makeover" of something theological. — Trans.

16. Husserl *Festschrift*, p. 112.

Thomas Aquinas see the essence of time in the *"hodie"* and the *"nunc,"* wherein one catches a glimpse of the *"hodiernum"* and *"nunc stans"* of God, so too for Husserl this "transcendental presence" is preceded by a "primordial now that occupies no place between the before and the after — an original presence, from which the flow of time gushes forth, but which does not itself flow along with it. The river of time, grasped in its deepest subjective interiority, flows from a timeless source."[17] Logically, this "most original depth of the life of consciousness is . . . no longer touched by the difference between *essentia* and *existentia*, but is instead the primordial ground out of which the bifurcation of fact and essence, actuality and possibility, individual and species, the one and the many first arises."[18] Thus, the egological "transcendental ego" and the monadological "transcendental world" ultimately converge in this "primordial ground," which logically one must now call the "transcendental God." The apparently "empty space" of Husserl's final analyses, which arises from the phenomenological "bracketing" of every reality (the reality of God, the world, and the ego), bears as its "transcendental structure" the classical metaphysical structure[19] that Thomas Aquinas and Nicholas of Cusa viewed as a "real structure": beyond the "intersubjectivity of a monadic cosmos"[20] the manuscripts present us with the notion of an "original ego"[21] that is prior to the difference between the "ego" (in Husserl's "transcendental ego") and the "alter ego" (in Husserl's "transcendental world"), and that first allows a plurality to break forth from itself. "Time is grounded in a presence that creates time but is not itself within time; the bifurcation of all beings *(essentia-existentia)* is grounded in a primordial unity, which is neither 'actual'[22] nor 'possible,' neither one nor many, neither an individual nor a species; the plurality of subjects is grounded in a depth of life that is prior to every individuation into egos."[23] Thus, "Husserl seeks to go back in thought to the formless ground from which formations emerge; he seeks to grasp the *apeiron*, the limitless."[24] But here there is an unconscious shift in Husserl from Thomas Aquinas and Nicholas of Cusa to the theognosis of the late Schelling and of the

17. Husserl *Festschrift*, p. 112.
18. Husserl *Festschrift*, p. 113.
19. *Das klassich Metaphysische.* — Trans.
20. Husserl *Festschrift*, p. 113.
21. *Ur-Ich.* — Trans.
22. *Faktisch.* — Trans.
23. Husserl *Festschrift*, p. 113.
24. Husserl *Festschrift*, p. 113.

Kabbalah;[25] for this "primordial ground" is an "origin"[26] that is conceived as a "rupture that tears the ground of life" and thus as a "negativity in the most original being" — a negativity that, as such, is "all-creative," "bringing forth time from timeless eternity," "the structure of the world from the conjunction of fact and essence," and "selves, subjects, in the self-ing[27] of absolute being."[28] But as Fink rightly points out, these three, previously unanticipated steps — from an egology to a monadology to a theosophical theology — do not mean that Husserl has a "system." Rather, everything leads into the "open," to an ever renewed searching understood as a "movement of endless reflection" — to that "brilliant, clear *aridity* [of] . . . spirit" of a "man who had no fixed formulas, but who possessed an immense capacity for wonder" and thus fulfilled the saying of Heraclitus, "the dry soul: the wisest and the best."[29] As the one who brings European idealism to its completion, it is precisely in the "empty space" of his radical and total "bracketing" of all real being that Husserl sees real being as Nicholas of Cusa did: between a divine *"complicatio"* and a creaturely *"explicatio,"* a cosmic origin and a cosmic unfolding. But he does not see it as a "system"; rather, he sees it in the functional medium of that genuinely Augustinian maxim, *"quaerere invenien-dum"* and *"invenire quaerendum,"* which is to say, in the medium of the *in infinitum* of "a searching for the sake of finding and a finding for the sake of searching." (There is therefore an internal reason for why he chose the Augustinian *"veritas,"* the "truth in itself," as the motto for his *Cartesian Meditations:* the truth that is found in infinite searching.) Accordingly, what we see in Husserl's philosophy is in the best sense: an "idealism" in the form of a "Romanticism of an unceasing quest of the origins."

In the case of Heidegger, not only can one not point to such a background: it is not even possible, because his practical existentialism is always strictly *"in actu,"* in a state of (spiraling) enactment. Here every objective content is simply a "limit concept" within the ever renewed, self-consuming (and therefore immanently circling) "spiral" of a genuinely Romantic searching for the sake of searching, and disintegration[30] (of apparent results) for the sake of disintegration (as one already sees in *Being and Time,* in

25. Cf. Gershom Scholem, *Major Trends in Jewish Mysticism* (New York: Schocken Books, 1941).
26. *"Ur-Grund," "Ur-Sprung."* — Trans.
27. *Selbstung.* — Trans.
28. Husserl *Festschrift,* p. 113.
29. Husserl *Festschrift,* pp. 114f.
30. *Zerfällen.* — Trans.

which every chapter simply winds up a new spiral that leads to nothing in particular, but merely initiates a new spiral). Heidegger's final statement thus far concerning an "advent of Being" or, more precisely, "Being as advent," is therefore simply a "limit-statement" appropriate to the functionalism of a "searching for the sake of searching." At the same time, this is precisely what frees up the space for the *Festschrift* to explore — along the lines of Heidegger's "Being as advent" in "searching for the sake of searching" — the basic features of a "Heideggerian worldview." Ernst Jünger sketches out a worldview defined by the periodic nature of the world's ages: from the primeval times of a "golden age" to the "mythical time of heroes" to the "historical age" to the coming into being of an age of "overweening Promethean audacity," with its "elemental, telluric, and titanic features,"[31] to the point "that the world's fate, in the form of its demise . . . is placed in man's hands," "in that he has assumed divinity into himself"[32] — though here it is not by virtue of "spirit" that he becomes God (as a "titan"), but by virtue of the "primal ground" of the "matter" of "mother earth."[33] This quintessentially Romantic worldview (which abjures the "above" of "spirit" and descends into the maternal "below" of "earthly origins") would seem to be the most extreme instantiation of "Being as advent." But Heinrich Schlier's surprising analysis of the prologue of John's Gospel signals the opposing position. Schlier takes Heidegger's "truth as the disclosure of what is hidden" within the ever renewed process of "unconcealment *(a-letheia)*" and renders it transparent: to Christ "whose incarnation as the Logos and truth in the flesh" has "fundamentally redeemed history from its constant and necessary dialectic of 'unconcealment and concealment' and liberated it for an encounter with present truth."[34] "History's dialectic has come to rest in *one* place, and in arriving at this place it arrives ever anew at its end. . . . The truth is now there in person," and "now that the truth is the truth in person, its original and characteristic claim again comes to light and is not lost."[35] In other words: whereas Ernst Jünger sees in Heidegger's dialectic between an unconcealing (of what is concealed) and a concealing (back into concealment) the "coming worldview"[36] of a materialism of mother earth as "origin," Heinrich Schlier is able to see in this same Heideggerian *Ur-Dialektik*

31. Heidegger *Festschrift*, p. 233.
32. Heidegger *Festschrift*, p. 337.
33. Heidegger *Festschrift*, p. 339.
34. Heidegger *Festschrift*, p. 200.
35. Heidegger *Festschrift*, p. 201.
36. *Weltbild in Kunft.* — Trans.

the lightning-flash of a classical idealism, that of a majestic "truth in itself." Both of these possible worldviews, each the age-old enemy of the other — that of a titanism of the earth as origin and that of a manifestation of eternal truth from above — belong, precisely in their mortal opposition to one another, to the inner "perspective" of Heidegger's "Being as advent" within a "searching for the sake of searching."

It thus becomes definitively clear, in view of these indissoluble interconnections between an intrinsically Romantic idealism (in Husserl) and an intrinsically idealist Romanticism (in Heidegger), that the "final hour of German philosophy," which they symbolize, has arrived. It is the hour that marks the fulfillment — but in the sense of the "plenitude" of the "end" — of the two great themes of German philosophy, symbolized respectively by Hegel and Jacob Böhme.[37] In Heidegger's "delving" thought (which delves down to earthly "primal roots") we see a genuine return of Jacob Böhme as the *philosophus teutonicus.*" In Husserl's "world-projecting" thought (which goes so far as to conceive of the pure ideality of a "transcendental God") we see a genuine return of Hegel's "ideative world," but a world that exists in a state of "free suspension" disengaged from every "dialectical schema," in keeping with a phenomenology unfettered by any system. The fact that Edith Stein wanted to see Husserl on the same plane as Thomas Aquinas, and that a group of Catholic and Protestant theologians, most recently Gustav Siewerth and Heinrich Ott,[38] is hopeful that a Heideggerian method will bring about a new and free encounter between critical philosophy and positive biblical theology — all of this could be taken to represent the Church at the deathbed of German philosophy, invisibly attending it in its "final hour" with the "viaticum" (in keeping with Husserl's dream that the "Church" would assume his legacy, and with Heidegger's placing himself in a time of distress under the protection of his archbishop). As for the possibility of a "Christian Husserl," however, Eugen Fink is right to point out that the dying Husserl declined the assistance of a Protestant clergyman with the words, "I have lived as a philosopher and wish to die as one."[39] And in no sense does Heidegger's development lead in the direction of a free encounter between critical philosophy and positive, biblical theology (as his Christian followers, claiming to

37. See by the author, "Thèmes anciens et modernes de la philosophie allemande," in *Les Études philosophiques* 11 (1956): 647-52; 12 (1957): 220-26; 12 (1957): 368-75.

38. See Gustav Siewerth, *Das Schicksal der Metaphysik von Thomas zu Heidegger* (Einsiedeln: Johannes Verlag, 1959), and Heinrich Ott, *Denken und Sein: Der Weg Martin Heideggers und der Weg der Theologie* (Zollikon: Evangelischer Verlag, 1959).

39. Husserl *Festschrift*, p. 115.

find support in Maréchal's *Point of Departure for Metaphysics,* would like to think). On the contrary, Heidegger's emphatically "secular philosophy" of a world closed in on itself increasingly assumes the features of a *"mythos,"* this being, so to speak, "immanent theology" (or better: theosophy) of this *one* "secular philosophy," which in itself is a "doctrine of salvation" — as a "theosophical cosmosophy."[40] This is not to deny that Heidegger's "Being as advent" betrays the influence of Albert Schweitzer's emphatically "eschatological Christianity" (as found in Schweitzer's works on the life of Jesus and Paul).[41] But it is an essentially secular and intra-worldly eschatology, stemming from his application of the prophetic element in Hölderlin to Trakl's tragic world of decline. If Husserl's final worldview (as we find it in his manuscripts) could be considered a positive eschatology (which ultimately envisions a "transcendental God"), then the currently emerging worldview of Heidegger could be described as a negative eschatology (one that stands under the symbol of the decadent, death-obsessed Western civilization depicted by Trakl: "seized with anxiety / eerie evening afterglow / in the storm clouds").[42] Beginning with Husserl and concluding with Heidegger we thus see the actual and categorical incompleteness of an essentially system-free phenomenology, which is precisely what reveals its inner face: philosophy "in its final hour."

40. *Theosophische Kosmosophie.* — Trans.

41. Cf. by the author, *Humanitas: Der Mensch gestern und morgen* (Nuremberg: Glock und Lutz, 1952), pp. 488ff.

42. *Gewaltig ängstet/schaurige Abendröte/im Sturmgewölk,* from Trakl's poem *Abendland.* — Trans.

Index

Adam, Karl, 16, 348-49, 352

America, 482-83

Analogia fidei, 10, 20n.23, 27, 29, 42, 45, 90-91, 92n.257, 93-95, 100, 101n.277, 102-3, 349, 397n.134, 429, 479, 575, 578

Anselm of Canterbury, 289n.402, 387, 417, 504-5, 508, 514, 530

Antichrist, 11, 22-23, 56, 83, 101n.278, 110n.301, 112, 358, 428, 579-80

Aquinas, Thomas, 4, 13-15, 19n.59, 21-22, 37-43, 44, 46, 47n.128, 48-49, 50, 58n.155, 64, 69, 74-75, 85, 87-88, 97, 101n.280, 102n.281, 113, 115, 127-30, 136-37, 142, 144, 147, 149-50, 158, 162, 170-71, 176, 185, 200-201, 212n.95, 213, 219-24, 229, 232, 236, 244-45, 260, 270-81, 286-87, 295-96, 299n.486, 302-11, 322, 339, 344n.48, 350-51, 359-62, 369-72, 375-76, 378, 387-88, 395-96, 401-3, 407, 410, 415-16, 418, 425-26, 431, 442, 451, 454, 457-58, 460, 467, 473-74, 476, 482-88, 504, 506, 509, 514, 524, 527-28, 530-32, 537, 540, 571, 586-88, 590, 594, 596-98, 601, 603, 605, 607, 613-14, 616, 618, 621

Areopagite. *See* Pseudo-Dionysius

Aristotle, 31-33, 35-39, 55, 64, 66, 70, 73n.202, 83, 107, 113, 119, 125-26, 129-30, 134, 137-38, 142, 145, 148, 150, 154, 161-62, 174, 198, 203, 205-6, 208, 210-12, 220n.127, 239, 245-60, 266, 269-71, 305, 308-9, 322, 343, 410-12, 416, 419-20, 423,

442, 450-54, 458, 460-61, 464, 469, 521-23, 526, 560, 584, 597, 599, 602-3

Augustine, 14, 16, 17n.54, 18n.58, 22, 24, 31, 46, 47n.130, 49n.133, 58, 59n.158, 60, 67-68, 75, 82, 89n.250, 90n.250, 101n.280, 106, 113, 129-30, 150, 174, 176-77, 179, 180-82, 185n.88, 186, 195, 199, 211, 213, 215, 217, 218n.119, 229, 232n.218, 234, 236, 239, 260, 262, 269-70, 278, 286-87, 305, 308, 312, 314, 346nn.54-57, 347n.58, 363, 368-69, 371-77, 384, 386-89, 398, 407, 410-11, 413, 415-17, 426, 429n.52, 434, 443-44, 450, 462, 467, 472, 476, 496, 499, 501-19, 524, 529, 530, 533, 566-68, 571, 577-91, 608, 617

Baader, Franz von, 14, 319, 359, 430, 445, 451, 481, 504, 521-22, 524, 528-29, 562, 570, 580, 581, 600, 602

Bakunin, Mikhail, 25, 523, 601-2

Balthasar, Hans Urs von, 1-3, 5-9, 11, 19n.61, 24-29, 31, 45, 56-58, 81, 83n.232, 84, 93-95, 101-5, 110n.301, 111n.306, 112-13, 114n.312, 351-52

Báñez, Domingo (Banezianism), 390n.118, 420, 428, 476

Barth, Karl, 3, 4, 11-12, 16-19, 21-25, 27, 29-30, 42n.42, 43n.120, 45n.125, 51n.138, 52, 55-58, 71, 75-76, 82, 83-85, 85-91, 91-93, 93-95, 95-101, 101-5, 105-14, 114-15, 150, 164n.24, 166n.26, 176n.46, 348-50, 352, 381, 397n.134, 428, 575

623

Beatific Vision, 235, 274, 280, 290, 366, 610

Behn, Siegfried, 29, 444n.23

Benedict, St. (Benedictine), 358-79, 451, 480, 575

Bergson, Henri, 128, 130, 319, 341, 389, 532

Bhagavad Gita, 451, 607

Böhme, Jacob, 521-22, 529, 535, 562, 570, 572, 580-81, 585, 617, 621

Buddha, Gautama (Buddhism), 53, 79, 450, 470, 503, 548-49, 608

Bulgakov, Sergei, 356n.38, 360

Bultmann, Rudolf, 28, 78, 445, 447, 455, 459

Cajetan, 4, 13, 30, 38, 39n.111, 73

Calvin, John (Calvinism), 58, 100n.276, 483, 575, 578

Casel, Odo, 358n.44, 445

Christ, 7-8, 10, 14, 25, 30, 41n.116, 43n.120, 44, 47, 61n.161, 81n.227, 90, 92-94, 97-98, 100-104, 106-14, 187, 262, 264, 267-68, 276, 296, 301, 304-5, 335, 337, 350, 353, 360, 366-72, 375-84, 386, 394, 396, 398, 399n.135, 403, 416, 424-25, 438, 443, 446-47, 449-50, 455, 458, 460, 462, 480-81, 488-89, 493-95, 512-15, 517-19, 532-36, 547, 552-54, 557, 563-64, 566-69, 571-74, 577-82, 592-94, 599, 609, 611, 620; and Cross, 10, 25n.72, 28, 81n.227, 108, 177, 184, 268, 305, 334-35, 338-39, 346, 352, 368-69, 373, 386, 403-4, 425, 443, 473, 484, 494, 496-97, 500, 517-19, 534-36, 539, 554-55, 580, 592, 596, 600, 604, 607-12; as Mediator, 90, 107, 110-11, 270, 301-3, 415, 436, 571; totus Christus, 30, 377, 380, 518

Christology, 276, 383, 514-15

Church, 5-10, 19-23, 25, 28, 42, 43, 45, 54, 61, 75, 84, 103, 106, 109, 115, 171-72, 190, 186-87, 276, 294, 346-47, 353-55, 357-60, 362n.61, 363, 366, 368, 371, 374, 375-80, 382-84, 388, 393-99, 403, 405, 417, 424, 435, 443, 462, 506, 515, 539, 550, 551, 554-55, 557, 577-78, 586, 592, 609-11, 616, 617n.14, 621; Magisterium, 171, 337, 380-81; mystical body, 112, 275, 381-82

Clement of Alexandria, 260, 366-67, 438, 504, 514

Coincidentia oppositorum, 273, 463, 473, 487, 492, 496, 514-15, 522, 528-30, 583, 585

Cortés, Donoso, 481

Council of Trent, 22, 374

Cusa, Nicholas of, 9, 273, 390, 444n.23, 463, 472-73, 483, 487, 515, 522, 524, 528-29, 557, 585, 590-91, 601, 604, 618-19

Cyril of Alexandria, 366

Dacqué, Edgar, 341

Deification, 368

Dempf, Alois, 428, 477

Descartes, René, 64, 120, 150, 168, 200-201, 309, 311, 321-23, 349, 405, 410, 416, 430, 452, 467-68, 475, 477, 501-2, 504-6, 508-9, 528, 540, 599, 601, 617

Dilthey, Wilhelm, 424, 464-66

Docetism, 98n.272, 512, 533

Donatism, 515

Duplex ordo, 54n.143, 109, 168, 187

Ebner, Ferdinand, 350, 471

Enlightenment, the, 50, 145, 148, 373-74, 381n.106, 388, 405, 408, 438, 445, 523, 525

Fichte, Johann Gottlieb, 202, 322, 506

Filioque, 356-57

Fourth Lateran Council, 9-10, 72-74, 113, 234, 349, 353, 356-57, 360-63, 369-70, 372, 374-75, 379, 384, 391, 393, 396-97, 399, 422, 429, 477-78, 499, 506-7, 526-27, 531, 545, 560, 602-3

Franciscan "Spirituals," 357, 359, 380

Gehlen, Arnold, 445-46

Giordano Bruno, 166, 583

Gnosis, 350, 352-53, 357-58, 360, 366-67, 369, 372, 395, 502, 504, 521, 618

Goethe, Johann Wolfgang von, 14, 482, 490, 542

Görres, Joseph, 14, 445, 600

Greek Orthodoxy, 350, 356-57, 372, 377, 379-81, 389

Gregory the Great, 215, 299n.481, 434, 522, 524, 589, 590nn.27-29, 591

Grisebach, Eberhard, 319, 471

Guardini, Romano, 9, 10n.33, 16, 348, 352, 443-44, 471, 535

Haecker, Theodor, 113, 319n.3, 349, 352, 428
Harnack, Adolf von, 17, 445, 533
Hartmann, Nicolai, 16, 325n.22, 333, 418, 443, 465, 599
Hegel, G. W. F., 16, 24, 45, 51n.139, 52n.140, 56, 68, 79, 81, 122, 130, 144, 146n.25, 150-51, 165, 180, 183, 184-85, 188-89, 193-96, 202-3, 309, 319-20, 322, 331-33, 351, 359-60, 390, 405, 407, 412, 416-17, 428, 430-31, 434, 439, 443-44, 450, 452, 458, 459-60, 464-68, 471, 473, 481-82, 495, 498, 502-6, 509, 511, 523, 524, 526, 528, 532, 570, 592, 597, 599, 601, 606, 617, 621
Heidegger, Martin, 1, 3, 4, 11n.37, 12, 27-28, 51n.138, 56, 57n.154, 62, 63n.168, 64n.169, 65, 71, 75, 76-83, 92, 120, 125, 129-30, 146n.25, 165, 193, 196, 202-3, 218, 229, 318, 324n.21, 333, 349-52, 409, 440, 447, 452n.74, 454-57, 459, 466, 470, 482, 504, 542n.8, 598, 600-601, 605, 613-22
Heiler, Friedrich, 16, 381
Heraclitus, 5, 32-34, 142, 159, 203-7, 210, 241, 308, 343, 419-20, 439, 445, 453, 457, 467, 471-42, 474-75, 487, 489, 522-23, 597, 601, 605-6, 619
Heresy, 343n.47, 357, 362n.61
Herrigel, Eugen, 129
Humanism, nuptial humanism, 57, 77, 388, 480-85, 487-89, 492-93, 496-97, 499-500
Humboldt, Alexander von, 481
Husserl, Edmund, 4, 11n.37, 15-17, 24-25, 61n.164, 62, 79, 140, 143, 153, 194, 201, 309, 322, 409-12, 416, 444, 459, 464, 466-69, 472, 474-75, 478, 502-4, 506, 508, 520, 524, 596-99, 601, 605, 607-8, 613-22

Icon, 112, 241, 380, 435-36, 471, 484, 523, 532, 535, 539, 540, 543, 550-51, 555, 557, 573, 578; iconoclasm, 76, 82; iconology, 478
Imago Dei, x, 108, 556-69
Irenaeus, 366, 386, 566, 571

Jansenism, 357, 359, 373, 375, 380, 393, 564

Jaspers, Karl, 318-19, 333, 600
Joachim of Fiore, 45, 56, 72, 113, 353, 356-64, 366, 370, 372-74, 376, 379, 423, 498
John of the Cross, 20n.62, 28, 425, 500, 519, 607-12
Judaism, 25n.75, 572, 597-98; Jewish messianism, 166
Jünger, Ernst, 443, 444, 614-15, 617, 620

Kant, Immanuel (Kantianism), 3, 15n.51, 16, 24, 56, 57, 62n.165, 64, 79, 120, 122, 126, 128-30, 133, 136-38, 141, 143, 147, 150, 166n.26, 200, 309, 322, 332-33, 349n.7, 405-6, 410, 416, 443, 452, 461, 466-67, 473, 476, 481-82, 495, 502, 506, 523-25, 528, 542, 583, 585, 589, 617
Kierkegaard, Søren, 24, 89n.250, 165, 166n.27, 195, 202, 242, 319-20, 428, 470, 601
Koepgen, Georg, 350

Lakebrink, Bernhard, 428, 477
Lamarckianism, 341
Leibniz, Gottfried Wilhelm, 57n.154, 77, 405, 443, 466-69, 506, 591, 615
Lombard, Peter, 353-54, 356, 363-64, 370, 375, 387
Lotz, Johannes B., 29, 351, 443, 613-14
Luther, Martin, 4, 18, 20, 45, 50-53, 75, 78-79, 88-89, 92, 115, 295n.453, 336, 343, 389, 428, 473, 476, 506, 523, 558, 567-69, 572, 594

Magisterium. *See* Church
Man and woman, 161, 485, 487, 490-92, 561-62, 565, 568-69
Manicheism, 448, 508-10, 516-17, 562
Maréchal, Joseph, 147, 349-51, 352, 622
Marriage, 60, 414-15, 488-89, 492, 499, 556, 581, 610-12. *See also* Humanism, nuptial humanism
Mary, 22, 28, 99, 493, 563, 568-69
Meister Eckhart, 143, 359, 363, 405, 415, 610
Modernism, 14, 371, 375, 379, 381, 385, 392-93, 396, 498, 532
Möhler, Johann A., 9, 381
Molinism, 101n.280, 102, 390n.118, 475-77
Müller, Adam, 481

Müller, Max, 350, 352

Mystery, 7, 47-49, 60, 66, 68-69, 81-83, 110, 113, 115, 161, 181-83, 185, 188-89, 231, 242, 245, 258-59, 263-66, 269, 278, 284, 304, 335-36, 338, 347, 354-55, 358, 364, 367-70, 376-78, 381n.106, 386, 389, 395, 397n.134, 398n.135, 404, 417, 420, 422, 426, 438, 443, 445, 447-49, 451, 454, 460, 472, 475, 478-79, 488, 493-96, 515, 518, 523, 530-31, 540, 551-52, 554, 562, 565, 569, 572, 575-78, 580-81, 588-89, 591, 598, 602, 607, 609-10; Dionysian mysteries, 166, 334, 336, 343n.47, 352, 406, 449-50, 452, 454, 594; Eleusinian mysteries, 449-50, 454, 576

Natural desire *(desiderium naturale)*, 69, 71, 227, 290-92

Natural theology *(theologia naturalis)*, 1, 3, 6, 23, 49, 53-58, 68, 75, 84-85, 88-93, 100n.276, 106, 113, 114n.313, 160, 280n.322, 373, 388, 402, 479, 528

Nature. *See Physis*

Nature and grace, 19n.61, 20, 42n.116, 74, 99, 101n.280, 109-10

Neo-scholasticism, 87, 101n.280, 173, 390n.118, 406, 416, 418, 477, 501

Newman, John Henry, 4, 10n.33, 14-16, 59n.158, 348, 350, 381-82, 390n.118, 472, 504, 507

New Testament, 457, 460, 492, 573, 578

Nietzsche, Friedrich, 3, 5, 14, 16, 24-26, 51-52, 78, 166, 242, 334, 336, 389, 406, 504, 523, 601

Nominalism, 341, 442, 469

Ockham, William of, 363

Old Testament, 6, 424, 457, 460, 481, 503, 547, 558, 572-74

Origen, 352, 357-59, 362n.61, 366, 454, 575, 578

Original sin, 103, 105n.291, 106-10, 115, 260, 266-67, 320, 323, 337-39, 343-46, 364n.63, 365, 368, 379, 381n.106, 386-87, 389, 394, 402-5, 407-8, 535, 563, 564-66, 569; and philosophy, 405-11

Otto, Rudolf, 18, 50n.137, 348, 580

Otto, Walter F., 435

Pantheism, 20n.61, 25, 44n.124, 46, 50-53, 59, 65, 92, 165-67, 219, 223, 230, 243, 353, 362, 373, 392, 399

Parable (παρα-βολή), 439, 440-42, 450-51, 461, 559

Paradox, 226, 240, 259-60, 373, 386, 496-97, 533-36, 552, 596, 601

Parmenides, 32-34, 142, 159, 203-7, 239, 240nn.9-13, 241, 308, 321-23, 343, 419-20, 467, 474, 597, 601, 605

Participation, 33, 40n.114, 67, 90, 105n.291, 108, 110, 112, 161-62, 177, 187, 200, 215, 234, 241, 246, 276, 299, 306, 337-38, 340-43, 346-47, 351, 354-55, 362-71, 373-77, 385-89, 391, 393-94, 398n.135, 400, 438, 563-64, 567-68, 571, 575, 612

Pascal, Blaise, 89, 350, 389, 472, 601

Paul (Apostle), 22, 25, 40, 412, 425, 432, 448, 454, 494, 515, 535, 572, 574, 611, 622

Pelagianism, 515, 516

Phenomenology, 4, 15n.51, 24, 44-45, 61n.164, 62, 79, 81, 83, 121, 134, 140, 193, 202, 325n.22, 348, 350, 405, 409, 412, 435, 452, 459, 463-79, 485, 488, 493, 502-4, 520, 597, 603, 607, 613-15, 621-22

Physis, 119-20

Plato, 31-35, 45, 51, 67, 75, 79-80, 83, 107, 125-26, 129-30, 133, 135, 137-38, 141, 148, 150, 153, 161, 166, 192, 194-95, 203, 211n.85, 221, 239-47, 250-52, 254-60, 264, 266, 269-72, 305, 308-10, 314, 317, 322, 330, 332-33, 342-43, 373, 400, 405, 406, 408, 410, 419-20, 437-38, 442, 451-53, 457-58, 460, 464, 467-70, 478, 484, 493, 495, 502, 504, 507-9, 522-24, 532, 538, 541, 543-45, 563n.23, 578, 597, 604, 615

Plotinus, 341, 510, 541, 607, 610

Pneumaticism, 358-60, 376-79, 384, 390n.118

Potentia oboedientialis, 20, 71, 92, 99, 105n.291, 176, 223, 227-28, 280, 310-11, 344, 367, 370, 386, 388

Pseudo-Dionysius, 14, 43, 46, 75, 81, 145, 271, 278, 283, 300, 412, 422, 432, 451, 475, 519, 522-24, 582, 604, 607-8, 610

Psyche (soul), 8, 59, 61n.161, 98, 99n.272, 119-20, 127-28, 174-75, 186, 203, 250, 252, 260-64, 275n.285, 287-88, 296, 301,

313n.23, 335, 401, 451, 514, 521, 608, 611n.49, 612, 619

Pythagoras, 314, 471, 540

Real distinction *(realis distinctio)*, 34, 39n.111, 46, 47n.128, 62, 68, 83, 340, 476-77

Reformation, 17, 22, 50-51, 52n.140, 164-65, 169, 267, 323, 333-36, 343, 350, 357, 359, 373-74, 378-80, 392, 408, 414, 416, 428, 459, 481, 506, 557, 564, 566, 571-72

Religion, 18n.55, 19, 40, 57-58, 62, 81, 97-98, 99n.272, 107, 110, 150, 180, 388, 394-95, 402, 409-29, 431-33, 445, 465, 467, 479, 490, 506, 528, 571n.5, 572, 578, 580; Greek and Roman, 413-14; in Old Testament, 414-15

Renaissance, 166, 388, 405, 408, 480-81, 483, 585, 590

Revelation, 18-19, 40, 44-45, 55-58, 60, 69, 75-78, 81, 87, 89-90, 96-98, 100, 103, 105-7, 110-11, 112n.306, 113n.312, 114n.313, 115, 161, 171-72, 174, 177, 179, 181n.66, 183, 188n.106, 235, 266-67, 269-70, 283, 293, 300-301, 348, 355, 358, 364, 367, 370, 372-73, 378, 383, 391, 393, 395, 397, 401, 413, 418, 423-24, 443, 444n.23, 445-47, 456, 462, 472-74, 479, 488, 492, 495-98, 510, 512, 520-21, 530-32, 557, 561, 570-71, 573, 575, 592-93, 602, 606, 610-11

Rhythm, 59, 79, 86, 113n.312, 126, 139, 185, 202, 208-9, 217, 240-41, 243, 257, 264-66, 291, 295-96, 308, 312, 314, 329, 333, 375, 383, 384n.5, 390, 392, 406, 411, 418-20, 432, 434, 438, 449n.57, 464-65, 474, 479, 484-85, 487, 507-8, 521-22, 527, 529, 552, 562, 589, 594, 599, 603, 605-6

Ritschl, Albrecht, 533

Romanticism, 12, 16, 375, 381n.106, 405, 433-34, 445, 451, 481, 507, 524, 600, 615, 619, 621

Rome (Roman), 27, 145, 172, 359, 413-14, 418, 480, 482, 489-94, 498n.31, 541-42, 545, 549, 574; Roman Catholic, 11, 23n.67, 83, 93, 100

Sacrifice, 186, 335, 414, 417, 425, 482, 573-74

Salvation, economy of, 109, 364, 416, 423, 479, 518

Scheler, Max, 4, 14-15, 24, 61n.164, 421, 443, 466, 470, 504

Schelling, Friedrich Wilhelm, 16, 202, 322, 359-60, 482, 524, 528, 570, 580-81, 618

Schleiermacher, Friedrich Daniel Ernst, 57, 62n.165, 88, 348, 350, 498, 533

Scholasticism, 5n.21, 13n.47, 15n.51, 24, 44n.123, 45, 50, 129, 138, 172, 174n.45, 317-18, 321, 358, 371, 373, 378-79, 382, 384, 387, 389, 391, 395, 398, 408, 458, 460, 470, 476, 532

Science, 37, 52, 57n.154, 69, 117, 123, 125, 130, 135, 137, 162n.17, 172n.43, 203, 249, 324-26, 329, 386-87, 394-95, 401-2, 405, 407, 457, 460

Scotus, Duns (Scotism), 22, 39n.11, 50, 79, 168, 179, 350, 353, 387, 389-90, 398, 469, 475-77, 529, 589, 594

Scripture, 27, 40, 42, 44, 64, 106, 306n.542, 364n.63, 365n.63

Siewerth, Gustav, 351-52, 621

Simmel, Georg, 14, 16, 464-65, 484, 598

Söderblom, Nathan, 16, 381

Söhngen, Gottlieb, 84, 93, 94, 113, 397n.134, 428

Sophiology (of the Greek Orthodox East, Gnostic), 356

Soul. *See Psyche*

Spinoza, Baruch, 52n.140, 150, 166

Spirit, 8, 10, 42, 98, 102, 104, 132, 139, 144-45, 201, 225, 227-28, 230, 262-63, 272, 283, 288, 297-300, 302, 304-5, 322, 335, 350-52, 357-60, 362, 366, 371, 376-78, 384, 399, 406, 412, 414, 416-17, 421, 426, 431, 438, 448, 461, 465, 467-68, 493-98, 500, 501, 503, 506, 511-12, 521, 528, 533, 541, 543, 545, 552-54, 557, 559, 577, 581, 590, 594, 608-10, 619-20; Holy Spirit, 72, 85, 91-93, 111, 112n.306, 185, 267, 279, 314, 337-38, 353, 354-60, 362n.61, 363, 365-69, 377, 381, 384, 407, 423, 479, 493-95, 500, 504, 511, 521, 569, 571

Stein, Edith, 4, 11n.37, 17, 25, 28, 31, 61n.164, 596-612, 613-14, 616, 621

Suárez, Francisco, 13, 30, 39n.111, 168, 428

Symbol, 21, 136, 145, 205, 251, 270-71, 380,

414-15, 430-62, 472, 480-500, 519, 525, 539, 541, 543, 557, 565, 569, 576, 578, 585, 587, 601, 612, 614, 622

Tao-Te-Ching, 451, 503
Theologia crucis, 369
Theopanism, 19-20, 44n.124, 46, 50-53, 65n.174, 72, 92, 165-67, 219, 223, 229-30, 243, 353, 362, 372-74, 388-89, 392, 399
Thomism, 49n.111, 50, 349-50, 353, 389-90, 396, 398, 399n.135, 468-69, 475-77, 594
Tragedy, 108, 333-39, 373
Transcendentals, 45, 64-65, 126-31, 132, 135n.3, 173, 209, 248, 281, 322, 406, 545; the beautiful, 44n.124, 64, 125-26, 128-31, 241n.17, 248, 251, 258, 286-87, 406-7, 420, 538, 541-46, 551-53, 555; the good, 44n.124, 64, 125-26, 128-31, 223n.156, 224n.157, 226, 247-49, 258n.168, 270n.249, 284, 286, 303n.516, 406-7, 448; the true, 44n.124, 64, 125-26, 128-31, 132-

33, 144, 217n.118, 247-49, 284-86, 322, 330, 406-7
Trinity, 90, 113n.312, 145n.24, 263, 278-79, 353, 356-57, 359, 361, 373, 416, 426, 442, 530-31, 575, 611; economic Trinity, 357, 416, 611; *imago Trinitatis,* 264, 266-67, 278, 359, 361, 407-8, 416-17, 426, 511; *relationis oppositio,* 500; rhythm of, 185, 202; Trinitarian Gnosis, 357-58, 360

Vatican Council (First), 113, 168, 172, 313, 375-76, 379, 381, 405, 497, 498n.29, 530
Victorines, 430, 442
Voluntarism, 50, 359, 405, 476

Weil, Simone, 11n.37, 28, 277n.304, 445, 580, 596-612
Whitman, Walt, 482
Wolfe, Thomas, 482
Wolff, Christian, 470, 476, 501